Henry Halleck's War

Major General Henry Wager Halleck

Henry Halleck's War

A Fresh Look at Lincoln's Controversial General-in-Chief

CURT ANDERS

GUILD PRESS OF INDIANA, INC.

HARDCOVER ISBN 1-57860-029-4
PAPERBACK ISBN 1-57860-071-5

Library of Congress
Catalog Card Number
99-71527

Printed and bound in the United States of America

Text design by Sheila Samson
Cover and dustjacket design by Steven D. Armour

On the cover:

Henry W. Halleck by Jacob H. Lazarus, oil on canvas
Courtesy of the West Point Museum Collection
United States Military Academy

Contents

Maps

Maps by Joan Pennington, based on sketches by the author.

A photograph section follows page 382, with portraits of the key figures in *Henry Halleck's War*: Don Carlos Buell; George B. and Mary Ellen McClellan; John Pope; Herman Haupt; John McClernand; Ambrose Burnside; Nathaniel Banks; William Rosecrans; Abraham Lincoln; Montgomery Meigs; Philip Sheridan; George Meade; Ulysses S. Grant; George Thomas; Edwin Stanton; Benjamin Wade; and William T. Sherman.

Introduction
and Acknowledgments

*If I do not survive the war, sufficient materials for a correct under-
standing of my acts are on record and will be found by the future
historian who seeks the truth.*[1]

SO WROTE UNION MAJOR GENERAL HENRY W. HALLECK to Major General William T. Sherman on October 1, 1863.

General Halleck did survive the war, but his reputation had been
shredded long before Appomattox. Almost a hundred years later, historian
Kenneth P. Williams would note, "Any argument about the Civil War, no
matter how spirited, will end amicably if one of the disputants has enough
presence of mind to say, 'But wasn't Halleck terrible?' Condemnation ranges
all the way from condescending remarks by academic historians with no
discernible basic military knowledge to sharp criticisms by soldiers who have
not troubled themselves to examine the full record."[2]

Williams had gone about as far as his failing health permitted toward
completion of Volume V of his *Lincoln Finds a General*. "A number of
reviewers have remarked that I have been kinder than other writers to
Halleck," he recalled in an appendix to the final volume. "Some have merely
noted the fact; others have implied censure. . . . The truth is that about no
one have I altered my views as much as about Halleck. A dozen years ago I
would have made the usual denunciations, pointing to bad orders that
Halleck gave, and leveling off with the charge of general unfitness. . . . I
could have stated that everyone said what I was saying, and that therefore it
must be true."[3]

Williams also wrote: "A competent study of Halleck is in my judgment a most needed book on the Civil War." That was in 1958, the year of his death. As if in response, in 1962 Stephen E. Ambrose's *Halleck: Lincoln's Chief of Staff* was published. It remains the only biography yet produced; fortunately, it is still in print.

This book, *Henry Halleck's War*, is not a biography; Ambrose presented about as much regarding Halleck's life as any scholar is likely to discover. My intent is summed up in the working title I used: *Some Notes Toward the Restoration of a Soldier's Good Name*.

"Reputations are the only things over which historians have power," Walter A. McDougall has observed.[4] While I am a student rather than an historian, it occurred to me more than ten years ago that if no one else followed Kenneth Williams' lead in taking a long, fresh look at the record on which Halleck was content to rely, I would. This book is the result of my curiosity.

My purpose is to present overlooked information which enables readers to make up their own minds regarding this highly controversial man. It will be obvious that I admire General Halleck and have the highest respect for him. If I make it to Valhalla I will be eager to cross trails with him. Yet, these "Notes" are not offered toward *vindicating* General Halleck. In my opinion, his own messages provide all the defense he ever needed. Neither do I seek to make a hero of him. He did not win the Civil War for the Union, but he may well have prevented Abraham Lincoln from *losing* it.

In fact, Henry Halleck should be considered the true author of this book. In 1863 he began the collection of messages, reports, and other documents that became the 128 volumes published between 1877 and 1901 known as *War of the Rebellion: Official Records of the Union and Confederate Armies*.[5] This Gargantuan supply of information is the source for a very large percentage of the 275,000 or so words in this book, and of those passages perhaps more than half were written by H. W. Halleck.

It seems to me that he revealed a great deal about himself in his messages, even the shortest ones, which is one reason for my having included so many of them—some at lengths that may strain readers' patience. Telegrams and letters written by others and sent to him are relevant here because they enable us to discern the quality of the thinking and expression that General Halleck employed in responding.

From exchanges with various generals—McClellan, Grant, Buell, Sherman, Rosecrans, Thomas, Burnside, Meade, Banks, Sheridan—and of course with Lincoln and Secretary of War Edwin M. Stanton, we can see relationships form, develop, and often deteriorate. In fact, here we have material for future studies of the influence of certain very important persons on the decisions and actions of others in high command.

Why has this kind of book—part biography, part an assemblage of significant messages, part history—not been written before?

Halleck was shunned by writers and publishers during the "Great Remembering" and has been ever since because he had the independence and personality of an afflicted dinosaur: qualities often found in authentic intellectuals. As a highly successful lawyer in San Francisco before Fort Sumter, he could ignore public opinion with impunity; clients needed his skills more than he needed clients. But once retained by Abraham Lincoln in Washington as general-in-chief of the Union armies, he continued to refuse to "go along to get along"—which offended everyone.

"We have no time to quibble and contend for the pride of personal opinion," he wrote his old friend Sherman on February 16, 1864. "Here we have too much party politics and wire-pulling. Everybody wants you to turn a grindstone to grind his particular axe; and if you decline, he regards you as an enemy and takes revenge by newspaper abuse."[6]

Also, Halleck had grown wealthy through the use of his mental powers—"Old Brains" was his only nickname—but he had not acquired a power base along the way. That had not mattered during his years in San Francisco. But he had to labor without support from anyone at all for three years in Washington, a city in which politics vied with odors from the inadequate sewage disposal system for atmospheric supremacy.

Finally, Halleck has been condemned or at best ignored by so many authors of books and articles on the Civil War in large part because anyone seriously interested in evaluating his contributions to the quelling of the rebellion had to have been daunted by the sheer bulk of the 128 thick volumes of the *Official Records*, even if a complete set could be located. Many of those volumes contained a thousand or more pages, which did not age well and which contained acres and acres of trivia completely unrelated to General Halleck.

Kenneth Williams, Herman Hattaway, Shelby Foote, Stephen Ambrose, and many other esteemed historians have made extensive use of the *Official Records* in their works, but as far as I know this book is the first to adopt any participant in the Late Unpleasantness as a central figure and call attention to his performance *as revealed by the O.R.* I hope, of course, that this makes Henry Halleck the winner in the gamble he took by refusing to respond to his horde of critics during his lifetime and to repose his confidence in the belief that in due course someone might compile some notes toward the restoration of his good name.

If I have made progress toward encouraging posterity to reconsider General Halleck's reputation, much of the credit is due Alan Aimone, Chief of Special Collections at the United States Military Academy's Library at West Point, who years ago introduced me to the *Official Records*. More recently I have had cause to be grateful for advances in technology—the personal computer, the CD-ROM—and especially to the talents of the people at Guild Press of Indiana who put all 128 volumes of the *Official Records* on *The Civil War CD-ROM*. Of those 128, I have drawn material from 57. My procedure was to search for, locate, and print those messages, letters, and reports I found relevant, apply a highlighter pen to passages I wanted to include, and then transfer those bytes to the text. When I had completed version 1.0 of this book, I stacked all of those printouts on the floor, placed a yardstick alongside, and took a photograph that showed an accumulation of sixteen inches of paper. Another measurement of the text's *Official Records* origins: of the 1,703 endnotes herein, 1,235 or 73 percent cite the *O.R.* as the source.

I have taken the liberty of breaking long messages into shorter paragraphs than the compilers of the *O.R.* chose to provide. Also, I have omitted the salutations and effusive closings. However, recalling that those messages and letters were written between 1861 and 1865 and that the terms used in referring to minorities and the spellings of many words are not the same as we employ today, I have retained usages current at the time as reflected in the *Official Records*. Otherwise, Clio would have been justified in banishing me from the ranks of her devotees.

Communications among the war managers in Washington and generals in the field need to be examined in context, of course, and to that end I have provided narratives of campaigns and battles based on works made available to me by a number of libraries—notably, West Point's and that of the Union League Club of New York, and especially the Desmond-Fish Library here in Garrison, New York, through which I was able to draw upon the resources of others in the vast mid-Hudson Valley network. To them, I am deeply grateful.

Nancy Baxter and Jenny Larner at Guild Press are due my special gratitude for the diligence and skill they devoted to editing the manuscript, and also for their graciousness in considering my dissents. Text designer and editor Sheila Samson, whose efforts and talents went so far toward making *Disaster in Damp Sand: The Red River Expedition* possible, earned more of my respect and appreciation by coping with this book, which is four times the length of its predecessor. All departures from good form herein are to be attributed exclusively to my squawks, and to my adherence to the Mayan belief that it is dangerously offensive to their lightning-wielding gods to create a *perfect* work of art. Speaking of art, again—as in *Disaster in Damp Sand*—Joan Pennington has provided the maps for this work, and for this I thank her very kindly. The fact that General Halleck's influence ranged over such vast geographic regions presented unusual challenges. Accordingly, Joan and I have included a mixture of maps that suggest the *span* of Old Brains' concerns and, where needed, close-ups of campaigns and engagements where graphics may be helpful.

To my niece Martha McBride Shaver and her husband, Bill, I wish to express my deep gratitude for wringing out California libraries' resources regarding Halleck's years and achievements in the Golden State. In so doing they developed more information about this segment of his life than, as far as I know, has been assembled earlier. As I hope to show, it was during the California period that he developed capabilities that led to the enviable pinnacle from which the erosion in his reputation took place during his wartime service. To the extent this fresh contribution adds to the restoration of General Halleck's good name, the credit is due Martha and Bill.

And then there is my West Point classmate Colonel George M. Crall, USMCR, who provided me with chapter-by-chapter corrections, comments, and admonitions. Not being a resident in the grove of academe, I needed someone knowledgeable enough and also tough-minded and candid enough to save me from literary sin. Of course George is not responsible for my lapses but he certainly won my gratitude for having prevented so many.

Finally, a personal point. Years ago, when first I expressed interest in investigating and reporting on the chance that General Halleck's performance during the Civil War had been grossly misapprehended, the reactions were so discouraging that I turned to other projects. Even in more recent years, "Lots of luck!" sums up the encouragement I received.

Well, it may be a blessing that I did not swim upstream until technology and Guild Press of Indiana made trying to do that feasible. And once I became immersed in Old Brains' messages, again I found myself recalling the declaration William Faulkner made in accepting the Nobel Prize for Literature in Oslo in 1950.

The writer, he said, must leave "no room in his workshop for anything but the old verities and truths of the heart, the old universal truths lacking which any story is ephemeral and doomed—love and honor and pity and pride and compassion and sacrifice. . . . The poet's, the writer's, duty is to write about these things. It is his privilege to help man endure by lifting his heart, by reminding him of the courage and honor and hope and pride and compassion and pity and sacrifice which have been the glory of his past. The poet's voice need not merely be the record of man; it can be one of the props, the pillars to help him endure and prevail."[7]

Of course, Henry Halleck was no poet. Yet many of the thoughts and values he put into the words of his soldier-to-soldier messages more than a century ago suggest that Old Brains and William Faulkner were kindred spirits. So I believe, and so I hope you will agree.

C. A.
Garrison, New York
Spring 1999

1 ★ Crucibles

*W*HENEVER IT HAS SEEMED THAT the United States of America could not possibly endure past the end of the year, much less into another decade, a man has emerged whose leadership not only prevented chaos but set examples that inspired those who came after him to go and do likewise.

George Washington established high standards, but most of his successors as president failed to meet them. From roughly 1850 onward, the experiment so nobly launched during the late 1780s was blighted so egregiously that in 1860, as the presidential elections approached, the country that had entered the year united in peace was in fact well down the slipperly slope toward being split asunder and civil war.

In that noonday of American innocence, so remote had such possibilities seemed that no one, apparently, had thought it important to raise the question of whether *any* presidential candidate was qualified to carry out the Constitutionally imposed duties of commander-in-chief of the armed forces.[1] Yet in the interval between the election of Abraham Lincoln and his inauguration, seven Southern states seceded and the Confederate States of America came into being.

Suddenly both North and South needed leadership of Washingtonian quality. The Confederates placed their hopes in former United States Senator Jefferson Davis of Mississippi, a graduate of the United States Military Academy who had commanded a regiment of volunteers with distinction in combat during the Mexican War and had served afterward as secretary of war.[2] By contrast, Lincoln's only military experience had been as a militiaman for several uneventful weeks during the Black Hawk War.[3] Moreover, "All we ask is to be let alone," Jefferson Davis had declared, which meant that his mission was to defend the South against federal coercion and invasion until the Union conceded the Confederacy's independence,[4] while the North's new president faced the task of restoring the Union.

But if Commander-in-Chief Lincoln was overmatched, the North itself was not. Soon after news of Fort Sumter's surrender reached San Francisco, Lieutenant James B. McPherson gave a concise summary of the federal advantages in a letter he sent Edward Porter Alexander in a vain effort to persuade Alexander not to resign from the army:

> *Now this is not going to be any 90 days or six months affair as some of the politicians are predicting. Both sides are in deadly earnest, & it is long & desperate & fought out to the bitter end.*
>
> *If you go as an educated soldier you are sure to be put in the front rank & where the fighting will be hardest. God only knows what may happen to you individually, but for your* cause *there can be only one possible result. It must be lost.*
>
> *The population of the seceding states is only 8 million while the North has twenty million. Of your 8 million over 3 million are slaves & may prove a dangerous element. You have no army, no navy, no treasury, no organisation & practically none of the manufacturers—the machine shops, coal & iron mines & such things— which are necessary for the support of armies & carrying on war on a large scale. You are but scattered agricultural communities & will be isolated from the world by blockades. It is not possible for your cause to succeed in the end & the individual risks you must run meanwhile are very great.*[5]

And Confederate Secretary of State Robert Toombs had pointed out the Union's superior war-making potential to his president and fellow cabinet members: "The firing on that fort [Sumter] will inaugurate a civil war greater than any the world has yet seen. You will wantonly strike a hornet's nest which extends from mountains to ocean, and legions now quiet will swarm out and sting us to death."[6]

Indeed, the North mobilized with astonishing rapidity. Obtaining war materiel was less a problem than paying for it. Actually, Abraham Lincoln's main challenge became one of finding the *intellectual* resources he needed to augment his own in order to cope with the awesome and unprecedented challenges he faced.

During and after the war much attention would be given to Lincoln's frustration as he searched for generals who could win victories for the Union. In fact, however, the most vexing shortage of military talent was at the Union army's highest command level.

Initially, Lincoln depended heavily upon General-in-Chief Winfield

Scott, the nation's most seasoned and highly respected soldier. But Scott was seventy-four and he was ill; he had been a general since the War of 1812 and he was worn out; and though he and his very small staff devoted their best efforts to supervising the expansion of the army from about seventeen thousand men to more than one hundred thousand in a matter of a few weeks, "Old Fuss and Feathers" was unable to persuade Lincoln to resist political pressures to commit the partially trained troops to combat. The result was a stunning Union defeat at the battle known in the North as Bull Run.

Acting on Scott's recommendation, Lincoln summoned Major General George Brinton McClellan to Washington from western Virginia to rebuild the shattered army. Half the general-in-chief's age, McClellan proved highly effective in training troops. But he was driven by ambition, and soon he was conducting a campaign marked by studied insubordination to drive Winfield Scott into retirement.

Realizing that his five decades as a soldier were ending, and fearing that McClellan might be selected to succeed him, General Scott urged the appointment of Major General Henry W. Halleck, instead. However, Halleck had only recently returned to active duty; he had been ordered to Washington, but he had not yet left San Francisco, where he had been practicing law for the past seven years.

Ultimately, the aged warrior's failing health forced him to give way. Lincoln replaced Scott with McClellan. About a week later, in mid-November, General Halleck reached Washington. Neither Lincoln nor McClellan knew much about this stranger from California. Why, they may have wondered, had General Scott held him in such high esteem?

2

DURING HIS TWO DECADES AS GENERAL-IN-CHIEF, Scott had been accused of giving preferential treatment to West Point graduates whose roots were in the South. It was true that he had offered command of the Union armies to Colonel Robert Edward Lee—like Scott, a Virginian—and that after Lee resigned he turned to Colonel Albert Sidney Johnston, who had served under Sam Houston in Texas' war for independence from Mexico in 1836.[7] But in calling for Henry Halleck to succeed him as general-in-chief, Old Fuss and Feathers had designated not only a Northerner but a member of a family whose history in New York State began on Long Island around 1640.[8]

Included among four earlier generations of American-born Hallecks was an armed vessel's commander killed in the Revolutionary War; Jabez Halleck who, in 1799, moved to Oneida County in upstate New York and lived to be 103; and Joseph Halleck, the general's father, who served as a lieutenant in the War of 1812. Henry Wager Halleck was born on the family farm near Westernville on January 16, 1815, the first of Joseph and Catherine Wager Halleck's thirteen children. But he disliked farming so much that at sixteen he ran away from a life that challenged only his physical stamina; thereafter Henry Wager, his maternal grandfather, sponsored his attendance at Fairfield Academy at Hudson, New York, and Union College in Schenectady. At Union he was one of five students who won the maximum mark in all their courses, and he was elected to Phi Beta Kappa.[9] Then, suddenly, in 1835 again Henry Wager Halleck made a surprising change: In July he entered the United States Military Academy at West Point as a cadet in the Class of 1839.[10]

Grandfather Wager had obtained an appointment from Oneida County's congressman for his young namesake, which explained how this change was made. Not clear, however, was why Henry Halleck decided to set aside the college-level work he had already done and the honors he had earned and to start all over again at an institution that gave him no credit for his achievements and would require him to complete four full years of study, no matter how brilliant he might be.

Moreover, West Point was controversial. Politicians of the populist persuasion considered the Military Academy "elitist" and clamored for its abolition. Justification for its continuance, reflecting the distinction its graduates would earn in combat during the Mexican War, was still a decade and more ahead. Superintendent Sylvanus Thayer had instituted academic and disciplinary reforms that would move West Point to the front rank as an engineering college and provide the growing nation with men who would design and build (among other things) its railroads, but—again—later on. In the meantime, about all that cadets could expect after commissioning was dreary and often deadly duty in the West fighting Indians, or drawing plans for proposed coastal defenses which Congress refused to authorize.

Why, then, would any young man well on his way to becoming an "intellectual" commit himself to such a place? Halleck provided no clues. But others who have attended West Point selected it because it was almost unique in giving all cadets—regardless of background, family wealth, or degree of preparation—an equal opportunity to develop their capabilities, and because the Academy's standards were not only extremely high but rigorously and equitably enforced. Also, within the Corps the cadets themselves have a curious way of inspiring each other to excel; this does not end at graduation, and it can extend for lifetimes.

During Halleck's four years as a cadet, the Corps was small enough for him to become acquainted with men in the classes ahead of him and those entering after 1835, as well as those in USMA '39. Among his contemporaries who achieved eminence were Montgomery C. Meigs, '36; Braxton Bragg, Jubal Early, and Joseph Hooker, '37; Pierre G. T. Beauregard and William J. Hardee, '38; George H. Thomas and Richard S. Ewell, '40; and William S. Rosecrans, John Pope, and James Longstreet, '42.[12]

Cadet Halleck was later described as "very quiet and studious." His roommate (and years later his brother-in-law) Schuyler Hamilton recalled that "he had few intimate friends, but they were of the best." Along the way Halleck acquired the nickname "Old Brains," and indeed his standings in academic subjects were mostly in single digits. But he was a cadet first sergeant in his third year and a cadet captain in the final one, indicating that his emergence as a soldier matched his performance as a student.[13]

At his graduation in July 1839, Henry Halleck stood third in his class of thirty-one survivors of the sixty-four who had entered four years earlier.[14] This enabled him to be commissioned a second lieutenant in the "elite" corps of engineers; but during his final year as a cadet he had been made an assistant professor of chemistry and engineering, and the Academy's academic board kept him on in that capacity and also as an instructor in French for a year after his graduation.[15]

It was in a West Point section room that Cadet Ulysses S. Grant (USMA 1843) and Halleck, then a faculty member, "a tall, solemn man of twenty-five, who viewed the world with wide-eyed, staring abstraction," first crossed trails.[16] Halleck's friendship with William Tecumseh Sherman had started much earlier, in 1836, when "Cump" entered the military academy one class behind him.[17] Reviews made subsequently of the records of men Halleck might have known, either as fellow cadets or as students, suggest that he, Grant, and Sherman contributed more to the success of the side they served during the Civil War than any other graduates within the 1836–1843 span.

3

IN MID-1840 LIEUTENANT HALLECK WAS ASSIGNED as an assistant to the Board of Engineers in Washington. But his duties must not have been arduous, for he found the time to produce a paper on "Bitumen: Its Varieties, Properties and Uses," which was said to have included all that was then known about the application of asphalt to military projects.[18]

After five years in the gorgeous but remote Hudson Highlands, Halleck seemed to relish the fast pace of life in the capital—albeit with some reservations. In the wake of President Martin Van Buren's defeat, he wrote a friend:

> *My own feelings have not been as warmly enlisted in this political campaign as probably they would have been had not my position in the army precluded my taking any part in this partizan* [sic] *warfare. Nevertheless, I deeply regret the change of administration, both on account of my political opinions and the loss of many friends here who must soon leave. . . . With the society here I am most pleased. We have had several delightful supper parties recently, to which twenty-five or thirty are invited. . . . We assemble about nine o'clock, chat, dance and partake of refreshments until one or two o'clock. Late hours are now kept in Washington.*[19]

As would become nigh-traditional, in the early 1840s the federal government of the United States was preparing to re-fight the War of 1812—to the extent that it was paying any attention or devoting any resources at all to national defense. This meant that being an officer in the "elite" corps of engineers, the honor Cadet Halleck had earned, obliged him to spend part of his career supervising the repair and maintenance of coastal forts. Such was the work Lieutenant Halleck was given to do when he was assigned to the defenses of New York Harbor. Lacking in glamor though this assignment may have been, however, apparently he preferred it to civilian life, for in 1843 he declined the professorship of engineering in Harvard's Lawrence Scientific School.[20]

Among the officers with whom he served was Robert Edward Lee, second man in West Point's Class of 1829 and a fellow engineer.[21] And among the senior army officers watching the progress of promising young graduates of the Military Academy was General Winfield Scott.

Exactly how Halleck attracted the favorable attention of the United States' senior soldier is not entirely clear, but in the fall of 1844 General Scott sent him to France. "Thus far my time has been most profitably spent in military fortifications and places of historical interest," he wrote his mother back in upstate New York, adding:

Paris, where I am at present, is the capital of France and among the world's largest cities. In beauty, it stands first of all. It contains about thirty thousand houses, some of which are extremely elegant. I was in the palace of the Tuileries a fortnight ago, and was presented to the King and Queen. They are both fine looking and advanced in years. The King conversed with me in English, which he speaks very well, but the Queen talked French, so that I was obliged to use the same language, which I had fortunately learned at West Point.[22]

Combining his experiences on New York harbor projects with what he had learned in France, upon his return Halleck produced his "Report on the Means of National Defense," which the Senate promptly published. So favorably impressed was the Lowell Institute of Boston by Halleck's work that it sponsored twelve lectures its author delivered to that very highly regarded learned society. Such, in essence, was the genesis of Halleck's *Elements of Military Art and Science,* published in 1846. At the time there was no comparable work in English. *Elements* soon became a textbook at West Point, and in years to come a revised edition would attract a host of readers North and South—including, notably, a man utterly bewildered by having to manage a civil war no one had expected: Abraham Lincoln.[23]

Henry Halleck's interest in the theoretical aspects of warfare had been stimulated by Dennis Hart Mahan, professor of military art and engineering at West Point during his years as a cadet. Mahan had returned from study in Europe enormously impressed by the works of Baron Henri Jomini, which were attempts to identify principles of war embedded in the history of Napoleon's campaigns. Among the lessons Jomini had derived and Professor Mahan had stressed were at least four, which Halleck would advocate: establishment of secure bases and maintenance of lines of communication with them, concentration of forces, use of interior lines, and exploitation of opportunities to strike fractions of the enemy's armies with superior numbers.[24]

In *Elements of Military Art and Science,* Halleck combined his re-collections of Mahan, his own study of Baron Jomini's works and Napoleon's battles, his language skills, his powers of observation and analysis, and his abilities to think matters through and then to state his conclusions in remarkably clear English. But at the time Halleck's book appeared, one might well have asked why its author had bothered. In an army of only a few thousand men and far fewer officers, and given the understandable indifference of other Americans to military subjects during a period in which attention was scattered everywhere else, who cared enough to wade through Halleck's prose?

Much more useful, it seemed for a time, were books such as one William J. Hardee produced in 1855, *Rifle and Light Infantry Tactics.* Hardee, a graduate of West Point in the class a year ahead of Halleck's, had also studied in France; indeed, some thought Hardee's work a mere translation of French manuals; and by the end of the Civil War, advances in weapons' accuracy and power had made his work obsolete.[25]

The contrast between the two authors and their books calls attention to the difference between intellectual pursuit and expedient response to ephemeral challenge. Halleck was sharing his findings *so far;* and in so doing, he was sharpening the skills that later would facilitate his advancement in the other disciplines (the law, business, finance) he would master during the rest of the 1840s and throughout the 1850s.

Whatever prestige *Elements* might have won for Halleck in 1846 was blown away in the spring of that year with the outbreak of the Mexican War. Hardee was already serving along the Rio Grande. Captain Robert E. Lee, Halleck's superior officer at Fort Hamilton guarding New York Harbor, was ordered to Texas. So would be West Point graduates George B. McClellan, Thomas J. Jackson, Joseph E. Johnston, Ulysses S. Grant, Pierre G. T. Beauregard, and George G. Meade, to name only a few. But not Henry Halleck: Monterey, California, would be his destination, and he would have to endure a seven-month voyage around Cape Horn to reach it.[26]

4

THE MEXICAN WAR RESULTED FROM A SERIES of breakdowns in negotiations, diplomatic blunders, and muddled politics—all of which led to fighting in May 1846 at Palo Alto and Resaca de la Palma north of the Rio Grande's mouth in South Texas, and a declaration of war by the United States at around the same time. Major General Zachary Taylor, senior officer in South Texas, advised against an advance toward Mexico City from where he was, but he did recommend a drive to Monterrey, Saltillo, and possibly San Luis Potosi with the objective of gaining control of Mexico's northern provinces.[27] At that early point in the war, General-in-Chief Winfield Scott's efforts were directed mainly toward raising volunteer forces and shipping them to Taylor.[28]

Amid the confusion in Washington, some thought was given to Alta (Upper) California, in part because British naval vessels were operating along the coastlines of Mexico's provinces fronting on the Pacific. United States naval and marine units were authorized to protect American settlers' interests in Monterey and San Francisco. Then-Colonel Stephen W. Kearny was ordered to seize Santa Fe, then march westward to Alta California. A regiment of New York volunteers was alerted for 'round-the-Horn shipment to San Francisco.[29] So was Company F, Third Artillery, which by late June was about to board the old supply ship *Lexington* with New York as its port of embarkation and Monterey as its destination.[30]

In June 1846, no one could have foreseen that there would be a significant difference between the amount of combat experience officers sent to northern Mexico were going to gain compared with those ordered to California. Cump Sherman, for example, made very strong efforts to be assigned to Company F, lest he have to spend the war in Ohio. "That I should be on recruiting service while my comrades are actually fighting is intolerable," he declared.[31] Whether First Lieutenant Henry Halleck (he was promoted while he was in Europe) also actively sought duty even in remote Alta California is not known, but that is what he got; and for purposes of the voyage he was attached to Company F and the *Lexington*.[32]

Built in 1826 as a sloop of war, the *Lexington* had been downgraded to a store ship in 1843. She was only 127 feet long with a 38-foot beam, but she was large enough to take seven officers and 113 enlisted artillerymen aboard on July 13, 1846. Understandably, *Lexington's* passengers spent as much time as they could on deck.[33]

Halleck, Sherman recalled, lived up to his nickname. "When others were struggling to kill time," he wrote, "he was using it in hard study. When the sea was high & ship rolling, the sky darkened so that daylight did not reach his state room, he stood on a stool, his book and candle on the upper berth and a bed strap around his middle secured to the frame to support him in the wild tossing of the ship."[34]

During the voyage Halleck also began his translation of Baron Henri Jomini's *Vie Politique et Militaire de Napoleon,* at the time available only in French.[35] But in September, when the *Lexington* reached Rio de Janiero and paused there for a week to refit, Old Brains joined Sherman and the others on trips into the city, as Cump reported, "as much to see the pretty girls as the flowers which they so skillfully made" out of shells, silks, and feathers. After sixty days of meals at sea consisting mainly of boiled ham and boiled rice, the tourists gleefully gorged themselves on steak, potatoes, omelets, ice cream, and "fruits of every variety and excellence, such as we had never seen before or even knew the names of."[36]

Blithely unaware that at the time Zachary Taylor's troops up in

Mexico were fighting their way through the streets of Monterrey, the fugitives from the *Lexington* attended the opera and made a trip out to the emperor's palace and botanical gardens. But "the thing I best recall," Sherman wrote many years later, "is a visit Halleck and I made to the *Corcovado,* a high mountain whence the water is conveyed to the city. We started to take a walk, and passed along the aqueduct which approaches the city by a series of arches. . . . Halleck and I continued our ascent of the mountain, catching from points [along] the way magnificent views of the scenery round about Rio [de] Janiero." After reaching the summit Sherman and Halleck "returned to the city by another route, tired but amply repaid by our long walk."[37]

In October the *Lexington* spent nearly a month in storms while rounding Cape Horn. Sixty days out of Rio de Janiero she reached Valparaiso, Chile. Halleck and another officer visited Santiago, sixty miles from where the ship was being restocked for the last segment of the voyage. Finally, on January 26, 1847, 198 days out of New York, the *Lexington* lowered anchor in Monterey Bay, Alta California.[38]

"Every thing on shore looked bright and beautiful," Sherman wrote, "the hills covered with grass and flowers, the live-oaks so serene and home-like, and the low adobe houses, with red-tiled roofs and whitened walls, contrasted well with the dark pine trees behind, making a decidedly good impression upon us who had come so far to spy out the land."[39] But admiring the scenery was about all that the newcomers would have to do, for United States forces had recently won control of all Alta California towns of any importance, and the only conflicts remaining had to do with whether the army or navy commander was authorized to be military governor.[40]

None of the engagements leading to Mexicans' apparent acquiescence in the United States' occupation of the region had involved very many men on either side. Most of them had ended not in a decisive manner but by default, with Mexican forces withdrawing; this war was a quarrel between corrupt politicians in Mexico City and inept ones in Washington, and native Alta Californians seemed willing to leave the glory-seeking (especially the dying) to their compatriots several hundred miles to the southeast.

During the period of disputes among the senior officers of the army and navy, otherwise ordinary problems had been made more complex and vexing by the presence in the region of explorer John Charles Frémont, *de facto* leader of Anglo settlers who were in rebellion against Mexican authority and had declared themselves citizens of the Bear Flag Republic. Frémont had caused more trouble than his forces had been worth, and when Halleck arrived at Monterey, "The Pathfinder" was about to be escorted back to United States territory (western Missouri) where he would be placed under arrest and tried by court-martial. Such a fate hardly bothered John Frémont: Jessie, his wife, was the daughter of powerful Senator Thomas Hart Benton of Missouri. Neither did it matter to Frémont that the government had ordered him to explore and survey regions far to the east of Mexican-owned Alta California. Ignoring that mission, he had crossed the Sierras—hoping to find, presumably, a new route westward for emigrants and their wagon trains. Unable to discipline himself, now The Pathfinder faced retribution.

Such may have been Henry Halleck's first opportunity to learn about the quirky nature of the man he would succeed in command of the Department of the Missouri at St. Louis fourteen years later. So resilient was Frémont, however, that in 1856 he would be the new Republican Party's candidate for President of the United States.[41]

By early February, two weeks or so after the *Lexington* arrived, most of the officers who had been engaged in controversies over control were on their way east or about to leave, and new commanders for both army and naval forces had taken over. Colonel Richard B. Mason brought with him orders from Washington making California's government the army's responsibility. On land the navy was in charge only of customs and port regulations; Commodore W. Branford Shubrick directed operations at sea.[42]

Among Lieutenant Halleck's first engineering projects were improvements in the provincial capital's defenses, mainly "a redoubt in the form of a bastion, on a hill commanding the anchorage and the town, mounting upon it 20 guns carrying 24-pound shot and four 8-inch mortar guns on platforms. Quarters for [Company F of the Third Artillery], consisting of two large two-story log houses, were erected, and in the rear of the redoubt a stone magazine."[43]

In February 1847, General Taylor was about to fight an army led by General Antonio Lopez de Santa Anna at Buena Vista, southwest of Saltillo in north-central Mexico.[44] General-in-Chief Winfield Scott was preparing to make an amphibious landing near Vera Cruz, with Mexico City as his objective.[45] Yet, in Alta California the war seemed over. Cump Sherman settled into his duties as quartermaster, and Halleck spent more and more time in administration, while other graduates of West Point were gaining battlefield experience elsewhere under the tutelage of the United States' most seasoned soldier.

Orders from Washington, calling for seizure of some point in Baja (Lower) California, changed the outlook. On July 21, 1847, the old *Lexington* put two companies of New York volunteers, led by Lieutenant

Colonel Henry S. Burton, ashore on the peninsula near the province's capital, La Paz. Attention then shifted to ports on the eastern shore of the Gulf of California. Marines landed by naval vessels occupied Guayamas in October. In the middle of that month, Commander Shubrick brought another task force down from Monterey to Cabo San Lucas, at the southern tip of Baja California. In a combined operation on November 10, United States troops landed near Mazatlan, southeast of Guayamas on Mexico's Gulf of California coast. Mexican defenders fled, whereupon Brevet Captain Halleck (he had been promoted in May) began laying out fortifications that discouraged thoughts of counterattack.[46]

Such as Mazatlan's seizure was, it had amounted to Henry Halleck's first exposure to combat, although he may have been involved in quelling scattered opposition on the Baja California peninsula. Certainly he was familiar enough with the situation around La Paz to help Commodore Shubrick deal with the plight of Mexicans in the province who had cooperated with occupation troops.

At the war's end Sherman was still a first lieutenant, and likely to remain one indefinitely, while George McClellan—six West Point classes behind him—was a captain. So great was Cump's discouragement that he was strongly tempted to resign. In 1848 Sherman had confirmed that a few rocks two settlers had brought to Colonel Mason's headquarters from Captain Johann Sutter's property near Sacramento *were* gold, yet he would not benefit from it—while lust for gold accelerated settlement, which not only advanced Halleck's career but drew it into new directions.[47]

In August 1846, before the *Lexington* reached Rio de Janiero, Commodore Robert F. Stockton at Monterey had issued a proclamation in which he declared that Alta California belonged to the United States by right of conquest. As soon as circumstances would permit, he said, the region would be governed by officers and laws similar to those of other territories of the United States. Meanwhile, military law would be in force and Stockton would act as governor.

Commodore Stockton's proclamation proved premature. Mexican resistance flared anew at several places. Also, there were disputes regarding whether Major John Charles Frémont or Brigadier General Stephen W. Kearny would replace Stockton as governor.[48] This was settled on May 31, 1847, when Colonel Richard B. Mason assumed command of the land forces and took over as governor.

Drawing upon the authority set forth in Stockton's proclamation, in mid-August Mason had selected Captain Henry Wager Halleck as his secretary of state. Halleck's duties, as prescribed earlier by Stockton,

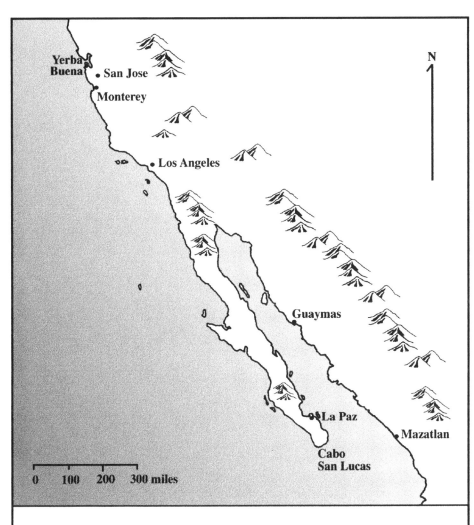

Yerba
Buena
• San Jose
Monterey
• Los Angeles
Guaymas
La Paz
Mazatlan
Cabo
San Lucas

0   100   200   300 miles

Alta y Baja California
en 1847

included recording and preserving the laws and proceedings of the executive and legislative departments, reporting them annually to the President of the United States and Congress, and acting for the governor in his absence.[49]

The constituency over which Mason and Halleck presided was a mixture of native *Alta Californios* of Spanish or Mexican descent and settlers who had crossed the Sierras from the eastern United States: "a people apart." Neither segment of the population had much understanding of the laws and political philosophies and instututions of the other. Both had strong aversions to military government—the *Californios* for obvious reasons, the Anglos because of the democratic traditions prevalent in "the States."[50]

Mason, who had been an army officer for thirty of his fifty years and described himself as a "simple soldier,"[51] was fortunate in having Old Brains as his principal assistant. Halleck, in turn, would benefit considerably from being obliged to learn Spanish, familiarize himself with Mexican as well as United States laws, become an expert on land titles, and provide counsel to Mason on matters ranging from the sources and applications of funds derived from import duties (and used to cover the cost of military government) to diplomacy.[52]

But Mason's limitations caused critics to complain about "ineffectual mongrel military rule."[53] And there were other impediments: the authorities in Monterey had to support operations in Baja California, and the discovery of gold led both to desertions as soldiers headed for the mines and to a heavy influx of people seeking instant riches. Even so, during 1847 and the early part of 1848, Mason—aided presumably by Old Brains—developed a body of laws designed to meet the needs of the "people apart." These statutes were never introduced, however, because before that could be done, the Treaty of Guadalupe Hidalgo ended the war and foreshadowed the replacement of military rule by a territorial or state government.[54]

Regarding desertions, Colonel Mason's report for 1848—which may well have reflected help from Halleck—made these observations:

> *I was in hopes that the news of the discovery of the gold mines in this country, together with its effects on the troops stationed here, would have reached* [Washington] *before any more were ordered out, for every day adds to my conviction that no soldier should be sent to California for some years to come, unless congress provide them pay bearing some proportion to the amount they can make in the country, and, at the same time, devise some laws by which deserters, and those who entice them away, employ them, and purchase from them their arms, accoutrements, clothing, and other public property,*

which they steal and carry off, can be more summarily and severely punished; the present laws being entirely inadequate, as long experience has proved.

Troops are needed here, and greatly needed; but of what use is it to send them, with the positive certainty of their running off to the gold mines as soon as they arrive, taking with them whatever public property they can lay their hands on?[55]

Immigrants from the States were accustomed to small grants of land, squatters' rights, and careful surveys based on fixed, or at least verifiable, boundaries. But native Californians, they found, owned great sections of the best lands and these Mexican grantees obstructed the newcomers' attempts to encroach.

In addition to taking part in the Baja California and Mazatlan operations, helping Colonel Mason prepare new laws, and monitoring the progress of local governments throughout the jurisdiction, Captain Halleck undertook a thorough study of land titles, grants, and transfers during the period of Mexican ownership of Alta California. On April 13, 1849, Old Brains issued his *Report on Land Titles in California* and sent copies off to Congress. His work was considered clear, accurate, and comprehensive. However, as anyone caught in the crossfire during a clash of cultures might have expected, controversy not only lingered on but proliferated.[56]

Halleck's conclusion was, in a word, *caution.* In a large number of California land titles, he discovered, boundaries were not definitely indicated. Some grants had been dated in advance or were otherwise fraudulent. Yet the Treaty of Guadalupe Hidalgo had called for the pre-existing property rights of Alta Californios to be respected. Very well, Old Brains seemed to be saying—actually, warning—but those claims ought to be tested because, in effect, the situation gave new meaning to *caveat emptor.*[57]

"The Californians tried to hope," wrote historian Hubert Howe Bancroft, "that their rights would be protected in a liberal spirit of equity, though what they knew or thought they knew of American methods was not reassuring."[58] Another historian, Josiah Royce, called attention to the "universal squatters' conspiracy against Mexican titles" versus "legalized meanness" and he added:

The squatter wants to make out that Mexican land grants, or at the very least all in any wise imperfect or informal grants, have in some fashion lapsed with the conquest. . . . The big Mexican grant was to [the squatters] *obviously an un-American institution, a creation of*

*a benighted people. What was the good of the conquest if it did not
make our enlightened American ideas paramount in the country?*[59]

After ratification of the Treaty of Guadalupe Hidalgo, Colonel Mason
and Captain Halleck had expected Congress to respond to Californians'
demands that Congress replace the military government with one for a
territory or a state. This amounted to overestimation of the objectivity of
that assemblage; Congress adjourned without taking any such action.
However, Missouri Senator Thomas Hart Benton, John Charles Frémont's
powerful father-in-law, did not remain idle.

Senator Benton had another son-in-law, William Carey Jones, and by
strange coincidence the federal secretary of the interior sent Jones to
California as a confidential agent to investigate the land questions. Three
months on the scene were all Jones needed, apparently, but he had access to
Halleck's findings and on March 9, 1850, (about a year after Old Brains'
warnings were published) he gave his sponsors in Washington his report.
Wrote Bancroft about Jones' conclusions:

> *While admitting the current belief and probability that fraudulent
> titles had been made since July 1846, he did not believe such to be
> many, extensive, or difficult to detect. He regarded the titles as for
> the most part perfect or equitable, that is, such as would have been
> fully respected under continued Mexican rule; and he advised [that]
> an authorized survey of the grants would be sufficient, the
> government reserving the right to take legal steps against suspicious
> titles.*[60]

Jones would later be prominent as an attorney in many of the
California land cases, historian Bancroft noted.[61] Also, there would come a
time when Senator Benton's other son-in-law, The Pathfinder, would have
less difficulty than might have been expected in acquiring title to the vast
and enormously valuable Las Mariposas acreage in California.[62]

In the course of searching the land title archives, Secretary of State
Halleck may well have identified some properties that he might acquire later
on.[63] It is also possible that he decided to become a lawyer at about this
time; certainly he must have been aware that attorneys seemed destined to
prosper considerably from decades of litigation over disputed grants.

In the spring of 1849, however, Washington sent two brigadier
generals to California to relieve Colonel Mason. Persifor Smith took command of military forces and made his headquarters in the San Francisco

vicinity. Bennett Riley took over as governor at Monterey on April 13.[64]

General Riley, like Mason, had made the army his career. But he was older by ten years, and his service record extended from the War of 1812 through the Black Hawk War and campaigns against the Seminoles to the landings at Vera Cruz and the subsequent battles of Cerro Gordo and Contreras in Winfield Scott's advance to Mexico City in 1847.[65] He was described as "a grim old fellow" (he was sixty-one) and "a fine, free swearer."[66] And no more than Mason was Riley equipped to act as a governor.

Of the departing Mason it would be said, "The record of his administration in California shows that his respect for order and justice was so exemplary as to dull markedly the sharp criticism of his detractors. He deserves high praise for having so administered the affairs of the country that when his successor arrived, adjustment to a civil form of government was relatively easy."[67]

Of course, Old Brains had contributed considerably to Mason's achievements. Among Governor Riley's earliest actions was reappointment of Henry Halleck as secretary of state. And one of Halleck's first services to his new superior was counsel in dealing with mischief generated by Senator Thomas Hart Benton.

"The treaty [of Guadalupe Hidalgo] with Mexico makes you citizens of the United States," the Missouri lawgiver told Californians in a letter published in the newspaper *Alta California.* "Congress has not yet passed the laws to give you the blessings of government, and it may be some time before it does so. In the meantime, while your condition is anomalous and critical, the temporary civil and military government established over you is at an end."[68]

Neither Mason nor Riley had been so advised by the secretary of war or the President, but Benton seemed to ignore such facts. "Having no lawful government," he continued, "nor lawful officers, you can have none that have authority over you except by your consent."[69]

Riley, surely with help from Halleck, tried to explain that the ultimate solution would have to come from Congress. But something more was needed to offset Benton's crass and inflammatory demagogery and to prevent movements toward an independent republic or anarchy. This response took the form of a proclamation General Riley issued on June 3, 1849, that was to serve as a map of the road to statehood.[70]

California historian William Henry Ellison provided this summary of the document:

[Governor Riley] *described the institutions and laws as they then existed, and pointed out the necessity of completing the organization of the civil government and the need for a convention to provide a state or territorial government in California subject to the approval of Congress. In explanation of what was proposed, he listed the various officials and outlined their functions. His scheme of civil government recognized Spanish forms fully, but it gave an American character to the administration by making the officers of the law elective instead of appointive.*

In the document, Riley ordered an election to be held on August 1, in which officials would be chosen to serve until January 1, 1850. He named the same date for an election of delegates to a convention, the purpose of which was to draw up a state constitution or to organize a territorial government, and he specified that thirty-seven delegates should be elected from the several districts, to meet at Monterey on September 1, [1849].[71]

Could anyone, no matter how perceptive or how fast a learner, have possibly gained so much familiarity with a complex and nigh-unique set of conditions and problems, and produced a reasonable plan of action, in only fifty-one calendar days? General Riley must have anticipated such a question, for he made a public acknowledgment of the "efficient aid" rendered him by Captain H. W. Halleck, his—and fortunately for California, Richard Mason's—able secretary of state.[72]

5

FORTY-EIGHT DELEGATES, NOT THIRTY-SEVEN, were admitted to the constitutional convention at Monterey on September 3, 1849; Governor Riley (or Secretary of State Halleck) had set a rule that every man who received over one hundred votes in his district should be a member. These were the most respected men in California at the time. Moreover, the variety of their origins, experience, and occupations suggested that virtually all interests would be represented.

"All were in the prime of life," wrote historian Bancroft, "all very much in earnest, and patriotic according to their light, albeit their light was colored more or less by local prejudices." Of the forty-eight, fourteen were lawyers, twelve were farmers or ranchers, and seven were merchants. Their ages ranged from fifty-three to twenty-five and averaged thirty-six. Twelve had been born in New York, six in California, and five abroad—two in France; one each in Spain, Switzerland, and Scotland.[73]

Henry Halleck, one of seven delegates elected from Monterey, was thirty-two, on his way to becoming a lawyer, New York-born, with more experience in dealing with the region's governmental problems than any of his colleagues. Others served as officers of the convention. But Old Brains was one of eighteen members of Chairman William M. Gwin's committee on the constitution, and the product reflected many of his contributions.[74]

"They did not pretend to originate a constitution," Bancroft wrote; "they carefully compared those of the several states with whose workings they were familiar, and borrowed from each what was best and most applicable, or could be most easily made to conform to the requirements of California, all of which, by amendments frequently suggested, became modelled into a new and nearly faultless instrument."[75]

Although Old Brains and anti-Riley delegate William Gwin disagreed on many if not most other questions, so closely did their positions regarding the location of California's eastern boundary seem that one alternative was called the Gwin-Halleck proposal. Had it been adopted, the northeastern corner of California would have been located north and east of the Great Salt Lake and the new state would have included modern Nevada and portions of Utah and Arizona.

"Old Gwin has hypnotized the Governor's own secretary to support some nefarious plot in preference to the Governor's own plan!" grumbled one delegate. As it turned out, however, Halleck persuaded Gwin to accept an amendment empowering the first of California's legislatures to change to the present Sierra Nevada border if Congress should so prefer.[76]

Another issue on which Halleck took a stand involved the rights of women. A section of the constitution offered this language:

All property, both real and personal, of the wife, owned or claimed by her before marriage, and that acquired afterwards by gift, devise, or descent, shall be her separate property; and laws shall be passed more clearly defining the rights of the wife, in relation as well to her separate property, as to that held in common with her husband.[77]

Opponents of the proposal argued that since nature had put women under the protection of men, the constitution should not experiment with that relationship. Halleck took a different view. Although he was "not wedded either to the common law or the civil law," he told the delegates, "nor as yet to a woman," he did have hopes of being wedded sometime. He advocated adopting this section as an "inducement for women of fortune to come to California." It was, he felt, "the very best provision for getting wives that we can introduce into the constitution" and he urged his fellow bachelors to vote for it.[78]

By October 13 the constitution (including the wealthy wife-attracting section) had been approved and signed by the delegates. After adjourning, they proceeded in a body to Governor Riley's home to thank him for his services to the people of California. "I never made a speech in my life—I am a soldier," he replied, whereupon the crowd gave him three cheers as governor and three more as "a gallant soldier, worthy of his country's glory." Then said General Riley: "I have but one thing to add, gentlemen, and that is, that my success in the affairs of California is mainly owing to the efficient aid rendered me by Captain Halleck, the Secretary of State. He has stood by me in all emergencies; to him I have always appealed when at a loss myself; and he has never failed me."

There followed three resounding cheers for Old Brains.[79]

That night the delegates celebrated at a ball "in which men of half a dozen nationalities, and almost as many shades of complexion, trod the giddy mazes of the dance with California señoras in striking costumes, whose dark splendors were relieved here and there by a woman of a blonde type and less picturesque attire."[80]

California's voters ratified the document on November 13 with 12,064 in favor and only 811 against.[81] The newly elected legislature met on December 15 and elected a governor three days later. On December 20 General Riley issued his last proclamation: "A new executive having been elected and installed into office, in accordance with the provisions of the Constitution of the State, the undersigned hereby resigns his powers as Governor of California"[82]

So ended Henry Halleck's service as secretary of state, but his name was one of seven considered by the legislature for the two seats in the United States Senate. Whether or not he declined to be a candidate would remain unclear; in any case, William Gwin and John Charles Frémont were elected.[83] But, mainly because of sharp controversies over slavery raging in the United States Congress, not until September 9, 1850, would California be admitted to the Union, and two more days had to pass before Senators Gwin and Frémont were sworn in.[84]

Former Governor Riley had remained at Monterey until July 1850. When he left, the town's citizens expressed their appreciation and esteem by giving him a massive gold medal—it weighed one pound—with "a heavy chain composed of nuggets of gold in their native shapes."[85] Henry Halleck's rewards, at the time, seemed doomed to remain intangible. Such would not be the case; but it would take ten more years of hard work and occasional controversy for Old Brains to reap the benefits of the experiences he had gained in the course of enabling Richard Mason and Bennett Riley to become ephemeral heroes.

6

FOR OLD BRAINS, ASSIGNMENT TO ALTA CALIFORNIA in 1846 had made—literally—a world of difference. Where else could he have found so great a need for such talents as he had, or so many opportunities to enhace and expand them?

By early 1850 he had achieved a prominence that had eluded men such as Sherman who were able, dedicated, and hard-working. But as the new decade opened, it seemed that Henry Halleck's career had peaked, that he was a specialist whose skills were now obsolescent—and as far as his army duties were concerned, that was true. He could look forward to little more than inspecting lighthouses and serving on the Board of Engineers for Fortifications on the Pacific Coast; Brevet Colonel Robert E. Lee and others senior to him were likely to be given the choice assignments elsewhere.[86]

Yet during all his years, one success had led to another. Situated as he was, in a region where the population was surging upward and economic activity was increasing at even faster rates, the question facing him was not *if* he could benefit from it, but how much and how soon.

When First Lieutenant Halleck had reached Monterey in January 1847, the village just southeast of the Golden Gate was known by most people as Yerba Buena. A year later, about eight hundred men and women lived there, and with increasing frequency the place was being called San Francisco. Its population grew to two thousand by February 1849, and to five thousand by the middle of that year; then there was a leap to twenty thousand inhabitants in 1850 and to about thirty-six thousand in 1852.[87]

With the waves of newcomers had come increased demand for land. This occurred just as the machinery ordained by Washington for the settlement of disputes over titles was clanking into motion. Lawyers were immediate beneficiaries of these developments. And the more of an expert on claims an attorney happened to be, the more wealth he was likely to acquire.

From the summer of 1847 until late in 1849, Halleck had been *de facto* attorney general of California. But the problems he had pointed out in the report on land titles, which he had prepared and sent to Congress in the spring of 1849, remained unsolved until March 1851, when the Land Commission Act became law. The three-member commission created under it did not begin to hold sessions in San Francisco until January 2, 1852.[88] Great years and high fees were inevitable for lawyers, but in 1850 such expectations seemed some distance away.

Meanwhile, Old Brains devoted some of his time to the post of director-general of the New Almaden Mine, near San Jose. Quicksilver (mercury) was the company's product—one that some observers thought to be more valuable than gold—and apparently engineer Halleck found some of the procedures and equipment being used outmoded, for in 1850 he supervised the replacement of retorts by furnaces.[89] His association with the New Almaden Mine would continue for most of the decade.

Statehood doomed Monterey to decline in importance. San Jose became California's new capital; control of army operations, such as they were, had long since been shifted to the San Francisco area; and at some point following General Riley's departure in 1850 and early 1853, Halleck moved to the city that had recently been a few adobe houses in a place known as Yerba Buena. During this interval he was admitted to the bar and began the practice of law. In 1853 he became a partner in San Fransico's most prominent law firm, Peachey & Billings. Given the advent of Land Commission operations early in 1852 and the ensuing surge in litigation over land claims, together with Old Brains' nigh-unique mastery of that complex and demanding field, before long he was the dominant lawyer in Halleck, Peachey and Billings.[90] He would remain head of California's most powerful and respected law firm until the spring of 1861.

One thing had always led to another with no serious setbacks for Henry Wager Halleck, and during his early years in San Francisco, the reputation he had earned while guiding California to statehood resulted in his becoming a director of two of the city's banks and president of the Pacific and Atlantic Railroad (which, despite its ambitious name, linked San Francisco only with San Jose). Even so, the brevet captain's devotion to such assignments as the army gave him resulted in his promotion, in July 1853, to the permanent rank of captain of engineers.[91]

Although West Point's mission had not been to produce financiers, during California's years under military rule, Captain Halleck had provided such adroit management of what was called the "Civil Fund"—the net of customs and similar revenue less expenses of governing—that General Riley had been able to turn a considerable sum over to the United States Treasury once taxation under the 1849 constitution changed arrangements. Never once had any impropriety been alleged, nor would any be subsequently.[92] And Old Brains was prudent in managing his own finances, as well, for in 1852 he emerged as a major participant in San Francisco's development.

At that time God was getting even with the city for its debauchery and licentious ways, or so preachers declared from atop beer barrels. Devastating fires seemed as regular as the seasons, and property owners were slow to rebuild after each one. Mining activity and purchasing power were declining, civic corruption and local taxes rising. Such were the reports Halleck received when he met with a group of citizens to discuss ways of restoring confidence and morale. Old Brains' suggestion: build a big building, an expensive building, one that would cost three million dollars.

"Halleck," he was told, "you're a fool!"[93]

What happened next was recorded by one of the city's historians:

> *Halleck went ahead without them, borrowing money wherever he could—from eastern financiers, from foreign banks, from the railroads—and late that year he put hundreds of Chinese coolies to work excavating for the foundation. Day after day they toiled . . . scooping up the tide-flat mud in baskets.*
>
> *When their work was finished, redwood logs, floated across the Bay from Contra Costa County, were fashioned into a huge mat and placed in position on the floor of the excavation. Crosswise over them was then laid another layer of redwoods, and, above that, a layer of twelve-by-twelve-inch ship's planking. Sidewalk superintendents, watching the progress of construction, shook their heads; the building would either sink out of sight into the mud, or else a good high tide and a strong blow would send it right out through the Gate. They called it "Halleck's Folly." Some wag offered a derisive alternative, "The Floating Fortress."*
>
> *But it kept on growing bigger. Into it went cement from England, glass from Belgium, France and Germany, iron fittings, beams, doors and balconies brought around the Horn from Philadelphia, and 1,747,800 bricks. When Halleck was through, he had the largest building on the Pacific Coast, the first earthquake-proof building in San Francisco and (it is said) the first commercial structure in the world to have inside rooms opening on an inner courtyard.*
>
> *It had taken fourteen months to build, and two days before Christmas 1853, "Halleck's Folly," or more formally, the "Washington Block," was opened to the public.*[94]

Members of the San Francisco bar promptly made Halleck's Folly headquarters for the legal profession; yet considering the controversies over titles to real property, it was hardly surprising that many of the building's tenants were lawyers.[95] By early 1854 the California Land Commission had spent two years validating some claims and denying others; many of them appealed to the District Court and some to the Supreme Court of the United States. When the Commission completed its work on March 3, 1856, it had considered 813 claims, roughly two-thirds of which were appealed.[96]

In certain cases bitter disputes would continue for decades. Even in some that were settled, the stench of political interference with justice lingered. Most of them provided lawyers with years of fees and enhanced their reputations. Halleck, of course, benefitted greatly. Of him it was said by a contemporary that few, if any, members of the San Francisco bar in the pursuit of their profession ever combined sounder mental powers with greater application and industry.[97]

With prominence and wealth also came criticism. In his "Pioneer Register" historian Bancroft remarked that "the positions held by [Halleck] are sufficent to show his abilities," but he added: "He was a cold-blooded, generally unpopular man; plodding rather than brilliant in all his efforts; arousing bitter enmity as well as profound admiration."[98] It should be noted, however, that Bancroft wrote *after* the Civil War, during which whatever esteem on the part of Californians Old Brains had earned and had taken east with him was eclipsed by allegations that destroyed his reputation.

No man would ever do more to ruin Henry Halleck than Edwin McMasters Stanton, secretary of war in the Lincoln administration, and it is curious that the two men first became adversaries in connection with California land title controversies in 1858. Stanton, born in Ohio, mentally unstable in his youth but later among the most highly regarded—and aggressive—lawyers in the east,[99] was retained by Attorney General Jeremiah S. Black as a special counsel for the federal attempt to overturn decisions in the claims cases that seemed to have impaired the interests of the United States in that fraud had been allowed to prevail. How this project was carried out and some of its results were summarized by historian William Ellison:

The voluminous records brought together were studied by Stanton and other able men. By using them and the evidence they yielded,

*and by comparing testimony, Black and Stanton were able to
determine with almost absolute certainty the truth or falsity of
almost any claim presented. So effective and persistent were they and
their aides in presenting the cases and convincing the courts, that
when Black made his report to the President he stated that more
than two-thirds of the forged land claims, valued at "probably no less
than $150,000,000" had been exposed and defeated.*[100]

One of the cases prosecuted by Stanton involved the New Almaden
Mine, of which Halleck had once been superintendent or director-general.
Apparently Stanton took testimony from Halleck, for he accused him of
perjury but he was unable to prove it.[101] This failure was hardly surprising,
given that Stanton, *et al.,* were following the trail Old Brains had blazed ten
years earlier. However, the perjury accusation suggests that Lincoln ordered
Halleck to Washington as general-in-chief of the Union armies in mid-1862
despite Stanton, by then the secretary of war.

7

WITHIN THE LAW FIRM OF HALLECK, PEACHY AND BILLINGS, Archibald
Peachy was the political partner; he served in both houses of the California
legislature.[102] Frederick Billings, a native of Vermont, would be best
remembered after the Civil War (during which he was California's attorney
general) as president of the Northern Pacific Railroad; Billings, Montana,
was named for him.[103]

Avoiding politics and insulated as he was from San Francisco's economic cycles by fees from land claim litigation, and despite his steadily
increasing prominence, during the second half of the 1850s Henry Halleck
attracted almost no attention from the press. About all that would become
known about his private life would be that on April 10, 1855, he married
Elizabeth Hamilton, the granddaughter of Alexander Hamilton and the
sister of Schuyler Hamilton, who had graduated two classes behind
Halleck's at West Point and who had been associated with him in California
in the New Almaden quicksilver mine organization. The Hallecks' only
child, a boy named for his father, was born in 1856.[104]

Successful though Halleck had been as a lawyer and corporate
executive, however, he seemed compelled to study and to write—by so
doing, to pass on to posterity what he had learned. In 1859 he published *A
Collection of Mining Laws of Spain and Mexico;* next, in 1860, a translation

of *Fundamental Principles of the Law of Mines* by J. H. N. de Fooz; and in 1861 *International Law, or Rules Regarding the Intercourse of States in Peace or War*.[105]

International Law was widely admired and in a condensed version was used in many law schools.[106] Also, by 1861 and the onset of the Civil War his *Elements of Military Art and Science*, first published before the Mexican War, was reissued with revisions Halleck had made after having studied that conflict.[107]

As a long-time supporter of Democrat Stephen A. Douglas, Henry Halleck could hardly have been encouraged by the election early in November 1860 of Abraham Lincoln.[108] And had he been aware of what was happening in in the North, as well as of the events in South Carolina and elsewhere in the South, well might he have agreed with Thomas Jefferson, who declared, "I tremble for my country when I consider that God is just."

Weakness at the top in Washington was a proximate cause of the Civil War. Lame duck President James Buchanan seemed bewildered by secession; to the extent possible, he left the problems it was causing to his successor. Abraham Lincoln, however, remained aloof from the deterioration occurring in the situation as Inauguration Day, March 4, 1861, approached. Even as he took the oath of office, he was not entirely sure that all of his nominees would serve in his cabinet. And on the next morning he found himself and the Union in much deeper trouble than he had expected: Major Robert Anderson, commander of Fort Sumter in Charleston Harbor, had reported that his provisions would be exhausted in about six weeks and that if he were not reinforced by twenty thousand troops he would be obliged to surrender.[109]

During the six weeks in which Sumter's food stocks dwindled, and despite attempts by Secretary of State William H. Seward to undercut his actions, Lincoln made strong but unsuccessful efforts both to find a peaceful solution and to resupply the fort's garrison. By April 30 news of the outcome had reached Old Brains in San Francisco, as he indicated in a letter to Senator Reverdy Johnson of Maryland:

> *We have much later news by the pony express—to the 18th inst.— giving full accounts of the attack and surrender of Fort Sumter, the President's proclamation, and the general arming, both North and South. Civil war seems now to be inevitable. This news has caused a deep feeling of regret here, and will have a very depressing effect on property and business.*

Whatever Virginia may have done or may do, I really hope that Maryland may not secede. If she goes there must result an immediate contest for the Capital. However, if no slave states remain in the Union, the North will become ultra antislavery, and I fear, in the course of the war will declare for emancipation and thus add the horrors of a servile to that of a civil war. But if Maryland should remain in the Union, slavery will still be recognized and protected under the Constitution, and the door be kept open for a compromise or reconstruction, if either should become possible. I, however, see very little hope of either till much of the bad blood of our present political leaders is drawn off by the sword and the cannon.

It is currently reported that a number of emissaries of Jeff. Davis have recently arrived here with overtures to prominent Southern men. Several officers of the army have resigned, and it is supposed will take commissions in the Confederate Army. I do not anticipate much trouble here at present, but still it may come sooner than we think. Our Governor, Downey, stands firmly up to the mark as a Union man; but who may next change no one can tell. The commander of the Pacific Division, General [Albert Sidney] *Johnston, a relative by marriage I believe of Jeff. Davis, resigned some three weeks ago, but is to remain, it is said, for the present upon this coast, and it is asked, for what purpose? Time alone can answer.*[110]

Added to all these anticipated troubles we already have a squatter rebellion in three counties and a suspension of the authority of the courts. In all probability a militia force will be ordered out, and it is possible that I may have to put on the old uniform. . . .[111]

Such a time came swiftly.

For Henry Halleck, as for uncounted millions of other Americans, news of Fort Sumter's surrender called for the setting aside of personal hopes and ambitions. He was already a major general of California militia. Duty and honor, instilled in him more than twenty years earlier at West Point, must have compelled him to volunteer to do more. Old General-in-Chief Winfield Scott had not forgotten or overlooked him, and by August 19, 1861, President Lincoln had commissioned Henry Wager Halleck a major general in the regular army.[112]

The end of Old Brains' golden years in the Golden State came on October 10, 1861, when—accompanied by his wife and child—he boarded a steamer bound for Panama.[113] Once there, a train would take the family across the isthmus to another vessel for the rest of the journey to Washington. This was a vast improvement over the old 'round the Horn route. But from his arrival in the capital onward, Henry Halleck would realize again and again how far he had left the good life behind.

2 ★ Games Grown Men Play

Months—years, in some instances—would pass before even a few people in the North would learn enough about what went on inside Lincoln's administration to link their heavy sacrifices and deep disappointments with the poor quality of war management that seemed to plague the Union at the highest levels. Soldiers committed to duty, honor, and country had sworn to obey the orders of the commander-in-chief, no matter who or how incompetent he might be. From their points of view, and from Henry Wager Halleck's in particular, the North's seeming indifference to the needs reality was imposing must surely have been appalling.

Congress was not in session when the Civil War broke out. To his credit, President Abraham Lincoln made use of powers he was not certain he had to mobilize militia units, call for ninety-day volunteers, add to the regular army, and impose a thirty-six-hundred-mile blockade (which he had too few ships to enforce) from Chesapeake Bay to the mouth of the Rio Grande.[1]

Mobilization plus the usual breaking-in every new administration requires led to chaotic conditions. Lincoln, grossly overloaded, could not cope with them.[2] Some of his cabinet members actually worked against his and the Union's interests: Secretary of War Simon Cameron, for one, was devoting most of his time to rewarding his old friends with lucrative deals and positions in procurement from which they could benefit.

Among the adverse consequences of Lincoln's inexperience was the scant attention he gave General Scott's proposal regarding Union grand strategy. Blockade of the Confederate coastline, the first element, the President had already ordered. Entirely fresh, however, was Scott's second recommendation: Restore the Mississippi River to Union control from

Minnesota to the Gulf of Mexico, thus cutting the Confederacy in two. Those things done, let Union troops ("the best regulars") squeeze the will to continue the war out of the rebels, he advocated. Scott's "Anaconda," the Northern press branded the concept and they ridiculed it. Even less acceptable was General Scott's warning that the war would last at least three years and require extensive training of men entering the Union army.[3]

Moreover, the commander-in-chief acted in too great haste in granting commissions as generals to politicians who were as lacking in qualifications to lead men in combat as was Lincoln. Among these were two former governors of Massachusetts, Benjamin F. Butler and Nathaniel P. Banks, both of whom would prove to be utter disasters. Another was John A. McClernand, congressman from Lincoln's home district in Illinois, whose incompetence resulted in heavy Union losses in virtually every battle in which his units were engaged.[4]

Early in July Lincoln had made a particularly serious mistake in selecting and assigning political generals—one that was to bring Henry Halleck into the war front and center. Some background:

After Fort Sumter's surrender and Lincoln's call for volunteers, all of the previously uncommitted "border" states except Delaware, Maryland, Kentucky, and Missouri had joined the Confederacy. Kentucky embraced neutrality. In Missouri, however, pro-Confederate and pro-Union factions resorted to violence that made the state a problem for both sides.

Francis P. Blair, Jr., and Brigadier General Nathaniel Lyon had secured St. Louis for the Union back in April and May. But the general commanding in the region was thought to be weak, and Lincoln considered Lyon too rash to replace him. Francis P. Blair, Sr., an advisor to presidents since Andrew Jackson's years, offered a suggestion: Make John Charles Frémont a general and send him out to Missouri. Lincoln accepted it.

At the time, The Pathfinder was in Europe. When news of Fort Sumter's fall reached him, acting without orders or authorization, Frémont started purchasing weapons. Upon being told that a commission as a brigadier general was waiting for him, he returned to Washington where he was appointed to command of the Department of the West, with headquarters at St. Louis. His mission: secure Missouri for the Union. "I have given you *carte blanche*," Lincoln told Frémont. "You must use your own judgment and do the best you can."[5]

When Frémont arrived in St. Louis in late July 1861, Nathaniel Lyon and about six thousand troops were in southwestern Missouri facing a Confederate force that outnumbered them by at least two-to-one. Lyon requested reinforcements, but The Pathfinder had other uses for the available units. First Lyon retreated, then he decided to attack. Early on the morning of August 10, having sent part of his men around east of the rebel camp along Wilson's Creek, Lyon struck from the front and rear; soon the Confederates rallied, however, and they gave the Yankees a sound whipping in which Lyon was killed.[6]

News of the defeat led to heavy criticism of Frémont for not having reinforced Lyon. But The Pathfinder had a history of generating controversy stretching back to 1846 and 1847 in Alta California; and although his residence in St. Louis had been brief, as August neared its end Frémont was again attracting attention—none of it favorable.

General Frémont had seemed to be doing his best to find the outer limits of Lincoln's *carte blanche*. For his headquarters he had leased, at $6,000 a month, a mansion on Chouteau Avenue. He imported many of his staff officers from central European armies. When he chose to venture out of his luxurious quarters, he was escorted by an entire squadron of cavalry.

Much of Frémont's support had come from Radical Republicans and other abolitionists, but in the wake of defeats at Wilson's Creek and elsewhere in Missouri, even they were expressing disappointment. To counter this erosion, on August 30 he issued a proclamation that created more problems than it solved. In order "to suppress disorder," he began, "to maintain as far as practicable the public peace, and to give security and protection to the persons and property of loyal citizens, I do hereby extend and declare established martial law throughout Missouri." And he continued:

> All persons who shall be taken with arms in their hands within [Union] *lines shall be tried by court-martial, and if found guilty will be shot.*
>
> *The property, real and personal, of all persons in the State of Missouri who shall take up arms against the United States, or who shall be directly proven to have taken an active part with their enemies in the field, is declared to be confiscated to the public use, and their slaves, if any they have, are hereby declared freemen.*[7]

If General Frémont's desire had been to rekindle the abolitionists' affection for him, his emancipation provision triggered more favorable response than he may have expected. Even newspapers normally friendly to Lincoln and his administration hailed The Pathfinder's initiative. But the general had encroached on presidential turf. Moreover, he had given his superior a nasty surprise.

In the circumstances, Lincoln's response on September 2 was remarkably restrained:

> *Two points in your proclamation of August 30 give me some anxiety.*
> *First. Should you shoot a man, according to the proclamation, the Confederates would very certainly shoot our best men in their hands in retaliation, and so, man for man, indefinitely. It is, therefore, my order that you allow no man to be shot under the proclamation without first having my approbation or consent.*
> *Second. I think there is great danger that the closing paragraph, in relation to the confiscation of property and the liberating slaves of traitorous owners, will alarm our Southern Union friends and turn them against us; perhaps ruin our rather fair prospect for Kentucky. Allow me, therefore, to ask that you will, as of your own motion, modify that paragraph so as to conform to the first and fourth sections of the act of Congress entitled "An act to confiscate property used for insurrectionary purposes," approved August 6, 1861, and a copy of which act I herewith send you.*
> *This letter is written in a spirit of caution and not of censure. I send it by special messenger, in order that it may certainly and speedily reach you.*[8]

The Pathfinder, however, had no intention of changing either the language or thrust of his proclamation. He took his time in preparing a reply, and when he had finished it he entrusted the letter to his wife, Jessie Benton Frémont, who caught a train bound for Washington. She arrived there on the evening of September 10 and immediately sent a note to the Executive Mansion requesting an appointment with the President. Back came a card: "Now, at once, A. Lincoln."

The greeting "General Jessie" received was terse: "Well?" She was not invited to sit down. Having handed the President the letter from her husband, all she could do was scan the walls of the Red Room while he read it.

Frémont opened with excuses:

> *I had not written to you fully and frequently, first, because in the incessant change of affairs I would be exposed to give you contradictory accounts; and, secondly, because the amount of the subjects to be laid before you would require too much of your time . . . I therefore went along according to my own judgment, leaving the result of my movements to justify me with you.*

Next, he turned to the proclamation:

Between the rebel armies, the [Missouri pro-Confederate] *Provisional Government, and home traitors, I felt the position bad and saw danger. In the night I decided upon the proclamation and the form of it. I wrote it the next morning and printed it the same day. I did it without consultation or advice with any one, acting solely with my best judgment to serve the country and yourself, and perfectly willing to receive the amount of censure which should be thought due if I had made a false movement. . . . If upon reflection your better judgment still decides that I am wrong in the article respecting the liberation of slaves, I have to ask that you will openly direct me to make the correction. . . . If I were to retract of my own accord, it would imply that I myself thought it wrong, and that I had acted without the reflection which the gravity of the point demanded. But I did not. I acted with full deliberation, and upon the certain conviction that it was a measure right and necessary, and I think so still.*[9]

That astonishing letter had been dated September 8, and so was another Lincoln received from The Pathfinder—one in which Frémont proposed military operations east and south of his department's boundary. Apart from the arrogance of the assumption that Lincoln was not going to sack him for having attempted to usurp powers that the President was not entirely sure *he* had, the general's effrontery led him to ask that his command be extended to include Indiana, Tennessee, and all of Kentucky.[10]

Neither the letters nor General Jessie's impassioned arguments moved Lincoln. She was equally ineffective the next day when she appealed to Francis P. Blair, Sr., to intervene on the general's behalf. "Madam," he told her, "I made your husband what he is, and I will unmake him."[11]

Concurrently, Lincoln was replying to the letter the Pathfinder's wife had delivered. "Your answer," he wrote Frémont, "expresses the preference on your part that I should make an open order for modification, which I very cheerfully do."[12]

2

SO *L'AFFAIRE FRÉMONT* STOOD IN MID-SEPTEMBER, and this was about as much as Major General Henry Halleck would have been able to learn about it from Eastern newspapers before his departure from San Francisco on October 10. Old Brains had taken John Charles Frémont's measure back in 1847 and subsequently, so he may have concluded that The Pathfinder's conduct had not changed materially over the years.

Even so, several shocks awaited General Halleck when he reported for duty in Washington on November 11, 1861. One was that about a week before, General Scott had requested retirement and received it, and that his successor as general-in-chief of the Union armies was George Brinton McClellan.[13] Another was that Frémont had been relieved of command of the Department of the West; Halleck was to replace him as soon as he could get to St. Louis.[14]

During their conference in Washington on November 11, General McClellan gave him a hint of the mess Frémont had left behind, and which Halleck was expected to clean up, in the orders he provided to the newcomer:

> *In assuming command of the Department of the Missouri, it is probably unnecessary for me to state that I have intrusted to you a duty which requires the utmost tact and decision. You have not merely the ordinary duties of a military commander to perform, but the far more difficult task of reducing chaos to order, of changing probably the majority of the personnel of the staff of the department, and of reducing to a point of economy, consistent with the interests and necessities of the State, a system of reckless expenditure and fraud, perhaps unheard of before in the history of the world.*
>
> *You will find in your department many general and staff officers holding illegal commissions and appointments not recognized or approved by the President or the Secretary of War. You will please at once inform these gentlemen of the nullity of their appointment, and see that no pay or allowances are issued to them until such time as commissions may be authorized by the President or Secretary of War.*
>
> *If any of them give the slightest trouble you will at once arrest them and send them, under guard, out of the limits of your department, informing them that if they return they will be placed in close confinement. You will please examine into the legality of the organization of the troops serving in the department. When you find any illegal, unusual, or improper organizations you will give to the officers and men an opportunity to enter the legal military establishment under general laws and orders from the War Department,*

reporting in full to these headquarters any officer or organization that may decline.

You will please cause competent and reliable staff officers to examine all existing contracts immediately, and suspend all payments upon them until you receive the report in each case. Where there is the slightest doubt as to the propriety of the contract, you will be good enough to refer the matter with full explanation to these headquarters, stating in each case what would be a fair compensation for the services or materials rendered under the contract. Discontinue at once the reception of material or services under any doubtful contract. Arrest and bring to prompt trial all officers who have in any way violated their duty to the Government. In regard to the political conduct of affairs you will please labor to impress upon the inhabitants of Missouri and the adjacent States that we are fighting solely for the integrity of the Union, to uphold the power of our National Government, and to restore to the nation the blessings of peace and good order.[15]

There was more—some vague instructions regarding military operations, an admonition to keep in touch. But such a detailed, to-the-point directive almost certainly could not have been written by McClellan, who had signed it.

The author was most likely Brigadier General Lorenzo Thomas, the army's adjutant-general, who had accompanied Secretary of War Simon Cameron on a trip to Missouri in order to investigate allegations of all sorts of wrongdoing by Frémont and his associates who operated out of the mansion on Choteau Avenue in St. Louis.

Among General Thomas' findings, as set forth in the report dated October 21, 1861, he gave President Lincoln:

- [General Samuel Curtis said that] *General F[rémont] never consulted him on military matters, nor informed him of his plans. . . . He deemed General Frémont unequal to the command of an army, and said that he was no more bound by the law than by the winds.*

- [At the Arsenal] *very few arms on hand; a number of heavy guns, designed for gunboats and mortar boats. Captain Callender said he heard that some person had a contract for making the carriages for these guns; that, if so, he knew nothing of it, and that it was entirely irregular, he being the proper officer to attend the case.*

• *Colonel Andrews, chief paymaster, represented irregularities in the Pay Department, stating that he was required to make payments and transfers of money contrary to law and regulations. Once, on objecting to what he conceived an improper payment, he was threatened with confinement by a file of soldiers.* [An] *abstract of payments was furnished, but not vouched for as reliable, to show the excess of officers of rank appointed to* [Frémont's] *body guard of 300 men; the whole number of irregular appointments was said to be nearly 200. . . . I saw an appointment given to an individual on General Frémont's staff as director of music, with the rank of captain of engineers. This person was a musician in a theater in St. Louis.*

• *Major Allen, principal quartermaster, reported great irregularities in his department. He was sending, under General Frémont's orders, large amounts of forage from St. Louis to the army at Tipton, where corn was abundant and very cheap. The distance was 160 miles. . . . It is the expressed belief that General Frémont has around him in his staff persons directly and indirectly concerned in furnishing supplies. . . . Captain Edward M. Davis, a member of his staff, received a contract by the direct order of General Frémont for blankets. They were examined by a board of army officers. The blankets were found to be made of cotton and to be rotten and worthless. Notwithstanding this decision they were purchased, and given to the sick and wounded soldiers in hospitals. . . . Amongst the supplies sent by General Frémont to the army now in the field may be enumerated 500 half-barrels, to carry water in a country of abundant supply, and 500 tons of ice.*

• *One week after the receipt of the President's order modifying General Frémont's proclamation, General Frémont by note to Captain McKeever required him to have 200 copies of the original proclamation printed and sent to Ironton for distribution throughout the country.*

• *At Tipton I saw General Hunter, second in command. He stated that there was great confusion, and that Frémont was utterly incompetent. . . .* [Hunter] *had just received a report from one of* *his colonels that but 20 out of 100 of his guns would go off. These were guns procured by General Frémont in Europe. . . . In conversation with Colonel Swords, just from California, he stated that Mr. Selover, who was in Europe with General Frémont, wrote to some friend in San Francisco that his share of the profit of the purchase of these arms was $30,000. . . . General Hunter stated that, though second in command, he was never consulted by General Frémont and knew nothing whatever of his intentions. . . . I have also been informed that there is not a Missourian on [Frémont's] staff, not a man acquainted personally with the topography and physical characteristics of the country or its people.*

- *The opinion entertained by gentlemen who have approached and observed [Frémont] is that he is more fond of pomp than of the stern realities of war; that his mind is incapable of fixed attention or strong concentration; that by his mismanagement of affairs the State has almost been lost, and that if he is continued in command, the worst results may be anticipated. This is the concurrent testimony of a very large number of the most intelligent men in Missouri.*[16]

Both the orders Halleck was given and General Thomas' report were lengthy, but he had plenty of time to study the documents on his long train ride westward to St. Louis. Certainly, they were specific enough to give him a perfectly clear idea of what Washington expected of him.

Curiously, Henry Halleck had already adopted the habit of asking persons who came to consult him, "Have you any business with me?"[17] A less-brusque way of putting it might have been, *What do you* want *of me?* for he had performed most effectively when he understood the callers' needs well enough to employ his talents, skills, and experience on their behalf.

Under both Richard Mason and Bennett Riley at Monterey he had known precisely what was expected of him. Much of that work had involved legal matters, and it was natural for him to have wanted to know what clients required of him when he began his law practice. George McClellan had been general-in-chief for only a week—hardly long enough for him to learn what *he* ought to do, much less how he should instruct Halleck regarding a situation about which McClellan was as ignorant as the newcomer. Fortunately, wise "Old Army" veteran Lorenzo Thomas had given Halleck what amounted to a checklist of very specific things to do.

Major General Halleck assumed command of the re-named Department of the Missouri—such districts were now being named for rivers—which included Missouri, Iowa, Minnesota, Wisconsin, Illinois, Arkansas, and Kentucky west of the Cumberland River—on November 19, 1861.[18] On the next day he issued General Orders No. 3—three sentences that would bring scathing condemnation upon him then and afterward:

> It has been represented that important information respecting the numbers and condition of our forces is conveyed to the enemy by means of fugitive slaves who are admitted within our lines. In order to remedy this evil, it is directed that no such persons be hereafter permitted to enter the lines of any camp or of any forces on the march, and that any now within such lines be immediately excluded therefrom.

So Halleck began. But as if he were anticipating that Frémont's supporters, Radical Republicans, and abolitionists all over the North would be infuriated, he added a sentence to make it clear that he was not aiming the order *only* at fugitive slaves:

> The general commanding wishes to impress upon all officers in command of posts and troops in the field the importance of preventing unauthorized persons of every description *from entering and leaving our lines, and of observing the greatest precaution in the employment of agents and clerks in confidential positions.*[19]

So intense and unfounded was the criticism Old Brains received that eventually he offered this correction:

> The object of this order is to prevent any person in the army from acting in the capacity of a negro catcher or negro stealer. The relation between a slave and his master, or pretended master, is not a matter to be determined by the military officers. . . . One object in keeping fugitive slaves out of our camp is to keep clear of all such questions. . . . The prohibition to admit them within our lines does not prevent the exercise of all proper offices of humanity, in giving them food and clothing outside, when such offices are necessary to prevent suffering.[20]

Having ignited a firestorm of anger and vituperation on the part of those who still cried for Abraham Lincoln's scalp—for the sins of stripping The Pathfinder's August 30 proclamation of its abolition and unlawful confiscation provisions, and also, later, for relieving him of command—Halleck gave further offense to his shrill detractors by launching vigorously into the tasks of stopping practices that had disgraced Frémont and the Union cause in Missouri, and then of trying to repair the damage.

"One week's experience," Halleck wrote General-in-Chief McClellan in a message dated November 28, 1861, "is sufficient to prove that everything here is in complete chaos. The most astonishing orders and contracts for supplies of all kinds have been made and large amounts purport to have been received, but there is nothing to show that they have ever been properly issued, and they cannot now be found."[21]

Halleck had detailed two brigadier generals to investigate the combat readiness of the troops west of St. Louis. "I have no officers to send to other points in the department," he told McClellan. Since most of the staff officers he had inherited had been "charged with being involved in the existing disorders," he asked for a few "regular officers of experience and worthy of confidence"[22]

On the day before, General Halleck had sent the general-in-chief a flash report:

> *Affairs here in complete chaos. Troops unpaid, without clothing or arms. Many never properly mustered into the service and some utterly demoralized. Hospitals overflowing with sick. One division of 7,500 has over 2,000 on sick list. . . .* [Confederates led by] *Price and McCulloch said to be moving north. . . . Have sent out strong reconnoitering parties. . . . Telegraph wires all work well, and I am in hourly communication with headquarters of divisions. All troops ordered to be in readiness to move. Price's forces estimated at from 15,000 to 23,000.*[23]

In another message to his superior that day, Halleck had said, "I am satisfied that the enemy is operating in and against this State with a much larger force than was supposed when I left Washington."[24] He might have said that *everything* was more chaotic than even Lorenzo Thomas' most appalling warnings had led him to expect.

3

MESSAGES SENT BY GENERAL HALLECK showed that he had no difficulty in moving directly into the duties of a general commanding a large military district, although he had never been directly in charge of anything but a law firm. From the start, he used the telegraph effectively. For example, Colonel Frederick Steele sent Halleck this message on November 23, four days after Old Brains assumed command:

> *I have what is deemed reliable information that Price is marching north with a large army at the rate of 30 miles a day. Force estimated at from 33,000 to 50,000. He will cross the Osage to-day at Huffman's Ferry. It is said that he is marching for this place* [Sedalia]. *The lines are down between this and Syracuse.*[25]

Five sentences; Halleck answered in one: "Make armed reconnaissances in sufficient force in the direction of the enemy's movement and keep me informed."[26] But if the major general commanding was slightly more verbose in replying to another wire from Steele on November 26, he was no less direct:

> *No orders have been given to fall back, nor is there any intention to do so. The only movement contemplated is an advance. I fully approve your views.*[27]

What commanders in the field such as Steele, Samuel Curtis, John Pope, and Samuel Sturgis wanted of Halleck were decisions and directions. Those, they got—usually in the terse manner of, and reflecting the will expressed in, his early messages to Steele.

Obliged as he was to operate from maps, and confined to St. Louis by the need to correct John Frémont's errors and lapses, the general commanding made no major changes in the dispositions of his divisions. But he wanted to know more about conditions in the field than he could learn *via* the telegraph. To gain information he turned to his old friend from the *Lexington* voyage and early California years, William Tecumseh Sherman.

Cump had found it difficult to get into the war, even with the influence of his well-connected foster father, Thomas Ewing, and his brother John, a United States Senator from Ohio. When offered the chief

clerkship in the War Department—by Postmaster General Montgomery
Blair, not Secretary of War Simon Cameron—he turned it down. But not
long afterward he was commissioned a colonel and placed in command of a
regiment, and he led a brigade in the battle of Bull Run (Manassas). By
October, Cump was a brigadier general commanding the Department of the
Cumberland, which included Kentucky. He was serving in that capacity
when Secretary Cameron and Adjutant General Lorenzo Thomas paused in
Louisville on their way back to Washington from the investigations they had
made of The Pathfinder's mismanagement in St. Louis.[28]

According to General Sherman's account: Cameron, Thomas, and
about six other men held a conference of sorts in Cump's room at the Galt
House. "I said I preferred not to discuss business with so many strangers
present," Sherman wrote in his *Memoirs.* "[Secretary Cameron] said, 'They
are all friends, all members of my family, and you may speak your mind
freely and without restraint.' " Cump did, describing a military situation he
considered extremely dangerous and pointing out that his 18,000 troops
were vastly outnumbered.[29] "On being asked the question what [Union]
force he deemed necessary," General Thomas wrote in his report,
"[Sherman] promptly replied 200,000 men. . . . The Secretary thought
General Sherman overestimated the number and power of rebel forces."[30]
Among Cameron's "family" was at least one reporter who concluded that
Sherman was insane, and then so described him to readers throughout the
North.[31]

"I know not whether it is insanity or not," declared a *Chicago Tribune*
writer, "but the General . . . indulged in remarks that made his loyalty
doubtful. He even spoke despondingly; said the rebels could never be
whipped; talked of a thirty years' war."[32] Indeed, Sherman had been tired
and discouraged. Even before the press' attacks he had requested a transfer.[33]
It came on November 13, two days after Henry Halleck had been ordered
to St. Louis: "Brig. Gen. W. T. Sherman, on being relieved from his present
command by Brig. Gen. D. C. Buell, will repair to Saint Louis, Mo., and
report to Maj. Gen. H. W. Halleck, for duty in the Department of the
Missouri."[34]

"Repair" was an apt choice of words, for on November 23 Old Brains
provided Cump with an assignment that was of genuine importance as well
as potentially therapeutic:

> *Brig. Gen. W. T. Sherman, having reported for duty in this depart-*
> *ment, will proceed at once to visit the different stations of the troops*
> *in this department, and will report* [among other matters]

*generally all things considered to give the commanding general an
idea of their real condition for service. He will also report upon the
routes of rivers or railway upon which these troops depend for their
supplies or transportation, and such other matters as may seem to
him proper to be communicated.*[35]

About a week later Brigadier Generals George W. Cullum and
Schuyler Hamilton joined General Halleck's staff. Both were graduates of
West Point, and both had been serving on Winfield Scott's staff in
Washington until his recent retirement as general-in-chief. As noted earlier,
Hamilton, Old Brains' brother-in-law, had been his roommate at West
Point and an executive at the New Almaden Mine in California. Cullum, an
engineer, was appointed chief of staff. Captain John C. Kelton was named
assistant adjutant general; he would remain on General Halleck's staff until
the end of the war.[36]

George McClellan had been prompt in sending Old Fuss and
Feathers' aides out to Halleck, but he did not respond to a message from
Old Brains dated November 20: "No written authority is found here to
declare and enforce martial law in this department. Please send me such
authority and telegraph me that it has been sent by mail."[37] Assuming
apparently (and correctly) that the general Northern newspapers had hailed
as "The Young Napoleon" was so preoccupied with his Army of the
Potomac that he had no attention to give to such messages, on November
25 Halleck sought help from Lorenzo Thomas:

*The commissioners appointed by the President have requested me to
bring before them certain persons and papers stated in sworn
affidavits to be necessary for them to prosecute their investigations
into certain alleged frauds. There are no civil authorities here to do
this. On their application I sent the telegram* [to McClellan].

*From a full investigation of this question I am satisfied that
the President has the power to confer this authority, and I feel unwilling to act, as requested by the commission and as the public good
seems to require, without it. It certainly is not right to leave a public
officer in a position where his duty requires him to exercise an
authority which his superior can, but is unwilling to, confer upon
him.*[38]

On the next day Old Brains tried again to get an answer. To McClellan
he wired: "If this authority be refused I shall not exercise it, no matter how

much the public service may suffer."[39] And on November 30 he put his case to the general-in-chief in the strongest possible terms:

> *There can be no doubt that the enemy is moving north with a large force, and that a considerable part of Northern Missouri is in a state of insurrection. The rebels have organized in many counties, taken Union men prisoners, and are robbing them of horses, wagons, provisions, clothing, &c. . . .*
>
> *To punish these outrages and to arrest the traitors who are organizing these forces and furnishing supplies, it is necessary to use the military power and enforce martial law. I cannot arrest such men and seize their papers without exercising martial law, for there is no civil law or civil authority to reach them.*
>
> *The safety of Missouri requires the prompt and immediate exercise of this power, and if the President is not willing to intrust me with it he should relieve me from the command. [This power] is and has been for months exercised here by my predecessors, but I cannot find any written authority from the President for doing so.*[40]

Lawyer Lincoln finally responded to lawyer Halleck's carefully structured brief by granting the desired authority on December 2, 1861, twelve days after Old Brains had asked McClellan to obtain it for him.[41]

General Halleck's difficulty in provoking officials in Washington into supporting his department persisted. On January 16, 1862, from Rolla, Brigadier General Samuel Curtis sent the general commanding a message in which he complained that his troops had not been paid in quite some time. Halleck replied the next day: "I regret to inform you that neither the Pay nor Quartermaster's Department have any money. . . . The truth is that Congress is so busy discussing the eternal [slavery] question that they fail to make any appropriations, and the financial departments are dead broke. No requisitions for money are filled." And in closing he added, "At present we have more difficulties to conquer with our own men than with the enemy."[42]

4

AT FIRST, CUMP SHERMAN'S PERFORMANCE had been no worse than disappointing. Hardly had he reached Sedalia on November 26 than he was telegraphing Halleck:

Look well to Jefferson City and the North Missouri Railroad. Price aims at both. He is gathering large numbers of recruits and is driving out all Union men as he comes north. I think McCulloch will threaten Rolla, whilst Price crosses the Osage, by large numbers of detachments, to assemble at some agreed point.[43]

Sherman sent another message similar in text and tone that day, another on the next, in which he told Halleck: "I have ordered forward the whole force from Lexington." Back shot the department commander immediately: "No forward movement of troops will be made. Only strong reconnoitering parties will be sent in the supposed direction of the enemy, the remainder of the troops being held in position till more reliable information is obtained."[44]

The text of Cump's next wire on the next day (November 28) suggested that he had missed a message. "I have ordered forward Pope's and Turner's divisions to-day," he reported from Sedalia, "but we cannot long stay here. The cold is intense on this naked prairie. We must move forward or back. Will you indicate your wishes?"[45]

Schuyler Hamilton replied: "General Halleck is satisfied, from reports of scouts received here, that no immediate attack on Sedalia is intended. You will therefore return to this city and report your observations on the condition of the troops you have examined."[46]

From Syracuse and John Pope soon came another telegram: "General Sherman ordered division from Tipton to this place, and both divisions were on the march to Sedalia when your dispatch arrived. Do I understand that I am in command of all forces west of Jefferson City and expected to post them for comfort and convenience at my discretion?"[47]

General Halleck answered Pope: "General Sherman has been directed to return to this city. I see no necessity for any movements of troops. I wish them left as they were and made as comfortable as possible."[48] Later on November 28 Halleck added: "If you deem movements necessary telegraph me, and I will order them."[49]

There were more reasons for Sherman's recall to St. Louis than what Halleck deemed his too-hasty initiatives and apparent failure to remember what his mission was. The press had continued to spread assurances that Cump was insane throughout the North. Angry and alarmed, Sherman's wife had arrived in St. Louis wanting to see him. Halleck sent Cump home with her, to Lancaster, Ohio, in the hope that a twenty-day leave in the midst of his loved ones would enable him to rest and recover his strength.[50]

General Halleck's compassion had mixed results—for him as well as for his old friend. His handling of the case was interpreted by the press (and, later, by anti-Halleck historians) as a hypocritical attempt to remove Sherman from his command lest his own reputation be in any way besmirched. Earlier, Halleck had drawn the fire of abolitionist newspapers by proclaiming camps within his jurisdiction off-limits to fugitive slaves. He had not been in St. Louis long enough to give Radical Republicans more cause to despise and revile him, but his being associated with "crazy" Sherman called their attention back to him.

For Cump, being taken home by his wife was something of a humiliation, one the newspapers took as confirmation that he had lost his mind. On December 11, 1861, the *Cincinnati Commercial* ran this item:

> ### GENERAL WILLIAM T. SHERMAN INSANE
> *The painful intelligence reaches us, in such form that we are not at liberty to disclose it, that General William T. Sherman, late commander of the Department of the Cumberland, is insane. It appears that he was at the time while commanding in Kentucky, stark mad. . . . When relieved of the command in Kentucky he was sent to Missouri and placed at the head of a brigade at Sedalia, when the shocking fact that he was a madman was developed by orders that his subordinates knew to be preposterous and refused to obey. He has, of course, been relieved altogether from command. The harsh criticisms that have now been lavished on this gentleman, provoked by his strange conduct, will now give way to feelings of deepest sympathy for him in his great calamity. It seems providential that the country has not to mourn the loss of an army through* [Sherman's] *loss of mind.*[51]

In war, someone once said, Truth is the first casualty.

Nothing in the *Cincinnati Commercial*'s mixture of horror and the shedding of crocodile tears was true. Understandably, it added to the weight of the press' previous gratuitous attempts to destroy Sherman. At a minimum, it almost persuaded him that the rabid jackals snapping at him were right. In a pathetic effort to find some alternative to that concession, on the day after the *Cincinnati Commercial* had consigned him to the asylum, he wrote Old Brains:

> *I believe you will be frank enough to answer me if you deem the steps I took at Sedalia as evidence of a want of mind.*

They may have been the result of an excess of caution on my part. . . . I set a much higher measure of danger on the acts of unfriendly inhabitants than most officers do because I have lived in Missouri and the South, and know that in their individual characters they will do more acts of hostility than Northern farmers or people could bring themselves to perpetrate. . . .

I write to you because a Cincinnati newspaper, whose reporter I imprisoned in Louisville for visiting one of my camps after I had forbidden him leave to go, has announced that I am insane, and alleges as a reason that at Sedalia my acts were so mad that subordinate officers refused to obey. I know of no order I gave that was not obeyed, except General Pope's, to advance his division to Sedalia, which order was countermanded by you, and the fact communicated to me.

These newspapers have us in their power, and can destroy us as they please, and this one can destroy my usefulness by depriving me of the confidence of officers and men.

I will be in Saint Louis next week, and will be guided by your commands and judgment.[52]

General Halleck replied on December 18:

The newspaper attacks are certainly shameless and scandalous, but I cannot agree with you, that they have us in their power "to destroy us as they please." I certainly get my share of abuse, but it will not disturb me.

Your movement of troops was not countermanded by me because I thought it an unwise one in itself, but because I was not then ready for it. I had better information of Price's movements than you had, and I had no apprehension of attack. I intended to concentrate the forces on that line, but I wished the movement delayed until I could determine upon a better position.

After receiving Lieutenant-Colonel [James B.] McPherson's report, I made precisely the location you had ordered. . . . As you could not know my plans, you and others may have misconstrued the reason of my countermanding your orders. . . .

I hope to see you well enough for duty soon. Our organization goes on slowly, but we will effect it in time.[53]

On December 23, 1861, General Halleck put Cump in charge of

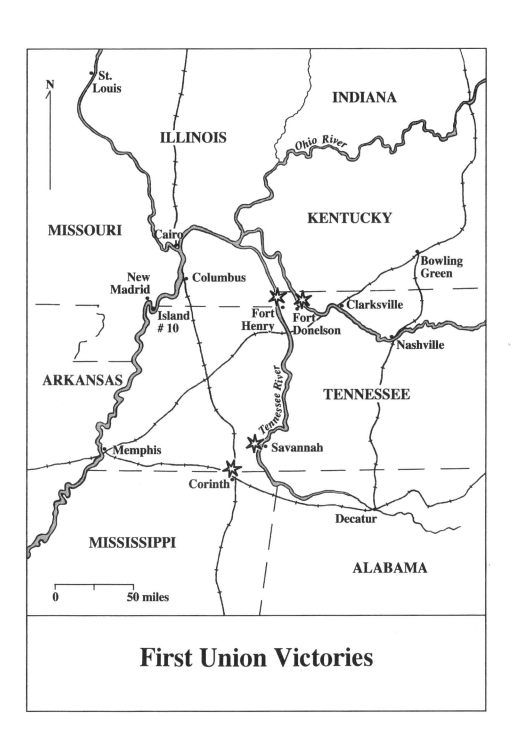

First Union Victories

Benton Barracks, near St. Louis.[54] This kind of position was ideal for him at the time; from troop training duties, at which he excelled, he gradually regained his confidence. His family continued to fret over him, but Old Brains treated him as though nothing had happened; to some that seemed callous, but what Sherman needed most of all was respect—and how General Halleck gave it was something Cump remembered years afterward:[55]

> [One night in late December, I was sitting in Halleck's] *room, on the second floor of the Planters' House, with him and General Cullum, his chief of staff, talking of things generally, and the subject then was of the much-talked-of 'advance,' as soon as the season would permit. . . . General Halleck had a map on his table, with a large pencil in his hand, and asked, "Where is the rebel line?"*
>
> *Cullum drew the pencil through Bowling Green, Forts Donelson and Henry, and Columbus, Kentucky. "That is their line," said Halleck. "Now, where is the proper place to break it?" And either Cullum or I said, "Naturally, the centre." Halleck drew a line perpendicular to the other, near its middle, and it coincided nearly with the course of the Tennessee River; and he said, "That is the true line of operations."*[56]

5

LATER IT WOULD SEEM THAT EVERYONE—including a lady named Anna Ella Carroll—had advocated the strategy Henry Wager Halleck adopted that night in December 1861 in his room at the Planters' Hotel.[57] Indeed, perhaps a month earlier Brigadier General Don Carlos Buell had suggested just such a plan in a message to General-in-Chief George McClellan dated November 27:

> *And now a plan of campaign. . . . First, to establish a sufficient force before Bowling Green to hold* [Confederate Brigadier General Simon Bolivar] *Buckner there, while a column moves into East Tennessee. . . . In conjunction with either of these should be the movement of two flotilla columns up the Tennessee and Cumberland* [Rivers], *so as at least to land and unite near the* [Kentucky-Tennessee] *State line, and cut off communication between Bowling Green and Columbus, and perhaps run directly into Nashville. . . .*

For the water movements means are necessary which I have not the
control of, that is, gunboats and transports. The troops which you
promise from Missouri could be used for the purpose, and ought to
move at my signal.[58]

Put differently: General Buell may well have considered the days-old
change of command in St. Louis an opportunity to persuade the Young
Napoleon, still a newcomer to the position of general-in-chief and nigh-
totally immersed in the task of increasing his Army of the Potomac's
strength, to move Buell's department's boundary westward at Halleck's
expense—*before* Old Brains could turn his attention away from the chaos he
had inherited from Frémont and toward the weakest portion of the
Confederates' "line."

Actually, back on November 7, McClellan had directed Buell to
"throw the mass of your forces by rapid marches, by Cumberland Gap or
Walker's Gap, on Knoxville, in order to occupy the railroad at that point,
and thus enable the loyal citizens of Eastern Tennessee to rise. . . ."[59] Cutting
the rebels' railroad between the Mississippi and tidewater Virginia would
benefit McClellan, who was under pressure to take his huge army "On to
Richmond." East Tennessee was of great importance to Lincoln because so
many of the region's people were pro-Union, and Radical Republicans in
Congress and elsewhere wanted them liberated from alleged Confederate
mistreatment.

Curiously, General Buell seemed to assign relatively low priorities to a
Knoxville campaign. Kentucky geography undoubtedly had much to do
with his reluctance, for the countryside between Louisville and Knoxville
was about as devoid of the characteristics favorable to Union military
operations as the mountains of the moon—especially in winter. But General
Buell shared his vision regarding the use of the Tennessee and Cumberland
as routes southward into the rebel heartland *only* with his close friend
McClellan. And at the time, the Young Napoleon had reasons of his own
that precluded him from passing Buell's suggestion on to Old Brains.

Radical Republicans in Congress, in particular, seemed determined to
banish the Young Napoleon from the Union high command. They held him
responsible for the embarrassing defeat of Brigadier General Charles P.
Stone's troops at Ball's Bluff on the Potomac back in October, the battle in
which Senator Edward D. Baker of Oregon had been killed. As a means of
channeling into action their fury over that whipping and the one at Bull
Run, together with their frustration over Lincoln's being beyond their reach,
they formed the Joint Congressional Committee on the Conduct of the

War, which called McClellan as its first witness. Recurrence of typhoid fever enabled the general-in-chief to postpone his appearance, whereupon the committee began interrogating his subordinates in the hope of building the case for his removal.[60]

General Halleck's instructions had been highly detailed regarding the task of repairing the damage The Pathfinder had done but vague regarding military goals. An obvious one was clearing Missouri of the Confederates led by Major General Sterling Price. To his credit, Frémont had placed forces at Cairo, Illinois, from which they might be employed in the western Kentucky portion of the department or in operations aimed at regaining control of the Mississippi. Of necessity, during his first few weeks in St. Louis, Old Brains had given almost all the attention available for military operations to meeting the challenges presented by Price's army and rebel sympathizers in northern Missouri. But at the close of a report to McClellan on December 26, 1861, Halleck included this uncommonly interesting sentence: "If I receive arms in time to carry out my present plans in Missouri I think I shall be able to strongly re-enforce Cairo and Paducah for ulterior operations by the early part of February."[61]

Hindsight suggested that "ulterior operations" meant the advance up the Tennessee and Cumberland rivers that Halleck, Cullum, and Sherman had considered that night in Old Brains' hotel room. Earlier, however, there had been several actions by McClellan and Buell indicating that they were moving toward the kind of riverborne assaults to seize Forts Donelson and Henry that Buell had proposed to the Young Napoleon on November 27.

On December 5, McClellan told Buell: "Give me at once in detail your views as to the number and amount of gunboats necessary for the water movement, the necessary land forces, &c. Would not [Brigadier General] C. F. Smith be a good man to command that part of the expedition? When would they move?" But later in the telegram McClellan recalled Buell's attention to his main mission: "Let me again urge the necessity of sending something into East Tennessee as soon as possible."[62] Also, on December 6, from Cairo Commodore Andrew H. Foote reported to Halleck: "Telegraphed to General McClellan that there are twelve gunboats, of which three are in commission and nine in the contractors' hands. . . ."[63]

"I assure you I will pursue your views [regarding East Tennessee's importance] with as much zeal and hopefulness, and perhaps more energy, than if I entirely concurred in them," Don Carlos Buell wrote McClellan on December 10. But again he turned to a familiar subject:

*And now for the other side of the field. I feel more anxiety about it
than any other, because I have less control over the means that ought
to bear on it, and have less knowledge of their details* [than] *if I had
the control. . . . The precise manner of conducting the expeditions
depends so much on local knowledge that I can hardly venture on its
details, but at least the expedition should go as rapidly as possible to
the nearest point to where the road crosses the peninsula; that is, to
Dover* [Fort Donelson] *and Fort Henry.*[64]

Along the way, Buell had replied to McClellan's query regarding C. F.
Smith as a possible leader of the proposed expedition by saying that he did
not share the high regard for him that others seemed to have. Even so, Buell
did not hesitate to ask the veteran soldier—a subordinate of Brigadier General U. S. Grant under General Halleck's command—for troop strengths
and other information. From those reports, Buell concluded that the
Confederates might build their number of men at Bowling Green to fifty
thousand or sixty thousand. "It is my conviction," he wrote the bed-ridden
general-in-chief on December 29, "that all the force that can possibly be
collected should be brought to bear on that front of which Columbus and
Bowling Green may be said to be the flanks. The center, that is, the
Cumberland and Tennessee where the railroad crosses them, is now the
[rebels'] most vulnerable point. I regard it as the most important strategical
point in the whole field of operations."[65]

6

ON LEARNING OF GENERAL HALLECK'S ASSIGNMENT to St. Louis, Confederate President Jefferson Davis wrote to a member of the new country's
Congress: "The Federal forces are not hereafter, as heretofore, to be
commanded by path-finders and holiday soldiers, but by men of military
education and experience in war. The contest is therefore to be on a scale of
very different proportions than that of the partisan warfare witnessed during
the past summer and fall."[66]

By contrast, Davis' opposite number in Washington did not seem to
know what kind of warfare, if any, his feverish general-in-chief intended to
wage. Exasperated, on the last day of 1861 Abraham Lincoln sent similar
messages to the men of military education and experience commanding at
St. Louis and Louisville. General Halleck read: "General McClellan is sick.
Are General Buell and yourself in concert? When he moves on Bowling

Green, what hinders it being re-enforced from Columbus? A simultaneous movement by you on Columbus might prevent it."[67]

Old Brains replied:

> *I have never received a word from General Buell. I am not ready to co-operate with him. Hope to do so in a few weeks. Have written fully on this subject to Major-General McClellan. Too much haste will ruin everything.*[68]

And General Buell admitted:

> *There is no arrangement between General Halleck and myself. I have been informed by General McClellan that he would make suitable disposition for concerted action. There is nothing to prevent Bowling Green from being re-inforced from Columbus if a military force is not brought to bear on the latter place.*[69]

Acting General-in-Chief Lincoln directed both generals to communicate with each other. On January 2, 1862, Old Brains wired Buell:

> *I have had no instructions respecting co-operation. All my available troops are in the field except those at Cairo and Paducah, which are barely sufficient to threaten Columbus, &c. A few weeks hence I hope to be able to render you very material assistance, but now a withdrawal of my troops from this State is almost impossible. Write me fully.*[70]

General McClellan was too ill to be interrogated by Ohio Senator Benjamin F. Wade's Committee on the Conduct of the War, but on January 3 he bestirred himself enough to make his contribution to the war effort out west. To Halleck he wrote:

> *It is of the greatest importance that the rebel troops in Western Kentucky* [Columbus] *be prevented from moving to support of the force in front of General Buell* [at Bowling Green]. *To accomplish this an expedition should be sent up the Cumberland River, to act in concert with General Buell's command. . . . It may be well also to make a feint on the Tennessee River, with a command sufficient to prevent disaster under any circumstances.*[71]

Halleck responded to the commander-in-chief's concerns on January 6. His letter was long but unusually rich in information—much of which he had furnished the Young Napoleon earlier. From it, Lincoln was able not only to grasp the situation but to appraise the quality of Henry Halleck's thinking and generalship:

> *In reply to your excellency's letter of the 1st instant, I have to state that on receiving your telegram I immediately communicated with General Buell and have since sent him all the information I could obtain of the enemy's movements about Columbus and Camp Beauregard.*
>
> *No considerable force has been sent from those places to Bowling Green. They have about 22,000 men at Columbus, and the place is strongly fortified. I have at Cairo, Fort Holt, and Paducah only about 15,000, which, after leaving guards at these places, would give me but little over 10,000 men with which to assist General Buell. It would be madness to attempt anything serious with such a force, and I cannot at the present time withdraw any from Missouri without risking the loss of this State. . . .*
>
> *I am satisfied that the authorities at Washington do not appreciate the difficulties with which we have to contend here. The operations of Lane, Jennison, and others have so enraged the people of Missouri, that it is estimated that there is a majority of 80,000 against the Government. We are virtually in an enemy's country. Price and others have a considerable army in the Southwest, against which I am operating with all my available force.*
>
> *[St. Louis] and most of the middle and northern counties are insurrectionary—burning bridges, destroying telegraph lines, &c.— and can be kept down only by the presence of troops. A large portion of the foreign troops organized by General Frémont are unreliable; indeed, many of them are already mutinous.*
>
> *They have been tampered with by politicians, and made to believe that if they get up a mutiny and demand Frémont's return the Government will be forced to restore him to duty here. It is believed that some high officers are in the plot. I have already been obliged to disarm several of these organizations and I am daily expecting more serious outbreaks.*
>
> *Another grave difficulty is the want of proper general officers to command the troops and enforce order and discipline, and especially to protect public property from robbery and plunder. Some*

of the brigadier-generals assigned to this department are entirely ignorant of their duties and unfit for any command.

I assure you, Mr. President, it is very difficult to accomplish much with such means. I am in the condition of a carpenter who is required to build a bridge with a dull ax, a broken saw, and rotten timber. It is true that I have some very good green timber, which will answer the purpose as soon as I can get it into shape and season it a little.

I know nothing of General Buell's intended operations, never having received any information in regard to the general plan of campaign. If it be intended that his column shall move on Bowling Green while another moves from Cairo or Paducah on Columbus or Camp Beauregard, it will be a repetition of the same strategic error which produced the disaster of Bull Run. To operate on exterior lines against an enemy occupying a central position will fail, as it always has failed, in ninety-nine cases out of a hundred. It is condemned by every military authority I have ever read.

General Buell's army and the forces at Paducah occupy precisely the same position in relation to each other and to the enemy as did the armies of McDowell and Patterson before the battle of Bull Run.

On January 10, 1862, when the President had read this letter, he added this note:

The within is a copy of a letter just received from General Halleck. It is exceedingly discouraging. As everywhere else, nothing can be done.[72]

In fact, however, Old Brains *was* doing something. On the same day he wrote Lincoln (the acting general-in-chief) he sent this order to Brigadier General Grant at Cairo:

I wish you to make a demonstration. . . . Let it be understood that Dover [Fort Donelson on the Cumberland] *is the object of your attack. But do not advance far enough to expose your flank and rear to attack from Columbus, and by all means avoid a serious engagement.*

Make a great fuss about moving all your forces towards Nashville, and let it be so reported by the newspapers.

*Take proper precaution to deceive your own men as well as the
enemy. Let no one, not even a member of your own staff, know the
real object. I will send you some forces to increase the deception. Let
it be understood that 20,000 or 30,000 men are expected from
Missouri. . . . The object is to prevent re-enforcements from being
sent to* [Bowling Green]. *Having accomplished this, you will slowly
retire to your former positions, but, if possible, keep up the idea of a
general advance.*

*Be very careful, however, to avoid a battle; we are not ready
for that; but cut off detached parties and give your men a little
experience in skirmishing.*[73]

7

ULYSSES GRANT MUST HAVE BEEN AMUSED by all the urgings and admonitions his one-time instructor at West Point had pressed upon him.
Possibly, General Halleck had forgotten an incident that had occurred
before he reached Washington back in early November 1861: Grant carried
out a raid at Belmont, Missouri, not far down the Mississippi from Cairo
and directly across the river from Columbus, Kentucky.

Years afterward, Grant had this to say about Belmont in his *Memoirs:*

*I gathered up all the troops at Cairo and Fort Holt, except suitable
guards, and moved them down the river on steamers convoyed by
two gunboats, accompanying them myself. . . . I had no orders
which contemplated an attack by the National troops, nor did I
intend anything of the kind when I started out from Cairo; but after
we started I saw that the officers and men were elated at the prospect
of at last having the opportunity to do what they had volunteered to
do—fight the enemies of their country.*[74]

Once ashore a few miles above Belmont, Grant's eager skirmishers
pushed the Confederates back into their camp and then down under the
bluff at the river's edge. While the Union troops paused for some looting,
rebel guns on the east bank opened fire. Lest the enemy under the bluff
move north and block the return to the transports, Grant ordered a withdrawal. "I announced that we had cut our way in," he wrote long afterward,
"and could cut our way out just as well." He was the last to reboard, riding
his horse up the gangplank.[75]

Since then, General Halleck's attention had been drawn to south-western Missouri and kept there. But with the new year had come the pressure from Washington to provide a demonstration to prevent the rebels from shifting troops from Columbus to Bowling Green, and Brigadier General Grant was in the right place to execute that mission.

"The weather was very bad," he recalled. "Snow and rain fell; the roads, never good in that section, were intolerable. We were out more than a week splashing through the mud, snow, and rain, the men suffering very much. [But the] object of the expedition was accomplished."[76]

Brigadier General C. F. Smith, who had been commandant of cadets while Grant was at West Point, had led the forces that had gone up the Tennessee as far as Fort Henry.[77] On his return he told Grant that he thought the place could be taken. "This report of Smith's confirmed views I had previously held," Grant wrote, "that the true line of operations was up the Tennessee and Cumberland Rivers." Obtaining leave to go to St. Louis, Grant meant to lay his plan for such a campaign before Halleck. "[But] I was received with so little cordiality that I perhaps stated the object of my visit with less clearness than I might have done, and I had not uttered many sentences before I was cut short as if my plan was preposterous. I returned to Cairo very much crestfallen."[78]

Of course, General Grant's proposal had been made well after Old Brains' session in his hotel room with Cullum and Sherman, and the department commander may have been venting his displeasure over Don Carlos Buell's awkward, recently uncovered attempt to encroach upon his turf. In any case, the direct resumption of the Halleck-Grant relationship was hardly auspicious.

Earlier, Brigadier General John Pope had been offended by his superior's curt rejection of his suggestions, and he had so stated in messages. Halleck had been equally abrupt in replying to Pope:

> *Your plans of campaign may be well adapted to the positions and numbers of the enemy as reported to you, but, judging from the information I am hourly receiving from other parts of the state, I do not think I would be justified in adopting them, nor do I think you would have proposed them if you had been fully advised on the subject. . . .*
>
> *General, your letters indicate a decided spirit of fault-finding and of a desire to place yourself in a position by various and conflicting suggestions to be able to say, in case of any disaster, that*

you advised differently. I am willing to believe, however, that such was not your intention.[79]

After a week and another letter from Pope, however, Halleck's next response was somewhat less abrasive: "I shall always be happy to receive suggestions as to operations and dispositions of any kind, but to criticize them after they have been ordered does not accord with my ideas of military discipline and subordination. . . . You are under a misapprehension as to my want of confidence in you. My assigning you to the largest command and the most important position in this State should be sufficient proof of the contrary."[80]

And in closing, General Halleck tried even harder to explain the facts of life as he understood them:

> *I have no desire, general, to prolong this correspondence, nor do I intend to resume it. I have thus far given to you the fullest confidence, and will do to you, and every other officer in my command, full and entire justice.*
>
> *At the same time I do not intend that you shall misunderstand my own position. I am acting under orders from my superiors, which I intend to obey, but which I am not at liberty to communicate to others.*
>
> *I hope, therefore, you will extend to me that charity and consideration which I extend to those placed over me. I am not always at liberty to adopt the suggestions of others even though I may approve them. Other circumstances, not known to the party making the suggestions, may and often do, prevent their adoption. Nevertheless, I shall always be happy to receive them and will give them due consideration.*[81]

Surely, General Grant would have returned to Cairo less crestfallen had Old Brains said something to that effect to him. But it was not in Henry Halleck's nature, apparently, to give much thought to the impression he was making on those with whom he was obliged to deal. As his explanation to John Pope implied, he was interested in being obeyed, not liked—just as, back in San Francisco, he seemed to have craved respect for his knowledge of the law and skill in applying it, not popularity. He had long since been widely recognized as an able lawyer, an able businessman, an able author in fields many considered arcane; now he was trying to establish himself as an able military commander at a very high level, and he was not allowing what people thought of him to muddy-up his thinking.

John Pope had been more fortunate than Ulysses Grant; indeed, about the only people who had much evidence from which to form opinions of Henry Wager Halleck were those who received telegrams or letters from him. Curiously, he came to high command just when the telegraph had made it possible for him to stay in communication with Samuel Curtis, who was leading troops out in the most distant part of Missouri from St. Louis, and Pope closer-in, and Grant down in Cairo. Absent the "wires," he would have had to wear out horse after horse riding from one endangered unit to another.

But California lawyer Halleck's new clients were the war managers in Washington. And until he won some morale-boosting victory in a battle, they would have to evaluate his performance as a major general commanding in a critically important post *mainly* on the basis of what they learned from reading his letters, reports, and messages on a very wide range of subjects other than the military attractiveness of using the Tennessee and Cumberland to break the Confederates' line.

When he reversed Frémont's policy by placing Union lines, and especially his troops' camps, off-limits to runaway slaves, General Halleck had steadfastly ignored all the Radical Republican and other abolitionists' professions of outrage laced with vituperation. Later, Thomas Ewing— Cump Sherman's foster father and also father-in-law—would be among the first persons outside the Department of the Missouri to learn that Halleck was equally adamant regarding enforcement of harsh provisions to deal with guerrillas. Responding to a letter from Ewing on New Year's Day, the general wrote:

> *I am satisfied that nothing but the severest punishment can prevent the burning of railroad bridges and the great destruction of human life. I shall punish all I can catch, although I have no doubt there will be a newspaper howl against me as a blood-thirsty monster. . . . I have determined to put down these insurgents and bridge-burners with a strong hand. It must be done; there is no other remedy. If I am sustained by the Government and country, well and good. If not, I will take the consequences.*[82]

Earlier, Halleck had issued Orders No. 24, establishing procedures whereby Confederate sympathizers living within Union lines would be assessed to pay for the care and support of the "suffering families driven by rebels from Southwestern Missouri which have already arrived [in St. Louis and which] have been supplied by voluntary contributions made by Union men."[83] On January 3, 1862, from Washington, Missouri Congressman Francis P. Blair, Jr., told Halleck in a letter: "Recently it was intimated from Saint Louis that an effort was being made by some of our Union friends in Saint Louis to induce you to relax the order, if not to recall it entirely. . . ."[84] Old Brains replied:

> *Don't trouble yourself about Orders No. 24. It will be rigorously executed in good time. . . . You have no idea of the character of the material I have to work with.*
>
> *The German troops are on the brink of mutiny. They have been tampered with by politicians, and made to believe that if they refuse to obey my orders and demand the return of Frémont the Government will be compelled to yield. . . .*
>
> *Don't be alarmed at an explosion. I am prepared for it, and will put it down. I have already cut off its legs, and soon will get its head.*
>
> *All I ask of my Washington friends is to keep cool and let me work out my plans. I understand the problem and will solve it in time.*[85]

Assuming that Abraham Lincoln was one of General Halleck's Washington friends, an action the President took in mid-January suggested that he was not entirely willing to let the department commander work out his plans regarding the dissident Germans without assistance. In any event, on January 21, 1862, Gustave Koerner arrived at Halleck's headquarters and handed him a letter signed A. Lincoln:

> *This will introduce Gov. G. Koerner of Illinois, who is my personal friend, and who calls to see you at my particular request. Please open the sealed letter he will hand you before he leaves you and confer with him as to its contents.*[86]

Lincoln had said:

> *The Germans are true and patriotic, and so far as they have got cross in Missouri it is upon mistake and misunderstanding. Without a knowledge of its contents Governor Koerner, of Illinois, will hand you this letter. He is an educated and talented German gentleman,*

as true a man as lives. With his assistance you can set everything right with the Germans. I write this without his knowledge, asking him at the same time, by letter, to deliver it. My clear judgment is that, with reference to the German element in your command, you should have Governor Koerner with you; and if agreeable to you and him, I will make him a brigadier general, so that he can afford to so give his time. He does not wish to command in the field, though he has more military knowledge than many who do. If he goes into the place he will simply be an efficient, zealous, and unselfish assistant to you. I say all this upon intimate personal acquaintance with Governor Koerner.[87]

Whatever Halleck's intimately personal reaction may have been, his answer reflected lawyerish restraint:

Your Excellency's letter of the 15th, by Governor Koerner, is just received. I nominated [him] *some time ago for appointment as aide-de-camp, with the rank of colonel, the highest authorized by law as a staff officer. Should Your Excellency see fit to make him a brigadier-general I will use my best endeavors to give him such employment as may best suit him.*

The difficulty with the Germans results from two causes: 1st, the want of pay, the pay department here being out of funds, which fact it is very difficult to explain to them. 2d, they are continually tampered with by designing politicians in and out of service in order to serve particular ends. A part of the scheme is the story about the ill-treatment of General [Franz] *Sigel, which is without the slightest foundation.*

All these difficulties are being satisfactorily arranged. A firm and decided course will end them forever. Any yielding on the part of the Government will only create new difficulties and give rise to new demands. Being a German myself by descent, I know something of the German character, and I am confident that in a few weeks, if the Government does not interfere, I can reduce these disaffected elements to order and discipline.[88]

Was this—A. Lincoln may well have wondered—Teutonic arrogance by descent? True, in his response Halleck had not been insubordinate. His obedience was indicated. But might his self-confidence have been a bit overstated?

The frustrated commander-in-chief already had one high-ranking general—McClellan—who had declared, "I can do it all!" yet who was proving every day that he could not, or at least not to anyone's satisfaction. Could Halleck be effective enough to justify "the Government" not interfering more than Lincoln already had?

General Halleck had made no promise to keep His Excellency *directly* informed of his progress in dealing with the dissident Germans. Instead, he returned the matter to strictly military channels by sending General-in-Chief McClellan a report, dated February 2, 1862, that indicated in Teutonic detail the actions Old Brains had taken and was still pursuing:

> *I inclose herewith extracts from General Sigel's letters, published in the German papers and translated. The German papers here are filled with anonymous attacks on the Government at Washington and on my administration here, coming, as it is well ascertained, from the German officers under General Sigel's command. They have also held a number of secret meetings in this city for the purpose of organizing a meeting among the foreign troops and an insurrection of the German population.*
>
> *I have succeeded in introducing police officers into some of these meetings, and their reports are conclusive as to the existence of this plot. I send you a copy of a report of a captain of police, who was present at a meeting of this kind on the 26th ultimo. . . .*
>
> *General Sigel's name is put forward first, but he is an instrument rather than the head of these revolutionists. Letters and papers which have fallen into my hands prove that the instigators of this movement are the emissaries of leading politicians of the Frémont party, and it is expected that the result will, by means of the newspaper press, be made to inure to his benefit as against the present administration.*
>
> *The plan, as discussed at one of these secret meetings, was to force the President to make Sigel a major-general, which would make him second in command in this department. He would then claim all the German regiments and the largest portion of the troops in this State. By this means, it was said, the Frémont party would be virtually restored to power here; and, by continually fomenting dissatisfaction among the German troops and German population, they could completely paralyze and control the action of the Government.*
>
> *Moreover, it was said that the German and Abolition press*

throughout the country would use Sigel as an instrument with which to attack me, and break down, or at least greatly weaken, my authority and influence in this State, so that, at the proper time, the press and the Germans throughout the country could demand my removal and the substitution of Sigel in the command.

This having been accomplished, Sigel, his army, and the German press would require the restoration of Frémont. By a joint movement in Congress, by mass meetings, &c., it was thought that the President would finally be forced to yield. I am also told that leading secessionists in this city are cognizant of these movements and assist them indirectly.

Any yielding on the part of the Government to the demands of Sigel's friends will only add to the mutiny and insurrection, for his promotion would be but a single step in the plan. Our only safety is to put it down with a strong hand, and, when we get sufficient proof, arrest the leaders and remove them out of the department. I am fully posted in the matter and am prepared for them, but I must have the support of the Government. . . .[89]

The irony, here, was excruciating. Halleck was obliged to operate through a general, McClellan, who Lincoln should not have appointed, in repairing damage caused by another general who Lincoln should not have commissioned: John Charles Frémont.

In mid-January 1862, Confederate Major General Sterling Price tried to win concessions on paper that he had not been able to obtain through force of arms. In a long letter to Halleck he complained about various harsh policies being applied by the Union's commander. But Price could derive no comfort or benefit from General Halleck's reply, dated January 22, in which the rebel commander's allegations were bluntly thrown back at him:

Where 'individuals and parties of men' violate the laws of war they will be tried, and if found guilty will certainly be punished, whether acting under your 'special appointment and instructions' or not. You must be aware, general, that no orders of yours can save from punishment spies, marauders, robbers, incendiaries, guerrilla bands, &c., who violate the laws of war. You cannot give immunity to crime.[90]

While showing Sterling Price that he was no Frémont, Old Brains also attempted to eliminate nonsense and negligence on the part of the Union's war management. On January 21, 1862, A. S. Baxter, assistant quarter-master at Cairo, had written his opposite number at St. Louis, Captain Lewis B. Parsons:

> *What does* [the] *Government intend to do? This department has been neglected in every way. No funds; no nothing, and don't seem as though we ever would get anything. Everybody, high and low, in this district is discouraged, and I assure you I had rather be in the bottom of the Mississippi than work night and day as I do without being sustained by* [the] *Government.*
>
> *I have written to Saint Louis and Washington and it avails nothing, and if my whole heart and soul was not in the cause I would never write another word on the subject, but let matters float, I assure you; and a few days will prove my assertion, that unless Government furnishes this department with funds, transportation, &c., the whole concern will sink so low that the day of resurrection will only raise it.*
>
> *Laborers have not been paid a dime for six or seven months; don't care whether they work or not. If they do, don't take any interest in anything. Government owes everybody and everything, from small petty amounts to large. Liabilities more plenty than Confederate scrip and worth less. Regiment after regiment arriving daily. Nothing to supply them with, and no funds to buy or men to work. No transportation for ourselves or any one else.*
>
> *To tell you the truth we are on our last legs, and I have made my last appeal in behalf of Government unless it's to a higher power, for it will kill any man and every man at the head of departments here the way we are now working. Is it possible that General Halleck does not know the situation of affairs here? If you think not, I hope you will inform him at once, for if he should come here he will be astonished and annoyed to find us in such a condition. The general commanding* [Grant] *and myself have done our best to bring about better results, but our wants are not supplied or even noticed.*[91]

On January 25, General Halleck added this endorsement and sent Baxter's letter to Washington:

> *Respectfully referred to Major-General McClellan for his perusal. Unless the quartermaster's department here is furnished with funds soon it will be impossible to organize the expedition from Cairo.*

[This letter shows] *the condition of affairs not only at Cairo but throughout the department.*[92]

8

HENRY HALLECK MAY WELL HAVE BEEN INCLINED to agree with Quartermaster Baxter that he "had rather be in the bottom of the Mississippi" than work night and day without being sustained by the Government. In fact, however, he had been sustaining Washington. When he had arrived, less than three months earlier, he found what his chief of staff, George Cullum, described as "a chaos of insubordination, inefficiency and peculation, requiring the prompt, energetic, and ceaseless exercise of his iron will, military knowledge, and administrative powers."[93] And in that short time, he had annulled fraudulent contracts, dismissed useless hangers-on, disbanded a colossal staff hierarchy that was long on fancy titles but woefully short on brains and military capacity, pruned complex organizations, and established himself as a competent and effective general officer, even though this former captain had spent the previous seven years in civilian clothes and civilian occupations.[94]

Among the issues the Department of the Missouri's commander had attacked were exclusion from Union army camps of fugitive slaves, assessment of Confederate sympathizers to fund support of pro-Union refugees, dissent by certain elements of the German population, and the application of law to rebels engaged in criminal activities. Less momentous but typical of Old Brains' approach to problems was his response to St. Louis women who wore red rosettes to show their sympathies for the Confederate cause: he bought a large quantity of rosettes and had them distributed to the city's streetwalkers.[95]

Even so, military success was what the people in the North expected of their major generals, no matter how adept they proved to be as chief magistrates of large, troubled jurisdictions. During his first three months Halleck had fought no battles, which was hardly surprising given the shortages that had inspired Quartermaster Baxter nigh unto eloquence. Yet he had strengthened the Union's position in Missouri immeasurably, and by mid-January he seemed ready to focus his efforts and resources on defeating Confederate forces first in southwestern Missouri, and then—after shifting troops eastward—in the southern reaches of the Tennessee and Cumberland rivers.

Halleck knew what he could do and what ought to be done, but he felt compelled to echo, in another context, Baxter, who asked: What does the Government intend to do? In a message to General-in-Chief McClellan dated January 20, 1862, Old Brains wrote:

I have received no information in respect to the general plan of campaign, and I therefore feel much hesitation in recommending any line of operations for troops which I may be able to withdraw from Missouri.

Of course this line must be subordinate to some general plan. I take it for granted, general, that what has heretofore been done has been the result of political policy rather than military strategy, and that the want of success on our part is attributable to the politicians rather than to the generals.

So far it seems to me the war has been conducted upon what may be called popper-box strategy—scattering our troops so as to render them inferior in numbers in any place where they can meet the enemy. Occupying the circumference of a great circle, with the enemy within that circumference and near the center, we cannot expect to strike any great blow, for he can concentrate his forces on any one point sooner than we can ours.

The division of our force upon so many lines and points seems to me a fatal policy. I am aware that you, general, are in no way responsible for this, these movements having been governed by political expediency and in many cases directed by politicians in order to subserve particular interests; but is it not possible with the new Secretary of War [Edwin McMasters Stanton] to introduce a different policy and to make our future movements in accordance with military principles?

On this supposition I venture to make a few suggestions in regard to operations in the West.

The idea of moving down the Mississippi by steam is, in my opinion, impracticable, or at least premature. It is not a proper line of operations, at least now. A much more feasible plan is to move up the Cumberland and Tennessee, making Nashville the first objective point. This would turn Columbus and force the abandonment of Bowling Green.

Columbus cannot be taken without an immense siege train and a terrible loss of life. I have thoroughly studied its defenses; they are very strong. But it can be turned, paralyzed, and forced to surrender. This line of the Cumberland or Tennessee is the great central line of the Western theater of war. . . .[96]

"I am ignorant of General Buell's forces or plans," Halleck added. But for that officer to move against Bowling Green from two directions, Old Brains suggested, is "always a hazardous operation, unless each of the exterior forces is superior to the enemy. Under any circumstances it is bad strategy, because it requires a double force to accomplish a single object"[97]

Abraham Lincoln, also, had been wondering about the Young Napoleon's "general plan of campaign." In Washington the major question was—and had been for three months—*What was McClellan planning to do with his huge Army of the Potomac?* Yet on January 13 the Young Napoleon had found time to write Major General Buell:

> *You have no idea of the pressure brought to bear here upon the Government for a forward movement. It is so strong that it seems absolutely necessary to make the advance into East Tennessee at once.*
>
> *I incline to this as a first step for many reasons. Your possession of the railroad there will surely prevent the main* [Confederate] *army in my front from being re-enforced and may force* [Albert Sidney] *Johnston to detach. Its political effect will be very great. Halleck is not yet in condition to afford you the support you need when you undertake the movement on Bowling Green.*[98]

East Tennessee had been a sensitive issue as far as McClellan was concerned since the exchange of messages between Buell and Lincoln that occurred while "Little Mac" was ill. "Have arms gone forward for East Tennessee?" the President had asked Buell in a telegram dated January 4.[99] Buell replied the next day:

> *Arms can only go forward for East Tennessee under the protection of an army. . . . While my preparations have had this movement constantly in view I will confess to Your Excellency that I have been bound to it more by my sympathy for the people of East Tennessee and the anxiety with which you and the General-in-Chief have desired it than by my opinion of its wisdom as an unconditional measure.*
>
> *As earnestly as I wish to accomplish it, my judgment has from the first been decidedly against it, if it should render at all doubtful*

the success of a movement against the great power of the rebellion in the West, which is mainly arrayed on the line from Columbus to Bowling Green, and can speedily be concentrated at any point of that line which is attacked singly.[100]

On January 6 General McClellan had changed the subject abruptly in a seemingly routine message to say to Buell:

I was extremely sorry to learn from your telegram to the President that you had from the beginning attached little or no importance to a movement in East Tennessee. I had not so understood your views, and it develops a radical difference between your views and my own, which I deeply regret.

My own general plans for the prosecution of the war make the speedy occupation of East Tennessee and its lines of railway matters of absolute necessity. Bowling Green and Nashville are in that connection of very secondary importance. . . . My own advance cannot, according to my present views, be made until your troops are solidly established in the eastern portion of Tennessee. If that is not possible, a complete and prejudicial change in my own plans at once becomes necessary.[101]

A week later, General Buell's attempt to carry sulfuric acid on both shoulders took this form: "I did not mean to be understood . . . as attaching little importance to the movement on East Tennessee; on the contrary, it is evidently of the highest importance, if thoroughly carried out; but I believe that if the other object were attained the same result would be accomplished quite as promptly and effectual. . . ."[102]

By contrast, it had never been necessary for Henry Halleck to make convoluted excuses or indeed excuses of any kind. Explanations, yes; but seldom, and then only in a straightforward manner.

Yet, as February approached, General Halleck was about to compound the risk he had assumed when he volunteered back in San Francisco. All of the merit he may have deserved for saving the Department of the Missouri from The Pathfinder's sins might be lost if he proved to have erred in placing the Tennessee-Cumberland operation in the hands of Ulysses Grant, a man known earlier as a four-finger whiskey drinker.

3 ★ *Primus, non docere*

*A*FTERWARD, ALMOST ALL ACCOUNTS of the Union forces' advances up the Tennessee River—and not many days later, the Cumberland—made it seem that General Halleck claimed undue amounts of credit for what was in fact the Union's first major victory of the war to date. True, he had set Brigadier General Ulysses S. Grant and Commodore Andrew H. Foote in motion. But he had done that while operating from his headquarters in St. Louis, where he had remained.

Well, what *were* Halleck's contributions to their successes, beyond that conference with Cullum and Cump Sherman over a map in his hotel room in St. Louis back in December, and all the telegraph traffic during January involving Abraham Lincoln, the Young Napoleon, and Don Carlos Buell?

General-in-Chief McClellan passed on to Halleck a report that Confederate General Pierre G. T. Beauregard, the hero to Southerners of Fort Sumter and Manassas, now second in command to General Albert Sidney Johnston in the West, was on his way to Fort Henry with ten thousand troops. On January 30, 1862, Halleck responded: "General Grant and Commodore Foote will be ordered to immediately advance, and to reduce and hold Fort Henry on the Tennessee River, and also cut the railroad between Dover [Fort Donelson] and Paris [southwest of Fort Henry]."[1] And to Buell: "I have ordered an advance of our troops on Fort Henry and Dover. It will be made immediately."[2]

Halleck also increased Grant's freedom of action in an aspect some might not have considered important:

> *You will organize your command into brigades and divisions, or columns, precisely as you may deem best for the public service, and will from time to time change such organizations as you may deem*

the public service requires, without the slightest regard to political influences or to the orders and instructions you may have heretofore received. In this matter the good of the service, and not the wishes of politico-military officers, is to be consulted.

Get all the troops you can from Illinois, and organize and supply them the best you can when you get them. Don't let any political applications about brigades and divisions trouble you a particle. All such applications are sheer nonsense and will not be regarded.[3]

Information General Buell had received from Halleck and McClellan evidently activated Don Carlos' excuse mechanisms, for on January 31 he asked Old Brains:

Do you consider active co-operation essential to your success, because in that case it would be necessary for each to know what the other has to do? It would be several days before I could seriously engage the enemy, and your operation ought not to fail.[4]

Halleck shot back: "Co-operation at present not essential."[5] His mind was on Grant, and to him—as though Old Brains had been carrying out missions like this one for years—he offered some coaching:

By using steamers on the river, and as the troops will not move far from their supplies and water transportation, much of the usual trains can be dispensed with for several weeks. Don't cumber up the expedition with too large a train. The object is to move rapidly and promptly by steamers, and to reduce the place before any large re-enforcements arrive.[6]

On February 2, Grant reported: "I leave at Cairo and defenses eight regiments of infantry, six companies of cavalry, two companies of artillery, and the sick of the entire command."[7] Apparently, Halleck thought that was too conservative. "Make your force as large as possible," he replied, adding: "I will send more regiments from here in a few days."[8]

From Paducah on February 3, Grant wired: "Will be off up the Tennessee at 6 o'clock. Command, twenty-three regiments in all." His next message was from "near Fort Henry" on February 4:

This morning the debarkation of one division, under General

McClernand, took place 3 miles below [downriver from] *Fort Henry, nearly in view of the rebel batteries. . . . I went up on the* Essex *this morning with Captain Porter, two other iron-clad boats accompanying, to ascertain the range of the rebel guns. From a point about 1 mile above the place afterwards decided on for the place of debarkation several shells were thrown, some of them taking effect inside the rebel fort. This drew the enemy's fire, all of which fell far short, except for one rifled gun, which threw a ball through the cabin of the* Essex. . . .*

I expect all the troops by 10 a.m. to-morrow. Enemy are represented as having re-enforced rapidly the past few days.[9]

"I am sending every available man from Missouri," Halleck wrote General-in-Chief McClellan. "I was not ready to move but deemed [it] best to anticipate the arrival of Beauregard's forces."[10] Lest Grant's attempt fail, he sent message after message to Buell and McClellan asking for more troops. Also, he changed his mind about co-operation. Such efforts achieved little, but in the process some interesting statements were made.

Replying to Halleck's request that he make a diversion by threatening Bowling Green, Buell said:

My position does not admit of diversion. My moves must be real ones, and I shall move at once unless I am restrained by orders concerning other plans. Progress will be slow for me. Must repair the railroad as we advance. It must probably be twelve days before we can be in front of Bowling Green.[11]

To McClellan, Buell wired: "I am unwilling to seem to swerve from the execution of your plan [East Tennessee] without advising you of the meaning of it and knowing that you will acquiesce in the necessity for it. . . . I hope General Halleck has weighed his work well."[12] And the Young Napoleon answered: "I need not urge you to delay the move on East Tennessee as little as possible."[13]

In another message, McClellan asked Buell: "If it becomes necessary to detach largely from your command to support Grant, ought you not to go in person?"[14] Evidently the proposal stunned Don Carlos, who offered this response of sorts:

The whole move, right in its strategic bearing, but commenced by General Halleck without appreciation—preparation or concert—

has now become of vast magnitude. I was myself thinking of a change of the line to support it when I received your dispatch. It will have to be made in the face of 50,000 if not 60,000 men and is hazardous. I will answer definitely in the morning.[15]

Concurrently, Halleck was telegraphing McClellan:

If you can give me in addition to what I have in this department, 10,000 men, I will take Fort Henry, cut the enemy's line and paralyze Columbus. Give me 25,000, and I will threaten Nashville and cut off railroad communication, so as to force the enemy to abandon Bowling Green without a fight.[16]

It proved unnecessary for General Buell to find another excuse for not assuming command of Grant's expedition, for while all the message-swapping had been going on, Ulysses Grant and Andrew Foote had been giving the Union its first victory of the war. "Fort Henry is ours," Henry Halleck reported to McClellan on February 7. "The flag of the Union is re-established on the soil of Tennessee. It will never be removed."[17] And in a message addressed to Brigadier General Grant or Flag Officer Foote at Fort Henry, Old Brains ordered: "Push the gunboats up the river to cut the railroad bridges. Troops to sustain the gunboats can follow in transports."[18]

2

AS IT HAD ELSEWHERE EARLIER AND WOULD many times subsequently in this strange, still-new war, water had shaped the outcome of the Union's attempt to seize Fort Henry. Confederates who had selected this site—on the Tennessee River's eastern bank, just south of the Kentucky-Tennessee state line—had been more mindful of respecting Kentucky's neutrality than of the terrain's vulnerability to flooding. Consequently, by early February 1862, six of Brigadier General Lloyd Tilghman's fifteen guns were under water and the rest, and also his powder magazine, were threatened with inundation. As historian Shelby Foote would later observe, "it had become a question of which would get there first, flood crest or the Yankees."[19]

General Grant might well have wondered if his troops could reach Fort Henry at all. Recalling the accuracy and range of Tilghman's six-inch rifle, which had damaged the gunboat *Essex* during his upriver reconnaissance voyage several days earlier, he had disembarked his men three miles downstream from their objective. Overflowing creeks and muddy trails between those bivouacs and the fort retarded their progress so severely that Flag Officer Foote ordered his four new ironclad "Pook turtles" to move up the river abreast, to be followed by his three wooden gunboats.[20]

Tilghman, recognizing that his infantry would be of no use, started the better part of the three-thousand-plus members of his garrison eastward on a twelve-mile march to Fort Donelson, on the Cumberland. Left behind were far less than a hundred artillerymen, and Tilghman returned to the doomed fort to share their fate. He asked the gun crews for one hour of resistance, so that the infantry column might get as far toward Donelson as muddy roads would allow. His men gave him two hours, during which they scored thirty-two hits on Foote's flagship and thirty on the ironclad to port of her; *Essex* took a round in her boiler and was swept out of the fight by the current. But Tilghman's six-inch rifle's tube had burst, and ammunition was running low. With only four guns still firing, he decided that the requirements of honor had been met and surrendered to Andrew Foote. General Grant arrived an hour later.[21]

Steamers carried news of the victory, but few details, down the Tennessee to Paducah and Cairo for relay by wire to St. Louis and the rest of the North. Initially, Grant had thought and said that he could "take and destroy Fort Donelson" in another two days. But it would take him more time than that, and in the interval General Halleck would both continue to seek reinforcements for Grant from every conceivable source, send him picks and shovels to prepare Fort Henry for defense against rebel counterattacks, and resume his war of words *via* the telegraph with the Young Napoleon in Washington and his neighbor east of the Cumberland, Don Carlos Buell.[22]

Such were the roots of the contention by almost everyone who would ever write about Henry Wager Halleck that he was driven so frantically by his desire to become the Union's supreme commander in the West that he resorted to conduct that was thought to be abominably self-serving, devious, and hypocritical. But what does the record show, and what different impressions might extracts from it reveal about Old Brains?

Abraham Lincoln's toleration of McClellan as general-in-chief, together with the Radical Republicans' and abolitionists' condemnation of Halleck for exposing their beloved hero Frémont as the disaster he certainly had been, were the forces that eroded such favorable notice as Old Brains had attracted to that point in the war.

McClellan ought to have been coordinating the operations of all the

Union's military departments. Lincoln discovered how abysmally Little Mac had failed to do that when—during McClellan's illness—Halleck and Buell professed utter ignorance of each other's situations and plans.

Don Carlos Buell revealed himself in his messages as a man fully as vain as McClellan, an empty uniform with an inability to focus his mind or act in accordance with any apparent principle. For all his protestations of willingness to help take Fort Henry, Buell in fact had done nothing at all— except to waffle pitifully when McClellan floated the idea of Don Carlos superseding Grant in command of Halleck's maneuvering element, then thought to be headed into combat.

Perhaps even more gratifying to Halleck than the taking of Fort Henry was the experience in generalship he had gained and the fresh appraisals he had been able to make of the men and conditions most relevant to his ability to perform successfully. He had attained his military goal, but he had not been able to control the timing; partially false information had nigh-stampeded him. It had come from the Young Napoleon, and many of the general-in-chief's other contributions had ranged from merely silly ones to evidence of minimal attention and unjustified favoritism shown Buell.

George McClellan, Halleck may well have decided, was not to be trusted. But for as long as Lincoln held back from sacking him, Halleck might *use* him.

Put bluntly, the federal high command's weaknesses had already cost thousands of Union lives and might be the fatal flaw that caused even more disasters unless more authority were granted to department commanders. Yet David Hunter in Kansas and Don Carlos Buell in Kentucky were mental and moral midgets who needed close and continuing direction—something neither McClellan nor Lincoln nor anyone else in Washington had been able to provide.

To Halleck, the solution was obvious: The entire West ought to be under the command of one officer, whose powers enabled him to carry out his missions on the basis of actual and potential regional combat realities as he—and not politicians and holiday soldiers in faraway Washington— deemed them.

Of course, anyone who proposed such a change risked being branded an ambition-crazed, power-hungry, would-be despot who was also an ego maniac or worse. Was the hard-core principle involved here important enough to advance and adhere to, no matter what the personal conse-quences might be? Why not merely tiptoe past this hornets' nest without striking it, gambling that someone else would advocate the correct solution?

Out in California, Henry Wager Halleck had not become a wealthy and widely respected attorney and authority on international law and a successful businessman by backing away from challenges. Regardless of which standards of measurement anyone might apply, he had earned everything—of whatever nature—he had amassed. He was a cold steel realist; he was not a politician and indeed had never been shy about expressing his contempt for them; and he had left none of these traits behind him.

3

IN A MESSAGE TO SECRETARY OF WAR STANTON dated February 8, 1862, General Halleck indicated the need to change the command system in his expanded department:

> *Brigadier-Generals Sherman, Pope, Grant, Curtis, Hurlbut, Sigel, Prentiss, and McClernand, all in this department, are of the same date* [of rank], *and each unwilling to serve under the other.*
>
> *If Brigadier-General E. A. Hitchcock could be made major-general of volunteers and assigned to this department it would satisfy all and reconcile all differences. If this can be done there should be no delay, as an experienced officer of high rank is wanted immediately on the Tennessee Line.*[23]

Next, Halleck turned to the larger question raised by the departments' boundaries and the need for a chain of command that could eliminate fumbling and waste. To General-in-Chief McClellan, on the same date, he wrote:

> *I have considered with due deliberation that part of your telegram of yesterday in relation to General Buell's coming to the Cumberland River and taking command of the expedition against Nashville. General Sherman ranks General Buell, and he is entitled to a command in that direction.*
>
> *I propose, with due deference to your better judgment, the following plan, as calculated to produce unity of action and to avoid any difficulties about rank and command. Create a geographical division, to be called the Western Division, or any other suitable name, and to be composed of three* [present] *departments. . . . General Buell would retain his present command, with a small addition. General Hunter could take the new Department of the*

Missouri, which, I have no doubt, would be more agreeable to him than his present position; and General Hitchcock, if you can get him appointed, could take the new Department of the Mississippi.

I have no desire for any larger command than I have now, but it seems to me that this would produce greater concert of action, give more satisfaction to General Hunter, and economize your labor, as all your orders for the West would go through a single channel. Moreover, where troops of different departments act together, as they must on the Cumberland and Tennessee and on the frontiers of Kansas, Missouri, and Arkansas, they would be under one general head. This would avoid any clashing of interests or differences of plans and policy.[24]

After all the thousands of words in telegrams that originated in Washington and Louisville regarding whether and how General Buell would or would not (and if not, why not) help Ulysses Grant take Fort Henry, it should have been obvious to all concerned that there had to be a better way to fight a war. Had George McClellan been a real general, he would very likely have called for precisely the same arrangement Halleck was proposing. Even Abraham Lincoln saw that cooperation was not working, and he had intervened—but not far enough.

As the commander most directly concerned, it was only natural for General Halleck to seek a remedy that was sound militarily. It was inevitable that his Radical critics and students of the era whose understanding of what was really happening was shallow, at best superficial, would call his initiative self-serving. What would they have had him do, given his determination to correct an apparent malpractice? Suggest someone else? Who? What other Union regular army major general had performed nearly as well or achieved even a fraction of what Halleck had—in St. Louis, out in southwestern Missouri, and now in Kentucky and Tennessee?

Having made his proposal, Halleck resumed his efforts to obtain reinforcements. Euphoria over Fort Henry soon gave way to awareness that capturing Fort Donelson would require twice the fifteen thousand troops Grant had commanded. The topography where the Cumberland's fortress was located gave the defenders several advantages Lloyd Tilghman and his men had not possessed. And as before, Beauregard was reported to be strengthening Donelson's garrison with Confederate troops drawn from every direction but north.

Indeed, the texts of messages being sent to and from St. Louis, Washington, and Louisville differed from those exchanged before Henry fell only as to their dates. Buell continued to share with the Young Napoleon his doubts regarding the feasibility of securing East Tennessee, while telling Halleck he might be of help in taking Donelson but not for ten, fifteen, twenty, or more days. Halleck told McClellan that Donelson was "the crisis of the war in the West," as though Little Mac's mind could focus on anything other than defying Lincoln's order that he use his huge, splendidly equipped Army of the Potomac to drive the rebels from the old Manassas battleground, just west-southwest of Washington. More often than not, the general-in-chief (in a rather off-handed manner) encouraged Buell to go over to the Cumberland and take charge; Halleck seconded the motion, mindful as he was of how much could go wrong if the rumors of Confederate troop movements were true.

Of the three generals, only Halleck appeared to be able to see the possibilities for smiting federal columns from the Confederate high command's point of view. "Have you fully considered the advantage which the [upper] Cumberland affords the enemy at Nashville?" he asked McClellan. "An immense number of boats have been collected [upstream], and the whole Bowling Green force can come down in a day, attack Grant in the rear, and return to Nashville before Buell can get half-way there."[25]

Later, some tellers of Henry Halleck's story would try to persuade posterity that Old Brains was so tightly gripped by panic that he tried to bribe General Buell by offering to cast Grant aside.[26] True, Halleck wrote him on February 11: "Can't you come with all your available forces and command the column up the Cumberland?"[27]

Overlooked were certain facts. Flag Officer Foote took Fort Henry, not Grant. To his credit, Grant had followed General Halleck's instructions; yet that was only to be expected, and his only claim to the command he held had been won at Belmont and by satisfactory performance subsequently. If Buell actually moved to the Cumberland—the department border he shared with Old Brains—with forces as large or larger than Grant's, as the situation seemed to require, how (short of incompetence, which in the circumstances Halleck could not prove) *could* Halleck have denied him command?

On February 13, again Halleck offered Buell the "bribe": "Why not come down and take the immediate command of the Cumberland column yourself? I will transfer Sherman and Grant to the Tennessee column."[28]

Wrote Buell to McClellan: "General Grant cannot any longer be in danger. From what I have heard within three days, he must have some 30,000 men. The only apprehension I have now is for his gunboats."[29]

While Don Carlos was sharing his thoughts with McClellan, Halleck was reading the general-in-chief's latest expression of his views:

Your proposition in regard to the formation of a Western Division has one fatal obstacle, viz, that the proposed commander of the new Department of Missouri [Hunter] ranks you. . . . If you do not go in person to the Tennessee and Cumberland, I shall probably write Buell to take the line of the Tennessee, so far as Nashville is concerned. If his advance on Bowling Green must be done, it may well be necessary to throw a large portion of the troops up the Tennessee, in which case he is entitled to the command.[30]

On the next day, February 15, Halleck reported to McClellan: "Enemy has completely evacuated Bowling Green, and is concentrating on the Cumberland. I must have more troops. It is a military necessity."[31] That was in mid-afternoon. At 8 p.m. Old Brains tried again to get the general-in-chief's attention:

General Buell telegraphs that he purposes to move on Bowling Green and Nashville. This is bad strategy. Moreover the roads are very muddy and all the bridges destroyed. His forces should come and help me to take Fort Donelson and Clarksville. . . . Nashville would then be abandoned, precisely as Bowling Green has been, without a blow. With troops in mass at the right points the enemy must retire, and Tennessee will be freed, as Kentucky has been; but I have not forces enough to make this new strategic move and at the same time observe Columbus. Give me the forces required, and I will insure complete success.[32]

And Halleck, as if he thought the Young Napoleon might have remembered that there were *two* campaigns in progress in the Department of the Missouri, added: "Price is still in retreat, with General Curtis in pursuit."[33]

McClellan responded that night with two messages, both of which made it clear that he was making a stronger than usual attempt to direct operations in the field from his desk in far-away Washington. "Buell will move in force on Nashville as rapidly as circumstances will permit," he said in one. And in the other: "The immediate possession of Nashville is very important. It can best be gained by the movement I have directed. . . . I do not see that Buell's movement is bad strategy, for it will relieve the pressure on Grant and lead to results of the first importance."[34]

Among George Brinton McClellan's many faults was his faith in strategic movement alone, making bloodshed unnecessary, to win victories.

Contrary to the real Napoleon's advice to leaders, *"l'audace, l'audace, tou-jours l'audace!"* he would not "depart from my intention of gaining success by maneuvering rather than by fighting; I will not throw these men of mine into the teeth of artillery & intrenchments, if it is possible to avoid it."[35] And he had demonstrated his sincerity at Rich Mountain in western Virginia in July 1861 by preparing to make a frontal attack on a rebel position while troops led by Brigadier General William S. Rosecrans struck it from the rear, then—after hearing gunfire from where Rosecrans was engaged—failing to launch his assault, leaving Rosecrans' maneuvering element to its fate.[36]

Such was the moral fiber of the man Lincoln had made general-in-chief. And in this instance, McClellan may well have set an example Old Brains would not forget, and most certainly would not emulate.

Curiously, on February 16, Abraham Lincoln in the Executive Mansion sent General Halleck this message:

> *You have Fort Donelson safe, unless Grant shall be overwhelmed from outside; to prevent which latter will, I think, require all the vigilance, energy, and skill of yourself and Buell, acting in full co-operation. Columbus will not get at Grant, but the force from Bowling Green will. They hold the railroad from Bowling Green to within a few miles of Fort Donelson, with the bridge at Clarksville undisturbed. It is unsafe to rely that they will not dare to expose Nashville to Buell. A small part of their force can retire slowly towards Nashville, breaking up the railroad as they go, and keep Buell out of that city twenty days. Meantime Nashville will be abundantly defended by forces from all South and perhaps from here at Manassas. Could not a cavalry force from General Thomas on the Upper Cumberland dash across, almost unresisted, and cut the railroad at or near Knoxville, Tenn.? In the midst of a bombardment at Fort Donelson, why could not a gunboat run up and destroy the bridge at Clarksville? Our success or failure at Fort Donelson is vastly important, and I beg you to put your soul in the effort. I send a copy of this to Buell.*[37]

In mid-February the commander-in-chief was extremely worried over the critical illness of his son, Willie. Not since McClellan's indisposition in December and January had there been a meeting of the minds between Lincoln and his general-in-chief on virtually any subject. And indeed, the references the President made to the proposed attempt to seize Nashville suggested that his strategic thinking may have been sharpened more than somewhat by his recent study of Halleck's *Elements of Military Art and Science*. Even so, he could not fail to mention East Tennessee.

A commander-in-chief might ignore channels, but Henry Halleck elected to respond through McClellan. In the first of two messages that day, Old Brains said:

> *I am perfectly confident that if Buell moves from Bowling Green on Nashville we shall regret it. Think of it before you approve. I am certain that if you were here you would agree with me. If I had any doubts I would not insist. Fort Donelson and Clarksville are the key-points. Since the evacuation of Bowling Green the importance of Nashville has ceased.*[38]

Later in the day he added:

> *Hard fighting at Fort Donelson on Thursday, Friday, and Saturday. At 5 p.m. yesterday we carried the upper fort, where the Union flag was flying last night. . . . I am still decidedly of the opinion that Buell should not advance on Nashville, but come to the Cumberland with his available forces. United to Grant we can take and hold Fort Donelson and Clarksville, and by another central movement cut off both Columbus and Nashville. Until Columbus is cut off we must retain large forces at Cairo, Bird's Point, Paducah, and Fort Henry. This is too great a loss of force on our side.*
>
> *Commander Foote cannot return for some days. Four gunboats badly disabled. . . . Can't expect much more aid from the Navy for several days. The mass of the force from Bowling Green are at Fort Donelson and threatening us from Clarksville. . . .*
>
> *Unless we can take Fort Donelson very soon we shall have the whole force of the enemy on us. Fort Donelson is the turning point of the war, and we must take it at whatever sacrifice. Our men are in excellent spirits and fight bravely.*[39]

Just as Lincoln could not abstain from advocating the liberation of Unionists in East Tennessee, the Young Napoleon could not cease insisting on taking Nashville. To Halleck he responded:

> *Should Donelson fall, you will move on Nashville by either route which may at the time be quickest. A part of the column moving*

*from Bowling Green towards Nashville might relieve Donelson, but
the direct move on Nashville is the most important.*[40]

It was somewhat ironic that while the telegraph was enabling Lincoln,
Halleck, McClellan, and Buell to exchange (variously) expressions of
concern, prudence, nonsense rooted in vanity, and excuses, the soldier that
Old Brains had ordered to take Fort Donelson was sending his men into the
teeth of the bastion's "artillery & intrenchments." What those four Union
war managers did not know was that on February 15, 1862, Ulysses Grant
had sent a terse message to Confederate Brigadier General Simon Bolivar
Buckner: "No terms except an unconditional and immediate surrender can
be accepted. I propose to move immediately upon your works."[41] Yet on the
next day, February 16—while those exchanges of messages regarding
Nashville had been heating the telegraph wires—Grant was able to start
genuine news toward St. Louis:

*We have taken Fort Donelson and from 12,000 to 15,000
prisoners, including Generals Buckner and Bushrod [R.] Johnson;
also about 20,000 stand of arms, 48 pieces of artillery, 17 heavy
guns, from 2,000 to 4,000 horses, and large quantities of com-
missary stores.*[42]

General-in-Chief McClellan's first message to Halleck on the morning
of February 17 was: "Please give me your reasons for objecting to Buell's
plan. Give facts on which your opinion is based."[43]

Old Brains' response: "Make Buell, Grant, and Pope major-generals of
volunteers and give me command in the West. I ask this in return for Forts
Henry and Donelson."[44]

4

IN FACT, GENERAL HALLECK HAD ALREADY RESPONDED to the general-in-
chief's demand that he give his reasons for wishing General Buell to march
on Clarksville. At the root of the dispute between St. Louis and Washington, however, was the mystery regarding what Confederate General
Albert Sidney Johnston was going to do now that Halleck's forces had taken
Fort Donelson as well as Fort Henry.

In the ensuing fog of war, Johnston succeeded admirably in making
McClellan think he would concentrate at Nashville and defend the place.

Old Brains became equally certain that Johnston would not fight for the Tennessee capital but might well attack Cairo and Paducah as part of a campaign aimed at recapturing Forts Henry and Donelson, using as a base the rebel stronghold at Columbus.

Whatever McClellan thought or did might as well be ignored, or so Old Brains seemed to have concluded. The Young Napoleon had done nothing but cause trouble and hamper cooperation; his citing a technicality as a reason for withholding approval of Halleck's Western Division proposal indicated that if Old Brains was going to be reinforced by more than token forces, he would have to persuade Don Carlos Buell to provide them. This Halleck tried to do in a message to Buell dated February 18, 1862:

> *To remove all questions as to rank, I have asked the President to make you a major-general. Come down to the Cumberland and take command. The battle of the West is to be fought in that vicinity. You should be in it as the ranking general in immediate command. Don't hesitate. Come to Clarksville as rapidly as possible. Say that you will come, and I will have everything there for you. Beauregard threatens to attack either Cairo or Paducah. I must be ready for him. Don't stop any troops ordered down the Ohio. We want them all. You shall have them back in a few days.*
>
> *Assistant Secretary of War Scott left here this afternoon to confer with you. He knows my plans and necessities. I am terribly hard pushed. Help me, and I will help you. Hunter has acted nobly, generously, bravely. Without his aid I should have failed before Fort Donelson. Honor to him.*
>
> *We came within an ace of being defeated. If the fragments which I sent down had not reached there on Saturday we should have gone in. A retreat at one time seemed almost inevitable. All right now. Help me to carry it out. Talk freely with Scott.*
>
> *It is evident to me that you and McClellan did not at last accounts appreciate the strait I have been in. I am certain you will when you understand it all. Help me, I beg of you. Throw all your troops in the direction of the Cumberland. Don't stop any one ordered here. You will not regret it. There will be no battle at Nashville.*[45]

Messages such as this one caused Halleck's detractors to assert that he was in panic, that to beg Buell was an indication of craven weakness. A more objective reading reveals a man so determined to protect the progress his troops had made that he would do anything to obtain Buell's support, given that Halleck had no authority to order Buell and hence no choice; he was forced not only to beg, but to beg Buell to disobey McClellan. And although it did not seem to be in Buell's nature to obey anyone without protest, delay, and contrived excuses, Halleck ought to have learned by then that he could not trust Buell even if he agreed to help—yet, what alternatives did Old Brains have?

Also, General Halleck was quite right in pointing out to Buell that Grant "came within a ace of being defeated." Confederate batteries had inflicted awesome damage on Flag Officer Foote's gunboats. A rebel attempt to break through McClernand's lines succeeded but Confederate confusion kept troops from escaping through it for long enough to enable Grant to close the gap. Cowardice on the part of political Brigadier Generals John B. Floyd and Gideon Pillow left it to third-ranking Simon Buckner to ask for terms. And, curiously, Albert Sidney Johnston had waffled as to whether Donelson should be abandoned or reinforced; had he resolved to hold the fort, and backed their resolve with the movement of troops from Bowling Green that Halleck expected, people throughout the North might not have had the opportunity to claim as their new hero, "Unconditional Surrender" Grant.[46]

Indeed, in the rush to give new meaning to Grant's initials, most observers lost sight of mistakes Jefferson Davis had made, despite his military background. It was not so much that Grant had won Donelson as that the Confederates had lost it.

Halleck appeared to have assumed that Johnston would make no more errors. This was not panic but prudence. But the problems created by the Union's unworkable departmental arrangement, mismanaged by an incompetent general-in-chief, continued to vex Old Brains. Earlier, McClellan had blithely dismissed the Western Division proposal on the grounds that David Hunter ranked Halleck; on February 19, Halleck replied:

> *I think Hunter will consent to go under me and command the central column. If not, leave him where he is. It was decided in the Mexican War that regulars ranked volunteers, without regard to dates. This decision, if sustained, makes everything right for the Western Division. Give it to me, and I will split secession in twain in one month.*[47]

He also took the time to devote a message to McClellan about a real hero:

Brig. Gen. Charles F. Smith, by his coolness and bravery at Fort Donelson when the battle was against us, turned the tide and carried the enemy's outworks. Make him a major-general. You can't get a better one. Honor him for this victory and the whole country will applaud.[48]

At about that time, General Grant was informing Cullum that the rebels had evacuated Clarksville and that he was sending Smith's division there. "If it is the desire of the general commanding the department," he added, "I can have Nashville on Saturday week."[49]

"The fall of Clarksville confirms my views," boasted the Young Napoleon in a message to Halleck the next day. "I think Cairo is not in danger, and that we must now direct our efforts on Nashville." Then McClellan let slip some interesting news: "In less than two weeks I shall move the Army of the Potomac, and hope to be in Richmond soon after you are in Nashville."[50]

Halleck in Nashville? Hadn't McClellan been pressing Buell toward Nashville in message after message? Similarly, Old Brains had said repeatedly that his main concern was keeping the Confederates at Columbus from taking Cairo and Paducah, his main supply bases for operations on the Tennessee and Cumberland. Exasperated, surely, by General McClellan's wispy statements, Halleck wasted no charm in his next telegram: "I must have command of the armies in the West. Hesitation and delay are losing us the golden opportunity. Lay this before the President and Secretary of War. May I assume command? Answer quickly."[51]

McClellan did: "Buell at Bowling Green knows more of the state of affairs than you at Saint Louis. Until I hear from him I cannot see the necessity of giving you entire command. . . . I shall not lay your request before the Secretary until I hear definitely from Buell."[52] And later on the same day, February 21: "What more have you from Columbus? You do not report either often or fully enough. Unless you keep me fully advised, you must not expect me to abandon my own plans for yours."[53]

With those last few words—*you must not expect me to abandon my own plans for yours*—George Brinton McClellan confessed his unfitness to be general-in-chief of the Union armies. In the circumstances, General Halleck must have been sorely tempted to express his understandable contempt for the Young Napoleon simply by ignoring him. Instead, he replied with restraint and in considerable detail, as though McClellan were still relevant:

For the events of the last two weeks I must refer you to my telegrams, having had no time to write. Our successes on the Tennessee and Cumberland and in the Southwest, together with the stringent measures taken here, have completely crushed out the rebellion in this city and State; no more insurrections, bridge-burnings, and hoisting of rebel flags. This enables me to rapidly increase my force in Tennessee. Nashville and Columbus must soon fall. I am, however, perfectly confident that if you had sent General Buell to the Cumberland to co-operate with me both would have been evacuated by this time.

I cannot possibly be mistaken in the strategy of the campaign. Threatened as I have continually been from Columbus, compelling me to keep a large force at Cairo and Paducah, I was too weak to act with promptness and efficiency on the Tennessee and Cumberland. The enemy made a terrible mistake in not falling back from Bowling Green on Clarksville, driving me out of Fort Henry, re-enforcing Fort Donelson, and connecting again with Columbus. It is true they would thus have exposed Nashville to Buell, but with their river communication they could soon have reoccupied Nashville—much sooner, I think, than Buell could have reached it on muddy roads.

They have lost the golden opportunity, and I believe they will fall back from Nashville, without a battle, either on Decatur or Memphis. I certainly should if I were in Johnston's place. If he should not, and General Buell should take the line of the Cumberland, so as to co-operate with me on the Tennessee, the enemy would be cut off and forced to surrender.

In your telegrams you complain of not getting returns from me of the numbers and positions of my troops. Certainly you do not expect to get information from me which I cannot obtain myself. I have worked hard for months, issuing order after order for returns, but the officers of this department are so negligent or ignorant of their duties in this respect that I find it impossible to obtain returns till long after they cease to be of any use, as everything in the meantime has changed. They became so negligent under the Frémont regime of all law, regulations, and orders that it will take time to bring about a reformation. I am doing everything in my power to effect it.[54]

Concurrently, Halleck telegraphed Assistant Secretary of War Thomas Scott at Louisville:

Advices just received from Clarksville represent that General A. S. Johnston has fallen back on Columbia, and that there is very little preparation for a stand at Nashville. General Grant and Commodore Foote say the road is now open and are impatient. Can't you come down to the Cumberland and divide the re-sponsibility with me? If so, I will immediately prepare to go ahead. I am tired of waiting for action in Washington. They will not understand the case. It is as plain as daylight to me.[55]

Evidently the need for approval of Old Brains' proposal for a Western Division had been plain as daylight to Scott, for—as a message to Halleck from Secretary of War Edwin Stanton dated February 21 indicated—Scott, significantly *not* General McClellan, had passed it along: "Your plan of organization has been transmitted to me by Mr. Scott," wrote Stanton, "and strikes me very favorably, but on account of the domestic affliction of the President I have not yet been able to submit it to him. The brilliant results of the energetic action in the West fills the Nation with joy."[56]

Washington, however, had gone into mourning with the first family the day before: The Lincolns' son Willie had died, and he would not be buried for three more days.[57] But Halleck must not have understood the nature, certainly not the gravity, of the domestic affliction to which Stanton had alluded. His reply:

One whole week has been lost already by hesitation and delay. There was, and I think there still is, a golden opportunity to strike a fatal blow, but I can't do it unless I can control Buell's army. I am perfectly willing to act as General McClellan dictates or to take any amount of responsibility. To succeed we must be prompt. I have explained everything to General McClellan and Assistant Secretary Scott. There is not a moment to be lost. Give me authority, and I will be responsible for results.[58]

Evidently the urgency Halleck's words reflected caused Stanton to intrude after all. On February 22 he replied:

Your telegram of yesterday, together with Mr. Scott's reports, have this morning been submitted to the President, who, after full consideration of the subject, does not think any change in the organization of the Army or the military departments at present desirable. He desires and expects you and General Buell to co-operate fully and zealously with each other, and would be glad to know whether there had been any failure of co-operation in any particular.[59]

And Halleck responded: "If it is thought that the present arrangement is best for the public service, then I have nothing to say. I have done my duty in making the suggestions, and leave it to my superiors to adopt or reject."[60]

5

HENRY HALLECK WOULD HAVE BEEN SUPERHUMAN had he not reflected his disappointment at Lincoln's rejection in the tone of his message that day to General Cullum, who was acting as an expediter temporarily at Cairo. Fumed Old Brains:

There is a screw loose in [the Cairo] *command. It had better be fixed pretty soon, or the command will hear from me. Nashville has been abandoned. General Buell marches in this afternoon without opposition. This enables me to withdraw my column from the Cumberland. I was holding the Cumberland forces to await Buell's movements. All O.K., and now for a decisive movement.*

Tell Flag Officer Foote not to move till I give him further orders. The sending of steamers to General Buell was all wrong. It disconcerted my plans. You should not have done it without my orders. If you can stop them by telegraph, do so, and order them to rendezvous at Paducah. You are too fast at Cairo. Consult me before you order any movement. I have held everything in check till I could have positive information about the abandonment of Nashville. It is now certain.[61]

Abrupt though those admonitions and instructions were, embedded within them was a hint that Halleck was about to strike out in another direction—one entirely within the boundaries of his Department of the Missouri, a move that he was confident he could make without any blessings from Washington or additional failures of Don Carlos Buell to cooperate. The uses of the Tennessee and Cumberland he, George Cullum, and Cump Sherman had identified during their map study back in December seemed exhausted, at least for the time being. Out in northwestern

Arkansas, Brigadier General Samuel Curtis had Sterling Price's forces pretty well intimidated. Now it was time to concentrate on the task old General-in-Chief Winfield Scott had advocated as the second element of his ridiculed Anaconda strategy: cutting the Confederacy in two by regaining control of the Mississippi River from Cairo to the Gulf of Mexico.

Until this point, however, General Halleck had used the divisions led by Curtis and John Pope to clear Missouri of rebels and he had relied on the forces under the command of Grant and Commodore Foote to serve as his maneuvering element. But in early March Old Brains changed this pattern, apparently for reasons that his critics would relish in perpetuity.

Perhaps the first ominous message in a series of them was one on March 2, 1862, from General Cullum at Cairo to General Grant, relayed through Sherman at Paducah. In it, Cullum attempted to bring Grant up to date:

> *General Halleck, February 25, telegraphed me:*
>
>> *Grant will send no more forces to Clarksville. General Smith's division will come to Fort Henry or a point higher up the Tennessee River. Transports will also be collected at Paducah. Two gunboats in Tennessee River with General Grant. Grant will immediately have such garrisons detailed for Forts Donelson and Henry and all other forces made ready for the field.*
>
>> *From your letter of the 28th I learn that you are at Fort Donelson and General Smith at Nashville, from which I infer you would not have received orders.*
>
> *Halleck's telegram of last night says:*
>
>> *Who sent Smith's division to Nashville? I ordered it across to the Tennessee, where they are wanted immediately. Order them back. Send all spare transports up Tennessee to General Grant.*
>
> *Evidently the general supposes you on the Tennessee. . . .*[62]

However, this was only the most recent instance of messages from St. Louis not reaching Grant and vice versa, mainly because direct telegraphic communication had not been established. As General Grant explained in his *Memoirs,* he went to Nashville on February 28 after having started a message on its way to St. Louis advising Halleck that he was going. The purpose of Grant's trip was to straighten out a mess caused by General Buell, one involving Buell's having ordered C. F. Smith's division to Nashville.[63]

On March 3 General Halleck expressed his frustration in a message to McClellan:

> *General Pope will attack New Madrid to-morrow. At the same time there will be a bombardment of Columbus.*
>
> *I have had no communication with General Grant for more than a week. He left his command without my authority and went to Nashville. His army seems to be as much demoralized by the victory of Fort Donelson as was that of the Potomac by the defeat of Bull Run. It is hard to censure a successful general immediately after a victory, but I think he richly deserves it. I can get no returns, no reports, no information of any kind from him. Satisfied with his victory, he sits down and enjoys it without any regard for the future. I am worn out and tired with this neglect and inefficiency. C. F. Smith is almost the only officer equal to the emergency.*[64]

The general-in-chief's response was immediate:

> *The future success of our cause demands that proceedings such as Grant's should at once be checked. Generals must observe discipline as well as private soldiers. Do not hesitate to arrest him at once if the good of the service requires it, and place C. F. Smith in command. You are at liberty to regard this as a positive order if it will smooth your way.*
>
> *I appreciate the difficulties you have to encounter, and will be glad to relieve you from trouble as far as possible.*[65]

It could be argued that Halleck's unburdening himself on the Young Napoleon was a greater lapse in judgment than undue haste in condemning Grant. Old Brains compounded his error, however, in his next message to McClellan:

> *A rumor has just reached me that since the taking of Fort Donelson General Grant has resumed his former bad habits. If so, it will account for his neglect of my often-repeated orders. I do not deem it advisable to arrest him at present, but have placed General Smith in command of the expedition up the Tennessee. I think Smith will restore order and discipline.*[66]

On March 10, 1862, Adjutant General Lorenzo Thomas asked General Halleck to do what he ought to have done earlier: determine whether General Grant left his command without authority. But Old Brains took the time that day to harangue McClellan again regarding the Western Division proposal:

> [The Tennessee River] *is now the great strategic line of the Western campaign, and I am surprised that General Buell should hesitate to re-inforce me. He was too late at Fort Donelson, as Hunter has been in Arkansas. I am obliged to make my calculations independent of both. Believe me, general, you make a serious mistake in having three independent commands in the West. There never will and never can be any co-operation at the critical movement; all military history proves it. You will regret your decision against me on this point. Your friendship for individuals has influenced your judgment. Be it so. I shall soon fight a great battle on the Tennessee, unsupported, as it seems, but if successful, it will settle the campaign in the west.*[67]

As it turned out, Old Brains need not have bothered, for on the next day, March 11, 1862, Commander-in-Chief Abraham Lincoln issued President's War Order No. 3:

> *Major-General McClellan having personally taken the field at the head of the Army of the Potomac, until otherwise ordered he is relieved from the command of the other military departments, he retaining command of the Army of the Potomac.*
>
> *Ordered further, That the two departments now under the respective commands of Generals Halleck and Hunter, together with so much of that under General Buell as lies west of a north and south line indefinitely drawn through Knoxville, Tenn., be consolidated and designated the Department of the Mississippi, and that until otherwise ordered Major-General Halleck have command of said department.*[68]

There was more: Lincoln, having risked the ire of the Radicals by giving Halleck supreme command in the West, sought balance by creating a Mountain Department east of Knoxville and giving the command of it to (of all people) Major General John Charles Frémont.[69] Yet Halleck may well have welcomed that development. Presumably, The Pathfinder would advance southwestward down the Alleghenies to free the Unionists in East Tennessee and thus be operating too far from Halleck's domain to do any damage.

Also, in issuing the President's War Order, Lorenzo Thomas told Halleck: "Major-General Hunter, whose date [of rank] is senior to yours, has been relieved from his command, and the Secretary of War directs that you place some other officer at Fort Leavenworth."[70]

Major General Halleck assumed command of the Department of the Mississippi on March 13, 1862.[71] The next day he reported to Secretary of War Stanton:

> *After several days' skirmishing and a number of attempts by the enemy's gunboats to dislodge General Pope's batteries at Point Pleasant, the enemy has evacuated his fort and intrenchments at New Madrid, leaving all his artillery, field batteries, tents, wagons, mules, &c., and an immense quantity of military stores. Brig. Gen. Schuyler Hamilton has occupied the place. This was the last stronghold of the enemy in this state. There is no rebel flag now flying in Missouri.*[72]

Before Old Brains could get on with his campaigns, there remained the task of setting the record straight, or as straight as he could amend it, regarding Ulysses S. Grant. From St. Louis on March 15, he wrote Lorenzo Thomas:

> *In accordance with your instructions of the 10th instant I report that General Grant and several officers of high rank in his command, immediately after the battle of Fort Donelson went to Nashville without my authority or knowledge. I am satisfied, however, from investigation, that General Grant did this from good intentions and from a desire to subserve the public interests.*
>
> *Not being advised of General Buell's movements, and learning that General Buell had ordered Smith's division of his (Grant's) command to Nashville, he deemed it his duty to go there in person. During the absence of General Grant and a part of his general officers numerous irregularities are said to have occurred at Fort Donelson. These were in violation of the orders given by General Grant before his departure, and probably, under the circumstances, were unavoidable.*

> *General Grant has made the proper explanations, and has been directed to resume his command in the field. As he acted from a praiseworthy although mistaken zeal for the public service in going to Nashville and leaving his command, I respectfully recommend that no further notice be taken of it.*
>
> *There never has been any want of military subordination on the part of General Grant, and his failure to make returns of his forces has been explained as resulting partly from the failure of colonels of regiments to report to him on their arrival and partly from an interruption of telegraphic communication. All these irregularities have now been corrected.*[73]

Had he been so inclined, General Halleck might have told Lorenzo Thomas that substantially all of the Frémont-era irregularities the adjutant-general had noted in his report, back in October, had been corrected, as well. In the process, Old Brains had directed Generals Curtis, Pope, and Grant in clearing northwestern Arkansas, Missouri, and western Kentucky of Confederate forces. The captures of Forts Henry and Donelson, carried out under his orders by forces led by General Grant and Commodore Foote, were the greatest victories the Union had won so far in the war. No other Union officer had achieved anywhere near as much.

In a mere 116 days—between November 19, when he assumed command at St. Louis, and March 15—Old Brains had evolved from a lawyer in an ill-fitting uniform who had never commanded troops in peace, much less war, into a commander who had earned the respect of his officers and men and elicited their best efforts. Along the way, he had taken heavy fire from abolitionists, Radical Republicans, and others who would never forget that he succeeded in cleaning the Augean Stables their hero Frémont had left behind. Forced to operate in a departmental framework under a general-in-chief whose guidance via telegraph was notable mainly for its uselessness, condemned to "co-operate" with a fellow department commander who seemed to think nothing was the best thing to do and usually followed his own advice, Henry Halleck had neither taken counsel of his fears nor allowed what others might think of him to hold him back from doing what he thought best. That he made mistakes—in the matter of Grant's old bad habits, for example—was not so remarkable as the fact that he did not make more.

But the past was prologue. Albert Sidney Johnston was concentrating west of the Tennessee. Confederate-held Island No. 10 still blocked the Mississippi below New Madrid. And now that Henry Halleck had all the fighting room and resources he had been seeking, he faced the task of demonstrating that Abraham Lincoln had been justified in giving him this fresh opportunity in which to excel.

6

IN REMOVING GENERAL MCCLELLAN from the position of general-in-chief, Abraham Lincoln not only did not name a successor but added those responsibilities to his other burdens. He had been able to limit the damage the Young Napoleon had done by relieving him, but who could force the commander-in-chief to step aside if he, too, failed?

Actually, no one really knew precisely what a general-in-chief was supposed to do. Winfield Scott had performed effectively in that role for twenty years, but hardly any precedents he had set applied to a Union army swollen from his seventeen thousand men to more than half a million. As Generals Halleck and Buell had learned, McClellan gave his highest priority to preparing his Army of the Potomac for battle; as a consequence, the attention he gave the Union's other field armies was sporadic; he grasped only fragments of his subordinates' situations, resulting in instructions that were often confusing and inconsistent. And if a West Point graduate who was the army's most senior major general could not command the generals heading his departments and coordinate their operations, what success could a midwestern lawyer with twenty-five-odd million constituents to govern possibly have hoped to achieve?

Was Lincoln confessing his inability to find a single general in his huge army who might concentrate his talent and experience on the task of supporting, encouraging, and in certain circumstances directing the Union's armies? Perhaps. He might have called upon Halleck, the only successful commander to date; however, Old Brains was just now being given the wider powers and fighting room he needed to quell the rebellion in the West; and there was, as yet, no general qualified to replace him.

Possibly President Lincoln thought he and the Union might be able to get along *without* a real general-in-chief: better a vacancy than—well, McClellan. Or the commander-in-chief may have expected that by being totally immersed in this new calling (as he had been, earlier, in farming and the practice of law) he could learn enough day-by-day at least to find out what a general-in-chief *ought* to do.

And from March 11, 1862—when Lincoln had confined McClellan to the command of the Army of the Potomac, given Halleck supreme command in the West, and restored Major General John Charles Frémont to active duty—until after the middle of May, it seemed that the acting general-in-chief had done no harm.[74] In the West General Halleck seemed to have firm control over generals who were fighting or getting ready to fight in places as widely separated as northwestern Arkansas, along the Mississippi below Cairo, and up the Tennessee south of what remained of Fort Henry. And George McClellan had proved magnificently able in moving his enormous Army of the Potomac down its namesake river and through Chesapeake Bay to Fort Monroe, at the tip of the long peninsula formed by two of Virginia's rivers; from that landing site, Little Mac meant to move up the long land bridge to and through the gates of Richmond.

But within the Confederacy, as spring 1862 opened, there was grim determination to stop losing. Critics of Jefferson Davis were howling for scalps, and General Albert Sidney Johnston was prompt in offering the President his. "The test of merit in my profession," he wrote his commander-in-chief, soldier-to-soldier, "is success. It is a hard rule, but I think it right."[75] Said Davis in reply: "My confidence in you has never wavered, and I hope the public will soon give me credit for judgment rather than continue to arraign me for obstinacy."[76]

But Davis was doing more. From a coastal defense mission in the Carolinas he called General Robert E. Lee to Richmond to be his military advisor.[77] Such was the first link in the chain of events in the Shenandoah Valley and east of Richmond that would put Acting General-in-Chief Lincoln's ability to *do it all* to tests more severe than he must have imagined probable back on March 11, 1862.

7

GENERAL HALLECK WAS NOT LIKELY to mourn the ejection of McClellan from the Union's high command. Neither Stanton nor Lincoln would present problems, or so he probably thought it safe to assume. Moreover, he had just spent a little under four months achieving *more* than Washington had asked of him *without* receiving much in the way of even basic support, including timely pay and reliable firearms for his men.

In fact, two of Halleck's most damaging errors had involved his communications with Washington. First, he had assumed the war managers there understood his problems well enough to accept his Western Division solution, when in fact they thought him both jealous of "Unconditional Surrender" Grant's sudden fame and unduly self-seeking when he asked for command in the West in return for Forts Henry and Donelson. Next, although the general commanding had every right to become irate over what appeared to be disobedience on Grant's part, he blundered tremendously by sharing his concern with Washington. If Grant was a problem, he was Halleck's problem; no good could possibly have come from involving the faraway War Department, and none did.

From early March onward, Grant had ended almost every message to General Halleck with words such as these: "There is such a disposition to find fault with me that I again ask to be relieved from further duty until I can be placed right in the estimation of those higher in authority."[78]

Two days after that message Halleck replied:

> *You cannot be relieved of your command. There is no good reason for it. I am certain that all that the authorities at Washington ask is that you enforce discipline and punish the disorderly. The power is in your hands; use it, and you will be sustained by all above you. Instead of relieving you, I wish you as soon as your new army is in the field to assume the immediate command and lead it on to new victories.*[79]

Having said those things, in his next message to Grant, General Halleck got back to business as usual, which in mid-March 1862 was selecting a base on the Tennessee River for use in preparing to attack Albert Sidney Johnston's army gathering at Corinth, Mississippi.

Far from expecting guidance from Washington, Halleck offered some to Secretary of War Stanton. Confederate General Braxton Bragg, thought to have been in the deep South, was at Memphis, he reported, and large reinforcements for Johnston were arriving from the South by rail. "If an attack on Mobile is intended," wrote Halleck, "now is the time. The capture of that place would assist us very much here."[80]

But Halleck was marshaling his own resources and providing his subordinates with strict, unambiguous orders. "Move your forces by land to the Tennessee as rapidly as possible," he telegraphed Don Carlos Buell, adding that Johnston's strength at Corinth was reported at sixty thousand. "Grant's army is concentrating at Savannah [on the Tennessee]. You must direct your march on that point, so that the enemy cannot get between us."[81] And to Grant:

> *As the enemy is evidently in strong force, my instructions not to advance so as to bring on a general engagement must be strictly*

obeyed. . . . General Buell is moving in [your] *direction, and I hope in a few days to send 10,000 or 15,000 more from Missouri. We must strike no blow until we are strong enough to admit no doubt of the result. . . .*[82]

The author of *Elements of Military Art and Science* was practicing what he had long ago preached: concentration—and at a point that could be supplied and supported by a line of reliable communications with resources in the rear. Albert Sidney Johnston was more soldier than military scholar but he, too, was concentrating. Since Donelson, Johnston had incurred the wrath of his countrymen by giving up Nashville and virtually all of central Tennessee. His honor as a soldier obliged him to strike a blow successful enough to redeem the recent Confederate losses and to reinvigorate the will of his depressed people to continue their war to repel invasion and punish Yankee coercion. But Henry Halleck intended to deny Johnston that opportunity by destroying him first.

Whether Pittsburg Landing on the Tennessee was selected as the Union army's concentration point by C. F. Smith or W. T. Sherman was less important than the fact that on March 19 Cump issued orders to arriving units for their occupation of campsites extending over a wide area from the river westward to a little Methodist church called Shiloh Chapel.[83] General Smith was ill—terminally, as it turned out—from a leg infection, and he would spend his last days at Savannah, six miles or so downstream, where General Grant was to make his headquarters.[84] Sherman, by then commanding a division, would be the senior officer present at Pittsburg Landing for the rest of March and a few days beyond.

By March's third week, then, the Department of the Mississippi's general-in-chief was dependent for success along the Tennessee upon Sherman, an officer he had restored to duty after Northern newspapers had condemned him as "hopelessly insane"; Grant, an officer he had wronged by passing along rumors and his own unfounded assumptions to Washington; and Major General Don Carlos Buell, whose record for making excuses for his failures to perform as promised was his most remarkable characteristic. Moreover, as Old Brains' territory and powers had been expanded, so had been his vulnerability to politicians' alarums and fevers. Wrote Andrew Johnson, military governor of Tennessee, and Horace Maynard to Stanton on March 14:

We see in the new arrangement of military departments Tennessee west of Knoxville falls under Halleck, east of Knoxville under

Frémont. We entreat that the State be not divided. Place it all under Halleck. This is most important. For God's sake do not divide East Tennessee into two military departments. We have suffered enough already from a conflict of military authorities.[85]

A week later, the secretary of war replied that the President "regards the existing arrangement as a paramount necessity."[86] Stanton also directed Halleck to "place at [Johnson's] disposal an adequate force."[87] Then Frémont, a political general who could always be counted upon to make trouble, pressed Stanton to assign political Brigadier General James A. Garfield to his department. Buell explained to the secretary that Garfield was to lead the force he was sending westward to aid Grant, but this flurry caused him to warn Halleck that the Confederates might "contemplate an advance upon Nashville and our position in middle Tennessee under certain circumstances—a thing which offers very strong inducements" and that some troops would have to be diverted from "offensive operations between the Tennessee and Mississippi."[88]

8

FORTUNATELY FOR GENERAL HALLECK and his cause, officers in command of the divisions and detachments west of the Mississippi had carried out their missions without adding to Old Brains' burdens. Throughout February, while the general commanding had been sparring over the telegraph with Buell and McClellan and suffering from lack of communication with Grant, Samuel Curtis had been clearing southwestern Missouri of Confederates without bringing on a general engagement. By early March, this seasoned soldier had pushed the rebels into the Boston Mountains of northwestern Arkansas, which was far enough for the time being, or so Washington, Halleck, and Curtis agreed. Curtis even withdrew northward a few miles, but he kept patrols active.

News that Confederate Major General Earl Van Dorn was massing forces in the mountains brought Curtis southward again, to a place about ten miles northeast of Bentonville called Elkhorn Tavern, just south of a long outcropping called Pea Ridge. Van Dorn approached from the west with about seventeen thousand troops, including Indians, but instead of attacking directly, he took forces led by Sterling Price eastward on an overnight march around to the north of Pea Ridge so that on the morning of March 7 they could strike Curtis' units southeast of it, while Brigadier

General Ben McCulloch advanced from Pea Ridge's western end.

General Curtis about-faced his divisions and conducted a two-day defense that ended with the rebels shattered and fleeing in panic in almost every direction. Apart from this victory's significance to the Unionists in southwestern Missouri, Samuel Curtis' quiet competence had enabled General Halleck to devote his attention to operations on the Tennessee and the Mississippi.[89]

Similarly, after Old Brains had honed-down some early rough spots, John Pope had developed into a general who considered St. Louis a destination for his detailed reports instead of a source of guidance. Columbus, the Confederate bastion on the Mississippi's Kentucky bank, had long been a threat to almost everything General Halleck was trying to do. Once it had become clear that Samuel Curtis could push Sterling Price's rebels around without help from elsewhere in Missouri, Old Brains had given Pope the mission of taking New Madrid, on the Mississippi's western bank, and Island No. 10 below it. Success would make Columbus untenable.

"I will not attempt to hamper you with any minute instructions," Halleck wrote Pope on March 21, thus drawing criticism from historians who apparently failed to read on: "The great object, you know, is to cut the enemy off from any chance of retreat by water. I leave you to accomplish this according to your own judgment, having full confidence in your ultimate success."[90]

General Halleck also shared with Pope information that would enable him to see his mission's relationship to other operations east of the Mississippi:

> *Buell will effect a junction with Grant and Smith by Monday. We shall then have 70,000 men at a single point on the Tennessee with which to cut the enemy's center, destroy their railroad connections, and thus cut off the retreat by land of Polk, McCown, &c. Unless the enemy is very much stronger at Corinth than reported, I can see no chance of failure. There will probably be a big battle somewhere in that vicinity.*[91]

Pope justified the confidence Halleck had shown in him by capturing New Madrid on March 14 following an eleven-day siege in which Union casualties were very low.[92] This enabled Old Brains to telegraph Stanton, "There is no rebel flag flying in Missouri."[93]

But Island No. 10 presented problems to Pope that would require measures far more complex than a siege. "General Pope is gradually working his way through the swamps south of New Madrid," Halleck reported to the secretary of war on March 23. "His progress is necessarily slow, but if the operation should be successful, it can hardly fail to produce important results."[94]

In that same message, General Halleck revealed that he had not been power mad when he first suggested creation of the Western Division and then advocated its adoption with what his bitter critics, then and afterward, considered deplorable audacity. Earlier, Stanton had asked Halleck to reinforce forces under Edward R. S. Canby, who was then retreating up the Rio Grande into northern New Mexico. "I am organizing a column for New Mexico as rapidly as possible," he assured the secretary, then he turned to command questions Stanton had raised:

> *I know* [then-Colonel] *Canby well. He is one of the best officers in the service.*[95] *I am certain that he will do everything possible to hold out until our re-enforcements reach him. I therefore do not deem it necessary, at least for the present, to attach New Mexico to this department. I am confident that* [Colonel] *Canby and myself can co-operate as well as if he were under my direct orders. Moreover, his command is so very distant that I could not well direct his movements, and by having an independent position he can act more freely.*[96]

Confirming Halleck's judgment of him, Canby cleared New Mexico of rebels within the next few weeks.

As April approached, however, General Halleck's main concern was how soon Don Carlos Buell's divisions would reach Grant. Excuses heated the wires. "The progress of the bridge over the Duck River has been much slower than I expected," Buell said on March 27 in a typical message, "but the difficulties have also been greater than I supposed."[97] On March 29 Buell raised another possibility, to which Old Brains replied: "There is no danger of the enemy's moving to Nashville. . . . I wish he would. I wish you to concentrate everything possible against the enemy's center. Don't fail in this, as it is all-important to have an overwhelming force there."[98]

Then, on March 30, Secretary Stanton telegraphed Halleck:

> *This Department has just received information that Nashville "has almost been left defenseless by General Buell." Governor Johnson and General Dumont, in command, are of the opinion that the force is*

inadequate to the security of that city. . . . You can appreciate the consequence of any disaster at Nashville, and are requested to take immediate measures to secure it against all danger.[99]

Halleck gave the mission to Buell: "Of course Nashville must be properly secured," he wrote. "This under no circumstances must be neglected."[100] Regarding concentration at Pittsburg Landing, in an earlier message he had said, "We must be ready to attack the enemy as soon as the roads are passable."[101] Apparently, he did not contemplate anything but taking the offensive.

9

JEFFERSON DAVIS' MIND WAS ALSO on Confederate attacks in the West. On March 12, 1862, not long after the loss of Fort Donelson, he wrote General Albert Sidney Johnston: "With a sufficient force, the audacity which the enemy exhibits would no doubt give you the opportunity to cut some of his lines of communication, to break up his plan of campaign, and, defeating some of his columns, to drive him from the soil as well of Tennessee as of Kentucky."[102] On March 18, Johnston replied that after evacuating Nashville,

> *I marched southward and crossed the Tennessee at this point* [Decatur, Alabama]*, so as to co-operate with General Beauregard for the defense of the valley of the Mississippi. The passage is almost completed, and the head of my column is already with General Bragg at Corinth. . . . Day after to-morrow, unless the enemy interrupts me, my force will be with Bragg, and my army nearly 50,000 strong.*[103]

General Johnston's letter reached Richmond on March 26, and President Davis replied immediately: "You have done wonderfully well, and now I breathe easier in the assurance that you will be able to make a junction of your two armies. If you can meet the division of the enemy moving from the Tennessee before it can make a junction with that advancing from Nashville the future will be brighter."[104] Eight days later, from Corinth, Johnston telegraphed this report to his commander-in-chief:

> *General Buell is in motion, 30,000 strong, rapidly from Columbia*

by Clifton to Savannah. Mitchel behind him with 10,000. Con-
federate forces, 40,000, ordered forward to offer battle near Pitts-
burg. . . . Hope engagement before Buell can form junction.[105]

Clearly, like Halleck, neither Davis nor Johnston had ever worked toward anything but "to offer battle." And to both sides, the time at which Buell's force reached Grant's might well be the key to which army would be the attacker.

Johnston's message was dated April 3. On that Thursday, General Grant, at Savannah, was passing word to Halleck that "[Buell's] advance will arrive probably on Saturday"[106]—the day on which, as it happened, Johnston then intended to launch his assault.

The Confederate advance was delayed by bad weather, but faulty planning and poor control of units on the march were also contributing factors. On Saturday night the rebel camps were only a few miles south of Sherman's at Shiloh Chapel. General Beauregard, Johnston's second in command, and other officers advocated canceling the attack and returning to Corinth; surely the Yankees were aware of their approach, and Buell might have raised their strength from forty thousand to seventy thousand. But Albert Sidney Johnston declared, "I would fight them if they were a million!" and he ordered an attack at daylight Sunday morning.[107]

Indeed, the leading division of General Buell's force was in camps across the river from Savannah on that Saturday night. But those troops—and also Ulysses Grant, on crutches from an accident that had left him with a sprained ankle—were too far away from Shiloh Chapel to be of any use when waves of Confederates came charging out of the south, catching the men in Cump Sherman's division cooking breakfast and driving many of them northeastward in panic.[108]

Afterward, almost everyone in the North from Abraham Lincoln on down wanted to know why it took Ulysses Grant until late the next day to drive the Confederates out of his camps and back on the roads to Corinth, why Union casualties were so high, and why the federal forces had been surprised. The best that could be said of Shiloh (or Pittsburg Landing) was that—thanks to the addition of Don Carlos Buell's divisions on Monday—Grant's army was not destroyed. When the guns had cooled, the Union forces were still in their camps and the rebels were at Corinth; despite the thinning of federal ranks by roughly thirteen thousand men and Confederates' by eleven thousand (including General Albert Sidney Johnson, killed in action on Sunday), the battle had settled nothing at all.[109]

Mainly because of the lack of telegraph communication linking

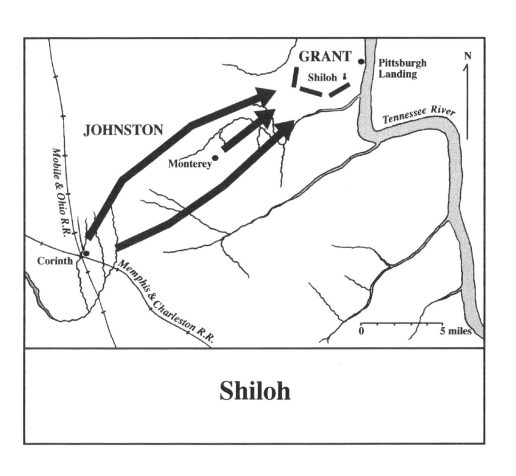

Shiloh

General Halleck's headquarters and Grant's, not until Tuesday, April 8, the day after the battle, was Old Brains able to send Secretary Stanton even this terse message: "The enemy attacked our works at Pittsburg, Tenn., yesterday, but were repulsed with heavy losses."[110] By contrast, Halleck had been able to follow John Pope's progress toward the seizure of Island No. 10 hour-by-hour, and on April 8 he informed Stanton that this Confederate strong point in the Mississippi River had been captured.[111] Pope's forces had taken seven thousand rebels prisoner without the loss of a man in combat, and the elimination of this riverblock extended Union control of the Mississippi southward almost to Memphis.[112] Yet news of this victory was all but eclipsed by the appalling accounts that emerged from the fighting near Pittsburg Landing on the Tennessee.

10

ON SATURDAY, APRIL 5, the day before Johnston's army attacked Grant's, General Halleck had telegraphed Flag Officer Foote: "I shall want a gunboat at Cairo ready to go up the Tennessee in the early part of next week."[113] This proved fortuitous, for Grant's near defeat was bound to raise all sorts of questions. And Old Brains had one of his own to ponder: Given his continuing desire to smite the Confederates at Corinth, now led by General Beauregard, should he bring John Pope's troops over to the Tennessee and add them to Grant's and Buell's, or order them to eliminate other rebel obstacles down the Mississippi?

To decide, he needed to see for himself the condition of his forces at Pittsburg Landing. Moreover, it was time for him to take direct command of his largest field army; he had already corrected most of the mistakes Frémont had made, and so there really was no compelling reason for him to remain in St. Louis any longer.

"Halleck was then in the prime of life," wrote James Grant Wilson, recalling his first sight of the general at Pittsburg Landing on April 11, 1862, "possessing robust health and great mental vigor, about five feet nine inches tall, and weighing perhaps one hundred and seventy or eighty pounds. He was carefully dressed in a new uniform, wearing his sword, and carrying himself erect, with a distant and somewhat austere manner, presenting, as he walked down the gangplank, altogether a striking contrast to General Grant. . . ."[114]

Three days after he reached Pittsburg Landing, the general wrote his wife:

I left St. Louis on Wednesday and arrived on Friday evening. The officers seemed very glad to see me, as according to all accounts and my own observations, this army is undisciplined and very much disorganized, the officers being utterly incapable of maintaining order. I have been very hard at work for the past three days endeavoring to straighten things out, and hope to succeed in time. The battles of the 6th and 7th were terrible slaughters, but our troops have suffered much less than the enemy. Gen. Albert S. Johnston, Mrs. Hepburn's brother-in-law, was killed on the field and is buried nearby. . . .

I have been living on a steamer since I arrived, but shall go into camp with the soldiers to-morrow. The Landing has only a few lone houses which are occupied by army stores, and I shall live in a tent. Living out this way is not very comfortable in rainy weather, but it always agrees with my health, and I rather like it, notwithstanding the inconveniences. Moreover, it will have a good effect upon the soldiers to camp out with them.[115]

However, Halleck's men were not impressed, wrote a biographer a century later, by his "high forehead and large, popping eyes. . . . In an amateurish manner, he tried to make the men like him" by living in a tent.[116] Such is the fate of men such as Old Brains who live too far ahead of their time: Sharing the miseries of the braves they commanded would come to be habitual, indeed characteristic of combat leaders who achieved superior results.

In any event, Henry Wager Halleck had not reached the station in life he by then enjoyed by currying favor with anyone. It was absurd to allege that he would suddenly adopt politicians' despicable hypocrisies. "I believe I can say it without vanity that I have talent for command and administration," Old Brains had written his wife from St. Louis back in mid-December. "At least I have seen no one here who can accomplish half so much in twenty-four hours as I do."[117]

General Halleck's file of outgoing messages on April 3, 1862, confirms what he wrote his wife. On that day, at widely separated points within his department, John Pope was moving closer to seizure of Island No. 10 and Grant was expecting the first of Buell's divisions to join him in two days, but Old Brains found the time to perform as chief magistrate in the region by replying to a St. Louis lawyer who had raised certain questions:

In answer to your inquiries I have to state that persons in arms against the United States under General Price can be received only as prisoners of war, and that they will be treated in the same kind and lenient manner as others have been who are willing to abandon a hopeless and unholy cause, take the prescribed oath of allegiance, and give satisfactory security for their future good conduct. Any one who voluntarily takes the oath and gives his parole of honor and afterwards violates it by aiding or abetting the enemy will most certainly be executed. A man who violates his military parole commits the most serious of all military offenses, and I will pardon no one who is guilty of that crime.

In regard to the wife of the reverend Captain Chaplain in General Price's army, who wishes permission to visit her husband, please inform her that no such permission can be granted. Nearly all the secessionists of this State who have entered the rebel service have left their wives and daughters to the care of the Federal troops. There is scarcely a single instance where this confidence has been abused by us. But what return have these ladies made for this protection? In many cases they have acted as spies and informers for the enemy and have been most loud-mouthed in their abuse of our cause and most insulting in their conduct towards those who support it. Under any other government they would for such conduct be expelled from the country or confined within the walls of a prison.

I am well aware that some good Union men in the interior of the State think that those now serving the rebel cause under General Price should be permitted to return to their homes without being considered prisoners of war, or, when taken prisoners of war, that they should be released simply on promise of future good conduct. Experience has satisfied me that such a course would neither be wise nor safe. Indeed, I find that the very persons who advocate a more lenient policy towards returned secessionists are also continually petitioning to have additional troops sent to their counties to protect them from the operations of these same rebels.[118]

But General Halleck would have little or no more time for jurisprudence now that he had assumed command of an army that was about to reach one hundred thousand men in size and would lead it in the offensive Shiloh had postponed. Once he had sent orders to Pope to load his forces on steamers and bring them up the Mississippi, Ohio, and Tennessee to Pittsburg Landing, he turned to the task of investigating questions such as this pair, posed by Secretary of War Stanton: "The President desires to know why you have made no official report to this Department respecting the late battle at Pittsburg Landing, and whether any neglect or misconduct of General Grant or any other officer contributed to the sad casualties that befell our forces on Sunday."[119]

Soon after his arrival Halleck had telegraphed Stanton:

> *It is the unanimous opinion here that Brig. Gen. W. T. Sherman saved the fortune of the day on the 6th instant, and contributed largely to the glorious victory on the 7th. He was in the thickest of the fight on both days, having three horses killed under him and being wounded twice. I respectfully request that he be made a major-general of volunteers, to date from the 6th instant.*[120]

But Old Brains had sent no such messages commending anyone else, and he had remained silent regarding Grant. To Stanton, he replied:

> *The sad casualties of Sunday, the 6th, were due in part to the bad conduct of officers who were utterly unfit for their places, and in part to the numbers and bravery of the enemy. I prefer to express no opinion in regard to the misconduct of individuals till I receive the reports of commanders of divisions. A great battle cannot be fought or a victory gained without many casualties. In this instance, the enemy suffered more than we did.*[121]

Clearly, Halleck had learned something from the hip shot he had taken at Grant after Donelson. Moreover, there were a number of perplexing mysteries and contradictions embedded in the accounts he had heard.

Had Sherman and the rest of the army been surprised or caught unprepared? Well, yes and no. As far back as Fort Henry, Halleck had ordered entrenchment and had furnished the shovels; but no defensive fortifications had been prepared at Shiloh, reflecting an Old Army belief that digging eroded soldiers' offensive spirit.[122] On Friday, April 4, some advance pickets had been captured and Cump sent a detachment to investigate. A skirmish ensued, and Sherman forwarded ten rebel prisoners to Grant's headquarters at Savannah.[123] On the same day, Sherman issued Orders No. 19:

> *I. In case of alarm, day or night, regiments and brigades should form promptly on their parade grounds and await orders. Of course, if*

attacked, the immediate commanders present must give the necessary orders for defense.

II. In case of an attack on the advance pickets they should fire and fall back. . . .[124]

Also on Friday, April 4, General Grant warned Sherman of a possible rebel attack at Purdy, downstream a few miles from Savannah. "I look for nothing of the kind," he wrote, "but it is best to be prepared. I would direct, therefore, that you advise your advance guards to keep a sharp lookout for any movement in that direction."[125]

Then, Sherman to Grant, Saturday, April 5, with Johnston's army only a few miles to the south: "All is quiet along my lines now. . . ." and, later that day:

I have no doubt that nothing will occur to-day more than some picket firing. The enemy is saucy, but got the worst of it yesterday, and will not press our pickets far. I will not be drawn out far unless with certainty of advantage, and I do not apprehend anything like an attack on our position.[126]

Concurrently, General Grant was starting a message to General Halleck *via* steamer to the nearest telegrapher: "The number of the enemy at Corinth and within supporting distance of it cannot be far from 80,000 men. . . ."[127]

Even so, on Sunday morning Cump Sherman did not seem to believe Jonhston's Confederates were actually attacking until the orderly standing next to him was shot dead. From then on, Sherman did his best to rally panicked troops. Grant arrived and shifted units to stem the rout. Yet at that Sunday's end, as Brigadier General William Nelson (leader of the first of Buell's arriving divisions) said in his report:

I found cowering under the river bank when I crossed from 7,000 to 10,000 men, frantic with fright and utterly demoralized, who received my gallant division with cries, "We are whipped; cut to pieces." They were insensible to shame or sarcasm—I tried both on them—and indignant at such poltroonery, I asked permission to open fire on the knaves.[128]

If General Nelson's account seemed a bit self-serving, consider the out-of-channels report political Major General John A. McClernand sent directly his old political friend, His Excellency Abraham Lincoln:

> *We have just passed through a terrible battle, lasting two days. My division, as usual, has borne or shared in bearing the brunt. I have lost in killed and wounded about every third man of my command. Within a radius of 200 yards of my headquarters some 150 dead bodies were left on the field, the proportion of rebels to Union men being about three to one. Among the killed is General A. S. Johnston (said to be), who fell within 30 yards of my tent. Part of a battery belonging to the enemy was taken within 150 yards of my tent, and some 30 or 40 horses were killed within the same distance. The largely superior number of the enemy enabled him to flank me all day Sunday (the 6th), yet I retook my camp twice, and checked the enemy by repeatedly changing front and meeting him until night-fall, which, together with the arrival of Buell's forces, enabled us to attack the enemy in turn next day and drive him back with great slaughter.*
>
> *It was a great mistake that we did not pursue him Monday night and Tuesday.*[129]

Subsequent events would make it clear that McClernand was one of the "officers who were utterly unfit for their places" General Halleck had in mind when he prepared his reply to Edwin Stanton. Among other—what? misleading claims? lies?—was the assertion that General Johnston "fell within 30 yards of my tent." Johnston did not fall *anywhere;* when shot leading a charge, he rode back to his own lines, dismounted, and bled to death, absent the surgeon he had sent earlier to take care of Union wounded.[130]

Reporting officially was an art form that seemed to encourage writers to launder and exaggerate. The process began at regimental and brigade levels, was repeated at divisions, and left senior commanders such as Ulysses Grant (who faced the task of writing his own report) awash in prose of questionable veracity. At this relatively early stage of the war, *primus non decere* seemed the guiding principle; only a fool would ever put in writing anything that might harm either his own post-war political career or that of anyone who might come after him with a loaded pistol publicly later on.

None of this was new to seasoned lawyer Henry Wager Halleck. From his earliest days in California, he had not only survived but prospered by developing the ability to suspect extravagant profession and apparent understatement—and, by holding his own writings to minimum length, he had usually avoided exposure to unexpected and embarrassing liability.[131] But the reports pouring in from the veterans of Shiloh surely must have strained Old Brains' skills in detecting truth from falsehood.

As it turned out, he rendered judgment in a way that was breathtakingly subtle. In turning to the next item on his agenda—preparing to attack Beauregard at Corinth—he gave command of the three wings of his expanded army to Don Carlos Buell, John Pope, and Brigadier General George H. Thomas, earlier one of Buell's most effective division commanders in the effort (long since abandoned) to free Unionists in East Tennessee. Thomas' forces were those Ulysses Grant had led previously; "Unconditional Surrender" was designated Halleck's second-in-command. Old Brains also assigned McClernand and certain other political generals to the lowest level of military limbo: his army's reserve.[132]

So matters stood, roughly five months after General Halleck had assumed command of the department Pathfinder Frémont had almost destroyed. And immediately ahead for Old Brains was the challenge to prove that he was something more than a military theoretician or a headquarters desk-driver: Corinth.

4 ★ From Shiloh to Corinth to Hell

WAR DEPARTMENT, May 24, 1862.

Major-General HALLECK,
    Near Corinth, Miss.

Several dispatches from Assistant Secretary Scott and one from Governor [Oliver P.] Morton, asking re-enforcements for you, have been received. I beg you to be assured we do the best we can. I mean to cast no blame when I tell you each of our commanders along our line from Richmond to Corinth supposes himself to be confronted by numbers superior to his own.

Under this pressure we thinned the line on the upper Potomac, until yesterday it was broken at heavy loss to us, and General Banks put in great peril, out of which he is not yet extricated, and may be actually captured. We need men to repair this breach, and have them not at hand.

My dear General, I feel justified to rely very much on you. I believe you and the brave officers and men with you can and will get the victory at Corinth.[1]

A. LINCOLN.

OF ALL THE MESSAGES THE ACTING general-in-chief wrote that month, this one may have been the most remarkable. On that Saturday, Lincoln had just returned from a short visit to Major General Irvin McDowell's corps' headquarters at Falmouth, Virginia. While there, thinking that Confederate

Major General Thomas J. Jackson's forces had left the Shenandoah Valley and no longer threatened Washington, he had ordered McDowell to "make a good ready" and start his corps southward on Monday, May 26, to reinforce McClellan.[2] But a telegram Major General Nathaniel P. Banks sent from Strasburg, out in the Valley, on Friday night was waiting for Lincoln at the War Department's telegraph room:

> *Our troops were attacked at Front Royal this afternoon, and, though making a vigorous resistance, were compelled by superiority of numbers to retire toward Middletown. The rebel force is reported at 5,000 and is said to intend advancing on the Middletown road. No definite information has yet been received, the telegraph line having been early destroyed. The force had been gathering in the mountains, it is said, since Wednesday. Re-inforcements should be sent us if possible. Railway communication with Manassas probably broken up.[3]*

This was the breaking of the line to which the President had alluded in his message to General Halleck. Lincoln spent most of that Saturday reading incoming wires and studying the map of Virginia. "Stonewall" Jackson's sudden reappearance at Front Royal placed him in a position to cut Banks' division at Strasburg off from Winchester and the Potomac. Yet Jackson seemed headed toward Washington—and if he were, it might be possible to trap him. The task before the acting general-in-chief, then, was one of ordering such forces as he had to suspend their current operations and move as he directed.

During that hectic Saturday, Lincoln sent messages to Major Generals Frémont, McDowell, and McClellan—and to Halleck, though Old Brains was clearly unable because of distance to send forces to the fight that was inevitable in the Shenandoah Valley. Indirectly expressing appreciation for Lincoln's having taken the time to contact him, he hastened to remove reinforcing him from the President's list of worries by telegraphing Stanton:

> *I have asked for no re-enforcements, but only whether any were to be sent to me. If any were to be sent, I would wait for them; if not, I would venture an attack.*
>
> *We are now in immediate presence of the enemy, and battle may occur at any moment. I have every confidence that we shall succeed, but dislike to run any risk, and therefore waited to see if any more troops can be hoped for.*
>
> *Permit me to remark that we are operating upon too many*

points. Richmond and Corinth are now the great strategically [sic]
points of the war, and our success at these points should be insured at
all hazards. My army is daily improving in health and discipline.[4]

For roughly three weeks Halleck's hundred-thousand-plus men had
been moving slowly toward Corinth, which was only twenty-five miles or so
south-southwest of Pittsburg Landing and the Shiloh battleground.
Newspapermen and other critics of Old Brains compared his progress to
that of a snail. His reputation was eroded almost daily by allegations of
lethargy and timidity. Particularly damning, to the ignorant, was Halleck's
insistence that the army entrench after each forward movement. Eventually,
Halleck's Corinth Campaign would be declared an example of how *not* to
conduct an operation, and he would be branded a disaster as a field
commander.

Some of the condemnation of Halleck was rooted in misunderstanding of his intent. Was he advancing on Corinth to seize and hold a
strategic railroad hub, or to destroy Beauregard's army?

Detractors of the strategic-place theory blamed him for not moving
aggressively enough to prevent the Confederates' escape from annihilation.
Those who perceived (as did Halleck) that capturing Corinth would deprive
the Confederacy of rail communication between Memphis and Chattanooga expected that success would cause some rebel units west of Corinth
and also east of there to die on the vine; as to Beauregard, the sheer size of
Henry Halleck's army suggested that the Creole might run but only for a
time.

"An irritated old maid, a silly school girl, a vacillating coquette,"[5] was
one reporter's characterization of the man who—in these circumstances—
was taking an approach to combat that Stonewall Jackson would shortly put
this way to a subordinate: "I am obliged to sweat [my men] tonight, that I
may save their blood tomorrow."[6]

Among other facts Halleck's judges chose to ignore were the
unprecedented size of his force in such an undeveloped part of the country,
the total absence of means of water transportation for supplies from
Pittsburg Landing southward to Corinth and, consequently, the army's
dependence on wagons, the region's variations in terrain and shortage of
roads, the effects of bad weather, and the difficulty of obtaining reliable
information about Beauregard's reactions to his advance and preparations to
block it. These and other conditions were revealed in his messages to
Stanton:

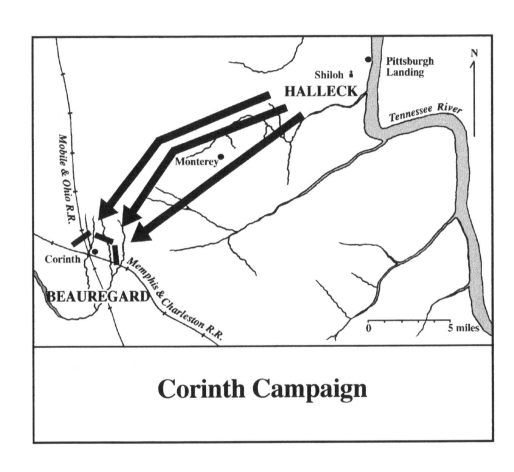

Corinth Campaign

PITTSBURG LANDING, May 2, 1862—11 a.m.

 The backwater of the Tennessee River from the flood has destroyed many of our bridges and overflowed the low lands and the creeks in our front. We have but few pontoons and no engineer troops. This greatly embarrasses our movement, as we cannot supply the army on the way. The river has begun to fall to-day, and we hope to move soon. We expect a terrible battle, but our men will fight well, and all are determined to have a victory.[7]

PITTSBURG LANDING, May 3, 1862.

 I leave here to-morrow morning, and our army will be before Corinth to-morrow night. There may be no telegraphic communication for the next two or three days.[8]

MONTEREY, May 6, 1862.

 The heavy rains of the 4th and 5th have destroyed some of our bridges and greatly injured the roads. We are rapidly repairing them. Our advance guards are within 6 miles of Corinth. Deserters report that Beauregard has received large re-enforcements from New Orleans, South Carolina, and Georgia, and is very confident of being able to repulse any attack we may make. This country is almost a wilderness and very difficult to operate in.[9]

FIVE MILES FROM CORINTH, Midnight, May 7, 1862.

 The advanced forces of the enemy, under Hardee, are 2 miles outside of the defenses at Corinth. The evidences are strong that the enemy are in force at Corinth. Pope's whole army will move forward in the morning to drive the enemy within his works. A severe battle will probably be fought.[10]

MONTEREY, May 13, 1862.

 We are gradually advancing on Corinth, but as the enemy is strongly intrenched, and his number equal if not superior to ours, it is necessary to move with great caution. Most of the country passed over is a thick forest, with numerous streams and deep marshes, which require corduroys and bridges. Our progress is necessarily slow.[11]

Monterey, barely north of the Tennessee-Mississippi state line, was about halfway between Pittsburg Landing and Corinth. General Halleck egregiously understated both the damage to the few roads in existence and the difficulty and time-consumption involved in corduroying them.

Moreover, critics seemed equally blind to the utter dependence of an army of more than a hundred thousand men on supply wagons which in turn were totally useless, unless and until adequate corduroying had been done— and often, done over and over. And the nearer to Corinth Halleck's army advanced, the longer the vitally important roads north to the Tennessee became and the more vulnerable this grotesquely massive army grew to the threats of starvation, ammunition depletion, or both.

The series of General Halleck's reports to Secretary of War Stanton continued:

> BEFORE CORINTH, *May 18, 1862.*
>   *Our whole line moved up yesterday to within 2 miles of enemy's works, driving back their advance guards, which made strong resistance. . . . The enemy apparently waiting our attack upon his works. Country is so wooded and marshy that we are obliged to feel our way step by step.*[12]

Many of the difficulties General Halleck was encountering were magnified by the presence of so many men. Concentration might afford advantages, but not during an approach to combat through terrain and in conditions that virtually confined units to a couple of poor roads; as a result, at times the huge three-wing army was advancing in two-abreast columns.

> CAMP, CORINTH ROAD, *May 22, 1862.*
>   *Daily skirmishing between our reconnoitering parties and the enemy. . . . The Sanitary Commission and State Governors carry away troops faster than I can recruit. Men only slightly unwell or feigning sickness are carried away without any authority.*[13]

So matters stood on May 24 when the acting general-in-chief telegraphed Halleck regarding the Confederates' sharp, surprising attack in the Shenandoah Valley. Lincoln set a trap for Jackson—but in so doing, he had fallen into one Stonewall and General Robert E. Lee had devised for him.

2

ALTHOUGH THERE WAS NO OBVIOUS CONNECTION between events in Washington, Virginia's Shenandoah Valley, and the forests and ravines north of Corinth, once again Pathfinder Frémont was creating problems that were to plague the Union's amateur acting general-in-chief.

On May 24, Lincoln had sent Frémont—at a place called Franklin in the Alleghenies, near where Jackson had given him a whipping back on May 8—an order that, curiously, he had Secretary of War Stanton sign. After replying to an administrative question Frémont had raised and then giving a summary of what was known about General Banks' situation, the message concluded:

> *You are therefore ordered by the President to move against Jackson at Harrisonburg, and operate against the enemy in such a way as to relieve Banks. This movement must be made immediately.*[14]

Harrisonburg, Frémont's objective on the Valley Turnpike, was about forty miles southeast of his camps at Franklin and roughly the same distance southwest of Strasburg. Once at Harrisonburg, Frémont's fifteen thousand men would be able to stop Jackson from retreating and also act as an anvil against which Banks' division or one of McDowell's could hammer the Confederates to pieces.

But acting General-in-Chief Lincoln was attempting to carry out the very operation the real Napoleon had described as the most difficult in war: *combining one's forces on the battlefield in the face of the enemy.* Worse, on Tuesday night, May 27, Lincoln received a message Frémont had sent him from Moorefield, a town in the opposite direction from Harrisonburg.[15] Angrily he wired back: "You were expressly ordered to march to Harrisonburg. What does this mean?"[16]

And The Pathfinder replied:

> *In executing any order received I take it for granted that I am to exercise discretion concerning its literal execution, according to circumstances. If I am to understand that literal obedience to orders is required, please say so. I have no desire to exercise any power which you do not think belongs of necessity to my position in the field.*[17]

The contemptuous, condescending, insolent tone of Frémont's response was reminiscent of that employed in his refusal to modify his emancipation proclamation back in August of the year before. Yet, in this instance, Lincoln had to concede that his order on Saturday had not been peremptory. Moreover, apparently the President had not seen or had forgotten about a message Stanton had sent The Pathfinder on Sunday:

General Banks fell back yesterday from Strasburg to Winchester. To-day he has been driven from Winchester toward Harper's Ferry. You must direct your attention to falling upon the enemy at whatever place you can find him with all speed. McDowell will also operate toward the same object with his force. You must not stop for supplies, but seize what you need and push rapidly forward; the object being to cut off and capture the rebel force in the Shenandoah.[18]

There was blame enough to go around, but Frémont's habit of going his own way obliged Lincoln to abandon the hope of smashing Jackson's forces against an anvil at Harrisonburg and to order a convergence of divisions at Strasburg. Such was part of the price he was paying for having made politicians Banks and Frémont generals and giving them command of combat forces; also, this was his reward for having given Frémont a second chance—and for, in so doing, having tried to appease the Radicals.

Concurrently, oblivious to the anxiety and anger and frustrations afflicting his superiors in the faraway War Department's telegraph room, General Halleck was continuing to provide progress reports:

CAMP ON CORINTH ROAD, *May 28, 1862.*
    Three strong reconnoitering columns advanced this morning on the right center and left, to feel the enemy and unmask his batteries. Enemy hotly contested his ground at each point, but was driven back with considerable loss. . . . The fighting will probably be renewed to-morrow morning at daybreak. The whole country is so thickly wooded that we are compelled to feel our way.[19]

Halleck might have commented as well about the fog of war being an impediment. If General Beauregard was not making his intentions known—conveying confusion, mostly—the reason may have been contained in a letter he wrote General Samuel Cooper, the Confederate Army's adjutant-general in Richmond, on May 19:

Since the battle of Shiloh, when I assumed command of the Western Department, . . . no instructions from the War Department . . . have been received by me.
    In the absence of such instructions I deem it advisable to lay before the Department . . . my reasons for still holding this position against a much stronger force of the enemy in my front, even at the risk of a defeat, instead of retiring into the interior of the country

along the Mobile and Ohio or Memphis and Charleston Railroad, which would draw him after me and increase the obstacles he would have to encounter in his march.

It is evident that Corinth, situated at the intersection of those two railroads, presents the advantage, besides its favorable local features for defense, of possessing those two main arteries for the supplies of a large army. By its abandonment only one of those roads could then be relied upon for that object.

If the enemy took possession of this strategic point, he would at once open his communications by railroad with Columbus and Paducah in his rear and Huntsville on his left flank, and thus relieve himself from the awkward position in which he is about to find himself by the rapid fall of the Tennessee River. . . .

It might be asked, why not retreat along the Memphis and Charleston Railroad toward the Mississippi River? The reason is obvious. Cut off from communication with the East, the State of Mississippi could not long support a large army.

It might also be asked, why not attempt to hold both the Memphis and Charleston and the Mobile and Ohio Railroads? Because, being already inferior in numbers to the enemy, should we divide our forces, it would not take him long to destroy both fractions.

Thus it becomes essential to hold Corinth to the last extremity, if the odds are not too great against us, even at the risk of a defeat.

Should the Department judge otherwise, however, I stand ready to carry its views into effect as soon as practicable, as my only desire is to save the cause and serve the country.[20]

Unwittingly, General Beauregard had paid considerable tribute to Old Brains' generalship. In fact, even General Lee, then military advisor to President Davis, seemed at a loss to recommend a course of action that would wrest victory away from the Yankees advancing at a snail's pace. But Lee tried, in a message to Beauregard sent from Richmond on May 26:

Should the superior numbers of the enemy force you back . . . it is hoped you will be able to strike a successful blow at the enemy if he follows, which will enable you to gain the ascendancy and drive him back to the Ohio.

The maintenance of your present position, with the advantages you ascribe to it, so long as you can resist the enemy and subsist your army, is of course preferable to withdrawing from it, and thus laying open more of the country to his ravages, unless by skillful maneuvering you can entice him into a more favorable position to attack. . . .[21]

Presumably, Lee's response had been reviewed and approved by President Davis. Before that letter left Richmond, however, Major General William J. Hardee had presented his analysis of the situation to the general commanding at Corinth, and it, like Beauregard's earlier "Thus it becomes essential to hold Corinth to the last extremity" statement, reflected acknowledgment that Halleck's strategy had all but succeeded. Moreover, in the study he forwarded to his commander on May 25, Hardee put considerable weight on the effectiveness of Old Brains' *tactics*—even entrenching:

The situation at Corinth requires that we should attack the enemy at once, or await his attack or evacuate the place, assuming that we have 50,000 men, and the enemy nearly twice that number, protected by intrenchments.

I am clearly of opinion that no attack should be made. Our forces are inferior, and the battle of Shiloh proves, with only the advantage of position, it was hazardous to contend against his superior strength; and to attack him in his intrenchments now would probably inflict on us and the Confederacy a fatal blow. Neither the number nor instruction of our troops renders them equal to the task.

I think we can successfully repel any attack on our camp by the enemy, but it is manifest no attack is meditated. It will be approached gradually, and [we] will be shelled and bombarded without equal means to respond. This will compel us to make sorties against his intrenched positions under most adverse circumstances or to evacuate the place.

The latter seems to me inevitable. If so, the only remaining question is, whether the place should be evacuated before, or after, or during its defense.

After fire is opened, or the place is actively shelled or bombarded, or during such an attack it will be difficult to evacuate the place in good order. With a large body of men imperfectly disciplined any idle rumor may spread a panic and inextricable confusion may follow, so that the retreat may become a rout.

The same objections would apply to any partial or feeble

defense of the place and an attempt to evacuate it in the mean time. If the defense be not determined or the battle decisive no useful result would follow, but it would afford an opportunity to our enemies to magnify the facts, give them a pretext to claim a victory, and to discourage our friends at home and abroad, and diminish, if not destroy, all claims of foreign intervention.

Under these circumstances I think the evacuation, if it be determined upon, should be made before the enemy opens fire, and not coupled with a sortie against his intrenchments or partial battle. It should be done promptly, if done at all. Even now the enemy can shell our camp. It should be done in good order, so as not to discourage our friends or give a pretext for the triumph of our enemies. . . .

If we resolve to evacuate, every hour of delay only serves to augment our difficulties. The enemy every day grows stronger on our flanks, and menaces more and more our communications. If he effects his designs, we must fight at every disadvantage or retreat disastrously. History and our country will judge us not by the movement, but its consequences.[22]

General Beauregard's response to Hardee came quickly:

I fully concur in the views contained in your letter of the 25th instant, received last night, and I had already commenced giving orders to my chiefs of staff departments for its execution.

But everything that is done must be done under the plea of the intention to take the offensive at the opportune moment. Every commandant of corps must get everything ready to move at a moment's notice, and must see to the proper condition of the roads and bridges his corps is to travel upon.[23]

But the Creole had neglected one detail in adopting deception: He did not inform Jefferson Davis, or anyone, that he no longer thought it "essential to hold Corinth to the last extremity."[24]

3

THAT GENERAL HALLECK REMAINED utterly ignorant of any change in Beauregard's intentions was evident in a message he sent Cump Sherman on

May 29, three days after the Confederate heeded Hardee's counsel:

> *I have just returned from Pope's. His battery of 20-pounder Parrotts opened about 10 o'clock, and soon compelled the enemy to abandon their advanced work. He [Pope] is of opinion that Price, Van Dorn, and Hardee marched their forces against him last night. This seems probable, but we must not trust to appearances. They may suddenly concentrate against you. I do not believe they will attack our right, but it is best to be prepared.*[25]

At 1:20 a.m. on Saturday, May 30, 1862, Halleck's headquarters received the first in a series of messages from General Pope that gradually dispersed the fog of war:

> *The enemy is re-enforcing heavily, by trains, in my front and on my left. The cars are running constantly, and the cheering is immense every time they unload in front of me. I have no doubt, from all appearances, that I shall be attacked in heavy force at daylight.*[26]

Next, at 6:00 a.m:

> *All very quiet since 4 o'clock. Twenty-six trains left during the night. A succession of loud explosions, followed by dense black smoke in clouds. Everything indicates evacuation and retreat.*
>
> *I am pushing forward my skirmishers in several directions toward Corinth. Will telegraph you again in a few minutes.*[27]

At 7:15 a.m:

> *I am in possession of the enemy's intrenched position, an embrasured work of seven guns. Four regiments are feeling their way into Corinth, and are now within three-quarters of a mile of the town. The whole country here seems to be fortified.*[28]

At 8:25 a.m:

> *The enemy evacuated yesterday and last night. They marched down the Mobile Railroad. Their sick went in the cars toward Memphis. I am pushing into town; my skirmishers are now in the outskirts.*[29]

Fifteen minutes later:

My advance, the Thirty-ninth Ohio and Forty-second Illinois, entered the town and planted the United States flag on the courthouse at 6.40 this morning. They were the first troops in the place. I am throwing my cavalry and artillery in pursuit. . . .[30]

And at 12:45 p.m. on May 30, Pope reported:

The advance of my cavalry detachment came upon the extreme rear guard of the enemy 8 miles from Corinth, on the Mobile and Ohio road, in the act of burning the bridge. They were at once dispersed, with loss of 40 prisoners. The fire was put out. The cavalry is pushing on.[31]

Major General John Pope's reward was a message that afternoon from Halleck that contained another mission:

Reports from Corinth respecting enemy's movements are so conflicting, it is very difficult to fix definitely now our plans. Buell thinks a body of the enemy has moved west to attack our right flank. If we advance under these circumstances it will be best to move cautiously, leaving Buell to act either on the right or left, as circumstances may require. You will move south and east, feeling the enemy as you advance. Your provision trains should follow. The distance of your advance must be decided hereafter. Should you be attacked by Price and Van Dorn in force, Buell will act as a reserve. The entire programme may be changed to-morrow. I have ordered my horse, and will meet you at your headquarters. Carry forward the telegraph with you.[32]

Toward the end of the day, General Halleck sent Stanton a preliminary report on Beauregard's departure:

Enemy's positions and works in front of Corinth were exceedingly strong. He cannot occupy stronger positions. In his flight this morning he destroyed an immense amount of public and private property—stores, provisions, wagons, tents, &c. For miles out of the town the roads are filled with arms, haversacks, &c., thrown away by his flying troops. A large number of prisoners and deserters have been captured, and estimated by General Pope at 2,000. General Beauregard evidently distrusts his army, or he would have defended so strong a position. His troops are generally much discouraged and demoralized. In all their engagements the last few days their resistance has been weak.[33]

And so it was that another victory had been won by a slow-moving, ugly, very cautious, goggle-eyed tortoise. Yet people throughout the Union would little note nor long remember, except in disparaging ways and pejorative terms, Old Brains' achievement as a field commander. Good news from Corinth was eclipsed by fears on the part of the war managers in the War Department's telegraph room that Pathfinder Frémont was about to doom Lincoln's revised plan to trap and destroy Stonewall Jackson to dismal and humiliating failure, and also by a development east of Richmond that was another consequence of Lee's and "Old Jack's" resolve to keep McDowell's corps from reinforcing the Young Napoleon's huge army menacing the Confederacy's capital.

Jefferson Davis was furious when he heard that instead of holding Corinth "to the last extremity," Beauregard had abandoned the place without a fight.[34] But Saturday, May 31, 1862, would not have been a good day for the Confederate commander-in-chief in any case. General Joseph Eggleston Johnston had told Lee that on May 31 he intended to attack two Union corps just east of Richmond that McClellan had left south of the Chickahominy River, which seemed to be a splendid thing to do since the Young Napoleon had deployed the greater portion of his enormous Army of the Potomac *north* of the rainstorm-flooded stream. But by afternoon no sounds of gunfire had been heard in the Confederate President's office in Richmond, so he rode eastward to Johnston's headquarters. He arrived just in time to see the general commanding and his aides gallop off toward what seemed a brisk, if belated, firefight. Joining General Lee, who was already mounted on his great gray warhorse, Traveller, old soldier Davis followed.[35]

Again, there was no apparent connection between a battle Johnston's subordinates had delayed, and then badly botched, and anything happening in Corinth, Mississippi. But on that Saturday afternoon, near a railroad station called Fair Oaks, General Johnston was seriously wounded. On the ride back into Richmond after darkness had suspended the firing, President Davis decided to place Robert E. Lee in command of Joe Johnston's army—which he did the next day.[36] Just under three months later, Henry Halleck would be wearing himself out trying to keep his old fellow engineer back in his New York Harbor fortifications years from destroying a Union army defending Washington on the old Manassas battlegrounds, a badly mauled force commanded by John Pope that may very well have been betrayed by George McClellan.

Another reason neither Abraham Lincoln nor Edwin Stanton had been paying much attention to General Halleck's incoming messages was that—as usual—John Charles Frémont was failing to obey direct orders. As a consequence—and also because acting General-in-Chief Lincoln had not directed McDowell's leading division to advance far enough westward—it appeared on that Saturday afternoon that while McClellan seemed about to lose two of his corps of his river-divided army, out in the Shenandoah Valley Stonewall Jackson might well slip southward through Strasburg *before* the jaws of Lincoln's revised trap could be slammed shut.

Not until early on that Saturday morning had Jackson ordered the forces that had been threatening Harpers Ferry on the Potomac, northwest of Washington, to withdraw. Yet his "foot cavalry" covered the nearly forty-two miles to Strasburg by late the next day.

A week later, up the valley at Cross Keys and Port Republic, Old Jack would compound Abraham Lincoln's humiliation. He did this by whipping first Pathfinder Frémont, and then turning around overnight to fight off a strong attack launched from nearly the opposite direction by the leading brigades of a division McDowell had been obliged to send westward, all the way from Fredericksburg, instead of southward to reinforce McClellan.[37]

Fair Oaks, the battle fought east of Richmond on May 31 and June 1, 1862, turned out to be one of those fights in which a great many young Americans were killed or wounded while settling nothing. General McClellan, who had taken no part in the engagement because of illness, blamed his brush with defeat on Lincoln's having reversed the decision to give him McDowell's corps.[38] Yet the Young Napoleon had been fortunate, in a sense. As far back as Sunday, May 25, so completely had Stonewall's threat dominated the acting general-in-chief's thinking that he had warned McClellan: "I think the time is near when you must either attack Richmond or give up the job and come to the defense of Washington."[39]

But Lincoln had left McClellan in Joe Johnston's path, and Frémont had behaved like Frémont, and—in part because of the amateur general-in-chief's bungling—Stonewall Jackson had been able to astonish the world with his audacity. Such was the background for the worst mistake Henry Wager Halleck ever made.

4

PIERRE GUSTAVE TOUSSANT BEAUREGARD, with perhaps fifty-five thousand men, had found Corinth an unhealthy place before Halleck's approach added battle casualties to the burdens being borne by Confederate medical personnel. Inadequate supplies of water, much of it polluted, amounted to a farewell gift from the Creole. Moreover, most of General Halleck's men were from more congenial climates north of the Ohio River, and this increased their vulnerability to Mississippi's often oppressive heat and humidity.

Understandably, Old Brains began thinking of dispersing his 120,000-man force almost as soon as his troops occupied Corinth. On that day, May 31, he revealed his intentions in a message to Secretary Stanton:

> *Main body of the enemy has moved south toward Okolona. General Pope, with 50,000, men is following him. I do not, however, propose to pursue him far into Mississippi. Having no baggage trains except railroad trains, he can move much faster than we can pursue. I propose to immediately open the railroad to Decatur, Ala., and to Columbus, Ky. The fall of the Tennessee River will soon render the use of this road necessary to us for supplies.*[40]

But General Halleck's capture of Corinth, with minimal combat casualties, was interpreted by some of the Union's war managers in Washington in terms of their priorities at the moment: trapping Jackson out at Strasburg, and keeping two-fifths of McClellan's Army of the Potomac from being destroyed in the fight east of Richmond near Fair Oaks. Telegraphed Assistant Secretary of War Thomas Scott to Halleck:

> *Have you obtained any reliable information from deserters or prisoners in regard to Beauregard's movements? Has Beauregard or any part of his army left for Virginia? . . . In the present state of affairs here information on this subject is of the utmost importance.*[41]

Quartermaster-General Montgomery Meigs, evidently pressed into duty as an aide to the beleaguered men in the telegraph room, added emphasis to Scott's concern. "Do the abandoned works at Corinth indicate a very large rebel force?" he asked Halleck. "Can they have begun the evacuation long enough since to have re-enforced Richmond by this time? Their attitude at Richmond has changed, and there have been rumors that Beauregard reached that city on Thursday week."[42]

Idle questions, those, for acting General-in-Chief Abraham Lincoln had no troops nearer Richmond's gates than recruits training near Washington with which to reinforce the Young Napoleon: Irvin McDowell's corps was out in the Shenandoah Valley, where Robert Lee and Old Jack had lured them. Even so, Old Brains sent his superiors a few words intended to dispel the fog of war: "If Beauregard has been at Richmond others have forged his signature, as I have received letters from him about exchange of prisoners, and nearly every day for this fortnight. . . ."[43]

Soon, however, armchair strategists in Washington and elsewhere consulted their maps and concluded that Halleck ought to have kept his 120,000 troops together and marched straight down to Vicksburg and captured the "Gibraltar of the West." Sending Don Carlos Buell's divisions eastward and some of George Thomas' westward to repair railroads would be added to their declarations that Halleck was excessively timid, entirely too cautious, a fool easily fooled.

But Henry Halleck had carried out operations on three or more fronts in Missouri, and his accomplishments there and more recently in the field demonstrated that he knew what he was doing and ignored those who did not. On June 4, 1862, he sent this report to Stanton:

> *General Pope, with 40,000, is 30 miles south of Corinth, pushing the enemy hard. He already reports 10,000 prisoners and deserters from the enemy and 15,000 stand of arms captured. Thousands of the enemy are throwing away their arms. A farmer says that when Beauregard learned that Colonel Elliott had cut the railroad on his line of retreat he became frantic, and told his men to save themselves the best they could. We have captured nine locomotives and a number of cars. One is already repaired and is running to-day. Several more will be in running order in two or three days. The result is all I could possibly desire.*[44]

Halleck's last sentence would often be cited as his reply to those who called his victory at Corinth hollow, his expression of satisfaction an empty bellow. Reactions of the men in the War Department's telegraph room, however, were different. First, Edwin Stanton's: "Your glorious dispatch has just been received, and I have sent it into every State. The whole land will soon ring with applause at the achievement of your gallant army and its able and victorious commander."[45] And then Abraham Lincoln: "Your dispatch of to-day to Secretary of War received. Thanks for the good news it brings." After the Young Napoleon's having been caught with his massive army astride the Chickahominy and mauled severely, and with Stonewall Jackson as yet unmolested as he withdrew up the Shenandoah Valley, the Union's acting general-in-chief needed some encouragement. "Have you anything from Memphis," he asked, "or other parts of the Mississippi River? Please answer."[46]

General Halleck replied:

> *General Pope's dispatch of yesterday assured me that the enemy was rapidly retreating south. At 10 o'clock this morning he telegraphed me that Beauregard was making a stand at Baldwin, 31 miles south, and was likely to attack his advance guard, under Generals Rosecrans and Hamilton. I immediately ordered General Buell with two divisions to advance in direction, and if he deemed necessary to assume the entire command, as the ranking officer. As the entire* [Union] *force on the Mobile and Ohio south of Corinth is nearly 60,000, no apprehension is felt for the result. The other divisions of the army are repairing the railroad to Decatur, Memphis, and Columbus, but can be immediately brought into position if required. It is believed that the enemy is making a demonstration merely to cover his retreat.*[47]

George Brinton McClellan apparently still thought of himself as removed only *temporarily* as general-in-chief, for four days after Joseph Johnston's under-managed, bungled attack at Fair Oaks had almost taken two of his corps out of the war he had the temerity to send this message to Lincoln:

> *May I again invite your excellency's attention to the great importance of occupying Chattanooga and Dalton* [nearby, in northwest Georgia] *by our Western forces? The evacuation of Corinth would appear to render this very easy. The importance of this move cannot be exaggerated.*[48]

Lincoln relayed McClellan's ingenuous effort to reassume direction of forces other than his own to Old Brains at 9:30 p.m. on June 5. Halleck's response on June 7 was typically terse, to the point, and impersonal:

> *Preparations for Chattanooga made five days ago, and troops moved in that direction.* [Union Brigadier General Ormsby] *Mitchel's foolish destruction of bridges* [over the Tennessee] *embarrassed me*

very much, but I am working night and day to remedy the error, and will very soon re-enforce him.[49]

Old Brains had taken McClellan's measure back in the winter, when the Young Napoleon had inadvertently revealed the appalling shallowness of his thinking in the messages the generals exchanged. But for such intramural nonsense to be recurring was a signal that absent any combat—Jackson wrecked Pathfinder Frémont's force on June 7 and then the one sent by Irvin McDowell the next day, ending the Valley Campaign several days after Lincoln had sent messages to both Union commanders to withdraw northward and chase Stonewall no more—prosecution of the war was returning to the usual weeks and weeks of boring trivia, interrupted occasionally by flashes of sheer, heart-stopping terror.

Among the first signs of insanity recurring was the lengthy but unbelievably revealing letter political Major General John A. McClernand sent General Halleck on June 1, while the guns Sherman's men and Pope's had fired from above Corinth were still cooling:

> *Now, since the evacuation of Corinth has partially relieved you of the perplexing cares and responsibilities lately pressing upon your attention, I trust I will be indulged in bringing to your notice a matter somewhat personal to myself.*
>
> *Since your reorganization of the forces of this department my position in the Army of the Tennessee has been one of actual inferiority, if not practical subordination, to that of other officers inferior to me in rank. A striking proof of this fact is to be found in the comparative smallness of my command, in its detached and separated condition, and its practical negation in the miscellaneous duties required of it of any distinctive character. . . . Other circumstances importing the same verity might be adduced, but I forbear to dwell upon them, out of regard for your valuable time and from a sense of personal humiliation in recounting them.*
>
> *Although not educated to the profession of arms, yet, having seen some service in the field in early life, I have seen still more recently, and trust that I have not proved myself unequal to others who, claiming the advantage of such an education, shared common trials with me in the progress of the war, or that I am unequal to them in public estimation of individual character or capability. . . .*
>
> *I have hastily recalled these incidents in no spirit of egotism or vainglory, but in justice to the humble part I have borne in the*

present unhappy drama and what I deem to be the rights and dignity of my rank. On the other hand, if an inferior rank had been assigned to me by those whose prerogative it is to dispense rank, having decided to accept it, I would have cordially submitted to all of its conditions and consequences. In that case not a murmur would have been heard from me.

Animated by no other feelings than high regard and profound respect for you, both personally and officially, I hope you will receive this communication in that spirit of kindness, generosity, and forbearance which it is intended to evoke, and which, I trust, is due its frankness, sincerity, and the justice of the case it presents.[50]

Henry Halleck and John McClernand would cross trails again, but Abraham Lincoln's political associate from Illinois was not alone in bothering the general commanding with matters of that ilk. Reflected in Old Brains' letter to Don Carlos Buell dated June 12 was patience, along with understandable irritation:

I have just been shown a letter from General Nelson complaining that newspapers have done him injustice in stating that the troops of General Pope and some of the troops of General Sherman were the first in Corinth. In my reports to the Secretary of War I stated precisely what was officially reported to me and in the order of time as reported. General Sherman was the first to report to me that his troops were inside of the enemy's intrenchments; next General Pope, stating the exact hour and minute his men raised the flag on the court-house in Corinth; next, but some time after, came General Nelson's report, indorsed by you.

All these were sent to the Secretary of War in the order in which they were received. I never inquired nor do I now know who was first in Corinth nor have I ever attempted to decide upon the conflicting claims. Probably if the question is one of any importance it can be determined when all the official reports have been received.

Certainly General Nelson can have no cause to think that I have done him any injustice by sending to Washington the several reports, his among others, immediately on my receiving them. His insinuation that my headquarters furnish newspaper articles is a gross injustice to my staff.

The explanation of the substance of telegraphic dispatches and reports getting into the newspapers is very plain. All officers are well aware that the substance of such dispatches and reports, when of interest as news which it is proper to publish, is posted up on a bulletin-board, where any one who chooses can copy and send them to the newspapers.

No newspaper reporter has ever been harbored in my camp and no one has been permitted to obtain news at my headquarters which was not public for all who wished it.

It has also been reported to me that General McCook felt aggrieved that, in telegraphing to the Secretary of War the opening of batteries on the evening before the evacuation of Corinth, his was not mentioned. At the time I had not been informed that he had opened or established any battery within breaching distance of the enemy's works. I learned that afterward.

Please inform these gentlemen that no intentional injustice has been done them, and that full credit will be given to them as soon as I receive your official report on the operations before Corinth. Nothing could possibly be further from my mind than the intention to praise one officer at the expense of another equally meritorious.[51]

Ulysses Grant wrote no letter, but his dissatisfaction over having been made Halleck's second-in-command led him to believe an injustice had been done him. Indeed, in years to come, historians would write habitually that Halleck denied Grant command of a combat unit because he was jealous of Unconditional Surrender's fame and distrusted him.

Actually, the assignment reflected Halleck's confidence in Grant's ability to command the large force in the event he could not continue to perform. The jealousy slur was preposterous, given the likelihood that no glory was to be won by anyone in a campaign such as Corinth; moreover, Halleck had obtained all the authority he had felt he needed and a victorious end to the war at the earliest possible time seemed his only desire. Indeed, to what more could he have aspired? Finally, officers who have experienced the incomparable satisfaction of having commanded units in battle *always* find boredom and envy natural consequences of service as second-in-command.

General Sherman persuaded Grant to forget about resigning.[52] No one in Old Brains' army afforded a more impressive example of bounce-back from adversity—the newspapers' allegations of insanity, relegation to rear-area assignments during Grant's seizures of Forts Henry and Donelson, criticism for not having enforced Halleck's order to entrench before hell broke loose at Shiloh—than Cump, and it may have occurred to Grant that if Sherman could thrive under Halleck's command, so might he.

Indeed, Sherman might have harbored some resentment over Halleck's having given wings of the army to John Pope and George Thomas while leaving him where he had been at Shiloh, commanding a division. But there was no evidence of that in the congratulatory message Cump wrote to his troops on the day they entered Corinth:

> *It is a victory as brilliant and important as any recorded in history, and every officer and soldier who has lent his aid has just reason to be proud of his part. No amount of sophistry or words from the leaders of the rebellion can succeed in giving the evacuation of Corinth under the circumstances any title other than that of a signal defeat, more humiliating to them and to their cause than if we had entered the place over the dead and mangled bodies of their soldiers. We are not here to kill and slay, but to vindicate the honor and just authority of that Government which has been bequeathed to us by our honored fathers, and to whom we would be recreant if we permitted their work to pass to our children weaned and spoiled by ambitious and wicked rebels.*[53]

Not from that day, May 31, 1862, onward would such a realistic evaluation of Henry Halleck's Corinth campaign be made.

5

AFTER A WEEKEND IN WHICH Stonewall Jackson had marched through the jaws of Lincoln's trap, Halleck had completed his nigh-bloodless seizure of Corinth, and Robert E. Lee had been given command of a Confederate army east of Richmond that had nearly deprived McClellan of up to forty thousand troops, the winds of civil war blew in relatively gentle gusts during the middle weeks of June 1862.

Out in northern Mississippi and southern Tennessee thousands of Halleck's men were learning a new trade: railroad repairing. General Lee, nicknamed the King of Spades, set his Army of Northern Virginia to digging more field fortifications south of the Chickahominy River. And in Washington, the Union's war managers—notably, the acting general-in-chief—attempted to wrap their minds around the complex, always vexing problem of what to try next.

From the points of view of the movers and shakers in both

belligerents' capitals, it seemed that the landscape was littered with generals who had failed: Frémont, Banks, Beauregard, Joseph E. Johnston, and apparently the amateur Lincoln. A few new names appeared and some familiar ones reappeared on the order of battle charts. Braxton Bragg replaced Beauregard, who had relieved himself of command after his retreat from Corinth ended at Tupelo, Mississippi. John Pope, victor of the little-noted encounters at New Madrid and Island No. 10 and Old Brains' point man in the pursuit of Beauregard southward from Corinth, was suddenly summoned to Washington. Halleck placed Ulysses Grant in command of the forces he sent into western Tennessee, toward Memphis. And in a report to Secretary of War Stanton, he commended the performance of Philip H. Sheridan, a former quartermaster he had reassigned to a combat cavalry unit, and recommended his promotion to brigadier general.[54]

On June 8, Lincoln extended Halleck's departmental lines to include all of Kentucky and Tennessee.[55] Old Brains ordered Sherman toward Memphis.[56] Halleck revoked the three-wing organization on June 10 and replaced it with one consisting of corps commanded by Major Generals Grant, Buell, and Pope.[57]

As had been the case in St. Louis since mid-November 1861, General Halleck was directing the operations of three widely separated forces from a headquarters desk. Dealing with mundane hazards threatening troops' welfare was not raw material for chronicles of heroes, and indeed it may have been an indication of how far removed from desire for personal acclaim Old Brains actually was when he filed this lengthy but revealing report, dated June 25, 1862, to Secretary of War Stanton:

> *On arriving at Pittsburg Landing just after the battle I found the sick lists in the armies of General Grant and General Buell enormous. An immediate change of position seemed of imperative necessity. . . .*
>
> *On reaching the higher land a few miles south of the plain of Shiloh a decided improvement was observed in the health of the command. The issue of whisky rations mixed with quinine, under the judicious advice of Dr. McDougall, assisted much in this change.*
>
> *Moreover the employment of the men in building roads, throwing up intrenchments, and doing picket duty in the face of an active enemy served as a diversion from the ordinary duty of camp, and contributed not a little to the diminution of the sick lists.*
>
> *Nevertheless, the injudicious conduct of State Sanitary Commissions and State Governors, who visited the regimental camps and*

publicly offered free passages home to all who were sick, took off thousands of soldiers who were either well enough at the time or would have been in a few days to perform their duties. I found it very difficult to remedy this evil without giving serious offense to men who came here, as they believed, on an errand of mercy and charity. Their intentions were undoubtedly good, but the effect was exceedingly injurious to the efficiency of the army.

Since the evacuation of Corinth and pursuit of the enemy south our army has been comparatively in good condition. The question now arises, can it be kept so during the summer? Or, in other words, can we carry on any summer campaign without having a large portion of our men on the sick list?

If we follow the enemy into the swamps of Mississippi there can be no doubt that our army will be disabled by disease. And yet to lie still, doing nothing, will not be satisfactory to the country nor conducive to the health of the army. I have therefore deemed it best under the circumstances to establish a strong corps of observation a few miles south of this place, on high limbered [sic] *ridges in the vicinity of clear streams and springs of water. . . .*

General Grant's army has been mainly occupied along the railroads to Memphis and Columbus and driving guerrilla parties out of West Tennessee. As soon as this work is completed they can best guard the railroads by occupying positions at or near Hernando, Holly Springs, and Ripley. These places are on a plateau which is said to be the most healthy part of Mississippi.

Re-enforcements have already been ordered to General Curtis on the White River [in Arkansas], *and others will soon be sent. . . .*

General Buell's army is moving east through a healthy region via Decatur, Huntsville, and Stevenson to Chattanooga and East Tennessee. Should he be able to penetrate into Georgia as far as Atlanta he will still be in a dry and mountainous country.

After a full consideration of the matter, on consultation with medical officers, I cannot think of a better disposition of the army so as to guard its health and at the same time make it useful. Of course this plan is based on the supposition that the enemy will not attempt an active campaign during the summer months; should he do so, or should he expose himself so that we can gain some decided advantage by a movement, the present dispositions must be varied to suit the change of circumstances.

In this arrangement I have not provided for a movement on

Vicksburg. It is hoped that the two flotillas united will be able to reduce that place. If not, it will probably be necessary to fit out an expedition from the army.

I have no doubt that with all possible care in adopting every sanitary precaution our troops will suffer considerably from sickness. In this climate it will be unavoidable. But under the advice of Dr. McDougall and his medical officers I think we can prevent the mortality from being greater than it was last winter in Missouri, Kentucky, and Tennessee.

If the War Department has any suggestions or instructions to give in the matter under consideration I shall be most happy to receive them.[58]

Arriving in the War Department's telegraph room as it did at an inopportune time, and reporting nothing really new regarding operations, it is likely that Halleck's (for him) lengthy, technical message attracted no attention. Certainly his critics, then and since, ignored it. Yet it indicated, clearly, that at this fairly early stage in the war, he was not only aware of the disproportionate number of non-battle casualties in his units but doing what he could to ameliorate the hazards.

Take care of your men and they will take care of you would later become standard admonition to combat leaders. Here, Henry Halleck was concerned only with conserving the well-being, indeed the lives, of his men—remarkable, for a lawyer with no previous troop duty only eight months away from his practice in San Francisco. Unfortunately, his example would be lost in the fog of war then enveloping the Atlantic seaboard from Washington to below Richmond.

6

IF GENERAL HALLECK EXPECTED TO SPEND the summer planning and preparing for a drive toward Vicksburg in the fall, he seriously underestimated the influence events in the East were to have on his future. Given the trends in Abraham Lincoln's thinking, which no man could discern at the time, it was inevitable that changes would be ordered by Washington.

After Stonewall Jackson wrecked both columns that had tried to trap him at Port Republic, squabbling broke out among the federal commanders in the Shenandoah Valley.[59] By then Lincoln recognized his inability to direct operations from the War Department's telegraph room. Concurrently, he was vexed by the Young Napoleon's steady flow of excuses for not seizing Richmond and his incessant demand for more troops. Senator "Bluff Ben" Wade and the other Radical Republicans had never stopped seeking McClellan's banishment, and their fellow abolitionist in Lincoln's cabinet, Treasury Secretary Salmon P. Chase, agreed that drastic action was needed. So did Secretary of War Edwin Stanton; his close friendship with McClellan had not survived the winter.[60]

Chase and his fellow-Ohioan Wade had been favorably impressed by the victories won in the West by Major General John Pope, the son of one of Lincoln's Illinois associates and son-in-law of a staunch Republican representative from Ohio, an escort on the President-elect's Washington-bound train back in February 1861. Moreover, Pope was known to be anti-slavery and anti-McClellan. Accordingly, Lincoln needed no persuasion when someone suggested that he send for Pope.[61]

Apparently, the acting general-in-chief saw in John Pope the solution to several problems. The young general could take command of the forces still in the Shenandoah Valley. But there was an additional possibility, one that prompted Secretary of the Navy Gideon Welles to write in his diary: "A part of this intrigue has been the withdrawal of McClellan and the Army of the Potomac from before Richmond and turning it into the Army of Washington under Pope."[62]

Adding to all this was a message from the Young Napoleon: "I would be glad to have permission to lay before Your Excellency, by letter or tele-graph, my views as to the present state of military affairs throughout the whole country."[63] Lincoln did want advice, but not from him. Instead of accepting McClellan's ingenuous offer, the President left Washington se-cretly for a conference with retired Brevet Lieutenant General Winfield Scott, who was spending the spring and summer at West Point. Presumably, among the matters they discussed was Lincoln's decision to give Pope a new field army, and also the suggestion Old Fuss and Feathers had made back in the fall of the year before: that the President make Henry Halleck general-in-chief.[64]

By coincidence, while Lincoln and Scott were reviewing "the present state of military affairs throughout the whole country" as they sat on a bench overlooking the gorgeous Hudson Highlands, down northeast of Richmond on that day—June 23, 1862—General Robert E. Lee was presenting a heart-stopping plan to his subordinates that would have considerable bearing on the decisions Lincoln was attempting to make and also on their timing.[65] Three days later, Lee's forces attacked the Union corps McClellan had left north of the Chickahominy after massing the rest of his

130,000-man Army of the Potomac south of the river in preparation for beginning the siege of Richmond.

While the Confederates were assaulting Major General Fitz-John Porter's fortifications along Beaver Dam Creek near Mechanicsville,[66] up in Washington Abraham Lincoln was issuing an order to create the Army of Virginia and appointing John Pope as its commander. "While protecting Western Virginia and the national capital from danger or insult," Lincoln wrote, "[the army] shall in the speediest manner attack and overcome the rebel forces of Jackson and Ewell, threaten the enemy in the direction of Charlottesville, and render the most effective aid to relieve General McClellan and capture Richmond."[67] Pope assumed command the next day, whereupon Pathfinder John C. Frémont telegraphed Secretary Stanton:

> *I respectfully ask that the President will relieve me of my present command. I submit for his consideration that the position assigned me* [corps commander in Pope's army] *by his recent order is subordinate and inferior to those hitherto conceded to me, and not fairly corresponding with the rank I hold in the army. . . .*[68]

Lincoln granted Frémont's request immediately.[69]

Overshadowing news of the end of The Pathfinder's military career on June 27, however, were reports arriving that night and during the next day that Fitz-John Porter's corps had been driven from a second very strong position on the Chickahominy's north bank by Lee's continuing assaults. On the day before, the Army of the Potomac's commander had informed Washington: "Victory of to-day complete and against great odds. I almost begin to think we are invincible."[70] Yet during the night he ordered Porter to abandon his nigh-impregnable three tiers of lines along Beaver Dam Creek and to withdraw several miles southeastward to the vicinity of a mill owned by a Doctor Gaines. General McClellan had spent that Thursday at Camp Lincoln, south of the river and well away from the fighting.[71] After midnight he sent his superiors in Washington a message that was—among other things—compelling and damning evidence of how unfit for *any* command the Young Napoleon really was:

> *I now know the full history of the day. On this side of the river (the right bank) we repulsed several strong attacks. On the left bank our men did all that men could do, all that soldiers could accomplish, but they were overwhelmed by vastly superior numbers, even after I brought my last reserves into action. The loss on both sides is terrible.*

I believe it will prove to be the most desperate battle of the war. . . .

I have lost this battle because my own force was too small. I again repeat that I am not responsible for this, and I say it with the earnestness of a general who feels in his heart the loss of every brave man who has been needlessly sacrificed to-day. . . .

In addition to what I have already said, I only wish to say to the President that I think he is wrong in regarding me as ungenerous when I said that my force was too weak. I merely intimated a truth which to-day has been too plainly proved. . . . As it is, the Government must not and cannot hold me responsible for the result.

I feel too earnestly to-night. I have seen too many dead and wounded comrades to feel otherwise than that the Government has not sustained this army. If you do not do so now the game is lost.[72]

There was more, but a quick-witted supervisor in the War Department's telegraph cut those two sentences from the end of McClellan's telegram lest the general be accused of treason: "If I save this army now, I tell you plainly that I owe no thanks to you or to any other persons in Washington. You have done your best to sacrifice this army."[73]

However, what Lincoln and Stanton *did* read was enough to—as Old Brains would put it later—stampede them. On Saturday, June 28, the day after Lee had mauled Fitz-John Porter's corps in the battle later called Gaines's Mill, Stanton sent General Halleck this message:

The enemy have concentrated in such force at Richmond as to render it absolutely necessary, in the opinion of the President, for you to immediately detach 25,000 of your force and forward it by the nearest and quickest route by way of Baltimore and Washington to Richmond. . . . But in detaching your force the President directs that it be done in such way as to enable you to hold your ground and not interfere with the movement against Chattanooga and East Tennessee. . . . The direction to send these forces immediately is rendered imperative by a serious reverse suffered by General McClellan before Richmond yesterday, the full extent of which is not yet known.[74]

7

GENERAL HALLECK'S REPLY was not what the distressed war managers at the War Department wanted to read:

Your telegraph of the 27th is just received, but it is so imperfect that parts of it cannot be deciphered till repeated. The object, however, is understood and measures will be immediately taken to carry it out. . . . I think under the circumstances the Chattanooga expedition had better be abandoned or at least be diminished. If not, I doubt our ability to hold West Tennessee after detaching so large a force as that called for.[75]

Whether intentionally or not, Halleck had struck a Lincolnian nerve. Replied the acting general-in-chief on June 30:

Would be very glad of 25,000 infantry—no artillery or cavalry, but please do not send a man if it endangers any place you deem important to hold or if it forces you to weaken or delay the expedition against Chattanooga. To take and hold the railroad at or east of Cleveland, in East Tennessee, I think fully as important as the taking and holding of Richmond.[76]

Stanton, in his order dated June 28, had given Halleck discretion to select the units to be sent.[77] Old Brains took the Secretary at his word. As if he expected to be the senior Union commander in the West for the rest of the war, he seized this opportunity to—in effect—remove some deadwood. On June 30, 1862, and possibly anticipating that there might come a time when John McClernand's good friend in the Executive Mansion might read what he wrote, he sent this order to the political general:

The defeat of General McClellan near Richmond has produced another stampede at Washington. You will collect as rapidly as possible all the infantry regiments of your division and take advantage of transportation by every train to transport them to Columbus and thence to Washington City. . . . The entire campaign in the West is broken up by these orders and we shall very probably lose all that we have gained. I will do all I can with the few forces left. You go to a new theater; success attend you.[78]

On the next day, July 1, Halleck acknowledged receipt of the corrected message Stanton had sent him on June 28 and summarized for the secretary the actions he had taken in compliance with it. But he added his analysis of potential consequences:

The enemy acts in a friendly country, requiring no guards for his depots, and has an immense rolling stock, so that he can in a few days concentrate on any one point. We cannot so concentrate. I am therefore satisfied that a detachment of 25,000 from this army at the present time will result in the loss of Arkansas or West Tennessee, and perhaps both. Those who have not the proper data have been disposed to underrate the force of the enemy and to overrate that of this army. Those who represent otherwise deceive you. Either the Chattanooga expedition must be postponed or a less force sent to Washington, or we have left the alternative of losing much that we have gained here in the West. . . .[79]

"Save your army at all events," acting General-in-Chief Lincoln had urged George McClellan on June 28. "Will send re-inforcements as fast as we can. . . . If you have had a drawn battle or a repulse it is the price we pay for the enemy not being in Washington. . . ."[80] And on July 2, after the Young Napoleon had retreated southward all the way to the banks of the James River and checked Lee at Malvern Hill, but then ordered that position abandoned in favor of safe haven at Harrison's Landing—Lincoln reiterated to Halleck his admonition against the endangerment of "any point you deem important to hold. . . ." Next came an intriguing question: "Please tell me, could you not make me a flying visit for consultation without endangering the service in your department?"[81]

Halleck's reply was immediate and characteristically to the point:

According to reports of scouts and deserters Bragg is preparing to attack us with the whole force of Beauregard's army. Under these circumstances I do not think I could safely be absent from my army, although, being somewhat broken in health and wearied out by long months of labor and care, a trip to Washington would be exceedingly desirable.[82]

Surely General Halleck suspected that his flying visit might turn out to be a one-way trip. Whether or not he knew that John Pope had been acting as an unofficial aide to Lincoln during the string of battles east of Richmond that came to be known as the Seven Days,[83] Old Brains might also have discerned the possibility that Pope had done some prompting; it seems doubtful that he could have known that Pope had accompanied the President on the secret visit to consult General Scott at West Point regarding (among other things) selection of a real general-in-chief.[84] But whatever Abraham Lincoln's motives and intent may have been, by inviting Halleck to the capital he had opened a new subject—and this could neither be turned away lightly nor ignored.

Lincoln was in the position of a lawyer representing the Union in *United States of America* v. *Confederacy*, a case he had not made much progress toward winning. Many of the steps he had taken—appointment of political generals, appeasement of Radicals by committing "green" troops to battle at Bull Run, replacement of Winfield Scott by McClellan, and toleration of the Young Napoleon's insolence combined with overestimation of his ability to direct field operations—had been mistakes. Now, to his credit, he seemed to realize that he needed help of a particular kind; he needed someone who could prevent him from making additional mistakes; yes, he needed a qualified general-in-chief, but he needed one who thought as he did, as a lawyer.

Henry Wager Halleck was the only man in the Union army who could meet Lincoln's unusual specifications. From his California years as senior partner of Halleck, Peachy and Billings he could recall that the ideal client is a rich man in trouble. Here, President Abraham Lincoln was plagued by problems—yet it was by no means clear that Old Brains wanted him as a client.

Moreover, the immediate issue was whether General Halleck could comply with the peculiar terms of Secretary Stanton's request for troops. Lincoln modified it somewhat in a message dated July 4, 1862: "You do not know how much you would oblige us if, without abandoning any of your positions or plans, you could promptly send us even 10,000 infantry. Can you not? . . ."[85]

Earlier, Halleck's contribution of John McClernand and that general's troops had been suspended.[86] Also, by July 4 McClellan's Army of the Potomac was safely penned-up on the riverfront plantation known as Harrison's Landing, and navy gunboats on the James were inhibiting the Confederates from attacking. Even so, the President's telegram required a reply, and on July 5 Halleck provided one:

> *I submitted the question of sending troops to Richmond to the principal officers of my command. They are unanimous in opinion that if this army is seriously diminished the Chattanooga expedition must be revoked or the hope of holding Southwest Tennessee abandoned. I must earnestly protest against surrendering what has cost us so much blood and treasure, and which from a military point*

of view is worth more than Richmond. It will be infinitely better to withdraw troops from the Shenandoah Valley, which at this time has no strategic importance.[87]

A point the acting general-in-chief had not seemed able to grasp was that the 120,000-man army Halleck had assembled for Corinth's capture had been dispersed in order to seize and hold a number of regions widely scattered throughout his vast department. To ask for troops while retaining their control of presently occupied territory in three states east of the Mississippi and three west of it was to demand of Old Brains an impossibility.

Given that awkward impasse, General Halleck turned his attention to matters within his own bailiwick. Regarding a newspaper report he telegraphed Grant:

The Cincinnati Gazette *contains the substance of your demanding re-enforcements and my refusing them. You either have a newspaper correspondent on your staff or your staff is very leaky. This publication did not come from these headquarters.*[88]

Evidently, Sherman had complained regarding supplies. On July 8, the general commanding responded:

Don't get angry; we are doing everything for you in the range of human possibility. If you knew how hard everybody here has been working you would not grumble. . . . McClellan has suffered severe losses, but holds his position and is being re-inforced. He will now use pick and shovel.[89]

"Excuse my growl," Cump replied. "I feel and appreciate the burden you carry, and I know no man in the country able to carry it but you. . . . The startle [McClellan's] seeming defeat has given the country must result in reawakening attention to the large army that still opposes us."[90]

That relaxed tone carried over into Halleck's exchanges with Don Carlos Buell, as well. "The President telegraphs that your progress [toward Chattanooga] is not satisfactory and that you should move more rapidly,"[91] Old Brains advised him. "I regret that it is necessary to explain the circumstances which must make my progress slow," Buell began in a long letter dated three days later, though he was a master of the art of making excuses, and he closed by confessing: "The displeasure of the President pains me exceedingly."[92] On July 12 Halleck sent Buell some reassurance:

> *I can well understand the difficulties you have to encounter and also the impatience at Washington. In the first place they have no conception of the length of our lines of defense and of operations. In the second place the disasters before Richmond have worked them up to boiling heat. . . . I will see that your movements are properly explained to the President.*[93]

Two days earlier, a civilian visitor had arrived in Corinth bearing a letter dated July 6, 1862, addressed to Major General Halleck and signed by A. Lincoln:

> *This introduces Governor William Sprague of Rhode Island. He is now Governor for the third time and Senator-elect of the United States. I know the object of his visit to you. He has my cheerful consent to go, but not my direction. He wishes to get you and part of your force, one or both, to come here. You already know I should be exceedingly glad of this if in your judgment it could be done without endangering positions and operations in the Southwest, and I now repeat what I have said more than once by telegraph:*
>
> > *Do not come or send a man if in your judgment it will endanger any point you deem important to hold or endangers or delays the Chattanooga expedition.*
>
> > *Still, please give my friend Governor Sprague a full and fair hearing.*[94]

"Governor Sprague is here," General Halleck wired the President late in the afternoon on July 10. "If I were to go to Washington I could advise but one thing: to place all the forces in North Carolina, Virginia, and Washington under one head and hold that head responsible."[95]

Put differently: there was no need for him to go all the way to Washington to point out the necessity of having the kind of supreme command in the East that he had earned, been obliged to demand, and ultimately won in the West. He had kept his advice terse, as was his wont, but he seemed to have assumed that Lincoln would continue to act as general-in-chief or that this issue was irrelevant, since the President had been commander-in-chief all along and would be until early March 1864, at the earliest.

Absent a transcript of Halleck's conversations with Governor Sprague, and assuming that on behalf of Lincoln the visitor had offered the post of general-in-chief to him, posterity would have to rely on Old Brains' record in order to weigh the arguments for and against his acceptance. On this basis there was absolutely nothing even to suggest, much less prove, that Henry Wager Halleck coveted that honor—or indeed any other position to which the President might call him. Moreover, it was simply absurd for anyone to write that when Lincoln asked him to make a flying visit to Washington, "Halleck played the part of a blushing girl, flattered by the attention but determined to remain virtuous."[96] On the contrary, everything that anyone knew about Henry Halleck's life to date reflected facts that strongly suggested that he would remain exactly where he was in the great scheme of things if it were at all possible for him to do so.

Major General Halleck had been the Union army's most successful soldier since he reached St. Louis in November 1861, roughly eight months before. Yet, in July 1862, he was still in many ways the strong-minded, brusque, often arrogant, goggle-eyed, pudgy, middle-aged man who had the habit of pacing the floor and rubbing his elbows when in contemplation that he had been in San Francisco, where he had become California's most respected lawyer.

Indeed, there had been a certain consistency in the record of Henry Halleck's achievements—from his entrance to Union College in upstate New York nearly thirty years before, through West Point, Monterey's constitutional convention, San Francisco's Montgomery Street landmark called Halleck's Folly, and the thriving in that city of his law firm. In his studies he had identified principles he believed in, and once adopted he adhered to them with uncommon fidelity, even ruthlessness. And in a breathtakingly short period of time, as his messages *via* telegraph from St. Louis and elsewhere reflected, he had concentrated all of his intellectual powers on performance of the duties he had voluntarily assumed toward quelling the rebellion.

Instead of managing the Pacific Coast's most powerful law firm, in mid-1862 General Halleck was the single most powerful man in the North American continent's heartland: Kansas, Missouri, Arkansas, Kentucky, parts of Tennessee, and stretches of northern Mississippi and Alabama. He had accomplished all of the missions the Young Napoleon and the other war managers had assigned him. In the process, by remaining faithful to the principles that had guided him all of his adult life and by not hesitating to impose them when he thought appropriate, he had earned the trust of his superiors and the respect of his officers and men.

General Halleck had gained much for the Union in terms of control over disputed real estate. Now he had authority to set his own strategic objectives, to organize his forces and either to concentrate or disperse them when and as he saw fit. Also, he had developed combat leaders such as Unconditional Surrender Grant, Cump Sherman, John Pope, George Thomas, young Philip Sheridan, James Birdseye McPherson, and John Schofield. And he could look forward with justifiable confidence to employing all of these resources in attaining the second goal of Winfield Scott's ridiculed Anaconda strategy: recovery of control of the Mississippi from Cairo to the Gulf of Mexico, thereby cutting the Confederacy in two.

What, then, could Governor Sprague have offered that could have been more attractive than the satisfaction that appeared imminent from successful prosecution of the campaigns in three directions that Halleck was already conducting? And what could be of more value to the government than restoring the rest of the Mississippi River to Union control, a mission he could undertake when amelioration of climactic conditions and improvements in supply line integrity and efficiency permitted?

For Sprague to have made the thousand-mile journey from Washington to bring back either General Halleck and some of his forces, or one or the other, implied a willingness to negotiate. One possibility: since Halleck was adamant about the Union holding onto all of the territory that he had brought under federal occupation, and was also determined to prevent the erosion of his army's strength through reassignments of its elements eastward, *what if* Lincoln agreed to leave the troops where they were in exchange for Halleck's going to Washington? Once there, as general-in-chief he could not only continue to direct operations in the West but—perhaps— provide those forces with greater support. Was this opportunity not even greater than the one he sought when he proposed the Western Division? On some occasions, he had offered sound suggestions to Stanton regarding operations in theaters beyond his departmental boundaries. How much more might he contribute to the rebellion's quelling as commander of *all* the Union armies?

It was a bargain from hell and Old Brains was wary of it. And no matter what Governor Sprague might actually have said, proposed, offered, or even threatened, at the end of the day on July 10, 1862, all that Abraham Lincoln would learn about their conversations was that General Halleck thought a supreme command equivalent to his in the West ought to be created in the East.

But to Old Brains on the next day, July 11, 1862, came this message from Secretary of War Stanton:

The President has this day made the following order, which I hasten to communicate to you:

> *Ordered, That Major General Henry W. Halleck be assigned to command the whole land forces of the United States, as general-in-chief, and that he repair to this capital as soon as he can with safety to the positions and operations within the department under his charge.*

> *You will please acknowledge the receipt of this order, and state when you may be expected here. Your early presence is required by many circumstances.*[97]

5 ★ Warfare on a Three-Dimensional Chessboard

*T*HE EVENTS OF THE LAST TWO WEEKS have been momentous," Henry Halleck wrote his wife, Elizabeth. He was referring to George McClellan's having been driven from his positions just east of Richmond to a refuge more than twenty miles away, for that disaster had cast shadows long enough to reach Corinth:

> *Two messengers were sent to me, one from the President and one from McClellan, inviting me to go to Washington and the President and Secretary of War both telegraphed me to the same effect, but I declined the invitation, knowing that the object was to involve me in the quarrel between Stanton and McClellan. One of the messengers said that I was the only man in the United States who could reconcile the present difficulties. I replied that if that was the case I was probably the only person in the United States who would have nothing to do with these Cabinet quarrels, and that I would not go to Washington if I could help it![1]*

Indeed, General Halleck owed absolutely no one in the capital anything. Everything that he had ever amassed in the way of prestige, or opportunity to grow intellectually or in wealth or in power, he had *earned*. Neither George McClellan nor Secretary of War Stanton nor even Abraham Lincoln had grasped the common sense of his proposed Western Division.

And now that the principles he had advocated had proved effective, the Union's war managers seemed to be blundering again by assuming that what had been, would be: that success on a larger scale was not only attainable but probable.

Also, it may have been that as a civilian lawyer and businessman out in California, Henry Halleck had enjoyed so many years of being his own man, of being the dominant and dominating person in every relationship he had chosen to enter, that he had deep misgivings about—in effect—accepting the President of the United States as a client. True, Abraham Lincoln was a powerful, even if not rich, man in deep trouble. But, mainly because of the Northern electorate's failure in 1860 to require candidates for the nation's highest office to be qualified to act as a commander-in-chief if necessary, Lincoln had made egregious errors in prosecuting *United States* v. *Confederacy*: hence, his attempt to retain special counsel. This was entirely understandable, and even if belated, commendable. Yet there was no assurance (and indeed there could have been none) that such a client would be responsive enough to Old Brains' efforts to avoid losing the war.

But General Halleck did not have much time in which to ponder such matters, for on July 11, 1862, the day after Governor William Sprague's visit, the summons to Washington reached him. To the President, Halleck replied:

> *Your orders of this date are this moment received. General Grant, next in command, is at Memphis. I have telegraphed to him to immediately repair to this place. I will start for Washington the moment I can have a personal interview with General Grant.*[2]

By issuing a peremptory order Lincoln had squelched all further discussion. Moreover, he seemed to have surprised Halleck by—as the general wrote in a letter to his wife—"putting me in General Scott's place."[3]

Ironically, George McClellan may have had more to do with Lincoln's abrupt decision than anyone else. Having reached Harrison's Landing at the end of the Seven Days, the Young Napoleon had infuriated the acting general-in-chief by declaring: "We have failed to win only because overpowered by superior numbers."[4] On July 3 the New York *Tribune* had printed an article in which a reporter described as a "crime against the nation" the administration's "refusal to reinforce McClellan."[5] The next day McClellan's chief of staff (and father-in-law), Brigadier General Randolph B. Marcy, reached Washington to plead for reinforcements even after the President had explained in a message to Little Mac: "When you ask for

50,000 men to be promptly sent you, you surely labor under some gross misstatement of fact. . . . I have not, outside of your army, 75,000 men east of the mountains. Thus the idea of sending you 50,000, or any other considerable force, is simply absurd."[6]

Such was the background for a three-day trip Lincoln made on the steamer *Ariel* to Harrison's Landing. Shortly after his arrival on July 8, it became apparent that he was more interested in McClellan's subordinates' answers to the question, "If it were desired to get the army away from here, could it be safely effected?" than in anything the Young Napoleon had to say. Lincoln's interrogations, historian J. G. Randall would later write, suggested "a lawyer who seeks in cross examination to produce a predetermined conclusion."[7]

Lincoln returned to Washington on July 10, the day Governor Sprague was visiting General Halleck in Corinth, and on the next he issued the peremptory order that would bring Old Brains to Washington. Henceforth, determining what should be done regarding George McClellan and his Army of the Potomac would be the responsibility of a *real* general-in-chief.

Later, Major General John Pope would offer a different account of Halleck's summoning. McClellan, Pope alleged, had not responded to his requests for information that might help him apply pressure on the Confederates imprisoning the federal forces at Harrison's Landing. "It became apparent," he wrote, "that, considering the situation in which the Army of the Potomac and the Army of Virginia were placed in relation to each other, and the absolute necessity of harmonious and prompt co-operation between them, some military superior both of General McClellan and myself should be called to Washington and placed in command of all the operations in Virginia."[8]

With problems he meant to hand off to General-in-Chief Halleck proliferating, on July 14 Lincoln telegraphed him: "I am very anxious—almost impatient—to have you here. Having due regard for what you leave behind, when can you reach here?"[9]

Old Brains replied the next day:

> *General Grant has just arrived from Memphis. I am in communication with General Buell and Governor Johnson in Tennessee. Hope to finally arrange disposition of troops and re-enforcements for General Curtis by to-morrow and to leave Thursday morning, the 17th.*[10]

That should have been reassuring; but only two days earlier, he had written Mrs. Halleck that his appointment "is certainly a very high compliment, but I doubt very much whether I shall accept the promotion. I fear it may bring me in conflict with McClellan's friends. Everybody who knows me, knows that I have uniformly supported him, and I do not wish to be placed in a false position. Nevertheless, I must obey my orders and shall start for Washington. . . ."[11]

In the end, the soldier in Henry Halleck prevailed over his misgivings. Curiously, however, he postponed the task of notifying all but Grant of the impending change until July 15. "I am ordered to Washington and shall leave day after to-morrow (Thursday)," he telegraphed to Don Carlos Buell. "Very sorry, for I can be of more use here than there."[12]

Another day passed before he wrote his oldest friend in the West, Cump Sherman; and even then, he opened his second paragraph *Confidential*:

> *I am ordered to Washington, and leave to-morrow (Thursday). I have done my best to avoid it. I have studied out and can finish the campaign in the West. [I] Don't understand and cannot manage affairs in the East. Moreover, [I] don't want to have anything to do with the quarrels of Stanton and McClellan. The change does not please me, but I must obey orders. Good-by, and may God bless you. I am more than satisfied with everything you have done. You have always had my respect, but recently you have won my highest admiration. I deeply regret to part from you.*[13]

Back in March, Sherman had said in a letter to a friend: "Halleck has been the directing genius. I wish him all honor and glory."[14] That Cump's opinion of Old Brains had not changed was reflected in his reply:

> *I cannot express my heartfelt pain at hearing of your orders and intended departure. You took command in the Valley of the Mississippi at a period of deep gloom, when I felt that our poor country was doomed to a Mexican anarchy, but at once arose order, system, firmness, and success in which there has not been a pause.*
>
> *I thank you for the kind expression to me, but all I have done has been based on the absolute confidence I had conceived for your knowledge of national law and your comprehensive knowledge of things gathered, God only knows how.*
>
> *That success will attend you wherever you go I feel no doubt,*

for you must know more about the East than you did about the West when you arrived at Saint Louis a stranger. And there you will find armies organized and pretty well commanded, instead of the scattered forces you then had. I attach more importance to the West than the East. The one has a magnificent future, but enveloped in doubt. The other is comparatively an old country. The man who at the end of this war holds the military control of the Valley of the Mississippi will be the man. You should not be removed. I fear the consequences.

Personally you will rule wherever you go, but I did hope you would finish up what you had begun, and where your success has attracted the world's notice.

Instead of that calm, sure, steady progress which has dismayed our enemy, I now fear alarms, hesitations, and doubt. You cannot be replaced out here, and it is too great a risk to trust a new man from the East. We are all the losers; you may gain, but I believe you would prefer to finish what you have so well begun.[15]

When General Grant received a blunt order to "repair" to Corinth back on July 11, he telegraphed to ask if he should bring his staff. "This place will be your headquarters," Old Brains replied, terse as ever in his communications with him, "you can judge for yourself."[16] Yet when answering an inquiry about Halleck from his congressman, Elihu Washburne, Grant wrote: "He is a man of gigantic intellect and well studied in the profession of arms."[17]

There remained the difficult task of bidding farewell to his army, which General Halleck did in Special Orders No. 162 on July 16, 1862, eight months after he had assumed command in St. Louis:

The major-general commanding the department in giving up the immediate command of the troops now in the field and heretofore constituting the Armies of the Ohio, Tennessee, Mississippi, and Southwest desires to express to them his appreciation of the endurance, bravery, and soldierly conduct which they have exhibited on all occasions during the present campaign. As separate corps [they] won the memorable victories of Milford, Mill Springs, Pea Ridge, Fort Donelson, New Madrid, and Island No. 10, and when partially united they defeated the enemy in the bloody battle of Pittsburg [Landing] and drove him from his intrenchments at Corinth. In the latter of these operations, and in the labor of repairing railroads which the enemy had destroyed, the commanding general bears personal testimony of the good conduct of the troops, and of the cheerfulness and alacrity with which they endured the fatigues and hardships necessary to secure the great objects of the campaign.

The soldiers of the West have nobly done their duty and proved themselves equal to any emergency. The general commanding desires to express to the commanders of corps and their subordinate officers his warmest thanks for their cordial co-operation on all occasions.

Soldiers, you have accomplished much toward crushing out this wicked rebellion, and if you continue to exhibit the same vigilance, courage, and perseverance it is believed that under the providence of God you will soon bring the war to a close and be able to return in peace to your families and homes.[18]

2

WHEN ABRAHAM LINCOLN TELEGRAPHED his newly appointed general-in-chief: "I am very anxious—almost impatient—to have you here," he greatly understated his condition. He had good reason to. Had General Halleck known how many and how vexing were the federal high command's problems, he might well have decided to head for San Francisco instead of Washington. And, as he had told his wife, he feared most of the items he would find on his agenda when he reached the capital were controversies involving Major General George Brinton McClellan.

A. Lincoln was still engaged in an increasingly acrimonious running message-fight with the Young Napoleon over the true size of the Army of the Potomac. Using numbers he had acquired during his visit to Harrison's Landing, the President calculated (and wrote McClellan) that of the 160,000 troops that had been sent to him, there must be "45,000 of your army still alive and not with it. If I am right, and you had these men with you, you could go into Richmond in three days," he declared. "How can they be got to you, and how can they be prevented from getting away in such numbers in the future?"[19]

"I can now control people getting away better," the warden of what was virtually a prison compound responded, "for the natural opportunities are better."[20] Such was the product of the pen that would have had posterity believe that he had withdrawn more than twenty miles away from where General Lee had attacked him because he had "retired to prevent the superior forces of the enemy from cutting me off and to take a different base of operations."[21]

And then there was a long letter Lincoln had received from Major General E. D. Keyes, commander of the Army of the Potomac's IV Corps. Anything General Keyes had to say deserved both attention and respect, for he was a West Point graduate whose career in the pre-war army had included his having been detailed *three times* as aide and military secretary to former General-in-Chief Winfield Scott.[22]

> [Keyes asked,] *Can this army remain here encamped at Harrison's Bar?*
>
> *Clearly not, since the confinement to a small space, the heat, and sickliness of this camp would nearly destroy the army in two months, though no armed force should assail it. Moreover, the enemy being in possession of both banks of the James River above and below us, he will shortly find the means to cut us off from our supplies, or shut us up by means of fortifications and his abundant artillery, in such a manner as will give him time, ample time, to capture Washington before we could possibly go to its rescue.*
>
> *Can this army leave its present camp to go and attack Richmond? No; it cannot. To make this army to march on Richmond with any hope of success it must be re-enforced by at least 100,000 good troops. No officer here, whose opinion is worth one penny, will recommend a less number. To bring troops freshly raised at the North to this country in the months of July, August, and September would be to cast our resources into the sea. The raw troops would melt away and be ruined forever. . . .*
>
> *When a large army reaches, or is placed in, a position where it cannot hold the enemy in check nor operate effectively against him, it is a military axiom to move that army without delay. . . . This army cannot be employed here, and the enemy may close its egress, for which reasons and many others I respectfully recommend that immediate instructions may be issued for its withdrawal.*[23]

Well, yes—but Lincoln already had an army near enough to Washington to protect it, and this called attention to a weakness in General Keyes' argument: He had specified no combat mission for the Army of the Potomac if it were returned to its "spacious, healthy" old camps near the capital. Yet he had made a strong case for removing McClellan's force from Harrison's Landing, and that course of action would be at the top of General

Halleck's list of possibilities to evaluate and problems to solve once he arrived.

Major General John Pope's name would also belong on that list, for he was one of the problems. Apparently, being called to Washington and having been given a field army to command had led him to consider himself higher on the totem pole than he actually was, or at least to behave in ways that were controversial. Actually, it had taken about a month to convert the Army of Virginia from a Lincolnian decree into a unit ready for fresh employment. This transition required little of General Pope's attention, so he was able to devote much of his time to charming the Radical Republicans on the Joint Congressional Committee on the Conduct of the War, acting as a volunteer aide to Lincoln during the Seven Days, and perhaps becoming a bit intoxicated by the political atmosphere of the capital.

However, by July 14, 1862, the general commanding the Army of Virginia felt compelled to address his men. With the aid of Secretary of War Edwin Stanton, some said,[24] Pope issued this message:

> *By special assignment of the President of the United States I have assumed the command of this army. I have spent two weeks in learning your whereabouts, your condition, and your wants, in preparing you for active operations, and in placing you in positions from which you can act promptly and to the purpose. These labors are nearly completed, and I am about to join you in the field.*
>
> *Let us understand each other. I have come to you from the West, where we have always seen the backs of our enemies; from an army whose business it has been to seek the adversary and to beat him when he was found; whose policy has been attack and not defense. In but one instance has the enemy been able to place our Western armies in defensive attitude.*
>
> *I presume that I have been called here to pursue the same system and to lead you against the enemy. It is my purpose to do so, and that speedily. I am sure you long for an opportunity to win the distinction you are capable of achieving. That opportunity I shall endeavor to give you.*
>
> *Meantime I desire you to dismiss from your minds certain phrases, which I am sorry to find so much in vogue amongst you. I hear constantly of "taking strong positions and holding them," of "lines of retreat," and of "bases of supplies."*
>
> *Let us discard such ideas. The strongest position a soldier should desire to occupy is one from which he can most easily advance*

against the enemy. Let us study the probable lines of retreat of our opponents, and leave our own to take care of themselves. Let us look before us, and not behind. Success and glory are in the advance, disaster and shame lurk in the rear. Let us act on this understanding, and it is safe to predict that your banners shall be inscribed with many a glorious deed and that your names will be dear to your countrymen forever.[25]

Pope's anti-McClellan bombast evoked sympathy for the Young Napoleon even from critics who had recently been denouncing him. Fitz-John Porter, no doubt reflecting the views of his army commander, commented:

I regret that Gen. Pope has not improved since his youth and has now written himself down as an ass. His address to his troops will make him ridiculous in the eyes of military men . . . and will reflect no credit on Mr. Lincoln who has just promoted him. If the theory [Pope] proclaims is practised you may look for disaster.[26]

General Pope amused Confederates by beginning his messages with *Headquarters in the Saddle,* but he infuriated them by issuing (again, with help from Stanton) a series of orders on July 18. Some, for example those requiring Virginians within a five-mile radius of any guerrilla-type damages to railroads or telegraph lines to repair them, were similar to measures General Halleck had taken out in Missouri. But Pope also proposed to subject civilians to unprecedented degrees of military coercion, with death by shooting among the penalties for disobedience. Calling this evidence of Yankee depravity, Southerners agreed with General Lee who declared John Pope a "miscreant" who ought to be "suppressed."[27]

3

ON JULY 13, 1862, GENERAL HALLECK had written his wife: "I declined the invitation [to go to Washington], knowing that the object was to involve me in the quarrel between Stanton and McClellan." Three days later, he said in his farewell letter to Cump Sherman, "[I] don't want to have anything to do with the quarrels of Stanton and McClellan."

If Halleck knew enough about their squabbling to be wary of it, he may well have foreseen the inevitability of vast, tragic unpleasantness ahead for him. No man could long endure the crossfire between his superior and his principal subordinate.

It would be surprising if Old Brains had not recognized the probability that by accepting the unsought, unwanted position—by acting in accordance with his sense of duty and honor and love of country—he was risking everything he had attained with nothing personally to gain by doing so. For a time in early July, however, it seemed that the Stanton-McClellan quarrels were at an end. To Little Mac, the secretary of war wrote: "There is no cause in my heart or conduct for the cloud that wicked men have raised between us for their own base and selfish purposes. No man ever had a truer friend than I have been to you and shall continue to be. You are seldom absent from my thoughts and I am ready to make any sacrifice to aid you."[28]

In his long and prompt reply, McClellan opened with a review of the cordiality of their association back in 1861. But soon the general's tone changed:

> *But from the time you took office, your official conduct towards me as* [general]*-in-chief of the Army of the U.S. and afterwards as commander of the Army of the Potomac was marked by repeated acts done in such manner as it be deeply offensive to my feelings and calculated to affect me injuriously in public estimation. After commencing the present campaign your concurrence in the withholding of a large portion of my force, so essential to my plans, led me to believe that your mind was warped by a bitter personal prejudice against me.*

Abruptly—in the next sentence—came another reversal: "Your letter compels me to believe that I have been mistaken in regard to your real feelings and opinions and that your conduct so unaccountable to my fallible judgment, must have proceeded from views and motives which I did not understand." And, in closing, McClellan wrote: "Let no cloud hereafter arise between us."[29]

Such were the conciliatory, hopeful, reassuring words exchanged between July 5 and July 8. Even so, only five days later, the Young Napoleon confided in a letter from Harrison's Landing to his wife, Mary Ellen Marcy McClellan:

> *I still hope to get to Richmond this summer—unless the Govt commits some* extraordinarily *idiotic act—but I have no faith in the administration & shall cut loose from public life the very moment*

the country can dispense with my services. . . . So you want to know
what I feel about Stanton, & what I think of him now? I will tell
you with the most perfect frankness. I think that he is the most
unmitigated scoundrel I ever knew, heard, or read of; I think that
(& I do not wish to be irreverent) had he lived in the time of the
Saviour, Judas Iscariot would have remained a respected member of
the fraternity of the Apostles, & that the magnificent treachery &
rascality of E. M. Stanton would have caused Judas to have raised
his arms in holy horror & unaffected wonder. . . .[30]

But the Young Napoleon was not done. "God grant that I am
wrong—for I hate to think that humanity *can* sink so low—but my opinion
is just as I have told you. He has deceived me once—he never will again. . . .
Enough of the creature! Faugh!!"[31]

General McClellan was less verbose, but almost as candid, in a letter
he wrote Samuel L. M. Barlow—a close friend, New York businessman,
fellow Democrat, and supporter—on July 15: "I do not believe that Stanton
will go out of office—he will not willingly, & the Presdt has not the nerve
to turn him out—at least so I think. Stanton has written me a most abject
letter—declaring that he has ever been my best friend etc etc!!"[32]

By July 18 the Army of the Potomac's general commanding must have
heard rumors of change in Washington, for on that date he wrote in a letter
to Ellen:

I am inclined now to think that the Presdt will make Halleck comdr
of the Army & that the first pretext will be seized to supersede me in
command of this army—their game seems to be to withhold
reinforcements & then relieve me for not advancing—well knowing
that I have not the means to do so. . . . If they appoint Halleck Comg
Genl I will remain in command of this army as long as they will
allow me to, provided the army is in danger & likely to play an
active part. . . . I owe no gratitude to any but my own soldiers
here—none to the Govt or to the country. I have done my best for my
country—I expect nothing in return—they are my debtors, not I
theirs.[33]

There was something in McClellan's letters to Ellen of a young boy's
riding a pony back and forth in front of his girlfriend's house while standing
on his head, it being planted on the saddle—in order to impress her, but he
did not hesitate to share *more* than his dire misgivings with another

powerful Democrat in New York, William H. Aspinwall, on July 19. "My main object in writing you," the general stated after a lengthy preamble, "is to ask you to be kind enough to cast your eyes about you to see whether there is anything I can do in New York to earn a respectable support for my family. . . ."

Such was the state of McClellan's mind, apparently, soon after Halleck had squelched his reluctance to get involved with the quarrels, and all his other reservations, and had made his way *via* St. Louis to Washington.

In a letter the Young Napoleon had handed Lincoln upon his arrival at Harrison's Landing back on July 8, he had advocated a number of measures that did not "strictly relate to the situation of this army or strictly come within the scope of my official duties." Nearing the end of it, McClellan had declared:

> *In carrying out any system of policy which you may form you will require a Commander-in-Chief* [sic] *of the Army—one who possesses your confidence, understands your views, and who is competent to execute your orders by directing the military forces of the nation to the accomplishments of the objects by you proposed. I do not ask that place for myself. I am willing to serve you in such position as you may assign me, and I will do so as faithfully as ever a subordinate served superior. . . . I may be on the brink of eternity, and as I hope forgiveness from my Maker, I have written this letter with sincerity toward you and from love for my country.*[34]

Yet, roughly one short week earlier, while—well in the rear—General McClellan was learning of the wrecking of Fitz-John Porter's virtually unreinforced corps by General Lee, he had telegraphed Abraham Lincoln and Edwin Stanton these subsequently censored words: "If I save this Army now I tell you plainly I will owe no thanks to you or any other persons in Washington—you have done your best to sacrifice this Army."[35]

Acting General-in-Chief Lincoln had not seen that language. But when he returned to Washington from his visit to the penned-up Army of the Potomac on July 11, among his first actions was preparation of the order making Henry Halleck general-in-chief of the Union armies *despite* Old Brains' hesitations. In so doing, he did not inform McClellan of the decision he had made and—summarily—acted upon. The Young Napoleon would have to learn of this development from newspapers.

Mrs. McClellan was quick to express her outage: "To have a man put over you without even *consulting* you is rather more than I can endure—&

if you don't resign, I will!! . . . I am indignant."[36] Samuel Barlow wondered if Halleck's appointment had been made with McClellan's "knowledge & sanction" or was "a slap in the face." The latter, McClellan replied.[37] Later in the month, in another letter to Barlow, he thundered:

> *I know that the rascals will get rid of me as soon as they dare—they all know my opinion of them. They are aware that I have seen through their villainous schemes, & that if I succeed my foot will be on their necks. . . . I do not believe there is one honest man among them—& I know what I say. . . . God will yet foil their abominable designs & mete out to them the terrible punishment they deserve.*[38]

By July 30, the date of the Young Napoleon's blanket condemnation, General Halleck was firmly established in McClellan's mind as a conspirator of the Lincoln-Stanton ilk. Yet on July 26 McClellan had acknowledged receipt of a letter from another New York friend, Joseph W. Alsop, that passed along a reported conversation "in the cars" between Halleck and a railroad official on July 21 while they were en route to Washington. "[Halleck] said *that McClellan was the ablest military man in the world,*" wrote Alsop. "This delighted me."[39]

Once the cars reached Washington on July 23, 1862, Old Brains soon found himself in a conference with Abraham Lincoln; Edwin Stanton; and, later, Major Generals John Pope and Ambrose Burnside.[40] The next day, Halleck and Burnside boarded a steamer for a quick voyage down the Potomac and Chesapeake Bay through Hampton Roads and up the James to Harrison's Landing.[41]

"General McClellan received me kindly," the new general-in-chief wrote his wife on July 28, after his return, "but our interview was from its nature necessarily somewhat embarrassing, especially as I was obliged to disagree with him as to the feasibility of his plans."[42]

Given adequate reinforcements, the Young Napoleon had proposed, he would cross to the James' south side, move westward and seize Petersburg, cut Richmond's lines of supply from the south, then capture the city. But their discussion degenerated into questions involving the size of General Lee's army (two hundred thousand men, insisted McClellan), the Army of the Potomac's true effective troop strength, and the general commanding's estimates of reinforcements required. General Halleck, apparently reserving judgment, reboarded the steamer, mulling over McClellan's assurance that another twenty thousand troops would be enough for him to go forward with capturing Richmond as his object.[43]

Yet Old Brains had returned with serious doubts as to General McClellan's grasp of realities—or so he revealed to Elizabeth Halleck in the letter he wrote after he was back in Washington: "It certainly was unpleasant to tell one who had been my superior in rank that his plans were wrong, but my duty to myself and the country compelled me to do so. If I had approved them I should have become responsible for them, and I could not in conscience do so."[44]

And, echoing the remark he had made to the railroad executive during their train ride, he added:

> *General McClellan is in many respects a most excellent and valuable man, but he does not understand strategy and should never plan a campaign. We can get along well together, if he is so disposed; but I fear that his friends have excited his jealousy and that he will be disposed to pitch into me. Very well. My hands are clean. When in command of the army* [in the West] *no one did more than I did to sustain him, and in justice to me and to the country he ought now to sustain me.*

"I hope he will," wrote the general-in-chief in closing, "but I doubt it."[45]

4

WHAT HENRY HALLECK COULD OR COULD NOT allow himself "in conscience" to do had shaped virtually all of his actions during his forty-seven years, and so it was not surprising that conscience apparently required him to make a special effort to reach an understanding with McClellan. Shortly after his return from Harrison's Landing, he wrote his host this letter:

> *You are probably aware that I hold my present position contrary to my own wishes, and that I did everything in my power to avoid coming to Washington; but after declining several invitations from the President I received the order of the 11th instant, which left me no option.*
>
> *I have always had strong personal objections to mingling in the political-military affairs of Washington. I never liked the place, and like it still less at the present time. But aside from personal*

feeling, I really believed I could be much more useful in the West than here. I had acquired some reputation there, but here I could hope for none, and I greatly feared that whatever I might do I should receive more abuse than thanks. There seemed to be a disposition in the public press to cry down any one who attempted to serve the country instead of party. This was particularly the case with you, as I understood, and I could not doubt that it would be in a few weeks the case with me.

Under these circumstances I could not see how I could be of much use here. Nevertheless, being ordered, I was obliged to come. In whatever has occurred heretofore you have had my full approbation and cordial support. There was no one in the Army under whom I could serve with greater pleasure, and I now ask from you that same support and co-operation and that same free interchange of opinions as in former days.

If we disagree in opinion, I know that we will do so honestly and without unkind feelings. The country demands of us that we act together and with cordiality. I believe we can and will do so. Indeed we must do so if we expect to put down the rebellion. If we permit personal jealousies to interfere for a single moment with our operations we shall not only injure the cause but ruin ourselves. But I am satisfied that neither of us will do this, and that we will work together with all our might and bring the war to an early termination. I have written to you frankly, assuring you of my friendship and confidence, believing that my letter would be received with the same kind feelings in which it is written.[46]

On August 1, promptly and cordially, McClellan replied:

My own experience enables me to appreciate most fully the difficulties and unpleasant features of your position. I have passed through it all and most cordially sympathize with you, for I regard your place, under present circumstances, as one of the most unpleasant under the Government. Of one thing, however, you may be sure, and that is of my full and cordial support in all things.

Had I been consulted as to who was to take my place I would have advised your appointment. So far as you are concerned I feel toward you and shall act precisely as if I had urged you for the place you hold. There is not one particle of feeling or jealousy in my heart toward you. Set your mind perfectly at rest on that score. No one of your old and tried friends will work with you more cordially and more honestly than I shall.

If we are permitted to do so, I believe that together we can save this unhappy country and bring this war to a comparatively early termination. The doubt in my mind is whether the selfish politicians will allow us to do so. I fear the results of the civil policy inaugurated by recent acts of Congress and practically enunciated by General Pope in his series of orders to the Army of Virginia.

At this point General McClellan reiterated many of the civil policy recommendations he had made in the letter he had handed to Abraham Lincoln when the President had arrived at Harrison's Landing earlier in the month. Then, toward the end, he returned to the question of cooperation:

I know that our ideas as to the concentration of forces agree perfectly. I believe that the principles I have expressed in this letter accord with your own views. I sincerely hope that we do not differ widely.

You see I have met you in your own spirit of frankness, and I would be glad to have your views on these points, that I may know what I am doing. We must have a full understanding on all points, and I regard the civil or political questions as inseparable from the military in this contest.

It is unnecessary for me to repeat my objections to the idea of withdrawing this army from its present position. Every day's reflection but serves to strengthen my conviction that the true policy is to re-enforce this army at the earliest possible moment by every available man and to allow it to resume the offensive with the least possible delay.[47]

Resolving the reinforce/withdraw question, however, was beyond the powers of the two men who had just professed their willingness to work together in harmony. At a meeting shortly after the Harrison's Landing trip, Halleck and Burnside conferred again with Lincoln and Stanton.[48] Removal of McClellan and his replacement by Burnside was considered, but the oddly bewhiskered general protested that he was not capable of commanding so large an army. While Old Brains had been talking with McClellan at Harrison's Landing, Burnside had discussed withdrawal with Little Mac's corps commanders, including Erasmus Darwin Keyes, author of the letter to the President advocating movement of the Army of the Potomac back to the banks of its namesake river as soon as possible. Also on the war managers' agenda, no doubt, was the response General Pope ought to make regarding reports that Stonewall Jackson had moved *north* of Richmond to Gordonsville.[49]

However, McClellan precipitated a decision by sending a message to the general-in-chief in which he announced that he would need *more* than twenty thousand reinforcements if he were to try again to take Richmond. Immediately, Halleck ordered the Young Napoleon to begin evacuating his sick and wounded.[50] And on August 3, 1862, he sent McClellan this message:

> *It is determined to withdraw your army from the Peninsula to Aquia Creek. You will take immediate measures to effect this, covering the movement the best you can. Its real object and withdrawal should be concealed even from your own officers. Your material and transportation should be removed first. You will assume control of all the means of transportation within your reach, and apply to the naval forces for all the assistance they can render you. . . .*[51]

By noon of the next day General McClellan had recovered from this shock enough to set forth his objections. "Your telegram of last evening is received," he began. "I must confess that it has caused me the greatest pain I ever experienced, for I am convinced that the order to withdraw this army to Aquia Creek will prove disastrous to our cause. I fear it will be a fatal blow. . . ." There followed a lengthy citation of the geographic disadvantages of moving to Aquia Landing, based on the assumption that seizing Richmond was still the Army of the Potomac's objective. That done, he turned to other considerations:

> *Add to this the certain demoralization of this army which would ensue, the terribly depressing effect upon the people of the North, and the strong probability that it would influence foreign powers to recognize our adversaries, and these appear to me sufficient reasons to make it my imperative duty to urge in the strongest terms afforded by our language that this order may be rescinded, and that far from recalling this army, it may be promptly re-enforced to enable it to resume the offensive.*
>
> *It may be said that there are no re-enforcements available. I point to Burnside's force; to that of Pope, not necessary to maintain a strict defensive in front of Washington and Harper's Ferry; to those portions of the Army of the West not required for a strict defensive*

there. Here, directly in front of this army, is the heart of the rebellion. It is here that all our resources should be collected to strike the blow which will determine the fate of the nation. All points of secondary importance elsewhere should be abandoned, and every available man brought here; a decided victory here and the military strength of the rebellion is crushed. It matters not what partial reverses we may meet with elsewhere. Here is the true defense of Washington. It is here, on the banks of the James, that the fate of the Union should be decided. . . .

If my counsel does not prevail, I will with a sad heart obey your orders to the utmost of my power, directing to the movement, which I clearly foresee will be one of the utmost delicacy and difficulty, whatever skill I may possess. Whatever the result may be— and may God grant that I am mistaken in my forebodings—I shall at least have the internal satisfaction that I have written and spoken frankly, and have sought to do the best in my power to avert disaster from my country.[52]

On August 5, the day after McClellan's cry of anguish reached Washington, Old Brains replied: "You cannot regret the order of the withdrawal more than I did the necessity of giving it. It will not be rescinded, and you will be expected to execute it with all possible promptness. . . ."[53]

Perhaps the most remarkable thing about the letter that Halleck sent dated August 6, 1862, was not so much its length or the speed with which he had thought through a variety of complex matters and then expressed his judgments, but the combination of precise legal reasoning and sound military doctrine the text reflects. Later, his reputation would suffer greatly because he refused to reply to critics. Yet he was perfectly capable of defending his decisions, as this letter to McClellan indicates:

I was advised by high officers, in whose judgment I had great confidence, to make the order immediately on my arrival here, but I determined not to do so until I could learn your wishes from a personal inter-view; and even after that interview I tried every means in my power to avoid withdrawing your army, and delayed my decision as long as I dared to delay it. I assure you, General, it was not a hasty and inconsiderate act, but one that caused me more anxious thoughts than any other of my life; but after full and mature consideration of all the pros and cons, I was reluctantly forced to the conclusion that the order must be issued. There was to my mind no alternative.

Allow me to allude to a few of the facts in the case. You and your officers at one interview estimated the enemy's forces in and around Richmond at 200,000 men. Since then you and others report that they have received and are receiving large re-enforcements from the South. General Pope's army covering Washington is only about 40,000. Your effective force is only about 90,000. You are 30 miles from Richmond, and General Pope 80 or 90, with the enemy directly between you, ready to fall with his superior numbers upon one or the other, as he may elect. Neither can re-enforce the other in case of such an attack.

If General Pope's army be diminished to re-enforce you, Washington, Maryland, and Pennsylvania would be left uncovered and exposed. If your force be reduced to strengthen Pope, you would be too weak to even hold the position you now occupy should the enemy turn round and attack you in full force. In other words, the old Army of the Potomac is split into two parts, with the entire force of the enemy directly between them. They cannot be united by land without exposing both to destruction, and yet they must be united. To send Pope's forces by water to the Peninsula is, under present circumstances, a military impossibility. The only alternative is to send the forces on the Peninsula to some point by water, say Fredericksburg, where the two armies can be united.

Let me now allude to some of the objections which you have urged. You say that the withdrawal from the present position will cause the certain demoralization of the army, "which is now in excellent discipline and condition." I cannot understand why a simple change of position to a new and by no means distant base will demoralize an army in excellent discipline, unless the officers themselves assist in that demoralization, which I am satisfied they will not. Your change of front from your extreme right at Hanover Court-House to your present position was over 30 miles, but I have not heard that it demoralized your troops, notwithstanding the severe losses they sustained in effecting it.

A new base on the Rappahannock at Fredericksburg brings you within about 60 miles of Richmond, and secures a re-enforcement of 40,000 or 50,000 fresh and disciplined troops. The change, with such advantages, will, I think, if properly represented to your army, encourage rather than demoralize your troops. . . . Besides,

[Fredericksburg] *is between Richmond and Washington, and covers Washington from any attack of the enemy. The political effect of the withdrawal may at first be unfavorable; but I think the public are beginning to understand its necessity, and that they will have much more confidence in a united army than in its separated fragments.*

But you will reply, why not re-enforce me here, so that I can strike Richmond from my present position? To do this you said at our interview that you required 30,000 additional troops. I told you that it was impossible to give you so many. You finally thought you would have "some chance" of success with 20,000. But you afterward telegraphed me that you would require 35,000, as the enemy was being largely re-enforced. If your estimate of the enemy's strength was correct, your requisition was perfectly reasonable, but it was utterly impossible to fill it until new troops could be enlisted and organized, which would require several weeks.

To keep your army in its present position until it could be so re-enforced would almost destroy it in that climate. The months of August and September are almost fatal to whites who live on that part of James River, and even after you received the re-enforcements asked for, you admitted that you must reduce Fort Darling and the river batteries before you could advance on Richmond. It is by no means certain that the reduction of these fortifications would not require considerable time, perhaps as much as those at Yorktown. This delay might not only be fatal to the health of your army, but in the mean time General Pope's forces would be exposed to the heavy blows of the enemy without the slightest hope of assistance from you.

In regard to the demoralizing effect of a withdrawal from the Peninsula to the Rappahannock I must remark that a large number of your highest officers, indeed a majority of those whose opinions have been reported to me, are decidedly in favor of the movement. Even several of those who originally advocated the line of the Peninsula now advise its abandonment.

I have not inquired, and do not wish to know, by whose advice or for what reasons the Army of the Potomac was separated into two parts, with the enemy between them. I must take things as I find them. I find the forces divided, and I wish to unite them. Only one feasible plan has been presented for doing this. If you or any one else had presented a better plan I certainly should have adopted it. But all of your plans require re-enforcements, which it is impossible to give you. It is very easy to ask for re-enforcements, but it is not so easy to give them when you have no disposable troops at your command.

I have written very plainly as I understand the case, and I hope you will give me credit for having fully considering the matter, although I may have arrived at very different conclusions from your own.[54]

From the time of General Halleck's having ordered McClellan to begin evacuating his sick and wounded men onward, Little Mac's references to the general-in-chief in his letters to Ellen grew progressively pejorative. On August 4: "Halleck has begun to show the cloven foot already."[55] On August 8: "I strongly suspect him of being a 'scalawag.' "[56] By August 10 the McClellan had received Halleck's long letter; and just as Old Brains had revealed a great deal about himself in that product, McClellan gave an astonishingly clear and candid forecast of how he intended to behave in the letter he wrote his wife that morning:

Halleck is turning out just like the rest of the herd—the affair is rapidly developing itself, & I see more clearly every day their settled purpose to force me to resign. I am trying to keep my temper and force them *to relieve me or dismiss me from the service. I have no idea that I will be with this army more than two or three weeks longer & should not be surprised any day or hour to get my "walking papers." I have a strong idea that Pope will be thrashed during the coming week—& very badly whipped he will be & ought to be— such a villain as he is ought to bring defeat upon any cause that employs him. . . .*

The absurdity of Halleck's course in ordering the army away from here is that it cannot possibly reach Washn in time to do any good, but will necessarily be too late—I am sorry to say that I am forced to the conclusion that H is very dull & very incompetent— alas poor country! . . .

I am satisfied that the dolts in Washn are bent on my destruction if it is possible for them to accomplish it—but I believe that Providence is just enough to bring their own sins upon their heads & that they will before they get through taste the dregs of the cup of bitterness. The more I hear of their wickedness the more am I surprised that such a wretched set are permitted to live much less to occupy the positions they do. . . .

Midnight. I received a very harsh & unjust telegram from Halleck this evening & a very friendly private *letter from the same individual—blows hot & cold. Halleck* writes *that all the forces in Virginia including Pope, Burnside etc are to be placed under my command—I doubt it, but will accept no less place. . . . I think the result of their machinations will be that Pope will be badly thrashed within two days & that they will be very glad to turn over the redemption of their affairs to me. I won't undertake it unless I have full & entire control. . . .*[57]

The night before, General Halleck had written his wife:

The President and Cabinet have thus far approved everything I have proposed. This is kind and complimentary, but it only increases my responsibility, for if any disaster happens they can say We did for you all you asked. The great difficulty now is to get the troops together in time. I have felt so uneasy for some days about General Pope's army that I could hardly sleep. I cannot get General McClellan to do what I wish. The President and Cabinet have lost all confidence in him and urge me to remove him from command. This is strictly entre nous. *In other words they want me to do what they were afraid to attempt! I hope I may never be obliged to follow their advice in the matter.*[58]

General Halleck's reluctance to sack the Army of the Potomac's commander—and his rejection of even the thought of currying favor with Lincoln and Stanton by performing that service on their behalf—may have been proof of a sort that his expressions of respect for McClellan had been genuine. More evidence to this effect was in the "very *friendly and private* letter" Old Brains had written McClellan on August 7:

I deeply regret that you cannot agree with me as to the necessity of reuniting the old Army of the Potomac. I, however, have taken the responsibility of doing so, and am to risk my reputation on it. As I told you when at your camp, it is my intention that you shall command all the troops in Virginia as soon as we can get them together; and with the army thus concentrated I am certain that you can take Richmond. I must beg of you, General, to hurry along this movement. Your reputation as well as mine may be involved in its rapid execution.

I cannot regard Pope and Burnside as safe until you re-enforce them. Moreover, I wish them to be under your immediate command

*for reasons which it is not necessary to specify. As things now are,
with separate commands, there will be no concert of action, and we
daily risk being attacked and defeated in detail.*[59]

Yet the Young Napoleon's reaction, as reflected in his letter to Mary
Ellen on the night he received Old Brains' letter, was: "I think the result of
[Lincoln's, Stanton's, Halleck's, *et al.*] machinations will be that Pope will be
badly thrashed within two days & that they will be very glad to turn over
the redemption of their affairs to me."

5

THRASHING JOHN POPE'S ARMY OF VIRGINIA was indeed the object of
General Lee's forces, nearly all of which he had shifted north of Richmond
during July's second half—in the process, showing his contempt for George
McClellan and the Yankee hordes he was leaving virtually unguarded at
Harrison's Landing. Instead of two hundred thousand men, Lee had only
about eighty thousand—not enough to do grievous harm to McClellan's
ninety thousand but more than Pope's fifty thousand. Moreover, the Army
of Northern Virginia was in a central position, able to strike Pope or block
McClellan without having to move very far, and its commander wanted to
wring all the benefit he could from that advantage as quickly as possible.[60]

Even before July 23, John Pope had been aware that Stonewall Jackson
had loaded his troops on the cars and moved northward. On that date, the
general Lee considered a miscreant sent his southernmost corps commander,
Major General Nathaniel Banks, a second warning:

> *There is no doubt that a large force of the enemy is at Louisa Court-
> House, Gordonsville, and perhaps farther west. Do you know what
> they are doing, and which way, if any, they are moving? There ought
> not to pass a day without your being advised of these movements
> through spies, scouts, and reconnaissances.*
>
> *As I have heard nothing from you for a day or two on the
> subject, I presume you have no advices. You are in the presence of an
> active, vigilant enemy. Omit no precautions and spare no expense in
> keeping yourself constantly posted as to his movements.*[61]

Immersed as General Halleck had been in determining whether the
Army of the Potomac should remain penned up or withdraw, on July 31 he

responded to a message from Pope regarding the Confederates' reported departures from Richmond: "The evacuation may be only a trick; take care and do not be caught in the trap."[62] On the next day, he ordered General Burnside to move his troops from Fort Monroe to Aquia Landing on the Potomac, and then to "take position near Fredericksburg, the movement to be made as rapidly as possible, and the destination to be concealed."[63] This was designed to put Burnside on Jackson's flank, and also to facilitate reinforcing Banks if necessary.

"Do not advance so as to expose yourself to any disaster," Old Brains telegraphed Pope on August 8, "unless you can better your line of defense, until we can get more troops up the Rappahannock. I hope to increase your forces very soon, but in the mean time you must be very cautious. Keep up your connection with General Burnside, and do not let the enemy get between you."[64] And on the next day, August 9, the general-in-chief telegraphed Burnside: "I fear the enemy may attack Pope in large force. Be ready at a moment's notice to co-operate with him."[65] Pope, in turn, ordered Banks to halt Jackson's advance so that the other Union corps could reach the Culpeper area. But in order to comply, Banks had to find Jackson.

As it turned out, on August 9, 1862, Banks' forces attacked a line Jackson had occupied on Cedar Mountain. The federal assault was vigorous; it penetrated the Confederate positions at several points; but Jackson, saber-drawn, led a counterattack, and Ambrose Powell Hill's division arrived and hit Banks' troops from the flank. At the end of the day's bloody fighting, Stonewall's men were pursuing the fleeing Yankees. Banks' casualties, roughly twenty-four hundred, were about a thousand more than Jackson's.[66]

Cedar Mountain was hardly the thrashing George McClellan had told Ellen he expected Pope to receive, so of course there was no call from Washington for the Young Napoleon to "redeem" anything. Pope had needed one more day to complete the assembly of his corps, as General Halleck had admonished him to do; but after a two-day impasse, Jackson backed off to Gordonsville.[67]

Even so, the indecisive blood-letting had enabled both sides to learn enough to discern the strategic possibilities and to plan their reactions to it. General Lee realized that he would have to suppress the miscreant Pope before McClellan's massive army could be moved down the James and up Chesapeake Bay and the Potomac to reinforce him. The farther westward Lee could draw Pope, the more distant from Aquia Landing and Alexandria—the Potomac's ports of debarkation—the Army of Virginia was obliged to move, the better the Confederates' chances would be for destroying the smaller federal force.

Old Brains had foreseen such a situation almost as soon as he had arrived in Washington. One of his reasons for ordering McClellan to abandon Harrison's Landing and move the Army of the Potomac to Aquia Creek forthwith had been to frustrate Lee should he threaten Pope. Put simply, the Union's success in the East depended primarily, indeed overwhelmingly, on how quickly McClellan could get his army back to the western banks of its home river.

6

IN EFFECT, ABRAHAM LINCOLN had drawn General Halleck into a chess match in which the men on the vast board were real and numbered nearly a million. And this was a contest not only with the South's *de facto* general-in-chief, Jefferson Davis, but with two field generals who seemed to be overcoming the lapses that prevented them from destroying McClellan's army during the Seven Days: Robert Edward Lee and the enigmatic but able Thomas Jonathan Jackson.

From the Confederate side of the vast strategic chessboard, Jefferson Davis was about to test Old Brains' ability to fight off two strong rebel initiatives on fronts as widely separated as eastern Kentucky and piedmont Virginia *at the same time.*

Halleck's move had been to order McClellan to reinforce Pope. Yet there was that other portion of the board, the West. "I am doing everything in my power to get new troops into the field," Old Brains wrote his wife not long after Cedar Mountain, "and the sky here is cleared. But at the West everything since I left has gone wrong. It is the strangest thing in the world to me that this war has developed so little talent in our generals. There is not a single one in the West fit for a great command."[68]

Curiously, Davis could have made the same remark. Albert Sidney Johnston had bled to death at Shiloh. Pierre Beauregard had invoked presidential wrath by abandoning Corinth without a fight. The Creole's successor, Braxton Bragg, was reputed to be somewhat eccentric. And while Edmund Kirby Smith had led a brigade with distinction at Manassas back in July 1861, how effective he would prove as the commander of the Department of East Tennessee in the high summer of 1862 remained to be demonstrated.

Bragg and Kirby Smith, equals not in rank but as department commanders, advised Davis that they would "cooperate" in a campaign to regain control of eastern Kentucky and Tennessee from the Yankee invaders.

And in not appointing either general as supreme commander in the West, Jefferson Davis was making a colossal blunder.

Even so, there were qualitative differences working. Davis had Lee and Jackson operating north of Richmond, but Halleck was having to direct McClellan and Pope, generals who held each other in contempt, in coping with the rebels' threat building in central Virginia. Worse, from a telegraph office nearly a thousand miles from Decatur, Alabama, Old Brains was obliged to rely on the lethargic Don Carlos Buell to respond to the strategic challenge Braxton Bragg and Edmund Kirby Smith seemed about to throw down to the Union in East Tennessee.

In these circumstances, *generalship* had to acquire new, multi-level meaning in the course of fighting everything out. Given the telegraph, gone forever were the years when kings or even barons commanded directly in the field—in the process, inspiring and motivating their troops more by their examples in battle as fighters than by words few of their soldiers could possibly have heard. Valor still made the difference, often, between victory and anything less. But now it was displayed by sergeants, captains, colonels—leaders whose shouts of "Follow me!" quickened the hearts of their men. And, as throughout military history, the missions of the generals were being accomplished by *their men.*

Words transmitted as if by magic over countless miles of copper wire were taking on inordinate importance at a time when strategic decisions were being made in the belligerents' capitals—often, several states distant from where they were to be implemented. The commander having superior skills not only in thinking complex and usually unexpected questions through in a matter of minutes, but also in communicating his instructions clearly and succinctly, had a decided advantage. Yet, until 1861, hardly anyone was aware of the need to operate in this new mode, much less prepared to excel in so doing.

Henry Halleck was an exception primarily because somewhere along his life's path, he had developed the ability to focus his mental powers on adapting to new and different conditions. Almost from the day he arrived in St. Louis, his telegrams reflected a style so unique that the addressees did not have to glance down at the signature line to know the name of the sender. Never from the outset of Halleck's message-writing would his terseness, sharp focus, and clear direction be matched, much less exceeded, by anyone on either side other than—occasionally—A. Lincoln.

It was as if Old Brains recognized that the telegraph would be his primary, and in many instances his *only*, means of exercising the considerable command authority he possessed. It was a resource, like time, never to be wasted. He could be succinct to the point of arrogance; sarcastic; sensitive to the feelings of the recipient, yet firm; conciliatory and even flattering when an occasion was important enough in his opinion of the Union's interest to justify stretching. And among the most impressive instances of his employment of the telegraph during the early period of his general-in-chiefship was his use of the wires during August and early September 1862.

One recipient of General Halleck's messages, however, was not pleased: George McClellan. On August 17, 1862, he complained:

> *I have had this morning a full conversation with General Burnside. To be perfectly frank with you, I must say that I did think from some of your recent telegrams that you were not disposed to treat me in a candid or friendly manner. This was the more grating to me because I was conscious that although I differed from you in opinion I had done so with entire frankness and loyalty, and that I had not delayed one moment in preparing to carry out your orders. I am glad to say that Burnside has satisfied me that you are still my friend; in return I think he can satisfy you that I have loyally carried out your instructions, although my own judgment was not in accordance with yours.*
>
> *Let the past take care of itself. So long as I remain in command of this army I will faithfully carry out the new programme.*[69]

Three days later, Halleck replied:

> *I have just received yours of the 17th by General Burnside.*
>
> *You can scarcely imagine the pressure on me for the last two weeks and the anxiety I have had in regard to your movements. When I felt that the safety of Washington depended on the prompt and rapid transfer of your army it is very probable that my messages to you were more urgent and pressing than guarded in their language. I certainly meant nothing harsh, but I did feel that you did not act as promptly as I thought the circumstances required.*
>
> *I deemed every hour a golden one, the loss of which could not be repaired. I think you did not attach so much value to the passing hours; but perhaps I was mistaken. I know that there are several little matters which have annoyed you; they could not be avoided. . . .*
>
> *My dear general, we must not let little things annoy us, but push right ahead to the great end in view.*
>
> *There is enough and more than enough for all of us to do,*

although none of us can do exactly what we could wish. That Lee is moving on Pope with his main army I have no doubt. Unless we can unite most of your army with Burnside and Pope, Washington is in great danger.

Under these circumstances you must pardon the extreme anxiety (and perhaps a little impatience) which I feel. Every moment seems to me as important as an ordinary hour.[70]

For Halleck to have responded at all was additional confirmation that his regard for McClellan was high. Moreover, had he not replied, or if he had told the Young Napoleon in effect to quit complaining and obey orders, McClellan might have delayed the movement of his army even more than he already had.

Concurrently, out west of Chattanooga, Don Carlos Buell was in the process of being outwitted by Braxton Bragg. Reports that the Confederates who had skedaddled from Corinth to Tupelo were being moved from there to Chattanooga by rail reached Buell at Huntsville, Alabama, as early as July 20, but not until that month's last day was General-in-Chief Halleck to read this message from General Buell:

My information is that Bragg arrived at Chattanooga Sunday evening, the 27th. Two trains, with troops, arrived the same day. Their railroad agent, it is said, has orders to furnish cars for 30,000 men as fast as he can. You can judge for yourself of the probability of the concentrating of a heavy force against Middle Tennessee, now that they have nothing to apprehend in Mississippi. The work of reenforcing here would be slow.[71]

In reply to Buell's wire came a prompt, equally typical one from Halleck: "I have ordered General Grant to be prepared to re-enforce you if you should find the enemy too strong at Chattanooga."[72] Grant's divisions were scattered from near Memphis southeastward into northern Mississippi.

Much of Buell's information, however, was correct. The rebel army's east-northeastward move of roughly 250 crow-flight miles was taking place along 776 miles of tracks *via* Mobile and Atlanta—a roundabout route, thanks to Old Brains' having seized Corinth.[73]

Tennessee's Confederate Governor Isham Harris wrote Andrew Ewing from Chattanooga on July 28 that "[Bragg] assures me that he will carry me to Nashville before the end of August. . . . If General Bragg succeeds in crossing the Tennessee River and marching rapidly through Middle

Tennessee it places him in rear of Buell's force, now threatening Chattanooga, and compels Buell to fall back, if indeed we do not cut him off."[74]

And on the same day, from Cullum Springs, Alabama, where he was recuperating, Pierre Gustave Toutant Beauregard was responding to his successor's request for his views. "Action, action, and action is what we require," the general who abandoned Corinth without a fight advised, adding: "[It] is evident that unless you re-enforce General E. K. Smith at Chattanooga he will be overpowered by Buell, and then our communications with the east and our supplies at Atlanta, Augusta, &c., will be cut off. . . ."[75]

On August 7, Buell had sent the general-in-chief an estimate of the situation that placed Confederate strength in East Tennessee at 90,000—twice his own 46,000—although he conceded that there might be only 60,000 rebels at Chattanooga and in Knoxville. He was prepared to resist Bragg, he assured Halleck, then he gave several reasons suggesting that it was "doubtful" whether he could cross the Tennessee and seize Chattanooga—after which he summed-up: "I shall march upon Chattanooga at the earliest possible day, unless I ascertain certainly that the enemy's strength renders it imprudent. If, on the other hand, he should cross the river I shall attack him, and I do not doubt that we shall defeat him."[76]

By August 10, Buell was relaying reports to Halleck that "the enemy has 60,000 men at Knoxville and that additional troops are arriving. The enemy is advancing in Kentucky."[77] At about the same time, Nathaniel Banks' corps of Pope's Army of Virginia was recovering from its collision with Stonewall Jackson's forces at Cedar Mountain, and George McClellan had only recently started to respond to Old Brains' peremptory order to withdraw from Harrison's Landing forthwith. Yet, busy as he was, on August 12 Halleck wired Buell simply but directly: "If the enemy are concentrating in East Tennessee you must move there and break them up. Go wherever the enemy is."[78]

Also dated August 12, 1862, was a letter to his former neighboring department commander that was unrelentingly candid:

> *I deem it my duty to write to you confidentially that the adminis-*
> *tration is greatly dissatisfied with the slowness of your operations. . . .*
> *So strong is this dissatisfaction that I have several times been asked*
> *to recommend some officer to take your place.*
> *   I have replied that I know of no more capable officer than*
> *yourself to recommend. To-day the matter has been urged on me very*

hard on the ground that you were accomplishing nothing, and I should not be surprised if a change of command should be ordered without again consulting me.

Permit me, General, to say in all kindness that the Government will expect an active campaign by the troops under your command, and that unless that is done the present dissatisfaction is so great your friends here will not be able to prevent a change being ordered.

There are several outside applications for command who are now urging their claims. Not one of these applicants, so far as I have learned their names, is competent to command a single division, much less a geographical department.[79]

How much better it would have been, Old Brains may well have wondered, if there had been in command there a Cump Sherman or even a Grant who would understand what he meant, *and act on it,* when he said, merely, *Go wherever the enemies are and break them up.*

By August 16, however, Braxton Bragg had apparently been replaced, at least in Don Carlos Buell's mind, as the main threat in the West. "Kirby Smith is advancing into Kentucky by the gaps west [of] Cumberland Gap with some 12,000 or 15,000 men. . . ." he telegraphed Halleck, adding:

I have repeated my requests to the Governors of Ohio and Indiana to forward troops with all dispatch, and have ordered General Nelson to command [in Kentucky]. . . . *I don't know when I can expect troops from General Grant, but they ought to be here immediately. If more troops could be spared they ought to come.*[80]

"[Ohio] Governor Tod telegraphs here that he will send five regiments into Kentucky by Wednesday, the 20th," the general-in-chief assured Buell on August 18. But the next two sentences were devoted to a different subject: "So great is the dissatisfaction here at the apparent want of energy and activity in your district, that I was this morning notified to have you removed. I got the matter delayed till we could hear further of your movements."[81]

Back, immediately, came Buell's response:

My movements have been such as the circumstances seemed to me to require. I beg that you will not interpose on my behalf; on the contrary, if the dissatisfaction cannot cease on grounds which I

*might think be supposed if not apparent, I respectfully request that I
may be relieved. My position is far too important to be occupied by
any officer on sufferance. I have no desire to stand in the way of
what may be deemed necessary for the public good. . . .*[82]

Secretary of War Edwin Stanton simplified Buell's life on August 19 by
assigning Major General Horatio Wright to command of all Union forces in
Kentucky—actually, of the Department of the Ohio, "consisting of the
States of Ohio, Indiana, Illinois, Michigan, Wisconsin, and Kentucky,
including Cumberland Gap and the forces there."[83] General Buell's
disappointing performances earlier suggested that he might prove incapable
of meeting even one challenge nearby—the one the presence of Bragg's
army in Chattanooga was posing—much less the other in Kentucky.

But was acceptance of Stanton's injection of Horatio Wright into the
command arrangement a concession Halleck had been obliged to make in
order to prevent Buell's sacking? If so, was this an indication that a split was
occurring between the administration and its general-in-chief? No, not
quite—or at least, not yet. Or so Old Brains' message to General Wright on
August 25 suggested:

> *The Government, or rather I should say the President and Secretary
> of War, is greatly displeased with the slow movements of General
> Buell. Unless he does something very soon I think he will be
> removed. Indeed it would have been done before now if I had not
> begged to give him a little more time. There must be more energy
> and activity in Kentucky and Tennessee, and the one who first does
> something brilliant will get the entire command.*
>
> *I therefore hope to hear very soon of some success in your
> department. I can hardly describe to you the feeling of dis-
> appointment here in the want of activity in General Buell's large
> army.*
>
> *The Government seems determined to apply the guillotine to
> all unsuccessful generals. It seems rather hard to do this where the
> general is not in fault, but perhaps with us now, as in the French
> Revolution, some harsh measures are required.*[84]

6 ★ Harder Rights, Easier Wrongs

$\mathcal{A}$ S KIRBY SMITH'S FORCES were bypassing George Morgan's at Cumberland Gap and surging northwestward into Kentucky out in the West, in northern Virginia, both the Union and Confederate armies were demonstrating once again how profoundly water—the presence and courses of rivers, in particular—could shape military operations. Not far west of Fredericksburg, the Rapidan, flowing eastward, joined the Rappahannock's waters coming down from the northwest. These streams were the northern and southern legs of a triangle whose apex was where the two met; the third leg, closing the eastward-pointing triangle on the west, was provided by the tracks of the Orange & Alexandria Railroad, which in happier years had been an important link in the system connecting Washington and Richmond.

In mid-August 1862, the O&A was the lifeline of Major General John Pope's Army of Virginia. But that force's commander had gained considerable experience in dealing with waterways during his campaigns along the Mississippi's western bank, and so it was perhaps natural for him to use rivers as reference points in reporting to General Halleck: "My whole force was advanced and is posted near the Rapidan," he wrote on April 16. "It is impossible, without crossing the river, to establish camps near it on account of low, wet ground. The hills are all on [the] south side. . . ." And so was substantially all of General Lee's Army of Northern Virginia. "Ac-cording to your instructions I shall not cross the Rapidan for the present," Pope said in his message to Halleck, "but will at least make a strong reconnaissance and demonstration. . . ."[1]

Shifting his attention from Kentucky eastward several hundred miles on that day, Old Brains replied: "I think it would be very unsafe for your army to cross the Rapidan. It would be far better if you were in rear of the Rappahannock [the triangle's northern leg]. We must run no risks just now, but must concentrate so as to secure [McClellan's] full co-operation. As soon as [his] force reaches Aquia Creek to sufficiently sustain itself it will be sent to the fork of the rivers [the apex of the triangle in which Pope had placed his army]." Do not let your left [eastern] flank be turned, the Union armies' senior soldier admonished Pope. "If threatened too strongly, fall behind [north of] the Rappahannock [the triangle's northern leg]." General Halleck closed with an expression of encouragement mixed perhaps with devout hope: "Every possible exertion is being made to increase our forces on that line."[2]

Henry Halleck's response to Pope was the kind of message that would drive his critics to fresh excesses of condemnation, in part because they understood neither the circumstances nor the writer. Although Old Brains had a map and could wring from it at least as much topographical information as Pope, lines and squiggles on paper were no substitute for viewing actual conditions on-site. The mapmaker had provided enough selected data to serve as a starting point—but only for comment and suggestion, not orders. Even had General Halleck not recognized that limitation, however, his thought processes reflected his training and experience as a lawyer as well as a soldier. And lawyers almost always *advise,* even when they are strongly convinced a client should take a certain course of action.

In this instance, Halleck appeared to have placed himself in General Lee's boots and concluded that the best place to strike Pope was just east of the triangle's apex, at the United States Ford, where the Rapidan merged with the Rappahannock—hence, Old Brains' *admonition* to prevent the turning of the Army of Virginia's left (eastern) flank.

As it turned out, wedging his forces between Pope's and those from Harrison's Landing arriving at Aquia Landing was exactly what Lee was planning to do. But Pope acted on the general-in-chief's opinion that "it would be better if you were in rear of the Rappahannock," and by withdrawing northward promptly from the triangular trap, the miscreant obliged Lee to devise another way of suppressing him.[3]

"I fully approve your move," the general-in-chief telegraphed Pope on August 18. "Stand firm on that line until I can help you. Fight hard and aid will soon come."[4]

John Pope displayed genuine cooperation by giving his superior

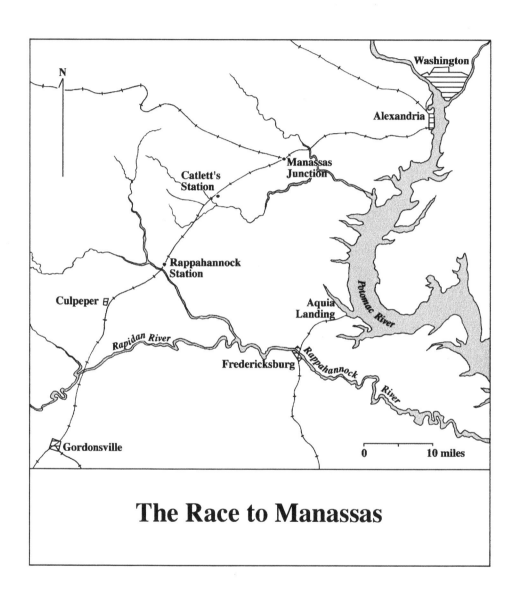

The Race to Manassas

helpful descriptions of terrain. "The line of the Rappahannock above its junction with the Rapidan is very weak," he reported on August 19, "as it is fordable almost everywhere and runs through a flat country. I must keep possession of the [O&A] railroad, and cannot draw farther downstream than I am now. An engagement with the enemy here will be simply a pitched battle in the open field, the river presenting scarcely any impediment, while the country is very open. . . ."[5]

General Lee agreed, apparently, for he decided to move northwestward along the Rappahannock's southwestern bank to draw Pope as far away from Aquia Landing as possible. Only if he could smash the Army of Virginia before McClellan could reinforce it, was there any hope for a Confederate success.

Disappointing Lee, then, took on greater urgency in the minds of the men in the Union's high command. Attaining that goal, however, depended upon how quickly the Young Napoleon actually delivered his army's five corps to Pope. "I have been pushing everything since I arrived here," he assured Halleck from Fort Monroe on August 20, "and shall continue to give it my personal attention."[6]

Indeed, in withdrawing his army from the Peninsula, General Mc-Clellan was demonstrating the same skills he had displayed back in March in moving it there from Alexandria. But in a confidential message to Ambrose Burnside, he described his achievement as a "retreat," and he declared that "it shall not be my fault if the troops do not arrive in time."[7] And during the next evening, he wrote Mary Ellen Marcy McClellan:

> *I believe I have triumphed!! Just received a telegram from Halleck stating that Pope & Burnside are very hard pressed—urging me to push forward reinforcements, & to come myself as soon as I possibly can! . . . Now they are in trouble they seem to want the "Quaker," the "procrastinator," the "coward" & the "traitor"!*[8]

2

AT TIMES, OF COURSE, GENERAL HALLECK could write orders in the peremptory manner as directly as anyone. Also, he was not above allowing his temper to drive his messages, as these examples dated August 19 and 20, 1862, both addressed to General Pope, show:

> *You will immediately remove from your army all newspaper re-*

porters, and you will permit no telegrams to be sent over the telegraph wires out of your command except those sent by yourself. You will also suspend the transmission of any mail matter other than that of official business.[9]

And:

I think your staff is decidedly leaky. The substance of my telegrams to you is immediately telegraphed back here to the press. Several of these telegrams have been intercepted. Clean out all such characters from your headquarters. It is useless to attempt any sending of orders if you permit them to be made public as soon as you receive them.[10]

"I am much surprised to receive your dispatch of 10:20 last night," Pope replied on August 21, and initially he blamed the leaking on the telegraph men. Later, he cited other suspects: "The several corps composing this army have until recently acted quite independently, and it is difficult to put a stop to practices which have prevailed hitherto. It is possible that the orders to which you refer have been made public by the army corps commanders to whom portions at least have been communicated."[11]

Two of those subordinates were Nathaniel Banks and Franz Sigel, both politicians who were likely to be courting press support.

Perhaps, but Old Brains was not satisfied—and he had cause: "My telegram to you was (or at least its substance) immediately telegraphed to New York and published. . . . I don't know where the leak is, but we must find it."[12]

The Union's general-in-chief would have been even more indignant if Mrs. McClellan had passed along to reporters some of the letters she was receiving from her husband. Still at Fort Monroe on August 22, McClellan wrote:

I think they are pretty well scared in Washn & probably with good reason. I am confident that the disposition to be made of me will depend entirely upon the state of their nerves in Washn. If they feel safe there I will no doubt be shelved. . . . I am truly & heartily sick of the troubles I have had & am not fond of being a target for the abuse & slander of all the rascals in the country. . . . To think that a man whom I so sincerely admired, trusted & liked as I did Stanton turning against me as he has—& that without any cause that I am aware of! Pah—it is too bad![13]

Halleck's interest, however, was in McClellan's troops. In a message intended to expedite their arrival, dated August 22 (as was the Young Napoleon's letter to Mary Ellen), he told their commander:

> *The great object now is to hold the line of the Rappahannock till we can get together sufficient forces to take the offensive. If forced to fall back, we must fight in retreat and dispute every inch of ground till we reach Manassas and the Occoquan* [Creek]. . . . *Of course no definite plan of offensive operations can be formed till we are strong enough to make the attack.*[14]

Clearly, Old Brains was scanning all possible moves on the chess board: hold, fall back, dispute, attack. And that Manassas was very much on his mind was suggested by a question he put to General Pope on the same day: "Would it not be well," he asked, to unload some of the troops arriving by rail from Alexandria at Warrenton Junction [not far southwest of the old battleground], "or somewhere in that vicinity, so as to act as a reserve and at the same time to threaten any movement of the enemy by the Springs [just west of Manassas]?"[15] And later on August 22:

> *The enemy is concentrating. it seems, near Manassas and Bull Run. You must look out for this and immediately break it up, for your supplies must come from Washington and you must fall back in this direction if compelled to retreat. Do not let him separate you from Alexandria. We will send some troops to meet you, but we are very short of transportation.*[16]

But General Halleck had not stopped considering offensive possibilities. In another message to Pope on August 22 he had said:

> *If you are satisfied that the enemy's main force is moving on Warrenton, mass your troops on the railroad and prepare to attack him in flank. If this should prove to be his move, we will take the offensive against his flank movement. You will readily understand my views.*[17]

Friday, August 22, 1862, however, would be memorable for much more than Old Brains' forebodings and telegraphed thought- and action-promptings. A visitor to General Pope's headquarters that day had been

Colonel Herman Haupt, who had been graduated from West Point in 1835 (the year Cadet Halleck had entered) but had resigned three months later to begin a career as a railroad builder. Haupt had wanted no part of the war, and he was facing financial ruin because of a dispute with Massachusetts politicians over reimbursements of costs he had borne in the course of constructing the five-mile Hoosac Tunnel in the Berkshires. But Stanton had prevailed upon him to come to Washington and serve as the superintendent of railroads the government was controlling. Haupt had agreed, provided that he would not have to accept a commission or pay, and he reserved the right to leave whenever he wished. He tolerated the effective rank of colonel only because it helped him get things done.[18]

Colonel Haupt was at Pope's headquarters on August 22 mainly because the army commander's quartermasters had been sidetracking unloaded boxcars and using them as warehouses, taking them as far out of service as the rebels might have had they blown them up. Every available rail car was needed back up the O&A's tracks at Alexandria to bring McClellan's arriving troops to reinforce Pope. That morning, Assistant Secretary of War Peter H. Watson had telegraphed General Pope:

> *Heintzelman's and Cox's troops are detained for want of cars. You have all the rolling stock and power* [engines] *at and near the Rappahannock. You can use the cars for either warehouses or for transportation, but not for both.*[19]

Herman Haupt, a kindred spirit of Henry Halleck's in that he tolerated no nonsense from anyone, demanded and got the release of some of the purloined rolling stock.[20] But he was still more of a soldier than he cared to admit. While Haupt was with Pope, the message flow from Old Brains up in Washington had been heavy, and those and other incoming reports prompted the visitor to ask the general commanding if the Confederates might be in the process of turning his western flank. Replied General Pope: "There is no danger."

However, during a stop at Manassas Junction on his way back to Alexandria that day, Haupt received a telegram from his recent host. Confederates were *indeed* moving around his western flank, the general reported, and he asked that the freight cars be moved out of the endangered area.

But it was too late for that. The train behind Haupt's had been fired upon and captured, and Major General James Ewell Brown Stuart was leading a cavalry raid at Catlett's Station on the O&A, only ten miles down the tracks from where Haupt was reading Pope's message.[21]

As part of General Lee's effort to lure Pope as far away from reinforcement and rescue as possible, he had ordered "Jeb" Stuart to destroy a bridge over Cedar Run near Catlett's so that Pope's army would be deprived of supplies stockpiled at Manassas Junction. Wet weather and stout timbers prevented Stuart from carrying out that part of his mission.

However, a man the Yankees called a contraband, who had declared that his heart was still with his "own folks," guided Stuart not merely to Pope's lightly guarded rear headquarters but to the absent general's own tent. From it and those of Pope's staff officers nearby, the raiders took back to General Lee the "miscreant's" order book, letters, and messages—including some interesting very recent ones from Washington and Fort Monroe—and also a Union army frock coat with the shoulder straps of a major general and a hat to match. And from the captured sheaf of telegrams, many of them signed H. W. Halleck, General Lee discovered how near he was to losing the race with McClellan.[22]

Late in the day on August 22, however, about all that Colonel Haupt knew when he reached Warrenton Junction was that the O&A Railroad had been cut at Catlett's Station. Soon came another message from the army commander who so recently had assured him that there was no danger:

> *Say to Generals Heintzelman, Cox, and Sturgis, as they come forward with their troops, to halt them at Warrenton Junction or on Cedar Creek, and take up a position there against any force of the enemy advancing to the direction of Warrenton.*
>
> *The enemy has succeeded, in greatly superior numbers, in turning our right in the direction of Sulphur Springs and Warrenton. . . . I have ordered a force back to Catlett's Station.*[23]

Even before Haupt had remarked to Pope that Lee might try to get around his western flank, General Halleck had warned him: "You must look out for this and immediately break it up. . . . Do not let [the enemy] separate you from Alexandria." Now, still thinking ahead, Old Brains wired Haupt at Warrenton Junction:

> *If you cannot get trains beyond Catlett's Station, land all the troops at that place and keep your rolling stock this side and out of danger. Expect large arrivals at Alexandria to-morrow, and make preparations to take them forward to General Pope.*[24]

3

TELEGRAMS REACHING GENERAL-IN-CHIEF Halleck's office in Washington from the West as well as from down the O&A's tracks and from George McClellan reminded him that he was engaged in a three-dimension chess match—a four-dimension one, if time be accorded its full importance. Moreover, out in the distant regions, Old Brains had even more generals looking to him for guidance than he did in the East. And adding to his burden was the variety of problems he was either asked or felt compelled to solve.

On August 23, 1862, for example, from Louisville came a message from Major General William Nelson:

> *I arrived here this morning, in obedience to orders from Major-General Buell, to assume command of the troops arriving in Kentucky to repel the threatened invasion of Kentucky and Tennessee north of the Cumberland River. . . . The rebel General Kirby Smith is moving in the direction of Burkesville, on the Cumberland River, with 15,000 good troops. My business was to meet him and drive him back. I find here Major-General Wright, who arrived in this city one hour before, and is announced to command the new Department of Ohio. Under these circumstances shall I return to my division? I solicit your orders in the premises.*[25]

One sentence was all General Halleck needed: "You and the officers under your command will remain in the new Department of the Ohio, and render all possible assistance to General Wright in driving the enemy from Kentucky."[26]

Earlier, rather abruptly, Old Brains had urged Wright to make his headquarters at Cincinnati. On August 23 he provided this explanation:

> *The reason why I advised against establishing your headquarters at Louisville is this: There are two factions there, the Speeds and the Guthries, very jealous of each other. It will be difficult if at Louisville for you to keep clear of these two factions, so as not to offend one or the other. Be on your guard against them even in Cincinnati.*[27]

Would—or could—General-in-Chief McClellan, or Lincoln, have set aside concern over the Confederate raid at Catlett's Station, only forty miles or so away, to explain such a suggestion? Perhaps, but here Halleck may have been recalling the destructive feud between William Gwin and David

Broderick during the 1850s; the Californian may have left the state, but he had brought much of California with him. At a minimum, he was supporting Wright in every way he could.

There was consistency, also, in Don Carlos Buell's implying that the challenges he faced were insurmountable. This was reflected in a long message he sent Halleck from Decherd, Tennessee, via Corinth on August 24—one that surely must have disturbed the general-in-chief in that it called only for actions on his part that were already being taken. Buell wrote:

The intimations of various kinds, which I have heretofore alluded to, of a design on the part of the enemy to attempt a formidable invasion of Tennessee are being verified, and there can be no doubt that Tennessee and Kentucky are in very great peril. It is impossible to ascertain with any certainty what the force of the enemy is. It probably is not less than 60,000 men, independently of irregular cavalry and the force operating toward Kentucky in rear of Cumberland Gap. They have crossed at Chattanooga, Harrison, Blythe's Ferry, and Kingston, and are marching on McMinnville.

Upon the receipt of this information I ordered the forces at Battle Creek to move up the Sequatchie River. . . . Owing to the mountainous character of the country, and perhaps some misapprehension, the concentration was not effected as I designed, and is not yet, though the troops are now in motion for that object. If not too late it will yet be made at Altamont and the enemy attacked on that route; but my impressions are that the enemy is already at Altamont.

If the junction cannot be affected there it may be necessary to fall back on Murfreesborough. More embarrassing than the force in front is the condition of things in the rear. Our communications have now been effectually cut for twelve days. I have had no force there sufficient to open and keep them open, and our supplies cannot last more than ten days.

This condition of things has determined me to withdraw the stationary force from the roads so as to increase the force at Nashville and in the rear, if possible, without reducing my active force, which after all cannot be brought up to more than about 30,000 men. The force is clearly insufficient, and ought to be increased without an hour's delay. The consequences may otherwise be of the most serious character.

I have been of this opinion for some time. Grant's troops have not crossed the river that I have heard of, and it must be several days before they can complete the march to form a junction even if they were already across. New troops, if they could move rapidly enough, are not suitable for the service required. We want cavalry very much.[28]

Even more distressing to Halleck and the war managers who were calling for General Buell's beheading was the tone of despair evident in another message he sent the next day:

The difficulties of the last two months in keeping open our communications make it plain that no permanent [Union] *advance into East Tennessee can be attempted without a much larger force than is at present under my command. While the enemy maintains his present attitude and strength every step in advance increases the demand for the main body to protect our lines. For the present no more can be attempted than to keep the enemy back by giving up some of our railroad lines.*

I hope to have a force about Nashville which will make the city secure against cavalry demonstration, reopen the road to Louisville, and still leave a concentrated force of about 30,000 men, but this force is altogether insufficient to render the State secure or exert much influence and control over the population.

The necessity for removing troops from points heretofore occupied is to be much regretted. The whole country swarms with irregular cavalry or guerrillas, who keep down anything like exhibition of loyalty. I attach so much importance to the only foothold we have in Alabama that I have determined to hold on to Huntsville and the road from there to Stevenson even at the great risk to the small force I can possibly spare, trusting to early reenforcements to make it more secure.[29]

The general-in-chief replied:

Two divisions of Grant's army were directed to report to you some time ago, and two more placed at Tuscumbia and Decatur as a reserve. He has also sent troops to reoccupy Clarksville and the Cumberland. I doubt if he can spare more, but will try. For want of cavalry, take all the horses you can find in the country and mount infantry.[30]

In short, Old Brains was saying, *Major General Buell, use your common sense.*

But there were limits to what a general-in-chief, no matter how highly motivated and willing he might be, could do. Halleck did not presume to try to solve everyone's problems, and when this was the case he was frank to admit it. Usually, however, he delegated powers to persons who were in positions to take action to correct whatever the dichotomy might have been between perceived need and actual fulfillment.

Some examples were generated while Braxton Bragg was inspiring Buell's depressing essays and Kirby Smith was driving toward the supplies-rich bluegrass in central Kentucky. Most of them involved Herman Haupt and rail movements of troops, but always in the background was the question of whether McClellan would continue to "push" his Army of the Potomac's elements near enough and early enough for them to enable John Pope to keep General Lee's Army of Northern Virginia from sweeping his own forces completely off the chess board.

Jeb Stuart's plundering of Pope's rear headquarters near Catlett's Station on August 22 had already disrupted telegraphic communications between the general commanding the Army of Virginia and almost everyone else. Late on the next afternoon, Haupt, from his headquarters in Alexandria's railroad yards, wired Halleck:

> As I receive no answer to my telegrams from General Pope, I wish to ask if all the troops are to be sent to Warrenton Junction. . . . I suppose it is your wish that commands should go as much as possible together. Have you directed that [Major General Samuel D.] Sturgis' command should take precedence over all others? . . . He says you gave peremptory orders that he should be sent after Kearny and before Hooker. Parts of Hooker's division have gone. Shall I send Sturgis ahead of the balance of Hooker's [division] and ahead of Kearny's batteries? . . .[31]

In response, Old Brains confessed his own limitations, but he did not leave Colonel Haupt without remedies: "It is impossible for me to direct the details of running the cars," he said. "General Pope must give the general directions, and General Heintzelman, or the officer highest in rank present of his corps. . . ."[32]

Sturgis, an officer General Halleck had inherited along with Ulysses Grant and John Pope from Pathfinder Frémont in Missouri, but who had long since been transferred eastward, had insisted on priority and had threatened to place Haupt under arrest if he did not provide trains immediately. Later, Haupt—a strict teetotaler—provided this account of his encounter with a general who, obviously, was not:

> *I replied that I was acting under the orders of General Halleck; that so far as my personal comfort was concerned, the arrest would be quite a relief. . . but that he must understand that he was assuming a very grave responsibility; the trains were filled with wounded; the surgeons with ambulances were waiting for them at the depot; the engines would soon be out of wood and water, and serious delays would be caused in the forwarding of troops to General Pope.*
>
> *The General exclaimed in an excited tone: "I don't care for John Pope a pinch of owl dung!"*
>
> *He then called for one of his staff and whispered something that I did not hear, but learned subsequently that he had sent an order to the engineers to cut loose from their trains, run to Alexandria for wood and water and then return. As there was but a single track and no one capable of the Munchausen feat of picking up the engines and carrying them around the trains, the order could not be executed.*
>
> *Soon after, an orderly rode up and delivered to me a dispatch from General Halleck in these words: "No military officer has any authority to interfere with your control over railroads. Show this to General Sturgis, and if he attempts to interfere, I will arrest him."*
>
> *I tried to make the General comprehend this, but he seemed to think the dispatch was from General Pope, and several times repeated his former declaration: "I don't care for John Pope a pinch," etc.*
>
> *At last [J. H.] Devereux took the paper from my hands and gave it to the Chief of Staff with the request that he try to make his chief acquainted with the contents.*
>
> *He was successful at length in conveying the information that the telegram was not from General Pope but from General Halleck. "Who did you say, General Halleck? Yes, I respect his authority. What does he say?"*
>
> *"He says if you interfere with the railroads he will put you in arrest."*
>
> *"He does, does he? Well, take your d——d railroad!"*[33]

Author Haupt added that the incident "deranged the trains for some time and kept at least 10,000 men out of the battle." Still, drunk or sober, Sturgis, who could easily have marched his men eighteen or so miles to join Pope, caused additional delays when his units' turns for rail movement did come.[34]

General Sturgis, at least, was *with* his troops. Most of the Young Napoleon's other division and corps commanders, newly arrived in the relaxation-encouraging Washington vicinity from having been penned-up for weeks by General Lee at Harrison's Landing, could not be located. Replying to one of Colonel Haupt's pleas for assistance in finding them, Assistant Secretary of War Watson offered some belated but sound advice: "Be as patient as possible with the generals. Some of them will trouble you more than the enemy."[35]

4

IN DUE COURSE, SAMUEL STURGIS would be gloriously flogged by Confederate "Wizard of the Saddle" Nathan Bedford Forrest. But Sturgis' imperfections may also have included his failure to pass along a report sent to him from Manassas Junction on August 23 by Colonel L. B. Pierce:

> From all I can learn there will be an effort made to-night to burn the commissary stores at this place, as also to capture large trains sent back to this place by General Pope. Colonel Halberd, of General Banks' staff, has just come in, and he informs me that the enemy at Catlett's are not guerrillas, but are from the main body of the enemy.
>
> He also states that they are crossing the Rapidan [sic] somewhere above in considerable force, both infantry and cavalry, and design coming down through Thoroughfare Gap and Warrenton, for the purpose of either flanking Pope or making a raid of some kind.
>
> All the military roads are open to these points, and nothing to prevent such a disaster.
>
> I think it absolutely necessary that we have a heavy force of infantry here at this point immediately. In view of what may be coming, General Banks has ordered his trains as far back as Centreville.
>
> Please answer immediately, with directions.[36]

Seldom in military history had a message such as the one Colonel

Pierce sent Sturgis been so timely or prescient, yet so often overlooked. Worth noting in this instance, in particular, is the apparent fact that this warning reached neither General Pope, who might have acted upon this threat to his army's vast supply stockpiles at Manassas Junction, nor General-in-Chief Halleck.

Concurrently, Old Brains was trying by telegraph and rhetorical questioning to convey to Pope his misgiving that the Army of Virginia's commander might be scattering his forces too much. Dangerous complacency had been reflected in Pope's shrugging-off the consequences of Jeb Stuart's raid: "I have just learned from one of my staff direct from Catlett's," the Army of Virginia's commander had assured the general-in-chief, "that the damage done by the enemy is trifling, nothing but some officer's [sic] baggage destroyed."[37]

Referring to two of McClellan's corps lately arrived at Aquia Landing, Halleck asked: "Cannot they move up along the Rappahannock so as to cover the fords in your rear, and also serve as a reserve to your main body?"[38] Then he continued: "Of course in all this, these matters of detail, you, from your local knowledge, are the best judge, and what I say is only in the way of suggestion."[39]

Old Brains had said much the same thing on earlier occasions and he would again. This was bedrock common sense as well as another reflection of his having trained himself to think as a lawyer should, basing his counsel on principle and not deviating from it. And, absent awareness of Colonel Pierce's warning to Sturgis of the Confederate threat to Pope's supply depot at Manassas Junction, General Halleck reiterated common sense counsel his *de facto* client, apparently, had not yet heeded: "By no means expose your railroad connection with Alexandria."[40]

Then, as if Old Brains did not already have enough to annoy him, at daybreak on Sunday, August 24, General McClellan reached Aquia Landing. By noon, however, he was somewhat peeved, or so the tone of a message he sent General Halleck suggested:

> *I telegraphed you at 6 a.m. this day that I had arrived here and respectfully reported for orders. . . . I took it for granted that I was to come here to receive orders and am ready to move in any direction, having my staff, &c., still on the steamers. . . . I regret to learn that General Pope last night abandoned Rappahannock Station without giving the slightest information to Morell and Sykes, who were within 6 miles of him. They discovered the fact accidentally by*

means of a patrol they sent out. No certain directions can be given to those divisions until the position and intentions of Pope are ascertained, which can only be done through you.[41]

At 12:30 P.M. General Halleck replied: "Porter and Reno should hold the line of the Rappahannock below Pope, subject for the present to his orders. I hope by to-morrow to be able to give some more definite directions. You know my main object, and will act accordingly."[42]

A little over an hour later, again the general-in-chief telegraphed McClellan:

I think Sumner's corps had better land at Aquia. We will then endeavor to get the forces together. . . . A portion of the enemy's forces crossed [the Rappahannock] *at Sulphur Springs and were attacked by Pope late yesterday afternoon. He expected to renew the fight this morning, but the enemy is retreating. You can either remain at Aquia or come to Alexandria, as you may deem best, so as to direct the landing of your troops.*[43]

But the Young Napoleon had not journeyed all that distance to carry out the duties of a quartermaster. Since Halleck seemed oblivious to his main concern, at 2:00 P.M. McClellan spelled it out for him. First, however, he asked "exactly where Pope is and what he is doing." Then he wrote:

Until I know what my command and position are to be, and whether you still intend to place me in the command indicated in your first letter to me and orally through General Burnside at the Chickahominy, I cannot decide where I can be of the most use. If your determination is unchanged I ought to go to Alexandria at once. Please define my position and duties.[44]

Not until near midnight did the general-in-chief answer, and his fatigue was showing. "You ask me for information I cannot give," Old Brains said. "I do not know either where General Pope is or where the enemy in force is. These are matters which I have all day been most anxious to learn."[45]

Evidently, McClellan could not leave it at that, for a few minutes later Halleck's patience ran out. "There is nothing more to communicate tonight," he telegraphed Little Mac. "I do not expect to hear from General Pope before to-morrow. Will telegraph you at Aquia. Good night."[46]

But the hectoring went on past midnight. "Are you in communication with Warrenton Junction," the Young Napoleon wanted to know, "and are Pope's forces in advance of Warrenton Junction?"[47]

Half an hour into the next day, as though he were trying to put his duty ahead of every other consideration despite McClellan's gratuitous provocation, General Halleck corrected him and then did his best to satisfy the man:

> *General Pope did not retreat from Rappahannock Station, but advanced and attacked the enemy near Sulphur Springs and is [now] in pursuit. What we intend is to hold the line of the Rappahannock until all our forces can get together. Your operations are to be directed to this object. Kearny is at Warrenton Junction, but Pope is near Waterloo Bridge. There is no telegraph line to him.*[48]

Down near the Rappahannock, General Lee had spent that Sunday morning studying the dispatch book Jeb Stuart had brought back from Friday's raid at Pope's rear headquarters at Catlett's Station. By noon, having read the reports of McClellan's progress toward reinforcing Pope, he had decided that his only course of action was to do the very thing General Halleck had been admonishing the Army of Virginia's commander to prevent: cut the Orange & Alexandria Railroad, isolating the Union forces from their supplies at Manassas Junction.

But this would be no mere raid. To Stonewall Jackson's headquarters Lee rode; once there, he told Old Jack to take all of his divisions early the next morning, move first to the northwest as though his columns were headed toward Luray in the Shenandoah Valley, and then hook around to the east and later the southeast, passing through Thoroughfare Gap, and finally to strike the O&A wherever his route took him. Later, General Lee said, he would bring James Longstreet's divisions over the same route to join Jackson somewhere near the old Manassas battleground. Meanwhile, Longstreet's mission was to hold Pope's forces where they were.

Put differently: General Lee was not only splitting his army in the face of an enemy outnumbering him substantially, but daring to attempt the Munchausen feat of landing his whole force deep in John Pope's rear and squarely across his supply lifeline. And, curiously, by so doing, Lee was paying tribute of a sort to John Pope's generalship. Since Cedar Mountain, especially since Old Brains had coached Pope north of the Rappahannock, the Union's field general had blocked every attempt Lee had made to get around him.[49]

As early as 8:00 on Monday morning, August 25, 1862, an aide to General Banks had seen wagon trains with infantry following. Forty-five minutes later, a Union acting signal lieutenant who signed his warnings merely "Taylor," observing from a place called Watery Mount, reported long lines of enemy infantry moving westward.[50]

Neither of those alerts reached Old Brains. By ironic coincidence, a Lieutenant Colonel H. L. Taylor, provost marshal at Alexandria, telegraphed him: "There is a great deal of drunkenness and disorder here, hundreds of soldiers loitering around. Brigade and regimental commanders seem to take no notice of it. The force at my disposal is insufficient."[51]

Tempted though Halleck may have been to order McClellan to Alexandria to help Colonel Taylor cope with Army of the Potomac soldiers' drunkenness and disorder and officers' indifference, the general-in-chief spent much of the day responding to the gadfly's telegrams from Aquia Landing by reiterating orders, information, and opinions he had sent earlier. Worse, in another ironic coincidence, Major General Pope found the time on August 25 to reveal in a long letter to Old Brains that he, like George McClellan, was peeved:

You wished forty-eight hours to assemble the forces from the Peninsula behind the Rappahannock, and four days have passed without the enemy yet being permitted to cross. I don't think he is yet ready to do so. . . . I had clearly understood that you wished to unite our whole forces before a forward movement was begun, and that I must take care to keep united with Burnside on my left, so that no movement to separate us could be made. This withdrew me lower down the Rappahannock than I wished to come.

I am not acquainted with your views, as you seem to suppose, and would be glad to know them as far as my own position and operations are concerned.

I understood you clearly that at all hazards I was to prevent the enemy from passing the Rappahannock. This I have done and shall do. I don't like to be on the defensive if I can help it, but must be so as long as I am tied to Burnside's forces, not yet wholly arrived at Fredericksburg.

Please let me know, if it can be done, what is to be my own command, and if I am to act independently against the enemy.

I certainly understood that as soon as the whole of our forces were concentrated you designed to take command in person, and that when everything was ready we were to move forward in concert.

I judge from the tone of your dispatch that you are dissatisfied with something. Unless I know what it is, of course I cannot correct it.

The troops arriving here come in fragments. Am I to assign them to brigades and corps? I would suppose not, as several of the new regiments coming have been assigned to army corps directly from your office. In case I commence offensive operations, I must know what forces I am to take and what you wish left and what connection must be kept up with Burnside.

It has been my purpose to conform my operations to your plans, yet I was not informed when McClellan evacuated Harrison's Landing, so that I might know what to expect in that direction, and when I say these things in no complaining spirit I think you know well that I am anxious to do everything to advance your plans of campaign.

I understood that this army was to maintain the line of the Rappahannock until all the forces from the Peninsula had united behind that river. I have done so. I understood distinctly that I was not to hazard anything except for this purpose, as delay was what was wanted.

The enemy this morning has pushed a considerable infantry force up opposite Waterloo Bridge and is planting batteries, and long lines of his infantry are moving up from Jeffersonville toward Sulphur Springs. His whole force, as far as can be ascertained, is massed in front of me, from railroad crossing of Rappahannock around to Waterloo Bridge, their main body being opposite Sulphur Springs.[52]

Clearly, emotions and ambitions could penetrate the fog of war while common sense counsel, repeated admonition, and forbearance were too easily set aside. Yet the proddings from McClellan and Pope for clarification of their missions and also of the roles General Halleck meant for them to have were perfectly proper in the circumstances. Moreover, both army commanders had assured him of their willingness to do as he directed.

But the general-in-chief was not yet ready, apparently, to make changes in existing command arrangements. Pope was in contact with the Confederates, and for as long as that was true his mission was simply to fight. McClellan was of no use except as an expediter of deliveries of reinforcements to Pope—for the time being, at least. True, at some point giving the Young Napoleon command of both armies might make sense. And it was possible that Halleck could take the field himself as generalissimo if that proved necessary in order to settle squabbling. But an actionable case for neither alternative to the *status quo* had yet been made by events.

Never even guessing that General Lee had recognized John Pope's skill by splitting his outnumbered army and gambling the Confederacy's future on the ability of Old Jack's foot cavalry to march fifty miles or more and cut the O&A, General Halleck added this tribute on August 26:

> *Not the slightest dissatisfaction has been felt in regard to your operations on the Rappahannock. The main object has been accomplished in getting up troops from the Peninsula, although they have been delayed by storms. Moreover the telegraph has been interrupted, leaving us for a time ignorant of the progress of the evacuation.*
>
> *Just think of the immense amount of telegraphing I have to do, and then say whether I can be expected to give you any details as to movements of others, even when I know them. . . . If possible to attack the enemy in flank do so, but the main object now is to ascertain his position. Make cavalry excursions for that purpose, especially toward Front Royal. If possible to get in his rear, pursue with vigor.*[53]

5

"ASCERTAIN, IF POSSIBLE," General Halleck had telegraphed Pope on Monday, August 25, "if the enemy is moving into the Shenandoah Valley."[54]

Back in May and early June, Old Brains' attention had been riveted to the requirements of capturing Corinth and then capitalizing on that achievement. During most of that time, Stonewall Jackson had been using his superior knowledge of the Valley of Virginia's terrain first to disrupt acting General-in-Chief Lincoln's plans for reinforcing McClellan east of Richmond with Irvin McDowell's corps, and later not only to escape the trap Lincoln had set but to wreck the Yankee forces pursuing him.

One major consequence of Jackson's having whipped him was the Union President's having summoned Old Brains to Washington. Careful student that Halleck was of facts bearing on any case he was entering, soon after his arrival surely he had made enough of an analysis of the Shenandoah Valley Campaign to view with alarm the possibility that Jackson might well use that obviously pro-Confederate real estate *again* to whip him.

General Pope's reply was to the effect that the rebel column, whose progress watchers had been reporting since early on that Monday, appeared to have turned to the northeast, toward Salem and Rectortown, around sundown. Pope continued:

> *I am induced to believe that this column is only covering the flank of the main body, which is moving toward Front Royal and Thornton's Gap, though of this I am not certain.*
>
> *I will push a strong reconnaissance across the river at Waterloo Bridge and Sulphur Springs early in the morning to ascertain whether* [the] *main body of the enemy has really left, and, if so, to push forward in their rear. There is certainly no force opposite Rappahannock Station.*

Then the army commander turned to another subject:

> *McDowell's is the only corps that is at all reliable that I have. Sigel, as you know, is perfectly unreliable, and I suggest that some officer of superior rank be sent to command his army corps. His conduct to-day has occasioned me great dissatisfaction. Banks' corps is very weak, not amounting to more than 5,000 men, and is much demoralized. Kearny's division is the only one* [of McClellan's] *that has yet reached me from Alexandria.*
>
> *I shall at all events push McDowell's corps and Kearny's division upon the enemy's rear if I find my suspicions confirmed in the morning. I shall also put Reno across the river at Rappahannock Station and direct him to move forward cautiously upon Culpeper. Banks' corps must be left somewhere in the rear to be set up again. Sigel's corps, although composed of some of the best fighting material we have, will never do much service under that officer.*[55]

Two conclusions, both unsettling, could be drawn from Pope's message. Apparently, he had lost the Confederates; until he regained contact, he could not make dispositions of his troops with certainty. Worse, even if he found the rebels, only a fraction of the forces in his Army of Virginia might prove effective in fighting them.

Whether General Lee was headed for the Shenandoah Valley or not, something had gone terribly wrong at nearby Manassas—or so a series of messages from Herman Haupt to the general-in-chief on Tuesday, August 26, indicated. First, in the evening:

The following telegram has just been received from Manassas:

No. 6 train, engine Secretary, was fired into at Bristoe by a party of cavalry—some say 500 strong. They had piled ties on the track, but engine threw them off. Secretary is completely riddled by bullets. Conductor says he thinks the enemy are coming this way.
McCRICKETT, Dispatcher.

The engine Secretary was being followed by four other trains, which are in great danger, as there is no communication. The wire is cut between Manassas and Warrenton. We have transportation for 1,200 men. This number might be sent to Manassas to protect the road while we repair it. I suppose the bridge at Bristoe will be destroyed.[56]

Next, at around 9 P.M:

In addition to the transportation for 1,200 men some other trains are coming and are this side of Mansassas. We may have in a few hours transportation for 3,000 or 4,000 men. They can be advanced as far as possible and then march forward.

I am just informed that the four trains following the Secretary are captured and that the rebels are approaching Manassas with artillery. These may be exaggerations, but the operator and agent are leaving, and prompt action is required. It is unfortunate that a portion of our forces did not march. I await instructions.[57]

Then:

Operator at Manassas just says: "I am off now, sure." I directed the agent to run the two engines at Manassas forward, wait until the last moment, and then escape on the engine, if a real necessity existed. Operator had just commenced message to headquarters of General Pope when wire was cut.

It is clear now that the railroad can be relied upon only for supplies. No more troops can be forwarded. By marching they will protect communication; in cars they are helpless. Our capacity by this raid will be much reduced.[58]

Actually, for once Colonel Haupt was wrong. It was not a raid that was in progress, but the arrival of Stonewall Jackson's troops at Bristoe Station.

After pausing for the night at Salem, Jackson's men had moved not westward into the Shenandoah Valley but southeastward, up through Thoroughfare Gap and then down to the tracks of the Orange & Alexandria, John Pope's lifeline. After driving off the few federal defenders of Bristoe Station, the rebels opened a switch that caused a northbound train's engine to tumble off an embankment, taking into the wreck half the cars it had been pulling. To the dismay of the Confederates, the cars were empty. But from citizens of Bristoe Jackson, they learned that only seven miles up the O&A was the vast Manassas Junction supply stockpile. To seize it Old Jack sent a brigade and Stuart's cavalry. Time was of the essence, for trains above and below the wreck were bound to be reporting the calamity to Pope in Warrenton and to Haupt in Alexandria.[59]

General Halleck responded to Haupt's messages by giving him authority to start corrective efforts. "General Smith, General Slocum, General Sturgis, or any other general officers you can find," he telegraphed Haupt, "will immediately send all the men you can transport to Bristoe Bridge or Manassas Junction. Show this order."[60]

At first, Colonel Haupt's tour of the Army of the Potomac's camps in the Alexandria area that night proved futile. "The attractions of Washington," he wrote later, "kept most of the General Officers in that city." Around midnight, however, he found Brigadier General Winfield Scott Hancock, who provided about three thousand men. Haupt reported Hancock's response to General Halleck, adding that he hoped that the troops and the construction crew he was sending could save the O&A's bridge over Bull Run.[61]

Brigadier General George W. Taylor was in command of the force Hancock sent toward Manassas. Instead of placing his men in positions to protect the bridge and the work crew, however, Taylor led his troops over the span and attacked part of Jackson's force—the rest were looting the square mile of warehouses, the brand-new freight cars loaded with supplies on sidings, and the sutlers' wagons filled with luxuries most of the Confederates had never enjoyed: canned oysters, Rhine wine, linen handkerchiefs, lobster salad, fine whiskey, "segars." Old Jack told his quartermasters to carry off all the ammunition, food, and other necessities that the wagons could haul. When the men had plundered the Yankee treasure houses to the limits of what haversacks could hold, Jackson ordered everything that had to be left behind put to the torch.[62]

Curiously, on that Wednesday morning no senior Union officer seemed aware of the orgy taking place at Manassas Junction except General Taylor, whose gallantry in trying to break it up would cost him his life. In a message from Warrenton Junction sent *via* Ambrose Burnside's head-quarters at Falmouth, John Pope informed the general-in-chief that "The enemy has massed his whole force at White Plains [northwest of Manassas Junction]" but that "a strong column penetrated by way of Manassas [Gap] Railroad last night. . . . My position at Warrenton is no longer tenable. I am now moving my whole force to occupy the line from Gainesville to railroad crossing of Cedar Creek on [the O&A]. . . ."[63]

Then Pope engaged in some speculation mixed with recollection of things past:

> *Whether the enemy means to attack us or not I consider doubtful [sic]; he never crossed the Rappahannock River, but masked every ford with heavy batteries, under cover of which he kept moving to my right close along the river. I never had the opportunity to attack him without forcing the passage of the river in face of very superior forces.*
>
> *I think it possible he may attempt to keep us in check and throw considerable force across the Potomac in the direction of Leesburg. Under all the circumstances I have thought it best to interpose in front of Manassas Junction, where your orders will reach me.*

So General Pope expected, ignorant—even as he wrote—of who was in possession of Manassas Junction and all its wonders, firmly interposed between him and Washington. Moreover, Pope apparently did not know that the Confederates at White Plains were Major General James Longstreet's divisions.

"I am pushing a strong column to Manassas Junction to open the road," Pope told General Halleck, adding some advice: "You had best send a considerable force to Manassas Junction at once, and forage and provisions, also construction corps, that I may repair the bridge and get the railroad trains in the rear."[64]

Doing that had occurred to Herman Haupt, of course, the night before—hence General Taylor's vain effort. But on that Wednesday morning Haupt, too, was unaware of who owned Manassas Junction or what was happening there. Yet, as had Pope, he had telegraphed Halleck: "I venture the suggestion: As soon as the cars return which carried the troops to Union Mills, I propose to load the whole with subsistence, put on top and inside 1,500 or 2,000 more men, and endeavor by all means to work the trains through. . . ."[65]

Quickly came Old Brains' reply: "If you can see General McClellan, consult him. If not, go ahead as you propose."[66]

Help us to choose the harder right instead of the easier wrong, later generations of cadets would pray. But even in Herman Haupt's years, West Point must have been instilling that thought. Trying to follow Halleck's instruction to the letter, Haupt took a rowboat out to a steamer in the Potomac River in order to "consult General McClellan."

The Young Napoleon listened to Haupt's plan, noted that it "would be attended with risk," then returned with the colonel to the rail yard at Alexandria. News of Taylor's defeat awaited them; it doomed Haupt's hopes. He wrote afterward: "My representations and arguments availed nothing; the General would not give his consent, or assume any responsibility, and would give no orders, instructions, or suggestions of any kind!"[67]

Soon General Halleck would learn that George McClellan had plenty of suggestions, most of which reflected his assumption that John Pope had *already* been defeated and that Washington had to be defended. Earlier that day, Old Brains had responded to Pope's estimates of his situation with these words—many of which were hardly new:

> *The enemy is concentrating, it seems, between you and Alexandria, near Manassas and Bull Run. You must look out for this and immediately break it up, for your supplies must come from Washington, and you must fall back in this direction if compelled to retreat. Do not let him separate you from Alexandria. We will send troops to meet you, but we are very short of transportation. Keep me advised, if possible.*[68]

In the circumstances, including the fog of war and the necessity of communicating *via* Falmouth, although Halleck and Pope were separated by only fifty miles or less and Jackson was even nearer, Old Brains' seemingly stale counsel was about all he could offer. Yet it was perhaps fortuitous that he had made that effort, for after Herman Haupt's rowboat brought McClellan to Alexandria and Little Mac's hectoring messages began pouring in, the general-in-chief must surely have been hard pressed to remember which world-ending crisis he ought to worry about, and prescribe palliatives for, next.

6

"HALLECK IS IN A DISAGREEABLE SITUATION," George McClellan wrote his wife on the morning of Wednesday, August 27, 1862. "[He] can get no information from the front either as to our own troops or the enemy. I shall do all I can to help him loyally & will trouble him as little as possible, but render all the assistance in my power without regard to myself or my own position."[69] And by 11:20 A.M., from Alexandria, he had sent the first of at least seven messages to the general-in-chief. In it was this indication of how his mind was really working:

> *If a decisive battle is fought at Warrenton a disaster would leave any troops on the Lower Rappahannock in a dangerous position. They would do better service in front of Washington.*[70]

"I have no means of knowing the enemy's force between Pope and ourselves," McClellan admitted in another telegram sent at 1:15 p.m. Even so, he seemed to take it for granted that Pope either had been whipped or that he was about to be:

> *Should not Burnside take steps at once to evacuate Falmouth and Aquia, at the same time covering the retreat of any of Pope's troops who may fall back in that direction? I do not see that we have force enough in hand to form a connection with Pope, whose exact position we do not know. Are we safe in the direction of the valley?*[71]

Why was it, Old Brains may well have wondered, that Major General McClellan could not keep his attention focused on his mission: to reinforce Pope? Actually, General Halleck had already been in communication with Burnside. But the Young Napoleon's flood of messages continued.

"I have just learned through General Woodbury," he telegraphed at noon, "that it was stated in your office last night that it was very strange that, with 20,000 men here, I did not prevent the raid upon Manassas. . . . I ask as a matter of justice that you will prevent your staff from making statements which do me such great injustice at a time when the most cordial co-operation is required."[72]

Halleck took the time to reply:

> *No remark was made by me, or in my hearing, reflecting on you, in relation to Manassas. I did remark to General Woodbury, on receiving news of the capture of the train, that there must have been great neglect in permitting 500 of the enemy to make the raid, when we had some 20,000 men in that vicinity (not vicinity of Alexandria), and added that many of the forces sent to Pope could not have been very far off. It would have been perfect nonsense to have*

referred to you, when you had just arrived and knew nothing of the disposition of the troops. Indeed, I did not blame any particular person, but merely said there must have been neglect somewhere. I think you must have misunderstood General Woodbury, for he could not possibly have drawn such an inference from anything I have said.[73]

At 2:40 on that busy Wednesday afternoon came more perfect nonsense from McClellan: "Have you received my messages of 1:15 and 1:35 P.M.? I am waiting here at your request."[74] Halleck's patience was surely strained, but it had not yet snapped. He responded:

As you must be aware, more than three-quarters of my time is taken up with the raising of new troops and matters in the West. I have no time for details. You will therefore, as ranking general in the field, direct as you deem best; but at present orders for Pope's army should go through me.[75]

Halleck's last sentence was uncharacteristically ambiguous—a reflection, perhaps, of how fatigued he was from days and nights of trying to prevent defeat in two widely separated theaters. *Of course* McClellan ought to have been empowered to act regarding details of how his forces were to be rushed to reinforce Pope. But it would have been better if Old Brains had made it clear that all orders *involving* Pope's army were to be cleared through him—specifically, that the Young Napoleon did *not* have discretion as to *if* or *when* his corps were to be hurried to General Pope.

Out in the West there were at least three places where hell seemed to be breaking loose. Kirby Smith had advanced far enough northward into Kentucky to discover that unless he pressed on from the barrens into the abundance of the bluegrass country *quickly,* his men and animals would face starvation. By August 27 his forces had reached a piece of high ground called simply Big Hill. From its summit, his men could see their goal. And all that stood in their way was a small Yankee unit, made up mostly of recruits, near the town of Richmond.

At Chattanooga, Braxton Bragg was finally leading his wing of the Confederates' western army out of its camps, his object to get northward in Tennessee or southern Kentucky far enough to cut the Louisville & Nashville Railroad before Don Carlos Buell could advance along it and protect it. Bragg's invasion shattered the illusion that Buell might eventually capture Chattanooga. However, Kirby Smith's need to move even more to the north to feed his troops and mules dashed the last wispy chances of his joining with Bragg to destroy Buell.

Such a combination of Confederate resources against Buell had been the aim of the "cooperation" agreement Bragg and Kirby Smith had reached weeks earlier. Any anxiety Jefferson Davis might feel now that his two armies were going their own ways, and for their own reasons, would be the price he was obliged to pay for having set aside two thousand years of military experience leading to the wise concept called chain of command and allowing the arrangement his distant subordinates had conceived in naiveté, if not in hell, to stand.[76]

But on August 27, the general-in-chief of the Union armies also had ample cause for anxiety. Having, like Davis, neglected to place someone in command of all his forces in the West, Halleck was obliged to wring all the fresh troops he could from the governors of Illinois, Indiana, and Ohio to reinforce the untried Horatio Wright in defending central Kentucky against Kirby Smith's drive; to prod Don Carlos Buell toward the roads Bragg was most likely to take; and to stimulate Ulysses Grant to expedite the shift of his divisions from northern Mississippi up to cover Nashville and fill the vacuum in Buell's wake—if any.

Of all these complex challenges to General Halleck, Little Mac knew nothing. Never had George McClellan paid much attention to the plights of others. And now, inadvertently, Old Brains had revealed his own vulnerability to the "ranking general in the field."

It would stand high among the worst mistakes Henry Wager Halleck ever made.

7

FOR DECADES AFTER HENRY HALLECK'S DEATH, historians writing about Second Manassas and its aftermath indicted him and, without trial of any sort, condemned him on at least two counts: The Union armies' general-in-chief broke under pressure and allowed himself to be betrayed by the wily McClellan, and he was never of much use afterward.

The facts may well have been otherwise. Taking the second count first, Old Brains' value to Abraham Lincoln—his usefulness—increased considerably during this period. As to the first, it is at least arguable that Halleck's "breakdown" did not, in fact, take place.

Something about Halleck that his detractors either missed or refused to concede was that he almost always knew exactly what he was doing and meant precisely what he said. Occasionally he mis-spoke himself, as folks used to put it, but when that happened he was usually both prompt and forthright in admitting his lapses and in correcting them. Accordingly, it was entirely possible that the admiration and respect for George Brinton McClellan he had expressed several times to several persons was genuine.

Moreover, the record is silent on whether Henry Wager Halleck ever sought revenge for any injustice any person ever inflicted upon him. Indeed he often avoided taking actions that might be considered unjust—for example, guillotining Don Carlos Buell as soon as the Union high command demanded his relief from command.

True, he was stern often to the point of rudeness. He had no time for fools and cared not how they took his abrupt rejections. Yet, even when he might have claimed he was much too busy to do so, Old Brains had written what he could to set matters as straight as possible with those who protested what they considered harsh treatment: Pope, John McClernand, Buell, George McClellan.

It was possible, also, that his regret at having been too quick to believe Ulysses Grant had resumed the role of four-finger whiskey drinker had caused him to err in the other direction—that is, to put too much weight on the good qualities of men with whom he dealt. Thus, in Henry Halleck's view, a general's potential contributions to the quelling of the rebellion tended to offset the facts of failures. He was not naive, nor was he an easy man to push around. But Old Brains may have been too forgiving, or insufficiently suspicious.

Duty and honor were what Henry Wager Halleck lived by. He did not seem to realize that other men did not.

Yet he was certainly not the only man George McClellan and Edwin Stanton had deceived. Only long after the war would anyone learn of the vast differences between the Young Napoleon's bland assurances in his official messages, and the nigh-treasonous sentiments he expressed in his letters to his wife. And Stanton's viciousness, duplicity, and ruthlessness did not emerge until after Abraham Lincoln was assassinated.

At the time, then, in 1862's high summer, it was not surprising that General Halleck seemed to be assuming that those with whom he was working were, fundamentally, as dedicated to the good of the service as he was. Indeed, if not on the basis of trust, how could a general-in-chief operate?

General Halleck could rely on the field-tested members of his staff he had brought east: George Cullum, J. C. Kelton, Schuyler Hamilton. John Pope had reverted to the plodding but diligent soldier he had been in the

West, and now that he had stood up to General Lee for two weeks, perhaps people would forget his earlier bombast. Don Carlos Buell wrote too much, or thought too little before he wrote, but he had saved Grant's career (and possibly his army) by reaching Pittsburg Landing just in time; moreover, it was not yet clear whether Horatio Wright would be even as effective as Buell as a regional commander. Herman Haupt, however, was proving to be every bit as tough-minded as the general-in-chief.

And then there was McClellan. General Halleck knew him mostly through what he read in messages. Vanity, ambition, touchiness were characteristics McClellan had revealed. Beyond words, it was also true that he had failed the tests of combat. But he had built the powerful Army of the Potomac, whose men adored him, and now how quickly their commander committed them to battle appeared to be the key to the future of the United States of America.

7 ★ *Disaster and Shame Lurk in the Rear; Treachery and Intrigue Make Defeat Hang Trembling in the Balance*

*B*Y LATE AFTERNOON ON WEDNESDAY, August 27, 1862, Major General Jackson's men had taken the Army of Virginia's huge supply depot at Manassas Junction completely out of the war. Prudently, Old Jack realized he had better remove his troops from the scene before the Yankees fell upon him from all points of the compass. He needed to do something not taught in any military academy in the world: to make his twenty-three thousand troops disappear. But, thanks to his memory of the old Manassas battle-grounds' topography, Stonewall accomplished that feat.

A mile or so east of Gainesville was the roadbed for a rail line extending from the Manassas Gap Railroad's track to the northeast. Roughly two miles along the unfinished spur and parallel to the Warrenton Turnpike (but several hundred yards northwest of it), an embankment provided Old Jack's divisions with a natural fortress concealed from view by trees. There he could await the arrival of General Lee and Longstreet's divisions, which were then following Jackson's roundabout route but still northwest of Thoroughfare Gap.

But General Jackson did not go directly to the roadbed-fortress. Instead, in the darkness that evening, he had his divisions march by several routes toward Centreville to create the impression he was concentrating there. That done, he turned his units back toward Groveton. By sunrise,

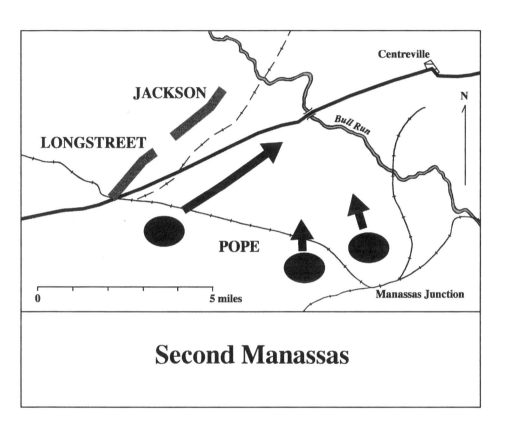

Second Manassas

almost all of his force was behind the embankment, as though he and his men had vanished from the face of the earth.[1]

General Halleck was entirely dependent on Herman Haupt for news of what was happening in Pope's area of operations, but Haupt's supply of information was limited to what telegraphers down the Orange & Alexandria's tracks were able to transmit. Understandably, much of that traffic was devoted to the progress that work crews from Alexandria were making. An example was this message sent from Fairfax Court House by an agent named Brayton:

> *I am convinced that we can do nothing at wreck without force to protect us. Rebels have a battery planted on hill and throw shells this side bridge. The railroad is lined with returning soldiers. One of our cavalry just in reports that rebel cavalry are in short distance of this place. I am not usually timid, but think there is no use of risking our two trains here to be captured. I await your order. I give you the best information I can get. The rebels are coming in now to this station.*[2]

Even A. Lincoln could learn only what Colonel Haupt had been told. At 4:20 on Wednesday afternoon Haupt replied to a query from the President:

> *Intelligence received within twenty minutes informs me that the enemy are advancing and have crossed Bull Run Bridge. If it is not destroyed it probably will be. The forces sent by us last night held it until that time.*[3]

General Pope inspected the smoldering ruins of the Manassas Junction depot around sunset.[4] By nine that evening he was at Bristoe Station telegraphing orders to his corps and division commanders. To Major General Philip Kearny, Pope began by waxing poetic:

> *At the very earliest blush of dawn push forward with your command with all speed to this place. You cannot be more than 3 or 4 miles distant. Jackson, A. P. Hill, and Ewell are in front of us. Hooker has had a severe fight with them to-day. McDowell marches upon Manassas Junction from Gainesville to-morrow at daybreak; Reno upon the same place at the same hour. I want you here at day-dawn, if possible, and we shall bag the whole crowd.*
>
> *Be prompt and expeditious, and never mind wagon trains or*

roads till this affair is over. Lieutenant Brooks will deliver you this communication. He has one for General Reno and one for General McDowell. Please have these dispatches sent forward instantly by a trusty staff officer, who will be sure to deliver them without fail, and make him bring back a receipt to you before daylight. Lieutenant Brooks will remain with you and bring you to this camp. Use the cavalry I send you to escort your staff officer to McDowell and Reno.[5]

General Pope's message to Irvin McDowell instructed him to leave Gainesville, where he had been in position to block General Lee's advance, suggesting that Pope was unaware of where *either* Confederate force was. But none of this mattered to General Halleck in Washington, for he would remain ignorant of what Pope was seeking to do for at least another twenty-four hours.

Confusion—some of it generated during that Wednesday night by Jackson's troops marching toward Centreville and then doubling back to the embankment near Groveton—compounded Union mistakes which made Thursday, August 28, a colossal waste of time and energy for the Army of Virginia. Lest it be one for the Confederacy, as well, that afternoon Stonewall Jackson decided to reveal his presence.

General Lee's object, Jackson surely recalled, was to suppress "the miscreant" Pope and his army before McClellan's masses arrived. But Lee and the rest of the Army of Northern Virginia were still up around Thoroughfare Gap somewhere. If Pope retreated past Centreville he might be beyond Lee's reach by the time the Confederate army was reunited. Worse, from Jackson's point of view, by then McClellan might have made the Union army too strong to attack.

Accordingly, Old Jack led some of his brigades down to the Warrenton Turnpike and surprised a strong Yankee column marching eastward by striking its long left flank. This sharp stand-up fight, like Kernstown back in late March,[6] settled nothing. But it did attract the Yankees' attention, and this time it caused John Pope to recognize that Jackson had not (as he had thought earlier) retreated or moved up to join Lee.

Thomas Jonathan Jackson was making life as difficult as possible for John Pope, and there was nothing the Union armies' general-in-chief could have done about it even had telegraph communication been restored— nothing, that is, beyond spurring General McClellan to do as he had long since been ordered: reinforce Pope. This prodding, of course, Old Brains had been doing for a month, since late in July. And now, with Old Jack displaying brilliant generalship and personal gallantry less than forty miles away from the Union Capitol's unfinished dome, the Young Napoleon seemed bent on making life as difficult as he could *not* for Lee or Jackson, but for Old Brains.

2

"I DON'T WANT TO HAVE ANYTHING TO DO with the quarrels of Stanton and McClellan," Halleck had written in his farewell letter to Cump Sherman back in July. So far, however, as had Lincoln, the secretary of war had left it to the new general-in-chief to deal with the Young Napoleon. But the closer General Lee's forces came to Washington, the more hours Stanton and the President spent in the War Department's telegraph office. And the more messages to Halleck from McClellan Edwin Stanton saw, the nearer he came to the boiling point. The result, on Thursday, August 28, was precisely the kind of involvement Old Brains had feared. To him Stanton wrote:

> *I desire you to furnish me information on the following points:*
>
> *1st. At what date you first ordered the general commanding the Army of the Potomac to move from James River.*
>
> *2d. Whether that order was or was not obeyed according to its purport and with the promptness which, in your judgment, the national safety required, and at what date the movement commenced.*
>
> *3d. What order has been given recently for the movement of Franklin's corps, and whether it was obeyed as promptly as the national interest required.*
>
> *4th. You will furnish me copies of the orders referred to in the foregoing inquiries.*[7]

Apparently, lawyer Stanton was about to wrap the mantle of prosecutor about him, and he was asking lawyer Halleck to provide evidence amounting to a cause of action against Little Mac in *Stanton* v. *McClellan*. In the circumstances—with Confederate threats demanding attention in Tennessee and Kentucky as well as roughly forty miles west of the War Department—Stanton's priorities and timing suggested that those who had doubted his sanity might have had a point. But the first duty of a soldier is to obey, and Henry Halleck was a soldier.

Stanton's timing was curious for at least two reasons. He may have known that McClellan had gone to Halleck's quarters in Washington around midnight and concluded that the two generals may have reached some sort of agreement favoring the Young Napoleon, an outcome the secretary of war certainly would not relish. Also, Stanton had made a pawn of Major General William Franklin in this odd side-game even though it was still possible that his corps would reach Pope's army in time to help whip Lee.

At a minimum, Stanton—perhaps acting for Lincoln—seemed to be anticipating efforts by Radicals in Congress and in the Northern press to blame the administration for the concurrent perils. Able lawyers never ask questions without knowing the answers; and able lawyer that Stanton was, surely he had already read most of the messages he was requesting and considered them a clear paper trail leading to conviction of McClellan as a scapegoat and justifying his removal forthwith.

Be all that as it might, General Halleck went about his work on August 28, 1862, as though only the demands of duty deserved his attention. To Franklin at Alexandria he telegraphed:

> *On parting with General McClellan, about 2 o'clock this morning, it was understood that you were to move with your corps to-day toward Manassas Junction, to drive the enemy from the railroad. I have just learned that the general has not yet returned to Alexandria. If you have not received his orders act on this.*[8]

That morning, aboard the steamer *Ariel,* McClellan used the scrap of time travel afforded to write his wife:

> *I am just about starting back for Alexandria. I came up here (Washington) last night—reached Halleck's house about midnight & remained talking with him until 3. . . . I find Halleck well disposed, he has much to contend against. I shall keep as clear as possible of the Presdt & Cabinet—endeavor to do what must be done through Halleck alone—so I shall get on better. . . .*[9]

Early that afternoon, from Alexandria, General McClellan reported that "the moment Franklin can be started with a reasonable amount of artillery he shall go."[10] Not long afterward, Little Mac sent the general-in-chief a long message that began with "impressions" he had picked up from various sources and led inexorably to self-serving counsel suggesting roots in cowardice or despair or treason:

I suggest that you take into consideration the propriety of Pope falling back . . .between the Occoquan [sic] and Potomac, . . . our best troops here advancing . . . to cover the movement. I do not think it now worth while to attempt to preserve the [O&A] railway. The great object is to collect the whole army in Washington, ready to defend the works and act upon the flank of any force crossing the upper Potomac.[11]

Halleck's reply was restrained and to the point: "Not a moment must be lost in pushing as large a force as possible toward Manassas, so as to communicate with Pope before the enemy is re-enforced. . . ."[12] But it was a waste of words, for—like Don Carlos Buell—McClellan's fund of excuses for not obeying was rich and inexhaustible. Late on that Thursday he telegraphed Halleck:

Neither Franklin nor Sumner's corps is now in condition to move and fight a battle. It would be a sacrifice to send them out now. . . . I still think that a premature movement in small force will accomplish nothing but the destruction of the troops sent out. . . . I repeat that I will lose no time in preparing the troops now here for the field, and that whatever orders you may give after hearing what I have to say will be carried out.[13]

Around sundown Old Brains made another effort:

There must be no further delay in moving Franklin's corps toward Manassas. They must go to-morrow morning, ready or not ready. If we delay too long to get ready there will be no necessity to go at all, for Pope will either be defeated or be victorious without our aid. . . .[14]

Twenty minutes after midnight McClellan's reply arrived. "Franklin's corps has been ordered to march at 6 o'clock to-morrow morning," he assured the general-in-chief, but he added: "Reports numerous, from various sources, that Lee and Stuart, with large forces, are at Manassas, that the enemy, with 120,000 men, intend advancing on the forts near Arlington and the Chain Bridge, with a view to attacking Washington and Baltimore. . . ."[15]

At about the same time that the Young Napoleon was trying to stampede Halleck into giving him supreme command, Major General John

Pope was sending the general-in-chief a calm, informative, soldierly report on how he and his Army of Virginia had spent that Thursday. It would not reach Old Brains until near sundown the next day, so what it said was less important than the warrior spirit it reflected. Pope had asked only for forage and provisions to be sent "as far as the railroad is unobstructed."[16]

3

"SO GREAT IS MY CONFIDENCE in General Lee," said Old Jack after the Seven Days, "that I am willing to follow him blindfolded."[17] And so great was Lee's confidence in T. J. Jackson that the Army of Northern Virginia's commander took his time in bringing James Longstreet's divisions along the route the foot cavalry had taken to Bristoe and Manassas Junction several days before.

On Thursday afternoon, August 28, at about the time Jackson—to hold John Pope's army within reach—was attacking the left flank of the Yankee brigades marching eastward on the Warrenton Turnpike, Lee was still west of Thoroughfare Gap. During an early dinner offered him by friends in a nearby home, the sounds of gunfire off to the east were heard. Yet the general remained in a genial mood even though, as an aide wrote afterward, "victory or defeat hung trembling in the balance."[18]

However, Lee was not showing his contempt for Pope. Jackson had covered the fifty-five miles in two days, but Longstreet could move no faster than the army's wagon trains, which included Old Jack's. Moreover, General Lee wanted Longstreet's men rested and the stragglers brought in so that he could smite the miscreant with his full force when he reached Jackson.

John Pope, meanwhile, was issuing orders aimed toward preventing Jackson from retreating. Absent direct telegraph communication with Washington, he knew no more about the progress (if any) General Halleck was making in rushing the Young Napoleon's troops to him than Old Brains knew about where Pope and his forces were and what they were doing.

General McClellan opened a message he sent the general-in-chief at 10:30 on Friday morning, August 29, by announcing that "Franklin's corps is in motion; started about 6 a.m." But, as was his wont, soon Little Mac was again behaving like Little Mac. "I do not think Franklin is in condition to accomplish much if he meets serious resistance," he added. "I should not have moved him but for your pressing order of last night."[19]

At least two other messages, however, did not reach the general-in-chief or indeed anyone who might have acted on them. Both were from cavalryman Brigadier General John Buford. The first, sent at 9:30 a.m. on that Friday to Brigadier General James B. Ricketts, reported that the Confederates were east of Thoroughfare Gap and moving: "Seventeen regiments, one battery, and 500 cavalry passed through Gainesville three-quarters of an hour ago." Later, to General McDowell: "A large force from Thoroughfare Gap is making a junction through Gainesville up the Centreville road with the forces in the direction of the cannonading."[20]

That firing had broken out early that morning along the unfinished railroad near Groveton where Stonewall Jackson's three divisions, behind three thousand yards of embankment, were being attacked by Franz Sigel's corps. Couriers had told Old Jack that General Lee and Longstreet's divisions were approaching, so all he had to do was hold his position.[21]

General Pope's forces, however, were still scattered—a circumstance that doomed him to commit them to the fight raging at Groveton piecemeal.[22] Instead of concentrating "to bag Jackson" in accordance with orders he had issued the night before, his corps had dispersed; and even the general commanding, for a time, had gotten lost in some woods.[23]

Lacking direct telegraph contact with Pope, the general-in-chief was still dependent on Ambrose Burnside to relay messages to and from the battle area. On Friday afternoon Burnside passed along this telegram Fitz-John Porter, one of McClellan's generals who shared his low opinion of John Pope, had sent him from "4 miles from Manassas":

> *All that talk of bagging Jackson, &c., was bosh. That enormous Gap (Manassas) was left open and the enemy jumped through, and the story of McDowell having cut off Longstreet had no good foundation. The enemy have destroyed all our bridges, burned trains &c., and made this army rush back to look after its line of communication and find our base of subsistence. . . . There is a report that Jackson is at Centreville, which you can believe or not. The enemy destroyed an immense amount of property at Manassas—cars and supplies. I expect the next thing will be a raid on our rear by way of Warrenton by Longstreet, who was cut off.*[24]

Late on that Friday afternoon, Burnside forwarded another message from Porter that contained this sentence: "I hope Mac is at work, and we will soon get ordered out of this."[25] Indeed, Mac was at work; in reply to a terse inquiry from A. Lincoln—"What news from direction of Manassas? What generally?"[26]—he replied:

The last news I received from the direction of Manassas was from stragglers, to the effect that the enemy were evacuating Centreville and retiring toward Thoroughfare Gap. This by no means reliable.

I am clear that one of two courses should be adopted: First, to concentrate all our available forces to open communications with Pope; Second, to leave Pope to get out of his scrape, and at once use all our means to make the capital perfectly safe.

No middle ground will now answer. Tell me what you wish me to do, and I will do all in my power to accomplish it. I wish to know what my orders and authority are. I ask for nothing, but will obey whatever orders you give. I only ask a prompt decision, that I may at once give the necessary orders. It will not do to delay longer.[27]

Such insolence, such nigh-treasonous arrogance must surely have appalled Abraham Lincoln and stunned Henry Wager Halleck—who, presumably, saw the telegraphed evidence of how deranged ambition had rendered the Young Napoleon's mind. But that he had acted consciously and deliberately was reflected in the letter he wrote Mary Ellen McClellan on Friday afternoon within minutes of his having sent those astonishing words to President Lincoln:

I was awake all last night & have not had one moment until now to write you. I have a terrible task on my hands now—perfect imbecility to correct. No means to act with, no authority—yet determined if possible to save the country & the Capital. I find the soldiers all clinging to me—yet I am not permitted to go to the post of danger! Two of my Corps will either save that fool Pope or be sacrificed for the country. I do not know whether I will be permitted to save the Capital or not—I have just telegraphed very plainly to the Presdt & Halleck what I think ought to be done—I expect merely a contemptuous silence. . . .[28]

Lincoln would treat McClellan's outrageous response with the contemptuous silence it deserved for a while. General Halleck, however, telegraphed Little Mac at 7:50 P.M:

I have just been told that Franklin's corps stopped at Annandale. . . . This is all contrary to my orders; investigate and report the facts of this disobedience. That corps must push forward, as I directed. . . .[29]

In fact, General-in-Chief Halleck had been ordering Franklin's corps to reinforce Pope "by forced marches" since Wednesday;[30] now, with Friday only four hours away from being all gone, McClellan added defiance to insolence:

> *By referring to my telegrams of 10.30 a.m., 12 m., and 1 p.m., together with your reply of 2.48 p.m., you will see why Franklin's corps halted at Annandale. His small cavalry force—all I had to give him—was ordered to push on as far as possible toward Manassas. It was not safe for Franklin to move beyond Annandale, under the circumstances, until we knew what was at Vienna.*
>
> *General Franklin remained here until about 1 p.m., endeavoring to arrange for supplies for his command. I am responsible for both these circumstances, and do not see that either was in disobedience to your orders. Please give distinct orders in reference to Franklin's movements of to-morrow. . . .*
>
> *In regard to to-morrow's movements I desire definite instructions, as it is not agreeable to me to be accused of disobeying orders when I have simply exercised the discretion you committed to me.*[31]

Then, as he had earlier that day, General McClellan took the time to write his wife. Toward the end of his letter he said:

> *I have no faith in anyone here & expect to be turned loose the moment their alarm is over. I expect I got in a row with Halleck tonight—he sent me a telegram I did not like & I told him so very plainly. He is not a refined person at all, & probably says rough things when he don't mean them. . . .*[32]

Well, no: Henry Halleck had disciplined himself even before he entered West Point to express himself with clarity and precision. Much of his success as a lawyer out in California had been due to his devotion to precision in thought as well as expression. The qualities in Halleck's messages that McClellan consistently overlooked—or was for some reason incapable of perceiving—were the honesty, the earnestness, the utterly absolute dedication to duty driving Old Brains.

For Abraham Lincoln to prepare a reply to the Young Napoleon's incredible suggestion that his commander-in-chief adopt as a course of action "To leave Pope to get out of his scrape. . . ." required the patience of

Job and the wisdom of Solomon. Posterity would be astonished at the restraint Lincoln applied on turbulent but understandable emotions that might have stimulated a lesser man to order George McClellan shot dead on sight, or arrested and charged with treason, or at the very least summarily relieved from command.

Yet, that Friday night—after roughly seven hours of contemptuous silence—the President responded:

> *I think your first alternative, to wit, "to concentrate all our available forces to open communication with Pope," is the right one, but I wish not to control. That I now leave to General Halleck, aided by your counsels.*[33]

4

ABRAHAM LINCOLN HAD DONE his reluctant general-in-chief no favor by allowing General McClellan even an advisory role even for the time being. Worse, this may have been the very first instance in which the President looked upon Henry Halleck, his armies' senior military officer, as a lightning rod for absorbing the inevitable criticism and condemnation Radicals would fling at him.

If so, such a deflection of controversy on Lincoln's part indicated an abysmally weak appreciation of how debilitating were the pressures on General Halleck as—concurrently—he fought two major and uncounted petty campaigns, body and soul, almost around the clock. And, notably, on Friday, August 29, 1862, from out in the West, Horatio Wright in Kentucky as well as Don Carlos Buell in Tennessee had added their problems to those of preventing the disaster only a few miles south and west of Washington that Little Mac had offered Lincoln as a possible course of action.

Predictably, General Buell's contribution seemed worded to discourage Old Brains with language conveying his own discouragement. From Dechard, Tennessee, on that Friday afternoon Don Carlos had telegraphed:

> *Every day renders it the more evident that we must abandon our extensive lines and concentrate at some point nearer our base of supplies, perhaps Murfreesborough. Our communications are interrupted almost daily and our detachments captured by superior*

numbers. Our communications are not yet opened with Louisville, and cannot be without putting a larger force on the road than can be spared.

I yield to this conviction with painful reluctance. I cannot collect at any point this side of Murfreesborough more than 30,000 men, and from that would have to be deducted something for convoys. It would be worse in advance of this point; and, besides, the character of the roads and of the country makes it impossible to subsist ourselves in the mountains.

I am therefore preparing to concentrate at Murfreesborough. I suppose General Grant's two divisions to have crossed the river, but I can get no information of their movements.[34]

Two messages from Horatio Wright in Cincinnati on that miserable and fatiguing Friday, August 29, arrived to burden the general-in-chief. In the first, General Wright passed along a warning sent him earlier that day:

General Nelson, at Lexington, asserts that Kirby Smith will assail General Buell in left and rear; that the condition of the latter is critical, and he is clamorous to be permitted to move at once upon Nashville to his relief. His opinion in regard to General Buell's condition is entitled to much weight, as he is recently from Tennessee. Kirby Smith's movements and strength are uncertain, none of the reports and rumors being reliable.

The troops we have at Lebanon and Louisville which might be available for this are entirely raw, and I am unwilling to make any forward movement as yet unless it is vitally necessary. . . . The largest part of our force so far assembled is at Lexington and in advance. The rest mainly at Lebanon, Louisville, and on the line of and guarding Louisville and Nashville Railroad at Munfordville and Bowling Green. . . .[35]

General Wright shared more of his concerns with Old Brains in another and even longer telegram:

Kentucky is in a much worse condition than I had been led to be-lieve. Guerrilla bands and recruiting parties parade the State under the very noses of the civil and military authorities, and thus far it has been next to impossible to put them down for want of a mounted force. The Governor and his officers I found cordially disposed, but they can do little. The full exercise of power has passed out of their hands in many parts of the State, and the civil authority is too slow in its operations for the present crisis.

Troops come in slowly. . . . I have used the telegraph freely in urging the Governors to hurry up their quotas, but they lack arms, equipments, clothing, and in some cases ammunition. They are doing the best they can, according to their own accounts. . . .

Nelson thinks Buell's case critical, and has urged to-day an immediate opening of the road [to Nashville]. *Perhaps we could do it, but I don't think so. . . . Our troops are utterly raw, remember; don't know how to march or fire, and can't be expected to do much in the way of fighting.*

Bear in mind that I have not been a week in the department as yet, and that an army can't be made in that time out of the raw material. If you say go, they go; but I shall not expect success except by chance, and I don't see yet that we won't gain by a little delay for necessary preparations. This of course supposes Buell not to be in extremities.

Nelson don't like serving in the department; it would be well to relieve him as soon as he can be replaced. In many respects he is a good officer, too changeable however, being influenced too much by every report that reaches him. This could be all overlooked if it were not for the rank and his consequent dissatisfaction.[36]

Oddly, Horatio Wright's last two sentences amounted to a fair description of George McClellan. Yet Little Mac was not changeable regarding William Franklin's corps. At around noon on that Friday, he had asked Halleck how far he wanted that force to advance.[37] Replied the general-in-chief:

I want Franklin's corps to go far enough to find out something about the enemy. Perhaps he can get such information at Annandale so as to prevent his going farther; otherwise, he will push on to Fairfax. Try to get something from direction of Manassas, either by telegram or through Franklin's scouts. Our people must move more actively and find out where the enemy is. I am tired of guesses.[38]

If Old Brains' temper was beginning to show in his words, he revealed one reason near the end of another message to McClellan. "General Cullum has gone to Harper's Ferry, and I have only a single regular officer for duty in this office."[39] More wrath was embedded at 7:50 on that Friday evening when General Halleck telegraphed McClellan:

> *I have just been told that Franklin's corps stopped at Annandale, and that he was this evening in Alexandria. This is all contrary to my orders; investigate and report the facts of this disobedience. That corps must push forward, as I directed, protect the railroad, and open our communications with Manassas.*[40]

Before the long day ended, however, General Halleck sent a few words of encouragement to John Pope. Responding to a relayed message, Old Brains wrote: "Yours of yesterday, 10 p.m., is the first I have received from you in four days. Live on the country as much as possible till we can supply you. Push the enemy as much as possible, but be sure to keep up your connection with Alexandria."[41]

Vague instructions? Yes, certainly; but they were an indication of how little the general-in-chief knew about the events within rifle range of Jackson's three divisions of Confederates deployed behind the embankment near Groveton.

Only a few of the units that General Pope had ordered, late on Thursday, to converge on the force that had ambushed the Iron Brigade and the one commanded by Abner Doubleday, actually struck the rebels early on Friday morning. As other Yankee outfits arrived, they, too, were repelled by the fierce resistance they encountered. Equally futile assaults throughout the day achieved nothing but lengthening federal casualty lists. Worse, from the Union point of view, while Jackson's men slaughtered the attackers—and suffered heavy losses themselves in the process—General Lee and Longstreet's thirty-two thousand men had started slipping into positions south of Old Jack's but adjoining them at a slight angle to it as early as ten o'clock on that Friday morning *without being noticed all day* by Pope.

Lee, noting the persistence of Pope's attackers and recalling the duration of Jackson's stout but costly defense, asked General Longstreet if he thought his five divisions just arrived should strike the Yankees in the flank. *No,* "Old Pete" replied, *not yet.*

Two more times General Lee raised the same question. Longstreet's only concession, late in the day, was to send Brigadier General John B. Hood's division on a reconnaissance southward to find out if any more federals were *en route* to the fighting going on past sundown at Groveton. There were some, Hood reported. With victory or defeat still undetermined, only darkness suspended the killing and maiming taking place along Jackson's embankment.[42]

5

APPARENTLY, GENERAL POPE HAD LEARNED a little by five o'clock on Saturday morning, August 30, for up front in a report to the general-in-chief he used the word *combined*. Not so accurate, however, was some of the other information his message contained:

> *We fought a terrific battle here yesterday with the combined forces of the enemy, which lasted with continuous fury from daylight until dark, by which time the enemy was driven from the field, which we now occupy. Our troops are too much exhausted yet to push matters, but I shall do so in the course of the morning, as soon as Fitz John Porter's corps comes up from Manassas.*
>
> *The enemy is still in our front, but badly used up. We have lost not less than 8,000 men killed and wounded, but from the appearance of the field the enemy lost at least two to one. He stood strictly on the defensive, and every assault was made by ourselves. Our troops behaved splendidly. The battle was fought on the identical battle-field of Bull Run, which greatly increased the enthusiasm of our men.*
>
> *The news just reaches me from the front that the enemy is retreating toward the mountains. I go forward at once to see. . . .*
>
> *I think you had best send Franklin's, Cox's, and Sturgis' regiments to Centreville, as also forage and subsistence.*
>
> *I received a note this morning from General Franklin, written by order of General McClellan, saying that wagons and cars would be loaded and sent to Fairfax Station as soon as I would send a cavalry escort to Alexandria to bring them out. Such a request, when Alexandria is full of troops and we fighting the enemy, needs no comment. . . .*[43]

And such a wry last sentence must have caused Old Brains' stern visage to relax just a bit when he read it.

But there was much work to do. To Nathaniel Banks he telegraphed: "General Pope is in want of ammunition, particularly for artillery. We will send from Alexandria as soon as possible. Cannot you send him some from Manassas?"[44]

To add clout, Halleck had an aide enlist Assistant Secretary of War Peter Watson's influence:

> *General Halleck desires me to say that General Pope wishes ammunition, and especially for artillery, to be sent at once to Centreville. The general has communicated this to General McClellan, General Banks, the chief of ordnance, and the chief quartermaster at Alexandria, and requests that you will do what you can to hasten and facilitate this matter.*[45]

As early as roughly half past nine that Saturday morning, the Young Napoleon offered this news to General Halleck:

> *Heavy artillery fire is now in progress in the direction of Fairfax Court-House* [well to the east of Groveton]. *There has been a good deal of it for two or three hours. I hear it so distinctly that I should judge it to be this side of Fairfax. Have not been able to ascertain the cause. It seems that the garrisons in the works on the north* [Washington] *side of the Potomac are altogether too small.*[46]

Fairfax was maybe fifteen miles nearer Washington than the actual battle area, but perhaps the reason General McClellan had not been able to ascertain the cause of the firing was simply that there had not been any fighting *at all* so far on that Saturday. John Pope had not yet marshaled his survivors of clashes with Old Jack to deliver the attacks that would annihilate the rebel defenders of the unfinished railroad's embankment. Again, scouts reported that Jackson had vanished.[47]

On a high summer day so hot and sultry that horses were no longer swishing their tails, General Jackson had moved most of his men back far enough from the previous day's killing grounds to enable them to rest. Only skeleton forces stood watch, ready to sound the alarm should the Yankees come at the embankment again.[48]

Confident now that he could finally "bag" Jackson—something acting General-in-Chief Lincoln had not been able to do in the Shenandoah Valley back in the spring—John Pope issued these orders at noon on that steamy Saturday:

> *The following forces will be immediately thrown forward in pursuit*

of the enemy and press him vigorously during the whole day. Major-General McDowell is assigned to the command of the pursuit:

Major-General Porter's corps will push forward on the Warrenton turnpike, followed by the divisions of Brigadier-Generals King and Reynolds. The division of Brigadier-General Ricketts will pursue the Hay Market road, followed by the corps of Major-General Heintzelman.

The necessary cavalry will be assigned to these columns by Major-General McDowell, to whom regular and frequent reports will be made. The general headquarters will be somewhere on the Warrenton turnpike.[49]

Yet there may have been some firing somewhere, however random or sporadic, for at around eleven o'clock that Saturday morning General Banks, the Waltham "Bobbin Boy," reported from Manassas in a message to Halleck:

There was a camp rumor as I came in from Bristoe that Jackson had moved [eastward] *toward Alexandria. Col. J. S. Clark, one of my aides, who has been out to the front, reports that Jackson has fallen back about five miles toward the mountains. He judges mainly by the sound of the guns.*

There has been an entire change of position, I judge. A scout reported to me at 10 a.m. that Jackson was at Gainesville with about 30,000. He said he saw and knew him.

My corps is moving up from Bristoe. No enemy near.[50]

Whether this amateur general's misinformation had any effect on John Pope's decision to order an attack to prevent Jackson from escaping *via* Thoroughfare Gap would never be known. Earlier, however, General Halleck had acted to give the Army of Virginia's commander all the fighting power he could.

"All of Sumner's corps on the south side of the [Potomac] river not actually required in [Washington's] forts should march to Pope's relief," Old Brains ordered McClellan. And for perhaps the twentieth time, he re-iterated: "Franklin should also be hurried to re-enforce Pope."[51]

By two o'clock that Saturday afternoon, General Halleck felt confident enough to send this assurance to John Pope:

All matters have been attended to. Thirty thousand men are march-

ing to your aid. Franklin should be with you now and Sumner to-morrow morning. All will be right soon, even if you should be forced back. Let your army know that heavy re-enforcements are coming.[52]

There, Old Brains said too much. On that Saturday morning, upon receiving McClellan's report of firing near Fairfax that had not in fact occurred, at 9:40 General Halleck had telegraphed the Young Napoleon:

I am by no means satisfied with General Franklin's march of yesterday. Considering the circumstances of the case, he was very wrong in stopping at Annandale. Moreover, I learned last night that the Quartermaster's Department could have given him plenty of transportation, if he had applied for it, any time since his arrival at Alexandria. He knew the importance of opening communication with General Pope's army, and should have acted more promptly.[53]

General Halleck's closing sentence suggested that Major General William B. Franklin's name might be added to Don Carlos Buell's on the list of candidates for replacement. And as if George McClellan might have paid some attention to tingling at the back of his own neck, he provided the general-in-chief with a wordy and evasive explanation that might have been written by the quartermasters, one that sought to exonerate all concerned. But, for once, Little Mac said something that was true. "The difficulty seems to consist in the fact that the greater part of the transportation on hand at Alexandria and Washington has been needed for current supplies of the [Washington] garrisons."[54]

Condescendingly, the Young Napoleon wrote in closing: "I take it for granted that this has not been properly explained to you."[55] But who had been building up the Washington garrisons? George Brinton McClellan.

Even so, at 2:10 p.m. on that Saturday, August 30, 1862, General Halleck had made one more attempt to spur Little Mac:

Franklin's and all of Sumner's corps should be pushed forward with all possible dispatch. They must use their legs and make forced marches. Time now is everything. Send some sharpshooters on the trains to Bull Run. . . . Give Colonel Haupt all the assistance you can. The sharpshooters on top of cars can assist in unloading the trains.[56]

Time had been everything for days; and even as General Halleck wrote, it was running out for John Pope. Still believing that Jackson had withdrawn from Friday's killing ground and was retreating by way of Thoroughfare Gap, at two o'clock he told his pursuers to move out. They did, only to be cut down by the rested Confederates who had never strayed very far from the embankment.

But more Yankees took the places of the fallen, and soon the fighting was as vicious as it had been the day before. When Confederates' ammunition ran out, they threw rocks at the attackers. Some federals got within a few yards of breaking through Stonewall's line, then were beaten back.

Curiously, Pope had focused his assaults on Jackson as though Longstreet's five divisions were over in the Shenandoah Valley. From different vantage points, Old Pete and General Lee had watched blue wave after blue wave surge westward, get shattered, then recede. Finally, from Old Jack came a request for a division. "Certainly," said General Longstreet, "but before the division can reach him the attack will be broken by artillery."

Fire from eighteen Confederate guns tore into the flank of the federals, stunning them with surprise as well as shredding them with hot scraps of metal. And by then, almost all of Pope's forces were within range.

Soon, to complete the wrecking of John Pope's army, General Lee sent all of his forces into a drive that smote the fleeing Yankees from their flank as well as their rear and continued northward over the old Manassas battleground's landmarks—Henry House Hill, the Stone Bridge, Bull Run—until fatigue and a thunderstorm slowed and then halted their advance.[57]

By sheer coincidence, out near Richmond, Kentucky, Confederate Major General Edmund Kirby Smith's troops were mauling two brigades of federal recruits who were the only Yankees standing between the invaders and the bluegrass country. Union Major General William Nelson lost roughly three out of every four of his seven thousand or so men; the rest fled. Nelson, six-foot five, weighing three hundred pounds, had tried to rally his green soldiers by shouting, "If they can't hit me, they can't hit anything." But rebel Minié balls nicked him twice, and he was obliged to join the rout to escape capture.[58]

General Halleck would not learn of either catastrophe for hours after each occurred. Presumably, he used the last scraps of time—before the appalling news began arriving—to prepare his reply to Secretary of War Stanton's request for answers to four questions regarding the performance (or lack of it) by Major General McClellan since the Seven Days; certainly it is unlikely that even Old Brains could have composed the report afterward. Halleck wrote:

In reply to your note of last evening I have to state:

1st. That on the 30th of July I directed General McClellan to send away his sick as quickly as possible, preparatory to his moving in some direction. Receiving no answer, the order was repeated August 2. On the 3d of August I directed him to withdraw his entire army from Harrison's Landing and bring it to Aquia Creek.

2d. That the order was not obeyed with the promptness I expected and the national safety, in my opinion, required. It will be seen from my telegraphic correspondence that General McClellan protested against the movement, and that it was not actually commenced till the 14th instant.

It is proper to remark that the reasons given for not moving earlier was the delay in getting off the sick. As shown in my correspondence, I was most earnestly pressing him to move quickly, for the reason that I felt very anxious for the safety of Washington. From all the information I could obtain I believed that the enemy intended to crush General Pope's army and attack this city.

I also believed that our only safety was to unite the two armies as rapidly as possible between the enemy and Washington. The object of pushing General Pope forward to the Rapidan was simply to gain time for General McClellan's army to get into position somewhere in rear of the Rappahannock.

This I at first hoped to accomplish by landing the troops of Generals Burnside and McClellan at Aquia Creek. But the time which elapsed between the arrival of these two armies compelled me to bring most of General McClellan's forces to Alexandria, as General Pope was then falling back from the Upper Rappahannock before the main body of the enemy.

When General McClellan's movement was begun it was rapidly carried out; but there was an unexpected delay in commencing it. General McClellan reports the delay was unavoidable.

3d. That on the 26th August, at 11.20, I telegraphed to Major-General Franklin, at Alexandria, to march his corps by Centreville toward Warrenton and to report to General Pope. Finding that Franklin's corps had not left, I telegraphed to General McClellan on the 27th, at 10 a.m., to have it march in the direction of Manassas as soon as possible. On the same day, at 12 m., I again telegraphed to General McClellan that General Porter reported a general battle imminent, and that Franklin's corps should move out

*by forced marches, carrying three or four days' provisions; to be after-
wards supplied, as far as possible, by railroad. I also gave him the
positions of General Pope's troops as well as I could ascertain them,
and suggested the possibility that the enemy would attempt to turn
his right. At 9 p.m. General McClellan telegraphed that he should
retain Cox with General Franklin till next morning, and would
visit my headquarters immediately. He came to my quarters soon
after midnight, and left about 2 o'clock in the morning of the 28th.*

*At our interview I urged on him the importance of pushing
forward Franklin as early as possible. Hearing about noon that General McClellan had not reached Alexandria, I telegraphed, at 12.40
p.m. (28th), to General Franklin, if he had not acted on General
McClellan's order to do so on mine, and move toward Manassas
Junction. At 1 p.m. General McClellan telegraphed to me that the
moment Franklin could be started with a reasonable amount of
artillery he should go forward. At 2.45 he telegraphed some rumors
he had heard about the enemy's movements, and expressed an
opinion that the troops sent from Alexandria should be in force, and
with cavalry and artillery, or we should be beaten in detail.*

*I replied at 3.30 p.m. that not a moment must be lost in
pushing as large a force as possible toward Manassas, so as to
communicate with General Pope before the enemy could be re-
enforced. He telegraphed back at 4.45 that Franklin's corps was not
in condition to move and fight a battle. At 8.45 I telegraphed to
him that there must be no further delay in moving Franklin's corps
toward Manassas—that they must go to-morrow morning, ready or
not ready. If we delay too long to get ready there will be no necessity
of going at all, for Pope will either be defeated or victorious without
our aid If there is a want of wagons, the men must carry provisions
with them till the wagons can come to their relief. At 10 he replied
that he had ordered Franklin's corps to move at 6 o'clock.*

*On the morning of the 29th, at 10.30, he telegraphed to me
that Franklin's corps had started at 6 a.m., and that he could give
him but two squadrons of cavalry. At 12 m. he telegraphed that
Franklin's corps was without proper ammunition and without
transportation; and again at 1 p.m. he telegraphed that in his
opinion Franklin ought not to advance beyond Annandale. At 3.10
p.m. I replied that I wanted Franklin's corps to go far enough to find
out something about the enemy; that perhaps he might get such
information at Annandale as to prevent his going farther; that*

otherwise he would push on toward Fairfax. I added that "our people must move more actively and find out where the enemy is. I am tired of guesses." Late in the afternoon I heard that Franklin's corps had halted at Annandale, and that he himself had been seen in Alexandria in the afternoon. I immediately telegraphed to General McClellan at 7.50 p.m. that his (Franklin's) being in Alexandria and his corps halting at Annandale was contrary to my orders; that his corps must push forward as I directed, protect the railroad, and open our communication with Manassas. General McClellan replied at 8 p.m., referring to his previous telegrams, and said that he had not deemed it safe for Franklin to march beyond Annandale, and that he was responsible for his being in Alexandria and his corps halting at Annandale.

Early on the morning of the 30th I made inquiries of the Quartermaster-General in regard to transportation, and telegraphed at 9.40 to General McClellan that I was by no means satisfied with General Franklin's march of yesterday (29th). Considering the circumstances of the case he was very wrong in stopping at Annandale. I referred to the fact that he could have obtained transportation if he had applied for it to the Quartermaster's Department, and added: "He knew the importance of opening communication with General Pope's army, and should have acted more promptly."

The foregoing is, I believe, a correct summary of the orders and instructions given by me in regard to the movement of General Franklin's corps, my expressions of dissatisfaction, and the reason alleged for the delays which in the result proved so unfortunate.

4th. Copies of letters, orders, &c., relative to your inquiries are sent herewith.[59]

"Halleck could be a master of objective reporting when he so desired," wrote his biographer, Stephen E. Ambrose, adding: "Stanton could not drop McClellan on the basis of his reply."[60] Well, yes; but it was only to be expected that lawyer Halleck would respond to lawyer Stanton with the facts substantiated and opinions so-labeled. It would have been completely out of character and practice for Old Brains to have seized the occasion in order to vent his outrage or to slant his response to support McClellan's relief.

Moreover, Stanton's request had been premature. If he truly wanted to justify the Young Napoleon's removal, and if McClellan continued to behave like McClellan, was it not probable that in due course the intended scapegoat would convict himself?

6

AT CENTREVILLE, AT 9:45 P.M. ON SATURDAY, August 30, 1862, Major General John Pope took the time to write a report on the whipping General Lee and his Army of Northern Virginia had just inflicted on him. It would not be the first information Halleck received regarding the battle—Old Brains would not receive it until late the next morning—and it would contain a number of inaccuracies, but it reflected a state of mind that was indeed remarkable in the circumstances. Pope wrote:

> *We have had a terrific battle again to-day. The enemy, largely re-enforced, assaulted our position early to-day. We held our ground firmly until 6 p.m., when the enemy, massing very heavy forces on our left, forced back that wing about half a mile. At dark we held that position.*
>
> *Under all the circumstances, both horses and men having been two days without food; and the enemy greatly outnumbering us, I thought it best to draw back to this place at dark. The movement has been made, in perfect order and without loss. The troops are in good heart, and marched off the field without the least hurry or confusion. Their conduct was very fine.*
>
> *The battle was most furious for hours without cessation, and the losses on both sides very heavy. The enemy is badly crippled, and we shall do well enough. Do not be uneasy. We will hold our own here.*
>
> *The labors and hardships of this army for two or three weeks have been beyond description. We have delayed the enemy as long as possible without losing the army. We have damaged him heavily, and I think the army entitled to the gratitude of the country. Be easy; everything will go well.*

And General Pope added this post-script: "We have lost nothing; neither guns nor wagons."[61]

Exactly when and how General Halleck first learned of the disaster would never be clear. George McClellan, however, knew enough about it to express his dismay in a message to the general-in-chief sent at 10:30 Saturday night.

As if he anticipated being charged with having shamelessly allowed "Pope to get out of his own scrape," he opened with a claim to the contrary:

"I have sent to the front all my troops with the exception of Couch's division, and have given the orders necessary to insure its being disposed of as you directed." That said, Little Mac got to the point:

> *I cannot express to you the pain and mortification I have experienced to-day in listening to the distant sound of the firing of my men. As I can be of no further use here, I respectfully ask that, if there is a probability of the conflict being renewed to-morrow, I may be permitted to go to the scene of battle with my staff, merely to be with my own men, if nothing more; they will fight none the worse for my being with them.*
>
> *If it is not deemed best to intrust me with the command even of my own army, I simply ask to be permitted to share their fate on the field of battle. Please reply to this to-night. . . .*[62]

General McClellan, reflecting impatience or perhaps fascination coupled with insomnia, provided the general-in-chief with another bulletin at 3:30 on the next morning, Sunday, August 31, 1862:

> *My aide just in. He reports our army as badly beaten. Our losses very heavy. Troops arriving at Centreville. Have probably lost several batteries. Some of the Corps entirely broken up into stragglers. Shall Couch continue his movement to the front? We have no other tried troops in Washington. Sumner between Fairfax and Centreville. Franklin now at Centreville—having fallen back from Bull's [sic] Run. Enemy has probably suffered severely.*[63]

Came the dawn on Sunday morning, and at 9:18 General Halleck replied with the precision of thought and brevity that called attention to McClellan's lack of those qualities:

> *I have just seen your telegram of 11.5 [sic] last night. The substance was stated to me when received, but I did not know that you asked for a reply immediately.*
>
> *I cannot answer without seeing the President, as General Pope is in command, by his orders, of the department.*
>
> *I think Couch's division should go forward as rapidly as possible and find the battlefield.*[64]

Go forward and find the battlefield.

By eleven o'clock General Halleck had received John Pope's report that had been written the evening before. "My Dear General," he began his reply, continuing:

> *You have done nobly. Don't yield another inch if you can avoid it. All reserves are being sent forward. Couch's division goes to-day. Part of it went to Sangster's Station last night with Franklin and Sumner, who must be now with you. Can't you renew the attack? I don't write more particularly for fear dispatch will not reach you. I am doing all in my power for you and your noble army. God bless you and it.*[65]

Can't you renew the attack?

At about the same time on that Sunday morning, George McClellan was working on a letter to Mary Ellen. "I telegraphed last evening asking permission to be with my troops," he told her, and "received a reply about half an hour ago from Halleck that he would have to consult the Presdt first!" Then, as usual, he put all such matters in his own perspective:

> *If they refuse to let me go out I think I shall be obliged to insist on a leave or something of the kind the moment the question of the existing battle is settled. I feel like a fool here—sucking my thumbs & doing nothing but what ought to be done by junior officers. . . .*
>
> *A short time since I saw the order defining commands etc.— mine is that part of the Army of the Potomac not sent to Pope—as all is sent, there I am left in command of nothing—a command I feel fully competent to exercise, & to which I can do full justice. I am going to write a quiet moderate letter to Mr. Aspinwall presently, explaining to him the exact state of the case, without comment, so that my friends in New York may know all. . . .*[66]

But the Young Napoleon did not confine his expression of personal and professional bruised feelings to that letter. In mid-afternoon on that Sunday, in a message to the general-in-chief, he complained: "Under the War Department order of yesterday I have no control over anything except my staff, some 100 men in my camp here, and the few remaining near Fort Monroe."[67]

Old Brains offered him no sympathy. Hours later he replied:

> *Since receiving your dispatch, relating to command, I have not been able to answer any* [message] *not of absolute necessity. I have not*

seen the order as published, but will write to you in the morning.
You will retain the command of everything in this vicinity not
temporarily belonging to Pope's army in the field.

　　　I beg of you to assist me in this crisis with your ability and
experience. I am utterly tired out.[68]

So Henry Wager Halleck wrote, and afterward he faced—without
complaint or excuses or even carefully reasoned explanation—the disparaging and discouraging criticism that ensued. It was as though he
expected his statement to be understood in the same context prevailing
when he had made it, near sundown on the day after two of the Union's
worst defeats so far in the war: Second Manassas and Richmond, Kentucky.
And, of course, hardly anyone but the pitifully few staff officers helping him
could possibly have known how many and varied and complex were the
pressures bearing on the general-in-chief, and that had been eroding his
stamina for uncounted days and nigh-sleepless nights.

Even so, posterity's judgments of Halleck would be warped to an
inordinate degree by the gross and widely and often-repeated error of
placing undue weight on an exhausted but honest and dedicated soldier's
freely offered, completely understandable, candid confession that he was
tired and needed help. "Halleck's cry of despair," biographer Ambrose called
it, placing pejorative spin on what may well have been nothing of the sort.
Worse, he offered the distorted criticism of Radical Republican, and
therefore committed enemy of both Halleck and McClellan, Secretary of
the Treasury Salmon P. Chase:

　　This telegram announced the surrender of Halleck to McClellan. It
　　saddens me to think that a Commander-in-chief [sic], *whose*
　　opinion of his subordinate's military conduct is such as I have heard
　　Halleck express of McClellan's should, in a moment of pressure, so
　　yield to that very subordinate.[69]

Would a man in the grip of despair have told McClellan he wanted
Darius Couch's troops to go forward and find the battlefield? Or have asked
Pope, *Can't you renew the attack?*

Moreover, General Halleck had worn himself out dealing as best he
could with often difficult people and situations, and fighting a war on
several fronts concurrently with little more than his brain and the telegraph
as his resources and weapons. Decades afterward, nigh-countless exchanges
of messages preserved in volumes of the *Official Records of the Union and*

Confederate Armies would document Halleck's responses to an astonishing variety of challenges. But, returning to the context of Old Brains' admission that he was "utterly tired out," consider some of the matters regarding which—often concurrently—he had recently been (or might soon be) obliged to render counsel or make decisions:

- In Tennessee, Bragg's invasion was causing Don Carlos Buell to abandon his campaign to seize Chattanooga and East Tennessee, thus risking the wrath of Lincoln.

- Also, raids on railroads, towns, and even Union garrisons in central Tennessee carried out by Confederate cavalry led by Nathan Bedford Forrest were bedeviling Buell, who claimed he lacked cavalry to oppose the "Wizard of the Saddle."

- Tennessee Military Governor Andrew Johnson was not happy with Buell for a number of reasons.

- Lincoln and Stanton wanted Buell relieved, but there was no general officer available who was fully qualified to replace him.

- Grant had agreed to loan at least four divisions to Buell, but Buell and Grant had experienced difficulty in communicating, and Buell was complaining to General Halleck.

- Given the threat created by Kirby Smith's invasion, Buell had sent William Nelson to command in Kentucky, but Washington had designated Horatio Wright commander of a new department including that state, leading to confusion Old Brains had to clear up.

- Wright seemed able, but he was new both to Kentucky and high command and needed time in which to train recruits he was asking governors of Illinois, Indiana, and Ohio to raise and send to Kentucky.

- Brigadier General J. T. Boyle, commanding a unit at Louisville, was helpful as a gatherer and forwarder of intelligence but his place in the Kentucky command structure was not clear.

- If Bragg moved northward, as seemed likely, Buell would almost certainly be obliged to follow him up the Louisville & Nashville Railroad into Kentucky and, if possible, head him off—thus complicating an already muddled command situation because of the administration's desire to guillotine Buell.

- Grant's stripping West Tennessee and northern Mississippi of divisions to assist Buell and Wright was making it more likely that Confederates would take advantage of his weakness.

- Nelson's complete defeat by Kirby Smith's forces at Richmond, Kentucky, on August 30 left the way open for the invaders to cross the Kentucky River and seize Lexington and Frankfort, driving the pro-Union government to Louisville and prompting Ohio's governor to make preparations for resisting rebel thrusts aimed at Cincinnati.

- Even before Lee's army swept Pope's from the old Manassas battlefield on Saturday, it was clear that Pope would have to replace Nathaniel Banks and Franz Sigel and return their corps to combat effectiveness—yet, from whence cometh able corps commanders?

- Fitz-John Porter's indications in messages to Burnside of unwillingness to serve under Pope, even in the emergency, suggested that McClellan's influence over some of his highest-ranking subordinates may have made the Army of the Potomac unreliable.

- McClellan's "leave Pope to get out of his scrape" proposal seemed certain to infuriate the Radical-dominated Joint Congressional Committee on the Conduct of the War, leading to more unwanted political interference in military operations.

- Stanton's call for answers to questions regarding McClellan's conduct suggested that the administration might relieve the Young Napoleon at a time when no qualified successor to command of the Army of the Potomac was in sight and his removal might cause his troops to turn against the government or refuse to serve.

- Bringing Ambrose Burnside's forces up to augment Washington's defenses might be necessary, but it would enable the Confederates to seize and occupy the federal bases at Aquia Landing, Falmouth, and Fredericksburg and might also give the rebels control of the lower Potomac—isolating Washington from Chesapeake Bay.

Sixteen or more problem areas are listed above in the simplest terms, yet these are only a small fraction of the vexations that sapped the stamina of the general-in-chief during the last two weeks of August 1862. Any one, or any number of them might have emerged as a challenge demanding immediate response the next time a telegraph decoder handed General Halleck an incoming message. Who would *not* be utterly tired out, merely from keeping all of these and other active problems in the correct mental pigeonholes?

And where in the record is the surrender to McClellan, according to Chase, that Halleck's telegram "announced"?

"You will retain the command of everything in this vicinity not temporarily belonging to Pope's army in the field," the general-in-chief had told McClellan on at least two earlier occasions. Halleck was answering a question McClellan had insisted on repeating, apparently in the hope of eventually stampeding Old Brains into adding to his powers. Here, Halleck appeared to be drawing upon his recollection of the recently issued War Department order that specified: "General McClellan commands that portion of the Army of the Potomac that has not been sent forward to General Pope's command."[70]

Moreover, McClellan's next telegram sent a few hours after Halleck's "I beg of you to assist me in this crisis with your ability and experience" message made no reference to any concession on the general-in-chief's part. Instead, after relaying some useless reports of the fighting's aftermath, Little Mac *complied* by offering some counsel in addition to his usual dire predictions:

> I recommend that no more of Couch's division be sent to the front, that Burnside be brought here as soon as practicable, and that everything available this side of Fairfax be drawn in at once, including the mass of the troops on the railroad. I apprehend that the enemy will or have by this time occupied Fairfax Court-House and cut off Pope entirely unless he falls back to-night via Sangster's and Fairfax Station. I think these orders should be sent at once.
>
> I have no confidence in the dispositions made as I gather them. To speak frankly—and the occasion requires it—there appears to be a total absence of brains, and I fear the total destruction of the army. The occasion is grave and demands grave measures. The question is the salvation of the country.
>
> I learn that our loss yesterday amounted to 15,000. We cannot afford such losses without an object. It is my deliberate opinion that the interests of the nation demand that Pope should fall back to-night if possible, and not one moment is to be lost. I will use all the cavalry I have to watch our right.

Please answer at once. I feel confident that you can rely upon the information I give you. I shall be up all night, and ready to obey any orders you give me.

Despite his earlier admission that he was utterly tired out, General Halleck was still at his office at 1:30 on the next morning, Monday, September 1, 1862. Far from writing as though he had ever even thought of surrendering anything to the Young Napoleon, he telegraphed him:

Burnside was ordered up very early yesterday morning. Retain remainder of Couch's forces, and make arrangements to stop all retreating troops in line of works or where you can best establish an outer line of defense.

My news from Pope was up to 4 p.m. He was then all right. I must wait for more definite information before I can order a retreat, as the falling back on the line of works must necessarily be directed in case of a serious disaster.

Give me all additional news that is reliable. I shall be up all night, and ready to act as circumstances may require. I am fully aware of the gravity of the crisis, and have been for weeks.[71]

Men who have had breakdowns, or who are suffering from despair or who are giving-in, do not do what Henry Halleck did in that terse text. Politely, but firmly, he put George Brinton McClellan in his place.

Critics' and historians' other allegation, that General Halleck was never worth much after Second Manassas shattered him, was equally false and malicious. Of course, many of Old Brains' detractors, particularly those of the ultra Radical Republican persuasion, had been condemning him since his earliest days as Pathfinder Frémont's successor at St. Louis. By smearing him, they were merely being consistent in their hypocrisy and demagoguery. And from Second Manassas onward, Henry Wager Halleck also was consistent—in his devotion to duty, honor, and the Union, as well as to his client in *United States v. Confederacy,* Abraham Lincoln.

7

AS THE DICHOTOMY WIDENED between reality and General McClellan's many professions of full support to General Halleck's efforts to reinforce Pope's Army of Virginia, pressure on Lincoln mounted to submit the Young

Napoleon's neck to the slicing device that was so widely, and so mindlessly, used in France during the Reign of Terror. That the pro-abolition Radical Republicans would be howling for McClellan's head was no surprise. Within Lincoln's cabinet, Jacobins (John Hay's term for the dissidents, drawn as were guillotine-related figures of speech regarding relief from command of generals from the French Revolution) Salmon Chase and Edwin Stanton were the most ardent advocates of removing McClellan forthwith.

As early as Saturday, August 30—the same day General Halleck had presented answers to the questions Stanton had raised regarding Little Mac's performance, even as Lee's Army of Northern Virginia was driving Pope's shattered forces all the way to Centreville—Stanton, Chase, and Attorney General Edward Bates had gone to the President to state their case. Lincoln reserved judgment. On Sunday morning, August's last day, Lincoln held a meeting of the full cabinet to discuss the battle, but no decisions were made.[72]

Although nothing would ever be known about any conversations the President may have had with his general-in-chief, Lincoln must have read the messages Halleck had exchanged with General Pope since direct telegraphic contact had been restored. He would have seen the calm, soldierly report Pope had sent Halleck from Centreville soon after the battle, and Old Brains' "You have done nobly" response. On Monday, September 1, the day of his meeting with the cabinet, Lincoln would have been able to see these additions to the file:

Pope to Halleck, Sunday, August 31, 1862:

> *Your dispatch of 11 a.m. has been received, and I thank you for your considerate commendation. I would be glad to have it in such shape that the army might be acquainted with it.*
>
> *We shall fight to the last. The whole secession army engaged us yesterday. . . . The plan of the enemy will undoubtedly be to turn my flank. If he does so he will have his hands full. My troops are in good heart.*
>
> *I need cavalry horses terribly. Send me 2,000 in lots and under strong escort. I have never yet received a single one.*[73]

Halleck to Pope, Sunday morning, September 1:

> *Yours of last evening was received at 4 a.m. I want to issue a complimentary order, but as you are daily fighting it could hardly be distributed. I will do so very soon.*

Look out well for your right, and don't let the enemy turn it and get between you and the forts. We are strengthening the line of defense as rapidly as possible. Horses will be sent to you to-day. Send dispatches to me as often as possible. I hope for an arrival of cavalry to-day.[74]

Pope to Halleck, Sunday, 8:50 A.M:

All was quiet yesterday and so far this morning. My men are resting; they need it much. Forage for our horses is being brought up. Our cavalry is completely broken down, so that there are not five horses to a company that can raise a trot.

The consequence is that I am forced to keep considerable infantry along the roads in my rear to make them secure, and even then it is difficult to keep the enemy's cavalry off the roads.

I shall attack again to-morrow if I can; the next day certainly.

I think it my duty to call your attention to the unsoldierly and dangerous conduct of many brigade and some division commanders of the forces sent here from the Peninsula. Every word and act and intention is discouraging, and calculated to break down the spirits of the men and produce disaster.

One commander of a corps, who was ordered to march from Manassas Junction to join me near Groveton, although he was only 5 miles distant, failed to get up at all, and, worse still, fell back to Manassas without a fight, and in plain hearing, at less than 3 miles' distance, of a furious battle, which raged all day. It was only in consequence of peremptory orders that he joined me next day.

One of his brigades, the brigadier-general of which professed to be looking for his division, absolutely remained all day at Centreville, in plain view of the battle, and made no attempt to join. What renders the whole matter worse, these are both officers of the Regular Army, who do not hold back from ignorance or fear.

Their constant talk, indulged in publicly and in promiscuous company, is that the Army of the Potomac will not fight; that they are demoralized by withdrawal from the Peninsula, &c. When such example is set by officers of high rank the influence is very bad amongst those in subordinate stations.

You have hardly an idea of the demoralization among officers of high rank in the Potomac Army, arising in all instances from personal feeling in relation to changes of commander-in-chief and others. These men are mere tools or parasites, but their example is producing, and must necessarily produce, very disastrous results.

You should know these things, as you alone can stop it. Its source is beyond my reach, though its effects are very perceptible and very dangerous. I am endeavoring to do all I can, and will most assuredly put them where they shall fight or run away.

My advice to you—I give it with freedom, as I know you will not misunderstand it—is that, in view of any satisfactory results, you draw back this army to the intrenchments in front of Washington, and set to work in that secure place to reorganize and rearrange it. You may avoid great disaster by doing so. I do not consider the matter except in a purely military light, and it is bad enough and grave enough to make some action very necessary.

When there is no heart in their leaders, and every disposition to hang back, much cannot be expected from the men.

Please hurry forward cavalry horses to me under strong escort. I need them badly—worse than I can tell you.[75]

While reading the file of messages, President Lincoln would also have found of particular interest those the general-in-chief had received from McClellan and Halleck's replies. Old Brains had closed the telegram that ended with his request for assistance at between ten and eleven o'clock on Sunday, August 31. What appeared to be a direct response from McClellan at around that time opened this series of exchanges in the file: McClellan (typically) to Halleck:

I am ready to afford you any assistance in my power, but you will readily perceive how difficult my undefined position, such as I now hold, must be. At what hour of the morning can I see you alone, either at your own house or the office?[76]

Before midnight on that Sunday, an aide replied: "General Halleck has gone to bed. I am directed to say he will see you at any time to-morrow morning that will suit your convenience."[77] Old Brains himself sent this inquiry to McClellan's headquarters at Alexandria at 10:20 on Monday morning, September 1: "Is the general coming up to Washington; and if so, at what hour? I am very anxious to see him."[78]

Trivial though some of this telegraph traffic may have seemed, from it (even from parts of it) Lincoln may have learned enough to listen, later that morning, to what his cabinet members had to say but to reserve judgment for at least two reasons: Halleck and Pope were of a mind to fight, and it would be interesting to see what, if anything, came of the supposed meeting between the general-in-chief and the man so many people in Washington had turned emphatically against. Also, it would take time to sort out Pope's allegations that something was rotten in the Army of the Potomac.

Indeed, even indirectly, John Pope had not been the first to call the President's attention to disaffection at the highest levels within McClellan's army. On August 25, from Yorktown, General Keyes had taken the liberty to write His Excellency the President of the United States. Keyes began by reminding Lincoln that he had advocated abandoning Harrison's Landing well before it occurred; had that move not been ordered, he said, sickness would have reduced the Army of the Potomac to not more than ten thousand men by the middle of September. But the thrust of Keyes' letter was that he felt that his earlier urging that the harder right course of action be followed, rather than the easier wrong, had (in effect) caused the Young Napoleon to leave him and his corps behind on the peninsula.

"I am disposed to complain of nothing but a want of opportunity," Keyes assured Lincoln near the close. His "habits," he added, would be of the greatest service "in the field."[79]

But on that Monday, September's first day, while the President was holding the Jacobins in his cabinet at bay by his unwillingness to be stampeded, McClellan indeed came to Washington. General-in-Chief Halleck, Little Mac wrote later in his official report, "instructed me verbally to take command of [Washington's] defenses, expressly limiting my jurisdiction to the works and their garrisons, and prohibiting me from exercising any control over the troops actively engaged in front under General Pope."[80]

Anent this and earlier developments, George McClellan had been less restrained when he wrote his wife:

> *I had just finished a very severe application for a leave of absence when I received a dispatch from Halleck begging me to help him out of the scrape & take command here—of course I could not refuse, so I came over this morning mad as a March hare, & had a pretty plain talk with him and Abe. . . . If when the whole army returns here (if it ever does) I am not placed in command of all I will either insist upon a long leave of absence or resign. . . .*[81]

During that interview with Halleck on September 1, McClellan stated in his official report, "I suggested to the General-in-Chief the necessity of his going in person or sending one of his personal staff to the army under

General Pope, for the purpose of ascertaining the exact condition of affairs." He sent Colonel J. C. Kelton."[82]

Whether or not the Young Napoleon meant to imply that he questioned Henry Halleck's courage, he may have been ignorant of many other problems that were demanding the attention of the general-in-chief. Details of Nelson's defeat at Richmond, Kentucky, while General Lee's army was suppressing Pope, were slow in arriving but appalled all who read them when they did. And, as had been the case for months, Old Brains was obliged to wonder how much of Don Carlos Buell's wordy combinations of speculation and excuses he could believe—and act upon. Two strong threats in the West remained as well as the one just a few miles west of Washington that General McClellan seemed engaged in manipulating to his advantage.

But after Lincoln's meeting with his cabinet ended, or so it seemed, concerns over McClellan's loyalty and that of his Army of the Potomac and of some of his corps commanders prompted the summoning of the Young Napoleon to General Halleck's quarters. General Pope, in a message to Halleck, had said—referring, of course, to the battle on Saturday—that "it would have been greatly better if Sumner and Franklin had been here three or four days ago."[83] True, but of even greater concern to the commander-in-chief than possible dereliction of duty may have been his doubts as to McClellan's fitness to command anything at all.

Significantly, Halleck had put heaviest weight on John Pope's willingness to fight. But he had recognized skills and advantages that Little Mac possessed and Washington might soon need. In the circumstances, it seems likely that Old Brains used such influence as he had to prevent Lincoln from handing the Young Napoleon over to the politicians.

Yet there was question of loyalty, and it was complex. Clearly, too many officers and men in the Army of the Potomac looked only to McClellan for leadership—which would benefit the Union if that force had to defend the capital. But could this man, who had put forth as a viable alternative to leave John Pope to get out of his own scrape, be trusted?

Yes, General Halleck had said, in effect, by giving McClellan command of Washington's defenses. Lincoln could have countermanded that action, but he did not. Even so, he needed more reassurance. And he sought it directly from Little Mac.

During that Monday afternoon, McClellan wrote in his report, he was again summoned to Halleck's quarters:

The President informed me that he had reason to believe that the Army of the Potomac was not cheerfully co-operating with and supporting General Pope; that he had "always been a friend of mine," and now asked me, as a special favor, to use my influence in correcting this state of things.

I replied, substantially, that I was confident that he was misinformed; that I was sure, whatever estimate the Army of the Potomac might entertain of General Pope, that they would obey his orders, support him to the fullest extent, and do their whole duty. The President, who was much moved, asked me to telegraph to "Fitz-John Porter, or some other of my friends," and try to do away with any feeling that might exist; adding that I could rectify the evil, and that no one else could.

I thereupon told him that I would cheerfully telegraph to General Porter, or do anything else in my power to gratify his wishes and relieve his anxiety; upon which he thanked me very warmly, assured me that he could never forget my action in the matter, &c., and left.

I then wrote the following telegram to General Porter, which was sent to him by the General-in-Chief:

> *I ask of you, for my sake, that of the country, and the old Army of the Potomac, that you and all my friends will lend the fullest and most cordial co-operation to General Pope in all the operations now going on. The destinies of our country, the honor of our arms, are at stake, and all depends now upon the cheerful co-operation of all in the field.*
>
> *This week is the crisis of our fate. Say the same thing to my friends in the Army of the Potomac, and that the last request I have to make of them is, that for their country's sake they will extend to General Pope the same support they ever have to me.*
>
> *I am in charge of the defenses of Washington, and am doing all I can to render your retreat safe, should that become necessary.*

To which he [Porter] sent the following reply:

> *You may rest assured that all your friends, as well as every lover of his country, will ever give, as they have given, to General Pope their cordial co-operation and constant support in the execution of all orders and plans. Our killed, wounded, and enfeebled troops attest our devoted duty.*

Neither at the time I wrote the telegram nor at any other time did I think for one moment that General Porter had been or would be in any manner derelict in the performance of his duty to the nation and its cause. Such an impression never entered my mind. The dispatch in question was written purely at the request of the President.[84]

So General McClellan reported, officially. But in drafting the message he sent Fitz-John Porter via the general-in-chief, after assuring Porter that he was "doing all I can to render your retreat safe, should that become necessary," he crossed-out: "I am now sure that the Presdt & the Genl in Chief neither wish nor intend that the Army shall remain in its present position one moment after its safety becomes jeopardized. It is desirable that it remain in its present position if it is reasonably safe to do so but it will never be sacrificed."[85]

Such editing was indeed prudent. Even as Lincoln, Halleck, and McClellan met in Washington for the second time on September 1, 1862, out near a place called Chantilly west-northwest of Centreville, Stonewall Jackson's foot cavalry—in the process of bypassing Washington's defenses, edging closer to the Potomac and Maryland beyond it—collided with a force General Pope had sent out to oppose it. Despite heavy rain, both sides slugged it out as if the war might be settled by the fight's outcome.

It might have been, if someone as gallant and audacious as Major General Philip Kearny had been in command of the Union armies resisting Lee. Earlier he had fought in Algeria, Mexico, (where he had lost an arm) and Italy. After helping to hold Malvern Hill on the last of the Seven Days, on being told that McClellan had ordered the retreat to Harrison's Landing he had told his division's staff: "I, Philip Kearny, an old soldier, enter my solemn protest against this order. . . . And in full view of the responsibility for such a declaration, I say to you all, such an order can only be prompted by cowardice or treason."[86]

But on this rainy Monday, he died shooting his way out of a ring of Confederates encircling him. General Lee sent his body to Union lines under a flag of truce; and later, at his own expense, he bought Kearny's horse and saddle and sent them to his old friend's widow.[87]

Also killed that afternoon was Major General Isaac Ingalls Stevens, first man in Henry Halleck's West Point class of 1839, who had picked up a regiment's colors from the hands of a dying man and was leading his troops in a charge when he was shot through the head. Long afterward,

Confederate veteran Edward Porter Alexander would write that at about that moment, "the authorities in Washington were about to supersede Pope, and place Stevens in command of the now united armies of Pope and McClellan."[88]

Maybe so; but with both Stevens and Kearny gone to Valhalla, at sundown on Monday, September 1, Abraham Lincoln and Henry Halleck were left with two related questions: How long John Pope could continue the active struggle, and how could the Radicals and their ilk be persuaded that prudence dictated entrusting Washington's defense to McClellan if, as, and when Pope could no longer blunt Jackson's—in fact, Lee's—drives.

8

CHANTILLY, OR OX HILL, or by whatever name Monday's fight west of Washington might be forgotten, was one of the (by then) many battles so far in this war that had settled nothing. Well, not quite; it marked the end of Lee's Second Manassas Campaign, and also of John Pope's conviction that he could still salvage some satisfaction for the Union through expenditures of not much more than valor and determination.

Earlier, General Pope had risked Old Brains' rebuke by advising that he "draw back this army to the intrenchments in front of Washington, and set to work in that secure place to reorganize and rearrange it," adding: "You may avoid great disaster by doing so." And on Monday, September's first day, General Halleck instructed Pope: "If the enemy moves as your last telegram indicates, and you engage him to-day without a decisive victory, I suggest a gradual drawing in of your army to Fairfax, Annandale, or if necessary, farther south, toward Alexandria."[89]

On the day before, from out in Louisville, Brigadier General Boyle had telegraphed President Lincoln:

> *News grows worse from vicinity of Lexington. Many of our troops captured. Rebels on the Lexington side of Kentucky River. Lexington will be in their possession to-morrow. We must have help of drilled troops unless you intend to turn us over to the devil and his imps.*[90]

"So hard it is to have a thing understood as it really is," Abraham Lincoln had remarked in a letter to the North's governors back in July. Now Kentucky's James K. Robinson was trying to help General Halleck perceive his state's plight. On that eventful Monday he telegraphed Old Brains:

From information received General Nelson in the fight at Richmond lost all his artillery. It is of the utmost importance that at least six well-trained batteries be sent immediately to Kentucky from Saint Louis or elsewhere. We ask you to order them without delay.[91]

Between meetings over what, if anything, to do about Generals Lee, Jackson, Pope, and especially McClellan, Halleck answered: "I have telegraphed to General Schofield to ascertain if he can spare any batteries. I await his reply."[92]

Henry Wager Halleck seemed to be operating that day and night as though his "I am utterly tired out" remark in a message to McClellan had been more rhetorical than either true or the breakdown and surrender to the Young Napoleon his detractors would brand it. But on Tuesday, September's second day, the first links were forged in a chain of events that would cause even greater erosion in his reputation than the best (or worst) efforts the Radicals had yet made.

"I was surprised this morning when at bkft by a visit from the Prsdt & Halleck," General McClellan wrote his wife at around noon, "in which [Lincoln] expressed the opinion that the troubles now impending could be overcome better by me than anyone else. Pope is forced to fall back on Washn & as he reenters everything is to come under my command again! A terrible & thankless task—yet I will do my best with God's blessing to perform it. . . ."[93]

In his official report, written much later, the Young Napoleon added a few details:

[The] *President informed me that Colonel Kelton* [Halleck's assistant adjutant general] *had returned from the front; that our affairs were in a bad condition; that the army was in full retreat upon the defenses of Washington; the roads filled with stragglers, &c. He instructed me to take steps at once to stop and collect the stragglers, to place the works in a proper state of defense, and to go out to meet and take command of* [Pope's] *army when it approached the vicinity of the works; then to place the troops in the best position— committing everything to my hands.*[94]

General Halleck was present, but McClellan made no reference to him beyond that fact. Yet if Lincoln had been as explicit in his instructions as Little Mac seemed to want posterity to believe, who other than Old Brains might have done the coaching?

Put differently: what might have Lincoln told McClellan if for any reason Halleck had not been available?

Such questions aside, clearly at least two changes were occurring in the Lincoln-Halleck relationship. Under the pressure of circumstances, and after weeks of abstinence, the President was again becoming directly involved in military decision-making. In so doing, he was accepting and applying what had to have been Old Brains' counsel. But it seems most unlikely that in the confusing conditions then prevailing Lincoln would have responded as he had if indeed he suspected that his general-in-chief had "gone to pieces."[95]

Presumably, after interrupting the Young Napoleon's breakfast the commander-in-chief reverted to his role as President and departed for the Executive Mansion for another meeting with the members of his by then highly agitated cabinet. And soon to arrive at the general-in-chief's office at the War Department was a message from Horatio Wright, in Louisville, that Halleck must have found ironic as well as distressing. "The reverse met with at Richmond," said Wright, "shows that the newly raised troops are not reliable, even with largely superior numbers, and I desire to suggest that a force of disciplined troops, who have seen service, be sent to this department."[96]

Well, fine, Old Brains may have been tempted to reply, *I will send you McClellan's Army of the Potomac.* Instead, he telegraphed Wright simply: "General Granger's division has been ordered from Corinth to Louisville, Ky. General Grant reports that this is the only division which can be spared from West Tennessee."[97]

And, predictably, from Don Carlos Buell in Nashville came a typical mixture of anguish, dismay, and uncertainty spiced with only dashes of news:

> *My whole force will be at Murfreesboro on the 5th, as I advised you. This move becomes necessary, both to accumulate from our extended lines a force sufficient to meet the force of the enemy threatening to advance on this city and to open our communications, now effectively closed.*
>
> *The condition of affairs in Kentucky seems to render something more absolutely necessary. I believe Nashville can be held and Kentucky rescued. What I have will be sufficient here with the defenses that are being prepared, and I propose to move with the remainder of my army rapidly against the enemy in Kentucky.*
>
> *The movements of the enemy [Bragg] from Chattanooga are*

still somewhat obscure, screened as they are by the mountains between us. That Bragg crossed the [Tennessee] *river with a force of 45,000 or 50,000 men is beyond question. He has been making demonstrations to cross the mountains for several days. Some circumstances however justify the suspicion that he is moving up the valley, with the object of getting into Kentucky.*

The wires are cut almost as soon as they can be repaired, and may at any moment be interrupted entirely.

One of Grant's divisions has arrived, but not the other. I expect it within a few days, though I have no certain knowledge when it crossed the [Tennessee] *river.*[98]

One terse sentence was all General-in-Chief Halleck sent Buell: "March where you please, provided you will find the enemy and fight him."[99]

Inadvertently but with heart-stopping accuracy, in those thirteen words—all but two, words of one syllable—Old Brains had summarized everything he had ever read or written in *Elements of Military Art and Science* or learned so far in this war or in fact believed. No other single statement would separate Henry Wager Halleck so distinctly from his contemporaries. Nor would such an order be both so overlooked or so misinterpreted by those, then and later, who found it either to their advantage or intellectual comfort to condemn Old Brains.

8 ★ The Appalling Cost
of Incompetence

SECRETARY OF WAR EDWIN STANTON had been busy collecting cabinet members' signatures to a document he and Salmon Chase had prepared for presentation to the President at Tuesday's meeting. General Halleck would not be present, but his answers to the questions Stanton had raised regarding General McClellan's performance gave considerable weight to the "memorial," in which Stanton had demanded that McClellan be removed.

Attorney General Bates persuaded the authors to moderate the language of the "remonstrance," making it declare that "it was not safe to entrust to Major General McClellan the command of any of the armies of the United States." Even so, Gideon Welles still refused to sign, considering the project a discourtesy to the President.

Abraham Lincoln astonished everyone present at the gathering—and infuriated Stanton and Chase—by announcing that Major General George B. McClellan had been given command of all Union forces in the Washington area. "We must use the tools we have," he added.[1]

Reports of what happened before and during that cabinet meeting vary widely, reflecting the range of participants' support for the Young Napoleon. Ultra-Radical Chase thought that retaining McClellan would "prove a national calamity." West Point graduate Montgomery Blair remained silent. According to one version, Lincoln told the group that at times he felt "almost ready to hang himself" but that he could not see who could do "the work wanted" as well as McClellan.[2]

Apparently to explain Lincoln's having taken an action that angered and appalled many of the men in his cabinet, historian David Herbert Donald would write:

> *Halleck insisted that only McClellan could turn back the invasion. Lincoln agreed reluctantly to restoring McClellan to full command, placing full responsibility on Halleck. "I could never have done it,"* the President explained [later] *to Welles, "for I can never feel confident that* [McClellan] *will do anything."*[3]

Halleck's biographer offered a version suggesting that Lincoln's having asked McClellan to assume "command of all the forces in the field" on that Tuesday morning "came as a surprise to Halleck," and that during the next few days, the President made statements that appeared designed to shift the blame for his highly unpopular decision to Old Brains. "Halleck made little effort to defend himself," wrote Stephen Ambrose, "there was nothing he could do." And he added:

> *McClellan was in command and nearly everyone blamed him* [Halleck]. *Welles characterized Halleck as a man with a "scholarly intellect and, I suppose, some military acquirements, but his mind is heavy and irresolute," and many shared his opinion.*[4]

So would other able, diligent scholars and historians in decades to come, including Margaret Leech, who seemed to want posterity to believe that "[Halleck's] armchair in the War Department held only an irritable bureaucrat."[5]

Missing from such appraisals, however, may well have been something that Abraham Lincoln had somehow perceived before he abandoned attempts at persuasion and peremptorily ordered Old Brains to Washington. Successful lawyers are not bureaucrats; they are fighters. They take definite positions on difficult questions rooted in controversy, and they maintain them with all the skill and vigor they possess. And in Henry Wager Halleck, the Union's President had the benefit of learned and experienced counsel from a man who may well have realized on the day he left San Francisco that in going east he had nothing to gain but everything to lose.

Lawyer Lincoln had been in many such scrapes out in Illinois. More recently, he may also have recognized anew that an attorney who represents himself in an action has a fool for a client, and he had made himself a more attentive listener.

Moreover, Henry Halleck had not become California's most successful and highly respected lawyer by allowing personal considerations—for example, resentment—to distort his reading of the facts of a case. True, on at least one recent occasion, Old Brains had employed sarcasm (or something like unto it) in the course of replying to McClellan's hectoring: "I am fully aware of the crisis and have been for weeks." Yet at no point along the long paper trail had he ever revealed limitations in his estimation of Little Mac more damning than what he had written weeks earlier in a letter to his wife: "General McClellan is in many respects a most excellent and valuable man, but he does not understand strategy and should never plan a campaign."[6]

Well, McClellan was not being asked to plan and conduct anything more than the defense of Washington. And, then and subsequently, Gideon Welles and Halleck's other detractors must not have haunted the War Department's telegraph room, as had Abraham Lincoln, or they would have seen and been depressed and disappointed by John Pope's reports to the general-in-chief on that Tuesday morning, September 2. First, from Fairfax Court House at 7:30:

> *We had another pretty severe fight last night, in which Reno's and Heintzelman's corps were engaged. The enemy massed his force to turn our position by breaking through at Fairfax, but so far without success. He was repulsed by Hooker and McDowell.*
>
> *As soon as the enemy brings up his forces again he will again turn me. I will give battle when I can, but you should come out and see the troops. They were badly demoralized when they joined me, both officers and men, and there is an intense idea among them that they must get behind the intrenchments.*
>
> *The whole force I had for duty yesterday morning was 57,000 men, exclusive of Couch's.*
>
> *The straggling is awful in the regiments from the Peninsula. Unless something can be done to restore tone to this army it will melt away before you know it. Part of Couch's command was detained, and is still so, at Alexandria.*
>
> *The enemy is still in our front. It is his undoubted purpose to keep on, slowly turning our position so as to come in on our right. You had best at once decide what is to be done. The enemy is in very heavy force and must be stopped in some way. These forces under my command are not able to do so in the open field, and if again checked I fear the force will be useless afterwards.*

If you knew the troops here and their condition I think it would be well. You had best look out well for your communications. The enemy from the beginning has been throwing his rear toward the north, and every movement shows that he means to make trouble in Maryland.

Wherever I have attacked him he is in greatly superior force. I would attack to-day, but the troops are absolutely unable.[7]

General Halleck replied:

You will bring your forces as best you can within or near the line of fortification. General McClellan has charge of all the defenses, and you will consider any direction, as to disposition of the troops as they arrive, given by him as coming from me. Do not let the enemy get between you and the works. It is impossible for me to leave Washington.[8]

Clearly, Old Brains had detected the erosion in John Pope's morale since his earliest assurances. "We shall fight till the last," Pope had said on Sunday, the day after his army's scourging by General Lee. And later that day: "I shall attack again to-morrow if I can; the next day certainly." Halleck may also have recalled something else Pope had said: "When there is no heart in their leaders, and every disposition to hang back, much cannot be expected from the men." He had been referring to certain of the Army of the Potomac's officers, but now the comment seemed equally applicable to him.

Only toward the end of General Pope's next message did he show any reaction to Halleck's having—in effect—guillotined him: "Your telegram of this date is just received, and its provisions will be carried out at once." The wire's most significant news—"The enemy has not renewed his attack this morning, but is evidently again beating around to the northeast"—tended to confirm the wisdom of the order Halleck had given.[9]

2

MAJOR GENERAL GEORGE B. MCCLELLAN'S restoration to command pleased most of the troops in the Army of the Potomac but hardly anyone else in the North. Much of the criticism was directed at the President, which was nothing new, but now he could and did point out that all the orders pertaining to the Young Napoleon's resurrection were signed by General-in-Chief Halleck.

Old Brains, however, seemed oblivious to the fact that he had acquired the additional duty of serving as Abraham Lincoln's lightning rod. Early on Tuesday, September 2, 1862, Henry Halleck had written his wife:

> *I have scarcely slept for the past four nights and am almost worn out. . . . General McClellan is now with me and co-operating heartily. Pope has had six days of severe fighting in front of Alexandria and must probably fight again today. We are doing all in our power to secure Washington, and everybody now admits that if I had not brought McClellan's army here when I did, we should have been lost. As it is we have every hope.*[10]

General Lee would most likely have agreed with "everybody" regarding Halleck's earliest key decision back in July. After the fight at Chantilly, he made no attempt to test the Union capital's defenses, manned as they were about to be by Pope's survivors of Second Manassas as well as the rest of McClellan's Army of the Potomac. However, hunger rather than mere prudence was the main reason Lee left the Yankees pretty much alone. "My men had nothing to eat," he explained much later,[11] and headed north and west, lured toward fords along the upper Potomac by Maryland's abundance.

By so doing, General Lee presented the Union's high command with a vexing question. Earlier, Lincoln had assured his secretary, John Hay, and perhaps others that McClellan's assignment was limited and even temporary. "We must use the tools we have," he had declared. "There is no man in the army who can man these fortifications and lick these troops of ours into shape half as well. . . . If he can't fight himself, he excels in making others ready to fight."[12] Well, yes—but who would lead the Union's reorganized and refitted eastern armies out of Washington's defenses to prevent the Confederates from invading the North?

Secretary of War Stanton provided an answer on Wednesday, September 3, 1862, that seemed crafted to protect the administration from liability through adroit use of his pen:

> *Ordered, that the General-in-Chief, Major-General Halleck, immediately commence, and proceed with all possible dispatch, to organize an army for active operations, from all the material within and coming within his control, independent of the forces he may*

deem necessary for the defense of Washington, when such army shall take the field.

By order of the President.[13]

This was about as far as any armchair bureaucrats could go toward insuring themselves against criticism if worse came to worst. Yet the suspicion lingers that lawyer Henry Halleck may well have advised his client Lincoln to back out completely *on paper.* If so, Old Brains may have recognized and indeed anticipated that—as in providing for the capital's defense—when the "army for active operations" was ready to "take the field," the only general officer anywhere near capable of commanding it would be George B. McClellan.[14]

Might Lincoln and Stanton have used the order as a signal that they wanted Halleck to assume command of the rebuilt eastern army? "Halleck cast a blind eye at the invitation and rewrote it for General McClellan," wrote a recent Young Napoleon biographer,[15] reflecting generations of anti-Halleck bias.

Facts: Lincoln had ordered Old Brains *away from* the only field command he really had wanted; absent Halleck's presence, Confederates had identified and were advancing through the weakest points in the West; coping with those threats required a real general-in-chief who could deal with two or more disasters at the same time; and if Halleck took the field in the east, no general officer was qualified to replace him, *and* Lincoln would still have to face the question of what to do with (or about) General McClellan.

That Stanton's action came as no surprise to General Halleck was suggested also by the "invitation" he rewrote and sent to the Young Napoleon before midnight on that Wednesday, even though he had not received Stanton's order until two hours earlier. Well-prepared, apparently, Old Brains worded the text so as to retain control of the desired operation but to elicit McClellan's cooperation during the essential preparations:

> *There is every possibility that the enemy, baffled in his intended capture of Washington, will cross the Potomac, and make a raid into Maryland or Pennsylvania. A movable army must be immediately organized to meet him again in the field. You will, therefore, report the approximate force of each corps of the three armies now in the vicinity of Washington, which can be prepared in the next two days to take the field, and have them supplied and ready for that service.*[16]

Surely Old Brains had not forgotten that it had taken him several weeks after Shiloh to combine Grant's, Buell's, and Pope's forces into the field army he led to Corinth, yet he was giving Little Mac only *two days* in which to comply with his order. Was Halleck starting a paper trail that might be useful if the Radical-dominated Joint Congressional Committee on the Conduct of the War later selected him for persecution? More likely, probably, was the respect he had gained since mid-August for the strategic and tactical skill and especially for the audacity of his long-ago brother engineer, Robert E. Lee.

George McClellan, too, had served with Lee on Winfield Scott's staff during the advance from Vera Cruz to Mexico City; and surely the wrecking of John Pope's army at Manassas was fresh in his mind. Also, Lincoln had been quite right in recalling that "[McClellan] excels in making others ready to fight."

But that Little Mac was confident that Halleck would give him command of the "active army" in due course was reflected in reports to the general-in-chief that included details of cavalryman Alfred Pleasanton's efforts to find the enemy and at least track him. Another indication that McClellan was no longer harboring suspicions that "the dolts in Washn" were bent on his destruction was his having opened a letter to Mary Ellen on September 3 by reporting only that "I am now about to jump into the saddle & will be off all day. . . ."[17]

For George McClellan, it was July and August of 1861 all over again: his mission was to restore a whipped army to combat effectiveness. But in getting out of his scrape without more than a fraction of the reinforcements Halleck had ordered McClellan to rush to him, Pope had maintained much stronger control over his troops after Second Bull Run than had Irvin McDowell in the first debacle a little over a year before. This simplified Little Mac's task; and later, Halleck helped him by suspending compliance with an order requiring relief from command of Major Generals Fitz-John Porter and William Franklin pending disposition of charges filed by General Pope calling for their trial by court-martial or boards of inquiry.[18]

3

WHILE TO HIS VERY GREAT CREDIT (from the Union's point of view) General McClellan was jumping into his saddle and making others ready to fight, out in Tennessee Don Carlos Buell was concentrating his forces to protect Nashville. Braxton Bragg, however, seemed headed directly for

Kentucky. Once he was well north of Buell, Bragg and Kirby Smith could join forces and either annihilate Buell's army or seize Louisville. But even by the end of September's first week, the Confederates' drives in the West could be considered successes; they had attracted so many federal units northeastward that large portions of regions Halleck had secured earlier—West Tennessee, northern Mississippi, and Alabama—were back under rebel control. And if in fact Bragg and Kirby Smith whipped Buell, the entire heartland would be lost.[19]

Coupled with the anxieties such actual and potential situations were causing in Washington was frustration. General Halleck, in particular, was unable to do more than encourage Buell to find Bragg and fight him. If Buell could not or would not do that, Old Brains' having persuaded the administration to postpone his beheading would appear to have been a colossal mistake. Yet what general could have been put in Buell's place?

Worse, a Confederate victory in the West might well be blamed on Halleck's having scattered his forces after he captured Corinth: Bragg had recognized the opportunity to defeat Halleck by attacking one of his army's fragments, and he had moved the better part of a thousand miles to do precisely that. Yet Buell's mission had been to bring East Tennessee's Unionists back under the Stars and Stripes—and that effort had been ordered by Abraham Lincoln and repeated frequently.

Major General Horatio Wright's plight was reflected in a message he sent Halleck from Cincinnati on September's fourth day: "Can you tell me in regard to the importance of holding the railroad from Bowling Green to Louisville? If garrisons are to be withdrawn, the sooner the better."[20]

General Halleck's reply was brief, blunt, and honest even if it was unsatisfactory:

> *As I know neither where Buell is nor the position of the enemy, I cannot advise in regard to the importance of holding Bowling Green. If the garrison is likely to be cut off, withdraw it of course. The great object should now be to concentrate your forces upon the best point to strike the enemy.*[21]

Abraham Lincoln, in early September a regular visitor to the War Department's telegraph room, asked General Boyle, in Louisville, "Where is Bragg? What do you know on the subject?"[22] In Tennessee, Boyle replied.[23]

Still curious, the President queried Horatio Wright in Cincinnati: "Do you know to any certainty where General Bragg is? May he not be in Virginia?"[24] No, replied Wright, "Nothing reliable about Bragg. . . . All

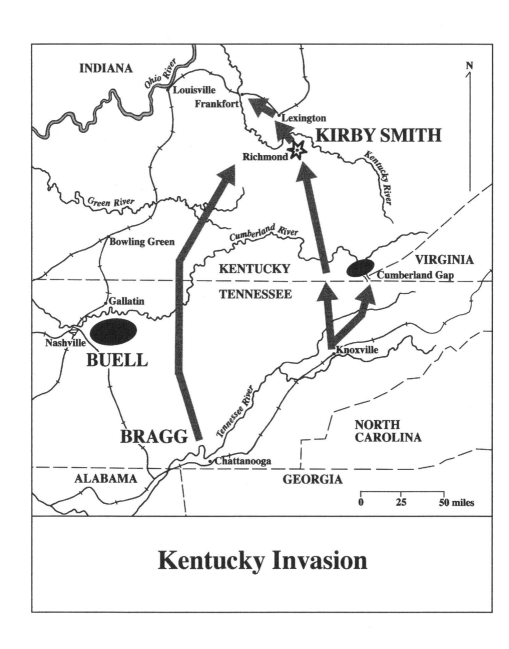

Kentucky Invasion

intelligence coming from the southward is very unreliable."[25]

Then General Boyle telegraphed Lincoln: "Intelligent persons who left Nashville on the 6th instant say that nothing is known of Bragg's army in Tennessee. There is some conjecture that Bragg may have joined the forces near Washington."[26]

Following that, the commander-in-chief addressed a curiously lawyer-like question to Don Carlos Buell, who ought to have known more about Braxton Bragg's whereabouts all along than anyone: "What degree of certainty have you that Bragg with his command is not now in the valley of the Shenandoah, Virginia?"[27]

The presumptive witness being interrogated was only partially responsive to the question. "Bragg is certainly this side of the Cumberland Mountains with his whole force," Buell replied, "except what is in Kentucky under Kirby Smith." That strong but unsubstantiated statement made, Don Carlos added to the fog of war:

> [Bragg's] *movements will probably depend on mine. I expect that for the want of supplies I can neither follow him nor remain here. Think I must withdraw from Tennessee. I shall not abandon Tennessee while it is possible to hold on. Cut off effectively from supplies, it is impossible for me to operate in force where I am; but I shall endeavor to hold Nashville, and at the same time drive Smith out of Kentucky and hold my communications.*[28]

Surely Lincoln and Halleck must have read Buell's telegram over and over, attempting to discern what, if anything at all, the general actually meant to do. Buell's last sentence, in particular, was nonsense:

- *". . . it is impossible for me to operate in force where I am;*
- *I shall endeavor to hold Nashville,*
- *and at the same time drive Smith out of Kentucky*
- *and hold my communications."*

And so it was that Lincoln's attempt to find out if Braxton Bragg had repeated his Munchasen feat of moving his army from Tupelo to Chattanooga by planting it within striking distance of Washington came to naught. Even so, from those futile exchanges of ignorance and confusion, Henry Halleck must have learned anew both how wrong it was for any war managers in a distant capital to try to control field armies' operations, and also how pitifully vulnerable the Union was to being defeated in battle because of its appalling deficiency in the quality of its general officers.

4

HAD THE ARMY OF THE POTOMAC been defeated in Maryland, George B. McClellan declared near the end of his life, "I would, no doubt, have been tried for assuming authority without orders, and . . . would probably have been condemned to death."[29] Perhaps. The only facts were, on the morning of Friday, September 5, 1862, President Lincoln and General Halleck visited McClellan's quarters; and soon thereafter, the Young Napoleon took the army he was rebuilding into the field against the enemy. Absent a written order giving McClellan command for the purpose of fighting Lee, the presumption was that either Lincoln or Halleck had given him instructions verbally; later, each claimed that the other had done it. Questions survived all of the participants.

Did it matter? No, except to the extent posterity would misinterpret a statement Halleck made to the effect that he did not know beforehand that Lincoln would give such an order.[30] The true point of interest, here, was the quality of the Halleck-Lincoln relationship, which may well have been better than connoisseurs of controversy allege.

Viewed from a legal standpoint, no formal order was necessary. McClellan's status as commander of the Army of the Potomac—hence, his authority to take his forces into the field—had not been changed by the shuffling of units before and after Second Bull Run. His missions to restore the armies to combat effectiveness and to defend Washington amounted to additional duties. Lawyer Halleck would have understood this to have been the case, and it was reasonable for him to have assumed that lawyer Lincoln concurred.

For the President to have reported that General Halleck gave McClellan the verbal order was consistent with his having directed Old Brains to sign the order that appeared to have returned McClellan to high command. Radicals and other foes of the administration were likely to object vehemently to any employment of McClellan. With a sturdy lightning rod available to absorb thunderbolts thrown by political opponents, why not use him?

Such, in early September, may have been the course the relationship was taking. Lincoln and Halleck agreed on most questions involving military operations. Similarly, now that John Pope was sidetracked, McClellan's messages to Old Brains reflected cordial cooperation; and as early as September 4, Halleck was relaying reports of Confederate movements near the Potomac to Little Mac as though it were already understood that he would take the army out to deal with Lee.[31]

In any event, Henry Halleck did not consider the morning's visit to McClellan's house important enough to mention in the letter he wrote his wife on that Friday, September 5. Instead, he opened by giving himself the credit he was unlikely to receive from any other source:

> *I hope and believe I have saved the capital from the terrible crisis brought upon us by the stupidity of others. I got McClellan's army here just in time—and barely that—to save us.*
>
> *Few can conceive the terrible anxiety I have had within the past month. I foresaw all that has occurred, but I feared to tell it to more than a few in strict confidence lest I should produce a panic. Generals Cullum, Meigs, the Secretary of War, and a few of the members of my staff were the only persons to whom I told what I considered our real danger—the capture of Washington. I think it is now past. . . .*
>
> *I hardly know myself how I am able to keep up amidst the excitement and labor of my office. The generals all around me are quarreling among themselves, while I am doing all in my power to conciliate and satisfy. It is sad to witness the selfishness of men at this time of sore trial. I have no ambition or hopes beyond my present position, and would resign that to-morrow if I could do so conscientiously. I want to go back to private life as soon as possible and never again to put my foot in Washington.*
>
> *We are organizing a new army as rapidly as possible and hope to do better next time. Pope was not defeated, but he failed to defeat the enemy. He is in ill-humor with everybody, and very likely will pitch into me. I think, however, he will again be my friend in a few days.*[32]

Around noon on that Friday, from Arlington, John Pope telegraphed Halleck:

> *I have received an order from General McClellan to have my command in readiness to march with three days' rations and further details of the march. What is my command, and where is it? McClellan has scattered it about in all directions, and has not*

informed me of the position of a single regiment. Am I to take the field under McClellan's orders?[33]

Soldier Halleck replied to soldier Pope simply and directly: "The armies of the Potomac and Virginia being consolidated, you will report for orders to the Secretary of War."[34]

That done, Old Brains informed McClellan of that and other changes:

The President has directed that General Pope be relieved and report to War Department; that Hooker be assigned to command of Porter's corps, and that Franklin's corps be temporarily attached to Heintzelman's. The orders will be issued this afternoon. Generals Porter and Franklin are to be relieved from duty till the charges against them are examined. I give you this memorandum in advance of the orders, so that you may act accordingly in putting forces in the field.[35]

During that Friday, Major General John E. Wool, veteran of the War of 1812, commanding the military district that included Harpers Ferry, had passed reports along to the general-in-chief suggesting that at least thirty thousand rebels had crossed the Potomac into Maryland near the mouth of the Monocacy River.[36] Old Brains replied:

I find it impossible to get this army into the field again in large force for a day or two. In the mean time Harper's Ferry may be attacked and overwhelmed. I leave all dispositions there to your experience and local knowledge. I beg leave, however, to suggest the propriety of withdrawing all our forces in that vicinity to Maryland Heights [just north of the village]. *I have no personal knowledge of the ground, and merely make the suggestion to you.*[37]

General McClellan's authority to take the field with his army, the subject of a meeting at his house earlier on that Friday, was confirmed in a telegram Halleck sent him: "I think there can be no doubt that the enemy are crossing the Potomac in force, and that you had better dispatch General Sumner and additional forces to follow. If you agree with me, let our troops move immediately."[38]

With General Lee invading Maryland, Braxton Bragg impossible to locate, and Kirby Smith menacing the Ohio River frontier, Abraham Lincoln was a very long way from any victory that would enable him to issue the emancipation proclamation which he had been drafting during quiet moments in the telegraph room.[39] But Washington had not been seized and pillaged by the Confederates, and the Union's high command had not been shattered by frictions within it. Heartened considerably by having read in the War Department's message file exhortations such as *March where you please, provided you find the enemy and fight him* and *let our troops move immediately,* the President could once again turn his thoughts to matters transcending the stupidity of others and the selfishness of men. At around this time, he wrote:

> *The will of God prevails. In great contests each party claims to act in accordance with the will of God. Both* may *be, and one* must *be wrong. God can not be for, and* against, *the same thing at the same time. In the present civil war it is quite possible that God's purpose is something different from the purpose of either party—and yet the human instrumentalities, working just as they do, are of the best adaptation to effect His purpose. I am almost ready to say that this is probably true—that God wills this contest, and wills that it shall not end yet. By his mere quiet power, on the minds of the now contestants, He could have either* saved *or* destroyed *the Union without a human contest. Yet the contest began. And having begun He could give the final victory to either side any day. Yet the contest proceeds.*[40]

5

HARDLY HAD THE FIRING CEASED in northern Virginia before the search for scapegoats began. Major General John Pope, of course, was an obvious candidate for the angled blade, and he invoked the military justice system in the hope of wreaking vengeance upon Fitz-John Porter and William Franklin. Summoning John Pope from the West back in June had been one of Abraham Lincoln's mistakes, but an earlier and more serious one had been his selection of George McClellan. Lincoln was beyond the mob's reach, and thanks to General Halleck, so was the Young Napoleon—at least for the time being. And Halleck? He had lost his first major battle as general-in-chief, or so it appeared; but at the moment, no replacement was in sight.

Primarily because Pope had consigned Major General Nathaniel Banks to duties in the rear, where he could do little or no harm, the Waltham Bobbin Boy—among the first politicians the abysmally unprepared commander-in-chief had empowered with high rank—was merely relieved of command of his corps and assigned to oversee Washington's defenses once McClellan's reorganized and refitted troops took the field. For Irvin McDowell, two whippings at Manassas were two too many; after surviving a court of inquiry, he would spend the rest of the war behind desks.

Pope had courted and won the Radicals' approval before he transferred his headquarters to the saddle. McDowell was a protege of Treasury Secretary Salmon Chase, the Jacobins' man in Lincoln's cabinet. Condemning McClellan's rescue from oblivion, Chase said, "I thought that there were brave, capable & loyal officers such as Hooker, Sumner, Burnside and many more who might be named, to whom the command of armies might be more safely & much more properly entrusted." Ohio Senator John Sherman, Cump's brother, was no Radical but even he declared that he considered Lincoln and General McClellan the country's worst enemies.[41] That Edwin Stanton and Henry Halleck did not stimulate more ultra Radical wrath was probably due to the Jacobins' tendency to go exclusively for the jugular.

While the political pot boiled, General McClellan was busy doing what Lincoln and Halleck knew he did best. In a minimum of time, he and members of his staff had repaired most of the damage Second Bull Run had inflicted on the armies, including their logistics and their troops' morale. By Friday, September 5, 1862, units leaving Washington on their way out to find and fight Lee's Army of Northern Virginia were cheering as they marched past McClellan's house—notably, not past the Executive Mansion.

On Saturday, though, Little Mac apparently grew tired of waiting for Old Brains to respond to the message he had sent him regarding his access to the services of Porter and Franklin. In a telegram marked *Confidential,* he went over Halleck's head to "Your Excellency." Lincoln, proving that he and his general-in-chief were singing from the same page of the same songbook, replied simply: "With entire respect, I must repeat that General Halleck controls these questions."[42]

Little Mac got the two generals he wanted, which must have put him in the mood to forgive and forget. To Mary Ellen on the afternoon of the next day, Sunday, September 7, he wrote:

> *I leave in a couple of hours to take command of the army in the field. I shall go to Rockville* [Maryland] *tonight & start out after the rebels tomorrow. I shall have nearly 100,000 men, old & new, & hope with God's blessing to gain a decisive victory.*

> *I think we shall win for the men are now in good spirits—confident in their General & all united in sentiment. Pope & McDowell have morally killed themselves—& are relieved from command—a signal instance of retributive justice. I have done nothing towards this—it has done itself. I now have the confidence of the Govt & the love of the army—my enemies are crushed, silent & disarmed—if I defeat the rebels I shall be master of the situation. . . .*[43]

Most people in the North would have meant the rebels when they wrote the word *enemies,* but George McClellan's priorities were as extraordinary as his letter-writing style was bizarre. The fact was, he did not seem to devote much thought to Confederates. He was so reluctant to attack Joe Johnston's army at Manassas in the fall and winter of 1861 that the Radicals suspected him of treason. Rather than use his heavy numerical superiority at Yorktown, he resorted to a long, nigh-bloodless, and ultimately futile siege. For weeks, at the gates of Richmond, he made no aggressive move. When Lee attacked in late June, McClellan's objective appeared to be merely to save his army. Defending the capital—not destroying the Confederate army threatening it—had seemed his main concern in the matter of Pope's recent scrape. And now, he saw defeating the rebels as a means of becoming "master of the situation," not of restoring the Union.

Actually, circumstances were making General Lee easier to whip with each passing day, each mile northward into Maryland his army advanced. Thousands of his men had refused to cross the Potomac. They were in the army to resist federal coercion, repel invasion, and secure their independence; moving into the North, they believed, would lower them to the level of the degenerate Yankees.

Such desertions cost Lee the equivalent of several divisions, and the men who drifted away could not be replaced. Moreover, he needed to shift his main line of communications westward, through the Shenandoah Valley. He could not do that, or indeed advance past Frederick, until he eliminated federal garrisons at Martinsburg and Harpers Ferry—which meant that he would have to split his army again, depleted as it was, this time into *four* elements instead of just two.

Such was the background for Special Orders No. 191, issued by Lee at Frederick on Tuesday, September 9, 1862. Stonewall Jackson was to move west and south to destroy the Union detachment at Martinsburg, then eastward to rid the war of the one at Harpers Ferry. Two other forces were to operate north of Harpers Ferry to prevent the Yankees from escaping.

Longstreet was to move from Frederick westward to Hagerstown, the point at which all of Lee's units were to reassemble for resumption of the offensive. All of the Confederate units went their separate ways on Wednesday, September 10.[44]

Two days earlier, General McClellan had opened his headquarters at Rockville, Maryland, about seventeen miles northwest of Washington. From there he reported to the general-in-chief:

> *I have ordered reconnaissances in all directions to-morrow, includ-ing one well to the north and northwest. I think that we are now in position to prevent any attack in force on Baltimore, while we cover Washington on this side. . . . Our information is still entirely too indefinite to justify definitive action. I am ready to push in any direction, and hope very soon to have the supplies and transportation so regulated that we can safely move, farther from Washington, and clear Maryland of the rebels. . . . As soon as I find out where to strike, I will be after them [the rebels] without an hour's delay.[45]*

Even more pleasing to Halleck must have been another message from Rockville that arrived less than two hours later: "After full consideration, I have determined to advance the whole force to-morrow. . . ."[46]

Politicians in Pennsylvania, however, had been driven to the edge of panic by reports of General Lee's advance. From Harrisburg, Governor Andrew G. Curtin bombarded Edwin Stanton with requests for troops and authority to direct certain military preparations in his state. To one such message, the secretary of war replied: "Your telegram of last night in regard to your proposed military operations was referred to the General-in-Chief, for such directions as he might deem proper under the circumstances. He will communicate with you."[47]

General Halleck did:

> *It is not deemed advisable to assemble troops at so many different points. For the present we want all troops sent here. We can protect Harrisburg better from this vicinity than to weaken our force by leaving [units] there. Should our communications be cut off, of course, we cannot get them here. Under these circumstances, I cannot consent to the retention of troops at Harrisburg, nor can we spare any to send there.[48]*

"I have just received your message," Curtin wired back. "You evidently

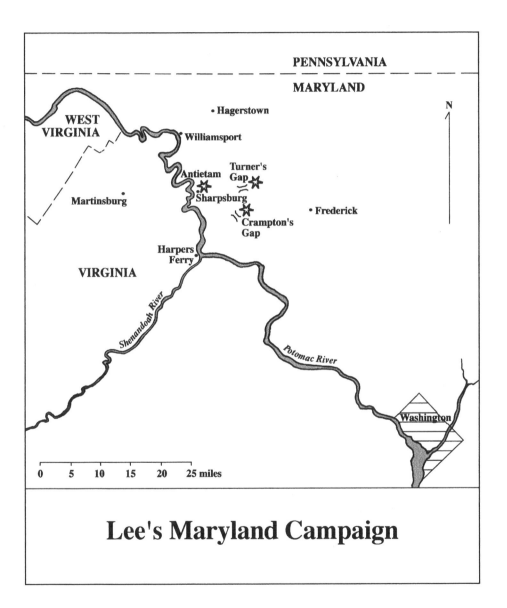

Lee's Maryland Campaign

do not understand my wishes on the subject."[49] Not likely; but soldier-lawyer Halleck had made his case, and both Stanton and Lincoln allowed Old Brains' judgment to prevail.

On the same day, Tuesday, September 9, 1862, to His Excellency the President came a communication from Thomas A. Webster, vice chairman of Philadelphia's Citizens' Bounty Fund Committee, enclosing a resolution passed by that body calling for "all of the aid in troops, arms, and material of war which can be spared for the defense of Philadelphia. . . ."[50]

Lincoln—by nature, experience, and position far more sensitive to political nuances than Halleck—responded to Webster, but he did so in words that may well have reflected some coaching in military art and science by Old Brains:

> *Your dispatch received and referred to General Halleck, who must control the questions presented. While I am not surprised at your anxiety, I do not think you are in any danger. If half our troops were in Philadelphia, the enemy could take it, because he would not fear to leave the other half in his rear; but with the whole of them here* [near Washington], *he dares not leave them in his rear.*[51]

Such, in the wake of Second Bull Run, were the ways in which relationships were developing among the three lawyers who were also the Union's land war managers: Lincoln, Stanton, and Halleck. But the secretary of war had failed to bring about McClellan's removal. Obliged as he was to recuse himself from dealing with the Young Napoleon, that burden had to be shared by the President and Old Brains.

By the afternoon of Thursday, September 11, 1862, General McClellan appeared to have reverted to a practice with which Lincoln was all too familiar. "Please send forward all the troops you can spare from Washington," he telegraphed the general-in-chief from Rockville, "particularly Porter's, Heintzelman's, Sigel's, and all the other old troops."[52]

Evidently, Halleck took the matter to the Executive Mansion. After reviewing the possible consequences, a reply signed by Lincoln was sent to McClellan at 6:00 p.m. "This is explanatory," the text began, implying that more thought should be given to the request. The commander-in-chief (or Halleck) continued:

> *If Porter, Heintzelman, and Sigel were sent you, it would sweep everything from the other* [south] *side of the* [Potomac], *because the new troops have been distributed among them, as I understand.*

Porter reports himself 21,000 strong, which can only be by the addition of new troops. He is ordered to-night to join you as quickly as possible. I am sending you all that can be spared, and I hope others can follow Porter very soon.[53]

Before McClellan could have received that answer, or so it seemed, he had composed a very long analysis of the situation—one that tended to support his request for more men but that also contained more references to the Union's enemies than had been his wont. Addressed to Halleck, he said in his text:

At the time this army moved from Washington, it was not known what the intentions of the rebels were in placing their forces on this side of the Potomac. . . . In view of this uncertain condition of things, I left what I conceived to be a sufficient force to defend the city against any army they could bring against it from the Virginia side of the Potomac.

This uncertainty, in my judgment, exists no longer. All the evidence that has been accumulated from various sources since we left Washington goes to prove most conclusively that almost the entire rebel army in Virginia, amounting to not less than 120,000 men, is in the vicinity of Frederick City. . . . Everything seems to indicate that they intend to hazard all upon the issue of the coming battle. They are probably aware that their forces are numerically superior to ours by at least 25 per cent.

This, with the prestige of their recent successes, will, without doubt, inspire them with a confidence which will cause them to fight well. The momentous consequences involved in the struggle of the next few days impels me, at the risk of being considered slow and overcautious, to most earnestly recommend that every available man be at once added to this army.

I believe this army fully appreciates the importance of a victory at this time, and will fight well; but the result of a general battle, with such odds as the enemy now appears to have against us, might, to say the least, be doubtful; and if we should be defeated the consequences to the country would be disastrous in the extreme.

Under these circumstances, I would recommend that one or two of the three army corps now on the Potomac, opposite Washington, be at once withdrawn and sent to re-enforce this army. I would also advise that the force of Colonel Miles, at Harper's Ferry, where it can be of but little use, and is continually exposed to be cut off by the enemy, be immediately ordered here. This would add about 15,000 old troops to our present force, and would greatly strengthen us.

If there are any rebel forces remaining on the other side of the Potomac, they must be so few that the troops left in the forts, after the two corps shall have been withdrawn, will be sufficient to check them; and, with the large cavalry force now on that side kept well out in front to give warning of the distant approach of any very large army, a part of this army might be sent back within the intrenchments to assist in repelling an attack.

But even if Washington should be taken while these armies are confronting each other, this would not, in my judgment, bear comparison with the ruin and disaster which would follow a signal defeat of this army. If we should be successful in conquering the gigantic rebel army before us, we would have no difficulty in recovering [Washington].

On the other hand, should their force prove sufficiently powerful to defeat us, would all the forces now around Washington be sufficient to prevent such a victorious army from carrying the works on this side of the Potomac, after they are uncovered by our army? I think not.

From the moment the rebels commenced the policy of concentrating their forces, and with their large masses of troops operating against our scattered forces, they have been successful. They are undoubtedly pursuing the same now, and are prepared to take advantage of any division of our troops in future.

I, therefore, most respectfully, but strenuously, urge upon you the absolute necessity, at this critical juncture, of uniting all our disposable forces. Every other consideration should yield to this, and if we defeat the army now arrayed before us, the rebellion is crushed, for I do not believe they can organize another army. But if we should be so unfortunate as to meet with defeat, our country is at their mercy.[54]

At 9 p.m. on that Thursday evening, Old Brains simply reiterated what he and Lincoln had told McClellan earlier: "General Fitz John Porter's corps has been ordered to move to-morrow to Brookville, via Leesborough [sic], to report to you for duty in the field."[55]

Brevity was characteristic of Henry Halleck's messages, but he may have been too stunned by McClellan's effusions to say more. "All the evidence that has been accumulated from various sources since we left Washington goes to prove most conclusively that almost the entire rebel army in Virginia, amounting to not less than 120,000 men, is in the vicinity of Frederick City," Little Mac had asserted. "Everything seems to indicate that they intend to hazard all upon the issue of the coming battle."

What evidence? What indications of intent?

Tough-minded lawyer that he was, General-in-Chief Halleck would surely have been quick to recognize something that Abraham Lincoln had perceived while Old Brains was still out West: George Brinton McClellan was no general, and maybe not even a soldier, but a man driven by fantasies.

Yet, Halleck had been highly instrumental in retaining him in a position in which he could do great harm. Earlier, he had said of the Young Napoleon in a letter to Mrs. Halleck, "he does not understand strategy and should never plan a campaign." Old Brains had been wrong: McClellan should never have been allowed anywhere near a war.

6

WAR, WROTE CLAUSEWITZ, *is the extension of politics by other means.* But politicians in the North were by no means willing to stand aside and let the generals and their armies fight it out until peace could be restored. Abraham Lincoln, of course, had a Constitutionally imposed duty to act as commander-in-chief of the Union's armed forces. But governors of states in harm's way were quick to seek roles involving control of military units and operations—one of the few legitimate functions of the federal government. And the more attention the Confederate drives in Maryland and in the West received, the hotter grew the wires linking state capitals with the War Department's telegraph room.

Pennsylvania's Governor Curtin had already discovered that General-in-Chief Halleck was not in awe of him. Yet Old Brains was considering each incoming gubernatorial squawk on its merits, as was shown in the dispute between politicians in Kentucky and Ohio over troops under the command of Major General Horatio Wright.

On Thursday, September 11, 1862, from Louisville, Kentucky's Governor James K. Robinson telegraphed General Wright at Cincinnati:

> *I have this morning reliable information that General* [Kirby]
> *Smith is now concentrating his troops at Frankfort for speedy attack*

on this place [Louisville]. . . . *There are not 5,000* [rebel] *troops in all in the direction of Cincinnati. The entire demonstration there is a delusion, rely upon it, and that city is in no danger.*

You have now 40,000 troops there and some 25,000 here, but troops are being ordered from here as fast as transportation can be obtained. This will be known to the enemy and will hasten his attack here and insure his success.

I most earnestly urge a reversal of this policy. If not done, in my opinion this city is lost and with it Kentucky. With all respect I am confident that you are misinformed and misled by those interested in and alarmed for Cincinnati. As the Governor of Kentucky I feel constrained to protest against a course which will result in an unnecessary sacrifice of this city and of my State.

My deep interest is my apology for this, my dispatch of yesterday being unanswered.[56]

Not having received a reply from Wright within the limits of his patience, Robinson then sent essentially the same text to the general-in-chief, closing with: "I feel constrained to appeal to you as my last effort to save Kentucky."[57] James Guthrie, a prominent Louisville citizen, also telegraphed his concern over "the fact that the possession of Louisville will give the State to the Confederates and lead to the capture of Buell's army. . . ." while the rebels' "designs in possession of Cincinnati could lead to no such consequences."[58]

Halleck wired Wright:

Governor Robinson reports that you are intending to remove the troops at Louisville to Cincinnati, and he and others protest against it. If possible do not abandon Louisville, for with it we lose Kentucky. I have no desire to interfere with your details, but we ought not to lose Louisville. Please answer where your troops are and what you intend to do.[59]

Wright had already replied to the governor's messages. "I stopped the further sending of troops from Louisville this morning in consequence of your dispatches of yesterday," he had written Robinson, "and not from a conviction that the information you forwarded was correct."[60] That done, and though it was almost midnight, he telegraphed Halleck:

I had no intention of abandoning Louisville or leaving it without strong protection. Cincinnati is seriously threatened, while the former is not. Two regiments only have been withdrawn from Louisville, leaving there twenty-three regiments of infantry, two of cavalry, and three complete and two incomplete batteries, to which should be added four or five more regiments and ten guns ordered in from Lebanon. It may be necessary to draw still further upon this force, but Louisville will be made safe.[61]

Brigadier General Boyle, a lawyer in peacetime, now commanding the military district of Louisville but more in the habit of communicating directly with "His Excellency" than of observing the chain of command, had sent the same sort of telegram to Lincoln on Thursday that Governor Robinson had sent Halleck.[62] On Friday the President replied to Boyle in a manner that must have surprised the general:

Your dispatch of last evening received. Where is the enemy which you dread in Louisville? How near to you? What is General Gilbert's opinion? With all possible respect for you I must think General Wright's military opinion is the better. He is as much responsible for Louisville as for Cincinnati. General Halleck telegraphed him on this very subject yesterday and I telegraph him now; but for us here to control him there on the ground would be a babel of confusion which would be utterly ruinous. Where do you understand Buell to be and what is he doing?[63]

Confusion is all Lincoln got in return.[64]

By Sunday, September 14, 1862, General Buell had moved the bulk of his army to Bowling Green, Kentucky, according to a message he sent from there on that day to General Halleck:

It has been apparent to me for some time that, on purely military grounds, the force in Middle Tennessee [Buell's] should fall back on its base [Louisville]. The political effect, however, of such a move occurred to me so serious that I have hesitated to execute it, still hoping that the force in Kentucky would be able to open my communications.

As that was not done it became absolutely necessary to fall back, with a portion of the force at least, to act against the enemy in Kentucky. I commenced that move Sunday last with five divisions, but its execution was delayed a couple of days by the reported movements of the enemy. I had expected that Bragg would detach a portion of his force to re-enforce Kirby Smith, while he, with the balance, would await the period of our starving out in Tennessee. It now appears that he is moving his whole force into Kentucky, and it is now concentrated, or nearly so, at Glasgow.

I have therefore ordered up all but one division from Nashville. They will arrive here on the 17th. I arrived here to-day with two divisions of the first force and shall commence to move against Bragg's force on the 16th.

You will not fail to observe that he is virtually between me and Louisville, and all communications by telegraph and railroad are cut off. I am not insensible to the difficulty and embarrassment of the position, but it must be so for him also, and I hope it may result in his discomfiture and not ours.

The danger is that he may form a junction with Smith. I apprehend that the latter may be moving for that object now. I am retaining only a nominal hold on Nashville and at the risk of losing the force (about 5,000 men) that I have there; but I trust to the belief that there is not for the present any organized force to come against it unless Price pauses longer, and I deem it better to do so than to undergo the political effect of entirely abandoning the place. I would like your instructions or views about it. It may still be possible to withdraw the remainder of the force.[65]

Well, possibly. Andrew Johnson, Tennessee's military governor, was even then telegraphing General Buell: "It is all-important that Major-General Thomas and his forces, as now assigned, should remain at Nashville. . . . If our strength is much reduced at this point [Bragg] will be induced to attack Nashville as a matter of course. . . ."[66]

Old Brains' instructions to Buell might well have been the same as he had given him earlier: *March where you please, provided you find the enemy and fight him.* The political effect of leaving only one division in Nashville, however, the general-in-chief would leave to the President to appraise.

7

"At last advices, Burnside's troops were within 2 miles of New Market," General McClellan informed Halleck in a wire received in Washington very early in the morning on Friday, September 12. "I have

ordered him to advance to-morrow, if possible, to Frederick and occupy it
. . . I am much obliged to you for sending me Porter's corps, and should like
the remainder of Keyes' corps as soon as possible. I shall follow up the rebels
as rapidly as possible."[67]

Fine, Old Brains may have thought, but *where were* those rebels?
Lincoln, too, had wondered, and on Thursday he had consulted Governor
Curtin in Harrisburg: "Please tell me at once what is your latest news from
or toward Hagerstown, or of the enemy's movements in any direction."[68]

Back came two replies. In the first, Curtin placed rebel cavalry in
Hagerstown but his message was otherwise too vague to be of much use.[69]
After it, though, came information of a "private" character: "The whole of
the rebel army has been moved from Frederick, and their destination is
Harrisburg and Philadelphia," Curtin reported, then he added some advice:

> *You should order a strong guard placed on the railway lines from
> Washington to Harrisburg to-night, and send here not less than
> 80,000 disciplined forces, and order from New York and States east
> all available troops to concentrate here at once. To this we will add
> all the militia forces possible, and I think that in a few days we can
> muster 50,000 men.*
>
> *It is our only hope to save the North and crush the rebel army.
> Do not suppose for one instant that I am unnecessarily alarmed. I
> believe I know all that I have stated to be true. . . .*
>
> *The enemy will bring against us not less than 120,000* [men],
> *with large amount of artillery. The time for decided action by the
> National Government has arrived. What may we expect?*[70]

On the next morning, Friday, September 12, Lincoln—probably with
some assistance from Halleck—replied:

> *Your dispatch asking for 80,000 disciplined troops to be sent to
> Pennsylvania is received. Please consider we have not to exceed
> 80,000 disciplined troops, properly so called, this side of the moun-
> tains, and most of them with many of the new regiments are now
> close in the rear of the enemy supposed to be invading Pennsylvania.*
>
> *Start half of them to Harrisburg and the enemy will turn
> upon and beat the remaining half, and then reach Harrisburg before
> the part going there, and beat it, too, when it comes. The best
> possible security for Pennsylvania is putting the strongest force
> possible into the enemy's rear.*[71]

Curtin's next message amounted to a surprise: "I have advices that Jackson is crossing the Potomac at Williamsport, and probably the whole rebel army will be drawn from Maryland."[72] The report was half-correct. Old Jack was complying with General Lee's Special Orders No. 191 by moving toward Martinsburg, Virginia, to eliminate the Yankee garrison from that point along the Valley Turnpike that Lee wanted as a link in his new supply line. Lincoln sent the whole text to McClellan, adding: "Please do not let him [Jackson] get off without being hurt."[73]

Correctly, McClellan surmised that if Jackson were south of the Potomac, his objective might be Harpers Ferry. "I think I can not only relieve [Colonel Dixon S. Miles, the garrison's commander], but place the rebels who attack him in great danger of being cut off,"[74] he assured General Halleck. And in another wire he said: "If Harper's Ferry is still in our possession, I think I can save the garrison, if they fight at all. If the rebels are really marching into Pennsylvania, I shall soon be up with them. My apprehension is that they may make for Williamsport, and get across the river before I can catch them."[75]

Elsewhere in McClellan's Army of the Potomac, Major General Joseph Hooker was expressing to McClellan's adjutant general a minority opinion of Governor Curtin's involvement:

> *I have just been shown an order relieving Brigadier-General* [John F.] *Reynolds from the command of a division in my corps* [for duty as sort of an aide to Curtin at Harrisburg]. *I request that the major-general commanding will not heed this order; a sacred Governor ought not to be permitted to destroy the usefulness of an entire division of the army on the eve of important operations.*
>
> *General Reynolds commands a division of Pennsylvania troops of not the best character; it is well known to them, and I have no officer to fill his place.*
>
> *It is satisfactory to my mind that the rebels have no more intention of going to Harrisburg than they have of going to heaven.*
>
> *It is only in the United States that atrocities like this are entertained.*[76]

Not far short of midnight on that Friday, the sacred governor relayed to the Union's war managers one more report from a "reliable gentleman" who had just returned from Maryland:

> *They* [the Confederates] *intend to cross about 70,000 men,*

forming their reserve at Williamsport, and occupy the Virginia shore as a general depot for all supplies they can gather. Part of this reserve to attack and capture Martinsburg and Harper's Ferry. The main rebel army to occupy Maryland between Williamsport and Hagerstown, from which they will move on Cumberland Valley and other points in Pennsylvania.

Their force in Maryland was about 190,000 men. That they have in Virginia about 250,000 men, all of whom are being concentrated to menace Washington and keep the Union armies employed there, while their forces in Maryland devastate and destroy Pennsylvania.[77]

In fact, General Lee had in his Army of Northern Virginia not more than fifty-two thousand "effectives" and possibly, after allowing for the desertions of men who thought it wrong to invade the North, as few as forty thousand—and they were scattered around western Maryland and northern Virginia in at least four fragments.[78]

8

ANDREW CURTIN SEEMED ABOUT TO OBTAIN the services of Major General John F. Reynolds as his personal link with the War Department, but the Honorable Alexander Henry in Philadeplphia was not so fortunate. To Henry's plea for "a competent general to take command" in Philadelphia, the President replied: "General Halleck has made the best provision he can for generals in Pennsylvania. . . . Philadelphia is more than 150 miles from Hagerstown, and could not be reached by the rebel army in ten days, if no hindrance was interposed."[79]

Instead of distance from danger as a reason for denying Henry's request, Lincoln might well have cited the Union's acute shortage of competent generals. McClellan's limited and specialized skills as an organizer and trainer did not equate to competence as a field commander, a fact Halleck had accepted—no more suitable general having been available. But Old Brains had misjudged the extent of the Young Napoleon's incompetence, as their disputes over the disposition of troops and Harpers Ferry indicate.

Before he took the Army of the Potomac out of Washington, according to a report McClellan composed later, he had asked Halleck to allow the garrison at Harpers Ferry to abandon the place and augment his forces. "No," the general-in-chief was said to have said. Then, on Wednesday, September 10, from Rockville he had telegraphed Halleck: "Colonel Miles is at or near Harper's Ferry, as I understand, with 9,000 troops. He can do nothing where he is, but could be of great service if ordered to join me."[80]

For once, Old Brains may have been too terse: "There is no way for Colonel Miles to join you at present," he said in opening his reply. "His only chance is to defend his works till you can open communication with him. When you do so, he will be subject to your orders."[81]

Perhaps Harpers Ferry's strategic importance was so obvious to Halleck that he assumed there was no need to point it out to Little Mac. The general-in-chief had never been there but George Cullum had, and surely his chief of staff had described the rugged but gorgeous terrain of the place where the waters of the Shenandoah flow into those of the Potomac, one Thomas Jefferson had called the most beautiful spot on the continent.

Maryland Heights loomed above the Potomac's north bank; Loudoun Heights to the southeast guided the Shenandoah to its junction with the Potomac; and Bolivar Heights to the southwest made the village itself appear to be in a pocket—for troops defending it, a death trap.

"I have no personal knowledge of the ground," Old Brains had confessed in a message to General Wool back on September 5, but—presumably, coached by Cullum—he had advocated "withdrawing all our forces in that vicinity to Maryland Heights."[82] Given the ability to defend themselves, to the Confederates the garrison's continuing presence was likely to serve as a burr under the saddle does to a horse: Lee was bound to do something about Harpers Ferry sooner or later, because he could not stay in Maryland or advance into Pennsylvania until that burr was removed.

Indeed, wresting control of Harpers Ferry was perhaps the main reason General Lee had taken pen in hand while pausing at Frederick on September 9 and had written Special Orders 191, among other things fragmenting his army and giving Jackson that particular mission. Guiding Lee's hand had been Old Brains' point in keeping Miles where he was.

But, apparently, it was a mistake to assume that the Young Napoleon was capable of grasping such basic elements of military art and strategy. "I would also advise that the force of Colonel Miles, at Harper's Ferry, where it can be of but little use, and is continually exposed to be cut off by the enemy, be immediately ordered here," McClellan had argued in his long, Buellesque message from Rockville back on Thursday, September 11. "This would add about 15,000 old troops to our present force, and would greatly strengthen us."[83] And two days later, he would advise Halleck:

This army marches forward early to-morrow morning, and will make forced marches, to endeavor to relieve Colonel Miles, but I fear, unless he makes a stout resistance, we may be too late. A report came in just this moment that Miles was attacked to-day and repulsed the enemy, but I do not know what credit to attach to the statement. I shall do everything in my power to save Miles if he still holds out.[84]

Earlier, McClellan and Halleck had been squabbling over the telegraph wires regarding the troops still manning Washington's fortifications. On the morning of Saturday, September 13, the general-in-chief actually scolded the Young Napoleon:

Until you know more certainly the enemy's force south of the Potomac, you are wrong in thus uncovering the capital. I am of opinion that the enemy will send a small column toward Pennsylvania, so as to draw your forces in that direction; then suddenly move on Washington with the forces south of the Potomac and those he may cross over.

In your letter of the 10th you attach too little importance to the capital. I assure you that you are wrong. The capture of this place will throw us back six months, if it should not destroy us.

Beware of the evils I now point out to you. You saw them when here, but you seem to forget them in the distance. No more troops can be sent from here till we have fresh arrivals from the North.[85]

Where that controversy might have led, the world would never learn. Even as Halleck was delivering his sermonette, the Young Napoleon was reading a copy of General Lee's Special Orders No. 191.

9

SIX MILES PER DAY WAS ALL the Army of the Potomac had averaged during its march northwestward from Rockville toward Frederick, partly because Marylanders along the way pressed upon them apples, pastries, tubs of water, even whiskey. But by Saturday morning, September 13, 1862, the troops were moving into campsites near Frederick, many of which the Confederates had left a few days earlier. General McClellan did not reach the headquarters his staff had prepared until around noon; he had been delayed by cheering, flower-throwing residents of Frederick, some of whom had held up babies for him to kiss.

Corporal Barton W. Mitchell, exploring the 27th Indiana's bivouac area, picked up a bulky white envelope and found three cigars inside, wrapped in a piece of paper that seemed to be a Confederate order of some sort. Pocketing the cigars, he started the wrapper up the chain of command.

McClellan was talking with some civilians when an aide called him aside and showed him the document. According to one of the visitors, the Young Napoleon grew very excited and said, "Now I know what to do!"[86]

McClellan's agitation was reflected in the scrambling of thoughts in the telegram he sent the President:

> *I have the whole rebel force in front of me, but am confident, and no time shall be lost. I have a difficult task to perform, but with God's blessing will accomplish it. I think Lee has made a gross mistake, and that he will be severely punished for it. The army is in motion as rapidly as possible. I hope for a great success if the plans of the rebels remain unchallenged [sic]. We have possession of Catoctin. I have all the plans of the rebels, and will catch them in their own trap if my men are equal to the emergency. I now feel that I can count on them as of old. All forces of Pennsylvania should be placed to co-operate at Chambersburg. My respects to Mrs. Lincoln. Received most enthusiastically by the ladies. Will send you trophies. All well, and with God's blessing will accomplish it.[87]*

More coherent was the message McClellan sent General Halleck a short time later. "An order from General R. E. Lee," he began, "addressed to General D. H. Hill, which has accidentally come into my hands this evening—the authenticity of which is unquestionable—discloses some of the plans of the enemy, and shows most conclusively that the main rebel army is now before us." He gave a few of the order's details, then wrote:

> *That this was the plan of campaign on the 9th is confirmed by the fact that heavy firing has been heard in the direction of Harper's Ferry this afternoon, and the columns took the roads specified in the order. It may, therefore, in my judgment, be regarded as certain that this rebel army, which I have good reasons for believing amounts to 120,000 men or more, and know to be commanded by Lee in person, intended to attempt penetrating Pennsylvania. The officers*

told their friends here that they were going to Harrisburg and Philadelphia.

Then McClellan returned to the subject of his desire to have more troops sent to him from Washington's defenses:

You will perceive, from what I have stated, that there is but little probability of the enemy being in much force south of the Potomac. I do not, by any means, wish to be understood as undervaluing the importance of holding Washington. It is of great consequence, but upon the success of this army the fate of the nation depends. It was for this reason that I said every thing else should be made subordinate to placing this army in proper condition to meet the large rebel force in our front.

Unless General Lee has changed his plans, I expect a severe general engagement to-morrow. I feel confident that there is now no rebel force immediately threatening Washington or Baltimore, but that I have the mass of their troops to contend with, and they [will] outnumber me when united.[88]

Seldom, if ever, in recorded military history had any commander been given such an enormous advantage over his enemy. "Now I know what to do!"—the remark the civilian visitor overheard—implied that Little Mac understood that Lee's army was fragmented and that he knew where those fragments were. Destroying enemy unit after separated unit before they could unite was (and is) every soldier's fondest dream. And a few days earlier McClellan had promised Old Brains, "As soon as I find out where to strike, I will be after them without an hour's delay."

At least seven hours passed before McClellan issued any orders at all, and they called for execution the next day. They did not include a task force to save Harpers Ferry's garrison.

During that Saturday night, General Lee was told that his Special Orders No. 191 was in McClellan's hands. He acted immediately to reassemble his army, but at Sharpsburg instead of Hagerstown.

Anticipating that McClellan would attempt to seize Turner's Gap and Crampton's Gap on South Mountain, Lee rushed forces to defend both of those passes and ordered Longstreet to move eastward to reinforce them. By so doing he sought to give Jackson time to complete the capture of Harpers Ferry and its garrison.

General Lee was making the most of the scraps of time; McClellan, as if stunned by too much good fortune, allowed his enormous opportunity to fade hour by hour. Inadvertently, both commanders were giving new meaning to the real Napoleon's often-quoted remark: "In war, the man is everything."

There was nothing Abraham Lincoln or Henry Halleck could do about the situation developing less than a hundred miles northwest of Washington, for they would not receive McClellan's messages until the next day, Sunday, September 14. By then, Confederate Major General Daniel Harvey Hill's troops were engaged in fierce firefights with Yankees from two corps attacking his position in Turner's Gap from north, south, and the east up the National Road. Because of the rugged and heavily wooded terrain, artillery was useless. But Harvey Hill's vastly outnumbered men still held the pass at sundown, when Longstreet's first units arrived.

Roughly eight miles south of Turner's Gap along South Mountain's spine, another federal column, commanded by William Franklin, finally managed to drive a rebel division out of Crampton's Gap, only to be inhibited by a fresh line Major General Lafayette McLaws' division had formed across Pleasant Valley. Not far south of there, mortally wounded Colonel Dixon S. Miles had surrendered more than 11,000 men to Stonewall Jackson.[89]

At around 9:40 on that Sunday evening, from "Three miles beyond Middletown, Md."—nearly thirty miles from the fighting—a message from the Army of the Potomac's commander to General in Chief Halleck reflected both a reduction in transmission time to only four hours and the distortion that occurs in the truth as information moves from the scene of the action to the rear:

> *After a very severe engagement, the corps of Hooker and Reno have carried the heights commanding the Hagerstown road. The troops behaved magnificently. They never fought better. Franklin has been hotly engaged on the extreme left.*
>
> *I do not yet know the result, except that the firing indicated progress on his part. The action continued until after dark, and terminated leaving us in possession of the entire crest.*
>
> *It has been a glorious victory. I cannot yet tell whether the enemy will retreat during the night or appear in increased force in the morning. I am hurrying up everything from the rear, to be prepared for any eventuality. I regret to add that the gallant and able General Reno is killed.*[90]

So had been more than three hundred other soldiers from the North.[91] But neither those sacrifices nor those of hundreds more wounded and missing men seemed to have bestirred the general commanding to recall that even as Sunday's sun set, Lee's Confederates *still* had to be scattered widely between Turner's Gap and Harpers Ferry and the Potomac River to the west.

Oddly, on Monday, September 15, while worrying about "any eventuality" instead of ordering his forces to find Lee's fragments and annihilate them, the Young Napoleon found the time to telegraph a message to the distinguished old soldier his studied disobedience had hounded into retirement nearly a year earlier, Winfield Scott, claiming that he had gained a "signal victory."[92] And Abraham Lincoln was moved to wire a friend in Illinois that "McClellan has gained a great victory over the great rebel army in Maryland. . . . He is now pursuing the flying foe."[93]

10

"WE WILL MAKE OUR STAND HERE," General Lee had declared on Monday, September 15, 1862, when he finished his ride over the ground west of Antietam Creek north, east, and south of the little village of Sharpsburg. That said, his desertion-depleted, vastly outnumbered, but reunited Army of Northern Virginia took appalling losses but inflicted even more on the Yankee corps George McClellan sent toward his thin lines piecemeal for fourteen hours of slaughter on Wednesday, September 17, 1862. Darkness stopped the killing and maiming, but not until Confederate marksmen and artillerymen had reduced McClellan's ranks by twelve thousand men.

General Lee had given battle to the Young Napoleon with the Potomac River only a short distance behind him. Had any of Little Mac's spasmodic attacks succeeded, the Army of Northern Virginia would surely have ceased to exist. As it was, on Thursday morning, September 18, Lee had only about twenty-six thousand men left. McClellan had twenty-four thousand or more troops available *who had not pulled a trigger* the day before.

Lee stood fast on that Thursday, defying McClellan to continue his attacks. None came. That night he began the withdrawal of his army over the nearby Potomac toward the lower Shenandoah Valley of Virginia.[94]

Instead of destroying the battle-weary Confederates facing him, George McClellan had elected to spend part of Thursday morning seated with pen in hand, reporting to General Halleck:

The battle of yesterday continued for fourteen hours, and until after dark. We held all we gained, except a portion of the extreme left, that was obliged to abandon a part of what it had gained. Our losses very heavy, especially in general officers. The battle will probably be renewed to-day. Send all the troops you can by the most expeditious route.[95]

Next, General McClellan wrote his wife:

We fought yesterday a terrible battle against the entire rebel army. The battle continued 14 hours & was terrific—the fighting on both sides was superb. The general result was in our favor, that is to say we gained a good deal of ground & held it. It was a success, but whether a decided victory depends upon what occurs today. . . . The spectacle yesterday was the grandest I could conceive of—nothing could be more sublime. Those in whose judgment I rely tell me that I fought the battle splendidly & that it was a masterpiece of art. I am well nigh tired out by anxiety & want of sleep. . . .[96]

During a brief lull in the battle on Wednesday, he had opened a wire to Halleck: "We are in the midst of the most terrible battle of the war—perhaps of history."[97] To the war managers in Washington, the few words he devoted to his actions merely heightened the craving for more details. The general-in-chief had already ordered Wool and others to send McClellan men and ammunition; there was nothing much more anyone could do but wait. And nothing more would come from the Young Napoleon himself until Friday morning:

But little occurred yesterday except skirmishing, being fully occupied in replenishing ammunition, taking care of wounded, &c. Last night the enemy abandoned his position, leaving his dead and wounded on the field. We are again in pursuit. I do not yet know whether he is falling back to an interior position or crossing the river. We may safely claim a complete victory.[98]

Also arriving that morning was a message from General Wool in Baltimore. "I have a dispatch," he telegraphed Halleck, "that the rebels have recrossed the Potomac. Look out for Washington. You are not out of the woods. The rebels are a day and a half in advance of McClellan."[99]

The general-in-chief had that warning in mind when he replied to McClellan shortly after noon on that Friday:

All available troops from railroad guards were sent to you yesterday. . . . So long as the river remains low there is much danger of a movement below your left. Letters received here give it as part of Lee's original plan to draw you as far as possible up the Potomac, and then move between you and Washington. Perhaps his defeat may be such as to prevent the attempt.[100]

The next communication from Little Mac that day was more of a declaration than anything else:

I have the honor to report that Maryland is entirely freed from the presence of the enemy, who have been driven across the Potomac. No fears now be entertained for the safety of Pennsylvania. I shall at once occupy Harper's Ferry.[101]

By Saturday, September 20, Old Brains' patience with McClellan was exhausted—and it showed. "We are still left entirely in the dark in regard to your own movements and those of the enemy," he complained. "This should not be so. You should keep me advised of both, so far as you know them."[102]

Not until that night did McClellan respond. "I telegraphed you yesterday all that I knew," he asserted, "and had nothing more to inform you of until this evening." What he offered then was hardly significant. Toward the end he scolded Old Brains: "I regret that you find it necessary to couch every dispatch I have the honor to receive from you in a spirit of fault-finding, and that you have not found leisure to say one word in commendation of the recent achievement of this army, or even to allude to them."[103]

George McClellan had not been so restrained in expressing his contempt for his superior officer in a letter he had written Mary Ellen that morning:

An opportunity has presented itself through the Governors of some of the states to enable me to take my stand—I have insisted that Stanton be removed & that Halleck shall give way to me as Comdr in Chief. I will not serve under him—for he is an incompetent fool—in no way fit for the important place he holds. Since I left

Washn Stanton has again asserted that I not Pope lost the battle of Manassas No 2! The only safety for the country & for me is to get rid of both of them—no success is possible with them. . . .[104]

That night, in another letter to his wife, he added: "I feel that I have done all that can be asked in twice saving the country. If I continue in its service I have at least the right to demand a guarantee that I shall not be interfered with—I know I cannot have that assurance so long as Stanton continues as Secy of War & Halleck as Genl in Chief. . . ."[105]

9 ★ Politicization Weakens the Union's War Efforts

S INCE CORINTH IN THE WEST and the Seven Days in the East, Robert E. Lee and Braxton Bragg had shown generalship of a high order. Stonewall Jackson and Edmund Kirby Smith had also won distinction. As 1862's high summer moved toward autumn, one Confederate army was in Maryland and two others seemed likely to cross the Ohio and invade the Union's Old Northwest within the near future.

Second Bull Run, however, may have marked the start of a new phase, one in which the Union high command's mistakes would be fewer and less costly and some of the initial errors would be corrected. Put differently, from September's first days onward Henry Halleck's client Abraham Lincoln would be more and more responsive to (and deriving more and more benefit from) the advice being provided by the special counsel he had retained.

Yet improvement in the Union's situation would not become apparent right away, nor would the reasons for it be discerned easily or clearly.

While General McClellan had been wasting his opportunity to destroy Lee's Army of Northern Virginia, the Union's military situation in the West deteriorated. Earlier, Halleck had incurred considerable risk by ordering Ulysses Grant to send troops from northern Mississippi to fill the vacuum being left by Buell's gradual shift from central Tennessee into Kentucky. By mid-September, Grant was weaker by at least three divisions, and Confederate Major Generals Earl Van Dorn and Sterling Price were attracted by his seeming vulnerability.

On September 14, while the battle for the gaps on South Mountain was raging in Maryland, Price's troops occupied Iuka, Mississippi, about twenty miles east of Corinth. Hoping to annihilate Price before Van Dorn joined him, Grant sent two divisions to regain possession of Iuka. Attacks from two directions on September 17 failed, and when they were renewed the next day the federals discovered that Price had withdrawn during the night.[1] Also on September 17, the day of the slaughter along Antietam Creek, Braxton Bragg's troops finessed the surrender of the Union garrison at Munfordville, Kentucky, a strong point on the Louisville & Nashville Railroad roughly forty miles north of Bowling Green—Buell's most recent stopping point—and about sixty-five miles south of Louisville and the Ohio River.

Major General Horatio Wright, in Cincinnati, had been far more responsive to Old Brains' counsel than Buell. To Wright, on September 20, Halleck telegraphed: "It seems to me of vast importance that the junction of Bragg and Kirby Smith should be prevented, or at least you and Buell should unite first."[2] But since *suggesting* seemed unlikely to produce the killing of a single Confederate, the general-in-chief came around to the views of Lincoln and Stanton on September 24 by issuing to an aide, Colonel J. C. McKibbin, orders whose execution was meant to result in an execution:

> *As the bearer of the accompanying dispatches you will proceed by the most practicable route to the army of General Buell in the field.*
>
> *The Secretary of War directs that if General Buell should be found in the presence of the enemy preparing to fight a battle, or if he should have gained a victory, or if General Thomas should be separated from him so as not to be able to enter upon the command of the troops operating against the enemy, these dispatches will not be delivered, and you will in either of the contingencies above mentioned telegraph to these headquarters for further instructions.*
>
> *If while en route to General Buell you should ascertain that either of these contingencies have occurred you will telegraph the facts and await orders.*
>
> *If neither of these events should occur you will present the dispatches to both General Buell and General Thomas and return to these headquarters.*
>
> *This mission is strictly confidential, and the nature of your instructions or object of your visit will not be communicated to any one.*

If by any accident you should fall into the hands of the enemy you will destroy your dispatches.[3]

Lawyer Halleck provided his messenger with a series of letters, beginning with one addressed to General Buell:

You will receive herewith the orders of the President placing Maj. Gen. G. H. Thomas in command of the Department of the Tennessee. You will therefore turn over your command to him and repair to Indianapolis, Ind., and await orders. All officers of your staff except your personal aides will report for duty to Major-General Thomas.[4]

Equally terse and to the point was the letter meant for General Thomas, if McKibbin found Buell idle:

You will receive herewith the order of the President placing you in command of the Department of the Tennessee.

I am directed to say to you that the Government expects energetic operations by the troops placed under your command. In your movements you will pay no regard to State or department lines, but operate against the enemy; find him and give him battle. If you form a junction with any troops belonging to the Department of the Ohio take command of them and use them.

Look well to the amount of your transportation and carry nothing with you which is not absolutely necessary. So far as you can, subsist your army on the country passed over. . . . The immobility of our armies results from the excess of transportation. This evil must be immediately remedied.

Send dispatches as often as possible giving information of your movements.[5]

Meticulously crafted though Halleck's guillotining procedure had been, events while McKibbin was en route westward and the existence of the telegraph combined to restrain the descent of the angled blade. On September 25, the day McKibbin left Washington, from Louisville Buell replied to Halleck's most recent hammering:

[Bragg] has had the advantage of many alternatives, none of which I could meet without giving him the advantage of time and

distance, and that at no time could I have forced a battle without yielding him greatly the advantage in point of numbers. It has not been possible to prevent his junction with Kirby Smith's forces except through the force in Kentucky, because he has been able all the time to move in a direct line, while I have been forced on a circuitous route.

I have been cramped because my communications have been effectually broken and beyond my control. I am not disposed generally to be very zealous in my own defense, but I ought perhaps to say this much. To enter into details would occupy time, perhaps uselessly.

The situation of affairs in Kentucky at present is this: Bragg has reached Bardstown; Smith is said to have reached Shelbyville this morning from Frankfort. This would seem to indicate an advance on this city, though I have doubted that they would attempt an attack if I formed a junction here. They could reach here to-morrow. I shall have seven divisions here by to-morrow morning. It will be safe to estimate the force of the enemy at about 60,000 inured and effective men.[6]

After nearly ten months of dealing with Don Carlos Buell, Old Brains must have been inured to his penchant for making excuses. But the fact that Buell had reached Louisville was interesting; apparently Bragg had not molested him along the way up from Bowling Green. Buell provided more information late the next day, September 26:

My troops are concentrated at [Louisville]. *They have made long and rapid marches, and require clothing, which is being issued to-day.*

I shall immediately advance against the enemy. I suppose his main force to be at Bardstown. Two brigades have arrived within 12 miles of this place to-day. I am not satisfied that it signifies an advance in force, but I shall be prepared.

I am exercising command of the whole force here, but something is necessary to make the command homogeneous.[7]

At about the same time, General Wright was calling for homogeneity or something of the sort. Also from Louisville, he telegraphed the general-in-chief:

General Buell is here with his army, and I have a force here of raw troops, somewhat superior in numbers. There is no doubt that for operations against the enemy these forces should be combined into one army. General Buell thinks it his duty to control the entire force, and that I have neither control nor responsibility in the matter of my own troops even. The question of the relations between us (he being my senior in date) should be at once decided, in order that the most effective steps may be promptly taken for operating against the rebel forces in Kentucky.[8]

Curiously, Horatio Wright had been overlooked in planning Buell's beheading. In his reply, Old Brains tried to make the best of an awkward situation:

General Buell having reached Louisville will by virtue of his rank exercise command of the army at that place. This, however, will not interfere with your general command of the department. The matter is complicated, but you must endeavor to work harmoniously.[9]

However, Halleck did not mention Wright in his message to Buell:

You will by virtue of your rank exercise command of the troops in Louisville until further orders. It is hoped that your force is now strong enough to enable you to immediately advance upon the enemy. There are many reasons—some of them personal to yourself—why there should be as little delay as possible.[10]

But these new circumstances made applying the chopper to Buell questionable, and on September 27 General Halleck telegraphed McKibbin: "Dispatches will not be delivered till further orders."[11] Again, two days later, "Await further orders before acting."[12] This time, the aide's reply was prompt:

The dispatches are delivered. I think that it is fortunate that I obeyed instructions. Much dissatisfaction with General Buell. There is no probability of a fight within a week. I shall await orders before leaving.[13]

Quickly, Old Brains sent McKibbin one: "You will return to Washington."[14]

Major General Buell's response to the execution of McKibbin's mission was brief, soldierly:

> *I have received your orders of the 24th instant, requiring me to turn over my command to Maj. Gen. G. H. Thomas. I have accordingly turned over the command to him, and in further obedience to your instruction I shall repair to Indianapolis and await orders.*[15]

But General Thomas' reaction must have jolted Halleck:

> *Colonel McKibbin handed me your dispatch, placing me in command of the Department of the Tennessee. General Buell's preparations have been completed to move against the enemy, and I therefore respectfully ask that he may be retained in command. My position is very embarrassing, not being as well informed as I should be as the commander of this army and on the assumption of such a responsibility.*[16]

General Halleck's position was far more embarrassing than Thomas' and it produced a reply that was, for him, unusual:

> *The order relieving General Buell was not made by me nor on my advice and I have no power to change it. It was made before General Buell arrived at Louisville, and Colonel McKibbin was twice telegraphed not to deliver the dispatches till further orders, but he received the telegrams too late.*
>
> *This statement is necessary to explain the telegrams sent by me to General Buell. Please show it to him.*
>
> *You may consider the order as suspended till I can lay your dispatch before the Government and get instructions.*[17]

A short time later on that Monday, September 29, the general-in-chief relayed the government's instructions to both Buell and Thomas:

> *General orders changing the command of the Department of the Tennessee and the troops at Louisville and my instructions based on those orders are, by authority of the President, suspended, and General Buell will act on my telegram of a later date.*[18]

And the next day, Buell wrote Halleck simply and admirably:

I received last evening your dispatch suspending my removal from my command. Out of sense of public duty I shall continue to discharge the duties of my command to the best of my ability until otherwise ordered.[19]

Monday, September 29, 1862, would have been a bad day for Don Carlos Buell in any case. After breakfast at Louisville's Galt House, Major Generals Jefferson C. Davis and William Nelson had engaged in a quarrel that resulted in Davis' borrowing a pistol and shooting Nelson dead.[20] Also at around that time, General Wright had left for Cincinnati, leaving behind a long report he had prepared for Buell on actions he had taken while commanding in Kentucky—one ending in a postscript: "Can you spare me General Sheridan for the cavalry force I hope to raise? I need him much."[21]

Buell kept Sheridan, the bandy-legged, bullet-headed fighter General Halleck had shifted from quartermaster to combat duties months earlier. Within a short time it would be clear that denying Wright "Little Phil's" services might have been the best decision Don Carlos Buell ever made.

2

SINCE MID-JULY, ABSENT ANY VALID PRECEDENT, lawyer Halleck had operated as general-in-chief as a prudent trustee might in administering all of the complex matters pertaining to the Union's armies. He had also acted as counsel to the President in *United States* v. *Confederacy*. Until roughly the end of September, most of the matters on which the general and the President worked together had been military, in part because of extraordinarily serious challenges presented by Robert E. Lee and Braxton Bragg. But with autumn came an increase in the President's political activities, and to the extent he mixed them and military operations, he added considerable complexity to the Lincoln-Halleck relationship.

This was ironic, for it had been Halleck's presence that had enabled Lincoln to devote more time to his purely presidential duties. The Emancipation Proclamation, which followed the bloody stand-off along Antietam Creek by a week, had been a product of this change. Yet its reception even in the North was decidedly mixed. And nowhere was opposition to it more likely to develop, or to have more serious implications if it did, than in Major General George B. McClellan's Army of the Potomac—mainly because the Young Napoleon had consistently maintained that slavery had nothing to do with the war or the conduct thereof.

As a lawyer, Henry Halleck may have had problems with the Proclamation similar to those expressed in London by the British Foreign Secretary:

> *There is surely a want of consistency in this measure. . . . If it were a measure of Emancipation it should be extended to all States of the Union. Emancipation is not granted to the claims of humanity but inflicted as punishment.*[22]

But as a soldier, General Halleck's only response could be to deal with the consequences if—with or without urging from its general commanding—the Army of the Potomac, or any portion of it, refused to fight any longer. A political thrust, though powered by desire to quell the rebellion, had pierced the veil that heretofore had tended to prevent military operations from being influenced by social policy or ideological factors. In the process of dealing with one problem, Lincoln had created a condition in which a host of others could proliferate.

Halleck was not a politician. He had no friends who *were* politicians—hence, no safety-net of support. And while he could obey orders with which he did not agree, he could not accept political expediency as justification for violating principles by which he lived.

But no damage had yet been done, and so he continued to concentrate on meeting the needs of his armies in the field: McClellan's in Maryland, Buell's in Kentucky, and Grant's in northern Mississippi. Problems presented by any of the three would have been enough to overwhelm him. In a few days, however, Lincoln was to inject politics into the planning and conduct of the campaign to bring the entire course of the Mississippi under federal control. And by early November, the President would begin an effort to achieve narrow political goals through military operations in what the Confederates called the Trans-Mississippi: Louisiana, Texas, and Arkansas.

Earlier, Halleck had been surprisingly successful in preventing the commander-in-chief from making military mistakes. He had also nudged Lincoln toward correcting some of his old ones. But saving the President from sins past, present, and future soon became nigh-impossible for Old Brains for at least two reasons: he was a soldier who meant to be nothing less and certainly nothing more, and no law said that a client had to be absolutely responsive to counsel. If Lincoln wanted to risk defeat by allowing unqualified "political" generals to undertake important missions for reasons of his own, all General Halleck could do—short of resigning—was to try to minimize the damage.

That he did not walk away from the threat of inevitable wrecks was among the other contributions to the Union's war effort that Henry Wager Halleck's many critics completely overlooked. So was his willingness to serve as President Lincoln's lightning rod. And both of these characteristics began to be tested anew as October 1862 opened.

Later, in his report to Secretary of War Stanton, the general-in-chief would state:

> *Soon after the battle of Antietam, General McClellan was urged to give me information of his intended movements, in order that if he moved between the enemy and Washington, re-enforcements could be sent from this place. On the 1st of October, finding that he purposed to operate from Harper's Ferry, I urged him to cross the [Potomac] river at once and give battle to the enemy, pointing out to him the disadvantages of delaying till the autumn rains had swollen the Potomac and impaired the roads. . . .*[23]

Actually, the quarrels of McClellan and Halleck had started getting acrimonious at least as early as September 26, when Old Brains responded to a somewhat grandiose proposal the Young Napoleon had submitted:

> *Your telegram in relation to reconstructing bridges at Harper's Ferry was received yesterday. As I telegraphed to you this morning, the War Department wishes to be informed more definitely of your plans before authorizing the expenditure of large sums of money for rebuilding bridges on the Potomac.*
>
> *Of course, your movements must depend in a measure upon the position and movements of the enemy; nevertheless they will be subordinate to a general plan. Without knowing your plan and your views on this subject, I cannot answer the questions which are asked me by the Government.*
>
> *I had hoped that, instead of crossing at Harper's Ferry (unless in the pursuit of a beaten army), you would be able to cross lower down the Potomac, so as to cover Washington by your line of operations, and thus avoid the necessity of keeping a large force here. In your present position the enemy threatens both your army and the capital.*
>
> *Will the crossing of your forces at Harper's Ferry relieve the*

latter? It will if the enemy is at Martinsburg; but will it if his main force falls back on Winchester? Moreover, his repairing the bridges over the Rapidan and Rappahannock would seem to indicate an attempt to reoccupy Manassas, or at least to threaten Washington from that direction. The number of troops to be left here will depend upon the amount of protection to be afforded by your army in the field. . . .

It seems to me that Washington is the real base of operations, and that it should not under any circumstances be exposed. Please state your plans as fully as possible.[24]

Abraham Lincoln, suspecting that the Young Napoleon had no plans, decided to get away from the vexing controversies his Emancipation Proclamation had provoked by spending a few days with the Army of the Potomac near Antietam Creek in western Maryland. Afterward he said, "I went up to the field to try to get [McClellan] to move." But while he was there, he had remarked to a friend as they gazed over the sea of tents, "That army is General McClellan's bodyguard."[25]

Accompanying the President on his trip were bodyguard Ward Lamon, Major General John A. McClernand and his aide, another Illinois politician, and a railroad president.[26] That Old Brains had not been included may or may not have been a reflection of several things. He and McClernand had never been on cordial terms out West. McClernand despised "elitist" West Pointers and longed for an opportunity to demonstrate the supposed superiority of home-grown generals. And according to telegrams reaching Halleck from Ulysses Grant, Confederates Earl Van Dorn and Sterling Price appeared to be threatening Corinth.

Not long after the tourists returned to Washington, however, it became abundantly apparent to Halleck that McClernand had bent Lincoln's ear often and effectively during the four days they spent as guests of Little Mac and his bodyguards. Presumably, McClernand and his good friend continued their deliberations, for on October 21, 1862, Secretary Stanton signed a document that was marked *Confidential*:

Ordered, That Major-General McClernand be, and he is, directed to proceed to the States of Indiana, Illinois, and Iowa, to organize the troops remaining in those States and to be raised by volunteering or draft, and forward them with all dispatch to Memphis, Cairo, or such other points as may hereafter be designated by the general-in-chief, to the end that, when a sufficient force not required by the operations of General Grant's command shall be raised, an expedition may be organized under General McClernand's command against Vicksburg and to clear the Mississippi River and open navigation to New Orleans.

The forces so organized will remain subject to the designation of the general-in-chief, and be employed according to such exigencies as the service in his judgment may require.[27]

The presence of the last paragraph suggests that General Halleck was involved in the drafting of the order. As matters stood, however, it appeared that Lincoln had enabled McClernand to harvest a bumper crop of political hay in the "Old Northwest" states and that Ulysses Grant's future role in regaining control of the Mississippi for the Union was uncertain.

Before and since the fight at Iuka, Mississippi, in mid-September, General Grant had been warning Halleck that Van Dorn and Price were behaving as though they meant to recapture Corinth. To Old Brains this was reassuring for at least two reasons: he did not want Price to threaten Nashville, which was all but undefended now that Buell had moved into Kentucky, and Grant seemed confident that he could whip the Confederates if they attacked. In fact, Grant and Cump Sherman were exchanging messages regarding possible strikes at rebel strong points in north central Mississippi and near the Yazoo River's mouth not far above Vicksburg.[28]

Van Dorn and Price interrupted the planning by joining forces at Ripley, southwest of Corinth, on September 28. Instead of moving directly to Corinth, however, the rebels marched northward as if they were bound for Bolivar, in Tennessee northwest of Corinth. But on October 3 the column turned eastward, and soon a battle was raging along the lines of fortifications Beauregard had prepared back in May as Halleck's army was approaching Corinth.

Major General William Starke Rosecrans was in command of the Union forces. He had called in nearby units, and this gave him a slight numerical advantage; Van Dorn had expected the Yankees to have roughly eight thousand fewer men. "Old Rosy" and his troops held off two days of determined rebel assaults—then watched as the Confederates melted away. Van Dorn had lost more than four thousand men, Rosecrans roughly twenty-five hundred.[29]

On September 26, Rosecrans had written Halleck to complain that the rank of major general, conferred upon him as of September 17—the date of the Iuka fight—should have been effective immediately following the "meritorious services in Western Virginia" that had earned him the promotion.[30] Did this matter? Well, yes; Old Rosy was under orders transferring him to Horatio Wright's army, where he would be junior to a number of generals. On October 1 the general-in-chief replied:

> *I know you are ranked by many of less capacity, and by some who have never rendered any services at all; but this cannot now be helped. I hope, however, that we may not be cursed with the appointment of any more political generals.*
>
> *We must all do the best we can for the country in our several positions. You have my entire confidence, and if it be possible I will give you a separate command. At present it is difficult to determine what will be done.*[31]

Rosecrans did not respond until three weeks later—after he had whipped Van Dorn and Price at Corinth, and Buell had fought Bragg at Perryville. From Corinth on October 22 he wrote a letter to Halleck that contained some passages the general-in-chief must have found disturbing:

> *I thank you for the kind expressions of confidence contained in your letter replying to mine. . . .*
>
> *Since then we had the stirring times here, and I think it probable* [we] *will have more of the same,.. but I am very sorry to say that ever since the battle of Iuka there has been at work the spirit of mischief among the mousing politicians on Grant's staff to get up in his mind a feeling of jealousy. They have at last so far succeeded that General Grant last evening telegraphed me that he thought certain leaky members of my staff and newspaper correspondents justified his insinuating that he thought I was getting up a spirit of division and trying to make my army appear independent of him.*
>
> *I dispatched, declaring that he had not had a truer friend or more loyal subordinate than myself; that no headquarters in these United States were less responsible for the sayings of newspaper writers and correspondents than mine, and that I wished it to be distinctly understood that this remark was especially applicable to what had been said about the affairs of Iuka and Corinth. After these declarations I said, "If you do not meet me with the frank avowal that you are satisfied, I shall consider that my ability to be useful in this department has ended." That now is my opinion.*
>
> *I am bending everything to complete the new defenses of Corinth so that we may hold it by a division against a very superior*

force. As soon as I finish this work and my report of the late battle and pursuit I shall hope for something that will settle this matter.

I am sure those politicians [in Grant's headquarters] *will manage matters with the sole view of preventing Grant from being in the background of military operations. This will make him sour and reticent. I shall become uncommunicative, and that, added to a conviction that he lacks administrative ability, will complete the reasons why I should be relieved from duty here, if I can be assigned to any other suitable duty where such obstacles do not operate.*

I forbear speaking of points in the operations here. . . .But I must close this personal letter, wishing you were here to command.[32]

Such, apparently, was the state of William Starke Rosecrans' mind on October 22, 1862. But on the next day, presumably before Halleck had received the general's letter, Old Brains telegraphed Grant: "You will direct Major-General Rosecrans to immediately repair to Cincinnati, where he will receive orders."[33] He sent Rosecrans much the same terse text, adding: "Telegraph your arrival. Go with the least possible delay."[34]

Both Grant and Rosecrans knew that Horatio Wright's headquarters were in Cincinnati. But neither knew why Halleck wanted Rosecrans to get there in such a hurry.

3

ABRAHAM LINCOLN'S FOUR-DAY ABSENCE during October's first week had given the general-in-chief an opportunity to give thought to the kind of problem that would never make headlines: what to do about regiments that had suffered horrendous losses in the Union's many defeats. Many, if not most, of the localities that had raised those units and sent them off to war could not replace their casualties. Had the time come to dilute the identities of those proud outfits with more recent recruits? Or should fresh regiments and brigades be organized to replace those whose ranks had been severely thinned?

These and related questions were neither new nor devoid of politics. Given the lack of a regular army worthy of the name at the war's outset, Lincoln had appealed to governors of the Northern states for troops. Congress had tinkered with the system, but ineffectually. By the early fall of 1862, General McClellan was offering solutions to the Adjutant-General designed to bolster the old units by taking a number of steps to recover men who had straggled, or been wounded, or detailed to non-essential duties.

"Nearly every measure recommended by you to fill up the old regiments has already been adopted," General Halleck informed him on October 7, 1862, then he made some rather un-lawyerlike remarks:

> *Straggling is the great curse of the army, and must be checked by severe measures. Whatever measures you adopt to accomplish that object, will be approved. I think myself that shooting them while in the act of straggling from their commands is the only effective remedy that can be applied. If you apply the remedy, you will be sustained here. . . .*
>
> *There is a decided want of legs in our troops. They have too much immobility, and we must try to remedy the defect. A reduction in baggage and baggage trains will effect something, but the real difficulty is, they are not sufficiently exercised in marching; they lie still in camp too long.*

But the real thrust of Old Brains' message on that occasion had been: "But you cannot delay the operations of the army. . . . It must move, and the old regiments must remain in their crippled condition. . . . The country is becoming very impatient at the want of activity in your army, and we must push it on."[35]

The want of activity in your army had driven General Halleck's first warning to Don Carlos Buell: the guillotine was waiting. George Thomas had stayed the angled blade's release in late September; but by October 2, he felt compelled to issue another admonition:

> *Much apprehension is felt here that unless a movement be made by you immediately the enemy may turn a portion of his force on Cincinnati, which is not in a condition to resist a very serious attack. I am directed to again urge upon you the importance of prompt action.*[36]

"My troops have been in motion since yesterday," Buell responded the next day, and he added a few brief details suggesting that contact with Bragg might be imminent.[37] During the next four or five days, three elements of Buell's army would be moving along three roads southeastward—a circumstance that would have horrified Halleck, believer in concentration that he was, and one that made a meeting engagement nigh-inevitable.

Water was exceedingly scarce in that part of Kentucky, and the

Confederates were deployed to protect their sources—among others, Doctors Creek, an almost dry tributary of the Chaplin River, near Perryville. A federal outfit made repeated attempts to seize those pools of stagnant water late on October 7, but the rebels held them until early the next morning when Little Phil Sheridan's brigade attacked and won possession not only of the creek but of a ridge between it and Perryville, a town bisected by the Salt River.

Such was the genesis of a strange, confusing battle on October 8 that reflected next to no credit on either side's generalship, added seventy-six hundred Americans' names to casualty lists, and, like so many others, seemed to have settled nothing at all. However, Bragg withdrew.[38]

General Buell had spent the battle recuperating from being thrown from a horse, so he knew about as little about it as Halleck did in faraway Washington. This was one reason news of the outcome did not reach Washington directly for several days.[39]

In the interim, however, the politicians among the Union's war managers had not been idle. For example, on October 8, while the armies were colliding out at Perryville, Secretary of War Stanton was sending the same telegram to the governors of seven states in the Old Northwest: "How many regiments of infantry and cavalry can you furnish and have ready in two weeks for an expedition against Vicksburg and to clear the Mississippi?"[40]

And on October 10, McClernand had sent Stanton a long memorandum in which he argued: "If the expedition should be limited at first to 20,000 troops, one-half or at least one-fourth of that number should be [experienced] troops."[41] Halleck would have been quick to note that the political general meant to take those veteran forces from Ulysses Grant and William Tecumseh Sherman. And Halleck may have insisted that the order Stanton issued on October 25, empowering McClernand to raise troops, include this key [italicized] phrase: " . . .to the end that, when a sufficient force *not required by the operations of General Grant's command* shall be raised, an expedition may be organized under General McClernand's command against Vicksburg. . . ."

And while General Halleck was having to watch his civilian superiors' moves regarding future Union operations aimed at reclaiming the Mississippi, and to devise ways of at least moderating the damages they might cause, he had to find time to try to budge McClellan from his resting place. Also, he had to conjure information from wherever it might be as to what had happened to Don Carlos Buell and his army.

From Louisville, Jeremiah Boyle had provided a blend of rumors and scraps of fact. But not until October 13—the better part of five days after Perryville—did Halleck receive word from the general commanding. The Confederates, Buell predicted, would withdraw from Kentucky with Bragg moving toward Nashville and Kirby Smith returning to Knoxville. "I shall direct the pursuit mainly against Bragg," he promised.[42] But in a message to Halleck sent near midnight on October 13, General Buell reverted to his habitual mixture of excuses and hopes:

> *Our loss in the battle of the 8th will sum up about 2,000 killed and wounded and some 400 prisoners, most of them taken in search of water, for the want of which our men suffered exceedingly.*
>
> *I have purposely abstained from reporting the embarrassment and suffering under which we labored from thirst and dust and the almost total want of water for nearly thirty-six hours previous to and during the battle. The country up to the position which the enemy held was destitute of water for such a force.*
>
> *The position which the enemy holds is exceedingly strong, in fact impregnable in front. Dick's River, from its mouth to Danville, runs between perpendicular cliffs, passable at only a few points, easily defended by a small force. I am moving to turn the position by their left.*[43]

By October 16, General Buell was able to take a broader—but not more hopeful—view of his situation, military and personal. To the general-in-chief he wrote:

> *You are aware that between Crab Orchard and Cumberland Gap the country is almost a desert. The limited supply of forage which the country affords is consumed by the enemy as be passes. In the day and a half that we have been in this sterile region our animals have suffered exceedingly. The enemy has been driven into the heart of this desert and must go on, for he cannot exist in it.*
>
> *For the same reason we cannot pursue in it with any hope of overtaking him, for while he is moving back on his supplies and as he goes consuming what the country affords we must bring ours forward. There is but one road and that a bad one. The route abounds in difficult defiles, in which a small force can retard the progress of a large one for a considerable time, and in that time the enemy could gain material advantage in a move upon other points.*

> *For these reasons, which I do not think it necessary to elaborate, I deem it useless and inexpedient to continue the pursuit, but propose to direct the main force under my command rapidly upon Nashville. . . .*
>
> *While I shall proceed with these dispositions, deeming them to be proper for the public interest, it is but meet that I should say that the present time is perhaps as convenient as any for making any changes that may be thought proper in the command of this army. It has not accomplished all that I had hoped or all that faction might demand: yet, composed as it is, one-half of perfectly new troops, it has defeated a powerful and thoroughly disciplined army in one battle and has driven it away baffled and dispirited at least, and as much demoralized as an army can be under such discipline as Bragg maintains over all troops that he commands. . . .*[44]

In his reply, Old Brains made no reference to Buell's having offered his neck to the French slicing device. "The rapid march of your army from Louisville and your victory at Perryville have given great satisfaction to the Government," he began. But his disagreement with General Buell regarding abandoning the pursuit and returning to Nashville compelled him to dwell on alternatives:

> *The great object to be attained is to drive the enemy from Kentucky and East Tennessee. If we cannot do it now we need never to hope for it. If the country is such that you cannot follow the enemy, is there not some other practicable road that will lead to the same result—that is, compel him to leave the country?*
>
> *By keeping between him and Nashville can you not cover that place and at the same time compel him to fall back into the valley of Virginia or into Georgia? If we can occupy Knoxville or Chattanooga we can keep the enemy out of Tennessee and Kentucky.*
>
> *To fall back on Nashville is to give up East Tennessee to be plundered. Moreover, you are now much nearer to Knoxville and as near to Chattanooga as to Nashville. If you go to the latter place and then to East Tennessee, you move over two sides of an equilateral triangle, while the enemy holds the third. Again, may he not in the mean time make another raid into Kentucky?*
>
> *If Nashville is really in danger, it must be re-enforced. Morgan's forces have been sent to Western Virginia, but we probably*

can very soon send some troops up the Cumberland. Those intended
for that purpose have been drawn off by the urgent appeals of
Generals Grant and Curtis. Cannot some of the forces at Louisville
be sent to Nashville?[45]

Henry Halleck's employment of plane geometry to make a point
regarding strategy was interesting. Three days earlier, he had inspired
Abraham Lincoln to urge General McClellan in a long letter to advance
directly southward east of the Blue Ridge rather than to waste time in the
Shenandoah Valley. "[Lee's] route is the arc of a circle," the commander-in-
chief (or Halleck) had written, "while yours is the chord."

But every soldier has only so much gold, someone once remarked, and
Don Carlos Buell had possessed very little of it even at the war's outset. His
supply had eroded steadily and not even his victory by default at Perryville
had halted it. From Indianapolis on October 21, Governor Oliver P.
Morton telegraphed His Excellency the President:

An officer just from Louisville announces that Bragg has escaped
with his army into East Tennessee, and that Buell's army is coun-
termarching to Lebanon. The butchery of our troops at Perryville
was terrible, and resulted from a large portion of the enemy being
precipitated upon a small portion of ours. Sufficient time was thus
gained by the enemy to enable them to escape.

Nothing but success, speedy and decided, will save our cause
from utter destruction. In the Northwest distrust and despair are
seizing upon the hearts of the people.[46]

Despair born of distrust was also seizing the minds of the Union's high
command regarding Major General Buell's fitness to remain in command of
his army. Undoubtedly, politician Morton redirected Lincoln's attention to
the eventual reactions of voters in the Old Northwest. And in perhaps the
longest message he ever wrote, on October 22 Buell gave numbers to his
departure from reality. Bragg had not less than sixty thousand men and
might increase his force to eighty thousand, he reported. Against this
background, he added a curious set of passages that had a valedictory tone
dashed with nigh-incoherence:

I could in an hour's conversation give you my views and explain the
routes and character of the country better than I can in a dispatch,
and perhaps satisfactorily; and if you think it worth while I can see

you in Washington without deferring my movements, provided you concur in the expediency of moving first in the direction of Nashville. . . .

We can give good reasons why we cannot do all that the enemy has attempted to do, such as operating without a base, &c., without ascribing the difference to the inferiority of our generals, though that may be true. The spirit of the rebellion enforces a subordination and patient submission to privation and want which public sentiment renders absolutely impossible among our troops.

To make matters worse on our side, the death penalty for any offense whatever is put beyond the power of the commanders of armies, where it is placed in every other army in the world. The sooner this is remedied the better for the country.

It is absolutely certain that from these causes, and from these alone, the discipline of the rebel army is superior to ours. Again, instead of imitating the enemy's plan (campaign) I should rather say that his failure has been in a measure due to his peculiar method. No army can operate effectually upon less than this has done in the last two months. A considerable part of the time it has been on half rations; it is now moving without tents, with only such cooking utensils as the men can carry, and with one baggage wagon to each regiment; but it must continue to do this during the cold, wet weather which must soon be expected, without being disabled by sickness.[47]

General Halleck replied:

It is the wish of the Government that your army proceed to and occupy East Tennessee with all possible dispatch. It leaves to you the selection of the roads upon which to move to that object; but it urges that this selection be so made as to cover Nashville and at the same time prevent the enemy's return into Kentucky.

To now withdraw your army to Nashville would have a most disastrous effect upon the country, already wearied with so many delays in our operations. To wait for the rising of the Cumberland for supplies will carry us into the rainy season, when the roads will be almost impassable and the campaign will terminate with no results.

Neither the Government nor the country can endure these repeated delays. Both require a prompt and immediate movement *toward the accomplishment of the great object in view—the holding of East Tennessee.*[48]

In fact, the Government's endurance had come to an end. This time the guillotining was not done by an aide but by a long message from the general-in-chief to General Rosecrans at Cincinnati. "You will receive herewith the order of the President placing you in command of the Department of the Cumberland and of the army of operations now commanded by General Buell," Old Brains began. "You will immediately repair to General Buell's headquarters and relieve him from the command." That said, Halleck gave Rosecrans a specific mission:

The great objects to be kept in view in your operations in the field are: first, to drive the enemy from Kentucky and Middle Tennessee; second, to take and hold East Tennessee, cutting the line of railroad at Chattanooga, Cleveland, or Athens, so as to destroy the connection of the valley of Virginia with Georgia and the other Southern States. It is hoped that by prompt and rapid movements a considerable part of this may be accomplished before the roads become impassable from the winter rains.

After outlining two means of reaching East Tennessee, Halleck provided summaries of the locations and operations of Union forces in West Virginia, Kentucky, and Mississippi. He also included a warning:

It is possible that Bragg, having failed of his object in Kentucky, may leave only a small force in East Tennessee and throw his main army into Mississippi against General Grant. His railroad communications from Knoxville to Holly Springs and Tupelo will enable him to make this movement with great rapidity. In that case a part of your forces must be sent to the assistance of General Grant, either by railroad to Decatur or by water, should the Cumberland be navigable, to Columbus or Memphis. Every effort should be made to ascertain Bragg's movements by pressing him closely.

Heed Buell's fate, Halleck seemed to be saying in closing: "I need not urge upon you the necessity of giving active employment to your forces. Neither the country nor the Government will much longer put up with the inactivity of some of our armies and generals."[49]

Even before Rosecrans could find Buell and relieve him, His Excellency the President received congratulations in a message signed by Governors Yates of Illinois and Morton of Indiana:

> *We were to start to-night for Washington to confer with you in regard to Kentucky affairs. The removal of General Buell and appointment of Rosecrans came not a moment too soon. The removal of General Buell could not have been delayed an hour with safety to the army or the cause. The history of the battle of Perryville and the recent campaign in Kentucky has never been told. The action you have taken renders our visit unnecessary, although we are very desirous to confer with you in regard to the general condition of the Northwest, and hope to do so at no distant period.*

4

IN FACT, THE BEHEADING OF MAJOR GENERAL BUELL did not take place exactly as General Halleck may have desired. Rosecrans did not reach Cincinnati until near noon on October 28, and he did not start in search of Buell until the next day.[50] Buell was in Louisville, and from there on October 29 he telegraphed General Halleck: "If as the papers report, my successor has been appointed, it is important that I should know it, and that he should enter on the command immediately, as the troops are already in motion."[51]

Also from Louisville came a protest by James Guthrie: "The renewed rumors of the removal of General Buell I hope are without foundation. . . . He has confidence of most, if not all, of his generals and of all thinking men here. . . . No general can now take his place without injury to the service and the cause. . . ."[52]

Governor David Tod of Ohio thought otherwise. "For the first time since my connection with the service I feel it my duty to advise as to the disposition of officers in the field," he wrote Secretary of War Stanton. "With one voice, so far as it has reached me, the army from Ohio demand the removal of General Buell."[53]

Curiously, General Halleck was getting advice as to the disposition of general officers from several sources. On October 25 from Cincinnati, Horatio Wright had sent the general-in-chief a long letter, most of which was devoted to a report on the military situation in Kentucky and ending with "please instruct me as to what shall be done with my available force." In the preceding paragraph, however, General Wright had advocated that "a commander of all the forces in the West should be appointed." He continued:

> *Until this is done it is certain but little can be accomplished. Leaving out of consideration and jealousies that may exist and arise, it is impossible that several independent commanders can act with the same effect as a single controlling head. It seems to me that I see every day the bad results of this want of unity of operations. You of course fully understand this, for your own experience while in command at the West must have been instructive on this subject. I only desire to add mine, though more limited. Who the man should be I do not know, but I am inclined to believe he is not now west of the Alleghenies.*[54]

On the next day from Jackson, Tennessee, Ulysses Grant also wrote the general-in-chief seeking direction. "As situated now, with no more troops," he said, "I can do nothing but defend my positions, and do not feel at liberty to abandon any of them without first consulting you." Toward the end of the letter, though, Grant referred to a dispute he was having with Samuel Curtis, whose jurisdiction included New Madrid, Missouri. "I would respectfully suggest," he concluded, "that both banks of the [Mississippi] river be under one command."[55]

Next, in a letter to Halleck sent on October 30, Major General George H. Thomas, Buell's second in command since the botched guillotining early in October, recalled his having stepped aside. "The order relieving [Buell] was suspended," he wrote, "but to-day I am officially informed that he is relieved by General Rosecrans, my junior. Although I do not claim for myself any superior ability, yet feeling conscious that no just cause exists for oversloughing me by placing me under my junior, I feel deeply mortified and aggrieved at the action taken in this matter. . . . I do not desire the command of the Department of the Tennessee, but that an officer senior to me in rank should be sent here if I am retained on duty in it."[56]

General Halleck's response:

> *I cannot better state my appreciation of you as a general than by referring you to the fact that at Pittsburg Landing I urged upon the Secretary of War to secure your appointment as major-general, in order that I might place you in command of the right wing of the army over your then superiors. . . .*
>
> *When it was determined to relieve General Buell another*

person was spoken of as his successor and it was through my repeated solicitation that you were appointed. You having virtually declined the command at that time it was necessary to appoint another, and General Rosecrans was selected.

You are mistaken about General Rosecrans being your junior. His commission dates prior to yours. But that is of little importance, for the law gives to the President the power to assign without regard to dates, and he has seen fit to exercise it in this and many other cases.

Rest assured, general, that I fully appreciate your military capacity, and will do everything in my power to give you an independent command when an opportunity offers. It was not possible to give you the command in Tennessee after you had declined it.[57]

Old Brains was receiving troubling squawks from West Point-trained commanders already in the field: Grant, Wright, Rosecrans, Thomas, Buell, and of course McClellan. But soon he found himself beset with additional problems caused by Abraham Lincoln's selection of Nathaniel Banks, a political general whose military record was even more dismal than John McClernand's or Benjamin F. Butler's, to assemble and head a secret force destined for service west of the Mississippi—notably, in Texas and Louisiana.

Abolitionists' agitation for a Union invasion of Texas was nothing new. But in the war's second year, shortages of cotton had stilled three-fourths of the spindles in New England's textile mills, and leaders of the anti-slavery movement had developed a program calling for the raising of troops in the region for the conquest of Texas with transfer of confiscated cotton-growing land to those soldiers as an incentive to volunteering. Success, of course, would be reflected in Lincoln's retaining New Englanders' political support in 1864's presidential election.[58]

Back in February 1862, General-in-Chief McClellan—at the time, massing all the resources he could in his Army of the Potomac—had declared:

The occupation of Brazos de Santiago and Brownsville [near the mouth of Texas' Rio Grande River border with Mexico] *is important and desirable for many reasons. It would not be prudent, however, to attempt it without force sufficient to hold points farther north and east* [i.e., much of the rest of Texas]. *We have not the disposable force at the present moment, nor would it do to risk a detached force in so remote a position, without retreat or succor, until certain that our foreign relations were satisfactory.*[59]

However, the Young Napoleon saw no harm in allowing Ben Butler to take army troops along in the operation that led to the navy's capture of New Orleans in May. "Spoons" Butler was still commanding the Department of the Gulf from the Crescent City in the fall of 1862.[60]

Just as Lincoln had not wanted to risk loss of New Englanders' votes and support for the war, neither had he been able to resist the pressure brought upon him by the governors of states in the Old Northwest, in particular by Indiana's Oliver P. Morton, to regain control of the region's main means of carrying on world trade: the Mississippi—hence, his approval of John McClernand's Vicksburg proposal. But with Lee's army only recently discouraged from remaining in Maryland, the forces led by Bragg and Kirby Smith still capable of menacing Kentucky, and Earl Van Dorn and Sterling Price pressing Grant, it was highly doubtful that Lincoln could please *both* the cotton-starved abolitionists on the Atlantic seaboard and the midwesterners demanding access to the Gulf of Mexico and worldwide markets. Even so, the President and Secretary Stanton gave the Northern public the impression that McClernand was headed for Vicksburg and Banks' destination was somewhere along Texas' Gulf Coast.

Perhaps aware of General Halleck's extreme abhorrence of the introduction of politics into military operations, apparently Lincoln used Stanton as the primary point of contact for the governors in New England. Massachusetts' John Andrew, long a leading advocate of the Texas invasion, telegraphed Stanton on October 31: "I assigned the three-years' (Forty-first) and seven nine-months' regiments to General Banks. . . . Shall Banks have any batteries and cavalry from Massachusetts?"[61] And Stanton replied: "Give General Banks all the infantry, cavalry, and artillery you can raise. Let Massachusetts show how liberal she can be to one of her own worthy sons."[62]

5

DURING MOST OF THIS BUSY PERIOD, General McClellan had inadvertently eased the general-in-chief's burdens slightly by spending much of it in a rented farmhouse near Harpers Ferry and Antietam Creek with Mary Ellen and their infant daughter. No one in Washington seemed to miss his petulant complaints or demands for more troops, more shoes, more of everything. That the angled blade would claim his head was all but certain; but when and how the slicing was to be carried out were open questions.

Earlier, the administration's pressures to relieve Don Carlos Buell from command had prompted lawyer Halleck to make certain that the paper trail fully justified severance. To that end, after Perryville Old Brains had sent the general a clear and stern admonition:

> *The capture of East Tennessee should be the main object of your campaign. You say it is the heart of the enemy's resources; make it the heart of yours. Your army can live there if the enemy's can. . . .*
>
> *I am directed by the President to say to you that your army must enter East Tennessee this fall, and that it ought to move there while the roads are passable. . . . He does not understand why we cannot march as the enemy marches, live as he does, and fight as he fights, unless we admit the inferiority of our troops and of our generals.*[63]

Abraham Lincoln directed a similar warning to General McClellan on October 13, 1862. Later, this unusually long and precisely crafted letter would be cited with admiration as evidence of his generalship. After Antietam and Perryville, a distinguished historian would write, "the President exhibited a growing mastery of military affairs. Getting little help from Halleck, who responded to inquiries by scratching his elbows and taking all sides on every question, Lincoln had to apply his good common sense to the problems of the army."[64]

Really? Anyone familiar with Old Brains' thinking—as reflected in the message to Buell (above) and hundreds of others—should be able to determine how much of the letter to McClellan (below) was contributed by Halleck and which words were likely to have been Lincoln's own:

> *You remember my speaking to you of what I called your over-cautiousness. Are you not overcautious when you assume that you cannot do what the enemy is constantly doing? Should you not claim to be at least his equal in prowess, and act upon the claim?*
>
> *As I understand, you telegraphed General Halleck that you cannot subsist your army at Winchester unless the railroad from Harper's Ferry to that point be put in working order. But the enemy does now subsist his army at Winchester, at a distance nearly twice as great from railroad transportation as you would have to do,*

without the railroad last named. He now wagons from Culpeper Court-House, which is just about twice as far as you would have to do from Harper's Ferry. He is certainly not more than half as well provided with wagons as you are.

I certainly should be pleased for you to have the advantage of the railroad from Harper's Ferry to Winchester, but it wastes all the remainder of autumn to give it to you, and in fact ignores the question of time, which cannot and must not be ignored. Again, one of the standard maxims of war, as you know, is to "operate upon the enemy's communications as much as possible without exposing your own." You seem to act as if this applies against you, but cannot apply in your favor.

Change positions with the enemy, and think you not he would break your communication with Richmond within the next twenty-four hours? You dread his going into Pennsylvania, but if he does so in full force, he gives up his communications to you absolutely, and you have nothing to do but to follow and ruin him. If he does so with less than full force, fall upon and beat what is left behind all the easier.

Exclusive of the water-line, you are now nearer Richmond than the enemy is by the route that you can and he must take. Why can you not reach there before him, unless you admit that he is more than your equal on a march?

His route is the arc of a circle, while yours is the chord. The roads are as good on yours as on his.

You know I desired, but did not order, you to cross the Potomac below instead of above the Shenandoah and Blue Ridge. My idea was that this would at once menace the enemy's communications, which I would seize if he would permit.

If he should move northward I would follow him closely, holding his communications. If he should prevent our seizing his communications and move toward Richmond, I would press closely to him; fight him, if a favorable opportunity should present, and at least try to beat him to Richmond on the inside track.

I say "try;" if we never try we shall never succeed.

If he makes a stand at Winchester, moving neither north nor south, I would fight him there, on the idea that if we cannot beat him when he bears the wastage of coming to us, we never can when we bear the wastage of going to him. This proposition is a simple truth, and is too important to be lost sight of for a moment.

> *In coming to us he tenders us an advantage which we should not waive. We should not so operate as to merely drive him away. As we must beat him somewhere or fail finally, we can do it, if at all, easier near to us than far away. If we cannot beat the enemy where he now is, we never can, he again being within the intrenchments of Richmond.*
>
> *Recurring to the idea of going to Richmond on the inside track, the facility of supplying from the side away from the enemy is remarkable, as it were, by the different spokes of a wheel extending from the hub toward the rim, and this, whether you move directly by the chord or on the inside arc, hugging the Blue Ridge more closely. The chord-line, as you see, carries you by Aldie, Hay Market, and Fredericksburg; and you see how turnpikes, railroads, and finally the Potomac, by Aquia Creek, meet you at all points from Washington; the same, only the lines lengthened a little, if you press closer to the Blue Ridge part of the way.*
>
> *The gaps through the Blue Ridge I understand to be about the following distances from Harper's Ferry, to wit: Vestal's, 5 miles; Gregory's, 13; Snicker's, 18; Ashby's, 28; Manassas, 38; Chester, 45; and Thornton's, 53. I should think it preferable to take the route nearest the enemy, disabling him to make an important move without your knowledge, and compelling him to keep his forces together for dread of you. The gaps would enable you to attack if you should wish.*
>
> *For a great part of the way you would be practically between the enemy and both Washington and Richmond, enabling us to spare you the greatest number of troops from here. When at length running for Richmond ahead of him enables him to move this way, if he does so, turn and attack him in the rear. But I think he should be engaged long before such point is reached.*
>
> *It is all easy if our troops march as well as the enemy, and it is unmanly to say they cannot do it.*[65]

Not having ever been a soldier, much less a graduate of any military academy, Lincoln must not have known that for a superior to instruct a subordinate in such strict ways is the equivalent of a direct, often a peremptory, command. And after more than a year of dealing with the Young Napoleon, he should have known better than to have added: "This letter is in no sense an order."[66]

Yet Lincoln did. And probable ghostwriter Halleck must have been as astonished as the commander-in-chief on October 22, a week later, when General McClellan left domestic pleasures long enough to reply: "After full consultation, I have decided to move upon the line indicated by the President in his letter of the 13th instant, and have accordingly taken steps to execute the movement."[67]

Well, fine, but McClellan's inherent—certainly, his consistent—fear of having his beloved Army of the Potomac smashed by General Lee seemed to inspire him to degrees of excellence in excuse-crafting never approached even by the master, Don Carlos Buell. On October 25, in a message to Halleck, Little Mac used a portion of a report submitted by Colonel Robert Williams, First Massachusetts Cavalry, to explain his inability to advance. Williams wrote: "I have in camp 267 horses . . .; of these, 128 are positively and absolutely unable to leave the camp. . . . The diseases are principally grease and sore-tongue. The horses, which are still sound, are absolutely broken down from fatigue, and want of flesh. . . ."[68]

A. Lincoln replied to McClellan: "I have just read your dispatch about fatigued and sore-tongued horses. Will you pardon me for asking what the horses of your army have done since the battle of Antietam that fatigues anything?"[69]

Little Mac responded at length, provoking His Excellency to telegraph him:

> *Yours in reply to mine about horses is received. Of course, you know the facts better than I; still, two considerations remain. Stuart's cavalry outmarched ours, having certainly done more marked service on the Peninsula and everywhere since. Secondly, will not a movement of our army be a relief to the cavalry, compelling the enemy to concentrate, instead of foraying in squads everywhere? But I am so rejoiced to learn from your dispatch to General Halleck that you begin crossing the* [Potomac] *river this morning.*[70]

McClellan's next about horses was even longer. "Someone has conveyed to your mind an erroneous impression in regard to the service of our cavalry," he wrote Lincoln, "for I know you would not intentionally do injustice to the excellent officers and men of which it is composed."[71]

By this point, the President may well have wished he had refrained from employing sarcasm and had left the horses question to Halleck. But McClellan had touched a Lincolnian nerve, and this could not be left unanswered:

Most certainly I intend no injustice to any, and if I have done any I deeply regret it. To be told, after more than five weeks' total inaction of the army, and during which period we have sent to the army every fresh horse we possibly could, amounting in the whole to 7,918, that the cavalry horses were too much fatigued to move, presents a very cheerless, almost hopeless, prospect for the future, and it may have forced something of impatience in my dispatch. If not recruited and rested then, when could they ever be? I suppose the river is rising, and I am glad to believe you are crossing.[72]

In a message sent later that day, October 27, McClellan changed the subject:

Your Excellency is aware of the very great reduction of numbers that has taken place in most of the old regiments of this command, and how necessary it is to fill up these skeletons before taking them again into action. I have the honor, therefore, to request that the order to fill up the old regiments with drafted men may at once be issued.[73]

Lincoln's weariness was reflected in his immediate reply:

Your dispatch of 3 p.m. to-day, in regard to filling up old regiments with drafted men, is received, and the request therein shall be complied with as far as practicable.

And now I ask a distinct answer to the question, Is it your purpose not to go into action again until the men now being drafted in the States are incorporated into the old regiments?[74]

One word—no—would have been a sufficient answer; instead, McClellan used 347 and exceeded Buell's ingenuity in inventing excuses. His reply, in part:

On the 11th instant I requested General Halleck to have the necessary order given. I received no reply to this, and learned this afternoon that no such order had been issued. In the press of business I then called an aide, and telling him that I had conversed with you upon the subject, I directed him to write for me a dispatch asking Your Excellency to have the necessary order given.

I regret to say that this officer, after writing the dispatch, finding me still engaged, sent it to the telegraph office without first submitting it to me, under the impression that he had communicated my views. He, however, unfortunately added "before taking them into action again." This phrase was not authorized or intended by me. It has conveyed altogether an erroneous impression as to my plans and intentions.

To Your Excellency's question I answer distinctly that I have not had any idea of postponing the advance until the old regiments are filled by drafted men.[75]

Curiously, in the first two sentences of this message to Lincoln, McClellan all but accused Halleck of negligence. This was a manifestation of the Young Napoleon's desire to regain the post of general-in-chief, as well as a reflection of his contempt for Old Brains. In late September, he had written his wife: "Stanton is as great a villain as ever & Halleck as great a fool—he has no brains whatever!"[76] A few days later: "I do think that man Halleck is the most stupid idiot I ever heard of—either that or he drinks hard—for he cannot even comprehend the English language."[77] And on October 29:

If you could know the mean & dirty character of the dispatches I receive you would boil over with anger—when it is possible to misunderstand, & when it is not possible, whenever there is a chance of a wretched innuendo—there it comes. But the good of the country requires me to submit to all this from men whom I know to be my inferiors socially, intellectually & morally! There never was a truer epithet applied to a certain individual than that of the "Gorilla."[78]

According to McClellan's biographer Stephen Sears, at around this time Little Mac sent Brigadier General John Cochrane to Washington to "tell the president that McClellan must be vested with 'more power and authority than he now has' or he would resign; he was unwilling to serve any longer under a general-in-chief who did not support him." Sears' account continued:

When he did discuss this with Lincoln, Cochrane recalled, the president acknowledged that such a plan had occurred to him, and he supposed another place could be found for Halleck so as to make room for McClellan. More specifically, it was the president's design, the political insider T. J. Barnett assured Samuel Barlow, to transfer Halleck to a western command "& promote Mc out of the Army of the Potomac & place Hooker there. . . . I presume Mc will be promoted as the pressure is intense. . . ."[79]

Be all that as it may, in a message to His Excellency on October 30, General McClellan nominated Old Brains to be the scapegoat for a disaster that had not yet occurred:

I ask your attention to my dispatches calling the notice of the General in Chief to the insufficiency of the preparations I leave behind me for resisting a raid, also to the fact that we are to have no reinforcements for the old Penna regts from the drafted men. . . . Please remember that I have clearly stated what troops I leave behind & that I regard the number insufficient to prevent a raid & that while the responsibility has been thrown upon me by Genl Halleck he has given me only limited means to accomplish the object. . . . I write this only to place the responsibility where it belongs & wish you to show this to Genl Halleck. . . .[80]

Among the referenced messages the hypocrite had sent Halleck was one that ended:

I leave the decision of these grave questions to the General-in-Chief. I know nothing of the number of troops at Baltimore, &c.
        An important element in the solution of this problem is the fact that a great portion of Bragg's army is probably now at liberty to unite itself with Lee's command.[81]

And the reply that had prompted the Young Napoleon to express his anguish to Lincoln was hardly an example of Halleck's rubbing his elbows and getting on all sides of the question:

Since you left Washington I have advised and suggested in relation to your movements, but I have given you no orders. I do not give you any now.
        The Government has intrusted you with defeating and driving back the rebel army in your front. I shall not attempt to control you in the measures you may adopt for that purpose.
        You are informed of my views, but the President has left you at liberty to adopt them or not, as you may deem best.
        You will also exercise your own discretion in regard to what

points on the Potomac and the Baltimore and Ohio Railroad are to be occupied or fortified. I will only add that there is no appropriation for permanent intrenchments on that line. Moreover, I think it will be time enough to decide upon fortifying Front Royal, Strasburg, Wardensville, and Moorefield when the enemy is driven south of them and they come into our possession.

I do not think that we need have any immediate fear of Bragg's army. You are within 20 miles of Lee's, while Bragg is distant about 400 miles.[82]

6

LINCOLN'S VISITS TO the telegraph office on October 25, 26, and 27 had resulted in substantial lengthening of the paper trail leading to McClellan's guillotining. Also, his associates in the Union's high command had made additions. Lincoln's sarcasm having failed to abash the general, on October 27 lawyer Stanton reverted to the idea of having lawyer Halleck provide documented answers to five questions:

It has been publicly stated [wrote Stanton] *that the army under General McClellan has been unable to move during the fine weather of this fall for want of shoes, clothing, and other supplies. You will please report to this Department upon the following points:*

1st. To whom and in what manner the requisitions for supplies to the army under General McClellan have been made since you assumed command as General-in-Chief, and whether any requisition for supplies of any kind has since that time been made upon the Secretary of War or communication had with him except through you.

2d. If you, as General-in-Chief, have taken pains to ascertain the condition of the army in respect to supplies of shoes, clothing, arms, and other necessaries, and whether there has been any neglect or delay by any Department or bureau in filling the requisitions for supplies, and what has been and is the condition of that army as compared with other armies in respect to supplies.

3d. At what date after the battle of Antietam the orders to advance against the enemy were given to General McClellan, and how often have they been repeated.

4th. Whether, in your opinion, there has been any want in the

army under General McClellan of shoes, clothing, arms, or other
equipments or supplies that ought to have prevented its advance
against the enemy when the order was given.

5th. How long was it after the orders to advance were given to
General McClellan before he informed you that any shoes or clothing
were wanted in his army, and what are his means of promptly
communicating the wants of the army to you or to the proper
bureaus of the War Department?[83]

Able attorney that Edwin Stanton was, of course he knew the answers
before he framed the questions. His intent seems to have been twofold: to
clear the War Department of any complaints made by McClellan or his
supporters, and to help make the case for the Young Napoleon's removal.

Providing the information the secretary craved was no problem for
Old Brains, thanks in part to the fact that all of McClellan's allegations had
been refuted by Quartermaster General Montgomery Meigs. A few excerpts
from his report, dated October 28, 1862, reflect the substance of the whole:

There has not been, so far as I could ascertain, any neglect or delay
in any Department or bureau in issuing all supplies asked for by
General McClellan or by the officers of his staff. Delays have
occasionally occurred in forwarding supplies by rail on account of
the crowded condition of the depots or of a want of cars, but,
whenever notified of this, agents have been sent out to remove the
difficulty. Under the excellent superintendence of General Haupt, I
think these delays have been less frequent and of shorter duration
than is usual with freight trains.

Any army of the size of that under General McClellan will
frequently be for some days without the supplies asked for, on
account of neglect in making timely requisitions and unavoidable
delays in forwarding them and in distributing them to the different
brigades and regiments. From all the information I can obtain, I am
of opinion that the requisitions from that army have been filled more
promptly, and that the men, as a general rule, have been better
supplied than our armies operating in the West. The latter have
operated at much greater distances from the sources of supply, and
have had far less facilities for transportation. In fine, I believe that
no armies in the world while in campaign have been more promptly
or better supplied than ours. . . .

In my opinion there has been no such want of supplies in the army under General McClellan as to prevent his compliance with the orders to advance against the enemy. Had he moved to the south side of the Potomac, he could have received his supplies almost as readily as by remaining inactive on the north side. . . .

The suffering for want of clothing is exaggerated, I think, and certainly might have been avoided by timely requisitions of regimental and brigade commanders. . . .

In regard to General McClellan's means of promptly communicating the wants of his army to me or to the proper bureaus of the War Department, I report that in addition to the ordinary mails he has been in hourly communication with Washington by telegraph.[84]

Having written what might prove the last chapter in *The Quarrels of Stanton and McClellan*, on October 30 General Halleck took the time to respond unofficially to an unofficial letter from Missouri's Governor H. R. Gamble regarding a federal-state disagreement. That subject disposed of, Old Brains provided his friend with a brief summary of where he stood:

I am sick, tired, and disgusted with the condition of military affairs here in the East and wish myself back in the Western army. With all my efforts I can get nothing done. There is an immobility here that exceeds all that any man can conceive of. It requires the lever of Archimedes to move this inert mass. I have tried my best, but without success. [But] I do not yet despair, and shall continue my efforts.[85]

General Halleck's discouragement raises the question, what did he mean by immobility? Actually, the case of *United States* v. *Confederacy* had been moved a considerable distance during October. Was he downhearted because he had not had more to do with the repelling of the rebels' many assaults at Corinth? Or with the turning back of Bragg's and Kirby Smith's invasions of Kentucky? Or was he unduly frustrated by his inability to get either Buell or McClellan to obey his peremptory orders?

In fact, at October's end Buell was gone and the Young Napoleon was going. No major Confederate force threatened any Union or Union-held city of any consequence. And the targets for the next federal military operations had been identified: Vicksburg, East Tennessee, not Richmond but the destruction of Lee's Army of Northern Virginia.

Perhaps the most alarming and depressing developments during the month had been Abraham Lincoln's politicization of the Union's war effort by entrusting military operations to McClernand and Banks, generals whose incompetence was utterly appalling. Moreover, these ventures had been launched if not behind Halleck's back, certainly by going *around* him. It was as though the President were reassuming the role of acting general-in-chief—not by default this time, but to use military resources for his own political ends. At a minimum, Old Brains had not succeeded in moving Lincoln's thinking and actions away from making egregious blunders.

Surely General Halleck was tempted to leave Lincoln to get out of his scrapes. Events such as the undercutting of Grant and the deceptions being employed in support of Banks suggested that Old Brains' first impulse—to refuse to come to Washington—had been the correct one. But he had allowed his sense of duty and of honor and of loyalty to his country to override his survival instincts, and now he was doomed to achieve little beyond minimizing the damage that seemed inevitable from the willful, yet totally unnecessary, mixing of politics and soldiers' blood.

"I do not yet despair, and shall continue my efforts," Halleck had written Governor Gamble on October 30, 1862. Concurrently, Edwin Stanton was telegraphing the governors of New York, Massachusetts, Rhode Island, Connecticut, New Hampshire, Maine, and Vermont this message:

> *General Banks has established his headquarters in New York to organize a Southern expedition. All the troops in your State not otherwise appropriated are placed at his command. You will please confer with him, answer his requisition, and render him every aid in your power in speedily organizing his command.*[86]

From Albany on November 1, the Bobbin Boy advised Halleck's chief of staff, Brigadier General George W. Cullum, that he had found "a very general and earnest feeling among all classes of citizens both in New York and New England in favor of the expedition intrusted to my charge. An unexpected expression of satisfaction has met me from all sides, and I have received evidences of hearty and prompt co-operation. . . ."[87]

On November 4, General Halleck acknowledged the wire addressed to Cullum and gave Banks a concise summary of actions taken in Washington on his behalf. In closing, he passed along this comment:

> *Our prospect for an early movement down the Mississippi is*

improving. In fact, while things remain in statu quo *here, where Archimedes with his longest lever could not move the army, at the West everything begins to look well again.*[88]

Archimedes had more success once the Congressional elections were over. Lincoln set politics aside for long enough to correct, finally, one of his worst mistakes. And during the next day or two, the general-in-chief put the finishing touches on the plan and documents to be employed in the severing of Major General George B. McClellan from his beloved Army of the Potomac.

10 ★ The Distressing Ending of a Dreadful Year

*H*ENRY WAGER HALLECK HAD MORE EXPERIENCE than anyone in a blue uniform in relieving generals from command, yet each occasion had been blighted in some way. Of course, no victim of the angled blade could have been expected to endure the modification with equanimity. Both John Pope and Irvin McDowell protested with vehemence and some cause that their severances were unjust. Don Carlos Buell's consignment to oblivion was marked by mistakes—twice. And the termination of any officer's career in the midst of a war was not to be undertaken lightly, no matter how disappointing his performance may have been.

Abraham Lincoln had brought George Brinton McClellan to prominence, and he was perhaps the last person in the Union government to decide that the Young Napoleon had to be removed from command. The Radical Republicans had been demanding his banishment for twelve months. In Lincoln's cabinet there had been considerable support for Secretary of War Stanton's "remonstrance" declaring it unsafe to entrust the command of any Union army to McClellan. General Halleck had advocated his retention after Second Bull Run, mainly because he saw no alternative.

Implementing the decision to relieve the general, however, entailed risks and required special care because of the strong affection the men of his Army of the Potomac were thought to have for their Little Mac. Refusal to fight under any other commander could not be ruled out. Also in jeopardy might be the continued support of the "War" Democrats, many of them close friends of McClellan.

Technically, removing general officers was a purely presidential prerogative. For political reasons, however, Lincoln confined his role in the process to the minimum, signing a directive on November 5, 1862:

> *By direction of the President, it is ordered that Major-General McClellan be relieved from the command of the Army of the Potomac; and that Major-General Burnside take command of that army. Also that Major-General Hunter take command of the corps in said army which is now commanded by General Burnside. That Major-General Fitz John Porter be relieved from the command of the corps he now commands in said army, and that Major-General Hooker take command of said corps.*
>
> *The General-in-Chief is authorized, in [his] discretion, to issue an order substantially as the above, forthwith, or so soon as he may deem proper.*[1]

Having been designated the Union's equivalent of Great Britain's Lord High Executioner, General Halleck put in motion secret procedures designed to prevent the kind of mistakes that had made Buell's removal so messy. Only two other officers were to be involved: Brigadier General Herman Haupt, who would provide a special train, and Brigadier General Catherinus P. Buckingham, the very important passenger. Buckingham was to find General Burnside and obtain his agreement to succeed McClellan; if Burnside refused—he had twice before—Buckingham was to return to Washington. If Burnside agreed, he and Buckingham were to go to McClellan's headquarters and deliver to him a piece of paper signed by General-in-Chief Halleck and containing this single sentence: "On receipt of the order of the President, sent herewith, you will turn over your command to General Burnside, and repair to Trenton, N. J., reporting, on your arrival at that place, by telegraph, for further orders."[2]

That the Young Napoleon had neither mended his ways nor suspected his supply of soldier's gold had run out was indicated by a message he sent from Rectortown to His Excellency (McClellan had long since stopped communicating with Halleck) at 4:00 p.m. on November 7, 1862:

> *The Manassas Gap Railroad is in such poor running order that I shall be obliged to establish my depot for supplies for the whole army at Gainesville until the Orange and Alexandria Railroad can be repaired beyond Manassas Junction. I am now concentrating my troops in the direction of Warrenton, and have telegraphed General Haupt to repair the Orange and Alexandria road to the line of the*

Rappahannock as soon as it can be covered by our troops. The [snow] *storm continues unabated.*[3]

More delay was in prospect, but this no longer mattered to anyone in Washington. Even as McClellan wrote, General Buckingham was nearing Warrenton on Herman Haupt's special train. From there, Buckingham rode through the early fall snowstorm to Ambrose Burnside's headquarters.

At first, Burnside refused—for the third time—and for the same reason: he did not feel qualified to command such a large force. Earlier, McClellan had agreed. In a letter to Mary Ellen on September 29, after complaining about having to write a report on the battle of Antietam, he said: "I *ought* to rap Burnside *very* severely & probably will—yet I hate to do it. He is very slow and is not fit to command a regiment."[4] But Buckingham's arguments proved persuasive, and at around eleven o'clock that night, he and Burnside rode through the snow to the army commander's tent to carry out the final step in the process General Halleck had prescribed.

McClellan had been writing Mary Ellen when the two officers arrived; afterward, he resumed:

> *11 ½ pm. Another interruption—this time more important. It was in the shape of dear good old Burnside accompanied by Genl Buckingham, the Secy's Adjt Genl—they brought with them the order relieving me of the Army of the Potomac, & assigning Burnside to the command. No cause is given. I am ordered to turn over the command immediately & repair to Trenton, N. J. & on my arrival there to report for further orders!! . . .*
>
> *Poor Burn feels dreadfully, almost crazy—I am sorry for him, & he never showed himself a better man or truer friend than now. Of course I was much surprised—but as I read the order in the presence of Genl Buckingham, I am sure that not a muscle quivered nor was the slightest expression of feeling visible on my face, which he watched closely. They shall not have that triumph. They have made a great mistake—alas for my poor country—I know in my innermost heart she never had a truer servant. I have informally turned over the command to Burnside—but will go tomorrow to Warrenton with him & perhaps remain a day or two there in order to give him all the information in my power. . . .*[5]

General Halleck had also armed Buckingham with a note to Burnside:

"Immediately on assuming command of the Army of the Potomac, you will report the position of your troops, and what you purpose doing with them."[6] On November 8, the new army commander closed a message to the general-in-chief with these words:

> *General McClellan had already given directions covering some two or three days, and during that time I will try to acquaint myself with the condition of his several staff departments, after which I will, as you request, give you a full statement of my plans.*[7]

This time the severance had been quick and sure.

2

AMBROSE BURNSIDE WAS PROMPT in keeping his promise. In a long and carefully crafted letter, he recommended to Halleck that Fredericksburg be his first objective, with Richmond the next, and he gave sound reasons not only to support his choices but also for rejecting alternatives. Moreover, the tone of his response was a welcome change, as his closing sentences reflected:

> *With an approval of these suggestions, I will endeavor with all my ability to bring this campaign to a successful issue. If they are not approved, I hope specific instructions will be given, and the General-in-Chief may rely upon a cheerful and implicit obedience. The General-in-Chief will readily comprehend the embarrassments which surround me in taking command of this army, at this place, and at this season of the year. Had I been asked to take it, I should have declined, but being ordered, I cheerfully obey.*
>
> *A telegram from you, approving my plans, will put us to work.*[8]

Soon after George McClellan had departed for Trenton, New Jersey, to await orders that would never come, General Halleck took Herman Haupt and Quartermaster General Montgomery Meigs with him on a visit to Burnside at Warrenton. In his proposal, the new army commander had devoted several paragraphs to means of supply—hence, the presence of Meigs and Haupt. For his part, Old Brains had some reservations that required discussion; also, the trip would be evidence of his desire to get Burnside off to a productive start.

In the lengthy Lincoln-Halleck paper His Excellency had sent McClellan on October 13, the authors invoked plane geometry in trying to persuade the Young Napoleon to drive straight to Richmond—though annihilating Lee's army was the grand object. Lest General Burnside's proposed dog-leg via Fredericksburg cause some furrowing of the presidential brow, Old Brains and his associates pressed for details. In the end, Halleck agreed to take Burnside's plan to his client in *United States* v. *Confederacy.* And within a short time he was able to report: "The President has just assented to your plan. He thinks that it will succeed, if you move very rapidly; otherwise not."[9]

Apparently, Abraham Lincoln had been happy to put the whole sordid and disappointing experience with McClellan behind him. Yet in correcting the mistake of having given too much power to an incompetent professional, concurrently he was compounding another earlier one not only by retaining an incompetent political general—Nathaniel Banks—but by expanding the Bobbin Boy's potential for producing fresh disasters.

Lincoln's reasons for doing something about Texas and cotton, of course, had been understandable. So had been his assurances to governors of the Old Northwest's states that General McClernand was going to reopen their constituents' access to world markets via the Mississippi. But Banks' activities could not be concealed forever, and lawyer Lincoln correctly perceived that a cloak of legality ought to be thrown over them.

Accordingly, lawyer Halleck, the President's lightning rod, caused an order to be prepared, dated November 8, 1862, declaring that: "By direction of the President of the United States, Maj. Gen. N. P. Banks is assigned to the command of the Department of the Gulf, including the State of Texas."[10]

In effect, Lincoln was subjecting the Radicals' beloved Ben Butler (another political general appointed by the panicked commander-in-chief in the war's earliest days) to the proverbial guillotine. Presumably, bureaucratic lethargy prevented the Jacobins from learning of this intended decapitation. But even more outraged would have been the abolitionists in New England, who were at that moment helping to recruit men for Banks' Texas expedition, had they known the contents of the directive Lincoln had caused General-in-Chief Halleck to prepare and send Banks. It was long and technical in a military sense, yet it would be more important over the long term than most documents that also cast long shadows:

The President of the United States having assigned you to command of the Department of the Gulf, you will immediately proceed with the troops assembling in transports at Fort Monroe to New Orleans and relieve Major-General Butler.

An additional force of some 10,000 men will be sent to you from Boston and New York as soon as possible.

The first military operations which will engage your attention on your arrival at New Orleans will be the opening of the Mississippi and the reduction of Fort Morgan or Mobile City, in order to control that bay and harbor. In these expeditions you will have the co-operation of the rear-admiral commanding the naval forces in the Gulf and the Mississippi River. A military and naval expedition is organizing at Memphis and Cairo to move down the Mississippi and cooperate with you against Vicksburg and any other points which the enemy may occupy on that river.

As the ranking general in the Southwest, you are authorized to assume control of any military forces from the Upper Mississippi which may come within your command. The line of division between your department and that of Major-General Grant is therefore left undecided for the present, and you will exercise superior authority as far north as you may ascend the river.

The President regards the opening of the Mississippi River as the first and most important of all our military and naval operations, and it is hoped that you will not lose a moment in accomplishing it.

This river being opened, the question will arise how the troops and naval forces there can be employed to the best advantage. Two objects are suggested as worthy of your attention:

> *First, on the capture of Vicksburg, to send a military force directly east to destroy the railroads at Jackson and Marion, and thus cut off all connection by rail between Northern Mississippi and Mobile and Atlanta. The latter place is now the chief military depot of the rebel armies in the West.*

> *Second, to ascend with a naval and military force the Red River as far as it is navigable, and thus open an outlet for the sugar and cotton of Northern Louisiana.*

> *Possibly both of these objects may be accomplished if the circumstances should be favorable. It is also suggested that, having Red River in our possession, it would form the best base for operations in Texas.*

It is believed that the operations of General Rosecrans in East Tennessee, of General Grant in Northern Mississippi, and of General Steele in Arkansas will give full employment to the enemy's troops in the West, and thus prevent them from concentrating in force against you. Should they do so, you will be re-enforced by detachments from one or more of these commands.

These instructions are not intended to tie your hands or to hamper your operations in the slightest degree. So far away from headquarters, you must necessarily exercise your own judgment and discretion in regard to your movements against the enemy, keeping in view that the opening of the Mississippi River is now the great and primary object of your expedition, and I need not assure you, general, that the Government has unlimited confidence not only in your judgment and discretion, but also in your energy and military promptness.[11]

Extravagant professions such as "I am, sir, with great respect, your most obedient servant" and similar effusions were commonplace, nigh-automatic at the end of messages—even those exchanged by men who would have horse-whipped or shot one another on sight. Old Brains was no behavioral maverick. Even so, wreathed in cigar smoke, he must have paced the floor and rubbed his elbows for a long time before signing a piece of paper that assured the Bobbin Boy that the Government had unlimited confidence not only in his judgment and discretion, but also in his energy and military promptness.

Obviously, Judge Lincoln was coming down on the side of his fellow Old Northwesterners. But lest he reveal *that* to cotton-starved New England's abolitionists, and risk losing their support in 1864's presidential election, his able counsel in *USA* v. *CSA* had included the passages regarding operations via the Red River in Louisiana aimed toward invading East Texas. Nothing in the military program Old Brains had suggested necessarily precluded any course of action Banks might adopt. Yet, at least for the time being, apparently it was thought best for the legal underpinnings of the Bobbin Boy's activities to be kept out of sight.

Prudent lawyers that they were, Lincoln and Stanton took another precaution in pursuance of their desire to avoid disrupting the recruiting efforts of either the governors in the Old Northwest to support McClernand, or of those in New England to fill Nathaniel Banks' ranks. Not General Halleck but Secretary of War Stanton, it was, who proclaimed on November 14, 1862, that Andrew Jackson Hamilton, a Texan Unionist in exile with no previous connection to the Union's or any other armies, was suddenly a brigadier general empowered to raise troops and command them—presumably, within the force Banks was attracting from New England.[12]

"You may rely upon the perfect confidence and full support of the [War] Department in the performance of your duties," Stanton assured Hamilton at the close of another directive the secretary prepared on November 14, 1862. It was typically wordy, but it was also a window into the mind of the man who was Henry Wager Halleck's immediate superior:

> *The commission you have received expresses on its face the nature and extent of the duties and power devolved on you by the appointment of Military Governor of Texas. Instructions have been given to Major-General Banks to aid you in the performance of your duty and the exercise of your authority. He has also been instructed to detail an adequate military force for the special purpose of a Governor's guard, and to act under your directions.*
>
> *It is obvious to you that the great purpose of your appointment is to re-establish the authority of the Federal Government in the State of Texas and to provide the means of maintaining peace and security to the loyal inhabitants of that State until they shall be able to establish a civil government. Upon your wisdom and energetic action much will depend in accomplishing that result.*[13]

Surely, Brigadier General-Military Governor Hamilton and his supporters in New England must have been gratified by Stanton's contribution to their case for General Banks'—actually, their—forces to be landed (where else?) somewhere along Texas' 500-plus mile-long Gulf of Mexico coastline. At the time, Banks was making his headquarters at New York City's Astor Hotel, where on November 15 he received this purely military admonition from the Union armies' general-in-chief:

> *There is no time to be lost, and you must move immediately with what troops you can get ready. The co-operating column [Mc-Clernand's] is nearly prepared. Delay may disarrange the plan. Moreover, this fine weather must not be lost.*[14]

Banks being Banks, only a week later, with recognizable help from Old Brains, Lincoln felt compelled to add his pressure:

Early last week you left me in high hope with your assurance that you would be off with your expedition at the end of that week or early in this. It is now the end of this, and I have just been overwhelmed and confounded with the sight of a requisition made by you which, I am assured, cannot be filled and got off within an hour short of two months.

My dear general, this expanding and piling up of impedimenta has been so far almost our ruin, and will be our final ruin if it is not abandoned. If you had the articles of this requisition upon the wharf, with the necessary animals to make them of any use, and forage for the animals, you could not get vessels together in two weeks to carry the whole, to say nothing of your 20,000 men; and, having the vessels, you could not put the cargoes aboard in two weeks more. And, after all, where you are going you have no use for them.

When you parted with me you had no such ideas in your mind. I know you had not, or you could not have expected to be off so soon as you said.

You must get back to something like the plan you had then or your expedition is a failure before you start. You must be off before Congress meets.

You would be better off anywhere, and especially where you are going, for not having a thousand wagons doing nothing but hauling forage to feed the animals that draw them, and taking at least 2,000 men to care for the wagons and animals, who otherwise might be 2,000 good soldiers.

Now, dear general, do not think this is an ill-natured letter; it is the very reverse. The simple publication of this requisition would ruin you.[15]

Such remarks, Old Brains may have mused after reading this indication that Lincoln had succumbed to impatience, confirmed at least two suppositions. First, the rich man in trouble who was his client had put too much faith in a demonstrated weakling. And second, his commander-in-chief had gone too far toward politicizing the Union's conduct of the war.

3

A. LINCOLN, HOWEVER, HAD ADVANCED not only Nathaniel Banks but

John McClernand as movers and shakers within the Union's war efforts in the West—in both instances for political reasons and apparently without regard to alternatives his general-in-chief might have offered. Given that the commander-in-chief was acting in accordance with his powers under the Constitution, at least two questions remained:

- Was Lincoln justified in risking the depletion of Union resources by entrusting them to generals whose records reflected nothing but incompetence?
- Was Halleck guilty of disloyalty to his president, or of acting against the best interests of his client, by protecting Ulysses Grant against politically driven encroachments on his turf?

Merely for such questions to exist was an indication that considerable erosion had occurred (and seemed likely to continue) in the Lincoln-Halleck relationship since Old Brains' arrival in Washington. Ironically, in the wake of the Young Napoleon's sacking and that of Don Carlos Buell, the general-in-chief was finding William Rosecrans and Ambrose Burnside to be vast improvements over the generals they had replaced—at least in terms of communicating and cooperation. But combat did not seem imminent in either Virginia or central Tennessee, so General Halleck had an opportunity to strengthen his ties to the man he had never quite gotten along with, Unconditional Surrender Grant.

As early as November's opening days, Grant had proposed and Halleck had approved drives aimed toward Holly Springs in northern Mississippi.[16] But as Grant was preparing to move, apparently he detected something ominous in a sentence in one of Halleck's messages to him: "Memphis will be made the depot of a joint military and naval expedition on Vicksburg."[17]

From La Grange, Tennessee, on the evening of November 10, 1862, General Grant asked three very good questions:

> *Am I to understand that I lie still here while an expedition is fitted out from Memphis, or do you want me to push as far south as possible? Am I to have Sherman move subject to my order, or is he and his forces reserved for some special service? Will not more forces be sent here?*[18]

Back to Grant the next day came one sentence that may well have been General-in-Chief Henry Wager Halleck's most important contribution to the quelling of the rebellion: "You have command of all troops sent to your department, and have permission to fight the enemy where you please."[19]

Notable by their absence were "By direction of the President . . ." or any other words at all. Having risked the termination of his own service, Halleck returned his attention to whatever telegrams from Nashville and the Astor Hotel in New York and Warrenton might require of him in the ways of decisions or guidance.

In stark contrast to Old Brains' Spartan literary effort that day, General McClernand delivered himself of two long, turgid, self-serving reports on the success to date of his recruiting efforts in the Old Northwest. In both, his claims were much the same. In the version he sent Halleck, sketchy details of those activities were all he offered. But in his message to Secretary of War Stanton, a kindred spirit, McClernand revealed much more about his motivation (and also his distressing lack of either discretion or respect for brevity) than he may have intended:

Passing from these details to a subject of a more prominent character, I wish to add that the avidity with which the Mississippi expedition is embraced by the people of the Northwest expose all who are charged with carrying it into effect to the consequences of popular fury if they should fail to do so.

As for myself I hardly need reiterate the deep and absorbing interest I feel in the enterprise and my entire willingness to do all in my power to promote it. Yet if, from obstacles such as opposed you in the beginning or for other causes, the expedition has become an uncertainty or must be long delayed I trust you will cut my supposed connection with it and order me to other duty in the field at once.

In the latter case my familiarity with the old troops of General Grant's command and the country in which he is operating would decide me, if I might be allowed a discretion, to prefer duty with him.

The blockade of the Mississippi River has left to the people of the Northwest but one outlet for their immense surplus of grains and live stock, and that by the lakes and railroads alone, to the East. . . . This evil operates most oppressively upon the energies and enterprise of the people of the Northwest on the one hand and most advantageously to capitalists in the East owning those roads and the manufacturing establishments furnishing the various fabrics required for the use of the Army and Navy on the other. The latter in a pecuniary aspect are deeply interested in continuing it.

What is seen? A comparatively insignificant obstruction has served to continue the blockade of the Mississippi River now for five months, covering a space during which the products of its valley are usually borne upon its waters to market, and the period of the investment of Vicksburg by a strong flotilla of gunboats.

In view of these facts, and the great addition which has been made to our armies under the late calls for volunteers, and the present inertness of the Mississippi Flotilla, the people so deeply interested are illy disposed to receive any excuse for further delay in removing that obstacle. Indeed, any further delay must produce consequences which will seriously complicate our national troubles by adding another geographical question to the one which is now undergoing the arbitrament of arms.

Already are there those who are beginning to look beyond the pale of Federal authority for new guarantees for the freedom of the Mississippi River. The late election, in some instances, affords unmistakable indications of this fact. . . . I am conscious that if something is not soon done to reopen that great highway that a new party will spring into existence, which will favor the recognition of the independence of the so-called Confederate States, with the view to eventual arrangements, either by treaty or union, for the purpose of effecting that object.

The resentments of the people will be inflamed by demagogical appeals designed to array the people of the West against the people of the East upon the pretended ground that the latter are in favor of continuing the war and the blockade of the Mississippi, as a means of fostering the interest of their trade, their manufactures, and their capital invested in both. This sentiment is reprehensibly wrong; nay, criminal.

Our first and highest duty under Heaven is to preserve the Union and the Government. This we must do; yet wise statesmen will not overlook the difficulties and dangers which surround them, but will avoid them by timely precautions.

In short, delay may bring another separation, and another separation will entail endless collisions, which, after wasting all the States, must sink them in anarchy and wretchedness, like that which drapes Mexico in misery and mourning.

Hence, in conclusion, let me appeal to you, and through you to the President, to do something, and that something quickly, to avert the rising storm, and insure a safe passage to our good and beloved Ship of State through the strait that now threatens her in the distance.

If I have spoken too freely, pardon my boldness. If I have said too much, charge it to an honest zeal for the welfare of my country, and forgive it.[20]

Not boldness but a flirtation with treason was embedded in John McClernand's nigh-interminable assertions. What General McClernand wanted, of course, was recognition in the form of orders specifying that he and not Grant was to be the man who took Vicksburg and opened the Mississippi. And in the middle of another long and tedious report to Stanton on December 1, he made his desires clear:

I trust it will meet with your views to order me forward to Memphis, or such other rendezvous as you may think preferable, in order that I may enter upon the more advanced work of organizing, drilling, and disciplining my command, preparatory to an early and successful movement, having for its object the important end of liberating the navigation of the Mississippi River.

Having worked early, assiduously, and zealously in this great enterprise, having it at heart, and the Governors and people of the Old Northwest having pronounced favorably upon it and, so far as I can hear, upon me as the executor of it, I trust that the Honorable Secretary of War will continue to encourage me by his sympathy and support.[21]

As had McClellan, John McClernand was ignoring the Union armies' general-in-chief. Actually, this not only spared Halleck the irritation of dealing with the influential windbag but gave him more time to devote to supporting Grant's efforts.

In mid-November Grant's plan called for Cump Sherman to join him in north-central Mississippi for a drive southward with Jackson, east of Vicksburg, as his objective.[22] Halleck, however, directed otherwise. "Operations in Northern Mississippi," he wrote Grant on November 15, "must be limited to rapid marches upon any collected forces of the enemy, feeding as far as possible upon the country. The enemy must be turned by a movement down the river from Memphis as soon as sufficient force can be collected."[23]

Had Old Brains been lured or coerced into McClernand's camp? Hardly. Despite the peremptory tone of his message, he approved Grant's advance to Holly Springs.[24] Meanwhile, acting on a suggestion made by Sherman, Rear Admiral David Dixon Porter had dispatched several gunboats to the mouth of the Yazoo River, not far upstream from Vicksburg.[25]

By December 4 Grant was asking Halleck: "How far south do you want me to go? We are now at Yocony, and can go as far as supplies can be taken. . . ." And the next day he telegraphed: "If the Helena [Arkansas] troops were at my command I think it practicable to send Sherman to take them and Memphis troops south of mouth of [Yazoo] River and thus secure Vicksburg and State of Mississippi."[26]

Halleck replied at once:

> *I think you should not attempt to hold the country south of the Tallahatchie [River]. The troops for Vicksburg should be back to Memphis by the 20th. If possible, collect at that place, for that purpose, as many as 25,000. More will be added from Helena, &c. Your main object will be to hold the line from Memphis to Corinth with as small a force as possible, while the largest number possible is thrown upon Vicksburg with the gunboats.*[27]

Two days later, he added: "The capture of Grenada may change our plans in regard to Vicksburg. You will move your troops as you deem best to accomplish the great object in view."[28]

Halleck was moving the case as though McClernand were irrelevant. By December 8, few questions remained. Grant asked one: "Do you want me to command the expedition on Vicksburg or shall I send Sherman?"[29]

But by ten o'clock that night, Grant had answered his own question— or so it seemed from a message he sent Halleck:

> *General Sherman will command the expedition down the Mississippi. He will have a force of about 40,000 men. Will land above Vicksburg, up the Yazoo, if practicable, and cut the Mississippi Central Railroad and the railroad running east from Vicksburg where they cross the Black River. I will co-operate from here, my movements depending on those of the enemy. . . .*[30]

Old Brains replied with some admonitions:

> *As it is possible that Bragg may cross [the Tennessee] at Decatur and fall upon Corinth, the security of that place should be carefully attended to. Do not make the Mississippi expedition so large as to*

endanger West Tennessee. I think 25,000 men, in addition to the forces to be added from Helena, will be sufficient, but send more if you can spare them. The President may insist upon designating a separate commander; if not, assign such officers as you deem best. Sherman would be my choice as the chief under you.[31]

In his next telegram, Grant reported: "A letter from General McClernand, just received, states that he expects to go forward in a few days. Sherman has already gone." And he closed with a gross understatement: "The enterprise would be much safer in charge of the latter."[32]

4

AT A TIME WHEN GENERAL HALLECK was having to deal with Burnside, Grant, and Banks almost concurrently, Rosecrans eased the general-in-chief's workload considerably by providing progress reports virtually devoid of problems. Mostly, "Old Rosy" was concentrating his forces near Nashville and sending scouts to monitor the movements of his Confederate adversaries—notably, Braxton Bragg. Typical of Rosecrans' messages was the one he sent Halleck on November 17:

News of to-day seems to confirm the impression of my last, save that some of the rebel generals are of opinion they will try to fight us on the tablelands near Tullahoma. I am trying to lull them into security, that I do not intend to move, until I can get the [Louisville & Nashville] road fully opened and throw in a couple of millions of rations here. Should the present rain raise the river, it will be of the greatest importance to have some gunboats for the Tennessee, for in that case, I shall throw myself on their right flank and endeavor to make an end of them. Let me entreat you to give us cavalry arms.[33]

General Rosecrans' mission, of course, was to liberate the Unionists in East Tennessee. But somewhere between Nashville and Knoxville he would have to eliminate Bragg's army, and possibly that of Kirby Smith as well, from the landscape. Confederate cavalrymen led by Nathan Bedford Forrest and John Morgan were capable of re-destroying bridges and tunnels along the L&N as soon as they were repaired, so Old Rosy considered himself justified in stockpiling as many millions of rations and other supplies at Nashville as he could before venturing forth to do battle.

General Halleck certainly understood that, but Lincoln apparently did not. On December 4, 1862, while he and Grant were exchanging messages regarding Vicksburg, Old Brains passed along this warning to Rosecrans:

The President is very impatient at your long stay in Nashville. The favorable season for your campaign will soon be over. You give Bragg time to supply himself by plundering the very country your army should have occupied. From all information received here, it is believed that he is carrying large quantities of stores into Alabama, and preparing to fall back partly on Chattanooga and partly on Columbus, Miss.

Twice have I been asked to designate some one else to command your army. If you remain one more week at Nashville, I cannot prevent your removal. As I wrote you when you took the command, the Government demands action, and if you cannot respond to that demand some one else will be tried.[34]

"I reply in few but earnest words," General Rosecrans began his response that night, but that was not to be:

I have lost no time. Everything I have done was necessary, absolutely so; and has been done as rapidly as possible. Any attempt to advance sooner would have increased our difficulty both in front and rear. In front, because of greater obstacles, enemies in greater force, and fighting with better chances of escaping pursuit, if overthrown in battle. In rear, because of insufficiency and uncertainty of supplies, both of subsistence and ammunition, and no security of any kind to fall back upon in case of disaster.

We should most probably have had a flying enemy to pursue, with a command daily frittered away by the large detachments required to guard forage and provision trains, and after all have been obliged to halt somewhere, to await the indispensable supplies, for which we have been waiting. Many of our soldiers are to this day barefoot, without blankets, without tents, without good arms, and cavalry without horses.

Our true objective now is the enemy's force, for if they come near, we save wear, tear, risk, and strength. . . .

If the Government which ordered me here confides in my judgment, it may rely on my continuing to do what I have been trying to—that is, my whole duty. If my superiors have lost confidence in me, they had better at once put some one in my place and let the future test the propriety of the change.

I have but one word to add, which is, that I need no other stimulus to make me do my duty than the knowledge of what it is. To threats of removal or the like I must be permitted to say that I am insensible.[35]

General Halleck might well have left the matter where it stood, but the only possible replacement for Rosecrans was George Thomas, who had declined command of the army earlier. Moreover, he was not ready to apply the ultimate remedy without making another attempt to persuade Rosecrans to save himself:

My telegram was not a threat, but merely a statement of facts. The President is greatly dissatisfied with your delay, and has sent for me several times to account for it. He has repeated to me time and again that there were imperative reasons why the enemy should be driven across the Tennessee River at the earliest possible moment. He has never told me what those reasons were, but I imagine them to be diplomatic, and of the most serious character. You can hardly conceive his great anxiety about it.

I will tell you what I guess it is, although it is only a guess on my part. It has been feared that on the meeting of the British Parliament, in January next, the political pressure of the starving operatives may force the Government to join France in an intervention. If the enemy be left in possession of Middle Tennessee, which we held last July, it will be said that they have gained on us.

We have recovered all they gained on us in Kentucky, Virginia, Missouri, Arkansas, and Mississippi, and in North Carolina, South Carolina, Florida, Louisiana, and Texas we have gained on them. Tennessee is the only State which can be used as an argument in favor of intervention by England.

You will thus perceive that your movements have an importance beyond mere military success. The whole Cabinet are anxious, inquiring almost daily. "Why don't he move?" "Can't you make him move?" "There must be no delay." "Delay there will be more fatal to us than anywhere else."

You will thus perceive that there is a pressure for you to advance much greater than you can possibly have imagined. It may be, and perhaps is, the very turning-point in our foreign relations.

It was hoped and believed when you took the command that you would recover all lost ground by, at furthest, the middle of December, so that it would be known in London soon after the meeting of Parliament. It is not surprising that our Government should be impatient and dissatisfied under the circumstances of the case. A victory or the retreat of the enemy before the 10th of this month would have been of more value to us than ten times that success at a later date.

No one doubted that General Buell would eventually have succeeded, but he was too slow to be in time. It was believed that you would move more rapidly. Hence the change.[36]

So matters stood three days later when Rosecrans received a long letter from James Guthrie, president of the L&N Railroad: Old Rosy's army's lifeline. Embedded in a plethora of excuses worthy of Don Carlos Buell were hints that deliveries of supplies to Rosecrans were likely to remain at disappointing levels for quite some time.[37]

5

"THE PRESIDENT HAS JUST ASSENTED to your plan," Old Brains had telegraphed Major General Burnside on November 14, 1862, following their conference at Warrenton. "He thinks that it will succeed if you move very rapidly; otherwise not."[38] Burnside got troops moving quickly, but their destination was Falmouth—not Fredericksburg, just south of there but across the Rappahannock. Did this matter? Well, at the Warrenton conference, Fredericksburg had been Burnside's recommendation, and his plan had been approved accordingly; moreover, if General Lee got there first, Burnside would have to fight for Fredericksburg sooner or later.

But Falmouth had been Burnside's headquarters and forward supply base for several months during the summer. Herman Haupt was repairing the docks at Aquia Landing and the railroad leading from there to Falmouth, the line's temporary terminal point until the bridge over the river into Fredericksburg could be rebuilt. Major General "Bull" Sumner had wanted to cross the Rappahannock and secure Fredericksburg when his corps reached the fords, but Burnside, fearing that forces on the Fredericksburg side might be marooned by an overflow, spurned his request.

Actually, General Lee was uncertain as to what Burnside was up to. Upon hearing that McClellan had been relieved, he had remarked to James

Longstreet: "We always understood each other so well. I fear they may continue to make these changes until they find someone I don't understand."[39] But he sent Longstreet's corps to Fredericksburg and they were in position on Marye's Heights west of the historic town before Burnside could have prevented it.[40]

Ambrose Burnside was in trouble for another reason: disloyalty, initially on the part of Major General Joseph Hooker. "Fighting Joe," as he was known because of an error in a newspaper story, had courted the favor of the Radical Republican-dominated Joint Congressional Committee on the Conduct of the War while recuperating from an ankle wound he received at Antietam. And, evidently, he had also formed close ties to Secretary of War Stanton, for it was to him that he wrote a distinctly out-of-channels letter on November 19, 1862.

"My position is at Hartwood," Hooker wrote, "4 miles from what is called the United States Ford, across the Rappahannock [upstream and west of Fredericksburg]. I have today requested Major-General Burnside to allow me to cross the ford" and drive on southward, perhaps even to Richmond. Mild enough, so far. But as Old Brains read the text Edwin Stanton shared with him, surely he perceived that dragon seeds were implanted in later passages:

> *This movement, made at once, will find the enemy unprepared, for they count on our delay in landing supplies, and also in crossing the Rappahannock, and, of course, if the movement could be continued to Richmond, we would find the enemy but illy prepared to receive us. We should, at least, avoid any position the enemy may assume for defense on our contemplated line of advance, which, God knows, we had enough of under McClellan. After the line of our operations is discovered, it seems to me that an invading army should do nothing but advance by the most rapid marches.*
>
> *The lateness of the season demands unusual vigor in the prosecution of the campaign. If Jackson was at Chester Gap on Friday last, we ought to be able to reach Richmond in advance of the concentration of the enemy's forces.*
>
> *I regret that the major-general commanding did not keep up the show of an advance on the line via Gordonsville, and even now I would recommend a demonstration, with a strong infantry and cavalry force, in that direction. It appears that the rebels are as much in the dark with regard to our movements as we have heretofore been of theirs.*

> *The enemy, it seems, have counted on the McClellan delays for a long while, and have never failed in their calculations. I feel more anxious concerning this movement, as I learn, informally, that we are to experience a delay of several days in the erection of bridges over the Rappahannock.*[41]

In fact, there would be a never-ending dispute over the delays in Burnside's operations attributed to the lack of the pontoon bridges General Halleck had promised the new army commander. And the absence of that equipment must have been all the more frustrating to Burnside as he contemplated the possibilities implied in the strategic questions Herman Haupt raised on November 22:

> *Several days must elapse before the railroad to Fredericksburg can be reconstructed; several days more before, in addition to daily supplies, ten or twelve days' rations can be accumulated in advance. . . .*
>
> *Suppose your whole army should be thrown on the south side of the Rappahannock, communicating by boat and pontoon bridges, would it not cover and protect the navigation of that stream? Could not supplies of all kinds be sent by water to Fredericksburg in greater quantity and in shorter time than in any other way? Could you not be prepared to advance much sooner than if dependent upon supplies exclusively by rail?*
>
> *If unsuccessful, could you not retire behind the Rappahannock, by which time a full depot would be formed at Falmouth? If successful, could you not draw supplies from White House or James River, while we reconstructed the road to Richmond, for the purpose of daily communication with Washington?*
>
> *I make these suggestions reluctantly. You have no doubt considered them already. If you have or have not, they can do no harm.*[42]

Haupt indicated that a copy was to be sent to General Halleck, which ought to have been detected by Burnside as a pretty strong hint that Old Brains concurred. Evidence that Halleck favored such an outcome was his note to Assistant Secretary of the Navy Gustavus Vasa Fox on November 21: "It is desirable that the Rappahannock should be opened as early as possible for quartermasters' vessels, for the supply of the army at Fredericksburg. I will notify you as soon as the heights below that town are occupied by our forces."[43]

While General Burnside awaited the arrival of the pontoon bridging trains, he considered crossing sites along the Rappahannock above and well below Fredericksburg. He was diligent in sending various plans to General-in-Chief Halleck. Inadvertently, Stonewall Jackson contributed to the variety of these schemes by bringing his corps down from the Shenandoah Valley and placing his divisions downstream along the Rappahannock.

By December 9, 1862, soon after the long-awaited pontoon bridges arrived, General Burnside settled upon a plan calling for seizure of Fredericksburg *via* river crossings at three sites, followed by assaults on the Confederate positions on Marye's Heights and the ridges south of there. After presenting the attack orders to his subordinates, near midnight the Army of the Potomac's commander telegraphed this message to Halleck's chief-of-staff, Brigadier General Cullum:

> *All the orders have been issued to the several commanders of grand divisions and heads of departments for an attempt to cross the river on Thursday morning. The plans of the movement are somewhat modified by the movements of the enemy, who have been concentrating in large force opposite the point at which we originally intended to cross.*
>
> *I think now that the enemy will be more surprised by a crossing immediately in our front than in any other part of the river. The commanders of grand divisions coincide with me in this opinion, and I have accordingly ordered the movement, which will enable us to keep the force well concentrated, at the same time covering our communications in the rear.*
>
> *I am convinced that a large force of the enemy is now concentrated in the vicinity of Port Royal, its left resting near Fredericksburg, which we hope to turn. We have an abundance of artillery, and have made very elaborate preparations to protect the crossing. The importance of the movement and the details of the plan seem to be well understood by the grand division commanders, and we hope to succeed.*
>
> *If the General-in-Chief desires it, I will send a minute statement by telegraph in cipher to-morrow morning. The movement is so important that I feel anxious to be fortified by his approval. Please answer.*[44]

General Halleck was horrified. "I beg of you," he wired Burnside the next morning, "not to telegraph details of your plans, nor the time of your

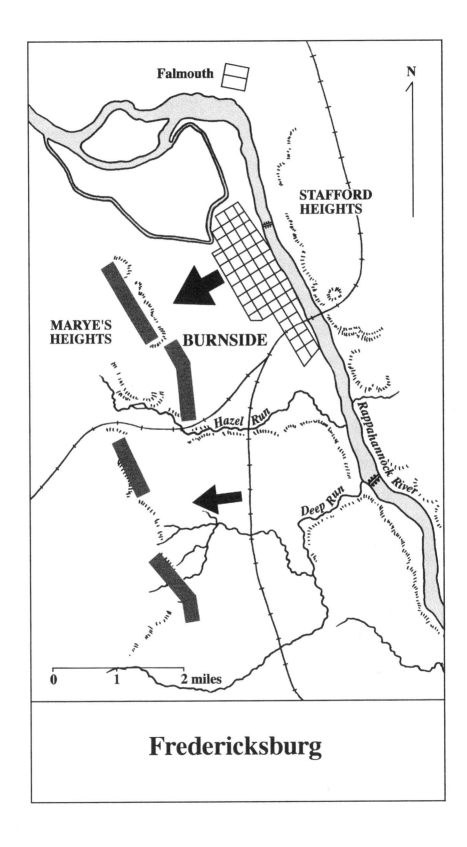

Fredericksburg

intended movements. No secret can be kept which passes through so many hands."[45]

Significantly, Halleck had not commented on the military merits of the orders Burnside had already given, nor had he given any indication of approval or disapproval.

6

KASSANDRA, RAPED BY ZEUS, was blinded by him but awarded the gift of prophecy—with a catch: she would be right, but no one would ever believe her. Thousands of years later, on the other side of the globe from Greece, Herman Haupt was destined to suffer Kassandra's fate in that he would often foresee developments and warn commanders, only to be ignored.

General Haupt was neither a physic nor a mystic. Nor was it clear that his education at West Point had equipped him for anything more than teaching mathematics, as he had at Gettysburg College, or building railroads. Yet, like kindred spirit Henry Wager Halleck, he had the ability to focus his intellect and combine it with common sense to a degree that was both remarkable and rare.

In August, while John Pope was moving northward along the upper Rappahannock in response to General Lee's advances, Haupt had asked the Army of Virginia's commander if he were considering the possibility that the rebels might sweep around to the north and east of him and plant themselves in his rear. Results: Second Manassas and General Pope's exile to fighting the Sioux in Minnesota.

Put simply, Haupt had seen the situation exactly as had General Lee. And now, in mid-December, shortly before the attacks Burnside had ordered were to be launched, again the latter-day Kassandra felt compelled to warn the general commanding of impending disaster.

Absent bridging equipment at the time, nothing had come of questions Haupt had raised earlier regarding seizure of Fredericksburg. Operating from Falmouth, Haupt had devoted his talents and energies to preparations for rebuilding the railroad bridge over the Rappahannock into Fredericksburg—a structure vital to the execution in the second stage of Burnside's plan, the one in which he would advance southward to Richmond.

While he was checking on that project's progress on December 11, General Haupt was appalled to see his workers skedaddling from heavy Confederate sniper fire coming from the Rappahannock's western bank.

And looking beyond the town across the river, he foresaw that the Confederates' fortifications on Marye's Heights—ground with which he was thoroughly familiar from work he had done earlier for Irvin McDowell— would make of the flatlands east of there the site of fearful slaughter.

Hoping to obtain soldiers to replace his departed crew so construction of the bridge could continue, Haupt went up to Army of the Potomac headquarters at the Phillips House. No, Burnside told him, no men could be spared, because the pontoon bridges were in place and troops were crossing. Haupt then expressed his opinion that Marye's Heights could not be taken except at appalling cost, and he strongly recommended that the orders to attack be canceled. Again, the army commander said no.

Haupt traveled to Aquia Landing on an engine he had commandeered and took a steamboat to Washington. He found John Covode, the Pennsylvania congressman who had summoned Haupt to Washington initially, and expressed his concern over what might happen down at Fredericksburg. Although it was by then around nine in the evening, Covode took Haupt to the Executive Mansion. As Haupt described the result:

> The President was much interested in my report, and asked me to walk with him to General Halleck's quarters. . . . When we arrived he requested Covode and the others present to step into the next room, as he desired to have a private conference, and then asked me to repeat the substance of my report to him, which I did.
>
> On its conclusion, the President asked General Halleck to telegraph orders to General Burnside to withdraw his army to the north side of the river. General Halleck rose and paced the floor for some time, and then stopped, facing the President, and said decidedly: "I will do no such thing. If we were personally present and knew the exact situation, we might assume such responsibility. If such orders are issued, you must issue them yourself. I hold that a General in command of an army in the field is the best judge of existing conditions."
>
> The President made no reply, but seemed much troubled. I then remarked that I did not consider the situation to be as critical as the President imagined, and proceeded to describe more in detail the topographical configuration. . . .
>
> When I finished, the President sighed and said: "What you say gives me a great many grains of comfort."[46]

President Lincoln sent no order to General Burnside. On December

13, 1862, General Lee's Army of Northern Virginia inflicted more than ten thousand casualties on Burnside's forces during a series of gallant but futile assaults the Army of the Potomac made. As Herman Haupt had foreseen, most of the killing and maiming took place on the flat ground west of Fredericksburg. Not a single Union soldier came within a hundred yards of the impregnable Confederate defenses at the base of Marye's Heights.

Burnside never had called-off the piecemeal attacks; Hooker had, later remarking in his report: "Finding that I had lost as many men as my orders required me to lose, I suspended the attack." At the end of that tragic day, the general commanding was not only ordering a resumption of the assaults the next morning but declaring his intention of leading his old IX Corps into the renewed fighting himself. His subordinates persuaded him to risk no more losses.[47] Finally, at 4:00 a.m. on December 16, two days after the battle, Burnside telegraphed the general-in-chief: "I have thought it necessary to withdraw the army to this side of the river, and the movement has progressed satisfactorily thus far."[48]

7

"IF THERE IS A WORSE PLACE THAN HELL," Abraham Lincoln exclaimed when he heard the news, "I am in it."[49] At his direction, on December 16 General Halleck telegraphed Burnside to "report the reasons for your withdrawal as soon as possible."[50]

His first response, sent to Halleck late that day, said it best: "The army was withdrawn to this side of the river because I felt the [Confederate] positions in front could not be carried, and it was a military necessity either to attack or retire. A repulse would have been disastrous to us."[51]

On the next day, December 17, however, Burnside must have felt compelled to answer questions not yet asked. To General Halleck he wrote:

> *I have the honor to offer the following reasons for moving the Army of the Potomac across the Rappahannock sooner than was anticipated by the President, Secretary, or yourself, and for crossing at a point different from the one indicated to you at our last meeting at the President's.*
>
> *During my preparations for crossing at the place I had at first selected, I discovered that the enemy had thrown a large portion of his force down the river and elsewhere, thus weakening his defenses in front; and also thought I discovered that he did not anticipate the*

crossing of our whole force at Fredericksburg; and I hoped, by rapidly throwing the whole command over at that place, to separate, by a vigorous attack, the forces of the enemy on the river below from the forces behind and on the crests in the rear of the town, in which case we should fight him with great advantages in our favor.

To do this we had to gain a height on the extreme right of the crest, which height commanded a new road, lately built by the enemy for purposes of more rapid communication along his lines; which point gained, his positions along the crest would have been scarcely tenable, and he could have been driven from them easily by an attack on his front, in connection with a movement in rear of the crest.

How near we came to accomplishing our object future reports will show. But for the fog and unexpected and unavoidable delay in building the bridges, which gave the enemy twenty-four hours more to concentrate his forces in his strong positions, we would almost certainly have succeeded; in which case the battle would have been, in my opinion, far more decisive than if we had crossed at the places first selected.

As it was, we came very near success. Failing in accomplishing the main object, we remained in order of battle two days—long enough to decide that the enemy would not come out of his strongholds and fight us with his infantry. After which we recrossed to this side of the river unmolested, and without the loss of men or property. . . .

Unlike McClellan, General Burnside did not try to disclaim blame for the tragic outcome or to shift it to anyone else:

The fact that I decided to move from Warrenton onto this line rather against the opinion of the President, Secretary, and yourself, and that you have left the whole management in my hands, without giving me orders, makes me the more responsible.[52]

Yet, taken out of context, that statement might have seemed to have the ring of complaint embedded within it. Good if not brilliant soldier that Ambrose Burnside was, however, it appears doubtful that he was employing either subtlety or sarcasm. More likely, if he loaded that sentence, it was to remind the Union's war managers that on three occasions he had professed his unfitness to command a major field army.

Inadvertently and indirectly, though, General Burnside had raised questions that went to the very heart of the morality, as well as the efficiency, of command. One, in stark terms, might be put this way: Had Henry Halleck been right or wrong to hold and declare that a general in command of an army in the field is the best judge of existing conditions?

Actually, Old Brains' assertion of this belief before the carnage at Fredericksburg was nothing new. Lincoln, in messages he had signed with or without prior consultation with Halleck, had said much the same thing. As recently as November 9, the general-in-chief—presumably with the President's approval—had assured Nathaniel Banks: "These instructions are not intended to tie your hands or to hamper your operations in the slightest degree. So far away from headquarters, you must necessarily exercise your own judgment and discretion in regard to your movements against the enemy. . . ."

Certainly, General Halleck's doctrine was not original. But seldom had it been applied so firmly, so unequivocally (some might say arrogantly), as he had on the night when he told Lincoln flat-out, "If such orders are issued, you must issue them yourself."

There, the lawyer in Henry Halleck was reasserting itself. A principle he was upholding had been challenged by his client, and he was saying—in effect—that its importance and applicability far transcended his apparent insubordination or even the accuracy of Herman Haupt's appraisals and reporting.

Granted, Old Brains had not been in a mood to tolerate intimidation or much else. Referring to Lincoln, "His fingers itch to be into everything going on," Halleck had remarked not long before.[53] And to a protege who had not yet escaped dull duty in backwater Missouri, John Schofield, he wrote:

> *I am sick and tired of this political military life. The number of enemies I have made because I would not yield my own convictions of right is already legion. If they would only follow the examples of their ancestors, enter a herd of swine, run down some steep bank and drown themselves in the sea, there would be some hope of saving the country.*[54]

Given a client, no matter how powerful, who proves unresponsive to counsel, a lawyer is usually justified in resigning from the case and leaving him to stew in his own juice. But neither the lawyer nor the soldier in Henry Wager Halleck would allow that—at least, not yet. The President had, after all, refrained from ordering Burnside to withdraw, as though the lawyer in Lincoln had recognized the propriety of Old Brains' fidelity to principle and had decided to join him in upholding it.

Also uncertain on that mid-December night in General Halleck's quarters was the future of the still-undefined position within the Union high command of any general-in-chief. Winfield Scott, rich in military experience, had been driven from the post by age, infirmity, and the studied insubordination of George Brinton McClellan. Neither the Young Napoleon nor Lincoln himself had proved able to "do it all."

Now, here in Washington by peremptory order, was Henry Halleck. And in what may well have been the most overlooked and yet critical incident during the entire civil war, Old Brains had abruptly defied his President.

Actually, the Halleck Doctrine presupposed that the general commanding an army in the field was competent, that he could be trusted. Herman Haupt described it this way: "He should be allowed full liberty to exercise his own discretion, and not be trammeled with orders from those who are not in a situation to know all the conditions which influence a decision."[55]

If Halleck or Lincoln had ordered Burnside to withdraw, at least two consequences might have been expected; perhaps, both. He might have gone on to commit an even more egregious blunder at another time and another place. And having had his authority and judgment overridden once, he would be unwilling from then on to undertake any important act without having the approval of Halleck, Stanton, and probably Lincoln.

Indeed, on several occasions Halleck and Lincoln had deliberately avoided approving or disapproving Burnside's proposals. General Halleck made this clear in a report he prepared on November 15, 1863:

> *General Burnside proposed to give up* [the] *pursuit of Lee's army toward Richmond, and to move down the north side of the Rappahannock to Falmouth, and establish a new base of supplies at Aquia Creek or Belle Plain.* This proposed change of base was not approved by me, *and in a personal interview at Warrenton I strongly urged him to retain his present base, and continue his march toward Richmond in the manner pointed out in the President's letter of October 13 to General McClellan.*
>
> *General Burnside did not fully concur in the President's views, but finally consented to so modify his plan as to cross his army by the*

fords of the Upper Rappahannock, and then move down and seize the heights south of Fredericksburg, while a small force was to be sent north of the river to enable General Haupt to reopen the railroad and to rebuild the bridges, the materials for which were nearly ready in Alexandria. I, however, refused to give any official approval of this deviation from the President's instructions until his assent was obtained.

On my return to Washington, on the 13th, I submitted to him this proposed change in the plan of campaign, and on its receiving his assent, rather than approval, *I telegraphed, on the 14th, authority to General Burnside to adopt it. I here refer, not to General Burnside's written plan to go to Falmouth, but to that of crossing the Rappahannock above its junction with the Rapidan.*

It has been inferred from the testimony of General Burnside before the Congressional Committee on the Conduct of the War, that his plan of marching his whole army on the north of the Rappahannock, from Warrenton to Falmouth, had been approved by the authorities in Washington, and that he expected, on his arrival there, to find supplies and pontoons, with gunboats to cover his crossing. In the first place, that plan was never approved, nor was he ever authorized to adopt it. *In the second place, he could not possibly have expected supplies and pontoons to be landed at points then occupied in force by the enemy. . . .*[56] [Emphasis supplied]

Was this merely lawyerish quibbling? No, there are substantial differences between the meanings of *approval* and of *assent*.

Then, in his message dated December 9, 1862, Burnside had written: "The movement [attacking Fredericksburg] is so important that I feel anxious to be fortified by [the general-in-chief's] approval." In reply, Halleck admonished Burnside regarding security.

A point the general's many critics missed at the time (and have ever since) was, neither Old Brains nor anyone else in his position could reasonably be expected to approve a plan without having *all* the knowledge of the situation the proposer possessed—an utter impossibility. In the circumstances, withholding approval was the only possible response; it most certainly was not the abhorrence of responsibility Halleck's detractors alleged. At a minimum, such charges reflected complete ignorance of how much he had accomplished, through his actions, toward defining the position of general-in-chief.

8

AMONG OLD BRAINS' ACQUIRED DUTIES, of course, was that of acting as A. Lincoln's lightning rod. But in performing it he did not feel compelled to waste time currying favor with politicians, and it was from this fact (among others) that he became known for his gruffness. Actually, out in San Francisco, lawyer Halleck had never bothered to conceal his contempt for fools, so this was just further confirmation that the only change in the man since Fort Sumter had been in the type of clothing he wore.

That Horace Maynard, who represented a Tennessee district in Congress, took umbrage at Halleck's lack of reverence for lawgivers was revealed in a letter he wrote on December 13, 1862, as Lee was wrecking Burnside's army:

> *At the special instance and request of the President, I called on you at your headquarters on the 11th instant, to confer with you, as the General-in-Chief, touching the lamentable condition of affairs among my people in East Tennessee. During the momentary interview with which you were pleased to favor me, among the crowd in your anteroom, you suggested that I reduce to writing what I wished to communicate. In a matter that concerns me so nearly as this, I waive, for the present, all considerations growing out of your place of reception and personal bearing, and adopt your suggestion by inclosing a statement which I hope will receive more attention than you accorded to the writer.*[57]

Nowhere in the statement's 2,321 words was General Halleck likely to have found anything he did not already know. Liberating East Tennessee had been at the top of A. Lincoln's priority list for a year; Don Carlos Buell had been relieved of command for failing to remove Confederate armies commanded by Braxton Bragg and Edmund Kirby Smith from his path; and presently, William Rosecrans faced sacking if he did not quit stockpiling and destroy Bragg's forces at Murfreesboro. But Maynard could brag to his constituents that he had smitten the ungracious general-in-chief hip and thigh with his eloquence, secure in the knowledge that Henry Halleck never responded to critics.

General Rosecrans, who had professed to be insensitive to threats, had continued to supply Halleck with reports of Bragg's movements toward concentration at Murfreesboro, not far southeast of Nashville. On December 15 he relayed some social notes:

Jeff. Davis attended John H. Morgan's wedding last night [at Murfreesboro], *was serenaded, and made a speech, in which he said Lincoln's* [emancipation] *proclamation put black and white on an equality. Urged them to fight to the death, and to hold Middle Tennessee at all hazards, until Grant could be whipped. . . . Things will be ripe soon.*[58]

Indeed, Grant was whipped—or half-whipped—on December 20, 1862, when Earl Van Dorn led his cavalrymen to Holly Springs and virtually destroyed the supplies Grant had amassed to support his drive southward from Grenada. This surprise raid forced him to cancel his advance. But John Morgan's wedding had not been the only one worthy of note: Major General McClernand had married an Illinois lady who (some said) had been his sister-in-law. His honeymoon gave Grant an opportunity to launch Cump Sherman's expedition to the mouth of the Yazoo above Vicksburg without interference by the bridegroom, so that portion of his plan could still be carried out.

With Christmas and 1863 fast approaching, activity at Headquarters of the Army accelerated to a bewildering pace. Among the developments General Halleck and his small staff were monitoring and trying to support—nigh-concurrently—were these:

• Nathaniel Banks' armada, filled with troops and a few politicians from New England who had believed they were bound for the Texas coast, reached New Orleans on December 14. "Not a soul here anticipated our arrival," the Bobbin Boy boasted to the general-in-chief, "and scarcely a man on board ship suspected our destination until we were steaming up the Mississippi." Banks did not mention the expressions of understandable outrage that emanated from the New Englanders he, Stanton, and Lincoln had been so successful in deceiving.[59]

• In Fredericksburg's wake, *Chicago Tribune* publisher Joseph Medill began referring to Lincoln's administration as the "Central Imbecility," and the *New York World* demanded that the President sack Treasury Secretary Salmon Chase, Edwin Stanton, and General-in-Chief Henry W. Halleck.

• William Rosecrans sent a Yuletide Eve present of sorts to Halleck:

I think the enemy is [as] *far committed to stand at Murfreesboro, to protect the* [Morgan] *raid into Kentucky, as they will be; and, having now the essentials of ammunition and twenty days' rations in*

Nashville, [I] shall move on them to-morrow morning at daylight. If they meet us, we shall fight to-morrow; if they wait for us, next day. If we beat them, I shall try to drive them to the wall. [The rebels'] detachment of Forrest to West Tennessee, and of Morgan, will materially aid us in our movement.[60]

• Halleck had not forgotten about Horatio Wright in Cincinnati. On December 17, Old Brains asked:

Is there any further danger of Eastern Kentucky; and cannot your forces act to best advantage on the Cumberland, or in concert with Rosecrans from Nashville? Is not the entire army of Bragg in front of Rosecrans? . . .[61]

Wright agreed that Rosecrans had a problem, and by December 30 he had one of his own. To Halleck he telegraphed: "I have information, on which I am inclined to rely, that in case the President issues his [formal] proclamation of emancipation on the 1st proximo, the Legislature of Kentucky, which meets on Monday next, will legislate the State out of the Union. . . ." He proposed a series of military precautions to cope with such an event and asked for approval or disapproval of each.[62]

Now it was General Wright's turn to learn that Henry Halleck held that a general in command of an army in the field was the best judge of conditions. And no way was the general-in-chief going to inject even an opinion in a situation as politically charged as this one.

• During December 17, 18, and 19 Halleck and the President tried to arrange a meeting with General Burnside at Aquia Landing if possible but in Washington if necessary.[63] Concurrently, Major Generals William B. Franklin and William F. Smith, Burnside's subordinates, were insubordinately preparing a letter to Lincoln that opened with the belief that "the plan of campaign which has already been commenced cannot possibly be successful. . . ." After presenting their reasons for disagreeing with their army commander, the authors offered a McClellanesque scheme that called for massing all federal forces in the East, shipping them *via* Chesapeake Bay up the James River, and attacking Richmond with units moving up both of that stream's banks.[64]

Appalled as he may have been by the generals' impudence, Halleck could not have been surprised by the idea. He had heard it proposed by the Young Napoleon at Harrison's Landing back in July, and Franklin was one of the corps commanders whose troops Little Mac had not sent John Pope to get him out of his scrape.

• By the day after Christmas, hell seemed to be breaking out again in the Shenandoah Valley, or so Old Brains telegraphed Burnside:

General Kelley reports that the enemy are reappearing in large force at Strasburg and Front Royal, and it is probable that he will take advantage of the inactivity of the Army of the Potomac to make another raid on Harper's Ferry. This is certainly very disheartening. I am almost at a loss what to say or do.[65]

"Take the whole of Slocum's corps, if you choose," Ambrose Burnside suggested.[66] But by December 30, another problem had taken that one's place. Lincoln—ignoring the Halleck Doctrine—wired him: "I have good reasons for saying you must not make a general movement of the army without letting me know."[67]

• Before Major General McClernand decided to suspend his efforts to reopen the lower Mississippi for long enough to get married, from Springfield, Illinois, he had showered Stanton and Lincoln with much the same question: "May I ask to be sent forward immediately?"[68] To Memphis, he meant, where the troops he had recruited had been assembling. Bureaucrat Stanton informed him his several queries had been passed along to the general-in-chief, who was at the time preoccupied with events at Fredericksburg, out in the Mississippi Valley, and near Nashville. General McClernand presumably swallowed his pride and telegraphed Halleck:

Having substantially accomplished the purpose of the order sending me to the States of Indiana, Illinois, and Iowa, by forwarding upward of 40,000 troops . . . I beg to be sent forward, in accordance with the order of the Secretary of War of the 21st of October, giving me command of the Mississippi expedition.[69]

That was on December 16, 1862. The next day, absent any reply from Halleck, McClernand wired his good friend in the Executive Mansion: "I believe I am superseded. Please answer."[70] He sent much the same text to

Stanton, who first professed his surprise and then replied some hours later at greater length:

> *There has been, I am informed by General Halleck, no order superseding you. . . . The operations being in General Grant's department, it is designed to organize all the troops of that department in three army corps, the First Army Corps to be commanded by you, and assigned to the operations on the Mississippi under the general supervision of the general commanding that department. General Halleck is to issue the order immediately.*[71]

General Halleck did, the next morning, December 18, but he sent it to Grant:

> *The troops in your department, including those from Curtis' command, will be divided into four army corps. It is the wish of the President that General McClernand's corps shall constitute a part of the river expedition and that he shall have immediate command under your direction.*[72]

Upon receipt, General Grant telegraphed McClernand:

> *I have been directed this moment by telegraph from the General-in-Chief of the Army to divide the forces of this department into four army corps, one of which is to be commanded by yourself, and that to form a part of the expedition on Vicksburg.*
> *I have draughted* [sic] *the order and will forward it to you as soon as printed. . . .*[73]

Nigh-concurrently, Grant sent a message *via* Columbus, Kentucky, to Cump Sherman, then at Memphis—where John McClernand's recruits had been sent:

> *Inform General Sherman that his army corps will be composed of Steele's forces and General Morgan L. Smith's division, and General McClernand's of the divisions of General A. J. Smith and Morgan, and that General McClernand and he will descend the river.*[74]

All of these messages flew hither and yon on December 18, but nowhere in the record is any reply—especially, any protest—from

McClernand until December 23. From Springfield on that day, he telegraphed Stanton a copy General Halleck had sent him of the order to Grant dated December 18 and commented: "Yet I am not relieved from duty here so that I may go forward and receive orders from General Grant. Please order me forward."[75]

Secretary Stanton obliged that evening:

> *It had not been my understanding that you should remain at Springfield a single hour beyond your own pleasure and judgment of the necessity of collecting and forwarding the troops. You are relieved of duty at Springfield, and will report to General Grant for the purpose specified in the order of the General-in-Chief.*[76]

Apparently, Grant's order to McClernand dated December 18 had not reached him. On Christmas Day, from Holly Springs, Grant's assistant adjutant-general sent this message to "Commanding Officer, Memphis, Tenn.":

> *Inclosed find communication for General J. A. McClernand, which you will deliver to him if he is at Memphis. If he has gone down the river, you will please forward it to him. The original letter was sent to the commanding officer at Cairo, with instructions to deliver it to General McClernand if he had not already passed that point going south, and if he had, to send it on to him at Memphis. Communication was cut off north and it probably did not reach him.*[77]

Another message that had been delayed reached General Halleck on Christmas Day. It was from Captain Henry S. Fitch in Cairo:

> *By direction of Major-General Sherman I telegraph you the fact that his expedition embarked from Memphis, December 20, in sixty transports, 22,000 strong. . . . The general expects to be . . .in all probability at the mouth of the Yazoo to-day. This dispatch should have been forwarded two days ago. . . .General Grant's communication has been cut off. . . .*[78]

Captain Fitch did not include the fact that among the troops Cump Sherman had loaded on the transports bound for the Yazoo were men General McClernand had recruited and was expecting to command in the Mississippi expedition. Curiously, the recent bridegroom made no reference to this in a message he sent General Grant from Memphis on December 28. Instead, he enclosed copies of the telegrams and orders comprising the paper trail from his scheme's earliest days, as if he meant to intimidate Grant by reference to evidence of Lincoln's and Stanton's intent regarding his role.[79]

Even as McClernand wrote, however, Cump Sherman was discovering that the Confederate defenses along Chickasaw Bluffs north of Vicksburg were too formidable to take by assault. In contrast to Ambrose Burnside, rather than incur losses greater than the seventeen hundred men already killed, wounded, or missing, he called off his attacks and withdrew to Helena, Arkansas.[80]

Both Grant and Sherman had been whipped by Confederate Lieutenant General John C. Pemberton's adroit use of his central position. Coming as they did so soon after the appalling disaster at Fredericksburg, those defeats strengthened demands by the Radical Republicans in Congress and other anti-administration forces that the Central Imbecility stop making mistakes.

Naturally, John McClernand could be expected to claim that the West Point clique had done him gross injustice. In fact, all of General Halleck's decisions and actions in the matter had been perfectly proper. So had been Grant's and Cump Sherman's, within the powers Old Brains had given Grant.

Few if any persons realized it at the time, but Henry Halleck had saved the careers of Ulysses Grant and William T. Sherman, and also of James B. McPherson and Frederick Steele. McClernand had not won a clear-cut victory over the elitist West Point clique; but the politician had been prevented from making Lincoln's decision to support him more costly than it might have been, and that was no small accomplishment.

- During 1862's last few days, General Rosecrans' army made good progress down the Nashville Turnpike toward Murfreesboro. Confederate Brigadier General Joseph Wheeler, emulating fellow cavalryman Jeb Stuart's exploits, led his troopers all the way around Rosecrans' columns, capturing some of his wagon trains and destroying others. But by nightfall on New Year's Eve, the Union and Confederate forces were facing each other near Stones River just north of Murfreesboro, and bands on both sides were serenading each other with "Home Sweet Home."
- And during that night, Ambrose Burnside would be riding through the rain to Washington to see Lincoln, not Halleck; but his visit would cause trouble for Old Brains anyhow.

11 ★ January 1, 1863, et seq.

$\mathcal{H}$ENRY HALLECK HAD NOT SPENT a New Year's Day in Washington in nearly twenty years. On January 1, 1862, he had been in St. Louis. And just as the war was not much of an observer of holidays, neither was he.

On this first day of 1863, there were to be receptions at the Executive Mansion and at the Stantons' home and elsewhere. He would have to attend the first two, but briefly: Rosecrans and Bragg were colliding north of Murfreesboro, Grant was assessing the damage done to Sherman's force at Chickasaw Bluffs, and (to revise an old saying about country boys) *you could take the general out of the West but you could not take the West out of this general.*

What General-in-Chief Halleck least expected that morning, probably, was to be summoned by the President several hours before the festivities were to begin. Another surprise was the presence in Lincoln's office of Major General Ambrose Burnside. Less of a shock, of course, was finding Secretary of War Edwin McMasters Stanton there.[1]

Lately, General Burnside had adopted George McClellan's and John McClernand's habit of bypassing him and communicating with the President directly, so Halleck may well have missed some of the recent exchanges of messages between Falmouth and Washington. But, apparently, there had been some other breakdown: Burnside had made the ride up from his headquarters to find out why Lincoln had telegraphed him: "I have good reasons for saying you must not make a general movement of the army without letting me know."[2]

If General Halleck had seen the vastly out-of-channels message dated December 20, 1862, that Major Generals William Franklin and William Farrar Smith had sent the President, he would surely have perceived that dissent, perhaps something bordering on insubordination, might be a proximate cause of Burnside's overnight ride and his own early morning summons. Franklin and Smith had opened their proposal to Lincoln with this sentence:

> *The undersigned, holding important commands in the Army of the Potomac, impressed with a belief that a plan of operations of this army may be devised which will be crowned with success, and that the plan of campaign which has already been commenced cannot possibly be successful, present, with much diffidence, the following views for consideration. . . .*[3]

Adopt George B. McClellan's scheme for taking Richmond using both banks of the James River, they had recommended to the commander-in-chief, not the general-in-chief.

But Old Brains may well have seen a long letter Quartermaster-General Montgomery Meigs had sent Burnside on December 30, 1862. Having, along with General Halleck and Herman Haupt, attended the conference with Burnside at Warrenton soon after Little Mac's decapitation, Meigs had standing to—as he put it—"say a few words to you which neither the newspapers nor, I fear, anybody in your army is likely to utter."

Meigs' words were not few, and in part they may have reflected deep discussions with Old Brains, but—coming as they did from an officer in the rear echelon—they were destined to be overlooked by historians. His meditations having been directed to General Burnside so recently, however, Meigs' counsel was almost certainly relevant to the matters discussed at the meeting held in the Executive Mansion on New Year's Morning:

> *In my position as Quartermaster-General much is seen that is seen from no other stand-point of the Army. . . .*
>
> *Every day's consumption of your army is an immense destruction of the natural and monetary resources of the country. The country begins to feel the effect of this exhaustion, and I begin to apprehend a catastrophe. Your army has, I suspect, passed its period of greatest efficiency, and, by sickness, disability, and discharge, is decreasing in numbers. The animals have been recruited by rest, and are in better condition than they will be a month hence. The weather and the roads will not in months be again as favorable as during the weeks which have elapsed since the battle of Fredericksburg. . . .*

General Halleck tells me that you believe your numbers are greater than the enemy's, and yet the army waits! Some officers talk of having done enough; of going into winter quarters. This I do not understand to be your thought, but I am told that you probably find opinions differ as to the possibility of any proposed movement.

In so great a matter, on which so much depends, there will be always differences of opinion. There are few men who are capable of taking the responsibility of bringing on such a great conflict as a battle between two such armies as oppose each other at Fredericksburg.

So long as you consult your principal officers together, the result will be that proverbial of councils of war. Upon the commander, to whom all the glory of success will attach, must rest the responsibility of deciding the plan of campaign.

Every day weakens your army; every good day lost is a golden opportunity in the career of our country—lost forever. Exhaustion steals over the country. Confidence and hope are dying.

While I have been always sure that ultimate success must attend the cause of freedom, justice, and government sustained by 18,000,000 against that of oppression, perjury, and treason supported by 5,000,000, I begin to doubt the possibility of maintaining the contest beyond this winter, unless the popular heart is encouraged by victory on the Rappahannock.

The Treasury fails not only to pay the troops, but to pay for the hire of the vessels and laborers employed in supplying them, and for the forage bought for your cavalry, artillery, and trains. Suppose the army broken up for want of rations and forage, what a prospect for the country!

Permit me to call your attention to the plan of operations, of which I spoke at Aquia.

While the retirement of the rebel army from your front, consequent upon any movement, would prolong the contest, and be a misfortune, even this would give some hope and heart to the country. But what is needed is a great and overwhelming defeat and destruction of that army. . . .

No battle fought with your back to the North or to the sea can give you such a victory. This enemy has shown his skill in retreat, and when he finds the day going against him he will retreat—will save the bulk of his army and compel a siege of Richmond, during which, as when McClellan invested it, he will gather up his forces for another struggle, and will cut your lines of supply and communication. In a desolated country, it will be almost impossible to support your army during a siege.

If by such a march as Napoleon made at Jena, as Lee made in his campaign against Pope, you throw your whole army upon his communications, interpose between him and Richmond, or even take a position to the southwest of the bulk of his army, and he fights, if you are successful, he has no retreat. His army would be dispersed, and the greater portion of it would throw down its arms. The artillery and baggage and camps would fall into your hands. The gain of the position would give you the strategic victory. Your troops, appreciating the means and the object of the march, would be confident of victory, while the rebels would be discouraged, and would expect defeat. . . .

It seems to me that the army should move bodily up the Rappahannock, cross the river, aim for a point on the railroad between the rebels and Richmond, and send forward cavalry and light troops to break up the road and intercept retreat. Your divisions marching within supporting distance, and ordered to march to the sound of battle, would concentrate upon any field, and compel a general engagement.

The result would be with the God of battles, in whose keeping we believe our cause to rest. Will we ever have a better opportunity? Do not we grow weaker every day? Can you not adopt this movement, which, if successful, promises the greatest results, and even if unsuccessful, leaves a practicable route of retreat?

If any other movement promises greater or readier results, let it be adopted; but rest at Falmouth is death to our nation—is defeat, border warfare, hollow truce, barbarism, ruin for ages, chaos!

To any plan you will find objections. Address yourself to the great work. Decide upon your plan and give your orders to each general to march by a certain road at a certain hour, and to expect that on his right or left such another will co-operate with him if he meets the enemy. Whatever advice they may give, you have no general in your army who will fail to march promptly on your order or to fight gallantly when brought face to face with the enemy.

The gallantry of the attack at Fredericksburg made amends for its ill success, and soldiers were not discouraged by it. The people, when they understood it, took heart again. But the slumber of the army since is eating into the vitals of the nation.

*As day after day has gone, my heart has sunk, and I see greater
peril to our nationality in the present condition of affairs than I
have seen at any time during the struggle.*

*Forgive me if I have written freely and strongly. I cannot
express as strongly as I feel our danger, and I know that you, as I
hope myself, have only one object—the success of our cause and
salvation of our country.*[4]

Against all of this background, or even part of it, General Halleck
must have sensed that this New Years' Morning meeting would most
certainly be no ordinary one. Yet, in fact, he could not have known at the
outset what had happened on December 29. Even Burnside had not known
until that morning, when Lincoln told him.

On December 29, two of Burnside's subordinates—names not
disclosed—had arrived in Washington in search of a certain senator who (as
it turned out) was out of town. But one of these political appointees recalled
his prior ties to Secretary of State William H. Seward, who was available.
Indeed, Seward felt their complaint important enough to take to the
President.

The two brigadier generals, Lincoln told Burnside, had stated that the
army lacked confidence in its general commanding and that it was in no
shape to be committed to an operation Burnside was about to launch: hence
the telegram that had brought Burnside to Washington.[5]

Lincoln, seconded presumably by Halleck and Stanton, persuaded
General Burnside to return to Falmouth and remain in command of the
army. Before leaving Washington, however, Burnside felt compelled to write
His Excellency:

*Since leaving you this morning, I have determined that it is my duty
to place on paper the remarks which I made to you, in order that you
may use them or not, as you see proper.*

*I am in command, as you know, of nearly 200,000 men,
120,000 of whom are in the immediate presence of the enemy, and
I cannot conscientiously retain the command without making an
unreserved statement of my views.*

*The Secretary of War has not the confidence of the officers and
soldiers, and I feel sure that he has not the confidence of the country.
In regard to the latter statement, you are probably better informed
than I am. The same opinion applies with equal force in regard to
General Halleck. It seems to be the universal opinion that the*

movements of the army have not been planned with a view to co-operation and mutual assistance.

I have attempted a movement upon the enemy, in which I have been repulsed, and I am convinced, after mature deliberation, that the army ought to make another movement in the same direction, not necessarily at the same points on the river; but I am not sustained in this by a single grand division commander in my command. My reasons for having issued the order for making this second movement I have already given you in full, and I can see no reasons for changing my views.

Doubtless this difference of opinion between my general officers and myself results from a lack of confidence in me. In this case it is highly necessary that this army should be commanded by some other officer, to whom I will most cheerfully give way.

Will you allow me, Mr. President, to say that it is of the utmost importance that you be surrounded and supported by men who have the confidence of the people and of the army, and who will at all times give you definite and honest opinions in relation to their separate departments, and at the same time give you positive and unswerving support in your public policy, taking at all times their full share of the responsibility for that policy?

In no positions held by gentlemen near you are these conditions more requisite than those of the Secretary of War and General-in-Chief and the commanders of your armies. In the struggle now going on, in which the very existence of our Government is at stake, the interests of no one man are worth the value of a grain of sand, and no one should be allowed to stand in the way of accomplishing the greatest amount of public good.

It is my belief that I ought to retire to private life. I hope you will not understand this to savor of anything like dictation. My only desire is to promote the public good. No man is an accurate judge of the confidence in which he is held by the public and the people around him, and the confidence in my management may be entirely destroyed, in which case it would be a great wrong for me to retain this command for a single day; and, as I before said, I will most cheerfully give place to any other officer.[6]

Later, there would be controversy over whether Halleck and Stanton were present when Burnside made his derogatory remarks regarding them. In any event, after the generals and Stanton left, and before getting ready for his New Year's Day reception, Lincoln sat down and wrote a note to General-in-Chief Halleck:

> *General Burnside wishes to cross the Rappahannock with his army, but his grand division commanders all oppose the movement. If in such a difficulty as this you do not help, you fail me precisely in the point for which I sought your assistance. You know what General Burnside's plan is, and it is my wish that you go with him to the ground, examine it as far as practicable, confer with the officers, getting their judgment and ascertaining their temper; in a word, gather all the elements for forming a judgment of your own, and then tell General Burnside that you do approve or that you do not approve his plan. Your military skill is useless to me if you will not do this.[7]*

At his reception, Lincoln gave the message to Stanton and requested him to see that General Halleck received it. Stanton complied. Old Brains went back to his office, wrote his reply, sent it to Stanton, and returned his attention to the war in the West.[8]

2

CERTAINLY ABRAHAM LINCOLN, as commander-in-chief, was entirely justified in asking General Halleck for help, but he erred *egregiously* in the way he went about it. It was obvious both from the curiously angry tone of the note and the specifications it contained that, in the circumstances, he had not thought the matter through.

General Halleck, however, was equally justified in refusing to accede to the President's demands as they had been stated. Lincoln had asked him, in effect, *to replace Burnside.* Amateur that he unfortunately was, the President apparently had not realized that if Halleck had done what he had specified, he would have undercut what little authority and respect Burnside still commanded.

True, back in July, Halleck had gone to Harrison's Landing at Lincoln's request to confer with General McClellan and settle an operational matter. Voluntarily, the general-in-chief had gone to Burnside's headquarters at Warrenton to discuss—again—operational questions. And in all likelihood, if Lincoln had asked Old Brains to go down to Falmouth and advise Burnside merely regarding the *operational* possibilities, he would have gone.

But Abraham Lincoln had appointed Ambrose Burnside on the assumption that he was capable of commanding the Army of the Potomac. Only the President could remove him, if he found the general incompetent. Indeed it was his duty to do so, given that Burnside evidently could not compel the unquestioned obedience of his subordinates. Ability to *command* was the question; and until that issue had been decided and acted upon, the opinion of the general-in-chief or anyone else regarding plans was irrelevant.

Put simply, Lincoln had demanded that Halleck settle the military equivalent of a nasty family squabble. But in his ignorance, he was making a *colossal* mistake—one that had the potential of destroying the effectiveness of command and discipline throughout the Union armies; for once it became known generally *how* General Burnside's authority had been undercut, the whole military structure would be doomed to rot and crumble.

What might have happened if Lincoln had simply asked Halleck what to do? Old Brains' response, most likely, would have been, *relieve Burnside forthwith and replace him with some commander who could and would clean up the mess McClellan left behind.*

But by seating himself and taking pen in hand, the President had foreclosed such a development. He had forced Henry Halleck to recall that a soldier's first duty is to obey. Inadvertently finding himself unable, by reason of fidelity to principles that he believed in, to obey his commander-in-chief in this instance, the only honorable course he could take was to ask that he be relieved.

It seems unlikely that Old Brains was either surprised or disturbed by Abraham Lincoln's having destroyed their relationship. If he had hoped to be able to keep his client from making mistakes, the involvement of John McClernand and Nathaniel Banks in military operations was evidence that the commander-in-chief had considered irrelevant any opinion his counselor may have had. Worse, as Lincoln's lightning rod, sooner or later Halleck would be obliged to absorb the bolts of justified criticism of failures he had been utterly unable to prevent.

Indeed, the President's note was—in essence—an unwitting confession that he wanted Halleck to take the actions he had specified, so that the general-in-chief would be the sole attractor of outrage if *l'affaire Burnside* turned into a fiasco. What Lincoln wanted was not military counsel, but protection from the effects of a potential *political* firestorm.

"If in such a difficulty as this you do not help me," the commander-in-chief had written, "you fail me precisely in the point for which I sought your assistance." Back in July, Lincoln seemed to have meant. And at the close, he had said, "Your military skill is useless to me if you will not do this."

Old Brains may have concluded that Lincoln considered his military skill useless in any case. If that be so, it followed that he had neither personal desire nor any other reason to remain in Washington as a politicized lightning rod. This attitude was reflected in a letter he wrote to Burnside on May 9, 1863:

> *Major General Franklin's pamphlet on the battle of Fredericksburg has been before the public for some weeks, and, no doubt, has attracted your attention.*
>
> *General Franklin states positively that after that battle you urged the President to remove from office the Secretary of War and General-in-Chief. In the absence of any contradiction of this positive statement, it must be presumed that it is correct.*
>
> *As you could have had no motives personal to yourself for giving this advice to the President, and as you were well aware that I was placed in my present position contrary to my own wishes, and that I had endeavored to be relieved from it, I am bound to believe that in my case you were actuated in giving the alleged advice to the President solely by a desire to confer a personal favor upon me.*
>
> *I look at the matter in this light, and sincerely thank you for using your influence with the President, in the manner stated by General Franklin, to have me relieved from a thankless and disagreeable position, which you knew I did not wish to occupy.*[9]

Such may well have been Old Brains' sentiments on New Year's Day, 1863, as he interrupted his attempts to find out what was happening out in Tennessee on the banks of Stones River, and wherever in Mississippi Grant and Cump Sherman were, to write a note addressed to Secretary of War Stanton:

> *From my recent interview with the President and yourself, and from the President's letter of this morning, which you delivered to me at your reception, I am led to believe that there is a very important difference of opinion in regard to my relations toward generals commanding armies in the field, and that I cannot perform the*

duties of my present office satisfactorily at the same time to the President and to myself. I therefore respectfully request that I may be relieved from further duties as General-in-Chief.[10]

3

FOR PRESIDENT ABRAHAM LINCOLN, January 1, 1863, had been a thoroughly unpleasant waypoint in a winter bringing more cause for discontent than anything else.

"If there is a worse place than Hell I am in it," he had declared after Fredericksburg. Before that shock had worn off, the Radical Republicans in Congress—Jacobins, acting on the chance to kick a man when he was down—tried to wrench control of the war from the executive branch.

General Grant had been blindsided by Confederates at Holly Springs, and Sherman was in trouble down the Mississippi at Chickasaw Bluffs. His supporters in New England were furious because Nathaniel Banks had disembarked at New Orleans instead of landing their troops anywhere along the Texas coast.

Moreover, something was happening southeast of Nashville, and the last thing Lincoln needed was news of another Union disaster. And only a short time before the President had been obliged to join his wife in his New Year's Day reception's receiving line, the distressed commander of the Union's largest and most prominent field army had tossed a greased pig into his lap.

After Lincoln finished shaking hundreds of visitors' hands and reciting the ritual greetings phrases innumerable times, Secretary of State William Seward had brought him the official copy of the Emancipation Proclamation to sign. That had required some ceremony.

Then came Edwin Stanton bearing General-in-Chief Halleck's response to the note Lincoln had dashed off that morning. On his copy of the message that had prompted Old Brains' request for relief, Lincoln scribbled: "Withdrawn, because considered too harsh by General Halleck."[11]

Belatedly, and fortunately for the Union, Abraham Lincoln had made the right decision for the wrong reason. Having been pressed too much by too many things early in the day when he had initiated this dispute, perhaps he had been too fatigued from playing all day a role immeasurably removed from rail-splitting or lawyering to care to participate in any more controversies.

In any case, "too harsh" was a reaction not reflected in a single word of Henry Halleck's message to Stanton. Too *revealing*, Old Brains may properly have felt when he had read the President's note.

But why had Lincoln not granted his general-in-chief's request?

Indeed, Halleck could be replaced. Herman Haupt had proved an extremely brilliant and efficient officer despite his having required Stanton to employ him on his own most unusual terms. Awaiting orders were generals far senior to Haupt: Buell, McDowell, Pope—and McClellan. Montgomery Meigs had shown an understanding of strategy that suggested his talents were hardly limited to those required for a quartermaster-general.

Perhaps Lincoln considered the Halleck matter so inconsequential that it might as well be postponed. However, his withdrawal tossed the greased pig back into the outward-bound general-in-chief's lap.

Henry Halleck had satisfied the requirements of honor, but there remained the demands of *duty*. He had succumbed to them back in July; and nearly six months later, that seemed to have been the worst mistake he had ever made in his life.

"Success is a duty" was the motto that Nathaniel Banks had adopted and observed from his days as a bobbin boy in a Waltham mill to the speakership of the United States House of Representatives and beyond. But that slogan reeked of politics, rigged elections, victory, and the spoils of office to be gained at any price. John McClernand behaved as though he shared Banks' guiding principle.

Now, on New Year's Day, 1863, Henry Wager Halleck demonstrated what duty meant to him by making the second worst mistake of his life: withdrawing his request to be relieved.

4

NEITHER LINCOLN NOR HALLECK REFERRED to the exchange and with-drawals of notes again, but the events of January 1, 1863, in Washington were to cast long shadows. In the new year's first few days, however, the fog of war was thicker than usual; news from Sherman and Rosecrans, in particular, was fragmentary and mostly incorrect.

Actually, on 1862's last day, Rosecrans had intended to attack Braxton Bragg's army but the Confederates struck first, bending the federal line's right but not breaking it despite waves of assaults. At a council of war held that night, Rosecrans was inclined to withdraw. "This army does not retreat!" said George Thomas, and it did not. Both armies rested in place on

New Year's Day, then Rosecrans skillfully blocked Bragg's renewed attacks on January 2. Faced with a draw, Bragg withdrew to Tullahoma the next day. Rosecrans occupied Murfreesboro, just south of the battlefield.[12]

On January 2, General Grant had opened a message to Halleck with "Sherman had not succeeded in landing at Vicksburg on Tuesday" but added no more about that.[13] Five days later, Old Brains was telegraphing Grant: "Richmond papers of the 5th and 6th say that Sherman has been defeated and repulsed from Vicksburg."[14] In fact, Sherman had broken off contact at Chickasaw Bluffs on December 29.[15] And on January 4, Major General McClernand had assumed command of the expedition, citing Grant's order dated December 18, 1862, as his authority; Sherman had been relegated to the position of corps commander.[16]

The *sturm und drang* of January 1 had not dissipated by January 4, however, for on the latter date General Burnside responded to a message from the general-in-chief with hints that all was still not well in Falmouth:

> *I think my movements will prevent the enemy from making any raid upon Alexandria or Harper's Ferry. If you think it advisable, I will send General Sigel to you. I cannot move as quickly as I could have done before I was stopped in my last movement. It is known that the President telegraphed me, and I am surrounded with greater difficulties than before. I will do my best.[17]*

Then, on the next day, January 5, General Burnside sent letters that were identical in part to both Lincoln and Halleck. First, the text sent to His Excellency:

> *Since my return to the army I have become more than ever convinced that the general officers of this command are almost unanimously opposed to another crossing of the river, but I am still of the opinion that the crossing should be attempted, and I have accordingly issued orders to the engineers and artillery to prepare for it. There is much hazard in it, as there always is in the majority of military movements, and I cannot begin the movement without giving you notice of it, particularly as I know so little of the effect that it may have upon other movements of distant armies.*
>
> *The influence of your telegram the other day is still upon me, and has impressed me with the idea that there are many parts of the problem which influence you that are not known to me.*
>
> *In order to relieve you from all embarrassment in my case, I*

inclose, with this, my resignation of my commission as major-general of volunteers, which you can have accepted, if my movement is not in accordance with the views of yourself and your military advisers.

I have taken the liberty to write to you personally upon this subject, because it was necessary, as I learn from General Halleck, for you to approve of my general plan, written at Warrenton, before I could commence the movement, and I think it quite as necessary that you should know of the important movement I am about to make, particularly as it will have to be made in opposition to the views of nearly all my general officers, and after the receipt of a dispatch from you informing me of the opinion of some of them who had visited you.

In conversation with you on New Year's morning, I was led to express some opinions which I afterward felt it my duty to place on paper, and to express them verbally to the gentlemen of whom we were speaking, which I did in your presence after handing you the letter. You were not disposed then, as I saw, to retain the letter, and I took it back, but I now return it to you for record, if you wish it.

I beg leave to say that my resignation is not sent in any spirit of insubordination, but, as I before said, simply to relieve you from any embarrassment in changing commanders, where lack of confidence may have rendered it necessary.[18]

Having presented Lincoln with an approve-my-plan-or-else situation, in his letter to Halleck, Burnside implied that his plan was not yet firm. Indeed, he specified the kind of help he needed from the general-in-chief to complete it:

I have decided to move the army across the river again, and have accordingly given the directions to the engineers and artillery to make the necessary preparations to effect the crossing.

Since I last saw you it has become more apparent that the movement must be made almost entirely upon my own responsibility, so far as this army is concerned; and I do not ask you to assume any responsibility in reference to the mode or place of crossing, but it seems to me that, in making so hazardous a movement, I should receive some general directions from you as to the advisability of crossing at some point, as you are necessarily well informed of the effect at this time upon other parts of the army of a success or a repulse.

You will readily see that the responsibility of crossing without the knowledge of this effect, and against the opinion of nearly all the general officers, involves a greater responsibility than any officer situated as I am ought to incur.

In view of the President's telegram to me the other day, and with its influence still upon me, I have written to him on this subject, and inclosed to him my resignation, directed to the Adjutant-General, to be accepted in case it is not deemed advisable for me to cross the river.

I send this resignation because I have no other plan of campaign for this winter and I am not disposed to go into winter quarters. It may be well to add that recent information goes to show that the enemy's force has not been diminished in our front to any great extent.[19]

Of Old Brains, Secretary of the Navy Gideon Welles had written in his diary: "[Halleck] originates nothing, anticipates nothing ... takes no responsibility, plans nothing, suggests nothing, is good for nothing."[20] And when asked why he kept such a disagreeable person around, Lincoln is said to have replied that Halleck amounted to little more than a first-rate clerk.[21] Well, perhaps, but evidence to the contrary was contained in the reply he sent General Burnside on January 7, 1863:

Your communication of the 5th was delivered to me by your aide-de-camp at 12 m. to-day.

In all my communications and interviews with you since you took command of the Army of the Potomac, I have advised a forward movement across the Rappahannock. At our interview at Warrenton, I urged that you should cross by the fords above Fredericksburg rather than to fall down to that place, and, when I left you at Warrenton, it was understood that at least a considerable part of your army would cross by the fords, and I so represented to the President. It was this modification of the plan proposed by you, that I telegraphed you had received his approval.

When the attempt at Fredericksburg was abandoned, I advised you to renew the attempt at some other point, either in whole or in part to turn the enemy's works, or to threaten their wings or communications; in other words, to keep the enemy occupied till a favorable opportunity offered to strike a decisive blow. I particularly advised you to use your cavalry and light artillery upon his communications, and attempt to cut off his supplies and engage him at an advantage.

In all our interviews I have urged that our first object was, not Richmond, but the defeat or scattering of Lee's army, which threatened Washington and the line of the Upper Potomac. I now recur to these things simply to remind you of the general views which I have expressed, and which I still hold.

The circumstances of the case however, have somewhat changed since the early part of November. The chances of an extended line of operations are now, on account of the advanced season, much less than then. But the chances are still in our favor to meet and defeat the enemy on the Rappahannock, if we can effect a crossing in a position where we can meet the enemy on favorable or even equal terms.

I therefore still advise a movement against him. The character of that movement, however, must depend upon circumstances which may change any day and almost any hour.

If the enemy should concentrate his forces at the place you have selected for a crossing, make it a feint and try another place. Again, the circumstances at the time may be such as to render an attempt to cross the entire army not advisable. In that case theory suggests that, while the enemy concentrates at that point, advantages can be gained by crossing smaller forces at other points, to cut off his lines, destroy his communication, and capture his rear guards, outposts, &c.

The great object is to occupy the enemy, to prevent his making large detachments or distant raids, and to injure him all you can with the least injury to yourself. If this can be best accomplished by feints of a general crossing and detached real crossings, take that course; if by an actual general crossing, with feints on other points, adopt that course.

There seems to me to be many reasons why a crossing at some point should be attempted. It will not do to keep your large army inactive. As you yourself admit, it devolves on you to decide upon the time, place, and character of the crossing which you may attempt. I can only advise that an attempt be made, and as early as possible.[22]

To this example of Henry Halleck's ability to impart military advice with a lawyer's logic and precision, A. Lincoln added this brief endorsement:

I understand General Halleck has sent you a letter of which this is a copy. I approve this letter. I deplore the want of concurrence with you in opinion by your general officers, but I do not see the remedy. Be cautious, and do not understand that the Government or country is driving you. I do not yet see how I could profit by changing the command of the Army of the Potomac, and if I did, I should not wish to do it by accepting the resignation of your commission.[23]

Here were very strong indications that, despite Fredericksburg and the vexing trouble his insubordinate subordinates had caused, Ambrose Burnside's superiors genuinely wanted him to succeed. So did Quartermaster-General Montgomery Meigs, who on January 12 sent the army commander a suggestion that his troops forage on the peninsula between the Potomac and the Rappahannock below Fredericksburg, thus easing the burdens of supplying his army from the North.

By mid-January, however, Burnside had decided to move his forces to Banks Ford about six miles west of Falmouth, cross to the south side of the Rappahannock, and lure General Lee out of Marye's Heights and onto terrain favorable for the Army of the Potomac to annihilate the Confederates or at least to cut Lee's communications with Richmond. The march began on January 20, and so did torrential rains that halted the advance well short of the crossing point. By the next morning the road was a quicksand-like bog, sucking the wheels of wagons and those of gun carriages to their axle-hubs. Double- and triple-teaming mule teams failed, and so did regiments of men pulling on ropes.

By the third day, Burnside was obliged to cancel the "Mud March." But getting back to Falmouth proved as difficult as reaching the turnaround point had been. Much damage had been done—not by the Confederates, who had watched from the south bank and found the whole thing hilarious—but by generals who had given newspaper reporters quotable quotes. "I came to the conclusion that Burnside was fast losing his mind," said William Franklin. Fighting Joe Hooker told a reporter that Lincoln was an "imbecile" and that the country needed a dictator. Many soldiers took the occasion to depart for their homes.[24]

"The character of [any] movement," Old Brains had cautioned Burnside in his letter of January 7, "must depend upon circumstances which may change any day and almost any hour." Accordingly, he may have been more disappointed than shocked when he learned of the fiasco.

Abraham Lincoln, however, received a severe jolt on January 24 when General Burnside appeared at the Executive Mansion bearing the draft of an order and demanding that the commander-in-chief allow him to issue it or—again—accept his resignation forthwith. Appalled, the President read:

> *GENERAL ORDERS, No. 8.*
> *HDQRS. ARMY OF THE POTOMAC,*
> *January 23, 1863.*
>
> *I. General Joseph Hooker, major-general of volunteers and brigadier-general U.S. Army, having been guilty of unjust and unnecessary criticisms of the actions of his superior officers, and of the authorities, and having, by the general tone of his conversation, endeavored to create distrust in the minds of officers who have associated with him, and having, by omissions and otherwise, made reports and statements which were calculated to create incorrect impressions, and for habitually speaking in disparaging terms of other officers, is hereby dismissed the service of the United States as a man unfit to hold an important commission during a crisis like the present, when so much patience, charity, confidence, consideration, and patriotism are due from every soldier in the field. This order is issued subject to the approval of the President of the United States.*
>
> *II. Brig. Gen. W. T. H. Brooks . . . for complaining of the policy of the Government, and for using language tending to demoralize his command, is, subject to the approval of the President, dismissed from the military service of the United States.*
>
> *III. Brig. Gen. John Newton . . . and Brig. Gen. John Cochrane . . . for going to the President of the United States with criticisms upon the plans of their commanding officer, are, subject to the approval of the President, dismissed from the military service of the United States.*
>
> *IV. It being evident that the following named officers can be of no further service to this army, they are hereby relieved from duty, and will report, in person, without delay, to the Adjutant General, U.S. Army. . . .*[25]

Among those listed were Major Generals Franklin and William Farrar Smith, Brigadier General Samuel D. Sturgis (who, before Second Bull Run, had declared: "I don't care for John Pope a pinch of owl dung."), and Cochrane, who had already been dismissed from the military service of the United States by Burnside in Paragraph II.[26]

Hasty draftsmanship aside, Burnside had forgotten that the power to relieve general officers from command belonged to the President alone. Burnside's reach had otherwise exceeded his grasp. Whether or not because of the January 1 unpleasantness, Commander-in-Chief Lincoln left Halleck out of the process, summarily consigned the oddly bewhiskered and truly unfortunate general to an administrative post, and dispensed justice to the other officers as he saw fit:

> *GENERAL ORDERS, No. 20.*
> *WAR DEPARTMENT, ADJT. GEN.'S OFFICE,*
> *Washington, D.C., January 25, 1863.*
> *The President of the United States has directed:*
> *1st. That Maj. Gen. A. E. Burnside, at his own request, be relieved from the command of the Army of the Potomac.*
> *2d. That Maj. Gen. E. V. Sumner, at his own request, be relieved from duty in the Army of the Potomac.*
> *3d. That Maj. Gen. W. B. Franklin be relieved from duty in the Army of the Potomac.*
> *4th. That Maj. Gen. J. Hooker be assigned to the command of the Army of the Potomac.*[27]

And so it was that the shadow of the disruptive events on New Year's Day stretched nearly all the way across the month of January, ending, or at least blighting, the career of one commander of the Army of the Potomac and enhancing that of the next. Just as Abraham Lincoln had not involved his general-in-chief in the removal of Ambrose Burnside, his selection of Joseph Hooker to replace him—made without consulting General Halleck[28]—had the appearance of a penalty he was imposing for Old Brains' having forced him to back down on January 1.

Having lost the opportunity to keep his client from making mistakes, Halleck turned his attention mainly to helping Grant get Vicksburg while he waited to see how well Lincoln coped with the task of being Fighting Joe's sole link to the War Department. To his credit, the President had inadvertently made Halleck's life simpler by assuming all of the responsibility for his astonishing decision in the letter he gave General Hooker:

> *I have placed you at the head of the Army of the Potomac. Of course*
> *I have done this upon what appears to me to be sufficient reasons,*

and yet I think it best for you to know that there are some things in regard to which I am not quite satisfied with you.

I believe you to be a brave and skillful soldier, which, of course, I like. I also believe you do not mix politics with your profession, in which you are right. You have confidence in yourself, which is a valuable, if not an indispensable, quality. You are ambitious, which, within reasonable bounds, does good rather than harm; but I think that during General Burnside's command of the army you have taken counsel of your ambition, and thwarted him as much as you could, in which you did a great wrong to the country and to a most meritorious and honorable brother officer.

I have heard, in such a way as to believe it, of your recently saying that both the Army and the Government needed a dictator. Of course, it was not for this, but in spite of it, that I have given you the command. Only those generals who gain successes can set up dictators. What I now ask of you is military success, and I will risk the dictatorship.

The Government will support you to the utmost of its ability, which is neither more nor less than it has done and will do for all commanders. I much fear that the spirit which you have aided to infuse into the army, of criticizing their commander and withholding confidence from him, will now turn upon you. I shall assist you as far as I can to put it down. Neither you nor Napoleon, if he were alive again, could get any good out of an army while such a spirit prevails in it.

And now beware of rashness. Beware of rashness, but with energy and sleepless vigilance go forward and give us victories.

Yours, very truly,
A. LINCOLN.[29]

5

HUMAN SUFFERING CAN NEVER BE QUANTIFIED, but—for nations as well as its citizens—it is worse at some times than at others. Having inadvertently elected a President utterly unqualified by education or experience to serve as a commander-in-chief in wartime, many people in the North had already recognized their error and wondered how much more sacrifice they would be obliged to make to atone for it.

Surely, Abraham Lincoln had been aware that any additional mistakes he might make would only increase his constituents' misery. His purpose in having summoned Major General Halleck to Washington, he had told one of Old Brains' many critics, was "to give me military advice."[30] Yet, on January 1, 1863, he had almost blocked himself from deriving any more benefits Old Brains might provide him. And by implying so very clearly in his letter of January 25 that General Hooker was to report directly to him, Lincoln had in effect gratuitously relieved his general-in-chief of the Union armies of concern for the largest, nearest, and most troubled army of them all.

General Halleck adjusted to this development mainly in two ways. "It is a military rule," he explained to Stanton, "that when a subordinate officer reports to and receives instructions directly from a superior, no one of intermediate rank can interfere. . . ." And he added:

> *I think it would be improper for me to interfere in any of General Hooker's plans or movements. All I know in regard to them is, that he told me he intended to make some movement. . . . Whatever that movement may be, I shall assist him to the best of my ability and means.*[31]

Old Brains' second adaptation reflected his belief that he must at least *monitor* developments regarding the Army of the Potomac because the operations of Fighting Joe's army had bearing on those commanded by Grant and Rosecrans. And in the months to come, General Halleck would coach and support his army commanders in the West and elsewhere in the light of what he was able to learn indirectly about what was happening down in Falmouth.

At the outset of his non-relationship with the Army of the Potomac, however, Old Brains provided its commander with a copy of his advice-filled letter dated January 7, 1863, to Burnside and endorsed favorably by A. Lincoln.[32] That done, many weeks passed with contact between Hooker and the general-in-chief limited to disputes Halleck could not in good conscience have avoided.

An example originated in a message Halleck sent Hooker on March 16, 1863:

> *Reports received here to-day, apparently more reliable than heretofore, indicate that the enemy has concentrated some 10,000 men near Strasburg [in the Shenandoah Valley], to threaten the Baltimore and Ohio Railroad. You have the only cavalry force to*

cope with that of the enemy, and it is expected that you will observe or occupy it so as to prevent any large body from moving toward Harper's Ferry.[33]

General Hooker's reply bordered on insolence:

This morning I dispatched 3,000 cavalry to attack and break up the cavalry camp of Fitzhugh Lee and Hampton in the vicinity of Culpeper. Is it ordered that the residue of my cavalry force shall be sent on to the Baltimore and Ohio Railroad, so as to prevent any large body from moving toward Harper's Ferry? Can no one tell me where all the enemy's cavalry come from?[34]

As a child might complain to his mother that his brother was pestering him, Fighting Joe turned to Secretary of War Stanton.[35] The incident, a false alarm, dwindled down to merely a spat. But it may well have taught the general-in-chief that President Lincoln's subordinate could not be counted upon to carry out a key portion of any Army of the Potomac commander's mission: to protect Washington.

By March 27, however, General Halleck had made enough progress toward smiting Confederates on other fronts to bend his abhorrence of interfering with the link between a superior and his subordinate. Blending information with a suggestion almost amounting to a prod, he telegraphed the inert Hooker:

Dispatches from Generals Dix, Foster, and Hunter, and from the west, indicate that the rebel troops formerly under Lee are now much scattered for supplies, and for operations elsewhere.

It would seem, under these circumstances, advisable that a blow be struck by the Army of the Potomac as early as practicable.

It is believed that during the next few days several conflicts will take place, both south and west, which may attract the enemy's attention particularly to those posts.[36]

Pearls cast before swine.

Another unnecessary dispute over whose duty it was to order forces to protect telegraph lines between Falmouth and Washington prompted General Hooker to send copies of his and Halleck's telegrams to Stanton, adding in his cover message: "I respectfully request that these should be laid before the President of the United States without delay."[37] The outcome:

General-in-Chief Halleck slapped Fighting Joe down in a message dated April 13, 1863:

> *I do not think that the safety of Washington depends upon the maintenance of communication with your army, but I think it is your duty to maintain your communications with Washington, and to keep the War Department advised of all your movements and intended movements. You therefore have my orders to keep up such communication.*[38]

Much earlier, reports reaching Washington from Falmouth had been decidedly mixed. Hooker's headquarters, wrote Charles Francis Adams, Jr., was "a place no self-respecting man wanted to go, and no decent woman could go. It was a combination of barroom and brothel."[39] This squared with Fighting Joe's reputation. However, in 1863's early months, the army commander—sobered, some said by the gravity of his new responsibilities and Lincoln's admonitions—had taken a number of actions to restore the morale of his men and to increase their combat effectiveness.

Hooker saw to it that the quality of his soldiers' food improved and that they got paid. He borrowed an idea the late and much-missed Phil Kearny had floated; he ordered each of his corps to identify its troops through the use of distinctive symbols, such as a crescent moon or a Maltese cross on cloth patches sewn onto their caps. Completely scrapped were the wing and grand division organization schemes of his two predecessors, replaced by one calling for seven army corps commanded by men he trusted.

Captain Adams' comments notwithstanding, President Lincoln took the First Lady and their son Tad along on an early April visit to Hooker's headquarters at Falmouth. After reviewing many of the units comprising the 133,000-man Army of the Potomac, the commander-in-chief could agree with Fighting Joe that it was "the finest army on the planet."[40]

Parades aside, Lincoln used the occasion to talk with many of Hooker's subordinates and presumably with the general commanding himself. In one conversation, he imparted some advice Henry Halleck might have given: "Next time, put all your men into the fight."[41]

6

NOT LONG AFTER LINCOLN'S RETURN to Washington, General Hooker modified whatever he had told the commander-in-chief earlier regarding his plans. On April 11, 1863, he wrote:

> *After giving the subject my best reflection, I have concluded that I will have more chance of inflicting a heavier blow upon the enemy by turning his position to my right, and, if practicable, to sever his connections with Richmond with my dragoon force and such light batteries as it may be deemed advisable to send with them.*
>
> *I am apprehensive that* [Lee] *will retire from before me the moment I should succeed in crossing the river, and over the shortest line to Richmond, and thus escape being seriously crippled. I hope that when the cavalry have established themselves on the line between him and Richmond, they will be able to hold him and check his retreat until I can fall on his rear, or, if not that, I will compel him to fall back by the way of Culpeper and Gordonsville, over a longer line than my own, with his supplies cut off.*
>
> *The cavalry will probably cross the river above the Rappahannock Bridge, thence to Culpeper and Gordonsville and across to the Aquia Railroad, somewhere in the vicinity of Hanover Court House. They will probably have a fight in the vicinity of Culpeper, but not one that should cause them much delay or embarrassment.*
>
> *I have given directions for the cavalry to be in readiness to commence the movement on Monday morning next. While the cavalry are moving, I shall threaten the passage of the river at various points, and, after they have passed well to the enemy's rear, shall endeavor to effect the crossing.*
>
> *I hope, Mr. President, that this plan will receive your approval. It will obviate the necessity of detaching a force from Washington in the direction of Warrenton, while I think it will enhance my chances for inflicting a heavy blow upon the enemy's forces.*
>
> *I sincerely trust that you reached home safely and in good time yesterday. We all look back to your visit with great satisfaction.*[42]

Evidently Lincoln offered no objection, for Fighting Joe sent his cavalry force west of Falmouth in accordance with his plan. But the weather and the streams flowing into the Rappahannock and the Rapidan were pro-Confederate, and spring overflows wrecked Major General George Stoneman's operation almost as soon as it started.[43] By April 15 the President was expressing "considerable uneasiness." And he added: "I greatly fear it is another failure already. Write me often. I am very anxious."[44]

Indeed, Lincoln was. On April 19 he went down to Aquia to confer with his army commander.[45] He was not surprised, presumably, when on April 21 Hooker reported: "The weather appears to continue adverse to the execution of my plans as first formed, as, in fact, for all others, but if these do not admit of speedy solution, I feel that I must modify them to conform to the condition of things as they are." His next movement, he concluded, would be one "in the execution of which I shall be able to exercise personal supervision."[46]

Fighting Joe did, and that proved to have been been a great mistake. After the battle of Chancellorsville he wrote: "I was not hurt by a shell, and I was not drunk. For once I lost confidence in Joe Hooker, and that is all there is to it."[47]

Well, yes, but the heartstopping audacity and superb generalship displayed by Generals Lee and Jackson during the last days of April and the first week of May 1863 had more than a little to do with the humiliating defeat the Army of Northern Virginia, with Longstreet and several divisions absent, inflicted on Hooker's Army of the Potomac. Fighting Joe would have obtained a few grains of comfort, however, had he known what mortally wounded Stonewall had said to someone riding in the ambulance wagon with him on the way to Guiney's Station on May 4, before the battle had ended:

> *It was, in the main, a good conception, sir, an excellent plan. But he should not have sent away his cavalry, that was his great blunder. It was that which enabled me to turn him, without his being aware of it, and to take him by his rear. Had he kept his cavalry with him, his plan would have been a very good one.*[48]

News of the disaster was slow in reaching Washington in large part because General Hooker had ordered his chief of staff, Major General Daniel Butterfield, back at Falmouth, to refrain from reporting anything. This was prudence rather than impudence, because Chancellorsville was such an unusual battle, with fighting taking place at several locations in the rather large battle area at the same time. Jackson and Lee smote Hooker first on one hip and then on his other thigh until Fighting Joe, rejecting the fervent pleas of his corps commanders to stay south of the U. S. Ford and continue the struggle, finally ordered his entire force to re-cross the Rappahannock and return, for the second time in less than four months, to their camps around Falmouth.[49]

Chief of Staff Butterfield broke the ominous silence on May 3 in a brief telegram to Lincoln: "Though not directed or specifically authorized to do so by General Hooker, I think it not improper that I should inform you that a battle is in progress."[50] It was just as well from the standpoint of the commander-in-chief's blood pressure that Butterfield had not revealed that his superior's Chancellorsville campaign was then in its *seventh* day.

Several hours after Hooker's chief of staff sent that message to Washington, he received one from Colonel Rufus Ingalls, the Army of the Potomac's chief quartermaster: "I think we have had the most terrible battle ever witnessed on earth. I think our victory will be certain, but the general told me he would say nothing to Washington, except that he is doing well. . . ."[51]

At 1:30 p.m. that day Butterfield sent His Excellency this message:

From all reports yet collected, the battle has been most fierce and terrible. Losses heavy on both sides. General Hooker slightly, but not severely, wounded. He has preferred thus far that nothing should be reported, and does not know of this, but I cannot refrain from saying this much to you. You may expect his dispatch in a few hours, which will give the result.[52]

In the middle of that afternoon, by then with most of his army penned into a defensive position protecting their only escape route over to safety on the Rappahannock's north bank, Fighting Joe made good on Butterfield's promise. To Lincoln he telegraphed:

We have had a desperate fight yesterday and today, which has resulted in no success to us. . . . I cannot tell when it will end. We will endeavor to do our best. My troops are in good spirits. We have fought desperately to-day. No general ever commanded a more devoted army.[53]

Three days later, Hooker advised the President: "Have this moment returned to camp. . . . Not to exceed three corps, all told, of my troops have been engaged. For the whole to go in, there is a better place nearer at hand. Will write you at greater length tonight."[54]

The next day, May 6, Secretary of War Edwin Stanton warned Hooker: "The President and General-in-Chief left here at 4 o'clock to see you. They are probably at Aquia by this time."[55]

Henry Wager Halleck was surely the last man on earth Fighting Joe wanted to see just then. Yet Lincoln must have had some other reasons for bringing Old Brains along. On the day of their return to Washington, May 7, he made heavy use of euphemisms and suggested no change in command relationships in writing Hooker:

> *The recent movement of your army is ended without effecting its object, except, perhaps, some important breakings of the enemy's communications* [by cavalry raids]. *What next?*
>
> *If possible, I would be very glad of another movement early enough to give us some benefit from the fact of the enemy's communications being broken, but neither for this reason nor any other do I wish anything done in desperation or rashness.*
>
> *An early movement would also help to supersede the bad moral effect of the recent one, which is said to be considerably injurious.*
>
> *Have you already in your mind a plan wholly or partially formed? If you have, prosecute it without interference from me. If you have not, please inform me, so that I, incompetent as I may be, can try and assist in the formation of some plan for the army.*[56]

The language of this message was so un-Lincolnian as to suggest that someone—Henry Halleck?—had attempted to put some steel into Lincoln's backbone and had failed. An alternate possibility: the commander-in-chief was building a case for relieving Hooker, which had to be done with care because Fighting Joe was a favorite of the Ultra-Radical Republicans in Congress and elsewhere.

"I suppose details are not wanted of me at this time," replied the Army of the Potomac's commander. "I have decided in my own mind the plan to be adopted in our next effort, if it should be your wish to have one made. It has this to recommend it: it will be one in which the operations of all the corps, unless it be a part of the cavalry, will be within my personal supervision."[57]

If Abraham Lincoln recalled his army commander's having said much the same thing after Stoneman's fiasco and before the tragedy of Chancellorsville, it must have chilled his blood. In the interval, 17,278 soldiers' names had been added to the Union's casualty rolls and—as had too often been the case—nothing at all had been gained.[58]

Such was one dimension of the shadow cast by the events of January 1, 1863.

Don Carlos Buell

George B. McClellan and
his wife, Mary Ellen.

John Pope

Herman Haupt

John A. McClernand

Ambrose E. Burnside

Nathaniel P. Banks

William S. Rosecrans

Henry Halleck's "client," President Abraham Lincoln.

Montgomery C. Meigs

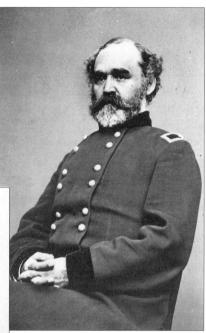

Philip H. Sheridan

George G. Meade

Ulysses S. Grant

George H. Thomas

Edwin M. Stanton

Benjamin F. Wade

William Tecumseh Sherman

12 ★ The Union's Spring of Discontent

IN MID-JULY OF 1862, LAWYER HALLECK had acquired as a client Abraham Lincoln, who by January 1, 1863, had become virtually unresponsive to counsel. But the Union armies were in dire need of Old Brains' legal skills, and by remaining as general-in-chief he was able to provide them.

No one anticipated how many questions would be spawned by such realities as guerrilla activities, exchanges of prisoners and paroles, application of martial law in occupied territories, and the frequent necessity to "live off the land." From his arrival at St. Louis in November 1861, General Halleck had encountered problems rooted in these and many other matters. Properly and promptly he sought guidance from the War Department in Washington. But little of it was forthcoming, in part because the complexity of modern civil war had been woefully underestimated. As a result, Old Brains was obliged to apply common sense along with his understanding of the principles of jurisprudence in dealing with the cases sent him by his subordinates.

Not content with improvising, he sent for a copy of a lecture on the laws of war given by Professor Francis Lieber of Columbia College. As it turned out, he and Lieber met when the professor came to visit his son who had been wounded at Fort Donelson.[1]

Although this was their first crossing of trails, the general and the educator were not exactly strangers. As a scholar, Lieber would have been familiar with Halleck's *International Law, or Rules Regulating the Intercourse of States in Peace and War,* published in 1861 before he left San Francisco.[2] And since both volumes of Lieber's *Legal and Political Hermeneutics* and his two-volume *Manual of Political Ethics* had been published as early as 1839, and his two-volume *On Civil Liberty and Self-Government* by 1853,[3] it would have been astonishing if anyone who had long since earned the nickname of Old Brains had not recognized the concerned father of the wounded soldier as a kindred spirit.

Lieber, older than Halleck by about fifteen years, had been born in Berlin, the tenth child of twelve. At the age of fifteen, he served under Blücher at the battle of Waterloo. In 1822 he went to fight for Greek independence but became disillusioned and lived for a time in Rome as tutor to the German ambassador's son. Back in Berlin his liberal political views caused him so many difficulties that he fled to England in 1826. A year later Lieber settled in Boston, where he founded the *Encyclopedia Americana* and formed friendships with a number of influential people. By 1835 Lieber was professor of history and political economy at South Carolina College. His most important writing was done there during the next twenty-one years; his books were the first systematic works on political science that appeared in this country. In 1857 he moved to New York City, where he was teaching at the war's outbreak. Two of Lieber's three sons served in the Union army; the other, a prominent geologist in the South, died of wounds received while he was a Confederate soldier.[4]

Early in their friendship General Halleck and Francis Lieber had agreed to collaborate in developing a code to cover the clusters of legal issues that had been raised in the course of this utterly unprecedented war. Union and Confederate disagreements regarding paroles and exchanges of prisoners, for example, needed to be settled, lest captured soldiers suffer from prolonged imprisonment, or units be deprived of men eligible for exchange and return to duty but held back by bureaucrats who could not comprehend existing regulations.

However, as general-in-chief, Halleck had discovered that the commanders of *all* the Union's field armies were having the same kinds of problems he had encountered in the West. This made it not only necessary but urgent for a code to be prepared and distributed. Accordingly, Old Brains appointed a commission, headed by Major General Ethan Allen Hitchcock and including Francis Lieber. The first product—General Orders No. 49—was issued on February 28, 1863, by order of the general-in-chief.

A remarkable feature of this document was the clarity of each of its twelve paragraphs, seven of which were only one sentence in length.

Confederate General Joseph E. Johnston thought so highly of it that he adopted it and had it distributed throughout the armies he was commanding in the West.

Yet Orders No. 49 had covered only paroles. Spurred by Halleck and guided by Lieber, the commission attacked many of the other subjects Old Brains had identified as in need of clarification. On April 24, 1863, Assistant Adjutant General E. D. Townsend wrote regarding General Orders No. 100:

> *The following instructions for the government of armies of the United States in the field, prepared by Francis Lieber, LL.D., and revised by a board of officers of which Maj. Gen. E. A. Hitchcock is president, having been approved by the President of the United States, he commands that they be published for the information of all concerned.*[5]

General Halleck was not mentioned, but his influence was apparent in the scope, organization, and precision yet simplicity of expression evident in General Orders No. 100. The document was in ten sections which contained a total of 157 paragraphs, including the twelve concerning parole that had been published in February. An idea of the broad span of matters on which officers and enlisted men throughout the Union armies could obtain guidance can be gained merely from the sections' headings:

I. *Martial law; Military jurisdiction; Military necessity; Retaliation.*

II. *Public and private property of the enemy; Protection of persons and especially women, of religion, the arts and sciences; Punishment of crimes against the inhabitants of hostile countries.*

III. *Deserters; Prisoners of war; Hostages; Booty on the battlefield.*

IV. *Partisans; Armed enemies not belonging to the hostile army; Scouts; Armed prowlers; War rebels.*

V. *Safe-conduct; Spies; War traitors; Captured messengers; Abuse of the flag of truce.*

VI. *Exchange of prisoners; Flags of truce; Flags of protection.*

VII. *The parole.*

VIII.[Missing from the Official Records.]

IX. *Assassination.* The complete text:

> *148. The law of war does not allow proclaiming either an*

*individual belonging to the hostile army or a citizen or a
subject of the hostile Government an outlaw who may be slain
without trial by any captor any more than the modern law of
peace allows such international outlawry; on the contrary it
abhors such outrage. The sternest retaliation should follow the
murder committed in consequence of such proclamation made
by whatever authority. Civilized nations look with horror
upon offers of rewards for the assassination of enemies as
relapses into barbarism.[6]*

X.   *Insurrection; Civil war; Rebellion.[7]*

"No work of this kind was in existence at that time in any language,"
a recent commentator has written. "It was accepted as standard by writers
on military law, was adopted by Germany in the conflict of 1870, and has
continued to be the basis of understanding on the conduct of war."[8]

Even so, General Orders No. 100 did not solve all disputes with
Confederates on these and other legal matters. Later, paragraph 109 in
Section VI—Exchange of prisoners—itself became controversial. It stated:

*The exchange of prisoners of war is a convenience to both
belligerents. If no general cartel has been concluded it* [exchange]
*cannot be demanded by either of them. No belligerent is obliged to
exchange prisoners of war. A cartel is voidable so soon as either party
has violated it.[9]*

With this as background, in his annual report to Secretary of War
Stanton, dated November 15, 1863, General-in-Chief Halleck wrote:

On the 22d of July, 1862, Major-General Dix and [Confederate]
*Major-General Hill entered into a cartel for the exchange of
prisoners during the existing war, specially stipulating when and
where exchanges should be made and how declared, defining the
meaning of a parole, and the rights and obligations of prisoners
under parole, and when and how they were to be released from these
obligations. . . .*

*Finding that the rebel authorities were paroling prisoners
contrary to these stipulations, they were notified on the 22d of May
last that all paroles not given in the manner prescribed by the cartel
would be regarded as null and void.*

Nevertheless, they continue to extort, by threats and ill-

treatment, from our men paroles unauthorized by the cartel, and also refused to deliver colored prisoners and their officers. It is stated that they sold the former into slavery and sentenced the latter to imprisonment and death for alleged violation of local State laws.

This compelled a resort to retaliatory measures, and an equal number of their prisoners in our hands were selected as hostages for the surrender of those retained by them.

All exchanges under the cartel, therefore, ceased. In violation of general good faith and of engagements solemnly entered into the rebel commissioner then proceeded to declare exchanged all his own paroled prisoners and ordered their return to the ranks of their regiments then in the field.

And we are now asked to confirm these acts by opening new accounts and making new lists for exchange, and the rebels seek to enforce these demands by the most barbarous treatment of our officers and men now in their hands.

Rebel prisoners held by the United States have been uniformly treated with consideration and kindness. They have been furnished with all necessary clothing and supplied with the same quality and amount of food as our own soldiers, while our soldiers who, by the casualties of war, have been captured by them have been stripped of their blankets, clothing, and shoes, even in the winter season, and then confined in damp and loathsome prisons, and only half-fed on damaged provisions, or actually starved to death, while hundreds have terminated their existence, loaded with irons, in filthy prisons. Not a few, after a semblance of trial by some military tribunal, have been actually murdered by their inhuman keepers.

In fine, the treatment of our prisoners of war by the rebel authorities has been even more barbarous than that which Christian captives formerly suffered from the pirates of Tripoli, Tunis, and Algiers; and the horrors of "Belle Isle" and "Libby Prison" exceed even those of "British Hunlks" [sic] or the "Black Hole of Calcutta." And this atrocious conduct is applauded by the people and commended by the public press of Richmond as "a means of reducing the Yankee ranks."

It has been proposed to retaliate upon the enemy by treating his prisoners precisely as he treats ours. Such retaliation is fully justified by the laws and usages of war, and the present case seems to call for the exercise of this extreme right. Nevertheless, it is revolting to our sense of humanity to be forced to so cruel an alternative. It is

hoped self-interest, if not a sense of justice, may induce the rebels to
abandon a course of conduct which must forever remain a burning
disgrace to them and their cause.[10]

Clearly, lawyer Halleck had not forgotten how to state a case. But impassioned, carefully crafted pleading was not enough. Populations of prisoners in camps such as Andersonville in the South and Point Lookout in the North soon far exceeded capacity and became the sites of incredible suffering.[11]

War, of course, is law enforcement by extraordinary means. Absent meetings of the minds regarding cartels for prisoner exchanges, it was up to General-in-Chief Halleck and the Union's field armies to punish the offenders. But Old Brains and his partner Francis Lieber had gone as far as their intellects could take them—at least for the time being.

Yet one wonders: What, if anything, might ever have been done to cut through the thick prevailing fog of ignorance and misunderstanding of legal issues if—instead of owl-eyed, pudgy, elbow-scratching Halleck—Professor Lieber had encountered the Young Napoleon when he went west to visit his wounded son?

2

ABRAHAM LINCOLN'S PARTIAL DISMISSAL of Halleck had enabled the general-in-chief to devote more time to work with Francis Lieber and others on what became General Orders No. 100. The President's selecting Fighting Joe Hooker to succeed Ambrose Burnside as commander of the Army of the Potomac, and his granting Hooker the privilege of reporting directly to him, also enabled Old Brains to concentrate his attention and his efforts on completing the tasks he had reluctantly left in mid-1862: capturing Vicksburg and re-opening navigation on the Mississippi all the way to the Gulf of Mexico.

But another project General Halleck could continue, now that he had decided (again) that duty compelled him to remain in Washington, was development and encouragement of commanders of field armies who were vast improvements over those they had replaced—generals who, in turn, would bring along promising youngsters to succeed *them.* Because of Lincoln's blunders in bestowing high rank (hence, seniority) on politicians early in the war, this could only be done gradually, subtly. Halleck's having been snubbed out of Hooker's operations, then, increased General Grant's ability to advance Cump Sherman and "Jamie" McPherson and General Rosecrans' chances of giving more opportunities to be of service to George Thomas and "Little Phil" Sheridan.

Yes, of course, all of these soldiers were graduates of the "elitist" United States Military Academy which the Radicals despised so vehemently. And Halleck had never concealed his reluctance to entrust the lives of Union troops to the likes of Nathaniel Banks, "Spoons" Butler, and John A. McClernand. Lacking any political support whatsoever himself, if Old Brains' efforts to increase the professionalism of the Union armies' officer corps failed, the guillotine awaited.

Accordingly, even before the twin Western disasters at Holly Springs and Chickasaw Bluffs, Halleck had bet the farm on Ulysses S. Grant's capturing Vicksburg. But in 1863's earliest days, the general-in-chief was indicating *also* that opening the Mississippi was the goal toward which he was focusing *all* the Union's resources in the West, as his wire on January 10 to Horatio Wright in Cincinnati reflected:

> *Are there not fractional regiments organized in Ohio, Indiana, and Illinois which can be consolidated by the Governors and imme-diately sent down the Mississippi? It is of vital importance that the army against Vicksburg be re-inforced as rapidly as possible. It is expected that you will use every exertion to accomplish that object. All our paroled prisoners taken prior to December 10 are declared exchanged. Get them back to their regiments in the field as rapidly as possible.*[12]

Halleck already knew that John A. McClernand was as vexing a problem for Grant as Vicksburg's batteries, and so he would not have been greatly surprised by a message from Grant he received on January 11: "General McClernand has fallen back to White River, and gone on a wild-goose chase to the Port of Arkansas. I am ready to re-inforce, but must await further information before knowing what to do."[13]

Might the utter candor of this simple message, which called for no help, have conveyed something more—that the old friction between the two men was entirely behind them, that their relationship was now completely straightforward?

General Halleck's reply the next day was equally direct: "You are hereby authorized to relieve General McClernand from command of the expedition against Vicksburg, giving it to the next in rank or taking it yourself."[14] But, sure of the general-in-chief's unqualified backing, Grant had not waited to hear back from him. On January 11 he had written McClernand:

> *I do not approve of your move on the Post of Arkansas. . . . It might answer for some of the purposes you suggest, but certainly not as a military movement looking to the accomplishment of the one great result, the capture of Vicksburg.*
>
> *Unless you are acting under authority not derived from me keep your command where it can soonest be assembled for the renewal of the attack on Vicksburg.*
>
> *Major-General Banks has orders from Washington to co-operate in the reduction of Vicksburg, and if not already off that place may be daily expected. You will therefore keep your forces well in hand at some point on the Mississippi River, where you can communicate with General Banks on his arrival. Should you learn, before you have an opportunity of communicating with him, that he is making an attack on Vicksburg, move at once to his support. Every effort must be directed to the reduction of that place.*[15]

McClernand's response was to send a letter to His Excellency on January 16, 1863, bringing to mind an old Southern saying: "It's the hit dog that yelps."

> *I believe my success here is gall and wormwood to the clique of West Pointers who have been persecuting me for months. How can you expect success when men controlling the military destinies of the country are more chagrined at the success of your volunteer officers than the very enemy beaten by the latter in battle?*
>
> *Something must be done to take the hand of oppression off citizen soldiers whose zeal for their country has prompted them to take up arms, or all will be lost.*
>
> *Do not let me be clandestinely destroyed, or, what is worse, dishonored, without a hearing. The very moment you think I am an impediment to the public service, upon the slightest intimation of it my resignation will be forwarded. Until then you may count upon my best endeavors, at whatever peril, to sustain the sacred cause for which we are contending.*
>
> *In addition to the reasons set forth in the copy of the dispatch inclosed for the Arkansas River expedition, I might assign the order*

of the Secretary of War, indorsed by you, to open the Mississippi River.

The Mississippi River being the only channel of communication, and that being infested with guerrillas, how can General Grant at a distance of 400 miles intelligently command the army with me? He cannot do it. It should be made an independent command, as both you and the Secretary of War, as I believe, originally intended.[16]

At about this time Ambrose Burnside's Mud March and his subsequent move toward banishing his dissenting subordinates to the outer darkness were higher on Lincoln's priority list than McClernand's childish whining. To the Secretary of War went the task of replying:

I think you need no new assurance of the sincere desire of the President and myself to oblige you in every particular consistent with the general interest of the service, and I trust the course of events will be such as will enable the Government to derive the utmost advantage from your patriotism and military skill.[17]

Lawyer Stanton had used fifty-six words to say nothing at all. But General Grant had not exercised his authority to relieve McClernand, and the dispute over command continued.

On January 20, from Memphis, Grant wrote Halleck:

I returned here last night from a visit to the expedition under General McClernand. I had a conversation with Admiral Porter, General McClernand, and General Sherman. The former and the latter, who have had the best opportunity of studying the enemy's position and plans, agree that the work of reducing Vicksburg is one of time, and will require a large force at the final struggle.

General Grant then proposed cutting a canal across one of the Mississippi's loops west of Vicksburg that would enable gunboats and other vessels to pass beyond the range of the rebel batteries. That done, he turned to other matters:

I would make no suggestions unasked if you were here to see for yourself, or if I did not know that as much of your time is taken up with each of several other departments as with this. As, however, I control only the troops in a limited department, and can only draw re-enforcements from elsewhere by making application through Washington, and as a demonstration made upon any part of the old district of West Tennessee might force me to withdraw a large part of the force from the vicinity of Vicksburg, I would respectfully ask if it would not be policy to combine the four departments in the West under one commander.

As I am the senior department commander in the West, I will state that I have no desire whatever for such combined command, but would prefer the command I now have to any other that can be given.

I regard it as my duty to state that I found there was not sufficient confidence felt in General McClernand as a commander, either by the Army or Navy, to insure him success. Of course, all would co-operate to the best of their ability, but still with a distrust. This is a matter I made no inquiries about, but it was forced upon me. As it is my intention to command in person, unless otherwise directed, there is no special necessity of mentioning this matter; but I want you to know that others besides myself agree in the necessity of the course I had already determined upon pursuing.[18]

In a second message, Grant gave Old Brains a relatively simple suggestion: "Both banks of the Mississippi should be under one commander, at least during present Operations."[19] Back the next day came the general-in-chief's reply, together with some advice:

The President has directed that so much of Arkansas as you may desire to control be temporarily attached to your department. This will give you control of both banks of the river.

In your Operations down the Mississippi you must not rely too confidently upon any direct cooperation of General Banks and the lower flotilla, as it is possible that they may not be able to pass or reduce Port Hudson. They, however, will do everything in their power to form a junction with you at Vicksburg. If they should not be able to effect this, they will at least occupy a portion of the enemy's forces and prevent them from re-enforcing Vicksburg. I hope, however, that they will do better and be able to join you.[20]

Now, apparently, Grant would have *two* incompetent political generals to beware of. The nearest one, John A. McClernand, seemed determined to prolong the tiresome dispute over command in the West, as was reflected at the end of a letter he sent his superior Grant on January 30, 1863:

> *I understand that orders are being issued directly from your headquarters directly to army corps commanders, and not through me. As I am invested, by order of the Secretary of War, indorsed by the President, and by order of the President communicated to you by the General-in-Chief, with the command of all the forces operating on the Mississippi River, I claim that all orders affecting the condition or operations of those forces should pass through these headquarters; otherwise I must lose a knowledge of current business and dangerous confusion ensue.*
>
> *If different views are entertained by you, then the question should be immediately referred to Washington, and one or the other, or both of us, relieved. One thing is certain, two generals cannot command this army, issuing independent and direct orders to subordinate officers, and the public service be promoted.*[21]

Armed with authority granted him by Old Brains earlier in the month, but—curiously—not using that part of it empowering him to relieve McClernand, General Grant issued General Orders No. 13 that same day, January 30. In this document he formally assumed command of the "expedition against Vicksburg," and he charged McClernand's corps with "garrisoning the post of Helena, Ark., and any other point of the west bank of the river it may be necessary to hold south of that place."[22]

Hardly had Orders No. 13's ink dried before McClernand erupted. "I hasten to inquire," he inquired, "whether its purpose is to relieve me from command of all or any portion of the forces composing the Mississippi River expedition, or, in other words, whether its purpose is to limit my command to the Thirteenth Army Corps. . . ." Referring to the section regarding his unit's mission, McClernand observed: "It is quite obvious that the whole or a large portion of the Thirteenth Corps must be absorbed by these garrisons if the purpose is to afford complete protection to all lawful vessels navigating the river, and thus, while having projected the Mississippi River expedition, and having been by a series of orders assigned to command of it, I may be completely withdrawn from it."[23]

General Grant set his subordinate straight the next day—or he tried to. "The intention of General Orders No. 13," he explained, "is that I will take direct command of the Mississippi River expedition, which necessarily limits your command to the Thirteenth Army Corps." Later in the message he added:

> *I regard the President as Commander-in-Chief of the Army, and will obey every order of his, but as yet I have seen no order to prevent my taking direct command in the field, and since the dispatch referred to in your note, I have received another from the General-in-Chief of the Army, authorizing me directly to take command of this army.*[24]

McClernand's reply:

> *Your dispatch of this date, in answer to mine of yesterday, is received. You announce it to be the intention of General Orders, No. 13, to relieve me from the command of the Mississippi River expedition, and to circumscribe my command to the Thirteenth Army Corps, and undertake to justify the order by authority granted by the General-in-Chief.*
>
> *I acquiesce in the order for the purpose of avoiding a conflict of authority in the presence of the enemy, but, for reasons set forth in my dispatch of yesterday, which, for anything disclosed, I still hold good, I protest against its competency and justice, and respectfully request that this, my protest, together with the accompanying paper, may be forwarded to the General-in-Chief, and through him to the Secretary of War and the President.*
>
> *I request this, not only in respect for the President and Secretary, under whose express authority I claim the right to command the expedition, but in justice to myself as its author and actual promoter.*[25]

On the same day, February 1, 1863, Grant did precisely what McClernand asked, by writing Colonel Kelton, General Halleck's Assistant Adjutant-General:

> *Herewith I inclose you copy of General Orders, No. 13, from these headquarters, and of correspondence between General McClernand and myself, growing out of it. It is due to myself to state that I am not ambitious to have this or any other command. I am willing to do all in my power in any position assigned me.*
>
> *General McClernand was assigned to duty in this department,*

with instructions to me to assign him to the command of an army corps operating on the Mississippi River, and to give him the chief command, under my direction. This I did, but subsequently receiving authority to assign the command to any one I thought most competent, or to take it myself, I determined to at least be present with the expedition.

If General Sherman had been left in command here, such is my confidence in him that I would not have thought my presence necessary. But whether I do General McClernand injustice or not, I have not confidence in his ability as a soldier to conduct an expedition of the magnitude of this one successfully. In this opinion I have no doubt but I am borne out by a majority of the officers of the expedition, though I have not questioned one of them on the subject.

I respectfully submit this whole matter to the General-in-Chief and the President. Whatever the decision made by them, I will cheerfully submit to and give a hearty support.[26]

Concurrently, Ulysses Grant could take considerable satisfaction from two letters he had received from General McPherson. The first, from northern Mississippi, had been written back on December 20, 1862, and most of it was devoted to reports on the situation in that area. At the end of it, though, Jamie had said:

In consequence of orders from Washington placing General McClernand in charge of the expedition under you, I would, if in your place, proceed to Memphis and take command of it myself. It is the great feature of the campaign, and its execution rightfully belongs to you.

In case you go I would like to accompany you with two divisions, Lauman's and Logan's, but I am ready for any position you may assign me.[27]

McPherson's second letter was sent to Grant from LaGrange, Tennessee, on January 16, 1863. It began:

I am just in receipt of orders assigning me to the command of a portion of the forces to operate against Vicksburg. I cannot express to you the gratification it gives me, and I shall most assuredly do my utmost to merit your confidence.[28]

Jamie McPherson was displaying exactly the attitude Cump Sherman had under Halleck a year earlier. And Grant was demonstrating his ability to confine McClernand's damage to the wasting of time and message paper. These may well have seemed small achievements, but Old Brains would have been fully justified if he took a few grains of satisfaction from them.

3

IN ALMOST ALL RESPECTS, William Starke Rosecrans was a vast improvement over Don Carlos Buell. He was a fighting general; at one point during the first day of Stones River, he had spurred his horse all along his lines to show his troops that he was not dead, telling them that the blood and brains on his uniform were not his but those of his chief of staff, Colonel Julius Garesché, who had been killed while riding beside him.[29] Yet Old Rosy resembled his predecessor in that his diligence in preparing for battle was often reflected in messages the war managers in Washington might easily misinterpret as excuses.

Having intimidated Braxton Bragg out of Murfreesboro and then occupied the town, Rosecrans began turning it into an advanced supply base. Bragg had withdrawn to Tullahoma and vicinity, a position from which he could strike Old Rosy's flank if his Yankee adversary moved either toward East Tennessee or southwestward to reinforce General Grant. Similarly, Rosecrans' positions near Murfreesboro tended to prevent Bragg from sending troops to Lee in Virginia or Pemberton at Vicksburg.

All fall and so far into the winter, however, Confederate cavalry led by Nathan Bedford Forrest and John Morgan had broken Rosecrans' long Louisville & Nashville Railroad supply line often enough to paralyze him. It was only natural, then, for Old Rosy to seek more cavalry from General Halleck, who responded to a number of his requests in a long letter dated February 3, 1863:

> *Your recent telegrams have been couched in terms implying a censure upon the Government for not properly supplying you with cavalry and cavalry arms. You are certainly under a grave misapprehension.*
>
> *You cannot be more anxious for success than the Government is for you to succeed; the Government is as desirous of giving you the means of success as you are to receive them; but yours is not the only nor the largest army in the field, and you are not the only general*

who is urgently calling for more cavalry and more cavalry arms. . . .

    For example yourself, Generals Grant, Sibley, Banks, Hunter, Foster, Dix, and Schenck are all urgently demanding "more cavalry." Of course, all cannot be supplied, nor, indeed, the full demands of any one. The Government has done everything in its power to raise and arm more cavalry, but if every regiment raised in the last few months in the whole country had been sent to you, to the exclusion of all others, your demands would not have been filled.

    The only alternative was to give you the authority which you asked for to mount a portion of your infantry. But you now bitterly complain of the want of better cavalry arms; that unless the Government supplies you with "revolving rifles in place of pistols," &c., you will not be prepared for coming emergencies. You also ask for the "best arms," "superior arms," &c. . . .

    Certainly you cannot expect that you can have all the best arms and other troops receive only those of a lower grade. In regard to "revolving rifles," "superior arms," &c., every one is issued the moment it is received. Those who cannot obtain these must use carbines, sabers, and pistols, or muskets. Even with these our cavalry is better armed than that of the enemy.

    Everything has been and will be done for your army which the Government can do without injustice to other troops. You cannot expect the best of arms or of anything else, to the exclusion of others, who need them as much as you do.[30]

Had Halleck's tone been too harsh? If so, was it the result of a difficult day, or the hemorrhoids that some said plagued him?[31] Or, recognizing that General Rosecrans was new to high command, was Old Brains trying to inculcate an understanding of the realities beyond the field general's experience or imagination?

    At a minimum, the general-in-chief seemed unusually eager to share information with Rosecrans that contributed to the distant commander's perspective. Only a few days before Halleck's letter regarding the shortage of cavalry, for example, he had mixed gossip with admonitions:

There is a general impression here that no troops have gone from Virginia to re-enforce Bragg, but, on the contrary, that a part of Bragg's forces have been sent to Port Hudson and Vicksburg, and I have been urged to send a part of your army down the Mississippi. I do not regard the reports of these changes as sufficiently reliable to authorize any change at present in the strength of your army. They are, however, of such a character as to render it exceedingly important that you should occupy the enemy in your front, and, as far as possible, feel him and keep yourself informed of his strength.

The continued inaction of the Army of the Potomac during the long and favorable season for field operations, which, it is feared, is now closed, has very greatly embarrassed the Government. It was expected that that army would at least drive the enemy from the vicinity of Washington and the Upper Potomac, and occupy the rebel army of Virginia south of the Rappahannock. This would have enabled us to detach sufficient forces to place the opening of the Mississippi beyond a doubt.

As things now are, we are hard pressed for troops for that purpose. Should the enemy succeed in holding your army in cheek with an inferior force while he sends troops to the Mississippi River, it is greatly to be feared that the time of many of our troops will expire without our having accomplished any important results.

In regard to [your request for] gunboats for the Cumberland and Tennessee Rivers, I regret that the entire control of these matters was taken from the War Department. We anticipated and predicted that just at the time and place where we most needed these boats, there would be no co-operation. Our only hope is for you to continually urge upon Admiral Porter the necessity of his keeping boats in these rivers, and I will continue to urge the matter upon the Navy Department here.

I have no doubt that there is every desire for a cordial co-operation, but this is very difficult to effect when the parties have different objects in view and act entirely independent of each other.[32]

In mid-February, however, Rosecrans introduced a new subject, one that gave Old Brains an opportunity to go a bit beyond General Orders No. 49, in which he and Francis Lieber, *et al.,* had dealt only with paroles, into a murky area everyone seemed queasy about acknowledging, much less facing. To Halleck on February 17, 1863, Old Rosy wrote:

The effect of the state of party agitation at the North is to encourage desertion.

To counteract this in my army, at least, I deem two things necessary: First, that I have the power of confirming and promptly executing sentence of death for desertion. Second, that I have the authority to send proper details of officers, and, if necessary, men, to arrest and bring back absentees, whether deserters, paroled prisoners, skulkers, convalescents, or stragglers.

I have once requested this of the War Department, but have not yet received a reply. I beg your attention to this matter, as one requiring immediate attention. There are 40,000 absentees from this army to-day.[33]

General-in-Chief Halleck's response was actually lawyer Halleck's, but it was the most straightforward statement of the status of remedies that anyone might have provided:

In your telegram of last evening you ask the power of confirming and promptly executing sentences of death for desertion. You must be aware, general, that no such power can be conferred upon you by the President or Secretary of War.

The law is positive that no such sentence shall be executed till approved by the President. The President cannot change this law, and it is his duty, as well as yours and mine, to obey the law.

I have advised the repeal of this statute, and there is a bill before Congress for that purpose. It may, or may not, pass. Until repealed, the law must be obeyed.

In regard to authorizing you to send officers and armed men into other departments than your own, to look up and arrest deserters, it is believed that such a measure would weaken rather than increase the numbers of your army, besides the risks of conflict between the civil authorities and indiscreet officers sent on that service.

The results of sending such parties from the Army of the Potomac, to arrest deserters, have proved that the plan is not a good one. The best way to prevent desertion here has been the sending out of patrols on the roads upon which deserters seek to return to their States.

There is a bill before Congress to provide means for arresting deserters, now absent from the army, without sending out military forces for that purpose. Should it not pass, or should it be found ineffectual, other means must be devised.[34]

Desertion covered, or at least patched, Rosecrans then drew Henry Halleck's attention to the complexities of the problems his troops were encountering in occupying territory inhabited by both Unionists and pro-

Confederates. Prompting this had been an eloquent letter from Major General J. J. Reynolds to George Thomas who had forwarded it to Rosecrans. In it, Reynolds had described both the plight of the loyal civilians and the actions of their rebel neighbors. General Reynolds' conclusion: "The remedy for this state of affairs appears very simple: Despoil the rebels as the rebel army has despoiled the Union men. Send the rebels out of the country, and make safe room for the return of loyal men."[35]

An eye for an eye, a tooth for a tooth? Well, perhaps, Old Brains implied, but he seized the occasion to apply his intellect to more than retribution. To General Rosecrans on March 5, 1863, he wrote:

> *The suggestions of General Reynolds and General Thomas in regard to a more rigid treatment of all disloyal persons within the lines of your army are approved. No additional instructions from these headquarters are deemed necessary.*
>
> *You have already been urged to procure your subsistence, forage, and means of transportation, so far as possible, in the country occupied. This you had a right to do without any instructions. As the commanding general in the field, you have power to enforce all laws and usages of war, however rigid and severe these may be, unless there be some act of Congress, regulation, order, or instruction forbidding or restricting such enforcement.*
>
> *As a general rule, you must be the judge where it is best to rigidly apply these laws, and where a more lenient course is of greater advantage to our cause. Distinctions, however, should always be made in regard to the character of the people in the district of country which is militarily occupied or passed over.*
>
> *The people of the country in which you are likely to operate may be divided into three classes. First. The truly loyal, who neither aid nor assist the rebels, except under compulsion, but who favor or assist the Union forces. Where it can possibly be avoided, this class of persons should not be subjected to military requisitions, but should receive the protection of our arms. It may, however, sometimes be necessary to take their property either for our own use or to prevent its falling into the hands of the enemy. They will be paid, at the time, the value of such property, or, if that be impracticable, they will hereafter be fully indemnified. Receipts should be given for all property so taken without being paid for.*
>
> *Second. Those who take no active part in the war, but belong to the class known in military law as non-combatants. In a civil war*

like that now waged, this class is supposed to sympathize with the rebellion rather than with the Government. There can be no such thing as neutrality in a rebellion. This term is applicable only to foreign powers. Such persons, so long as they commit no hostile act, and confine themselves to their private avocations, are not to be molested by the military forces, nor is their property to be seized, except as a military necessity. They, however, are subject to forced loans and military requisitions, and their houses to billets for soldiers' quarters, and to appropriation for other temporary military uses. Subject to these impositions, the noncombatant inhabitants of a district of country militarily occupied by one of the belligerents are entitled to the military protection of the occupying forces; but, while entitled to such protection, they incur very serious obligations— obligations differing in some respects from those of civil allegiance, but equally binding.

For example, those who rise in arms against the occupying army, or against the authority established by the same, are war rebels, or military traitors, and incur the penalty of death. They are not entitled to be considered as prisoners of war when captured. Their property is subject to military seizure and military confiscation. Military treason of this kind is broadly distinguished from the treason defined in constitutional and statutory laws, and made punishable by the civil courts. Military treason is a military offense, punishable by the common law of war. Again, persons belonging to such occupied territory, and within the military lines of the occupying forces, can give no information to the enemy of the occupying power, without proper authority. To do so, the party not only forfeits all claim to protection, but subjects himself or herself to be punished either as a spy or a military traitor, according to the character of the particular offense.

Our treatment of such offenses and such offenders has hitherto been altogether too lenient. A more strict enforcement of the laws of war in this respect is recommended. Such offenders should be made to understand the penalties they incur, and to know that these penalties will be rigidly enforced.

Third. Those who are openly and avowedly hostile to the occupying army, but who do not bear arms against such forces; in other words, while claiming to be non-combatants, they repudiate the obligations tacitly or impliedly incurred by the other inhabitants of the occupied territory. Such persons not only incur all the *obligations imposed upon other non-combatant inhabitants of the same territory, and are liable to the same punishment for offenses committed, but they may be treated as prisoners of war, and be subjected to the rigors of confinement or to expulsion as combatant enemies.*

I am of opinion that such persons should not, as a general rule, be permitted to go at large within our lines. To force those capable of bearing arms to go within the lines of the enemy adds to his effective forces; to place them in confinement will require guards for their safe keeping, and this necessarily diminishes our active forces in the field.

You must determine in each particular case which course will be most advantageous. We have suffered very severely from this class, and it is time that the laws of war should be more rigorously enforced against them. A broad line of distinction must be drawn between friends and enemies, between the loyal and the disloyal.

The foregoing remarks have reference only to military status and to military offenses under the laws of war. They are not applicable to civil offenses under the Constitution and general laws of the land. The laws and usages of civilized war must be your guide in the treatment of all classes of persons of the country in which your army may operate, or which it may occupy; and you will be permitted to decide for yourself where it is best to act with rigor and where best to be more lenient. You will not be trammeled with minute instructions.[36]

In view of the extraordinary length and detail of this letter, and considering that General Halleck, Francis Lieber, and others were working on General Orders No. 100 at the time, it seems highly likely that what Old Brains sent Rosecrans was, except for the opening paragraph, an adaptation of a position paper he had prepared. Whatever its genesis, this document reflects powers of analysis and clarity of expression seldom found even in first-rate clerks.

However, at times Halleck could be too terse. An example is the telegram he sent Grant, Hooker, Wright, and Rosecrans on March 1, 1863: "There is a vacant major-generalcy in the Regular Army, and I am authorized to say that it will be given to the general in the field who first wins an important and decisive victory."[37]

General Rosecrans expressed his umbrage in a telegram on March 6:

As an officer and a citizen, I feel degraded to see such auctioneering of honor. Have we a general who would fight for his own personal benefit, when he would not for honor and the country? He would come by his commission basely in that case, and deserve to be despised by men of honor. But are all the brave and honorable generals on an equality as to chances? If not, it is unjust to those who probably deserve most.[38]

A week later, Old Brains replied:

The names of yourself and others were presented to the War Department for major-generals in the Regular Army. The Secretary decided that he would not fill the vacancy till some general could claim it as a reward for a complete and decisive victory. This decision was briefly announced to you and others whose names had been urged.

To this note you, on the 6th, return an indignant answer, characterizing the announcement of the Secretary's decision as an "auctioneering of honors." If this be so, the general order of the President announcing that he would appoint brigadier and major generals only for distinguished services in the field is also an "auctioneering of honors," and should have incited equal indignation.

Before receiving your letter, I had not supposed that a Government which offered and bestowed its highest offices for military success either depreciated patriotism, encouraged baseness, or bartered away honor. When last summer, at your request, I urged the Government to promote you for success in the field, and, again at your request, urged that your commission be dated back to your services in Western Virginia, I thought I was doing right in advocating your claim to honors for services rendered.[39]

General Rosecrans went back to requesting cavalry and advanced weapons. "No restriction is placed on your mounting infantry," Halleck advised him, "and cavalry arms and equipments are sent to you as fast as they can be procured, but it is believed you weaken your force by adding too many. Mounted infantry are neither good infantry nor good cavalry."[40] That said, Old Brains turned his attention to trouble in Cincinnati.

4

ON MARCH 15, Horatio Wright wrote to Brigadier General Cullum, Halleck's chief of staff:

> *The recent action of the Senate, in refusing my confirmation as major-general, of which I presume there is no doubt, can be looked upon only as a condemnation of my administration of the affairs of this department, and will naturally occasion in the public mind a want of confidence which will seriously impair my usefulness in my present position.*
>
> *In this view of the case, I feel bound to suggest to the military authorities at Washington my removal from this command, by the assignment thereto of some one who shall fully command the confidence of the people and the troops in the department, and to ask that no unnecessary delay be permitted in adopting this suggestion. . . .*[41]

General-in-Chief Halleck took Wright at his word. On the next day, he gave Ambrose Burnside this order: "By direction of the Secretary of War, you will resume command of the Ninth Army Corps, and immediately relieve General H. G. Wright of the command of the Department of the Ohio."[42] And a week later, on March 23, Old Brains sent Burnside a letter of instructions that also contained a summary of the situation in his new command and elsewhere:

> *On assuming command of the Department of the Ohio, one of the first things to which your attention will be called is the expected raid of the enemy from East Tennessee into Kentucky. That the enemy is collecting a force in East Tennessee is very probable, and it is also very probable that he will attempt a raid into Kentucky as soon as the season is sufficiently advanced to make the roads practicable; but I do not think that the forces already collected amount to more than a few thousand, as the armies of Generals Rosecrans and Grant have in their fronts nearly all the troops that are available in the Southwest.*
>
> *Three plans will suggest themselves to you for counteracting this project of the enemy: First. To assume the offensive, by moving the mass of your forces into East Tennessee, and giving the enemy sufficient occupation there.*

If this were practicable, it would certainly be preferable not only in a military point of view, but would serve to relieve the loyal people of East Tennessee. But it is said that there are almost insuperable obstacles to this plan; that the country from the Kentucky Blue Grass Region to the valley of the Tennessee is almost barren, and would afford your army no supplies of provisions or forage; that a wagon could hardly carry forage enough for its own animals, much less provisions for men and forage for artillery and cavalry horses; moreover, it is said that East Tennessee has been so stripped by the enemy of forage and provisions that no adequate supplies can be procured there, even if we were to take away the means of support from the loyal or non-combatant inhabitants of that already impoverished country. I cannot say that these statements are entirely correct, but you will be able to determine on your arrival in Kentucky.

Second. To seize and fortify the different gaps in the mountains which separate Kentucky from East Tennessee. Unfortunately for this plan, there are so many practicable roads that it would require a large force to accomplish this object, and it would then be so scattered as to be incapable of concentration on any one point.

Again, the difficulty of supplies is very great. The passes to be occupied are at a very considerable distance from your base, and can be reached only by dirt roads which are impracticable most of the year.

Third. To concentrate your forces at some point in Central Kentucky, say Lebanon, Danville, or Richmond, from which point they can operate against an invading force, to meet or cut it off before it can reach any supplies, and while its men are short of provisions and its animals suffering for want of forage.

This plan is objected to on the ground that it leaves too many important points unprotected, and does not serve as a check to disloyalists now scattered through Kentucky. To accomplish this last object, it is urged that a considerable body of troops must be distributed through the country.

You will very probably find it impracticable to adopt either of these plans exclusively; indeed, I am of opinion that it will be preferable to combine the first and last; that is, to hold your main force in some central position, and at the same time to annoy the enemy and threaten his communications, by making cavalry raids into East Tennessee. In this way you will be able to feel the enemy to ascertain his movements, and to operate with your main body so as to thwart his plans.

The movements of your own troops will depend in no small degree upon those of the army under General Rosecrans. You will, therefore, frequently consult with him in regard to his intended operations. His first object is to occupy and injure as much as possible the army in his front, and, secondly, to rescue the loyal inhabitants of East Tennessee, or, rather, the latter is the ultimate object or his campaign. After the closing of the navigation of the Cumberland, all his supplies must reach him by rail from Louisville. It is, therefore, of vital importance that the line of the railroad is well protected. . . . These precautionary measures . . .have been too much neglected by our generals.

Another matter, to which I would particularly call your attention, is the retention, under various excuses, of troops in Ohio, Indiana, and Illinois, and more particularly in the latter State. With the exception of the necessary guards at the camps of prisoners, all troops should be immediately brought into the field. You will receive numerous and urgent solicitations to retain troops in various parts of these States for the purpose of overawing and restraining disloyalists, &c. You will find, however, that these representations are made to subserve some local or private interests, and should not be yielded to.

Partly for the same reasons, and partly from the real fears of loyal persons, you will be solicited to establish garrisons in nearly every town in Kentucky. To satisfy all these local solicitations would require an army of 100,000 men. In regard to your treatment of the inhabitants of Kentucky, you will be guided by your own good judgment; occurring events will cause this treatment to vary at different times and in different localities.

My own views upon this subject are pretty fully set forth in my letter of the 5th instant to Major-General Rosecrans, a copy of which is inclosed herewith. These views are formed from my own experience in Missouri and Tennessee.[43]

To this heavy load of guidance, Old Brains added more in a letter he sent Burnside on March 30:

Your headquarters are fixed nominally at Cincinnati, but it is not

intended that you should confine yourself to that place. If your troops
are concentrated in Central Kentucky (as I have advised), I think it
would be more satisfactory to the Government if you go there in
person to take the command. The principal objection to General
Wright was that he avoided the field, where his presence might have
been of great advantage.[44]

Ulysses Grant needed no guidance. His mission was simple though accomplishing it was not, mainly because his campaign was one of those in which the outcome was to be shaped as much or more by waters—the Mississippi, Yazoo, and countless bayous and lakes—as by Confederate actions.

John McClernand's long-range political ambitions continued to compel him to seek opportunities to operate independently. In mid-February he had written Grant: "If not inconsistent with your plans, I would ask that you would permit me, with a force of 20,000 infantry, including those of that arm here and at Helena, together with proper complements of artillery and cavalry, to move against the enemy at Pine Bluff [Arkansas] and capture or disperse him."[45] The department commander responded immediately and in a manner reminiscent of Old Brains:

In answer to your note of this date, suggesting an attack on Pine
Bluff, Ark., after reflection, I see but one objection to it. The
objection is that all the forces here now to operate with are assigned
to looking to the one great object, that of opening the Mississippi,
and to take off the number of men suggested would retard progress.[46]

Grant had tried to cut canals across the peninsulas formed by the river's loops, but the Big Muddy had not behaved as he wished. He had sent gunboat-escorted troops up the bayous on the east bank well upstream, hoping to connect with the Yazoo and get on the flank of defenders on Haines' Bluff, but either geography or Pemberton's rebels had blocked them.

By early April it took the fingers of both hands to count Grant's disappointments, all of which were reported in Northern newspapers. Murat Halstead, on the Cincinnati *Commercial*, wrote Radical Salmon Chase:

You do once in a while, don't you, say a word to the President, or
Stanton, or Halleck, about the conduct of the war? Well, now, for
God's sake say that Genl Grant, entrusted with our greatest army, is

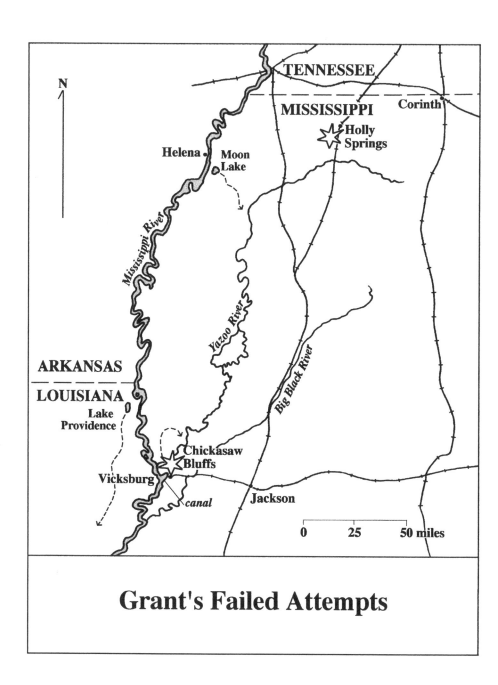

N

TENNESSEE

MISSISSIPPI   Corinth

Holly
Springs

Helena   Moon
Lake

Mississippi River

Yazoo River

ARKANSAS

Big Black River

LOUISIANA
Lake
Providence

Chickasaw
Bluffs

Vicksburg

canal   Jackson

0   25   50 miles

Grant's Failed Attempts

a jackass in the original package. He is a poor drunken imbecile. He is a poor stick sober, and he is most of the time more than half-drunk, and much of the time idiotically drunk. . . . Grant will fail miserably, hopelessly, eternally. You may look for and calculate his failures, in every position in which he may be placed, as a perfect certainty.[47]

The Treasury Secretary took the letter to Abraham Lincoln, who remarked: "If I knew what brand of whiskey he drinks, I would send a barrel or so to some other generals."[48] Stanton dispatched observers on phony missions to investigate allegations Halstead and others had made. Old Brains ignored the controversy, concentrating instead on supporting Grant's efforts and offering, occasionally, advice. An example:

Your letter of March 7 is received. It is the first communication from you for some time which has reached here. It is very desirable that you keep us advised of your Operations, in order that proper instructions may be sent to General Banks, General Rosecrans, &c. Send telegrams to Memphis by every opportunity.

In operating by the Yazoo, you have, no doubt, fully considered the advantages and dangers of the expedition. Our information here on that subject is very limited and unsatisfactory. There is one point, however, which has been discussed, and to which I would particularly call your attraction; it is the danger, on the fall of the water in the Mississippi, of having your steamers caught in the Upper Yazoo, so as to be unable to extricate them. In the present scarcity of steamers on the western rivers, this would be a very serious loss.

Another danger is, that the enemy may concentrate a large force upon the isolated column of McPherson without your being able to assist him. I mention these matters in order that you may give them your full attention.

When the Operations of an army are directed to one particular object it is always dangerous to divide forces. All accessories should be sacrificed for the sake of concentration. The great object on your line now is the opening of the Mississippi River, and everything else must tend to that purpose.

The eyes and hopes of the whole country are now directed to your army. In my opinion, the opening of the Mississippi River will be to us of more advantage than the capture of forty Richmonds. We shall omit nothing which we can do to assist you.[49]

Several days later, on April 2, 1863, Old Brains added:

What is most desired, and your attention is again called to this object, is that your forces and those of General Banks should be brought into co-operation as early as possible. If he cannot get up to co-operate with you on Vicksburg, cannot you get troops down to help him on Port Hudson, or at least can you not . . . destroy Grand Gulf [south of Vicksburg] *before it becomes too strong?*

I know that you can judge of these matters there much better than I can here, but as the President, who seems to be rather impatient about matters on the Mississippi, has several times asked me these questions, I repeat them to you.[50]

By March 29, however, General Grant had outlined what would be his eighth attempt to get at Vicksburg to Admiral David Dixon Porter. On the same day, the commander of the Mississippi Squadron replied:

I am ready to co-operate with you in the matter of landing troops on the other side, but you must recollect that, when these gunboats once go below [Vicksburg's batteries], *we give up all hopes of ever getting them up again. . . . If I do send vessels below, it will be the best vessels I have, and there will be nothing left to attack Haynes' Bluff in case it should be deemed necessary to try it.*[51]

Indeed Grant was concentrating every resource he had on opening the Mississippi, although not exactly in the sense General Halleck probably intended. Back in mid-February, for example, the department commander had suggested to Major General Stephen A. Hurlbut at Memphis: "It seems to me that [cavalryman Colonel Benjamin] Grierson, with about 500 picked men, might succeed in making his way south and cut the railroad east of Jackson, Miss. The undertaking would be a hazardous one, but it would pay well if carried out."[52] Now, Grierson would be pounding through Pemberton's rear, drawing rebel cavalry away from landing sites south of Vicksburg, while Grant was crossing the Mississippi.

General Halleck was not in the habit of prodding Grant, so prodding from Lincoln must have been the reason Old Brains reiterated points from earlier messages in what he wrote Grant on April 9:

You are too well advised of the anxiety of the Government for your

success, and its disappointment for the delay, to render it necessary to
urge upon you the importance of early action. I am confident that
you will do everything possible to open the Mississippi River. In my
opinion this is the most important operation of the war, and nothing
must be neglected to insure success.[53]

It most likely was not coincidental that by April 9 the President and
his family had returned from a visit to the headquarters of Hooker's Army
of the Potomac and that Lincoln had told General Halleck that Fighting Joe
was about to strike General Lee's forces. In theory, it would help Hooker if
Grant were attacking Pemberton concurrently—hence, Lincoln's pressure.
Yet Old Brains may have meant to advise Grant that doing it *right* was
preferable to doing it *now* by admonishing him that "nothing must be
neglected to insure success."

5

IF HENRY WAGER HALLECK HAD EVER craved popularity, he succeeded
admirably in concealing it. His high standing in West Point's Corps of
Cadets had been earned; his early achievements as a writer set him apart as
an intellectual. On the long voyage around Cape Horn to California, he had
evaded boredom by translating Henri Jomini's *Vie Politique et Militaire de*
Napoleon, and in the late 1850s and 1861 he had offset the tedium and
strains of business and practicing law by writing.

It was hardly surprising, then, for the hard-pressed general-in-chief of
the Union armies to turn for diversion to his old Jomini translation project
on nights when his presence in his office was not required. When word
leaked out that he was completing and revising the task he had started
seventeen years earlier, he was accused of shirking his duty and selling his
soul for a nickel a page—an allegation he might well have found amusing,
considering the wealth he had accumulated in San Francisco.[54] *Life of*
Napoleon would be published in four volumes in 1864, with no damage
having been done to the Union's war effort by its completion.[55]

In wartime Washington, only Francis Lieber and Herman Haupt were
his intellectual equals. Union College, where young Henry Halleck had
studied before he entered West Point, had added an LL.D. in 1862 to the
degree it had awarded him while he was still a cadet. But academic honors
counted for nothing in Washington's miasmal political swamp. And more
often than not, when Halleck used his writing talents to correct a sub-

ordinate, he contributed to the body of evidence his critics were amassing to condemn him.

General-in-Chief Halleck did not endear himself to Edwin Stanton, for one, by delivering a rebuke to General Rosecrans regarding a trivial matter and making it clear that the remonstrance had been coerced:

> *My attention has frequently been called to the enormous expense to the Government of your telegrams, as much or perhaps more than that of all the other generals in the field. I have avoided writing to you on the subject, lest you might misconceive my motives, but as the habit with you seems to be increasing, and is really injuring you in the estimation of the Government, I feel it my duty to you as a personal friend to call your attention to the matter.*
>
> *The truth is, you repeat again and again the same thing by telegraph, at a very great expense to the Government, without the slightest necessity. For example, you have telegraphed at least a dozen, and, perhaps, twenty times in the last few months that you require more cavalry.*
>
> *The Government is fully aware of your wants, and has been doing all in its power to supply them. It certainly was not necessary to remind it every day and every hour of its duty.*
>
> *Again, you telegraph continually about matters which require no immediate action or reply, and which might be communicated through the mails without any delay or injury to the public service and with great saving to the public treasury.*
>
> *The Secretary of War directs me to call your attention particularly to one peculiar feature in your telegrams and reports. You are very particular in mentioning all your successes and all captures from the enemy, but you do not inform the Government of your defeats and losses. These we learn only through the reports of the enemy and your requisitions for re-enforcements and supplies. A moment's reflection will convince you of the impropriety of this course. In order to act understandingly, the Government should be advised of your losses as well as your gains.*
>
> *This letter is not written in a spirit of fault-finding, but from a sense of duty to you and to the Government.*[56]

Presumably Old Brains sent the wrist-slap by mail or courier, for not until April 26 did General Rosecrans respond—and then, indirectly. On that date he opened a message to Adjutant General Lorenzo Thomas:

> *Inform the General-in-Chief I have it from a letter of Colonel Hill, commanding brigade in rebel army, that Joe Johnston has got 18,000 re-enforcements, of which 5,000 had already arrived on the 19th instant, and that he would have 30,000 in all by the 7th proximo. He says it is the intention of the rebels to advance on us, if we do not advance on them. . . .*

The rest of his text also covered matters of interest only to General Halleck. At the very end, though, Rosecrans thumbed his nose at his direct superior by adding: "[My] report [will come] by mail, under late instructions, to save expense."[57]

Rosecrans' direct response, also dated April 26 but sent presumably by mail, showed that he was, after all, still on speaking terms with General Halleck:

> *Your letter of the 20th instant is received. If I have used the telegraph freely, it has been through an anxious desire to do my duty, and to insure that by no fault of mine should things go unattended to, which my experience has shown may be the case even with the most able and zealous officers, without reminders.*
>
> *That I am very careful to inform the Department of my successes and of all captures from the enemy is not true, as the records of our office will show. That I have failed to inform the Government of my defeats and losses is equally untrue, both in letter and spirit.*
>
> *I regard the statement of these two propositions by the War Department as a profound, grievous, cruel, and ungenerous official and personal wrong. If there is any one thing I despise and scorn it is an officer's blowing his own Trumpet, or getting others to do it for him. I had flattered myself that no general officer in the service had a cleaner record on this point than I have.*
>
> *I shall here drop the subject, leaving to time and Providence the vindication of my conduct, and expect justice, kindness, and consideration only from those who are willing to accord them.*
>
> *Accept for yourself, personally, my cordial thanks for your kindness, both personal and official.*[58]

Ignoring both slurs and sarcasm, the general-in-chief was mindful of other lapses from perfection on Old Rosy's part, and on April 28 he shared them with him:

> *I regret very much to notice the complaining tone of your telegrams in regard to your supply of horses.*
>
> *You seem to think the Government does not do its duty toward your army. You have been repeatedly informed that every possible authority has been given to the quartermaster of your army, and to all quartermasters in the West, to purchase all the animals they possibly can for you. If any of them have neglected to do their duty in this respect promptly and thoroughly, why do not you report them for dismissal or other punishment?*
>
> *As you have reported none, it is presumed that they have all done their duty. Indeed, it appears from reports that you have been furnished since you took command of that army thirty-odd thousand additional horses, and this has been done to the neglect of other points but little, if any, less important than your own position. . . .*
>
> *But you ask for authority to go into loyal States and seize horses which the owners will not sell, or to purchase them at any price and in any manner. I do not precisely understand why you so often urge me to give you authority to violate the law. If you wish to violate the law, you certainly should not throw upon me the responsibility of your illegal acts. That certainly would be very unfair, to say the least.*
>
> *I have never found it necessary to do anything contrary to what I deemed the law authorized me to do. If I shall ever find it necessary to do what I consider an illegal act, I shall expect to assume the responsibility myself.*
>
> *But you will say that you want the especial authority of the Government.*
>
> *The Government gives you, and has given you, all the authority in its power. It cannot violate a law of Congress in regard to purchases, nor can it authorize any officer to violate such a law. . . . I venture to say that for no other army has greater care and solicitation been felt or given. Indeed, I think the returns will show that you now have a larger number of animals in proportion to your forces than any other general in the field.*[59]

Rather heavy chastisement. Was it justified? Or was the general-in-chief suffering from his annoying ailment? Well, three days later

Quartermaster-General Montgomery Meigs, another brilliant friend of Halleck, sent Old Rosy an extremely long letter backing-up Old Brains' remonstrance. Meigs said, in part:

> *The large number of horses you have sent back to Louisville, over 9,000, shows that you have had more horses than your troops have been able to take care of.*
>
> *You say that there has been great mortality, for want of long forage, which could not be furnished for want of transportation. Were there then so many animals in the department that they could not transport their own foods?*
>
> *When our army reaches this limit, what is the remedy? Is not every additional horse another subject for starvation? Or is the deficiency of transportation on the part of the railroad? Could it not transport enough food and forage to the depot of the army?*
>
> *How do the rebels, without water transportation, in a country destitute in a great measure of hay-producing grasses, support the immense mounted force which you report? Lieutenant-Colonel Taylor reports 11,478 cavalry and 3,339 artillery horses on hand on 31st March, say 12,000 mounted men. You say the mounted rebels outnumber you five to one, and this I do not take to be a careless expression, for I find it repeatedly used in your dispatches to the General-in-Chief and to myself. Have they 60,000 mounted men?*
>
> *How do they find food for them? How can long forage—cornstalks, the only long forage of the South—be conveyed in bulk to this immense force? I cannot but think you are mistaken in your estimate, and that their activity, the result of the same necessity which keeps the buffalo traveling, makes them appear in various places, and thus causes their numbers to be exaggerated. A herd of buffalo resting for four months on a prairie in one place would starve. They must travel to feed, and so with the rebel cavalry. . . .*
>
> *The main body of the cavalry should, it seems to me, be thrown upon the rear of the enemy, to live upon the country, cut his communications, and harass the country generally; take every horse seen, good or bad; shoot all those that cannot follow, and thus put the rebels to straits while mounting your own men.*
>
> *There can be no great bodies of troops at any interior points, and 1,500 cavalry and mounted infantry could, it seems to me, force their way as far south as Jackson, and cut all the telegraphs and railroads from near that point to Milledgeville, not attacking the*

large towns, running from every large body of troops, but living on the plantations, destroying all military stores and railroads and common road bridges, and sickening the people of a war which made their homes unsafe. . . .

When in good order, start them, a thousand at a time, for the rebels' communications, with orders never to move off a walk unless they see an enemy before or behind them; to travel only so far in a day as not to fatigue their horses; never to camp in the place in which sunset found them, and to rest in a good pasture during the heat of the day; to keep some of their eyes open night and day, and never to pass a bridge without burning it, a telegraph wire without cutting it, a horse without stealing or shooting it, a guerrilla without capturing him, or a negro without explaining the President's proclamation to him. Let them go any way so that it is to the rear of the enemy, and return by the most improbable routes, generally aiming to go entirely round the enemy, and you will put Johnston and Bragg into such a state of excitement that they will attack or retreat to relieve themselves; they will not be able to lie still.

You gained a great success at Murfreesborough by your persevering courage and endurance. The same qualities will enable you to conquer in the next struggle, but this long inactivity tells severely upon the resources of the country. The rebels will never be conquered by waiting in their front. Operate on their communications; strike every detached post; rely more upon infantry and less upon cavalry, which in this whole war has not decided the fate of a single battle rising above a skirmish. . . .[60]

Some generals, of course, did not appreciate coaching from Washington. But at times Old Brains' long essays served several purposes. Writing them helped him focus and refine his thinking on particular subjects, especially policy matters. Sending them enabled him to warn generals unofficially when it became apparent that rebukes might be forthcoming from Lincoln or Stanton. And at times Halleck could throw out statements the respondent could think about, develop, and perhaps act upon later.

General Halleck's letter to Ulysses Grant dated March 31, 1863, had all of these characteristics:

It is the policy of the Government to withdraw from the enemy as much productive labor as possible. So long as the rebels retain and employ their slaves in producing grains, &c., they can employ all the whites in the field [of combat]. *Every slave withdrawn from the enemy is equivalent to a white man put* hors de combat.

Again, it is the policy of the Government to use the negroes of the South, as far as practicable, as a military force, for the defense of forts, depots, &c. If the experience of General Banks near New Orleans should be satisfactory, a much larger force will be organized during the coming summer; and if they can be used to hold points on the Mississippi during the sickly season, it will afford much relief to our armies.

In the hands of the enemy, they are used with much effect against us; in our hands, we must try to use them with the best possible effect against the rebels.

It has been reported to the Secretary of War that many of the officers of your command not only discourage the negroes from coming under our protection, but by ill-treatment force them to return to their masters. This is not only bad policy in itself, but is directly opposed to the policy adopted by the Government.

Whatever may be the individual opinion of an officer in regard to the wisdom of measures adopted and announced by the Government, it is the duty of every one to cheerfully and honestly endeavor to carry out the measures so adopted.

It is expected that you will use your official and personal influence to remove prejudices on this subject, and to fully and thoroughly carry out the policy now adopted and ordered by the Government. That policy is to withdraw from the use of the enemy all the slaves you can, and to employ those so withdrawn to the best possible advantage against the enemy.

The character of the war has very much changed within the last year. There is now no possible hope of reconciliation with the rebels. The Union party in the South is virtually destroyed. There can be no peace but that which is forced by the sword. We must conquer the rebels or be conquered by them. The North must conquer the slave oligarchy or become slaves themselves—the manufacturers mere "hewers of wood and drawers of water" to Southern aristocrats.

This is the phase which the rebellion has now assumed. We must take things as they are. The Government, looking at the subject in all its aspects, has adopted a policy, and we must cheerfully and faithfully carry out, that policy.

I write you this unofficial letter simply as a personal friend and as a matter of friendly advice. From my position here, where I can survey the entire field, perhaps I may be better able to understand the tone of public opinion and the intentions of the Government than you can from merely consulting the officers of your own army.[61]

From what Old Brains was saying in the above paragraph regarding the changed *character* of the war, to the concept of *total* war was a very short step, and in the near future both Grant and Cump Sherman would take it.

6

"OPERATIONS HERE ARE BECOMING INTERESTING," General Halleck remarked to Burnside on May 2, 1863, at the end of a short message.[62] Was he referring to General Hooker's having launched his Chancellorsville operation? Perhaps, although much later he would learn that late on that day, Stonewall Jackson would complete his march around Fighting Joe's flank and wreck Major General Oliver O. Howard's XI Corps, opening the way for General Lee to smite the rest of the Army of the Potomac hip and thigh. But William Starke Rosecrans was doing nothing interesting at Murfreesboro. What Halleck may well have been referring to was the solid progress General Grant was making toward taking the rebel Gibraltar of the West out of the war, *combined with* the hoped-for success in the East.

After months of discouraging and frustrating failures, since mid-April everything General Grant had attempted had succeeded. Admiral Porter's gunboats ran past the batteries at Vicksburg, losing only one vessel. While troops moved down the Mississippi's west bank to the point below Vicksburg where they were supposed to cross, Porter took Grant on a reconnaissance that convinced them that Grand Gulf's defenses were too strong; prudently they selected Bruinsburg, downstream, as a viable landing site.

Back on April 12, shortly before Porter's gallant running past Vicksburg's vaunted batteries, General Grant had ended a report to Halleck:

The embarrassments I have had to contend against on account of extreme high water cannot be appreciated by anyone not present to witness it. I think, however, that you will receive favorable reports of the condition and feeling of this army from every impartial judge and from all who have been sent from Washington to look after its welfare.[63]

And to make sure I was not hopelessly, idiotically drunk, Grant might have added, but did not. Meanwhile, Grierson—a music teacher in peacetime who hated horses because one had once kicked him in the head—was drawing Pemberton's cavalry eastward, away from Grant's landing site, and also tearing-up railroads on his way from southern Tennessee toward Jackson, Mississippi. Indeed, Grierson was doing precisely the things Montgomery Meigs had urged Old Rosy to do in his long letter on horses.

Attractive to Grant and Porter as Bruinsburg seemed, however, the army commander wanted to give John McClernand's corps, which would have the honor of leading the crossing, every possible advantage. Accordingly, he telegraphed Cump Sherman on April 27:

> *If you think it advisable, you may make a reconnaissance of Haynes' Bluff, taking as much force and as many steamers as you like. . . . The effect of a heavy demonstration in that direction would be good so far as the enemy are concerned, but I am loth to order it, because it would be so hard to make our own troops understand that only a demonstration was intended, and our people at home would characterize it as a repulse.*
>
> *I therefore leave it to you whether to make such a demonstration. If made at all, I advise that you publish your order beforehand, stating that a reconnaissance in force was to be made for the purpose of calling off the enemy's attention from our movements south of Vicksburg, and not with any expectation of attacking.*[64]

Cump's reply must surely have warmed General Halleck's heart when, long afterward, a copy reached him:

> *We will make as strong a demonstration as possible. The troops will all understand the purpose, and will not be hurt by the repulse. The people of the country must find out the truth as they best can; it is none of their business. You are engaged in a hazardous enterprise, and, for good reasons, wish to divert attention; that is sufficient to me, and it shall be done.*[65]

By noon on April's last day, the leading elements of Grant's troops were crossing to the Mississippi's east bank as rapidly as steamers could ferry them. By May 2, when Old Brains had told Burnside that "things here are getting interesting," he may well have been glad he had bet the farm on Unconditional Surrender Grant.

From the Bruinsburg base, Jamie McPherson's corps led the way northeastward to Jackson, east of Vicksburg. Grant left Sherman's corps there to destroy the railroad crossings and other facilities, then turned westward. Despite McClernand's bungling during a battle at a place called Champion's Hill, Grant pressed on—driving Pemberton's forces inside the eastern trenches of the Confederates' impregnable Gibraltar of the West. After an unsuccessful army-strength assault on Pemberton's fortifications, spoiled in large part by a grossly misleading dispatch to him from McClernand, on May 22, 1863, General Grant decided to institute siege operations.[66]

All of which had been especially reassuring, coming as it had in the wake of Fighting Joe's appalling disaster at Chancellorsville. But Commander-in-Chief Abraham Lincoln owned more than a few shares of blame for that debacle, and this fact raised the question of *how*—absent Old Brains' counsel, summarily rejected earlier—he was going to cope with the impending Confederate threat to the North, one that would prove the most critical of all to the Union's survival.

13 ★ When the Man Had To Be Everything

$\mathcal{M}$AY 1863 WAS A MIXED MONTH for the Union. By the end of the first week, Generals Lee and Stonewall Jackson had given Fighting Joe Hooker's "best army on the planet" a humiliating whipping at Chancellorsville. Before May ended, however, forces led by Ulysses Grant had trapped John Pemberton's army inside Vicksburg's fortifications and were conducting a siege.

By selecting General Hooker and presuming to direct him, Abraham Lincoln had denied himself protection from blame for Chancellorsville that his lightning rod Henry Halleck might otherwise have absorbed. Offsetting that blunder to some extent, however, was his having allowed the general-in-chief to support Grant and William Rosecrans.

For the Union, May's results reflected the armies' increasing professionalism as well as the folly of depending upon commanders appointed for political reasons. Yet this was neither a *Halleck* v. *Lincoln* nor a *West Pointers* v. *Citizen Soldiers* outcome. It was more that certain generals who owed their commands to political considerations failed, while senior officers seasoned by education and experience in warfare did not.

Oh? Was Fighting Joe not a graduate of West Point and a veteran of the Mexican War and all of the battles fought in this one under the Young Napoleon and Ambrose Burnside? True, most of them had been lost—some catastrophically. But in the course of those calamities, had he not been hardened, had he not learned anything?

Many of Hooker's subordinates at Chancellorsville had records similar to his. On May 1, when Fighting Joe sent an order to those who were fighting Jackson, and driving him, to withdraw and fortify the terrain around the Chancellor mansion, they objected as vehemently as they could. Wrote Major General Darius N. Couch afterward:

> *Proceeding to the Chancellor House, I narrated my operations in front to Hooker, which were seemingly satisfactory, as he said: "It's all right, Couch, I have got Lee just where I want him; he must fight me on my own ground." The retrograde movement had prepared me for something of the kind, but to hear it from his own lips that the advantages gained by the successful marches of his lieutenants were to culminate in fighting a defensive battle in that nest of thickets was too much, and I retired from his presence with the belief that my commanding general was a whipped man.*[1]

In war, said the real Napoleon, *the man is everything.*

Ambrose Burnside had known he was not capable of commanding a unit as huge and complex as the Army of the Potomac; he had said so, on at least three occasions; and he had proved it at Fredericksburg and subsequently. Hooker had been reasonably competent as a division and corps commander (as had been Burnside), and the improvements he had made in the army were commendable. Like Burnside, he had not sought command of so large a force. But he had not objected when Lincoln—partly to appease the Radicals—all but shoehorned him into the post. And Joseph Hooker too had failed the stern test of combat.

Even so, the Union's commander-in-chief kept General Hooker in command of the Army of the Potomac. Although the guidance the President offered in a message to Fighting Joe dated May 14 was hardly firm, the tone was supportive:

> *When I wrote on the 7th, I had an impression that possibly by an early movement you could get some advantage from the supposed facts that the enemy's communications were disturbed and that he was somewhat deranged in position. That idea has now passed away, the enemy having re-established his communications, regained his positions, and actually received re-enforcements.*
>
> *It does not now appear probable to me that you can gain anything by an early renewal of the attempt to cross the Rappahannock. I therefore shall not complain if you do no more for a time than to keep the enemy at bay, and out of other mischief by menaces*

and occasional cavalry raids, if practicable, and to put your own army in good condition again.

Still, if in your own clear judgment you can renew the attack successfully, I do not mean to restrain you. Bearing upon this last point, I must tell you that I have some painful intimations that some of your corps and division commanders are not giving you their entire confidence. This would be ruinous, if true, and you should therefore, first of all, ascertain the real facts beyond all possibility of doubt.[2]

Secretary of War Stanton entered the picture on May 17 by asking General-in-Chief Halleck to ascertain the number of troops that could be spared from Washington's defenses to reinforce the Army of the Potomac "in case of necessity." On the next day Old Brains responded in a typically thorough report. After answering Stanton's question in some detail, he added some observations that suggest that Lincoln wanted to know how Halleck appraised the situation in the East without asking for such counsel openly and directly:

In regard to sending the movable corps of 8,600 men into the field, I would remark that, if this should be done, it will be necessary to abandon the line of the Bull Run and the Occoquan, to destroy the Alexandria Railroad, and withdraw all troops south of the Potomac to the line of fortifications. Moreover, we should then have no movable force to throw upon any point which should be seriously threatened.

If the Army of the Potomac should cross the Rappahannock above Fredericksburg, this force could be moved out to co-operate as a reserve. If that army should cross at or below Fredericksburg, it would, in my opinion, be exceedingly hazardous to remove this force from the vicinity of Washington. This remark equally applies to the supposition that the Army of the Potomac remains inactive in its present position.

If that army should cross the Rappahannock and win a victory, there would be no apprehensions for the safety of Maryland and Washington. If it should be defeated, then there would be good cause for such apprehensions. But judging the future from the past, there is likely to be a third contingency, that is, that the Army of the Potomac may for some time remain inactive.

It is proper to consider the consequences of this inactivity. In that case, Lee's army will have three plans from which to choose:

1. To cross the Rappahannock, attack Hooker's army, and risk the result of a general battle. Lee is as prudent as able, and I do not think he will run this risk.

2. To make a demonstration on Washington, Maryland, or Harper's Ferry, and seek to regain possession of Norfolk. This is by no means improbable.

3. To make a feint upon Norfolk, and a real movement in force on Washington, Maryland, or Harper's Ferry. Such an operation, with an active army and an energetic commander, in the position now occupied by the Army of the Potomac, would be exceedingly hazardous. Nevertheless it may be attempted, as Lee's army can move with much greater rapidity than ours.

It is also very probable that Lee will maneuver so as to leave us in doubt what his real intentions are. While he makes demonstrations in both directions, we shall probably know his real intentions only after the blow is actually struck.

Under these circumstances, I think it my duty to urge the retention of the present force in Washington or its vicinity.

When I visited Falmouth with the President, I informed General Hooker (in the presence of the President) what troops we had here, and told him that, in my opinion, he could calculate upon no re-enforcements from this place, unless upon the line of the Upper Rappahannock. He then said, most emphatically, that he had all the troops he wished, and all he could use with advantage. He also said that, notwithstanding the losses of the battle of Chancellorsville and the discharge of troops whose services were about expiring, he would have left about 100,000 men, which was all he could employ to advantage.

It is proper to remark in this place that General Hooker has never estimated General Lee's forces over 70,000 men. Others, who have had the best opportunities of observation, do not think they have exceeded 60,000. Nevertheless they have defeated very superior numbers on our side. It may be mortifying to do so, nevertheless it is our duty to provide for the contingency of a defeat upon a decisive point, notwithstanding the fact that we concentrate superior forces upon that point.

It is now conceded that most of Longstreet's force did not arrive *in time to take part in the battle of Chancellorsville. A part of them are probably now in Richmond, to guard that place from General Dix's forces at West Point.*

You will remember that before General Hooker made his movement across the Rappahannock, you offered him the general control of General Dix's command, in so much as concerned co-operation. This he declined. When, at General Hooker's camp, I offered to move General Dix's available force wherever it could assist him most, whether upon the York or Rappahannock, he then thought best to leave it where it is for the present. It will hold in check equal numbers in Richmond, and, perhaps, be able to cut the enemy's communications should he be again attacked by General Hooker.

I deem it proper to state here that I have no information in regard to the intended movements of the Army of the Potomac. General Hooker reports directly to the President, and receives instructions directly from him. I was not informed by General Hooker when, where, or how he intended to operate when he crossed to fight the battle of Chancellorsville. It is a military rule that when a subordinate Officer reports to and receives instructions directly from a superior, no one of intermediate rank can interfere.

Under present circumstances, I think it would be improper for me to interfere in any of General Hooker's plans or movements. All I know in regard to them is, that he told me he intended to make some movement immediately. Whatever that movement may be, I shall assist him to the best of my ability and means.[3]

Here, Old Brains was at the top of his form, combining legal, military, analytical, and writing skills with respect for the amenities. Remarkable, also, was his having produced such a cogent and important document overnight.

On the next day, May 19, Stanton passed General Halleck's report on to the President. Shortly thereafter, the secretary received a letter from one Thomas Prince, a citizen of Baltimore, relaying a report that "the rebels intend to invade Maryland [and] endeavor to capture Baltimore and Washington" in about three weeks "unless something should be done to frustrate their intended movement."[4] This squared with two of the three possible courses of action Old Brains had suggested General Lee might take. Accordingly, on May 23 Stanton again asked the general-in-chief to answer four questions, "in view of the possibility of an early raid by the enemy."[5]

Halleck replied the same day—as before, responding to the inquiries directly. Stanton's fourth query had asked for "any other suggestions you deem proper to make. . . ." but Old Brains respectfully declined to offer any regarding the Army of the Potomac, referring Stanton to his report of May 18.[6] Before sending Halleck's second report to Lincoln, the secretary of war closed his indorsement with a sentence containing some interesting (and for lawyer Stanton, rare) ambiguity: "As General Halleck, for reasons stated, does not deem himself authorized to give orders to General Hooker, it is submitted to the President whether the circumstances do not require him to give such directions as upon consideration of the within report may appear to be necessary."[7]

Then, on May 27, General Hooker telegraphed a request to Stanton for a copy of Halleck's first report. And on the same day, Fighting Joe forwarded to the general-in-chief a summary of information received regarding General Lee's army. Items 8 and 9 were of particular interest:

> *8. The Confederate army is under marching orders, and an order from General Lee was very lately read to the troops, announcing a campaign of long marches and hard fighting, in a part of the country where they would have no railroad trans-portation.*
>
> *9. All the deserters say that the idea is very prevalent in the ranks that they are about to move forward upon or above our right flank.*[8]

Apart from all the rumors, omens, and portents pointing toward a challenging change, was it possible that Old Brains was about to be called back as counsel in *Lincoln, Stanton, Hooker* et al. v. *Lee*?

2

NATHANIEL P. BANKS, THE ONE-TIME Waltham bobbin boy whose pre-war political career had been as illustrious as his military service had been lackluster, was fortunate during May 1863, in that—unlike Ulysses Grant—he was operating in a backwater where his blunders attracted next to no notice. Actually, Abraham Lincoln and Edwin Stanton had intended for both Major Generals Banks and McClernand to be key figures in the opening of the Mississippi. But the "elitist West Point clique" had relegated McClernand to the command of a mere corps, and almost every directive

Banks received from Washington called upon him to cooperate with Grant.

Unfortunately for the Union, and despite the marvels of the telegraph, Halleck and Banks could not communicate without appalling lapses of time between sendings and receipts of messages—which is to say, they could not communicate effectively at all. An example: On May 19, 1863, the general-in-chief telegraphed Banks:

> *I learn from the newspapers that you are in possession of Alexandria* [Louisiana, on the Red River to the west of Port Hudson], *and General Grant of Jackson. This may be well enough so far, but these operations are too eccentric to be pursued.*
>
> *I must again urge that you cooperate as soon as possible with General Grant east of the Mississippi. Your forces must be united at the earliest possible moment. Otherwise the enemy will concentrate on Grant and crush him.*
>
> *Do all you can to prevent this. I have no troops to re-enforce him. Both Burnside and Rosecrans are calling loudly for re-enforcements. I have none to give either. . . .*
>
> *We shall watch with the greatest anxiety the movements of yourself and General Grant. I have urged him to keep his forces concentrated as much as possible, and not to move east till he gets control of the Mississippi River.*[9]

Not until much later would General Halleck learn that on the day before, Banks had started a message toward him that said his troops had left Alexandria on May 14 and were, on May 18, concentrating at Simmesport, on the Mississippi's west bank, roughly across from Port Hudson.[10] Meanwhile, Old Brains may well have been pardoned for pacing the floor and scratching his elbows over the question: Why had Banks wasted days, perhaps weeks, splashing westward from New Orleans through bayou country and then hooking northward to Alexandria? How could *that* contribute to accomplishing his mission, opening the Mississippi?

As if he were anticipating General Halleck's question, from Simmesport on May 21, the Bobbin Boy wrote him: "Recent occupation of this country [Louisiana's Red River Valley] as far north as Natchitoches gives us reason to believe that at no distant day it can be permanently occupied and held with a small force, controlling substantially the entire northern part of the State. With the aid of transports and gunboats of light draught, this could be done without difficulty."[11] Later, this seemingly innocuous statement would make Banks wish he had not made it. But he was in trouble enough for the time being, as an irate message from General-in-Chief Halleck dated May 23 reflected:

> *Your dispatches, dated Opelousas May 2 and 4, are just received.* [!]
>
> *I regret to learn from them that you are still pursuing your divergent line to Alexandria, while General Grant has moved on Jackson, instead of concentrating with him on the east side of the Mississippi, as you proposed in your previous dispatch, and as I have continually urged.*
>
> *If these eccentric movements, with the main forces of the enemy on the Mississippi River, do not lead to some serious disaster, it will be because the enemy does not take full advantage of his opportunity.*
>
> *I assure you the Government is exceedingly disappointed that you and General Grant are not acting in conjunction. It thought to secure that object by authorizing you to assume the entire command as soon as you and General Grant could unite.*
>
> *The opening of the Mississippi River has been continually presented as the first and most important object to be attained. Operations up the Red River, toward Texas, or toward Alabama, are only of secondary importance, to be undertaken after we get possession of the river, and as circumstances may then require. If we fail to open the river, these secondary operations will result in very little of military importance.*
>
> *I have continually urged these views upon General Grant, and I do hope there will be no further delay in adopting them.*
>
> *If Grant should succeed alone in beating the enemy and capturing Vicksburg, all will be well, but if he should be defeated and fail, both your armies will be paralyzed and the entire campaign a failure. I can well understand that you have had great obstacles to overcome, with inadequate means; but you have had all the means we could possibly give you, and, if you succeed, the glory will be so much the greater.*[12]

By May 25 a message from Halleck to Banks reflected more impatience. Grant seemed likely to take Vicksburg without Banks' help, Old Brains reported, adding: "Nevertheless, the Government is exceedingly uneasy at your separation. . . . But I have so often called attention to this matter that it seems useless to repeat it."[13]

Well, yes, but Henry Halleck had never been comfortable with the prospect of Grant and Banks being near enough in space for the Bobbin Boy's Lincoln-bestowed seniority to give the Confederates an advantage. But General Grant shattered the fantasy of cooperation on May 31, over a week after he put Vicksburg under siege, by writing Banks: "While I regret the situation . . .and clearly see the necessity of your being re-enforced in order to be successful, the circumstances by which I am surrounded will prevent my making any detachments at this time."[14]

Ulysses Grant was being polite regarding Banks' need for reinforcements. When the Bobbin Boy attacked Port Hudson on May 27, his forces outnumbered the Confederate defenders by three to one. "Banks tried assault too soon," wrote his biographer, Fred Harvey Harrington, "before his officers had made a good reconnaissance, before his army was assembled. The result was a severe repulse, the Union losing four hundred and fifty dead and missing, and over fifteen hundred wounded." Professor Harrington continued:

> *Banks blamed superiors ("My force is too weak for the work it has to do"). He blamed subordinates ("Had they not failed we should have carried the works). He blamed the defenses ("perhaps the strongest in the country"). He did not add that he had erred in ordering the advance, and had blundered further in not giving detailed instructions to his officers. The attack was not even timed—Banks simply said to start "at the earliest hour practicable."*[15]

Ironically, Banks' greatest losses occurred on a patch of land called Slaughter's Field.[16] Back in August 1862, Slaughter Mountain was another name for Cedar Mountain, where Stonewall Jackson had whipped him the second time.

For John McClernand, also, May was a disaster. At Champion's Hill on May 16, his failure to engage the rebels to his front enabled them to reinforce their units to their north, which obliged Grant to take heavy casualties in winning that fight. Then, during Grant's assault on John Pemberton's fortifications east of Vicksburg on May 22, McClernand again caused needless grief. "The whole loss for the day will probably reach 1,500 killed and wounded," Grant wrote General Halleck. It was, actually, 3,199. "General McClernand's dispatches misled me as to the real state of facts, and caused much of this loss. He is entirely unfit for the position of corps commander, both on the march and on the battlefield. Looking after his corps gives me more labor and infinitely more uneasiness than all the remainder of my department."[17]

Soon thereafter, General McClernand was relieved and sent to serve under Major General Nathaniel Banks, another citizen-soldier. Banks' Department of the Gulf was becoming known as the "Brigade of Elephants" because of the War Department's practice of using it as a place of exile.[18]

3

POLITICAL GENERALS WERE NOT the only kind banished to Banks' Brigade of Elephants. Major General William B. Franklin, who finished first in West Point's Class of 1843, earned his trip to New Orleans by incurring the wrath of Ambrose Burnside during and after Fredericksburg. Not knowing what else to do with Brigadier General Charles P. Stone, USMA 1845, after his release from solitary confinement at Fort Lafayette prison in New York Harbor without ever having had the benefit of due process of law, the war managers gladly granted Banks' request for his assignment to the Department of the Gulf as his chief of staff. And for a time, it seemed possible that Army of the Cumberland commander William Starke Rosecrans, USMA 1842, might soon join the ranks of Banks' cast-offs.

During May 1863, both Halleck and Rosecrans incurred considerable telegraph expense by exchanges of messages that had advanced the quelling of the rebellion not one iota. Before Stones River, the general-in-chief had been obliged to warn Rosecrans that relief from command loomed in his future if he did not attack Bragg at Murfreesboro. Now, after nearly half a year of stockpiling, whining over his lack of cavalry, and providing Buellesque excuses, Old Rosy was again in peril of decapitation. Old Brains' report on the Tullahoma Campaign picked up the controversy:

> *While General Grant was operating before Vicksburg, information, deemed reliable, was received from captured rebel official correspondence that large detachments were being drawn from Bragg's army to re-enforce Johnston in Mississippi. Re-enforcements were sent to General Grant from other armies in the West, but General Rosecrans' army was left intact, in order that he might take advantage of Bragg's diminished numbers and drive him back into Georgia, and thus rescue loyal East Tennessee from the hands of the rebels, an object which the Government has kept constantly in view from the beginning of the war.*
>
> *I therefore urged General Rosecrans to take advantage of this opportunity to carry out his long-projected movement, informing*

him that General Burnside would co-operate with his force, moving from Kentucky to East Tennessee. For various reasons he preferred to postpone his movement until the termination of the siege of Vicksburg.

In order to avoid any misunderstanding of the orders given to General Rosecrans on this subject, I submit the following correspondence:

Rosecrans to Halleck, June 11, 1863:

I am preparing to strike a blow that will tell; but, to show you how differently things are viewed here, I called on my corps and division commanders and generals of cavalry for answers, in writing, to these questions: 1st. From your best information, do you think the enemy materially weakened in our front? 2d. Do you think this army can advance, at this time, with reasonable prospect of fighting a great and successful battle? 3d. Do you think an advance advisable at this time?

To the first, eleven answered no; six yes, to the extent of 10,000. To the second, four yes, with doubts; thirteen no. To the third, not one yes; seventeen no.

Not one thinks an advance advisable until Vicksburg's fate is determined. Admitting these officers to have a reasonable share of military sagacity, courage, and patriotism, you perceive that there are graver and stronger reasons than probably appear at Washington for the attitude of this army.

I therefore counsel caution and patience at headquarters. Better wait a little to get all we can ready to insure the best results, if by so doing we, per force of Providence, observe a great military maxim, not to risk two great and decisive battles at the same time.

We might have cause to be thankful for it; at all events, you see that, to expect success, I must have such thorough grounds that when I say "forward," my word will inspire conviction and confidence, where both are now wanting.

I should like to have your suggestions.

Halleck to Rosecrans, June 12, 1863:

I do not understand your application of the military maxim "not to fight two great battles at the same time." It will apply to a single army, but not to two armies acting independently of each other.

Johnston and Bragg are acting on interior lines between you and Grant, and it is for their interest, not ours, that they should fight at different times, so as to use the same force against both of you. It is for our interest to fight them, if possible, while divided.

If you are not strong enough to fight Bragg with a part of his troops absent, you will not be able to fight him after the affair at Vicksburg is over and his troops return to your front.

There is another military maxim, that "councils of war never fight."

If you say that you are not prepared to fight Bragg, I shall not order you to do so, for the responsibility of fighting or refusing to fight at a particular time or place must rest upon the general in immediate command. It cannot be shared by a council of war, nor will the authorities here make you fight against your will.

You ask me to counsel them "caution and patience." I have done so very often; but after five or six months of inactivity, with your force all the time diminishing, and no hope of any immediate increase, you must not be surprised that their patience is pretty well exhausted.

If you do not deem it prudent to risk a general battle with Bragg, why can you not harass him, or make such demonstrations as to prevent his sending more re-enforcements to Johnston?

I do not write this in a spirit of fault-finding, but to assure you that the prolonged inactivity of so large an army in the field is causing much complaint and dissatisfaction, not only in Washington, but throughout the country.

Rosecrans not having replied by June 16, Halleck wired him:

Is it your intention to make an immediate movement forward? A definite answer, yes or no, is required.

General Rosecrans' response:

In reply to your inquiry, if immediate means to-night or to-morrow, no. If it means as soon as all things are ready, say five days, yes.

Rosecrans to Halleck, June 21, 1863:

In your favor of the 12th instant you say you do not see how the maxim of not fighting two great battles at the same time applies to the case of this army and Grant's.

Looking at the matter practically, we and our opposing forces are so widely separated that for Bragg to materially aid Johnston he must abandon our front substantially, and then we can move to our ultimate work with more rapidity and less waste of material on natural obstacles.

If Grant is defeated, both forces will come here, and then we ought to be near our base.

The same maxim that forbids, as you take it, a single army fighting two great battles at the same time (by the way, a very awkward thing to do), would forbid this nation's engaging all its forces in the great West at the same time, so as to leave it without a single reserve to stem the current of possible disaster. This is, I think, sustained by high military and political considerations.

We ought to fight here if we have a strong prospect of winning a decisive battle over the opposing force, and upon this ground I shall act. I shall be careful not to risk our last reserve without strong grounds to expect success.

Rosecrans to Halleck, June 24, 1863, 2:10 A.M:

The army begins to move at 3 o'clock this morning.

So ended a remarkable but useless debate—remarkable for Old Brains' forbearance, useless because Rosecrans ought to have recalled from the outset that a soldier's first duty is to obey.

In the remainder of General-in-Chief Halleck's report, he gave Old Rosy full credit for an advance almost to Chattanooga that had been very light in Union casualties. Twice the Army of the Cumberland's sassy commander had been spared removal. Might he evade it a third?

4

DURING MAY'S SECOND HALF it had appeared that the President, through Stanton, was wringing counsel from Old Brains by requesting answers to specific questions related to the post-Chancellorsville plight of Washington and of the Army of the Potomac. Seasoned as he had been out in California by experience in dealing with politicians, and subsequently by his immersion in Washington's cesspool, surely General Halleck had perceived that his civilian superiors were playing games. Yet he had responded within the ridiculous rules, for a thoroughly whipped brother officer and the huge field army he commanded were in dire need of help that the commander-in-chief had been unable to provide.

As May turned into June, however, a change as difficult to detect as the turning of the tide occurred. Apparently, Abraham Lincoln realized that he had made a great mistake by selecting Joseph Hooker and had compounded it by shutting the general-in-chief out of the chain of command. The results spoke for themselves: Generals closely affiliated with the President had failed, while Grant and Rosecrans—Halleck's professional lieutenants—had not.

For the second time, Lincoln was obliged to concede that he could not "do it all," that he needed his first-rate clerk, possibly even that he could not get along without him. At a minimum, he had missed having Halleck available as a lightning rod.

In ancient Greek tragedies, the gods punished kings guilty of *hubris*, the sin of pride (reaching too far). Now, newspapers helped perform that function. Given one more Chancellorsville, the voters might well guillotine *him* in 1864.

For once, then, all the arrows pointed in the direction of restoring Old Brains to *Lincoln, Stanton, Hooker,* et al. v. *Lee*. That the President had adopted this course of action, however, was apparent only in the gradual increase in his messages to Fighting Joe of language and ideas that suggested that Old Brains had supplied him with a first draft that was converted into Lincolnian style. Secretary Stanton flashed a more direct signal on May 29 when he responded to a long wire from Fighting Joe regarding reports that General Lee was concentrating his cavalry at Culpeper. "If Stoneman had not almost destroyed one-half of my serviceable cavalry force [during Chancellorsville]," the Army of the Potomac's commander concluded, "I would pitch into [Lee] in his camps, and would now, if General Stahel's cavalry were with me for a few days."[19]

Stanton replied:

> *Your telegram of last evening, addressed to me, was submitted to the President and also Generals Halleck and Heintzelman. General Halleck reports as follows:*
>> *There is no other cavalry force about Washington than that of*

General Stahel, which is now engaged on scouting duty toward Bull Run Mountains, and in picketing Bull Run and Occoquan Rivers. If he is removed, there will be no force in front to give notice of enemy's raids on Alexandria or Washington.[20]

On June 5, however, General Hooker sent His Excellency a message that gave the commander-in-chief an opportunity to phase Halleck in a bit faster:

Yesterday morning appearances indicated that during the night the enemy had broken up a few of his camps and abandoned them. . . . He must either have it in mind to cross the Upper Potomac, or to throw his army between mine and Washington, in case I am correct in my conjecture. . . .

As I am liable to be called on to make a movement with the utmost promptitude, I desire that I may be informed as early as practicable of the views of the Government concerning this army. Under instructions from the major-general commanding [Halleck], dated January 31, I am instructed to keep "in view always the importance of covering Washington and Harper's Ferry, either directly or by so operating as to be able to punish any force of the enemy sent against them."

In the event the enemy should move, as I almost anticipate he will, the head of his column will probably be headed toward the Potomac, via Gordonsville or Culpeper, while the rear will rest on Fredericksburg.

After giving the subject my best reflection, I am of opinion that it is my duty to pitch into his rear, although in so doing the head of his column may reach Warrenton before I can return. Will it be within the spirit of my instructions to do so?

In view of these contemplated movements of the enemy, I cannot too forcibly impress upon the mind of His Excellency the President the necessity of having one commander for all of the troops whose operations can have an influence on those of Lee's army. Under the present system, all independent commanders are in ignorance of the movements of the others; at least such is my situation. I trust that I may not be considered in the way to this arrangement, as it is a position I do not desire, and only suggest it, as I feel the necessity for concert as well as vigorous action.

It is necessary for me to say this much that my motives may not be misunderstood.[21]

That afternoon Lincoln replied:

Yours of to-day was received an hour ago. So much of professional military skill is requisite to answer it, that I have turned the task over to General Halleck. He promises to perform it with his utmost care.

I have but one idea which I think worth suggesting to you, and that is, in case you find Lee coming to the north of the Rappahannock, I would by no means cross to the south of it. If he should leave a rear force at Fredericksburg, tempting you to fall upon it, it would fight in intrenchments and have you at disadvantage, and so, man for man, worst you at that point, while his main force would in some way be getting an advantage of you northward.

In one word, I would not take any risk of being entangled upon the river, like an ox jumped half over a fence and liable to be torn by dogs front and rear, without a fair chance to gore one way or kick the other.

If Lee would come to my side of the river, I would keep on the same side, and fight him or act on the defense, according as might be my estimate of his strength relative to my own. But these are mere suggestions, which I desire to be controlled by the judgment of yourself and General Halleck.[22]

These things said, Old Brains wrote Hooker:

The President has directed me to reply to your telegram to him of 10 a.m. to-day. My instructions of January 31, which were then shown to the President, left you entirely free to act as circumstances, in your judgment, might require, with the simple injunction to keep in view the safety of Washington and Harper's Ferry.

In regard to the contingency which you suppose may arise of General Lee's leaving a part of his forces in Fredericksburg, while, with the head of his column, he moves by Gordonsville or Culpeper toward the Potomac, it seems to me that such an operation would give you great advantages upon his flank to cut him in two, and fight his divided forces. Would it not be more advantageous to fight his movable column first, instead of first attacking his intrench-

ments, with your own forces separated by the Rappahannock?

Moreover, you are aware that the troops under General Heintzelman are much less than the number recommended by all the boards for the defenses of Washington. Neither this capital nor Harper's Ferry could long hold out against a large force. They must depend for their security very much upon the co-operation of your army.

It would, therefore, seem perilous to permit Lee's main force to move upon the Potomac while your army is attacking an intrenched position on the other side of the Rappahannock.

Of course your movements must depend in a great measure upon those made by Lee. There is another contingency not altogether improbable—that Lee will seek to hold you in check with his main force, while a strong force will be detached for a raid into Maryland and Pennsylvania. . . .

General Heintzelman and General Dix are instructed to telegraph directly to you all the movements which they may ascertain or make. Directions have also been given to forward military information which may be received from General Schenck's command. Any movements you may suggest of troops in these commands will be ordered, if deemed practicable.

Lee will probably move light and rapidly. Your movable force should be prepared to do the same.

The foregoing views are approved by the President.[23]

Clearly, Old Brains was making the transition from game-playing to reality easier for his civilian superiors by departing not an inch from his manner of conducting his relationships with them—or with the generals commanding field armies, including Fighting Joe Hooker. But on June 10, smitten by the desire to present a new idea, Hooker sent a long message to—as usual—His Excellency:

General Pleasonton, by telegram forwarded to the major-general commanding the army this morning, reports that he had an affair with the rebel cavalry yesterday near Brandy Station, which resulted in crippling him so much that [the enemy] will have to abandon his contemplated raid into Maryland, which was to have started this morning.

I am not so certain that the raid will be abandoned from this cause. It may delay the departure a few days. I shall leave the cavalry, which is all that I have mounted, where they are, near Bealeton, with instructions to resist the passage of the river by the enemy's forces. If to effect this he should bring up a considerable force of infantry, that will so much weaken him in my front that I have good reason to believe that I can throw a sufficient force over the river to compel the enemy to abandon his present position. If it should be the intention to send a heavy column of infantry to accompany the cavalry on the proposed raid, he can leave nothing behind to interpose any serious obstacle to my rapid advance on Richmond.

I am not satisfied of his intention in this respect, but from certain movements in their corps I cannot regard it as altogether improbable.

If it should be found to be the case, will it not promote the true interest of the cause for me to march to Richmond at once? From there all the disposable part of this army can be thrown to any threatened point north of the Potomac at short notice, and, until they can reach their destination, a sufficiency of troops can be collected to check, if not to stop, his invasion.

If left to operate from my own judgment, with my present information, I do not hesitate to say that I should adopt this course as being the most speedy and certain mode of giving the rebellion a mortal blow. I desire that you will give it your reflection. . . . I now have two bridges across the Rappahannock, ready to spring over the river below Fredericksburg, and it is this, I believe, that causes the enemy to hesitate in moving forward. . . .

It would be of incalculable service to this army to be transferred to some more remote point from Washington and Alexandria. The stampedes in those towns, gotten up, no doubt, by people in the rebel interest, have their influence on my men, for many of them have no means of knowing whether they are with or without cause. They think there must be some fire where there is so much smoke.[24]

"Beware of rashness," the President had admonished Hooker in the letter he sent him when he appointed him to command of the Army of the Potomac. Apparently, however, the general had forgotten the warning—and also, his and his army's mission. Lincoln replied:

Your long dispatch of to-day is just received. If left to me, I would not go south of Rappahannock upon Lee's moving north of it. If you had Richmond invested to-day, you would not be able to take it in twenty days: meanwhile your communications, and with them your army, would be ruined.

I think Lee's army, and not Richmond, is your sure objective point. If he comes toward the Upper Potomac, follow on his flank and on his inside track, shortening your lines while he lengthens his. Fight him, too, when opportunity offers. If he stays where he is, fret him and fret him.[25]

Hooker may not have received enough messages from the general-in-chief to be able to recognize the presence in this one of Old Brains' guidance. That Halleck was very much involved, however, was underscored the next day by a short wire from him to Fighting Joe:

The President has just referred to me your telegram and his reply of yesterday, with directions to say to you whether or not I agree with him. I do so fully.[26]

A field army commander's concerns extended far beyond the weird and mysterious goings-on among the Union's war managers, of course, and so it was not surprising that most of the message traffic between Fighting Joe and General Halleck would involve nothing much more than swaps of rumors. On June 14, though, Lincoln prodded Hooker: "If the head of Lee's army is at Martinsburg and the tail of it on the Plank Road between Fredericksburg and Chancellorsville," he noted, "the animal must be very slim somewhere. Could you not break him?"[27]

This was the President's way of reminding Hooker of something General Halleck had advised earlier: "In regard to the contingency which you suppose may arise of General Lee's leaving a part of his forces in Fredericksburg, while, with the head of his column, he moves by Gordonsville or Culpeper toward the Potomac, it seems to me that such an operation would give you great advantages upon his flank to cut him in two, and fight his divided forces." But Fighting Joe's reply suggested that Lincoln had touched a raw nerve:

I do not feel like making a move for the enemy until I am satisfied as to his whereabouts. To proceed to Winchester and have him make his appearance elsewhere would expose me to ridicule.[28]

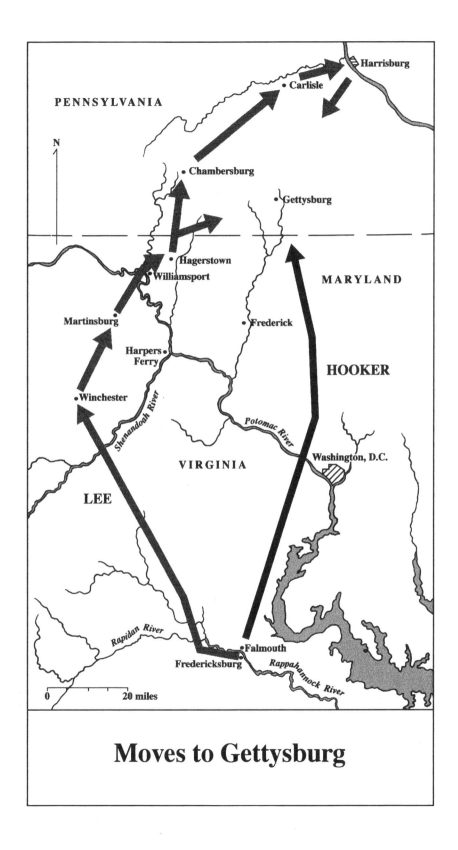

PENNSYLVANIA

N

• Harrisburg

• Carlisle

• Chambersburg

• Gettysburg

• Hagerstown

Williamsport

MARYLAND

• Martinsburg

• Frederick

Harpers
Ferry

HOOKER

• Winchester

Shenandoah River

Potomac River

VIRGINIA

Washington, D.C.

LEE

Rapidan River

0   20 miles

• Falmouth

Fredericksburg

Rappahannock River

Moves to Gettysburg

Heaven forfend! Halleck tried to stir the Army of the Potomac's ultrasensitive commander by taking a different approach:

> *Your army is entirely free to operate as you desire against Lee's army, so long as you keep his main army from Washington. It is believed that Longstreet and Stuart are crossing the Potomac above and below Harper's Ferry. They certainly should be pursued. The force needed for that purpose must depend on your information of movements or position of the remainder of Lee's army. Leesburg seems about the best point to move on first.*[29]

If Old Brains seemed very close to telling Hooker what to do, it may be that he had detected in Fighting Joe an unwillingness to take any initiative—lest Lee smash him again—combined with dislike of having anyone, including the President, to try to direct him away from doing exactly as he pleased. Worse, in two messages (both to Lincoln) on June 15, Hooker seemed nigh-incoherent:

- *"Your telegram . . . seems to disclose the intentions of the enemy to make an invasion, and, if so, it is not in my power to prevent it. I can, however, make an effort to check him. . . . On so short reflection, I am not prepared to say this is the wisest move, nor do I know that my opinion on this subject is wanted."*
- *"[Lee] has more to accomplish, but with more hazard, by striking an easterly direction after crossing* [the Potomac] *than a northerly one. . . . It is an act of desperation on his part, no matter in what force he moves. . . . I do not know that my opinion as to the duty of this army in the case is wanted; if it should be, you know that I will be happy to give it."*[30]

Why, one may well wonder, had General Hooker not given his opinion earlier, or then? That Lee was most likely heading for Maryland and possibly Pennsylvania had been obvious for days. After Chancellorsville, Fighting Joe had written a friend: "I was not hit by a shell, and I was not drunk. For once I lost confidence in Joe Hooker, and that is all there is to it." Had he lost confidence in Joe Hooker again?

5

HENRY HALLECK'S GOOD FRIEND Herman Haupt, the brilliant railroad builder, operator, and repairer who was also the Union's Kassandra, visited General Hooker on June 16, 1863, at the Army of the Potomac's headquarters at Fairfax Station on the Orange & Alexandria. Afterward, Haupt recalled:

> *I found him in a decidedly bad humor. He said that he did not intend to move at all until he got orders, and would then obey them literally and let the responsibility rest where it belonged; that he had made various suggestions that had not been approved by the powers that be in Washington, and if he could not carry out his own plans, others must give orders, and if disaster ensued his skirts would be clear, or words to that effect.*
>
> *I was greatly surprised at the spirit exhibited, and at the close of the interview returned as rapidly as possible to Washington and reported the situation to General Halleck, stating that General Hooker would not move until he got orders, and that action ought to be taken immediately.*
>
> *General Halleck replied that some of the statements of General Hooker were not in accordance with the facts, and then, opening his desk, he took out a bundle of papers and read to me, from the copies in his possession, part of the correspondence between General Hooker and the President, from which it appeared that Hooker's plan was to take advantage of the absence of Lee's army to capture Richmond. . . .*
>
> *After reading the letters to me, General Halleck put on his cap and left the office. I remained in conversation with his chief of staff, General Cullom [sic], for more than half an hour, when General Halleck returned, threw his cap on the table, and remarked: "Hooker will get his orders."*[31]

At about the same time, Hooker was telegraphing His Excellency: "You have long been aware, Mr. President, that I have not enjoyed the confidence of the major-general commanding the army, and I can assure you so long as this continues we may look in vain for success, especially as future operations will require our relations to be more dependent upon each other than heretofore."[32]

At ten o'clock that evening, Abraham Lincoln wired Hooker:

To remove all misunderstanding, I now place you in the strict military relation to General Halleck of a commander of one of the armies to the general-in-chief of all the armies. I have not intended differently, but as it seems to be differently understood, I shall direct him to give you orders and you to obey them.[33]

Such were the orders that General Hooker got; surely they were not what he craved; and if he found the position the President had taken more than slightly ingenuous, he may have been justified. Lincoln had spoiled him, and that was all there was to it.

While the commander-in-chief was extricating himself from one "misunderstanding," another surfaced. On June 16 General Halleck telegraphed Hooker:

I do not think there is reliable information that the enemy has crossed the Potomac in any force. Where his main corps are is still uncertain, and I know of no way to ascertain, excepting through your cavalry, which should be kept near enough to the enemy to at least be able to tell us where he is. My suggestion of yesterday, to follow the enemy's advance, by moving a considerable force first to Leesburg, and thence as circumstances may require, is the best one I can make. Unless your army is kept near enough to the enemy to ascertain his movements, yours must be in the dark or on mere conjecture. . . .[34]

Later on the same day he added:

There is now no doubt that the enemy is surrounding Harper's Ferry, but in what force I have no information. General Schenk says our force there is much less than before reported, and cannot hold out very long. He wished to know whether he may expect relief. He can hope for none, excepting from your army.[35]

That evening, Fighting Joe replied: "In compliance with your directions, I shall march to the relief of Harper's Ferry. . . ."[36]

Not many hours earlier, Herman Haupt had told Halleck that Hooker had said that he did not intend to move at all until he got orders, and would then obey them only literally and let the responsibility rest where it belonged. Now, Hooker seemed to have mistaken Old Brains' suggestions for orders. The irate general-in-chief telegraphed him at 10:15 P.M:

> *I have given no directions for your army to march to Harper's Ferry.*
> *I have advised the movement of a force, sufficiently strong to meet*
> *Longstreet, on Leesburg, to ascertain where the enemy is, and then*
> *move to the relief of Harper's Ferry, or elsewhere, as circumstances*
> *might require.*
>
> *With the remainder of your force in proper position to support*
> *this, I want you to push out your cavalry, to ascertain something*
> *definite about the enemy.*
>
> *You are in command of the Army of the Potomac, and will*
> *make the particular dispositions as you deem proper. I shall only*
> *indicate the objects to be aimed at. We have no positive information*
> *of any large force against Harper's Ferry, and it cannot be known*
> *whether it will be necessary to go there until you can feel the enemy*
> *and ascertain his whereabouts.*[37]

It is only fair to General Hooker to wonder if he had been laboring in ignorance of the Halleck Doctrine, that "a general in the field is the best judge of conditions." Also, Halleck's stern correction reached Fighting Joe at roughly the same time as His Excellency's message that ended, "I shall direct [Halleck] to give you orders and you to obey them." Two such jolts in a short interval were among the consequences of Lincoln's having excluded the general-in-chief from the chain of command for nearly five months.

During the next few days, Hooker and Halleck exchanged rumors and requests for enlightenment. Typical was this message from Old Brains to the Army of the Potomac's commander:

> *I can get no definite information of the enemy other than that sent*
> *to you. Rumors from Pennsylvania are too confused and*
> *contradictory to be relied on. Officers and others are on a big*
> *stampede. They are asking me why does not General Hooker tell*
> *where Lee's army is; he is nearest to it. There are numerous*
> *suppositions and theories, but all is yet mere conjecture. I only hope*
> *for positive information from your front. . . .*[38]

None was forthcoming, but by June 26 General Hooker's headquarters were a few miles north of the Potomac, at Poolesville, Maryland. At about this time, Harpers Ferry became the subject of a controversy that had most of its roots somewhere else—not an uncommon phenomenon in this strange war. To the general-in-chief, Hooker telegraphed:

> *Is there any reason why Maryland Heights* [north of Harpers Ferry] *should not be abandoned after the public stores and property are removed?*
>
> *I propose to visit the place to-morrow, on my way to Frederick, to satisfy myself in that point. It must be borne in mind that I am here with a force inferior in numbers to that of the enemy, and must have every available man to use on the field.*[39]

Major General George B. McClellan had signed a similar message not long before Antietam the year before. At the time, Old Brains insisted that Harpers Ferry be held if possible, because it was on the eastern flank of General Lee's supply route and because Lee would have to pause and divert troops to eliminate it before moving very far onward into Maryland. This strategic reality led to Lee's Special Orders No. 151, the fragmentation of his army, loss of his advance's momentum, and the battle at Sharpsburg. Now, as General Halleck saw it, Harpers Ferry had the same value. This time, however, Union forces would hold Maryland Heights—the high ground from which Stonewall Jackson had bombarded the federal garrison into surrender.

On the afternoon of June 27, General Hooker revealed his findings to the general-in-chief:

> *I have received your telegram in regard to Harper's Ferry. I find 10,000 men here, in condition to take the field. Here they are of no earthly account. They cannot defend a ford of the river, and, as far as Harper's Ferry is concerned, there is nothing of it.*
>
> *As for the fortifications, the work of the troops, they remain when the troops are withdrawn. No enemy will ever take possession of them for them. This is my opinion.*
>
> *All the public property could have been secured to-night, and the troops marched to where they could have been of some service. Now they are but a bait for the rebels, should they return.*
>
> *I beg that this may be presented to the Secretary of War and His Excellency the President.*[40]

Before General Halleck could either settle the Harper's Ferry dispute or comply with Hooker's request, another telegram from Fighting Joe reached him:

> *My original instructions require me to cover Harper's Ferry and Washington. I have now imposed upon me, in addition, an enemy in my front of more than my number. I beg to be understood, respectfully, but firmly, that I am unable to comply with this condition with the means at my disposal, and earnestly request that I may at once be relieved from the position I occupy.*[41]

How, one may well wonder, could an army commander whose troops in fact far outnumbered those of the elusive Lee, and who possessed every advantage in terms of weapons and secure sources of ammunition and other supplies, *possibly* base a request for his own guillotining on such flimsy grounds?

Once again, Joe Hooker had lost confidence in Joe Hooker—and that was all there was to it.

Five hours later, General-in-Chief Halleck replied:

> *Your application to be relieved from your present command is received.*
>
> *As you were appointed to this command by the President, I have no power to relieve you. Your dispatch has been duly referred for Executive action.*[42]

6

ABSENT EVEN CAVALRY CONTACT with General Lee's army, Major General Hooker had taken counsel of his fears regarding the Confederate forces' size, location, and potential for providing his Army of the Potomac with another whipping. Actually, by June 27, 1863, rebel corps commanded by Major Generals James Longstreet and A. P. Hill were in Chambersburg, Pennsylvania, and Richard Ewell's divisions had passed through Gettysburg and reached York, just west of the Susquehanna River. Lee's troop strength in Pennsylvania was not more than 75,000, Hooker's in Maryland perhaps 105,000. But the Army of Northern Virginia's audacious commander had made an egregious blunder on June 25 by allowing Jeb Stuart to take substantially all of his cavalry on a sweep eastward and then northward aimed at severing Hooker's lifelines' connections to Washington.

Hooker had been "blind" since he had left Falmouth. On June 27, 1863, no one could have known that Stuart's departure would leave General Lee blind for nearly a week. But, given Fighting Joe's request to be relieved and despite the density of the fog of war prevailing in Washington, the Union's war managers acted swiftly to grant the boon he craved.

This time around, the deed was done swiftly and surely. General Halleck recommended that Major General George Gordon Meade succeed Hooker; the President approved, whereupon lawyer Halleck drew up the papers and sent them up to Army of the Potomac headquarters at Frederick by an aide instructed to deliver them to Meade, not Hooker.

Colonel James A. Hardie reached Meade's tent at three o'clock on the morning of June 28, 1863. "General," Hardie is said to have said, "I'm afraid I've come to make trouble for you."[43] Meade read:

> *You will receive with this the order of the President placing you in command of the Army of the Potomac. Considering the circumstances, no one ever received a more important command; and I cannot doubt that you will fully justify the confidence which the Government has reposed in you.*
>
> *You will not be hampered by any minute instructions from these headquarters. Your army is free to act as you may deem proper under the circumstances as they arise. You will, however, keep in view the important fact that the Army of the Potomac is the covering army of Washington as well as the army of operation against the invading forces of the rebels. You will, therefore, maneuver and fight in such a manner as to cover the capital and also Baltimore, as far as circumstances will admit. Should General Lee move upon either of these places, it is expected that you will either anticipate him or arrive with him so as to give him battle.*
>
> *All forces within the sphere of your operations will be held subject to your orders. Harper's Ferry and its garrison are under your direct orders.*
>
> *You are authorized to remove from command, and to send from your army, any officer or other person you may deem proper, and to appoint to command as you may deem expedient.*
>
> *In fine, general, you are intrusted with all the power and authority which the President, the Secretary of War, or the General-in-Chief can confer on you, and you may rely upon our full support.*
>
> *You will keep me fully informed of all your movements, and*

the positions of your own troops and those of the enemy, so far as known. I shall always be ready to advise and assist you to the utmost of my ability.[44]

"Well," said the Army of the Potomac's new commander, "I've been tried and convicted without a hearing, and I suppose I shall have to go to execution."[45]

After sunrise, Meade informed Hooker of the change. Fighting Joe cheerfully assured his successor of his full cooperation in making the transition, and later he shared all of the information and plans he had. At seven o'clock that morning, Meade telegraphed the general-in-chief:

> *The order placing me in command of this army is received. As a soldier, I obey it, and to the utmost of my ability will execute it.*
>
> *Totally unexpected as it has been, and in ignorance of the exact condition of the troops and position of the enemy, I can only now say that it appears to me I must move toward the Susquehanna, keeping Washington and Baltimore well covered, and if the enemy is checked in his attempt to cross the Susquehanna, or if he turns toward Baltimore, to give him battle.*
>
> *I would say that I trust every available man that can be spared will be sent to me, as from all accounts the enemy is in strong force. So soon as I can post myself up, I will communicate more in detail.*[46]

"I fully concur in your general views as to the movements of your army," Old Brains replied that afternoon. "All available assistance will be given you. . . . It is most probable that Lee will concentrate his forces this side of the Susquehanna."[47]

On June 29 General Meade sent a long message to the general-in-chief regarding the situation and his plans, but it was delayed a day in reaching Washington because rebels had cut his telegraph wires and killed one of his couriers. Actually, direct communication between Meade and Halleck would not be restored until well after it had been needed most. But on June 30 Herman Haupt was able to get through to General Halleck, *via* railroad telegraph lines from Harrisburg, with this information:

> *Lee is falling back suddenly from the vicinity of Harrisburg, and concentrating all his forces. York has been evacuated. Carlisle is being evacuated. The concentration appears to be at or near Chambersburg. The object apparently a sudden movement against*

Meade, of which he should be advised by courier immediately. A courier might reach Frederick by way of Western Maryland Railroad to Westminister.[48]

"You will not be hampered by any minute instructions from these headquarters," Old Brains had assured Meade. "Your army is free to act as you may deem proper under the circumstances as they arise." In effect, the Halleck Doctrine was in force: *A general in the field is the best judge of conditions.*

He had applied it before and after Fredericksburg, in preventing Rosecrans from being relieved on the grounds that he was too diligent in amassing supplies, and in defending Ulysses Grant against charges such as Murat Halstead's prediction: "Grant will fail miserably, hopelessly, eternally. You may look for and calculate his failures, in every position in which he may be placed, as a perfect certainty."

Never had Henry Halleck retreated from his position. Yet, as of June 30, 1863, no general that he had shielded from distant, amateurish, rear-echelon interference had produced a clear-cut victory.

"In war," the real Napoleon had declared, "the man is everything." McClellan, Buell, Butler, Banks, McClernand, Burnside, and lately Hooker were mistakes President Abraham Lincoln had made. William Rosecrans had been Halleck's choice to replace Don Carlos Buell, and Ulysses Grant had been the general to whom Old Brains had bequeathed the mission of eliminating Vicksburg and restoring the entire length of the Mississippi River to Union control.

With Lincoln and Stanton standing aside (but not very far away), and with a Confederate invasion reaching the very heartland of Pennsylvania, General-in-Chief Halleck entrusted the task of protecting Washington and Baltimore to a general he knew only by reputation. Earlier, Halleck had bet the farm on Grant. Now, with telegraph lines out and message relays unreliable, Old Brains was betting almost everything the Union had left to lose on Major General George Gordon Meade and on his ability "to act as you may deem proper under the circumstances as they arise"—*and to win.*

14 ★ *Missions Unaccomplished*

*I*N THE ENTIRE RECORDED HISTORY OF WARFARE, seldom—if ever—
had any nation won *three* victories, each of major strategic importance, at
widely separated locations on virtually *the same day.* Such, however, was the
Union's distinction as of July 4, 1863, plus or minus a few hours.

Major General Meade, employing the nigh-unlimited discretion
General-in-Chief Henry Halleck had given him, had advanced enough
units northward to some interesting high ground just south of Gettysburg,
Pennsylvania, just in time to resist the series of attacks General Lee had
ordered and Longstreet had bungled until, on July 4, both sides' troops had
been utterly fought-out and Lee prepared to withdraw toward the Potomac
and Virginia's Shenandoah Valley.

Also on July 4, 1863, Major General Grant, having driven the
Confederate defenders of Vicksburg into their fortifications and having
conducted a siege for six weeks or so, put an end to the suffering and
approaching starvation of the Gibraltar of the West's garrison and trapped
civilians by accepting the unconditional surrender of Lieutenant General
John Pemberton and the troops he had commanded.

And by July 4, 1863, Major General William Rosecrans was halting
the advance that had maneuvered Braxton Bragg's forces out of their strong
defensive positions at Wartrace, Shelbyville, and Tullahoma and into
positions shielding Chattanooga.

Generals Meade, Grant, and Rosecrans had produced these results
exactly as General-in-Chief Halleck had intended: "without any minute
instructions from these headquarters." Yet, ironically, no one in the War

Department's telegraph room learned anything much about the events of July 4, 1863 until, in some instances, *days* later.

After the Union armies' appalling defeats at First and Second Bull Run, during the Seven Days, at Fredericksburg and Chancellorsville, in the ghastly stand-off along Antietam Creek in the East, and at the indecisive slaughters at Shiloh and Stones River in the West, surely the people in the North who had sacrificed so much for so little were entitled to celebrate now that so much seemed to have been accomplished in so short a time.

Even so, once the Union's war managers had finally received the messages reporting these triple triumphs, General-in-Chief Halleck recognized that victory seemingly achieved can quickly become victory rendered meaningless unless the victors *on the scene* exploit it rapidly and ruthlessly. Absent information, however, Old Brains and his civilian superiors were obliged to wait to order anyone to do anything until fresh reports of developments near Gettysburg and Vicksburg and Chattanooga burned off the dense fog of war blanketing the United States east of the Mississippi.

As was his wont, Brigadier General Herman Haupt had been at the right place at the right time in order to discern the probable unfolding of events and to warn those in harm's way. From Harrisburg, Pennsylvania's capital, on July 1 he telegraphed General Halleck:

> *Information just received, 12:45 a.m., leads to the belief that the concentration of the forces of the enemy will be at Gettysburg rather than Chambersburg. The movement on their part is very rapid and hurried. . . . Meade should by all means be informed, and be prepared for a sudden attack from Lee's whole army.*[1]

At six o'clock that morning Haupt followed up this flash dispatch with a more detailed message:

> *It appears to have been the intention of the enemy to attack Harrisburg yesterday. Our forces, supposed to be Pleasonton's, were resisting their movements, and, T. A. Scott said, had actually succeeded in retarding the advance on Harrisburg, and compelled a retreat.*
>
> *I thought I saw a much more decisive and important move on the tapis. Lee had received information of the removal of Hooker, and the substitution of Meade. He knew also that Meade's communications were cut by Stuart; that some confusion must exist from*

the change of commanders; that Meade could not at once get his forces in hand, and that, by suddenly concentrating and falling upon Meade, he could be crushed, when Washington, Baltimore, and Philadelphia would all be at the mercy of the enemy.

I mentioned to Scott my opinion, in which he at once concurred, and I immediately sent the telegrams to you and General Schenck last night.[2]

General Haupt went on to relay detailed information Assistant Secretary of War Scott had acquired regarding the strength and artillery firepower of each of General Lee's corps and also reports of their movements.

For the next two days, as the armies met and fought just south of Gettysburg, Haupt and his railroad repair and train crews rushed supplies to Meade over rail lines into towns east and south of the battle area—a region he knew well: Haupt had helped build a railroad from Gettysburg to the Potomac, and he had been professor of mathematics at Pennsylvania College in Gettysburg from 1845 to 1847.[3]

At 8:30 a.m. on July 4, General Meade had started a message on its way to General Halleck by telegraphing Major General Darius Couch in Harrisburg:

The enemy has withdrawn from his positions occupied for attack. I am not yet sufficiently informed of his movement. He was repulsed yesterday in his attack on me. . . . Until I get further information, I cannot decide as to the character of the movements or the enemy's intentions.[4]

Earlier, a newspaperman named Homer Byington had succeeded in sending a telegram to Washington,[5] but not until Meade's message arrived did President Lincoln—who had been starved for news—feel confident enough to release any. But at 10 a.m. on the Fourth of July he relented:

The President announces to the country that news from the Army of the Potomac, up to 10 p.m. of the 3d, is such as to cover that army with the highest honor; to promise a great success to the cause of the Union; and to claim the condolence of all for the many gallant fallen, and that for this he especially desires that on this day, he, whose will, not ours, should ever be done, be everywhere remembered and ever reverenced with profoundest gratitude.[6]

Neither General Meade nor Abraham Lincoln had claimed victory, which was prudent—among other reasons, because of what Herman Haupt was reporting to General Halleck at 11:00 p.m. on July 4 from Oxford, seven miles east of the battlefield:

> *Persons just in from Gettysburg report the position of affairs. I fear that while Meade rests to refresh his men and collect supplies, Lee will be off so far that he cannot intercept him. A good force on the line of the Potomac to prevent Lee from crossing would, I think, insure his destruction.*[7]

2

EVEN BEFORE THE ARRIVAL in Washington of the Union Kassandra's most recent warning, General-in-Chief Halleck had been acting upon his analysis of what General Lee might do if indeed George Meade had whipped him. At 11:00 a.m. on July 4, he telegraphed Brigadier General B. F. Kelley at Cumberland, Maryland:

> *Intercepted messages from Jeff. Davis show that the country between Lee's army and Richmond is entirely stripped of troops. You will push forward ... with all possible rapidity, and concentrate your available forces at Hancock, as near as possible, so as to be in a position to attack Lee's flanks, should he be compelled to recross the Potomac. Having so concentrated, hold your troops in readiness for a rapid movement. No time to be lost.*[8]

"Send everything forward to Frederick," Halleck telegraphed Major General Robert Schenck, commanding at Baltimore, on July 5. "The enemy is in retreat, and Baltimore is in no possible danger. Give General Meade all the aid in your power."[9] And twice on July 5 he spurred Kelley.[10]

That day, Haupt reached Meade's headquarters and obtained confirmation of his suspicion that *resting* was uppermost in his West Point classmate's mind. He argued that unless Meade moved quickly, Lee would escape. The general commanding thought otherwise, pointing out that the Potomac was swollen by recent rains and that Lee had no bridging equipment.

"Do not place confidence in that," Haupt warned Meade. "I have men who could construct bridges in forty-eight hours sufficient to pass that army, if they have no other materials than such as they can gather from old buildings or from the woods, and it is not safe to assume that the enemy cannot do what we can do."[11]

Leaving Meade, Haupt took an engine over his newly repaired track to Washington. On July 6 he reported to Old Brains and the President the substance of his conversation with the Army of the Potomac's commander.[12] This time, his warnings were heeded—at least, in Washington. As soon as communication with General Meade was restored on July 7, Old Brains telegraphed him: "It gives me great pleasure to inform you that you have been appointed a brigadier-general in the Regular Army, to rank from July 3, the date of your brilliant victory at Gettysburg."[13] Next, the general-in-chief urged Meade:

> *You have given the enemy a stunning blow at Gettysburg. Follow it up, and give him another before he can reach the Potomac. When he crosses, circumstances will determine whether it will be best to pursue him by the Shenandoah Valley or this side of Blue Ridge. There is strong evidence that he is short of artillery ammunition, and if vigorously pressed, he must suffer.*[14]

On July 7 Halleck sent Meade two more messages mentioning the importance of fighting Lee again before he could cross the Potomac, then he passed along a note signed *A. Lincoln*:

> *We have certain information that Vicksburg surrendered to General Grant on the 4th of July. Now, if General Meade can complete his work, so gloriously prosecuted thus far, by the literal or substantial destruction of Lee's army, the rebellion will be over.*[15]

The President's words had added considerably to the pressure on General Meade, in part because of a passage in the glowing congratulatory message the army commander had issued to his troops on the afternoon of July 4. Near the end he had told them: "Our task is not yet accomplished, and the commanding general looks to the army for greater efforts to drive from our soil every vestige of the presence of the invader."[16]

From the Soldiers' Home northwest of Washington, to which the Lincoln family went every summer to escape the capital's heat and humidity, on the evening of July 6 the commander-in-chief wired General Halleck:

I left the telegraph office a good deal dissatisfied. You know I did not like the phrase, in Orders, No. 68, I believe, "Drive the invaders from our soil."

Since that, I see a dispatch from General French, saying the enemy is crossing his wounded over the river in flats, without saying why he does not stop it, or even intimating a thought that it ought to be stopped.

Still later, another dispatch from General Pleasonton, by direction of General Meade, to General French, stating that the main army is halted because it is believed the rebels are concentrating "on the road toward Hagerstown, beyond Fairfield," and is not to move until it is ascertained that the rebels intend to evacuate Cumberland Valley.

These things all appear to me to be connected with a purpose to cover Baltimore and Washington, and to get the enemy across the river again without a further collision, and they do not appear connected with a purpose to prevent his crossing and to destroy him. I do fear the former purpose is acted upon and the latter is rejected.

If you are satisfied the latter purpose is entertained and is judiciously pursued, I am content. If you are not so satisfied, please look to it.[17]

General Meade responded to Washington's exhortations on July 8 in this message to Halleck:

General Couch learns from scouts that the train at Williamsport is crossing very slowly. So long as the river is unfordable, the enemy cannot cross.... My army is assembling slowly. The rains of yesterday and last night have made all roads but pikes almost impassable. Artillery and wagons are stalled; it will take time to collect them together. A large portion of the men are barefooted. Shoes will arrive at Frederick to-day, and will be issued as soon as possible. The spirit of the army is high; the men are ready and willing to make every exertion to push forward.

The very first moment I can get the different commands, the artillery and cavalry, properly supplied and in hand, I will move forward. Be assured I most earnestly desire to try the fortunes of war with the enemy on this side of the river, hoping through Providence and the bravery of my men to settle the question, but I should do wrong not to frankly tell you of the difficulties encountered.

I expect to find the enemy in a strong position, well covered with artillery, and I do not desire to imitate his example at Gettysburg, and assault a position where the chances were so greatly against success. I wish in advance to moderate the expectations of those who, in ignorance of the difficulties to be encountered, may expect too much. All that I can do under the circumstances I pledge this army to do.[18]

Concurrently, apparently, Halleck was telegraphing Meade: "There is reliable information that the enemy is crossing at Williamsport. The opportunity to attack his divided forces should not be lost. The President is urgent and anxious that your army should move against him by forced marches."[19]

Meade replied:

My information as to the crossing of the enemy does not agree with that just received in your dispatch. His whole force is in position between Funkstown and Williamsport. I have just received infor-mation that he has driven my cavalry force in front of Boonsborough.

My army is and has been making forced marches, short of rations, and barefooted. One corps marched yesterday and last night over 30 miles. I take occasion to repeat that I will use my utmost efforts to push forward this army.[20]

Realizing, perhaps, that Meade's reputed hot temper was nearing the boiling point, Old Brains added reassurance to his prodding in his response:

Do not understand me as expressing any dissatisfaction; on the contrary, your army has done most nobly. I only wish to give you opinions formed from information received here.

It is telegraphed from near Harper's Ferry that the enemy have been crossing for the last two days. It is also reported that they have a bridge across. If Lee's army is so divided by the river, the im-portance of attacking the part on this side is incalculable. Such an opportunity may never occur again.

If, on the contrary, he has massed his whole force on the Antietam, time must be taken to also concentrate your forces. Your opportunities for information are better than mine. . . .

You will have forces sufficient to render your victory certain.
My only fear now is that the enemy may escape by crossing the
river.[21]

By July 8 General Haupt had given up hope. "I do not believe we can prevent Lee's army from crossing," he said in a message to Quartermaster General Montgomery Meigs. "I could build trestle-bridges of round sticks, and floor with fence rails. It is too much to assume that the rebels cannot do the same."

Yet, characteristically, Herman Haupt had a suggestion:

If they get across, we should not follow at their heels, but strike at once for White Plains, use the railroad from that point, and head them off at Staunton.

It seems to me that every effort must be made by the rebels to save Lee by sending him supplies via the Shenandoah Valley. If we could find force enough to occupy the passes of the Blue Ridge, we could capture supply trains, and reduce the rebels to such a state of destitution as would compel a surrender.

Our course seems to me to be a clear one, and, if you concur in this opinion, I hope you will talk it over with General Halleck.[22]

Haupt and Meigs and Old Brains were speaking the same language, but the general-in-chief was busy mobilizing support for Meade. "Can you not squeeze out some more troops to send to Harper's Ferry?" he asked General Schenck.[23] And to Kelley: "If Lee gives battle, do not be absent, but come in and help General Meade gain a victory."[24] And to Major General John Dix at Fort Monroe: "It is important that the troops be pushed forward with all possible dispatch, and also that they arrive here ready for the field."[25]

And to General Meade: "Do not be influenced by any dispatch from here against your own judgment. Our information here is not always correct."[26] Surely, such an admission of rear-echelon fallibility must have put a rare grin on the face of the "Old Snapping Turtle."

General Halleck had never had an opportunity to make his Doctrine known to Hooker. In his message on June 30, he had told Meade he would not be hampered by instructions from on high. His addition on July 9 may well have been intended to amplify the notion that a general in the field is the best judge of conditions.

But by then, General Meade was belatedly trying to decide how strong

General Lee's defenses were and whether he could amass enough troops to attack without fear of repulse. "I think it will be best for you," Halleck advised on July 10, "to postpone a general battle till you can concentrate all your forces and get up your reserves and re-enforcements. . . . Beware of partial combats. Bring up and hurl upon the enemy all your forces, good and bad."[27]

However, Old Snapping Turtle took his time studying the situation. It had been ten days since gallant Brigadier General Lewis Armistead, with his cap on the tip of his saber, had led the charge erroneously known as Pickett's and had died embracing a cannon in a federal battery whose commander had been shot through the mouth while shouting a command.[28] On July 13, Meade informed Halleck: "In my dispatch of yesterday I stated that it was my intention to attack the enemy to-day, unless something intervened to prevent it. Upon calling my corps commanders together and submitting the question to them, five out of six were unqualifiedly opposed to it."[29]

Again, a field army commander's lack of familiarity with Henry Halleck's *weltanschauung* had exposed himself to rebukes Ulysses Grant and Cump Sherman had much earlier learned better than to invite. Sparks flew from Old Brains' immediate response:

> *You are strong enough to attack and defeat the enemy before he can effect a crossing. Act on your own judgment and make your generals execute your orders. Call no council of war. It is proverbial that councils of war never fight. Re-enforcements are pushed on as rapidly as possible. Do not let the enemy escape.*[30]

Words alone, as General Halleck had long since learned, do not win battles. George Meade added confirmation on July 14:

> *On advancing my army this morning, with a view of ascertaining the exact position of the enemy and attacking him if the result of the examination should justify me, I found, on reaching his lines, that they were evacuated. I immediately put my army in pursuit, the cavalry in advance.*
>
> *At this period my forces occupy Williamsport, but I have not yet heard from the advance on Falling Waters, where it is reported he crossed his infantry on a bridge. Your instructions as to further movements, in case the enemy are entirely across the river, are desired.*[31]

Indeed, it had been as Kassandra Haupt had foretold.

In the circumstances, General Halleck's reply reflected remarkable restraint:

> *The enemy should be pursued and cut up, wherever he may have gone. . . . I cannot advise details, as I do not know where Lee's army is, nor where your pontoon bridges are.*
>
> *I need hardly say to you that the escape of Lee's army without another battle has created great dissatisfaction in the mind of the President, and it will require an active and energetic pursuit on your part to remove the impression that it has not been sufficiently active heretofore.*[32]

Whereupon Meade responded:

> *Having performed my duty conscientiously and to the best of my ability, the censure of the President conveyed in your dispatch of 1 p.m. this day, is, in my judgment, so undeserved that I feel compelled most respectfully to ask to be immediately relieved from the command of this army.*[33]

Presumably, because it was the correct thing to do, Old Brains referred Meade's request to Lincoln. His reaction was reflected in the draft of a message to the Army of the Potomac's commander:

> *I have just seen your dispatch to Gen. Halleck, asking to be relieved of your command, because of a supposed censure of mine. . . . But I was in such deep distress myself that I could not restrain some expression of it. . . .*
>
> *I am sorry to be the author of the slightest pain to you. You fought and beat the enemy at Gettysburg, and of course, to say the least, his loss was as great as yours. He retreated, and you did not, it seems to me, pressingly pursue him. You had at least 20,000 veteran troops with you and as many more within supporting distance, all in addition to those who fought with you at Gettysburg; while it was not possible that [Lee] had received a single recruit, and yet you stood and let the river run down, bridges be built, and the enemy move away at his leisure without attacking him.*
>
> *Again, my dear General, I do not believe you appreciate the magnitude of the disaster involved in Lee's escape. He was within*

your easy grasp, and to have closed upon him would, in connection with our other successes, have ended the war. As it is the war will be prolonged indefinitely. . . . Your golden opportunity is gone, and I am immeasurably distressed because of it.[34]

But Lincoln recognized that the public and the soldiers of the Army of the Potomac would not understand how he could charge a victorious general with such lapses without relieving him from command, which he was not prepared to do. He decided not to send the letter.[35]

Instead, lawyer and lightning rod Henry Halleck dealt with the offended army commander:

My telegram, stating the disappointment of the President at the escape of Lee's army, was not intended as a censure, but as a stimulus to an active pursuit. It is not deemed a sufficient cause for your application to be relieved.[36]

3

WORTH NOTING HERE is the close cooperation, indeed a meeting of two powerful minds, of Abraham Lincoln and Henry Wager Halleck. For them, but for them only, Gettysburg appeared to have been an unremarked burying of the ashes of January 1, 1863. Indeed, their tacit reconciliation was reflected in the uneasiness both seemed to share over their treatment of General Meade and their unwillingness to leave an offense on their part uncorrected.

On the morning of July 29, 1863, Lincoln sent a note from the Executive Mansion to his general-in-chief, who promptly telegraphed it to the Army of the Potomac's commander:

Seeing General Meade's dispatch of yesterday to yourself, causes me to fear that he supposes the Government here is demanding of him to bring on a general engagement with Lee as soon as possible. I am claiming no such thing of him. In fact, my judgment is against it; which judgment, of course, I will yield if yours and his are the contrary.

If he could not safely engage Lee at Williamsport, it seems absurd to suppose he can safely engage him now, when he has scarcely more than two-thirds of the force he had at Williamsport, while it must be that Lee has been re-enforced. True, I desired General Meade to pursue Lee across the Potomac, hoping, as has proved true, that he would thereby clear the Baltimore and Ohio Railroad, and get some advantage by harassing him on his retreat.

These being past, I am unwilling he should now get into a general engagement on the impression that we here are pressing him, and I shall be glad for you to so inform him, unless your own judgment is against it.[37]

Later on July 29, Old Brains sent Meade a letter marked *Unofficial:*

I take this method of writing you a few words which I could not well communicate in any other way.

Your fight at Gettysburg met with the universal approbation of all military men here. You handled your troops in that battle as well, if not better, than any general has handled his army during the war. You brought all your forces into action at the right time and place, which no commander of the Army of the Potomac has done before.

You may well be proud of that battle. The President's order, or proclamation, of July 4, showed how much he appreciated your success.

And now a few words in regard to subsequent events. You should not have been surprised or vexed at the President's disappointment at the escape of Lee's army. He had examined into all the details of sending you re-enforcements, to satisfy himself that every man who could possibly be spared from other places had been sent to your army. He thought that Lee's defeat was so certain that he felt no little impatience at his unexpected escape.

I have no doubt, general, that you felt the disappointment as keenly as any one else. Such things sometimes occur to us without any fault of our own. Take it altogether, your short campaign has proved your superior Generalship, and you merit, as you will receive, the confidence of the Government and the gratitude of the country.

I need not assure you, general, that I have lost none of the confidence which I felt in you when I recommended you for the command.[38]

General Meade replied twice. On July 30 he began a long review of the situation and his possible courses of action with a confession: "The impression of the President is correct. I have been acting under the belief, from your telegrams, that it was his and your wish that I should pursue Lee and bring him to a general engagement, if practicable. . . ."[39] Then, on July's last day, Meade sent an unofficial response to General Halleck's unofficial letter:

> *I thank you most sincerely and heartily for your kind and generous letter of the 28th instant, received last evening. It would be wrong in me to deny that I feared there existed in the minds of both the President and yourself an idea that I had failed to do what another would and could have done in the withdrawal of Lee's army. The expression you have been pleased to use in your letter, to wit, "a feeling of disappointment," is one that I cheerfully accept and readily admit was as keenly felt by myself as any one.*
>
> *But permit me, dear general, to call your attention to the distinction between disappointment and dissatisfaction. The one was a natural feeling, in view of the momentous consequences that would have resulted from a successful attack, but does not necessarily convey with it any censure. I could not view the use of the latter expression in any other light than as intending to convey an expression of opinion on the part of the President that I had failed to do what I might and should have done.*
>
> *Now, let me say, in the frankness which characterizes your letter, that perhaps the President was right; if such was the case, it was my duty to give him an opportunity to replace me by one better fitted for the command of the army. It was, I assure you, with such feelings that I applied to be relieved. It was not from any personal consideration, for I have tried in this whole war to forget all personal considerations, and have always maintained they should not for an instant influence any one's actions.*
>
> *Of course you will understand that I do not agree that the President was right, and I feel sure when the true state of the case comes to be known, that however natural and great may be the feeling of disappointment, no blame will be attached to any one.*
>
> *Had I attacked Lee the day I proposed to do so, and in the ignorance that then existed of his position, I have every reason to believe the attack would have been unsuccessful, and would have resulted disastrously. This opinion is founded on the judgment of numerous distinguished officers, after inspecting Lee's vacated works and position. . . .*

The idea that Lee had abandoned his lines early in the day that he withdrew, I have positive intelligence is not correct, and that not a man was withdrawn till after dark.

I mention these facts to remove the impression, which newspaper correspondents have given the public, that it was only necessary to advance to secure an easy victory. I had great responsibility thrown on me. On one side were the known and important fruits of victory, and, on the other, the equally important and terrible consequences of a defeat.

I considered my position at Williamsport very different from that at Gettysburg. When I left Frederick, it was with the firm determination to attack and fight Lee, without regard to time or place, as soon as I could come in contact with him; but after defeating him, and requiring him to abandon his schemes of invasion, I did not think myself justified in making a blind attack simply to prevent his escape, and running all the risks attending such a venture.

Now, as I said before, in this, perhaps, I erred in judgment, for I take this occasion to say to you, and through you to the President, that I have no pretensions to any superior capacity for the post he has assigned me to; that all I can do is to exert my utmost efforts and do the best I can; but that the moment those who have a right to judge my actions think, or feel satisfied, either that I am wanting or that another would do better, that moment I earnestly desire to be relieved, not on my own account, but on account of the country and the cause.

You must excuse so much egotism, but your kind letter in a measure renders it necessary. I feel, general, very proud of your good opinion, and assure you I shall endeavor in the future to continue to merit it.[40]

Curiously, at about the same time that Old Brains was saying what he could to General Meade, USMA 1835, to clear the air, he was attempting to persuade a *political* general to withdraw his letter of resignation. To Major General Stephen A. Hurlbut, an old friend of Lincoln from their years as lawyers in Illinois who had served under Halleck and Grant at Shiloh and Corinth and had performed admirably at Memphis in supporting Grant's Vicksburg campaign,[41] on July 30, 1863, the general-in-chief wrote:

Your letter of resignation has been received at the War Department. I have also seen your private letter to the President on the subject.

I admire the tone of these letters, and fully appreciate your motives in writing them. The reasons for your wishing to return to your profession and business are weighty, but not more so than those which I and many other officers could offer.

We all must make sacrifices for our country.

The truth is, general, the war is not so near its end as you seem to suppose. The enemy will now make a desperate effort to repair his losses. He will force into his ranks every man capable of bearing arms. His fellow traitors and copperhead coadjutors at the North will do all in their power to help him by opposing the draft, which is the only possible means of supplying the loss of our forces by the expiration of the terms of those enlisted for nine months and two years. The patriotism of some of our old Democratic friends seems to have been destroyed by the heat of party spirit.

If the North were as united as the South, and would fill up our ranks now, we could soon end the war. But unfortunately the enemies of the Administration make themselves the enemies of the country, and will ruin the latter for the sake of defeating the former. The draft will be enforced, but it will take time. Under these circumstances we cannot consent to dispense with your services.

General officers who obey orders, who perform their duties faithfully, who do not quarrel with those temporarily placed over them, who neither protect thieves nor steal themselves, are not so numerous that we can well spare one, who, like you, has faithfully, honestly, and ably performed every duty. The President and Secretary of War are both anxious you should remain in service.[42]

Hurlbut's fellow Illinois politician John McClernand would never receive such a letter from the general-in-chief, nor would Major General N. P. ("Nothing Positive") Banks. After the costly failure of his sadly mismanaged assaults against Port Hudson's thinly defended fortifications on May 27, the Bobbin Boy—emulating Grant, upriver at Vicksburg—had employed siege operations.

By June 13, however, General Banks had decided to try again to take the place. Unfortunately for his reputation, he revealed the assininity of his plan in a message of that date to Rear Admiral David Farragut aboard his flagship, the *U.S.S. Monongahela:*

I shall open a vigorous bombardment at exactly a quarter past eleven this morning, and continue it for exactly one hour. I respectfully request that you will aid us by throwing as many shells as you can into the place during that time, commencing and ceasing fire with us. The bombardment will be immediately followed by a summons to surrender. If that is not listened to, I shall probably attack to-morrow morning; but of this I will give you notice.[43]

Seasoned naval warrior David Glasgow Farragut saw all the way through the Bobbin Boy's foolish scheme, but he confined his reply to a few words:

I will be ready for the bombardment at the time specified. I [think] *there is but little use in the demand for surrender. Although some may think they may, I do not—that is, General* [Franklin] *Gardner will not. The men may be very willing.*[44]

Amply warned by Bank's and Farragut's bombardments followed by the call for surrender, which Gardner promptly rejected, on June 14 Port Hudson's garrison prepared for attacks that the Bobbin Boy never launched.[45] And as he had after his earlier failure before Port Hudson's vulnerable fortifications, General Banks blamed everyone in sight but himself. To General-in-Chief Halleck on June 18 he complained:

The reduction of Port Hudson has required a longer time than at first supposed. First, because it is a stronger position. Secondly, because a large part of my force consists of nine-months' men who openly say they do not consider themselves bound to any perilous service. . . .[46]

On June 27, by which time Old Brains had almost quelled his fury, he replied:

The defection of your nine-months' men on the field of battle was a most criminal military offense, which should have been promptly and severely punished, in order to prevent a repetition of it by other troops.

*   When a column of attack is formed of doubtful troops, the proper mode of curing their defection is to place artillery in their rear, loaded with grape and canister, in the hands of reliable men, with orders to fire at the first moment of disaffection. A knowledge of such orders will probably prevent any wavering, and, if not, one*

such punishment will prevent any repetition of it in your army.

You will be fully sustained in any measures you may deem necessary to adopt to enforce discipline.

The reasons given by you for moving against Port Hudson are satisfactory. It was presumed that you had good and sufficient reasons for the course pursued, although at this distance it seemed contrary to principles and likely to prove unfortunate. . . .

The discharge of nine months' and two-years' men has so reduced our forces that we can hardly defend Washington and Baltimore. The effect of the Copperhead disaffection at the North has prevented enlistments, and the drafting has not yet been attempted. We have been forced to resort to State militia, most of whom refuse to be mustered into the service of the United States. Notwithstanding that Pennsylvania is invaded by a large army, the militia of that State positively refuse to be mustered. This is the work of the politicians.[47]

So was federal inability to take Port Hudson. That event finally occurred formally on July 9, 1863, but only after General Gardner had been given proof that Vicksburg's garrison had surrendered to Grant five days earlier.

Banks was obliged to rush troops back down the reopened Mississippi, lest Confederate Major General Richard Taylor isolate them far out of position to defend New Orleans. Before skedaddling from Port Hudson, however, on July 8 the Bobbin Boy had shared with General Grant his thoughts regarding his next strategic move:

The enemy [Gardner's nigh-starved garrison] *in my rear disposed of, I earnestly desire to move into Texas, which is now denuded of troops. The enemy here is largely composed of Texans. We hope to capture them.*

Will it be possible for you to spare me for this expedition, which should be closed in two months from this date, a division of 10,000 or 12,000 men? I know the claims upon your force. I see that you will hope to strengthen our armies in the east, and propose my request with hesitation, but there is no point where the same number of men could do so much good. I want Western men.[48]

This last was a politic thing for Banks to say to a Western general, although knowledge of it would hardly have endeared the former bobbin boy to the voters up in cotton-starved New England; they had furnished the troops he had recruited in the fall of 1862 for the purpose of invading Texas. Curiously, General-in-Chief Halleck's thinking after Port Hudson was parallel in several respects, or so it might seem from his message to Banks on July 24:

> *I have nothing from you since the 8th.*
>
> *I suppose the first thing done by your army after the fall of Port Hudson was to clean out the Teche and Atchafalaya countries. That being accomplished, your next operations must depend very much upon the condition of affairs.*
>
> *Texas and Mobile will present themselves to your attention. The navy are very anxious for an attack upon the latter place, but I think Texas much the most important. It is possible that Johnston may fall back toward Mobile, but I think he will unite with Bragg.*
>
> *While your army is engaged in cleaning out Southwestern Louisiana, every preparation should be made for an expedition into Texas. Should Johnston be driven from Mississippi, General Grant can send you considerable re-enforcements. The organization of colored troops should be pushed forward as rapidly as possible. They will serve as part of the garrisons of the forts on the river and interior posts, and some of the older regiments will do well in the field.*[49]

At about this time, as if he were reluctant to do or say anything that might disrupt the newly restored counselor-client relationship, A. Lincoln sent a curious note to Secretary of War Stanton:

> *Can we not renew the effort to organize a force to go to Western Texas?*
>
> *Please consult with the General-in-Chief on the subject.*
>
> *If the Governor of New Jersey shall furnish any new regiments, might not they be put into such an expedition? Please think of it.*
>
> *I believe no local object is now more desirable.*[50]

Equally as odd as the President's paragraphing was an abrupt reversal in General Banks' preferences. In a long letter to General Halleck from New Orleans on July 30, he opined: "While the rebel army in the east is occupied at Charleston and at Richmond by our forces, it would be impossible for them to strengthen Mobile to any great extent. It seems to be the favorable opportunity for a movement in that direction."[51]

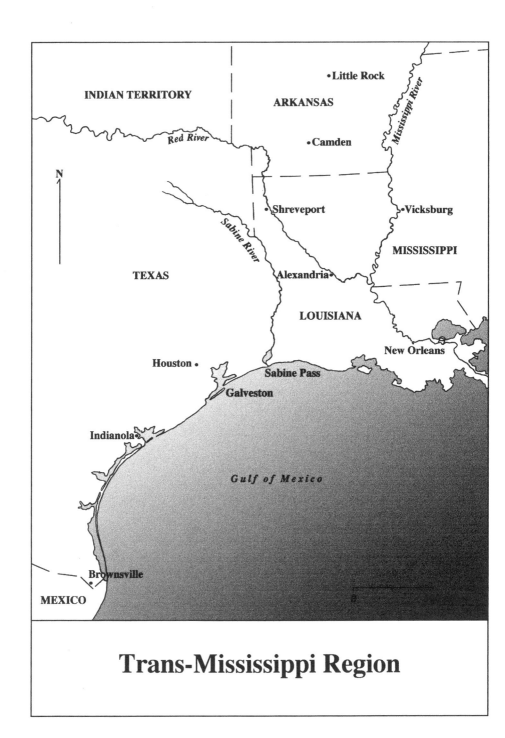

Trans-Mississippi Region

Well, maybe, but just then the message exchanges between New Orleans and Washington were woefully out of comment-and-reply synchronization. Before the Bobbin Boy's letter advocating Mobile as his next objective reached Washington, General Halleck had pressed on in the belief that Banks preferred Texas. On July 31, 1863, Old Brains wrote him:

It is important that we immediately occupy some point or points in Texas. Whether the movement should be made by land or water is not yet decided. We shall await your answer to my dispatch of the 24th. In the meantime every preparation should be made. If by water, Admiral Farragut will co-operate.[52]

On August 1, the next day, the Bobbin Boy was in Vicksburg—visiting General Grant, presumably. From there he sent the general-in-chief a long and detailed series of reasons for moving against Mobile, including his plan of approach and concluding:

The operation need not last more than thirty days, and can scarcely interfere with any other movements east or west. I understand it to meet with General Grant's approval, if it be consistent with the general plans of the Government, upon which condition only I urge it.[53]

Then, suddenly, on August 6, General-in-Chief Halleck sent an order to Banks that was as almost as peremptory as any he ever gave:

There are important reasons why our flag should be restored in some point of Texas with the least possible delay. Do this by land at Galveston, at Indianola, or at any other point you may deem preferable. If by sea, Admiral Farragut will co-operate. There are reasons why this movement should be as prompt as possible.[54]

4

SO FAR, THE UNPLEASANTNESS BETWEEN THE STATES had been entirely a domestic war. True, the Confederacy had tried to gain British and French recognition and support, and the Union had sought to prevent that; General Lee's invasions of Maryland and Pennsylvania had been undertaken in part to demonstrate to Europeans the Second American Revolution's viability. While the Union had been preoccupied with the task of quelling the rebellion, Napoleon III's forces had all but converted Mexico into a French colony. This was a gross violation of the Monroe Doctrine—which President Abraham Lincoln had the duty to enforce.

On June 10, 1863, the invaders took Mexico City and launched a fresh campaign to drive Benito Juarez' troops toward sanctuary in the Sierras and possibly Texas. But the Union was not prepared to fight more than one war at a time, hence the State Department's pressure on the War Department to show the Stars and Stripes north of the Rio Grande.

Recalling that a soldier's first duty is to obey, on August 6, 1863, General Halleck had ordered Nathaniel Banks (in effect) to forget about Mobile and plant some troops somewhere in Texas forthwith. Whether or not he remembered that Banks—in deference to furious New Englanders who understandably felt betrayed by his having taken most of their troops to New Orleans—had put a force ashore on Galveston Island back on Christmas Eve in 1862 only to have it ejected on New Year's Day, Old Brains had no choice but to rely on the Bobbin Boy.

Apparently, General Halleck considered flag-planting to be silly, naive, a nigh-criminal use of military and naval resources in the circumstances. And this may be why he followed-up his brief peremptory order of August 6 with a long, purely military advisory message four days later:

> *In my dispatch to you of the 6th instant, sent by the direction of the Secretary of War, it was left entirely to your own discretion to select any point for occupation in Texas, either on the seaboard or in the interior, the only condition imposed being that the flag of the United States should be again raised and sustained somewhere within the limits of that State.*
>
> *That order, as I understood it at the time, was of a diplomatic rather than of a military character, and resulted from some European complications, or, more properly speaking, was intended to prevent such complications.*
>
> *The effect and force of that order are left precisely as they were at its issue. The authority conferred on you by it is not in the slightest degree changed. You will, therefore, consider the following remarks as suggestions only, and not as instructions.*
>
> *In my opinion, neither Indianola nor Galveston is the proper point of attack. If it be necessary, as urged by Mr. Seward, that the flag be restored to some one point in Texas, that can be best and most safely effected by a combined military and naval movement up Red*

River to Alexandria, Natchitoches, or Shreveport, and the military occupation of Northern Texas.

This would be merely carrying out the plans proposed by you at the beginning of the campaign, and, in my opinion, far superior in its military character to the occupation of Galveston or Indianola.

Nevertheless, your choice is left unrestricted.

In the first place, by adopting the line of the Red River, you retain your connection with your own base, and separate still more the two points of the rebel Confederacy. Moreover, you cut Northern Louisiana and Southern Arkansas entirely off from supplies and re-enforcements from Texas. They are already cut off from the rebel States east of the Mississippi.

If you occupy Galveston or Indianola, you divide your own troops, and enable the enemy to concentrate all of his forces upon either of these points or on New Orleans.

I write this simply as a suggestion and not as a military instruction.[55]

Noteworthy, here, was the general-in-chief's adherence to the Halleck Doctrine even when this particular general in the field had demonstrated his incompetence whenever he had been obliged to exercise military judgment. Moreover, in suggesting a drive up the Red River, Old Brains might have been influenced by a statement the Bobbin Boy had made in a message dated July 23: "It is reported to us from Alexandria that the rebel troops there, expecting a movement from Port Hudson, and learning that the gunboats were ascending Red River, had abandoned the place and retreated to Natchitoches."[56]

On August 15 General Banks replied twice, first in a telegram and then in a letter:

Measures have been already taken to carry into effect your orders. We shall plant the flag in Texas within a week, I hope.

My plan has been to move against Galveston upon the land side, via the Sabine Pass, and from Berwick Bay, via Vermillionville and Niblett's Bluff, to Houston and Galveston, for the trans-portation and artillery. We shall be ready, I think, as soon as General Grant's corps can reach us. The route indicated is that followed by the Texans in their invasions of Western Louisiana.

We can move 8,000 men at once to the Sabine Pass, and thence concentrate rapidly on Galveston, fortifying and holding a position on the mainland or the island only, as may be deemed expedient. From thence operations are practicable in any direction to the interior or to the Rio Grande.

From Galveston, when strongly fortified, I would move a force of 5,000 or more to the Rio Grande, where one or more positions can be so fortified as to be held by a much less force, while we hold Galveston or the interior of the State. This has been my view of operations in Texas from the beginning.

Well, yes; never mind that federal forces had failed to hold their lodgment on Galveston Island once before. Banks went on, in a manner reminiscent of Don Carlos Buell, to provide excuses in advance should he fail:

No movement can be made from the Gulf against Galveston with a certainty of success. Our naval forces are not strong enough, and the enemy's works are too extensive and thorough. The enemy fears only an attack from the land, via Niblett's Bluff, the route I propose, or Alexandria. From that point our success is certain. We learned this from intercepted letters while at Alexandria, in May.[57]

"Mexican and French complications render it exceedingly important," General Halleck telegraphed Banks on August 20, "that the movement ordered against Texas be undertaken without delay."[58] To his credit, the Bobbin Boy developed a plan and marshaled his units in a remarkably short time. "I have made all possible exertions to get a sufficient force into the field to execute the order," he wrote the general-in-chief on August 26, 1863, "but encounter serious difficulties in the preparation." After reciting some of them, he devoted a long passage to his objections to the Alexandria-Shreveport alternative, a subject that was by then irrelevant and extraneous because of "the present low stage of the rivers."

A movement against the Sabine River frontier with Texas provided more than six advantages, strategist Banks argued in that message and again in another one bearing the same date.[59] Evidently, he was covering the contingency that his Sabine Pass plan would fail and that he would be blamed for not having given due thought to Halleck's suggestion.

Fail, the Bobbin Boy's task force most certainly did. At the end of September's first week, four gunboats reached a rendezvous point in the Gulf of Mexico and were joined by twenty-two transports bearing about eight thousand troops under the command of Major General William B. Franklin. What happened at Fort Griffin on the Texas side of the Sabine

River's mouth on September 8 was best and most accurately told by Lieutenant "Dick" Dowling, in happier times a Houston saloon keeper, who commanded the less than fifty Texans who spoiled the Bobbin Boy's operation. On September 9, Dowling reported:

> *On the morning of the 8th, the U.S. gunboat* Clifton *anchored opposite the light-house, and fired twenty-six shells at the fort, most of which passed a little over or fell short; all, however, in excellent range, one shell being landed on the works and another striking the south angle of the fort, without doing any material damage. The firing commenced at 6.30 o'clock and finished at 7.30 o'clock by the gunboat hauling off. During this time we had not replied by a single shot.*
>
> *All was then quiet until 11 o'clock, at which time the* [Confederate] *gunboat* Uncle Ben *steamed down near the fort. The U.S. gunboat* Sachem *opened on her with a 30-pounder Parrott gun. She fired three shots, but without effect, the shots all passing over the fort and missing the* Ben.
>
> *The whole fleet then drew off, and remained out of range until 3.40 o'clock, when the* Sachem *and* Arizona *steamed into line up the Louisiana channel, the* Clifton *and one boat, name unknown, remaining at the junction of the two channels. I allowed the two former boats to approach within 1,200 yards, when I opened fire with the whole of my battery on the foremost boat (the* Sachem*), which, alter the third or fourth round, hoisted the white flag, one of the shots passing through her steam-drum.*
>
> *The* Clifton *in the meantime had attempted to pass up through Texas channel, but receiving a shot which carried away her tiller rope, she became unmanageable, and grounded about 500 yards below the fort, which enabled me to concentrate all my guns on her, which were six in number—two 32 pounder smoothbores; two 24-pounder smoothbores; two 32-pounder howitzers. She withstood our fire some twenty-five or thirty-five minutes, when she also hoisted a white flag. During the time she was aground, she used grape, and her sharpshooters poured an incessant shower of Minie balls into the works.*
>
> *The fight lasted from the time I fired the first gun until the boats surrendered; that was about three-quarters of an hour. I immediately boarded the captured* Clifton, *and proceeded to inspect her magazines, accompanied by one of the ship's officers, and*

discovered it safe and well stocked with ordnance stores. I did not visit the magazine of the Sachem, *in consequence of not having any small boats to board her with. The C. S. gunboat* Uncle Ben *steamed down to the* Sachem *and towed her into the wharf. Her magazine was destroyed by the enemy flooding it.*

Thus it will be seen we captured with 47 men two gunboats, mounting thirteen guns of the heaviest caliber, and about 350 prisoners. All my men behaved like heroes; not a man flinched from his post. Our motto was "victory or death."[60]

"This seems to me to be the most extraordinary feat of the war," wrote Major General John B. Magruder, commanding the District of Texas, New Mexico, and Arizona; and "Prince John" of Yorktown fame provided a few more details. After losing two gunboats and watching a third flee from the fight, the Yankee task force "then backed out and sailed east." Dowling's Texans suffered no casualties.[61]

"It is with regret that I am obliged to report that the effort to effect a landing at Sabine Pass was without success," General Banks reported to Old Brains on September 13, and then—predictably—he opened his profusion of excuses. After citing the "misapprehension of the naval authorities of the real strength of the enemy's position, and the insufficient naval force with which the attempt was made," Banks went on to dismiss the loss of the *Sachem* and the *Clifton:* "The boats were unreliable for any service, on account of their decay and weakness both of hull and machinery." He did not disclose that his armada was turned back by a force of less than fifty Texans, none of whom were hit or taken—but perhaps he was unaware of those damning dimensions of his task force's utterly humiliating repulse.[62]

Banks' intention was to try the land route to Niblett's Bluff on the Sabine and west-southwest from there to Houston and the Rio Grande, or so he told the general-in-chief near the end of his report.[63] Halleck's response on September 30 was surprisingly mild. "The failure," he wrote, "is only another of the numerous examples of the uncertain and unreliable character of maritime descents. The chances are against their success."[64]

General Halleck was referring to seaborne operations, not the kind Grant had conducted at Belmont and up the Tennessee and Cumberland. But he must have fought-off the temptation to remark that, like the *Sachem* and the *Clifton,* the Union leadership employed in the Sabine Pass fiasco had been "unreliable for any service. . . ."

"I do not regard Sabine City in the same light as you do," Old Brains said, adding:

Instead of being "the very center of the circle" of the enemy's operations, it seems to me to be upon the very circumference of his theater of war west of the Mississippi. The center of this theater is some point near Marshall or Nacogdoches. The enemy's line extends from near Little Rock to the mouth of the Rio Grande. The occupation of Sabine City neither cuts this line nor prevents the concentration of all his forces on any point of it which he may select. Nevertheless, as the objects of your expedition are rather political than military, and do not admit of delay, you may be able to accomplish the wishes of the Government by the route you have chosen sooner than by any other.[65]

5

ANY GENERAL-IN-CHIEF, of necessity operating from a desk in Washington, had to find ways of communicating effectively with the distant commanders of the Union's field armies. The Young Napoleon, preoccupied with building his Army of the Potomac, never bothered to make the effort. His successor by default, the amateur Lincoln, may not have realized that such a requirement existed and had failed before he finally perceived it.

It had taken a lawyer with years of experience in dealing with all sorts of eccentric tycoons in a frontier environment to cope with the steady flow and wide range of challenges the field armies' commanders presented. Yet Henry Halleck had never tried to be all things to all men. *Au contraire,* he attracted criticism for adhering staunchly and consistently to principles and relying on them in his dealings with all men. Of course Old Brains had his favorites (Grant and Cump Sherman), and he seems to have been quite comfortable with other men who put principle first (Haupt, Lieber, and Meigs). Even so, he managed to operate with reasonable success with generals whose quirks made it all but impossible for him to respect them (McClellan, Buell, McClernand, Burnside, Hooker, and Banks).

William Starke Rosecrans, however, being neither a political nor a Western general (in the sense that Grant and Sherman were), was a soldier with whom General-in-Chief Halleck apparently found it unusually difficult to reach agreement. At times Old Rosy seemed bent on picking wire-fights with Halleck for the sheer hell of it. On some occasions, however, Rosecrans was right.

Secretary of War Edwin Stanton ignited the fuse of Rosecrans' powder keg by adding two sentences too many in this message on July 7, 1863:

We have just received official confirmation that Vicksburg surrendered to General Grant on the 4th of July. Lee's army overthrown, Grant victorious. You and your noble army now have the chance to give the finishing blow to the rebellion. Will you neglect the chance?[66]

With candor characteristic of Halleck, Old Rosy replied:

Just received your cheering dispatch announcing the fall of Vicksburg and confirming the defeat of Lee. You do not appear to observe the fact that this noble army has driven the rebels from Middle Tennessee, of which my dispatches have advised you. I beg in behalf of this army that the War Department may not overlook so great an event because it was not written in letters of blood. . . .[67]

Just so: Gettysburg had been so near Washington that Meade's victory had eclipsed Grant's partially and William Rosecrans' totally. The absence of any commendation from General Halleck may have been due to the strong efforts Old Brains was obliged to make at roughly the same time to encourage Meade to annihilate General Lee north of the roaring Potomac.

From Tullahoma on July 11, however, Rosecrans wired the general-in-chief:

It is important to know if it will be practicable for Burnside to come in on our left [northern] *flank, and hold the line of the Cumberland* [River]*; if not, a line in advance of it and east of us. . . . The operations now before us involve a great deal of care, labor, watchfulness, and combined effort to insure the successful advance through the mountains on Chattanooga.*[68]

Obviously, General Rosecrans was emitting signals that a third period of build-up of supplies was in the offing—implying, in effect, that it would be a waste of telegraph resources to spur him onward to Chattanooga for a while. Halleck's response two days later was to goad Burnside:

I must again urge upon you the importance of moving forward into

East Tennessee, to cover Rosecrans' left. Telegraph what you are doing toward this object, so that we can have definite information to act upon.[69]

That done, he telegraphed Rosecrans:

General Burnside has frequently been urged to move forward and cover your left by entering East Tennessee. I do not know what he is doing. He seems tied fast to Cincinnati.[70]

"Poor Burn," as McClellan referred to him, was pleasing no one. In a message marked PRIVATE from Cincinnati on July 20, 1863, Captain J. M. Cutts, judge-advocate of Burnside's Department of the Ohio, said to His Excellency Abraham Lincoln:

I advise you to relieve Maj. Gen. A. E. Burnside from command of the Department of the Ohio immediately by telegraph. He has been plausibly pursuing a policy hostile and adverse to your wishes and instructions and those of the Secretary of War and General-in-Chief.

Send some thoroughly brave man to take his place. I cordially recommend Hooker, who is a brave man, and will be very popular.

We are on the eve of important events, which require you to pursue the course I suggest. We are threatened with mobs and riots and bloodshed throughout our entire Western country. Orders 38 has kindled the fires of hatred and contention, and Burnside is foolishly and unwisely excited, and, if continued in command, will disgrace himself, you, and the country, as he did at Fredericksburg.

Please acknowledge the receipt of this dispatch. I am absolutely right. [Stephen] Douglas was my preceptor.[71]

His Excellency allowed the opportunity to subject General Burnside to a second sacking to pass, perhaps in part because Poor Burn had relieved Captain Cutts earlier that day, "to take effect the 23d of June last."[72]

By July 24, however, General Halleck had done his best to press Meade, and he shifted his momentum to Rosecrans in two exhortations bearing the same date:

You must not wait for Johnston to join Bragg, but must move forward immediately against the latter. Take with you hard bread, sugar, coffee, and salt, and push forward rapidly, supplying yourself with forage, bacon, beef, and mutton in the country. Organize supply parties under your quartermasters and commissaries, and live as much as possible on the country. Reduce your trains to the lowest point possible, and move rapidly.

There is great disappointment felt here at the slowness of your advance. Unless you can move more rapidly, your whole campaign will prove a failure, and you will have both Bragg and Johnston against you.[73]

Surely those words were written with the record in mind. Not content with that effort, Old Brains followed it up with a telegram marked PRIVATE AND CONFIDENTIAL:

The tone of some of your replies to my dispatches lately would indicate that you thought I was unnecessarily urging you forward. On the contrary, I have deemed it absolutely necessary, not only for the country but also for your own reputation, that your army should remain no longer inactive.

The patience of the authorities here has been completely exhausted, and if I had not repeatedly promised to urge you forward, and begged for delay, you would have been removed from the command. It has been said that you are as inactive as was General Buell, and the pressure for your removal has been almost as strong as it was in his case.

I am well aware that people at a distance do not appreciate the obstacles and difficulties which they would see if nearer by; but, whether well founded or without any foundation at all, the dissatisfaction really exists, and I deem it my duty, as a friend, to represent it to you truly and fairly; and I think I ought to do so, if for no other reason, because it was at my earnest solicitations that you were given the command.[74]

Telegraphed at nine o'clock the next morning, General Rosecrans' reply was both polite and firm:

Your views accord with my own. All your suggestions about baggage and rations have been anticipated and carried out from the beginning of our movement, and are now being carried out with all the energy of which we are capable. We never think of moving with any but the minimum baggage, nor of taking anything but essential parts of rations; but to move our troops beyond our means of supply would but break down and disable both men and horses without results. This, I am sure, you do not desire.

Any disappointment that may be felt at the apparent slowness of our movements would be readily removed by a knowledge of the obstacles and a true military appreciation of the advantages of not moving prematurely. I confess I should like to avoid such remarks and letters as I am receiving lately from Washington, if I could do so without injury to the public service.

You will, I think, find the officers of this army as anxious for success, and as willing to exert themselves to secure it, as any member of the Government can be. As to subsistence being drawn from the country over which we are to travel to Chattanooga, it was always barren—with but few fertile spots. Those spots have been gleaned and scraped by rebels with a powerful cavalry force ever since last winter. We shall get some hay and cattle in the region of Fayetteville, Huntsville, and south of there—none south or east of us. We shall move promptly, and endeavor not to go back.

What movements of General Grant will affect us?[75]

Not yet having reached a meeting of the minds with Grant, and perhaps noting that Rosecrans seemed to be drifting away into details, that afternoon Old Brains again tried to return the Army of the Cumberland's commander's attention to his mission:

The great object you will have in view is to drive Bragg from East Tennessee before he can be re-enforced by Johnston. It is said that supplies will be found abundant in the valley, if the enemy is not allowed time to take them away; and, moreover, that there is a large loyal population ready to declare for the Union.

The President has repeatedly promised these people relief, and has repeatedly and repeatedly urged that forces for this purpose be pushed forward. The pressure for this movement at this time is so strong that neither you nor I can resist it. Unless it is made while Grant's army occupies Johnston, there probably will not be another opportunity this year.[76]

General Rosecrans' one-sentence response bordered on insolence: "Assure the President that whatever prudence and energy we have shall be put to work to save and hold that region [East Tennessee], but these must go together, or the last state of those loyal men will be worse than their present condition."[77]

General-in-Chief Halleck hardly bothered to conceal his exasperation in his reply:

> *I perceive from the tone of your dispatch to-day that you are displeased at my urging you to move forward your army against Bragg. In other words, general, while I am blamed here for not urging you forward more rapidly, you are displeased at my doing so.*
>
> *Whatever I have written or telegraphed to you on this subject has been from motives of kindness and friendship. It was my only desire to impress upon you the wishes and expectations of the Government, in order that you might be fully acquainted with those wishes.*
>
> *Having now explained to you frankly that you can have no possible grounds for your tone of displeasure toward me, I shall not again refer to this matter.*[78]

It may well have been that General Rosecrans was reminding Old Brains of the Young Napoleon and Don Carlos Buell—both of whom had melted the telegraph lines with their inexhaustible supplies of excuses for failures not yet experienced. Also, after the effusions of blood along Stones River, Old Rosy had shown a preference for maneuvering Bragg's army out of his way. And his eclipsed but successful and nigh-bloodless Tullahoma Campaign was precisely the sort of operation closest to McClellan's heart's desire.

The phony Napoleon, however, had displayed a reluctance bordering on cowardice to fight in any circumstances. Even before Lincoln summoned him to Washington after the First Bull Run disaster, out in western Virginia McClellan had balked instead of leading an attack intended to make it easier for Rosecrans to strike the Confederates opposing them in the rear; by tearing into the defenders anyway Old Rosy had saved Little Mac's bacon that day, yet his superior got all the credit.[79] General Rosecrans' personal courage may have saved his army on Stones River's first day. But had his success in employing McClellanesque maneuvers against Bragg in the Tullahoma Campaign deluded him into setting aside Old Brains' urgings to concentrate his forces and *destroy* the enemy, not merely to provoke him into withdrawing to his fall-back positions?

For Old Brains to have hammered Rosecrans so severely suggests that he was losing confidence in the general he had placed in command of Buell's army. Also, George Thomas had made the key moves that had driven Braxton Bragg's forces into Chattannoga's defenses—and "Old Pap" was in place if the Union's war managers decided to give him a second chance to replace a superior.

But if Halleck's friendly proddings could not budge Old Rosy, what might?

Spurring Ambrose Burnside had also been on General Halleck's list of things to do on July 25. In replying to Poor Burn's inquiry regarding the return of his IX Corps troops from service under Grant, he said:

Whether the Ninth Corps will be returned to your department or sent to General Rosecrans will depend upon the enemy's movements. General Rosecrans' advance will force Bragg to withdraw the rebel troops from East Tennessee. This is the time for your troops to advance and occupy that country, where, it is said, there are thousands ready to join our ranks.

The present opportunity must not be lost. The column must be immediately organized and moved forward. It must not be stopped or called back by petty raids. The militia and Home Guards must take care of these raids.

Telegraph where the 6,000 troops for East Tennessee now are, and how you intend to move them. I wish these particulars, as there must be a concert of action with other forces.[80]

Like Rosecrans, at times Ambrose Burnside did not seem to take the general-in-chief of the Union armies seriously. Halleck's message had been only a few words short of being a direct order to move—yet Poor Burn's reply, on July 28 (three days later) was nigh-totally unresponsive:

The indications are that a considerable force of the enemy is advancing into Kentucky. Will inform you of their movements from time to time, and do the best we can with the force at hand. It is reported that it is a portion of Bragg's army, but not entirely reliable. The forces in East Tennessee, I am satisfied, have been underestimated.[81]

Evidently, however, during the passage of a few days Halleck's other problem general had given much thought to Old Brains' series of admonitions. In a message marked PRIVATE and dated August 1, 1863, William Rosecrans wrote him at great length but very much to the point:

I thank you for your notes of the 24th and 25th instant [ultimo], and for your support and confidence hitherto. These letters relieve my mind from a growing apprehension that the injustice which I have experienced from the War Department was extending to you.

But as my ambition is something like your own—to discharge my duty to God and our country—I say to you frankly that whenever the Government can replace me by a commander in whom they have more confidence, they ought to do so, and take the responsibility of the result. Meanwhile let me call your attention to the conditions of the problem before this army:

1st. Our base at Louisville is 264 miles distant from our present position.

2d. We are 83 miles from our principal depot—Nashville.

3d. We must transport all our subsistence, our clothing, camp and garrison equipage, wagons, animals, ammunition, and most of our forage over these distances by raft.

4th. We have before us 60 or 70 miles of barren mountain country, destitute of forage and subsistence, traversed by a few difficult roads, over which to advance.

5th. We have to cross the difficult defile of the Tennessee, a river from 600 to 1,000 yards wide, in the face of a powerful enemy, and maneuver or fight him from an intrenched position, in a mountainous country with several lines of retreat; the nearest points of this position being from 26 to 45 miles from our railroad over mountains.

6th. To advance in the face of these obstacles is not the only nor even the most important point in the problem. We must so advance as never to recede. The citizens say, and not without justice, "Whip our armies, and then, when we no longer fear their return to power, we will show you that we are satisfied to be in the Union; but until you do that, we are not safe from proscription."

7th. Not only so, but this must be done in view of the possibility of Joe Johnston joining Bragg.

These are the conditions of the first problem. The preliminaries to its successful solution are, first, to open the railroad, establish and provide for guarding depots at the nearest accessible points, and, secondly, to provide means of crossing the river and maintain communication over it.

To these ends every effort is now being bent. Rest assured these

things would have to be done by any commander, and I think we are
doing them as rapidly as our means will admit.[82]

General Halleck did not reply until August 4, three days later, suggesting that A. Lincoln and his secretary of war may have consumed some time in pondering Rosecrans' appraisal of his situation. Old Brains' response was terse: "Your forces must move forward without further delay. You will daily report the movement of each corps till you cross the Tennessee River."[83]

Rosecrans' reply was discouraging evidence of how far from concurrence he and Halleck actually were—and also that the Army of the Cumberland's commander had long since forgotten that a soldier's first duty is to obey. Telegraphed Old Rosy to his general-in-chief:

> *As I have been determined to cross the [Tennessee] river as soon as practicable, and have been making all preparations, and getting such information as may enable me to do so without being driven back like Hooker, I wish to know if your order is intended to take away my discretion as to the time and manner of moving my troops?*[84]

No answer could have been more direct than Halleck's the next day: "The orders for the advance of your army, and that its movements be reported daily, are peremptory."[85]

That message sent, the general-in-chief telegraphed Burnside in Cincinnati:

> *You will immediately move with a column of 12,000 men by the most practicable roads on East Tennessee, making Knoxville or its vicinity your objective point.*
>
> *As soon as the Ninth Corps arrives, it will serve as a reserve, and follow you as rapidly as possible. . . . You will report by telegraph all the movements of your troops.*
>
> *As soon as you reach East Tennessee, you will endeavor to connect with the forces of General Rosecrans, who has peremptory orders to move forward. The Secretary of War repeats his orders that you move your headquarters from Cincinnati to the field, and take command of the troops in person.*[86]

George McClellan had once remarked in a letter to his wife that

"Burn" was slow, or something to that effect, and the oddly bewhiskered general inadvertently confirmed Little Mac's judgment in his reply on August 6, 1863, to Halleck's direct order:

> *Your dispatch is received, and your order will be obeyed, for I had already determined to commence the movement, as you had been informed by my dispatches of July 24 and August 4.*
>
> *The Secretary of War has never, to my knowledge, ordered me to leave Cincinnati. . . . I have never willfully disobeyed an order of the Secretary of War, or any other order since this war commenced, but have given the Government an honest and unselfish support. I have submitted of late, without complaint, to your uniform refusal of my requests, which were made for the good of the public service in this department, but I am not willing to let the imputation that I have disobeyed orders go unnoticed.*
>
> *Your general instructions, as I understand them, leave me at liberty to do just what I have done without them; that is, to use my own judgment as to combination of forces, route, &c. The concentration is being made as rapidly as possible.*[87]

Stunned as Old Brains may understandably have been by the apparent workings of Ambrose Burnside's mind, surely he received a similar discouraging jolt the next day, August 6, when General Rosecrans' response to Halleck's peremptory order reached him:

> *My arrangements for beginning a continuous movement will be completed and the execution begun by Monday next. . . . To obey your order literally would be to push our troops at once into the mountains on narrow and difficult roads, destitute of pasture and forage, and short of water, where they would not be able to maneuver as exigencies may demand, and would certainly cause ultimate delay and probably disaster.*
>
> *If, therefore, the movement which I propose cannot be regarded as obedience to your order, I respectfully request a modification of it, or to be relieved from the command.*[88]

Even so, reflecting the patience of Job for which Abraham Lincoln would later be granted American sainthood, General Halleck made what may have been intended as his last effort to jar William Starke Rosecrans into obedience:

I have communicated to you the wishes of the Government in plain and unequivocal terms. The object has been stated, and you have been directed to lose no time in reaching it. The means you are to employ, and the roads you are to follow, are left to your own discretion.

If you wish to promptly carry out the wishes of the Government, you will not stop to discuss mere details. In such matters I do not interfere.[89]

General-in-Chief Halleck's forbearance and extra efforts were greeted only with defiance: "I can only repeat the assurance given before the issue of the [peremptory] order," Rosecrans telegraphed him. "This army will move with all the dispatch compatible with the successful execution of our [preparatory] work."[90]

Even then, Halleck refused to remove Rosecrans and give the Army of the Cumberland to George Thomas. On August 9, 1863, in another message marked PRIVATE, the general-in-chief demonstrated how far he was willing to go to reach an understanding with Old Rosy:

After my private notes of the 24th and 25th of July, I did not intend to write any further, urging your advance; I will, however, add a few words in answer to yours of the 1st instant.

If you suppose the Secretary of War has any personal hostility to you, or would not rejoice at your success as much as that of any other general, I think you are mistaken. I do not think he would willingly do you any injustice, but, as I have before written, neither the President nor the Secretary have been satisfied with your long delays.

This has been more particularly the case since detachments were sent from Bragg's army to re-enforce Johnston. Since then they have both repeatedly urged me to push your army forward into East Tennessee. They have seen all my dispatches to you and all of yours to me on this subject. In my communications I have in no case exaggerated the feeling of disappointment and dissatisfaction which has been manifested to me.

In your official dispatches, as well as in your private notes, you seem to be laboring under the impression that the authorities here were making war on you. There never was a greater mistake. I know of no one here who has not the kindest and most friendly feelings for you.

Nevertheless, many of your dispatches have been exceedingly annoying to the War Department. No doubt such was not your intention, but they certainly have been calculated to convey the impression that you were not disposed to carry out the wishes of the Department, at least in the manner and at the time desired. It is said that you "do not draw straight in the traces, but are continually kicking out or getting one leg over."

No one doubts your good intentions and your great interest in the cause, and your desire to secure its success.

I have endeavored in this matter to do my duty fully to you and to the Government, by endeavoring to convey to you the wishes of the Government as expressed to me, and there I must leave the matter.[91]

6

WHETHER GENERAL HALLECK'S prodding finally had some effect, or Rosecrans' build-up of supplies reached a level he considered satisfactory, on August 17, 1863, the Army of the Cumberland left its camps south of Tullahoma bound for Chattanooga. Concurrently, Ambrose Burnside's forces headed for Knoxville. Those departures marked the end of what may have been the most productive periods of General-in-Chief Halleck's service since his arrival in Washington just over a year earlier.

Given the Union armies' triple victories on or near July 4, 1863, Halleck had faced what turned out to be five challenges:

- To determine what to do with Grant's army after Vicksburg
- To persuade Meade to destroy Lee's army north of the Potomac, and then to keep him from resigning
- To cure Rosecrans' resentment over the war managers' failure to give him much credit for his Tullahoma Campaign, and then to spur him on toward Chattanooga
- To provoke Ambrose Burnside into advancing toward East Tennesse and, in so doing, to support Rosecrans' much-desired thrust to Chattanooga
- To chill Nathaniel Banks' ardor for seizing Mobile and redirect it into a campaign whose object was planting the Stars and Stripes in Texas

Henry Halleck responded to each of these challenges as though it were the only one he was attempting to advance. In fact, on almost every day of the six weeks or so of his second summer as the Union armies' general-in-chief, he was dealing with two or more of those complex cases at the same time.

Moreover, although Old Brains' relationship with A. Lincoln had improved remarkably, pressure imposed on him by the President and Edwin Stanton often compelled him to stretch the Halleck Doctrine to the outer limits of its elasticity. Although he certainly agreed with kindred spirit Herman Haupt that Meade ought not to have been so sluggish after Gettysburg and that he ought not to have let General Lee's army reach Virginia without enduring another mauling, Halleck had been obliged to apply coercion to the point where General Meade sought relief from command. Meade, the field general on the scene, was the best judge of conditions—not Halleck or even Haupt and certainly not Abraham Lincoln.

Similarly, Western service veteran Halleck had to have understood, much more clearly than Lincoln or Stanton, Rosecrans' need to amass huge stockpiles before sending his men into the complex terrain of southeastern Tennessee; yet, with Grant's, Meade's, Burnside's, and Banks' cases hanging in the balance, the general-in-chief could hardly have *again* told Lincoln, "I hold that the General in the field is the best judge of conditions," saying, in effect, *If you want Rosecrans removed, do it yourself.*

Actually, though no one else seemed to realize it at the time, by his day-to-day actions and his willingness to take on and cope with all sorts of challenges concurrently, Old Brains was defining the position of general-in-chief. In so doing, however, he was setting a standard of personal performance that could be matched only by another seasoned lawyer used to advancing a number of cases at the same time who was also a soldier steeped in military art and science.

That Henry Wager Halleck was a *soldier* was another point easily overlooked. As a lawyer, hardly anyone would have thought him wrong if he had resigned from such a tangled relationship and left his client in *United States* v. *Confederacy* swinging in the wind. Old Brains would probably not have passed inspection had he turned out for a parade. He was, however, unfailingly aware of his duty to his commander-in-chief despite Lincoln's faults, and he maintained the highest standard of the Government's honor as well as his own; in every decision he made he put his country first.

Henry Halleck said it best, as usual, in a letter to Cump Sherman on February 16, 1864:

The great difficulty in the office of General-in-Chief is, that it is not understood by the country. The responsibility and odium thrown upon it do not belong to it.

I am simply a military adviser of the Secretary of War and the President, and must obey and carry out what they decide upon, whether I concur in their decisions or not. As a good soldier I obey the orders of my superiors. If I disagree with them in opinion I say so; but when they decide, it is my duty faithfully to carry out their decision.

Moreover, I cannot say to the public I approve this and I disapprove that. I have no right to say this, as it might embarrass the execution of a measure fully decided on. My mouth is closed except when officially called on to give such opinion.

It is my duty to strengthen the hands of the President as Commander-in-Chief, not to weaken them by factious opposition. I have, therefore, cordially co-operated with him in every plan decided upon, although I have never hesitated to differ in opinion.

I must leave it to history to vindicate or condemn my own opinions and plans.[92]

15 ★ Halleck's Lieutenants

$\mathcal{A}$ s STONEWALL JACKSON LOOKED UPON THE WAR from Valhalla during the high summer of 1863, he must have been fascinated—at times amused, at others utterly appalled, but always fascinated—by what was happening on both sides.

Lieutenant General Jackson had been able to fight as part of a concentration, independently as Lee's maneuvering element, and in defense (Fredericksburg and Antietam). But his finest moments may have been when he was jerking Acting General-in-Chief Lincoln's forces from tidewater Virginia to the Shenandoah Valley and then whipping one fragment of them after another in battles fought on ground of his choosing; or bewildering John Pope by flailing around in the Yankees' rear; or by wrecking Oliver O. Howard's corps west of Chancellorsville, dooming Fighting Joe Hooker's campaign to be recorded as still another federal disaster.

Old Jack achieved, through maneuver and hard fighting, the results the Young Napoleon sought to obtain (at least on paper) through grandiose strategic envelopments and no bloodshed to speak of, but never did. As an afficianado of sweeps, General Lee's right arm might had approved and even applauded Rosecrans' Tullahoma Campaign, during which Old Rosy had not only split his army but had intimidated Bragg into withdrawing from one position after another. Jackson might also have relished the irony of Rosecrans' having turned General-in-Chief Henry Halleck's customary advocacy of concentration on its head—and having gotten away way with it.

But from Valhalla, Old Jack, who never had shown much respect for the Confederate war managers (except General Lee) anyway, surely would have noted with distress that (except Lee) all of his former superiors, Braxton Bragg, and Bragg's insubordinate subordinates, were shooting themselves in their feet by *squabbling.* Jefferson Davis and almost all of the generals involved were West Point graduates who knew better. But once Bragg had allowed his corps commanders to obey only those of his direct orders they choose to, Jackson could not have been surprised by the outcome.[1]

Absent Lieutenant General Jackson's presence, by the heartbreaking end of his Gettysburg Campaign, General Lee had discovered to his sorrow that the gods of war are not to be ignored with impunity. Splitting his army—as Lee had at Second Manassas, before Sharpsburg, and on several occasions during Chancellorsville—had been his responses to necessity as well as manifestations of his nigh-matchless audacity. But his successes prior to Gettysburg may have caused the Army of Northern Virginia's commander to try once too often to accomplish too much with too few troops and no leaders comparable to the late and much-missed Old Jack.

And so it was that in mid-August 1863, Rosecrans appeared to be repeating the strategy he had employed in his Tullahoma Campaign: using his four corps as separate maneuvering elements, bypassing Chattanooga, and pursuing Bragg into the mountainous terrain of Northwestern Georgia. Would the gods of war allow Rosecrans to mock them a second time?

Unwittingly, General Rosecrans endorsed the Halleck Doctrine while expressing his contempt for rear echelon thinking in a message dated August 22, almost a week after he launched his campaign to maneuver Bragg into withdrawing to Atlanta. Old Rosy wrote Halleck:

> *The contempt for our opinions, apparent from the War Department, arises from a want of knowledge of the circumstances. But you know what it is to advance with a great army, even over 25 miles of miry barrens; but when it comes to 30 miles of barrens, 70 miles of mountains, and two small rivers, and, finally, the great Tennessee—as broad here as at Pittsburg Landing—you know the magnitude of the work.*
>
> *I therefore expect consideration from the General-in-Chief. I ask it for the brave, true, and earnest officers of this command.*
>
> *But, general, the course of the War Department toward these officers' opinions, and the contemptuous silence with which our success was treated, has produced a feeling that the Secretary is unjust. As for myself, I am quite sure you, even you, wholly misunderstand me. You take my remonstrances and importunities for complaints. I know that from your dispatches last autumn.[2]*

McClellanesque, this was, and it called to mind two ancient sayings: *Pride goeth before a great fall*, and *Whom the gods would destroy, they first make mad*. Yet in the last days of August and the opening weeks of September, it seemed that Old Rosy's scorn of concentration had wrought another victory over Braxton Bragg. Rosecrans' northernmost corps took Chattanooga without a fight, and the three federal columns rampaging through the passes and valleys south and east of there managed to penetrate so far and so widely that they were separated from each other by up to forty miles.

This was not strategy; it was an indication that the army commander had lost control of his campaign. Rosecrans stood to lose all three of his maneuvering elements; he had given Bragg a marvelous opportunity to whip them one at a time. And so it might have been if the Confederate chain of command had not rusted and broken.

But Rosecrans ordered a concentration just in time. While his men had been admiring the scenery along their various routes, Braxton Bragg had been receiving reinforcements—concentrating, drawing in forces from Joe Johnston's survivors of the belated attempt to lift the siege of Vicksburg and even Lieutenant General James Longstreet's corps from General Lee's army in central Virginia.

General-in-Chief Halleck had decided as early as September 11, 1863, that sooner rather than later Rosecrans would probably need every man he could get, whereupon he ordered almost every general within reach of telegraph wire to rush troops to cover potential threats to Rosecrans' flanks at points along the Tennessee River downstream and upstream from Chattanooga; Burnside he directed to move from Knoxville, which he had occupied recently, down to help Old Rosy in every way possible.

Ironically, both contending armies confronted each other near the course of the Chickamauga River, a tributary of the Tennessee about twenty miles or so southeast of Chattanooga: *Chickamauga* was an Indian name meaning river of death. On September 19, 1863, Bragg opened attacks westward into Rosecrans' hastily prepared log fortifications but failed to achieve anything worthy of the day's effusion of blood. But by the next morning, Longstreet's divisions had completed their train ride covering nearly a thousand round-about miles over five railroads, instead of the one of perhaps 550 miles that they could have used if Burnside had not taken Knoxville.[3] And on the second day, Longstreet massed his troops into a fist that struck and shattered the Yankee lines at the spot where Rosecrans had just moved a division out of its position toward another. In the ensuing panic and utter rout of the troops who had been in the southern half of the Union line, the Roman Catholic army commander crossed himself and told

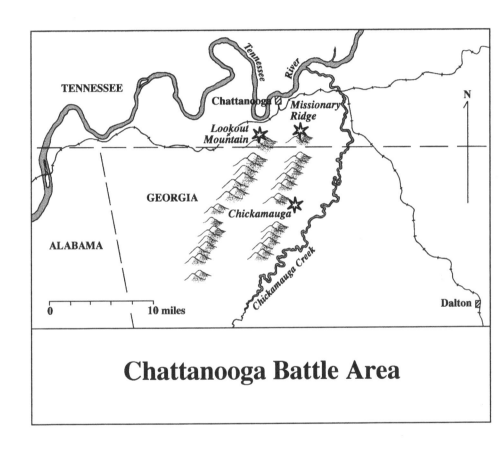

Chattanooga Battle Area

the officers gathered around him at his headquarters: "If you care to live any longer, get away from here!"[4]

Chattanooga became the destination toward which Rosecrans, Little Phil Sheridan, and other federals by the tens of thousands scrambled. But while they were clogging the few roads, George Thomas held his corps solidly in place—blocking the Confederate pursuit and earning the nickname, "the Rock of Chickamauga."

Whatever pride Stonewall Jackson may have experienced from Valhalla as he had watched Longstreet smite the Yankees hip and thigh and win Bragg's battle, however, was dashed by the Confederate army commander's incredible refusal to exploit "Old Peter's" success that night or indeed for another day or two. "You have played the part of a damned scoundrel and are a coward," cavalryman Nathan Bedford Forrest told his commanding officer, "and if you were any part of a man I would slap your jaws and force you to resent it. . . . I say to you that if you ever again try to interfere with me or cross my path it will be at the peril of your life."[5]

Meanwhile, Rosecrans—the only Union army commander ever to have been completely stampeded from a battle still in progress—pulled Old Pap Thomas' gallant corps inside Chattanooga's defenses. There, ironically, Rosecrans, who had twice barely escaped being relieved for too much stockpiling, was obliged to endure the added humiliation of putting his men on short rations and watching his draft animals die of starvation while Braxton Bragg's troops undertook a siege.

By early October 1863, almost all of General Bragg's subordinates shared Forrest's opinion of him. Longstreet, however, had sensed from the moment of his arrival that if he were going to accomplish anything, he had better do it on his own—hence Rosecrans' whipping. Old Pete's regard for Bragg went straight down from there, and his animosity was reciprocated. Before long, Bragg would send Longstreet's division up to drive Ambrose Burnside out of Knoxville. This, ironically, would make it easier for the Union's war managers to cope with situations near both cities in ways Braxton Bragg would find deplorable and that would also cast some very long shadows.

2

IN THE COURSE OF TELEGRAPHING commanders throughout the Union to rush reinforcements to Rosecrans, General Halleck had been obliged to send essentially the same message to five or more destinations and monitor the results. "As three separate armies were now to operate in the same field," Old Brains wrote in his Annual Report for 1863, "it seemed necessary to have a single commander. . . . General Grant, by his distinguished services, and his superior rank to all the other generals in the West, seemed entitled to this general command, but, unfortunately, he was at this time in New Orleans, unable to take the field."[6]

Halleck, underestimating Rosecrans' ability to get in trouble, had authorized Grant's trip south. While in the Crescent City, however, Grant fell from his horse and suffered three broken ribs, paralysis of one side, and concussion.[7]

But making Ulysses Grant supreme commander in the West was too good an idea to set aside any longer than his recuperation required, and in the meantime another positive development emerged in Washington in the wake of Rosecrans' disgrace at Chickamauga. On the night of September 23, 1863, at a conference at which the Union's war managers were joined by two cabinet members, General Hooker, and a few other officials, the discussion turned to ways of getting reinforcements to Rosecrans in the shortest possible time. Secretary of War Stanton argued that by taking control of the railroads, he could move thirty thousand troops from Meade's Army of the Potomac to the vicinity of Chattanooga in five days. Halleck, Lincoln, and Fighting Joe doubted that so many men could be moved that far in so short a time. But Stanton's suggestion was adopted, and before midnight he had sent telegrams to railroad executives summoning them to Washington or requesting information about availability of rolling stock. At 2:30 a.m. the next morning, September 24, General-in-Chief Halleck telegraphed Meade:

> *Please answer if you have positively determined to make any immediate movement. If not, prepare the Eleventh and Twelfth Corps to be sent to Washington, as soon as cars can be sent to you. The troops should have five days' cooked provisions. Cars will probably be there by the morning of the 25th.*[8]

This massive troop movement, of course, emulated the two the Confederates had conducted—Bragg's shift of his army from Tupelo via Mobile and Atlanta to Chattanooga the year before, and Longstreet's corps' long, roundabout train ride from Virginia to Chickamauga. Stanton's achievement took a little longer than he had predicted, and along the way Major General Joseph Hooker was placed in command of the troops. When they arrived at Stevenson, Alabama, downstream from Chattanooga, they were given the mission of opening a supply line into the besieged city.

Meanwhile, in Knoxville Ambrose Burnside, who had never quite understood the Halleck Doctrine, was learning that A. Lincoln fully supported it—and its author. On September 27, 1863, Poor Burn sent Halleck a long telegram in which he sought clarification of orders but also provided complaints and excuses worthy of the master of those arts, Don Carlos Buell. And concurrently, as if to make sure he got the general-in-chief's attention, he sent His Excellency a note: "I have just telegraphed General Halleck very fully, asking an explanation of your order [to reenforce General Rosecrans], and anxiously await a reply."[9]

Burnside's messages were received at around 6:00 p.m. Within an hour Lincoln had sent him the first of two replies, both reflecting opinion and style contributed by Old Brains. In it, he (or they) said:

> *Your dispatch just received. My order to you meant simply that you should save Rosecrans from being crushed out, believing if he lost his position you could not hold East Tennessee in any event; and that if he held his position, East Tennessee was substantially safe in any event. This dispatch is in no sense an order. General Halleck will answer you fully.*[10]

Then, at 8:00 p.m., Lincoln signed the second reply:

> *It was suggested to you, not ordered, that you should move to Rosecrans on the north side of the river, because it was believed the enemy would not permit you to join him if you should move on the south side. Hold your present positions, and send Rosecrans what you can spare in the quickest and safest way. In the mean time hold the remainder as nearly in readiness to go to him as you can consistent with the duty it is to perform while it remains. East Tennessee can be no more than temporarily lost so long as Chattanooga is firmly held.*[11]

Finally, at 8:30 that evening General Halleck provided Poor Burn with chapter and verse:

> *Your orders before leaving Kentucky, and frequently repeated since, were to connect your right with General Rosecrans' left, so that, if the*

enemy concentrated on one, the other would be able to assist. General Rosecrans was attacked on Chickamauga Creek and driven back to Chattanooga, which he holds, waiting for your assistance.

Telegram after telegram has been sent to you to go to his assistance with all your available force, you being the judge of what troops it was necessary, under the circumstances, to leave in East Tennessee. The route by which you were to reach General Rosecrans was also left to your discretion.

When he was forced to fall back on Chattanooga you were advised (not ordered) to move on the north side of the Tennessee River, lest you might be cut off by the enemy on the south side. The danger of the latter movement being pointed out to you, you were left to decide for yourself.

The substance of all telegrams from the President and from me is, you must go to General Rosecrans' assistance, with all your available force, by such route as, under the advices given you from here and such information as you can get, you may deem most practicable. The orders are very plain, and you cannot mistake their purport. It only remains for you to execute them.

General Rosecrans is holding Chattanooga and waiting reinforcements from you. East Tennessee must be held at all hazards, if possible.

The President has just shown me his telegram, which is added, and in which I fully concur.[12]

3

STONEWALL JACKSON HAD TAKEN Ambrose Burnside's measure at Fredericksburg, and so he may not have been too shocked to discover, as he watched from Valhalla, that the general with the strange facial adornments had not grown either in intelligence or obedience. There was nothing much else to look at until early in October when General Lee made a feeble thrust up to Bristoe Station on the Orange & Alexandria toward a Third Manassas, only to be thrown back. But, man of few words that he had been, Old Jack must have relished the manner in which Halleck responded when General Meade confessed that Lee had again eluded him. Old Brains wired Meade merely: "When King Joseph wrote to Napoleon that he could not ascertain the position and strength of the enemy's army the Emperor replied: 'Attack him and you will soon find out.' "[13]

Had General Jackson found a kindred spirit in Halleck, a man who was so very different from him in almost every respect?

All combat soldiers in every war have looked upon the rear echelons of their armies with scorn and contempt, but Old Jack in particular may well have been very interested in the progress of a Yankee bureaucrat's efforts to spur his army commanders to locate the forces opposing them *and fight them*. General Lee, temporarily occupying a position in the spring of 1862 similar to Halleck's, had provided exactly that kind of encouragement to Jackson: hence the Shenandoah Valley Campaign. And once Lee took command of the Army of Northern Virginia, he needed no guidance from Richmond. But, having no Lees, what might Old Brains achieve?

Major General George Gordon Meade, having all but ignored the real Napoleon's advice to King Joseph, the general-in-chief of the Union armies tried again on October 15 to prod the Old Snapping Turtle:

> *Reports from Richmond make Lee's present force only 55,000. Is he not trying to bully you, while the mass of the rebel armies are concentrating against Rosecrans? I cannot see it in any other light. Instead of retreating, I think you ought to give him battle. From all the information I can get, his force is very much inferior to yours.*[14]

Such was the situation as viewed from Washington, but on that same day's evening, one of Meade's ablest corps commanders, Major General Gouverneur K. Warren, telegraphed his army commander:

> *I think Lee's game is blocked, and that he will retreat when pressed. It may be, though, that he still contemplates an advance around our right. I believe we can whip him in any fair fight even by attacking. If you wish, I can push forward again and see what is going on in my front, if you are still in doubt about the enemy's movements.*[15]

On the next day Lincoln shared his thoughts with the general-in-chief in this note:

> *Doubtless in making the present movement, Lee gathered in all the available scraps, and added them to Hill's and Ewell's corps, but that is all, and he made the movement in the belief that four corps had left General Meade, and Meade's apparently avoiding a collision with him has confirmed him in the belief.*
>
> *If General Meade can now attack him on a field no more than*

equal for us, and will do so with all the skill and courage which he, his officers, and men possess, the honor will be his if he succeeds, and the blame may be mine if he fails.[16]

On October 18, a short message from Halleck to Meade contained this suggestion:

If Lee has turned his back on you to cross the mountains, he certainly has seriously exposed himself to your blows, unless his army can move 2 miles to your 1. Fight him again before he draws you out at such a distance from your base as to expose your communications to his raids.[17]

Meade replied promptly: "It is impossible to move this army until I know something more definite of [the] position of the enemy. . . ."[18] Halleck wired back:

Lee is unquestionably bullying you. If you cannot ascertain his movements, I certainly cannot. If you pursue him and fight him, I think you will find out where he is. I know of no other way.[19]

This was more than the Old Snapping Turtle could bear. That night he telegraphed Halleck:

If you have any orders to give me, I am prepared to receive and obey them, but I must insist on being spared the inflictions of such truisms in the guise of opinions as you have recently honored me with, particularly as they were not asked for. I take this occasion to repeat what I have before stated, that if my course, based on my own judgment, does not meet with approval, I ought to be, and desire to be, relieved from command.[20]

What General Meade needed, obviously, was a two weeks' leave in some of Joe Hooker's favorite places in Washington. What he got the next day, however, was this from the general-in-chief:

General Rosecrans continually reports arrival of troops from Lee's army. . . . He thinks the enemy's main force is concentrating there.
    Under these circumstances it is continually urged upon me

that you ought to ascertain Lee's force and position, in order that the Government might at least know the actual facts. As you could not ascertain otherwise, I have repeated the suggestion made to me of the necessity of giving battle.

If I have repeated truisms it has not been to give offense, but to give you the wishes of the Government. If in conveying these wishes, I have used words which were unpleasing, I sincerely regret it.[21]

"Your explanation of your intentions is accepted," the Army of the Potomac's commander responded, "and I thank you for it."[22]

4

OF COURSE, HALLECK WANTED TO KEEP General Meade as commander of the Army of the Potomac. "Meade has thus far proved an excellent general," he had remarked in a letter to Ulysses Grant in July, "the only one who has ever fought the Army of the Potomac well. He seems the right man in the right place. Hooker was more than a failure. Had he remained in command, he would have lost the army and the capital. . . . I sincerely wish I was with you in the West. I am utterly sick of this political hell."[23]

In a similar mood, the general-in-chief wrote Major General John M. Schofield in St. Louis: "So long as we can gain success, the interference of politicians in military matters can be resisted; but on the first disaster they press upon us like a pack of hungry wolves."[24]

Apparently, Halleck prevented or at least moderated the howling after Chickamauga by referring to the high command's intention to place General Grant in charge of all operations in the West as soon as he returned to duty. Old Brains' task was not so much to superintend the removal of Rosecrans but to obtain for Grant the broad authority he would need. And in carrying this out, he employed more than usual secrecy.

On October 3 he ordered Grant to proceed from Vicksburg first to Memphis and then to report from Cairo by telegraph, but Grant did not receive the directive until October 9. His pause at Memphis on October 14 was brief, but he managed to send General Sherman some instructions. Cump's reply to Grant indicated that he suspected something was going on:

Accept the command of the great army of the center; don't hesitate. By your presence at Nashville you will unite all discordant elements and impress the enemy in proportion. All success and honor to you.[25]

At Cairo on October 16 General Grant received this order from Halleck:

> *You will immediately proceed to the Galt House, Louisville, Ky., where you will meet an officer of the War Department with your orders and instructions. You will take with you your staff, &c., for immediate operations in the field. Wait at Louisville for the officer of the War Department.*[26]

Years later, Grant recalled: "I left Cairo within an hour or so of receiving this dispatch, going by rail via Indianapolis. Just as the train I was on was starting out of the depot at Indianapolis a messenger came running up to stop it, saying the Secretary of War was coming into the station and wanted to see me."[27]

Stanton dismissed the special train that had brought him from Washington and joined the general for the ride to Louisville. Grant continued:

> *Soon after we started the Secretary handed me two orders, saying that I might take my choice of them. The two were identical in all but one particular. Both created the "Military Division of the Mississippi," (giving me the command) composed of the Departments of the Ohio, the Cumberland, and the Tennessee, and all the territory from the Alleghenies to the Mississippi River north of Banks' command in the southwest. One order left the department commanders as they were, while the other relieved Rosecrans and assigned [George H.] Thomas in his place. I accepted the latter.*[28]

At Louisville Grant found a letter from Halleck dated October 16. "You will immediately proceed to Chattanooga and relieve General Rosecrans," Halleck said, but it was "left optional with you to supersede General Rosecrans by General G. H. Thomas or not."[29]

From Louisville on the afternoon of October 20, Stanton telegraphed Halleck:

> *Sunday night General Grant issued his orders taking command. Generals Burnside, Rosecrans, and Thomas reported last night. General Grant has gone forward with General Meigs, and will reach Chattanooga to-night or to-morrow.*
>
> *Thomas says if the supply wagons now on the road arrive*

safely they will be all right till November 1, at least. General Grant ordered him to hold Chattanooga at all hazards. He replied: "I will hold the town till we starve."[30]

"In compliance with my promise," wrote Old Brains to Grant that day, "I now proceed to give you a brief statement of the objects aimed at by General Rosecrans' and General Burnside's movement into East Tennessee, and of the measures directed to be taken to attain these objects." What followed was hardly brief—in all, Halleck used nearly twelve hundred words—but it amounted to a clear history of Union operations in the region reaching back to Buell's failure to seize East Tennessee in early 1862. Along the way Halleck noted that Burnside had been ordered *fifteen* times to aid Rosecrans but had not done so. The general-in-chief concluded:

> *Whatever measures you may deem proper to adopt under existing circumstances, you will receive all possible assistance from the authorities at Washington. You have never heretofore complained that such assistance has not been afforded you in your operations, and I think you will have no cause of complaint in your present campaign.*[31]

During 1863's first half, the Union's armies had been obliged to deal with General Lee in the East, plus Bragg, Johnston, and Pemberton in the West. Now, with Vicksburg fading into history and most of the forces engaged in that long campaign redirected by Halleck toward Bragg's army around Chattanooga, the remaining confrontations were reduced merely to *Meade* v. *Lee* and *Grant*—not Rosecrans or Burnside—v. *Bragg*.

Any development that facilitated the focusing, the concentration, of the Union's enormous superiority in combat resources on the fewest bodies of resistance, could have only the worst possible consequences for the South. Having brought *Union* v. *Confederacy* this far, it might seem that Old Brains had achieved about as much as any man could in circumstances that had often been nigh-intolerably adverse.

"I am utterly sick of this political hell," Halleck had told Grant, and with good reason. Was it time to leave settling the case to others and go home to California?

Well, no, not quite. He had promised to support both Meade and Grant. Meade and Lee seemed about to quit sparring and go into winter quarters, but Grant's immediate problem was to prevent Rosecrans' Chicka-mauga veterans from being starved out of their place of refuge.

5

IN FACT, THE OVERALL MILITARY SITUATION in the early fall of 1863 included several "sideshows." For the better part of the summer, a joint army-
navy task force had been trying to blast its way into Charleston Harbor, but
without success. There had been cavalry raids and guerrilla activities in a
number of places and they were continuing. The only sideshow to which the
general-in-chief was obliged to give much of his attention, however, was the
operation Abraham Lincoln had entrusted to Nathaniel Banks almost a year
earlier.

"We have more to fear from our friends," the Bobbin Boy had told a
subordinate during Jackson's Shenandoah Valley Campaign, "than from the
bayonets of our enemies." That may explain General Banks' tendency to
explain and explain and explain his failure to plant the flag anywhere in
Texas in the weeks following the fiasco at Sabine Pass. A simple recitation of
the facts had satisfied General Halleck, whose expectations had been low
given that the venture had been political in origin. Banks was apprehensive,
however, lest his good friend in the Executive Mansion abandon him, as he
had John McClernand—or so it would seem from the letter Banks wrote
His Excellency from New Orleans on October 22, 1863:

> *Dispatches from the General-in-Chief impress me with the belief*
> *that my plan of action in the movement to the Sabine Pass is not*
> *perfectly understood by the Government. It was not intended for the*
> *occupation of Sabine City, nor was it, indeed, the purpose to land at*
> *that point except it could be done without serious resistance.*
>
> *The landing contemplated and referred to in the orders given*
> *to General Franklin, as an alternative for that of Sabine Pass, was*
> *upon the coast, 10 or 12 miles below. Had the landing been*
> *accomplished either at the Pass or below, a movement would have*
> *been immediately made for Beaumont from the Pass, or for Liberty*
> *if the landing had been made below, and thence directly to Houston,*
> *where fortifications would have been thrown up, and our line of*
> *communication and supplies immediately established at the mouth*
> *of the Brazos River, west of Houston, until we could have gained*
> *possession of Galveston Island and City.*
>
> *I should have had in ten days from the landing 20,000 men*
> *at Houston, where, strongly fortified, they could have resisted the*
> *attack of any force that it was possible to concentrate at that time.*
> *Houston would have been nearly in the center of the forces in and*

about Louisiana and Texas, commanding all the principal communications, and would have given us ultimately the possession of the State.

The movement to the Sabine was made upon the reports furnished by the naval officers, who were perfectly confident of their success in being able to destroy the enemy's guns. The grounding of two boats, and the withdrawal of the other two boats, caused the failure to effect a landing and the return of the army. In my judgment, the army should not have returned, but should have continued to the point indicated for landing upon the coast, as contemplated in the instructions. . . .

It was impossible to repeat the attempt, the failure having given notice to the enemy of our purposes, and enabled him to concentrate his forces against us. I therefore directed the movement of the troops across Berwick Bay, with a view to an overland movement into Texas. The deficiency of transportation, the removal of the numerous obstructions to the navigation of the Teche, and the difficulty of obtaining supplies, made it impracticable for us to reach Opelousas until this date.

We are now in position for a movement westward into Texas and northward to Northeastern Texas, by the way of Shreveport. The resources of the whole of this country are completely and thoroughly destroyed by the enemy. To the Sabine, we have a march from Opelousas and Vermillionville of between 100 and 200 miles, without water, without supplies, and without other transportation than by wagons. At Niblett's Bluff, on the Sabine, we shall encounter all the possible force of the enemy in the State of Texas, and a powerful enemy hanging upon our rear throughout the whole march, which is now waiting for us between Alexandria and Opelousas. From the Sabine to Houston is 100 miles, making altogether a march of from 250 to 300 miles. By the way of Alexandria and Shreveport to Marshall, which is the nearest point on the other route, we have a march of from 350 to 400 miles in that direction, without other communication than by wagon train, and through a country utterly depleted of all its material resources.

Either of these routes present almost insuperable difficulties. It is not good policy to fight an absent enemy in a desert country, if it can be avoided.

While the army is preparing itself for one or the other of these *movements, I propose to attempt a lodgment upon some point on the coast from the mouth of the Mississippi to the Rio Grande. . . . If it is successful, the results must be far more important than could be obtained by getting possession of the town of Marshall in Northeastern Texas.*

I have therefore determined to make an expedition for the purpose of landing between Sabine and the Rio Grande, most probably at the latter point. The expedition will sail to-morrow morning (23d) at 9 o'clock. The troops, about 3,500 in number, are under the command of Major-General [Napoleon Jackson Tecumseh] *Dana. I accompany the expedition myself, and am confident of its success.*[32]

Stonewall Jackson would not have worried about the Texans in harm's way, knowing that the expedition would be led by a Yankee political general he had whipped twice. Lincoln, however, had cause to be concerned over the thinking reflected in Banks' long and nigh-useless letter, apart from the fact that the Bobbin Boy had made the same comments regarding Sabine Pass and the Red River alternative in a message to General Halleck six days earlier—a letter Old Brains surely had passed along to the President.[33]

During the first week in November 1863, General Banks' force landed at the mouth of the Rio Grande River and occupied Brownsville, Texas. From there, using the wide discretion granted him under the Halleck Doctrine, he wrote Brigadier General James H. Carleton, commander of the Department of New Mexico, to ask if it might be possible for their troops to cooperate in advances toward San Antonio from Santa Fe and Brownsville. An idea of the concept's absence of the realities can be gained from the fact that it took from November 5 to December 24 for Banks' letter to reach Carleton, who on Christmas Day 1863 replied in polite terms that the scheme was hare-brained.[34] Meanwhile, the Bobbin Boy had moved up the coast and planted flags at Aransas Pass and Corpus Christi.[35]

Back in New Orleans by December 4, the conqueror of the lower Gulf Coast of Texas informed His Excellency of the capture of Pass Cavallo: "This gives us possession of the Bay of Matagorda, which enables us to control the State at our pleasure, and the occupation of every important point on the coast, excepting Galveston." Well and good; but, true to form, Banks went on to answer questions not yet asked and to mourn anew his failure at Sabine Pass:

It has been impossible, within any reasonable time, to gain a foothold in Texas, excepting by the sea, at this season. The march by Louisiana, either to the Sabine or by Alexandria or Shreveport, would cover from 300 to 500 miles to any important point in Texas, over a country without water or supplies of any kind; without other transportation, in the present stage of the rivers, than that of wagon trains, and against the constantly retreating, but steadily concentrating forces of the enemy, who could not fail, by their superiority in numbers of mounted troops, to inflict upon our columns, trains, and communications serious and irreparable injury.

I appreciated the perils of coast descents in winter; but, after the failure to effect a landing on the Sabine coast, which would have enabled me to place a force of from 15,000 to 17,000 men at Houston, in the very center of all the rebel forces of Louisiana and Texas, there was nothing left but a failure to re-establish the flag in Texas or an effort to occupy the western coast of the State. The results of the expedition thus far have been communicated to you at earlier dates; other important results will follow immediately.[36]

What other important results, Lincoln may well have wondered, for—as Henry Halleck had foreseen back in August—General Banks' having stabbed some sand dunes with flagstaffs had made no impression on anyone, foreign or domestic. "Brownsville had its uses," wrote Banks' biographer Fred Harvey Harrington, "but the other places seized served for little save to provide commands-in-exile for Banks' surplus generals."[37]

Moreover, while the Bobbin Boy had been exploring the Texas littoral, the attention of the Union's war managers and just about everyone else east of the Mississippi had been riveted to dispatches from Chattanooga and its environs. There, Halleck's Lieutenants—Grant, Thomas, Sherman, Little Phil Sheridan—were engaged in a campaign that seemed as though it might settle something.

6

"WE WILL HOLD THE TOWN till we starve," General Thomas had assured Grant upon assuming command at Chattanooga. But, thanks to a project Old Pap had backed, soon even the loss of animals due to exhausted fodder supplies ceased.

Major General William Farrar Smith had some rafts built on which troops floated down the Tennessee one night and surprised the light rebel force holding Brown's Ferry. Concurrently, Fighting Joe Hooker attacked eastward from the Union supply base, opened the road, and secured what the hungry men in Chattanooga called the "Cracker Line."

General Halleck had started Sherman's corps toward Rosecrans earlier, but Cump's progress had been slow because of the need to rebuild the railroad eastward from Corinth. By mid-November, however, Grant had a plan to break Bragg's siege and annihilate the Confederate force. Also, it was at about this time that Bragg simplified Grant's task by sending Longstreet's corps up to keep Burnside at Knoxville from reinforcing Grant.

"Damn the battle!" General Grant is said to have said after George Thomas' Army of the Cumberland drove Bragg's wrecked army down the reverse slope of Missionary Ridge. "I had nothing to do with it!"[38]

His plan had called for Sherman's Army of the Tennessee to sweep around the northeastern end of Bragg's fortifications along Missionary Ridge and cut off the enemy force from its supply base in Atlanta, while Hooker's corps seized Lookout Mountain west of Grant's objective and Thomas merely made demonstrations in the Union line's center.

Lieutenant General Jackson, who knew something about envelopments, might have warned the mortals in blue that there was more risk involved in such ventures than met the eye. Indeed, heavy rains made the Tennessee so difficult for Cump to cross that Bragg discovered the threat and put Major General Pat Cleburne's division in position to block Sherman when he finally did get across. Thomas' troops, eager to exact revenge for Chickamauga, began the battle as demonstrators but won it by attacking directly up the face of Missionary Ridge and routing its defenders.[39]

If General Grant thought the battle botched, the people of the North certainly did not. On the morning of November 25, 1863, A. Lincoln telegraphed the victor: "Well done. Many thanks to all."[40] And Old Brains wired Grant:

> *I congratulate you on the success so far of your plans. I fear that General Burnside is hard pressed* [by Longstreet] *and that any further delay may prove fatal. I know that you will do all in your power to relieve him.*[41]

In fact, Grant had. On that day he had alerted Cump Sherman to move toward Knoxville, then changed his mind: "On reflection, I think we will push Bragg with all our strength tomorrow. . . . His men have manifested a strong desire to desert for some time past, and we will now give them a chance. I will instruct Thomas accordingly."[42]

Two days later, Halleck warned General Meade:

> *General Grant's operations to-day will probably cut Longstreet's line of communication with Bragg. If Burnside holds his position at Knoxville a few days longer, Longstreet will be obliged to retire up the line of the Virginia and Tennessee Railroad to rejoin Lee. If the Army of the Potomac does not act soon, it may find Lee re-enforced by Longstreet's army.*[43]

The general commanding the Army of the Potomac did not act. Confederate President Jefferson Davis ordered Longstreet to break-off his attack against Knoxville's defenses and to rejoin Bragg—which Old Pete promptly found he could not do with Cump Sherman in the way. Utterly frustrated, Longstreet withdrew into the mountains northeast of Knoxville to wait for spring.[44]

Indeed, for the next few months it would seem that the whole war was waiting for spring. It was as though 1863's battles had drained the willingness of *both* sides' armies to undertake any more war-winning operations until the passage of time restored the reserves of energy that power fighting men.

7

HENRY HALLECK HAD NOT BEEN ANYWHERE near combat since Corinth. For nigh-on sixteen months, however, he had been absorbing friendly fire and enduring barrages of the other kind from his critics. He, too, needed a chance to replenish his inner resources. But he would not get one; instead, he was obliged during the fall and early winter to cope with the wear and tear two and a half years of war had produced in the ranks of his armies' senior officers.

Herman Haupt's exercise of his right to return to solving problems with which Massachusetts' politicians had plagued him amounted to a loss that may have impacted Halleck more painfully than any that would follow, for the railroad genius with a gift of prophecy was a close friend as well as a valued contributor to the quelling of the rebellion. Moreover, it was unsettling to find that Secretary of War Edwin Stanton's streak of treachery, quiescent earlier, was recurring.

True, the circumstances of Haupt's recruiting had been highly unusual. In the spring of 1861, he had been engaged in a bitter fight with Massachusetts' Governor John A. Andrew over compensation for the work Haupt had done toward completion of the Hoosac Tunnel on the Troy and Greenfield Railroad. The Boston and Albany, a competing line, had raised questions regarding financial arrangements made by the Commonwealth of Massachusetts in connection with the tunnel project. Investigations cleared Haupt of wrongdoing and the legislature authorized settlement of his claims, but outgoing Governor Nathaniel P. Banks neglected to sign the bill and his successor, Andrew, refused to approve it.[45]

Heeding Stanton's call to Washington jeopardized Haupt's ability to protect his interests against Andrew, but the secretary of war did not object to the terms Haupt specified:

> *I would expect to continue only so long as public exigencies demanded it. . . . I have no military or political aspirations, and am particularly averse to wearing the uniform; would prefer to perform the duties without military rank if possible. . . . Pay I do not require or care about. If I take the position you have so kindly offered, it will be with the understanding that I can retire whenever, in my opinion, my services can be dispensed with, and that I will perform no duties on the Sabbath unless necessity imperatively requires it.*[46]

Having the rank of colonel, Haupt found, facilitated the achievement of his missions. In recognition of his services during Second Bull Run, he was promoted to brigadier general on September 5, 1862. Not having sought promotion, however, Haupt declined to accept it formally.

General Haupt continued to perform brilliantly during and after Gettysburg. But in August, Andrew came to Washington and visited Stanton. It was arranged, according to War Department sources, for Stanton to force Haupt to accept his commission unconditionally; that done, Haupt would be given some assignment that would preclude his returning to Boston to protect his interests in the Hoosac Tunnel controversy.

That information seemed authentic, for on September 1, 1863, Stanton ordered that all commissions would be vacated if they were not formally accepted within five days. On September 5, General Haupt wrote Stanton:

> *I have uniformly declined to accept military rank unconditionally, and have given you my reasons for it. I cannot part with control of*

my time and of my freedom of action to so great an extent as I must do if I accept a commission unconditionally.

    Interests involving more than a million dollars; the private fortunes of my associates and myself, my reputation as an engineer and a man, are in jeopardy from the effects of active and unscrupulous enemies. They can be saved only by my personal exertions. . . . Even while I have been in Washington parties in Massachusetts, to whom I have not been legally or equitably indebted a single dollar, have brought suit on fictitious claims of which I have had no notice, and from my non-appearance have obtained judgment, taken execution and seized upon personal property.[47]

Damaged though Haupt had been, he was still willing to serve as a civilian. To discuss that alternative, he went to see Stanton. Tempers flared. The result was a two-sentence order to Haupt dated September 14, 1863:

You are hereby relieved from further duty in the War Department.
    You will turn over your office, books, papers, and all other property under your control belonging to the United States to Colonel D. C. McCallum, Superintendent of Military Railroads.[48]

John Covode and other members of Senator Wade's Joint Congressional Committee on the Conduct of the War protested to Stanton. Haupt was told that parties in Congress would try to remove the secretary if he would help. But he had "absolutely no inclination to engage in such a contest," he explained, "even had I believed it could succeed."[49]

Stanton's treatment of Herman Haupt was reprehensible on many counts. Henry Halleck, for one, would hardly have found that surprising. For a time Old Brains would continue to serve as a loyal subordinate. And in due course, the perfidious, despicable secretary of war would do even greater harm to *him.*

Major General Ambrose Burnside was the next officer holding an important position to depart, albeit under other circumstances. On October 27, 1863, he wrote Lincoln:

I deem it my duty to say to you that the state of my health is such that I may at any moment become unfit for duty in the field. I have been suffering more or less ever since the Mexican war with chronic diarrhea, but having a remarkable constitution the effects of disease have not been apparent to any save those intimately connected with me. This is one of the reasons why I have been so anxious to quit the field, and I am now suffering very much from it, and therefore deem it my duty to let you know this that you may think of the possibility of making other arrangements for the command of the department.

I do not ask to be relieved during the present emergency, and shall continue at my post as long as it is possible and desirable for the interests of the public service.[50]

General Halleck may well have wondered how different the course of recent military history might have been if Poor Burn had told the Union high command of his malady a year earlier, before Fredericksburg.

John G. Foster, who had served under Burnside in the Roanoke Campaign in the spring of 1862 and was then in the Department of the Ohio, succeeded him on December 11, 1863. Foster, a West Point graduate in the Class of 1846, was severely wounded during the battle of Molino del Rey during the Mexican War and he had been at Fort Sumter when its surrender marked this war's beginning. But most of his assignments had been administrative until Longstreet's siege of Knoxville, so Burnside's respect for him apparently made up for his lack of combat experience since Roanoke Island.[51]

As if the command of the Department of the Ohio and the Army of the Ohio were snakebit, only two weeks after Major General Foster had assumed those responsibilities, he felt compelled to send this message to the general-in-chief:

I regret to have to inform you that the lameness from which I was suffering when I left Washington was so much increased by the ride over the mountains as to prevent my riding or moving about, except with great pain. I determined, however, to get along as well as I could, but on the 23d my horse, in passing over an inclined ledge of rocks, fell and caught my wounded leg under him. This has disabled me so that it is impossible to perform the duties on the field, made necessary by the presence of the active enemy in front.

I am, therefore, forced to ask to be relieved, and wish that it may be done as soon as possible for the purpose of having an operation performed, which the surgeon informs me is necessary to obviate the bad effects likely to result from the present condition of my leg.[52]

Soon after Halleck received this message, he wired General Grant:

Major-General Foster has asked to be relieved from his command, on account of disability from old wounds. If his request is granted, who would you like as his successor? It is possible that General Schofield will be sent to your command.[53]

That Old Brains had high regard for the young commander of his old Department of the Missouri was reflected in a letter he wrote Schofield on October 5, 1863—an unusual one in that the general-in-chief seldom shared so much of his thinking so candidly with anyone. Halleck said:

Yours of September 30 is just received. I have read the [anti-Schofield] *article to which you referred me in the Leavenworth* Conservative *of September 24. It is very difficult to advise in such a case, as it is one upon which judgments will differ.*

I have made it a rule of my life never to notice newspaper abuse, and I don't think this is as abusive of you as articles which almost daily appear in the Herald, World, Intelligencer, *and German radical papers are of me. The only ground upon which I would stop a newspaper is that of giving aid and comfort to the enemy by publishing improper information, inciting desertions, mutiny, riots, &c. And even in such cases I would avoid all appearance of any personal grievance, as would be charged in this case.*

Such gross abuse seldom does much harm. An old Quaker once said to me in regard to such attacks, "I never saw clubs in a poor apple tree; if I see clubs in a tree I am certain that the fruit is good."

What is required in your department is a steady, firm, energetic rule, entirely independent of all factions or factional in-fluences. Nothing helps a newspaper or faction more than the cry of persecution. I know that the President was very much embarrassed by General Burnside's against the newspaper press. I have not heard the President say anything about the representatives of the mammoth committee, but I don't think they did you much harm. They have the support of the ultra-radicals, but not of the leading men in the Cabinet. The whole thing is regarded as a political attack on the President, and your name is used merely as a cloak to strike at him.[54]

And so it was that two generals' disabilities led to the appointment, in February 1864, of Major General John Schofield as commander of the Department of the Ohio and of the Army of the Ohio. Clearly Schofield, like Grant, Sherman, McPherson, and Little Phil Sheridan, was a full-fledged member of Halleck's Lieutenants.

Earlier, it had seemed that General Meade—the only Union commander who had ever defeated General Lee—might nevertheless become a victim of the guillotine. Meade had been Halleck's choice to succeed Fighting Joe Hooker; but since Gettysburg, the performance of the commander of the Army of the Potomac had been disappointing and Meade had on several occasions asked to be relieved following prods from the general-in-chief.

Replacing Meade was among the subjects covered in a report to General Grant prepared on December 21, 1863, by Charles A Dana, Stanton's roving investigator. Dana had just completed talks in Washington with Lincoln, Stanton, and Halleck. After some comments about plans for 1864, Dana wrote:

> To my suggestion that the surest means of getting the rebels altogether out of East Tennessee is to be found in the Army of the Potomac, the reply is, that that is true, but from that army nothing is to be hoped under its present commander. This naturally led to your second proposition, namely, that either Sherman or W. F. Smith should be put in command of that army.
>
> To this the answer is such as to leave but little doubt in my mind that the second of these officers will be appointed to that post. Both Secretary of War and General Halleck said to me that as long as a fortnight before my arrival they had come to the conclusion that when a change should be made General W. F. Smith would be the best person to try.
>
> Some doubts which they seemed to have respecting his disposition and personal character I think I was able to clear up. Secretary of War has also directed me to inform him that he is to be promoted on the first vacancy. President, Secretary of War, and General Halleck agree with you in thinking that it would be, on the whole, much better to select him than Sherman.
>
> As yet, however, nothing has been decided upon. . . .[55]

Dana may well have tried to clear up doubts regarding William Farrar Smith's "disposition and personal character," because the general was thought to have exceeded the bounds of propriety in criticizing Burnside's conduct of the battle of Fredericksburg; for that offense, he had been exiled to the West. Recently, however, Smith had attracted Grant's admiration by having had the rafts built at Chattanooga and by directing the troops that rode them down the Tennessee to capture Brown's Ferry, thus contributing greatly to the opening of the "Cracker Line" and saving the Army of the Cumberland from starvation.

Given Halleck's long friendship with General Sherman, however, how could his acceptance of Smith in preference to Cump as Meade's successor be justified?

Well, Old Brains may have recalled that the soldiers in the Union's eastern armies had never accepted Westerner John Pope. Might not the men in the Army of the Potomac respond more favorably to a commander who had already served with them?

Moreover, General Halleck is likely to have foreseen that—sooner or later—Grant was going to be elevated to higher command, in which case Sherman ought to be available on the scene to succeed him in command of the Western armies. Certainly, Old Brains held Sherman in the highest esteem. As he had with Schofield, on October 1, 1863, Halleck paid Cump the rare compliment of writing to him man-to-man and friend-to-friend:

> *I have received and read with interest yours of September 17. I fully concur with you that this rebellion must be put down by military force; it cannot be by compromise and offers of peace, as proposed by Northern copperheads. The conquered territory must also be governed by military authority until the time arrives for reconstruction.*
>
> *I have always opposed the organization of a civico-military government, under civilians. It merely embarrasses the military authorities without effecting any good. Nevertheless, if the people of any section will organize locally against the Confederacy and in favor of the Union it would give us great assistance. General Banks thinks that this can be done in Louisiana. Perhaps he is too sanguine.*
>
> *In asking the views [on reconstruction] of yourself, General Grant, and others who have had full and personal experience with these people, I hoped to be able to give the President correct opinions whenever he should ask them. The advice of politicians generally on this question I regard as utterly worthless—mere Utopian theories.*
>
> *Your letter in regard to General Buell hits the nail on the head. I have never had other than friendly feelings toward Buell,*

and saved him several times when the Government had determined on his removal. Instead of any gratitude for this, he and his friends have not ceased to abuse me and to claim for him credit he does not deserve. He never once suggested the operations on Forts Henry and Donelson and up the Tennessee River, but strenuously opposed the plan, and I could get no assistance from him till I appealed to the President.

The same with McClellan. I did everything in my power to prevent his removal after I arrived here. This he knew perfectly well. Instead of any gratitude for this, he and his friends then and ever since have done all in their power to injure me.

I have made no reply to their misstatements and abuse, nor do I intend to so long as the war lasts or I am in command. If I do not survive the war, sufficient materials for a correct understanding of my acts are on record and will be found by the future historian who seeks the truth.

We all have enough to occupy us in the present, without discussing the past or seeking for premature fame. Those who indulge most in personal discussions will find it worse for them in the end.

Duty, Duty, Duty is the only proper motto now for military officers.

I am sorry to say that many of the generals commanding armies exhibit a very bad spirit. They seek rather to embarrass the Government and make reputations for themselves than to put down the rebellion. General Grant and a few others are most honorable exceptions.

Your ranks cannot be filled by the present draft. It is almost a failure, as nearly everybody is exempt. It takes more soldiers to enforce it than we get by it. A more complicated, defective, and impracticable law could scarcely have been framed. Moreover, the copperheads of the North have done everything in their power to render it inoperative.[56]

As it turned out, Meade remained in command of the Army of the Potomac. This suggested that, at least as far as the general-in-chief was concerned, Charles Dana's defense of "Baldy" Smith had not been as effective as he had believed.

With George Meade's retention no longer at risk, General-in-Chief Halleck could enter 1864 with the assurance of having as army commanders professional soldiers of his own selection or development. Here was another indication of how much the unpleasantness back on January 1, 1863, had receded as a factor in his relationship with Abraham Lincoln.

Even so, the conversion of all the Union armies to immunity from the inadequacies of political generals was not complete—nor would it be, given Lincoln's new determination to use Louisiana and Arkansas as test regions for application of his recently announced Proclamation of Amnesty and Reconstruction and his retention a year earlier of Major General Nathaniel P. Banks as his agent.

8

IN THAT PROCLAMATION THE PRESIDENT offered full pardon "with the restitution of all rights of property, except slaves," to all rebels (except high-ranking Confederate officials) who took an oath of future loyalty to the Constitution and pledged to obey federal laws. A state would obtain recognition when ten percent of its voters in the 1860 election took the oath and then elected a pro-Union governor and delegates to a convention where a new constitution would be written. With a new state government in place, duly elected persons would be sent to the Congress and—in 1864—to the Democrat and Republican conventions to nominate presidential candidates.[57]

At a minimum, Abraham Lincoln wanted a real-world test given to his approach to restoration in Louisiana and Arkansas. He also wanted to be re-elected in 1864. And in both states, the greater the geographic extent of Union military occupation, the more likely Lincoln's political objectives were to be attained.

As far back as early November 1862, General-in-Chief Henry Halleck had pointed out Louisiana's Red River as the best line for military operations aimed toward invading Texas. At that time no attention was given to Arkansas in connection with Banks' possible movements. For much of 1863, Major General Frederick Steele was aiding Grant in regaining control of the Mississippi. Toward the end of the year, however, Steele had been attacked in central Arkansas by Confederate Major General Sterling Price.

From these developments evolved the idea of having Steele drive southwestward from Little Rock to Shreveport as Banks headed toward that city *via* the Red River. Once the federal forces met, they would drive westward into East Texas. And along the way to the Shreveport rendezvous, both Steele and Banks would enroll oath-takers and engage in other actions to promote Lincoln's amnesty and restoration plan.

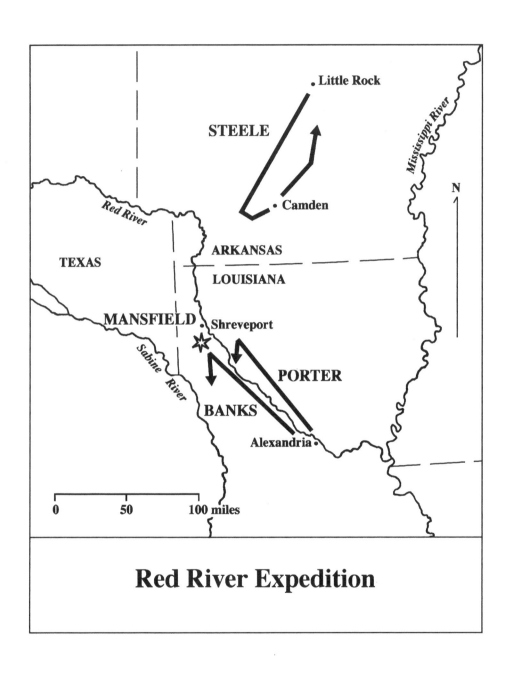

Red River Expedition

General Banks had repeatedly rejected Old Brains' suggestions regarding the Red River alternative. But that had not mattered to Halleck, who just as often had told Banks (in effect) that a general in the field is the best judge of conditions.

Now, as in Lincoln's earlier obsession with liberating Unionists in East Tennessee, it seemed that political considerations were again driving military operations. Put differently, about all General Halleck could do was try his best to minimize the damage in a situation where his client seemed to be making a truly colossal error. Accordingly, the general-in-chief's main challenge was to do everything possible to support both Lincoln and the Bobbin Boy *without* shattering the Halleck Doctrine.

How the general-in-chief viewed the situation in the West as it stood on December 11, 1863, is revealed in the message he sent Ulysses Grant that day:

> *General Steele reports that the rebel forces under Price and from Texas are advancing upon Little Rock. It is also reported that they are seriously threatening West Tennessee and the Mississippi River. Admiral Porter reports that Port Hudson is also threatened.*
>
> *Would it not be well under these circumstances to send back some troops to Hurlbut, so that the troops detached from Steele and Schofield to West Tennessee may be returned, and also instruct McPherson to assist, if necessary, General Banks' forces on the Lower Mississippi?*
>
> *Rebel papers received here indicate that an effort will be made to reclose the Mississippi River during the absence of your army and that of General Banks. The movement of the latter on the Rio Grande was unexpected and contrary to the advice of the Government.*[58]

Halleck's telegrams from Nathaniel Banks, however, suggested that the Bobbin Boy was very pleased with his accomplishments along Texas' Gulf coastline and wanted to improve upon them. On December 12, 1863, he wrote Halleck:

> *My desire is to occupy Galveston Island, if it can be done within reasonable time. This will give us the entire coast, and relieve the blockading squadron, which numbers now over thirty war vessels, enabling us to direct this naval force against the enemy on the Mississippi or any other part of the Gulf coast.*

> *If this can be accomplished, it will be of very material advantage. If we move in that direction, I shall concentrate on the Brazos all the disposable force at my command for a decisive and very short campaign. Eastern Texas offers us recruits, horses, forage, and supplies of every kind. All other parts of this department have been stripped by the two armies of everything necessary for their support.*
>
> *If this movement is made, the force under General Franklin on the Teche will be withdrawn and concentrated in Texas. I do not intend to divide my forces by the occupation of numerous positions. With the exception of Brazos Santiago [at the Rio Grande's mouth] it will be unnecessary to hold any other post, except it be upon Matagorda or Galveston Bay.*
>
> *Either of these positions will be sufficient for the permanent occupation of the coast, and for an entrance into the interior whenever it shall be deemed expedient. So far as the occupation of the State is concerned, Matagorda Bay, which is now in our possession, gives us the key to the greater part of it, which we can occupy whenever we please.*[59]

In effect, Nathaniel Banks' stubborn adherence in this message to advocating Galveston as an objective amounted to his shooting himself in the foot at least twice:

- First, taking the island city would do nothing to advance the success of President Lincoln's policies aimed at restoring Louisiana and Arkansas (and their electoral votes) to the Union; *au contraire,* more operations on the Texas coast or inland would draw resources *away* from achieving Lincoln's goals.
- Second, pitiful as well as fatuous was this claim Banks made: "So far as the occupation of [Texas] is concerned, Matagorda Bay, which is now in our possession, gives us the key to the greater part of it, which we can occupy whenever we please."

Cump Sherman had a better idea, which he expressed in a letter to Halleck written on December 26 at Lancaster, Ohio, during a leave. "With General Grant's consent," he began, "I have come here for a few days to comfort my family, almost heart-broken at the death of our oldest boy and at the declining health of Mr. and Mrs. Ewing." Later, Cump said:

> *The whole of the Mississippi from Cairo to the Balize should be in*

one command. Ought not General Grant's command to be extended accordingly, and give General Banks all of Texas, with of course, the right of deposit at New Orleans?

I do not believe in holding possession of any part of the interior. This requires a vast force, which is rendered harmless to the enemy by its scattered parts. . . . [In holding] inferior points on the Mississippi, and the interior of Louisiana, a large army is wasted in detachments.

I had a long conversation with General Grant at Nashville on these points, and he agreed I might write to you on the subject.[60]

Alas, Cump must not have been aware that General Banks was Abraham Lincoln's chosen instrument. Indeed Banks seemed to have forgotten that fact, along with his political mission, for on December 30, 1863, he provided the general-in-chief with another analysis of the military situation in his department, one that again seemed slanted toward his proposed seizure of Galveston:

In reference to the report made by General Steele, that General Price, with a portion of the rebel troops, was moving toward Little Rock, I beg to suggest that but a small force of Texas troops can be moving in that direction. The greater portion are in Texas or in Central Louisiana. . . .

The rivers are not yet deep enough to enable us to advance toward the Red River, excepting by wagon communication, which is impracticable. The country is without supplies of any kind.

It is my desire, if possible, to get possession of Galveston. This, if effected, will give us control of the entire coast of Texas, and require but two small garrisons, one on the Rio Grande and the other on Galveston Island, unless it be the wish of the Department of War that extensive operations should be made in the State of Texas.

A sufficient number of men can probably be recruited in that State for the permanent occupation of these two posts. It would relieve a very large number of naval vessels, whose service is now indispensable to us on the Mississippi and in the Gulf.

This can occupy but a short time, and, if executed, will leave my whole force in hand to move to any other point on the Red River or wherever the Government may direct. Once possessed of Galveston, and my command ready for operations in any other direction, I shall await the orders of the Government, but I trust that this may be accomplished before undertaking any other enterprise.

It is impossible at this time to move as far north as Alexandria by water. The Red River is not open to the navigation of our gunboats, and it is commanded by Fort De Russy, which has been remounted since our occupation of Alexandria. This position must be turned by means of a large force on land before the gunboats can pass.

To co-operate with General Steele in Arkansas, or north of Red River, will bring nearly the whole rebel force of Texas and Louisiana between New Orleans and my command, without the possibility of dispersing or defeating them, as their movement would be directed south and mine to the north. It is necessary that this force should be first dispersed or destroyed before I can safely operate in conjunction with General Steele.

Once possessed of the coast of Texas, and the naval and land forces relieved, I can then operate against the forces in Louisiana or Texas, and I can disperse or destroy the land forces in Louisiana, and safely co-operate with General Steele or with any other position of the army of the United States. . . .[61]

"Your dispatch of December 23 is just received," Old Brains began his reply on January 4, 1864. In that long letter, Banks had seemed to be anticipating being blamed for something, for the substance of his text was a recitation of his actions since August 1863 and his defense thereof.[62] But in it he had asked for reinforcements, and—tactfully—General Halleck had seized upon that subject to open his response:

General Steele's forces, in Arkansas, were directed to advance toward Shreveport, so as to co-operate with you on Red River. He went as far as Arkadelphia, when, hearing of your movement into Western Texas, he deemed it unsafe to attempt alone the occupation of the line of Red River.

General Grant was urged to send back to the Mississippi River a part of his command as soon as he could spare the troops. General Sherman has been detached for that purpose, and he will move down the river as rapidly as practicable. He is instructed to give you all the aid in his power. I have also ordered to New Orleans several detached regiments and batteries both in the West and in the East.

I enter into these details in order that you may know that no efforts have been spared to give you all possible assistance.

Generals Sherman and Steele agree with me in opinion that the Red River is the shortest and best line of defense for Louisiana and Arkansas and as a base of operations against Texas. If this line can be adopted most of the troops in Arkansas can be concentrated on it; but, as before remarked, Steele cannot alone attempt its occupation. His movements must, therefore, be dependent in a great measure upon yours.

If as soon as you have sufficient water in the Atchafalaya and Red Rivers you operate in that direction, Steele's army and such forces as Sherman can detach should be directed to the same object. The gun-boats should also co-operate.

If, on the other hand, your operations are mainly confined to the coast of Texas, Steele must make the Arkansas River his line of defense, and most of Sherman's force may be required to keep open the Mississippi.

So long as your plans are not positively decided upon, no definite instructions can be given to Sherman and Steele.

The best thing, it would seem, to be done under the circumstances is for you to communicate with them, and also with Admiral Porter, in regard to some general co-operation, and all agree upon what is the best plan of operations, if the stage of water in the rivers and other circumstances should be favorable; if not, it must be modified or changed.[63]

Nowhere in General Halleck's message was there comment on Banks' proposed Galveston operation. Moreover, in accordance with the Halleck Doctrine, he abstained from *ordering* the Bobbin Boy to abandon his fantasies and prepare to take his forces up the Red River.

But having suggested that Banks write General Steele and others, Old Brains practiced what he had preached. In a letter to Steele dated January 7, 1864, informing him that he was to command the newly created Department of the Arkansas within General Grant's zone of responsibility, he made this reference to cooperation with Banks: "It is hoped that measures may hereafter be concerted between yourself, General Sherman, and General Banks to drive the enemy entirely out of Arkansas and then occupy the line of the Red River, which is shorter and probably easier of defense."[64]

Afterward, critics and historians who blamed General Halleck for the dismal outcome of Nathaniel Banks' Red River Expedition of 1864 overlooked the Arkansas dimension. Quite apart from Lincoln's political interests, operations to remove Confederate threats to Missouri and Arkansas were fully justified and may well have had greater weight in Old Brains' highly qualified advocacy of the Red River line than has ever been recognized.

General Halleck implied as much in the confidential letter he wrote Grant on January 8, 1864. "In regard to General Banks' operations against Texas," he began, "it is proper to remark that it was undertaken less for military reasons than as a matter of State policy." He continued:

> *I allude to this matter here, as it may have an important influence on your projected operations during the present winter. Keeping in mind the fact that General Banks' operations in Texas, either on the Gulf coast or by the Louisiana frontier, must be continued during the winter, it is to be considered whether it will not be better to direct our efforts, for the present, to the entire breaking up of the rebel forces west of the Mississippi River, rather than to divide them by also operating against Mobile and Alabama.*
>
> *If the forces of Smith, Price, and Magruder could be so scattered or broken as to enable Steele and Banks to occupy Red River as a line of defense, a part of their armies would probably become available for operations elsewhere. General Banks reports his present force as inadequate for the defense of his position and for operations in the interior; and General Steele is of opinion that he cannot advance beyond the Arkansas or Saline unless he can be certain of cooperation and supplies on Red River.*
>
> *Under these circumstances it is worth considering whether such forces as Sherman can move down the Mississippi River should not co-operate with the armies of Steele and Banks on the west side. Of course operations by any of your troops in that direction must be subordinate and subsequent to those which you have proposed for East and West Tennessee. I therefore present these views, at this time, merely that they may receive your attention and consideration. . . .*[65]

By January 11, 1864, the general-in-chief had received Banks' letter of December 30, the second in which he had given the impression he meant to make a landing near Galveston. In responding, Halleck ignored that scheme; instead, he brought General Banks up to date on the Red River alternative:

I am assured by the Navy Department that Admiral Porter will be prepared to co-operate with you as soon as the stage of water in the Southwest will admit of the use of his flotilla there. General Steele's command is now under the general orders of General Grant, and it is hoped that he and General Sherman may also be able to co-operate with you at an early day. . . .

It has never been expected that your troops would operate north of Red River, unless the rebel forces in Texas should be withdrawn into Arkansas. But it was proposed that General Steele should advance to Red River, if he could rely upon your co-operation, and he could be certain of receiving supplies on that line. Being uncertain on these points, he determined not to attempt an advance, but to occupy the Arkansas River as his line of defense.

The best military opinions of the generals in the West seem to favor operations on Red River, provided the stage of water will enable the gun-boats to co-operate. I presume General Sherman will communicate with you on this subject. If the rebels could be driven south of that river, it would serve as a shorter and better line of defense for Arkansas and Missouri than that now occupied by General Steele; moreover, it would open to us the cotton and stores in Northeastern Louisiana and Southern Arkansas.[66]

So far in this letter, General Halleck had made no mention of Banks' political mission. He spoke of improving Steele's situation in Arkansas and Missouri, implying that operations on the Red River were means to that end. And he had indicated that he was aware of reports that New England's textile interests, many of whose mills were operating well below their capacities, were desperate for cotton.

Old Brains continued:

I am inclined to think that this gives us a better field of operations than any other for such troops as General Grant can spare during the winter. I have written to him, and also to General Steele, on this subject.[67]

For months—indeed, since his arrival in New Orleans more than a year earlier—General Banks had been deeply involved in various plans directed toward acquiring cotton in Louisiana beyond federal lines and selling it, either to New England mill operators or British firms. Many of those schemes were designed to benefit the Union government; Banks thought he could cover all of the costs of maintaining his Department of the Gulf; but most of the civilians seeking permits to deal with rebel cotton owners—and even with the general commanding the Confederate Trans-Mississippi Department, Edmund Kirby Smith—were open in their use of bribes and political influence to wring profits from the situation. No evidence was ever produced suggesting that General Banks was guilty of any wrongdoing. But his efforts to obtain cotton and channel it to his political supporters in New England and his desire to replace Lincoln as the Republican presidential candidate in 1864 seemed to make a neat fit.[68]

And then, just when General Halleck may well have supposed that Banks was proceeding with his Galveston venture, the general-in-chief received a letter from the Bobbin Boy dated January 23, 1864, reflecting an astonishing reversal in his thinking. Banks wrote:

> *I am much gratified to know that General Sherman is instructed to co-operate with the commands on the Mississippi. With the forces you propose, I concur in your opinion, and with Generals Sherman and Steele, "that the Red River is the shortest and best line of defense for Louisiana and Arkansas, and as a base of operations against Texas," but it would be too much for General Steele or myself to undertake separately. With our united forces and the assistance of General Sherman the success of movements on that line will be certain and important. I shall most cordially co-operate with them in executing your orders.*[69]

What *orders?* General Halleck had never given Banks any orders except to assume command of the Department of the Gulf, back in November 1862, and in August 1863, when Secretary of State Seward directed that the flag be planted in Texas forthwith. Suggestions? Yes, plenty of them. But no orders regarding movements: "A general in the field is the best judge of conditions."

Banks continued:

> *With my own command I can operate with safety only on the coast of Texas, but from the coast I could not penetrate far into the interior, nor secure control of more than the country west of San Antonio. On the other line, with commensurate forces, the whole State, as well as Arkansas and Louisiana, will be ours, and their*

people will gladly renew their allegiance to the Government.

The occupation of Shreveport will be to the country west of the Mississippi what that of Chattanooga is to the east, and as soon as this can be accomplished the country west of Shreveport will be in condition for movement into Texas. I have written to General Sherman and General Steele, in accordance with these views, and shall be ready to act with them as soon as the Atchafalaya and Red River will admit the navigation of our gun-boats. . . .

I inclose to you with this communication a very complete map of the Red River country and Texas, which embraces all the information we have been able to obtain up to this time. It has been prepared by Maj. D. C. Houston, of the engineer corps, and will show that we have not overlooked the importance of this line. Accompanying the map is a memoir, which exhibits the difficulties that are to be overcome. To this I respectfully ask your attention. . . .

I shall be ready to move to Alexandria as soon as the rivers are up, most probably marching by Opelousas. This will be necessary to turn the forts on Red River and open the way for the gun-boats. From that point I can operate with General Steele north or south of Red River, in the direction of Shreveport, and from thence await your instructions.[70]

Historian Ludwell H. Johnson, to whom all students of the ensuing operation are indebted, correctly considered Banks' letter the end of a beginning. But Johnson indicated that he had missed or misunderstood much of the record when he erred in writing:

At this juncture, however, the personal predilections of the general-in-chief entered the picture, and Halleck made use of the momentum prior events had given the Texas invasion, and of the influence of his official position, to implement his own strategic inclinations for an attack on Texas by way of the Red River. Helped by various political factors, he finally succeeded in securing the assent and cooperation of General Banks, and the result was that series of marches and battles known as the Red River expedition.[71]

Far from confirming Professor Johnson's horseback judgments, in the reply Halleck made on February 1, 1864, to Banks' letter of January 23, Old Brains seemed to be offering the Bobbin Boy more than a few excuses for *again* changing his mind:

[Major Houston's] *report and map contain very important and valuable information. The geographical character of the theater of war west of the Mississippi indicates Shreveport as the most important objective point of the operations of a campaign for troops moving from the Teche, the Mississippi, and the Arkansas Rivers. Of course the strategic advantages of this point may be more than counterbalanced by disadvantages of communication and supplies.*

General Steele reports that he cannot advance to Shreveport this winter unless certain of finding supplies on the Red River, and of having there the co-operation of your forces or those of General Sherman. If the Red River is not navigable (and it will require months to open any other communication to Shreveport), there seems very little prospect of the requisite co-operation or transportation of supplies.

It has therefore been left entirely to your discretion, after fully investigating the question, to adopt this line or substitute any other.

It was proper, however, that you should have an understanding with Generals Steele and Sherman, as it would probably be hazardous for either of these officers to attempt the movement without the co-operation of other troops. If the country between the Arkansas and the Red Rivers is impassable during the winter, as has been represented, it was thought that a portion of General Steele's command might be temporarily spared to operate with Sherman from the Mississippi. The Department of Arkansas was therefore made subject to the orders of General Grant.

It is quite probable that the condition of affairs in East Tennessee, so different from what General Grant anticipated when he detached General Sherman, may have caused him to modify his plans, or at least to postpone their execution. This may also prevent your receiving the expected aid from Sherman. . . .

So many delays have already occurred, and the winter is now so far advanced, that I greatly fear no important operations west of the Mississippi will be concluded in time for General Grant's proposed campaign in the spring. This is greatly to be regretted, but perhaps is unavoidable, as all our armies are greatly reduced by furloughs, and the raising of new troops progresses very slowly. Re-enforcements are, however, being sent to you as rapidly as we can possibly get them ready for the field.

Have you not overestimated the strength of the enemy west of the Mississippi River? All the information we can get makes the whole rebel force under Magruder, Smith, and Price much less than ours under yourself and General Steele. Of course you have better sources of information than we have here.[72]

"*It has therefore been left entirely to your discretion, after fully investigating the question,*" Old Brains had told Banks, "*to adopt this line or substitute any other.*" And *this* was the true end of the beginning of the Red River Expedition of 1864.

9

IN FACT, CHANGES OF ONE KIND or another had marked the high summer and fall of 1863 and the early weeks of 1864. John Schofield had been ordered to report to General Grant, and William Rosecrans was designated his successor as head of the Department of the Missouri.[73] Soon thereafter, Schofield replaced General Foster as commander of the Department of the Ohio; Foster's predecessor, Ambrose Burnside, was returned to his old IX Corps and assigned to Meade's Army of the Potomac. And John A. McClernand was transferred from one limbo to another: he was given command of some of Nathaniel Banks' troops on a sand bar off the Texas Gulf Coast.[74]

More important by far than any other development during the lull in the fighting after Missionary Ridge, however—certainly the most far-reaching one—was the increasing prominence Ulysses S. Grant was attaining in the opinions of his countrymen, especially those in the United States Congress. The main question seemed to be, in what manner could the greatest honor be bestowed upon him. Promoting Grant to lieutenant general, a rank not held by any American soldier since George Washington (Winfield Scott had held it only by brevet) appeared to be a solution no politician could resist, save one: Abraham Lincoln. Once Grant's assurances that he had no interest in politics had been obtained, however, no other barrier existed.[75]

All of which Henry Halleck had been well aware of and had supported as best he could. With Grant's elevation in rank would come his appointment as general-in-chief. To be relieved of that burden was a consummation devoutly to be wished, in Old Brains' view, which may have been why he had used every opportunity to prepare to hand over to Lieutenant General Grant an army that was as professional as he had been able to make it. True, Jamie McPherson and Little Phil Sheridan had yet to emerge. But they clearly belonged with Grant and Sherman and Thomas and Meade to the group of fighting generals that ought to be remembered as Halleck's Lieutenants.

If indeed the time had come for Old Brains to leave Washington's miasmal political swamps for whatever new post the incoming general-in-chief designated, he could do so knowing his duty to his country had been well-performed and with his honor intact. Glory being both ephemeral and hollow, no real soldier could—or can—hope for more than that.

16 ★ Duty, Duty, Duty

*F*OR ALL OF THOSE CRITICS who had been eagerly awaiting the ejection from the Union's high command of Major General H. W. Halleck once Lieutenant General Grant arrived and took over as general-in-chief, what actually happened must have been a dismaying disappointment. Old Brains not only survived the change, he gained more from it than anyone else involved.

Soldiers have a way of understanding each other which—if not unique—is still a remarkable phenomenon. This is one factor in the surprising ease with which the change in generals-in-chief was made. Brigadier General John A. Rawlins, Grant's chief of staff, foreshadowed such an outcome in a letter to Congressman Elihu Washburne, who, from the war's outset, had been Grant's strongest (and at times *only*) supporter in Washington:

> *I see by the papers the bill creating a Lieutenant General is still un-disposed of. So far as General Grant may be regarded in connection with it, I can only say that if the conferring of the distinguished honor upon him would be the taking of him out of the field, or with a view to the superseding of General Halleck, he would not desire it, for he feels that if he can be of service to the Government in any place it is in command of the army in the field, and there is where he would remain if made a Lieut. General; besides he has great confidence and friendship for the General-in-Chief, and would without regard to rank be willing at all times to receive orders through him. . . .*[1]

And in General Halleck's letter to Cump Sherman dated February 16, 1864, Old Brains had written:

> *You have probably seen the attempt in the newspapers to create difficulties and jealousies between me and General Grant. This is all for political effect. There is not the slightest ground for any such assertions. There cannot and will not be any differences between us. If he is made lieutenant-general, as I presume he will be, I shall most cordially welcome him to the command, glad to be relieved from so thankless and disagreeable a position. . . .*[2]

Since Missionary Ridge, Generals Halleck, Grant, and Sherman had been exchanging letters devoted to proposals for military operations in 1864—other than those driven mainly by politics and led by Banks and Fred Steele (with support from Rear Admiral David Dixon Porter) in Louisiana and Arkansas. Mobile and North Carolina seemed to be much on Grant's mind. Cump was less interested in *where* in the South Union armed forces should be employed than he was in their strategic effect, proposing that destroying the rebels' resources and will to resist justified conducting what much later generations would term *total* war.

What a difference a year had made! At the beginning of 1863 Grant's planned drive southward through central Mississippi had been wrecked by Earl Van Dorn's cavalry raid at the Holly Springs supply base; Sherman had been forced to abort his attempt to seize Chickasaw Bluffs near Vicksburg; and Old Brains had barely survived a bruising encounter with Abraham Lincoln. Now, however, General Halleck had—for the first time in nearly three years of war—the luxury of leaving the heavy lifting that planning required to subordinates he had brought along.

Moreover, even before Grant's promotion to lieutenant general seemed inevitable, Old Brains gradually eased into dealing with him much as he had with his client Lincoln and, earlier, with General Riley out in California: as mentor to a person whose duty obliged him to wield far more power than Halleck had ever aspired to, yet who still needed help in (among many other matters) avoiding traps. This rare skill was evident in the length to which the general-in-chief, normally a man of few words, went in a letter introducing the idea that any course of military action—however meritorious—that Grant might propose was subject to modification by the President. On February 17, 1864, Halleck wrote Grant:

> *The condition of affairs in East Tennessee and the uncertainty of*

General Banks' operations in Texas and Louisiana have caused me to delay answering your former communication in regard to the operations of the [1864] *campaigns.*

In one of these you suggest whether it might not be well not to attempt anything more against Richmond and to send a column of 60,000 men into North Carolina. In the first place, I have never considered Richmond as the necessary objective point of the Army of the Potomac; that point is Lee's army. I have never supposed Richmond could be taken till Lee's army was defeated or driven away.

It was one of Napoleon's maxims that an army covering a capital must be destroyed before attempting to capture or occupy that capital. And now, how can we best defeat Lee's army—by attacking it between here and Richmond, on our shortest line of supplies, and in such a position that we can combine our whole force, or by a longer line and with a force diminished by the troops required to cover Washington and Maryland?

Such movement through North Carolina alluded to by you, and also one from Port Royal on Savannah and into Georgia, have been several times suggested here, and pretty fully discussed by military men. It is conceded by those suggesting these expeditions that neither of them can be safely undertaken with a less force than that estimated by you, viz, 60,000 effective men. Some require a still larger force.

If we admit the advantage of either of these plans, the question immediately arises, where can we get the requisite number of troops?

There is evidently a general public misconception of the strength of our army in Virginia and about Washington. Perhaps it is good policy to encourage this public error. The entire effective force in the fortifications about Washington and employed in guarding the public buildings and stores, the aqueduct, and railroads does not exceed 18,000 men. . . . Considering the political importance of Washington, and the immense amount of military stores here, it would be exceedingly hazardous to reduce it still further.

The effective force of the Army of the Potomac is only about 70,000. General Meade retreated before Lee with a very much larger force, and he does not now deem himself strong enough to attack Lee's present army.

Suppose we were to send 30,000 men from that army to North Carolina, would not Lee be able to make another invasion of Maryland and Pennsylvania? But it may be said that by operating in North Carolina we would compel Lee to move his army there. I do not think so. Uncover Washington and the Potomac River, and all the forces which Lee can collect will be moved north, and the popular sentiment will compel the Government to bring back the army in North Carolina to defend Washington, Baltimore, Harrisburg, and Philadelphia. I think Lee would to-morrow exchange Richmond, Raleigh, and Wilmington for the possession of either of the aforementioned cities.

But suppose it were practicable to send 30,000 men from Meade's army to North Carolina, where shall we get the other 30,000? We have there now barely enough to hold the points which it is necessary to occupy in order to prevent contraband trade. Very few of these would be available for the field. Maryland is almost entirely stripped of troops, and the forces in Western Virginia are barely sufficient to protect that part of the country from rebel raids.

The only other resource is South Carolina. Generals Foster and Gillmore were both of opinion at the commencement of operations against Charleston that neither that place nor Savannah could be taken by a land force of less than 60,000 men. Large land and naval forces have been employed there for nearly a year without any important results. I had no faith in the plan at first, and for months past have ineffectually urged that 10,000 or 15,000 men from Gillmore's command be sent against Texas or Mobile. And now these troops are sent upon another expedition which, in my opinion, can produce no military result.

I always have been, and still am, opposed to all these isolated expeditions on the sea and Gulf coast. It is true they greatly assist the Navy in maintaining the blockade and prevent contraband trade, but I think the troops so employed would do more good if concentrated on some important line of military operations. We have given too much attention to cutting the toe nails of our enemy instead of grasping his throat.

You will perceive from the facts stated above that there are serious, if not insurmountable, obstacles in the way of the proposed North Carolina expedition. Nevertheless, as it has much to recommend it, I shall submit it with your remarks to the consideration of the President and Secretary of War as soon as troops enough return from furlough to attempt any important movement in this part of the theater of war.

Lee's army is by far the best in the rebel service, and I regard *him as their ablest general. But little progress can be made here till that army is broken or defeated. There have been several good opportunities to do this, viz, at Antietam, at Chancellorsville, and at Williamsport, in the retreat from Gettysburg. I am also of opinion that General Meade could have succeeded recently at Mine Run had he persevered in his attack.*

The overthrow of Lee's army being the object of operations here, the question arises, how can we best attain it?

If we fight that army with our communications open to Washington, so as to cover this place and Maryland, we can concentrate upon it nearly all your forces on this frontier, but if we operate by North Carolina or the Peninsula, we must act with a divided army and on exterior lines, while Lee, with a short interior line, can concentrate his entire force on either fragment.

And yet, if we had troops enough to secure our position here, and at the same time to operate with advantage on Raleigh or Richmond, I would not hesitate to do so, at least for a winter or spring campaign. But our numbers are not sufficient, in my opinion, to attempt this, at least for the present. Troops sent south of James River cannot be brought back in time to oppose Lee, should he attempt a movement north, which I am satisfied would be his best policy.

Our main efforts in the next campaign should unquestionably be made against the armies of Lee and Johnston, but by what particular lines we shall operate cannot be positively determined until the affairs of East Tennessee are settled, and we can know more nearly what force can be given to the Army of the Potomac. In the mean time, it will be well to compare views and opinions. The final decision of this question will probably depend, under the President, upon yourself.

It may be said that if General McClellan failed to take Richmond by the Peninsula route, so also have Generals Burnside, Hooker, and Meade failed to accomplish that object by the shorter and more direct route. . . . These facts in themselves prove nothing in favor of either route, and to decide the question we must recur to fundamental principles in regard to interior and exterior lines, objective points covering armies, divided forces, &c.

These fundamental principles require, in my opinion, that all our available forces in the east should be concentrated against Lee's army. We cannot take Richmond (at least with any military ad-

vantage), and we cannot operate advantageously on any point from the Atlantic coast, till we destroy or disperse that army, and the nearer to Washington we can fight it the better for us.

We can here, or between here and Richmond, concentrate against him more men than anywhere else. If we cannot defeat him here with our combined force, we cannot hope to do so elsewhere with a divided army.

I write to you plainly and frankly, for between us there should be no reserve or concealment of opinions. As before remarked, I presume, under the authority of the President, the final decision of these questions will be referred to you. Nevertheless, I think you are entitled to have, and that it is my duty to frankly give, my individual opinion on the subject. . . .[3]

This was pure Halleck: a soldier's comprehensive (if protracted) analysis of facts bearing on what ought to be done *combined with* the precision in thought and presentation he had mastered as a lawyer. If this letter was the longest Old Brains had ever put into the record, it may also have been his best.

2

"THE BILL REVIVING THE GRADE of lieutenant-general in the army has become a law," General Grant wrote Sherman on March 4, 1864. He had been ordered to report to Washington "immediately and in person," he said. "I leave in the morning to comply with the order, but I shall say very distinctly on my arrival there that I accept no appointment which will require me to make that city my headquarters."[4]

On March 10 Cump sent Grant a private and confidential reply:

Don't stay in Washington. Halleck is better qualified than you to stand the buffets of intrigue and policy. Come West; take to yourself the whole Mississippi Valley. Let us make it dead sure, and I tell you the Atlantic slopes and Pacific shores will follow its destiny as sure as the limbs of a tree live or die with the main trunk.

We have done much, but still much remains. Time and time's influences are with us; we could almost afford to sit still and let these influences work.

Even in the seceded States your word now would go further

than a President's proclamation or an act of Congress. For God's sake and your country's sake come out of Washington.

I foretold to General Halleck before he left Corinth the inevitable result, and I now exhort you to come out West. Here lies the seat of the coming empire, and from the West, when our task is done, we will make short work of Charleston and Richmond and the impoverished coast of the Atlantic.[5]

General Orders No. 98, dated March 12, 1864, made the changes official:

The President of the United States orders as follows:

I. Maj. Gen. H. W. Halleck is, at his own request, relieved from duty as General-in-Chief of the Army, and Lieut. Gen. U.S. Grant is assigned to the command of the armies of the United States. The headquarters of the army will be in Washington, and also with Lieutenant-General Grant in the field.

II. Maj. Gen. H. W. Halleck is assigned to duty in Washington as Chief of Staff of the Army, under the direction of the Secretary of War and the lieutenant-general commanding. His orders will be obeyed and respected accordingly.

III. Maj. Gen. W. T. Sherman is assigned to the command of the Military Division of the Mississippi, composed of the Departments of the Ohio, the Cumberland, the Tennessee, and the Arkansas.

IV. Maj. Gen. J. B. McPherson is assigned to the command of the Department and Army of the Tennessee.

V. In relieving Major-General Halleck from duty as General-in-Chief, the President desires to express his approbation and thanks for the able and zealous manner in which the arduous and responsible duties of that position have been performed.[6]

In the middle of March 1864, the North's attention, particularly that of the denizens of Washington's miasmal political swamp, was so sharply focused on Grant that, for a time, even Lincoln was all but eclipsed. The new lieutenant general, having observed the amenities, departed from the capital as quickly as he could. His destination was Major General George G. Meade's headquarters down the Orange and Alexandria Railroad near Culpeper, Virginia, where he took up residence—confirming General Rawlins' prediction that he wanted no part of Washington and that he meant to command all the Union armies from a tent in the field.

"Where Lee goes," Grant had told his host, the Army of the Potomac's commander, "there you will go, also."[7] And there, also, the new general-in-chief would go.

General Halleck had written his friend Francis Lieber that he would have preferred to command the Western army, but that duty came first:

> *I am perfectly willing to labor wherever the Prest., Secy of War &*
> *Genl Grant decide that I can be the most useful. As the latter has*
> *determined to remain in the field some one must be here to attend to*
> *the vast amounts of military-administrative duty connected with the*
> *war Dept & Head Qrs of the Army.*[8]

So completely and so amicably had the two soldiers reached a meeting of the minds that Abraham Lincoln had had next to nothing to do with it. True, given Halleck's request for relief from the post he had held since mid-1862, it would have helped the President politically to seize this opportunity to be rid of the man he considered no more than a first-rate clerk. It would be reaching too far to conclude that Lincoln recognized that he could not get along without Halleck. Yet, if Old Brains had dropped out at this convenient and attractive point and returned to California, where might Lincoln have found counsel more able to assist him than Henry Wager Halleck?

Major General Nathaniel P. Banks' projected Red River Expedition was one example of Lincoln's utter dependence on General Halleck—and also of Old Brains' devotion to duty. Grant had wanted no such "sideshows"; Banks' forces, he felt, should be used to seize Mobile; and by removing himself to Meade's headquarters, he had demonstrated (among other things) his total aversion to supporting a venture justified only by political objectives: the success of Lincoln's amnesty and restoration projects in Louisiana and Arkansas and his re-election in November.

Apart from General Halleck's acute discomfort over having the duty of aiding and abetting an incompetent field army commander in the execution of an operation utterly lacking in military usefulness, he was plagued with Banks' seemingly studied refusals to accept the Halleck Doctrine—hence the sharp tone of his letter to Banks back on February 11, 1864:

> *Your dispatches of January 29 and February 2 are received. In the*
> *former you speak of awaiting orders and instructions in regard to*
> *operations on Red River.*

> *If by this it is meant that you are waiting for orders from Washington, there must be some misapprehension. The substance of my dispatches to you on this subject was communicated to the President and Secretary of War, and it was understood that while stating my own views in regard to operations, I should leave you free to adopt such lines and plans of campaign as you might, after a full consideration of the subject, deem best.*
>
> *Such, I am confident, is the purport of my dispatches, and it certainly was not intended that any of your movements should be delayed to await instructions from here. It was to avoid any delay of this kind that you were requested to communicate directly with Generals Sherman and Steele, and concert with them such plans of co-operation as you might deem best under all the circumstances of the case.*[9]

Again, Professor Ludwell Johnson surrendered to his prejudices, his apparent ignorance of the Halleck Doctrine, and the consensus opinion regarding Old Brains when he wrote:

> *It seems quite evident that this was all Halleck's idea—to transfer to a subordinate all responsibility for decisions and for any possible reverses that might occur. . . . In short, Halleck's condition was normal: he was trying to avoid the responsibility involved in giving orders.*[10]

Why was it so difficult, and why has it been so difficult subsequently, for people to grasp the fact that it was impossible for General Halleck or anyone else to give direct orders from a desk in Washington to a field army commander operating a thousand miles or more away? Indeed, Old Brains had been utterly unable to control any of John Pope's movements when Second Bull Run was taking place less than forty miles from the War Department's telegraph office.

"If we were personally present [at Fredericksburg]," Henry Halleck had told the President before that tragic battle, "and knew the exact situation, we might assume such responsibility"—responsibility for giving orders to Ambrose Burnside, he meant.[11] "I hold that a General in command of an army in the field is the best judge of existing conditions."[12] Lincoln grasped the point. So had Grant, who was going into the field indefinitely to see exactly what General Meade saw. But why have so few others comprehended the Halleck Doctrine, then and ever since?

Ludwell Johnson was on much firmer ground, however, when he pointed out the folly of conducting an operation of the Red River Campaign's complexity without an overall commander. "Nobody assumed to give orders," Banks later complained to Bluff Ben Wade's notorious Joint Congressional Committee on the Conduct of the War.[13] But this had not been negligence on the distant general-in-chief's part; all of Halleck's Lieutenants had been busy elsewhere. "The difficulty is," Old Brains had explained in a letter to Sherman, "to get a suitable commander. General Banks is not competent, and there are so many political objections to superseding him by Steele that it would be useless to ask the President to do it."[14]

Clearly, how wise General-in-Chief Ulysses Grant had been to put as many miles as he could between himself and Washington.

3

LIEUTENANT GENERAL GRANT SETTLED the question of what the Army of the Potomac was going to do by assigning himself to it for rations and quarters. Meade's mission was merely to annihilate General Lee's Army of Northern Virginia. In Washington the chief of staff's duty was to make certain that the Army of the Potomac had all the men, weapons, and supplies required—and also, as before, to provide assurance to the President that Ulysses Grant knew what he was doing.

But in war, nothing is ever as simple as it may appear. Between mid-March and early May, General Grant made trips every week or so to Washington; Mrs. Grant was in residence there, but so were Lincoln and Halleck.

"Fundamental principles," Old Brains had written Grant back in mid-February, "require, in my opinion, that all our available forces in the east should be concentrated against Lee's army." Even so, the final plan for operations in the East included two of the "sideshows" General Grant professed to abhor. One was a landing on the James River roughly twenty miles south of Richmond to be made by troops commanded by Major General "Spoons" Butler. The second venture, also intended to distract Lee and weaken him by obliging him to detach units to meet the sideshows' challenges, was a drive up the Shenandoah Valley of Virginia to be led by Major General Franz Sigel.

Both of these elaborations had the smell of Abraham Lincoln's lamp about them. If so, however, this was hardly astonishing, given that 1864 was a presidential election year. Sigel had demonstrated his incompetence often enough to have merited reassignment to Arizona but, presumably, German-American voters throughout the North might think otherwise. "Beast" Butler may well have qualified for an extended prison sentence but he, too, had a political following in New England that Lincoln could not offend with impunity.

"I always have been, and still am, opposed to isolated expeditions," Old Brains had told Grant in his mid-February letter. "We have given too much attention to cutting the toe nails of our enemy instead of grasping his throat." But Halleck had to leave it there and turn his efforts toward making a needlessly complex scheme succeed, and so did the general-in-chief.

Such may well have been Lieutenant General Grant's *real* welcome to Washington.

By contrast, and in large part because of the relative remoteness of the West from the Union capital's *sturm und drang,* William Tecumseh Sherman was justifying the faith his old friend Halleck had long had in him by scourging swaths of Mississippi from ten to twenty miles wide in his Meridian raid. Beyond keeping many of his troops busy during the winter, Cump was applying his belief that Confederate civilians had to be discouraged from continuing to support the rebellion.

For all the devastation Sherman's troops inflicted, however, that expedition was a failure. Cump had ordered a Union force at Memphis to intercept Nathan Bedford Forrest's cavalry, but the Wizard of the Saddle turned it back, thereby precluding the continuation of the federal advance into Alabama. Yet, during the winter of 1864 much of Sherman's thinking, like Grant's, had been devoted toward operations that might end the war.

Adopting the principle General Halleck had tried to apply the previous spring—forward movement by all the Union armies at the same time, to prevent the Confederates from borrowing forces from any one point to reinforce another—the new general-in-chief meant for Meade and Sherman to open their offensives in late April or early May. Grant had agreed with Old Brains that Meade's object was annihilating General Lee's Army of Northern Virginia and nothing else. Sherman's goal had evolved into destroying Confederate resources (notably, those in Atlanta), with elimination of Joe Johnston's army from the war a task to be achieved along the way. Those matters settled, except for details, Chief of Staff Halleck turned to providing the field armies with whatever it might require to quell the rebels opposing Grant, Sherman, Spoons Butler, and Franz Sigel.

Once Major General Banks had embraced the idea of moving up the Red River to meet Frederick Steele's column from Little Rock at Shreveport, he acted quickly to work out arrangements with Sherman, who agreed to loan the Bobbin Boy ten thousand troops for thirty days; with Admiral David Dixon Porter, whose Mississippi Squadron's gunboats would provide massive mobile firepower as they escorted the steamers transporting Sherman's men from Vicksburg to the Red River battle area; and with Steele.[15] Accordingly, during the expedition's formation, Old Brains was left free to concentrate on doing what he could to strengthen the armies with the heaviest clout: Meade's and Sherman's.

At few times during the entire war did gaps in the telegraph's linkages isolate any active combat zone from Washington more or for longer than did those separating Generals Banks and Halleck in the spring of 1864. From his observation post in Valhalla, however, Lieutenant General Jackson could have witnessed events along the Red River and in central Arkansas that the Union's war managers would not learn about for weeks. Such as:

- Alexandria, the first town of any size on the Red River above its mouth, was designated the assembly point for Banks' forces, Porter's gunboats, and the transport-borne contingent Sherman had sent down under the command of Brigadier General A. J. Smith. The rendezvous date was to be March 17, 1864. Only Porter and the army troops on the steamers with him met the schedule; General Banks, having tarried in New Orleans to complete his work in Abraham Lincoln's political interest, did not arrive until March 24—only to find that the navy had seized all the Confederate cotton for miles around as a prize of war, that his own infantry was not yet up, and that very little water was trickling over a mile or so of exposed rock that in happier times had been a rapids.

- Jackson's subordinate during the Shenandoah Valley Campaign of 1862, Dick Taylor, seemed to be recalling how his mentor had given ground in order to lure Yankees onto terrain of his own choosing, where his smaller forces could trap a fragment of the federal army and wreck it. That was exactly what Taylor was doing: withdrawing toward Shreveport, as Banks—accompanied by gunboats and transports Porter was able to get past the rocky impediment—moved up the river's west bank.

- At Natchitoches, Banks spent more time than he could afford administering oaths as part of Lincoln's program and holding a grand review, which included his one thousand wagons. To suggestions that he have some of his cavalry find out if there was a road following the Red River's western bank, Banks replied that there was no time for that. On April 6 he sent his forces toward Mansfield on a road that diverged from the river. Admiral Porter, steaming upstream, would not see Banks' column again until they both neared Shreveport. Banks' route would be beyond the range of any covering fire the gunboats were along to provide.

- On April 8, General Taylor, having found exactly the kind of terrain Old Jack would have selected at a clearing called Sabine Crossroads a few miles south of Mansfield, drew the Union cavalry and infantry into an ambush and smashed the Yankees from three directions, driving the survivors back the way they had advanced. Additional panic prevailed during the chaotic rout, because wagons were too far forward in Banks' column and the thick woods prevented the teamsters from turning them around.

- Taylor attacked Banks' oddly deployed units at Pleasant Hill the next afternoon, but the Jacksonian wide envelopment he tried was not wide enough. Even so, during the night, Banks issued orders to retreat all the way back to Natchitoches.

- Not far south of Shreveport, at Loggy Bayou where Porter and Banks were to rejoin forces, the admiral learned of the disaster that had occurred in the trap south of Mansfield that Taylor (or Jackson?) had devised and reversed his armada's course forthwith.

- At about the same time, Frederick Steele's column, moving from Little Rock toward Shreveport, had been stalled at Camden, Arkansas, not so much by Confederate opposition as by the threat of starvation. Soon after Banks skedaddled toward Alexandria, General Steele had no choice but to turn his troops back toward Little Rock.[16]

Old Brains had long since feared that any expedition with Nathaniel Banks as its stemwinder was snakebit. But, absent wire linkage from Alexandria to Washington, many days would pass before any of the Union's war managers would learn how utterly appalling a thrashing Dick Taylor's pitifully few Louisianans and Texans, using captured weapons mostly, had inflicted on Abraham Lincoln's commander of the Department of the Gulf.

4

ON MARCH 19, 1864, WHILE DAVID DIXON PORTER'S sailors were stealing all the cotton they could find in and around Alexandria, Chief of Staff Henry Halleck was sending Cump Sherman his commission as a brigadier general in the Regular Army. "My only regret," he wrote, "is that it is not for a higher grade, but I think that will not be very long delayed." Then he added an admonition:

> There are, however, some elements in the higher grades [Hooker?] that may give you trouble unless you are continually on your guard against these intrigues. Be very cautious in what you say and do, for they will be ever ready to take all possible advantage.[17]

General Sherman replied on April 2 in one of those letters that conveys a great deal about a broad range of subjects:

> I wish you to say to the President that I would prefer he should not nominate me or any one to the vacant major-generalship in the Regular Army. I now have all the rank necessary to command, and I believe all here concede to me the ability, yet accidents may happen, and I don't care about increasing the distance of my fall. The moment another appears on the arena better than me, I will cheerfully subside.
>
> Indeed, now my preference would be to have my Fifteenth Corps, which was as large a family as I feel willing to provide for, yet I know General Grant has a mammoth load to carry. He wants here some one who will fulfill his plans, whole and entire, and at the time appointed, and he believes I will do it. I hope he is not mistaken. I know my weak points, and thank you from the bottom of my heart for past favors and advice, and will in the future heed all you may offer with the deepest confidence in your ability and sincerity.
>
> I will try and hold my tongue and pen and give my undivided thoughts and attention to the military duties devolving on me, which in all conscience are enough to occupy usefully all my time and thoughts. I hope you noticed that it was my troops that captured Fort De Russy [on their way up Red River to Alexandria]. Now, if the Red River be high, admitting our iron-clads up to Shreveport, I advise that place to be reduced, but if they cannot pass the rapids at Alexandria my part of the joint expedition should go no further at this time. . . .
>
> I hope to have by May 1 an army on the Tennessee, with a reserve of provisions, forage, and ammunition that will enable me to whip Joe Johnston or drive him back of the Chattahoochee, and

leave my right flank clear to sweep down between Georgia and Alabama. . . .

With Thomas as my center, McPherson on the right, and Schofield on the left, I will have an army that will do anything within the range of human possibility.[18]

General-in-Chief Grant gave Sherman and his armies their mission two days later, on April 4. "It is my design," his letter began, "if the enemy keep quiet and allow me to take the initiative in the spring campaign, to work all parts of the army together and somewhat toward a common center. For your information I now write you my programme as at present determined upon."[19]

That Grant wrote from Washington suggested that what followed had the blessing of Chief of Staff Halleck and President Lincoln. His "programme" also reflected the assumption that General Banks would reach Shreveport:

I have sent orders to Banks by private messenger to finish up his present expedition against Shreveport with all dispatch; to turn over the defense of the Red River to General Steele and the navy, and return your troops to you and his own to New Orleans; to abandon all of Texas except the Rio Grande, and to hold that with not to exceed 4,000 men; to reduce the number of troops on the Mississippi to the lowest number necessary to hold it, and to collect from his command not less than 25,000 men; to this I will add 5,000 from Missouri. With this force he is to commence operations against Mobile as soon as he can. It will be impossible for him to commence too early.[20]

Well, fine. But as Grant wrote, General Banks was at least eighty miles south of Shreveport in Natchitoches, winding up his political work, watching his troops (and wagons) parade past him, and preparing to take the inland road to his goal *via* Mansfield.[21] The day before, April 3, he had written Grant that "we hope to be in Shreveport by the 10th of April," adding:

I do not fear concentration of the enemy at that point; my fear is that they may not be willing to meet us there. If not and if my forces are not weakened to too great an extent, I shall pursue the enemy into the interior of Texas for the purpose of destroying his forces.[22]

Many days later Abraham Lincoln read this mixture of Buellesque excuse-planting and bombast reminiscent of the Young Napoleon with dismay. "The next news we hear from there," he predicted, "will be of defeat."[23]

But in early April, Grant had been general-in-chief for only three weeks, and in his earlier service he had had even less contact with Franz Sigel or "Spoons" Butler than with Banks. "With the long line of railroad Sigel has to protect," he commented, "he can spare no troops, except to move directly to his front. In this way he must get through to inflict great damage on the enemy, or the enemy must detach from one of his armies a large force to prevent it. In other words, if Sigel can't skin himself he can hold a leg whilst some one else skins."[24]

Having summarized his instructions to the two eastern sideshow operations' commanders, General Grant returned to Cump's mission:

> *You I propose to move against Johnston's army, to break it up and to get into the interior of the enemy's country as far as you can, inflicting all the damage you can against their war resources.*
>
> *I do not propose to lay down for you a plan of campaign, but simply to lay down the work it is desirable to have done, and leave you free to execute in your own way. Submit to me, however, as early as you can, your plan of operations.*[25]

Curiously, Grant did not mention Meade. "I will stay with the Army of the Potomac," he wrote Sherman, "and operate directly against Lee's army wherever it may be found."[26]

Clearly, Ulysses Grant had not only absorbed the Halleck Doctrine, he was *applying* it. General Sherman, too, gave evidence that he recognized the unwritten limitations inherent in high command. Earlier, Cump had suggested to General Halleck that there were too many departments in the West and that consolidation of authority under one officer was a remedy worth considering. In reply, Old Brains had drawn upon his pre-Washington experiences, pointing out that the enormous administrative burden would preclude any true soldier in such a position from giving proper attention to his *primary* duty: fighting.

"I see the points you make," Sherman responded to his old friend and mentor on April 16, "and admit their full force." Cump continued:

> *The division of a large command into departments, coupled with the fact that the law confers on the department commanders the*

power of discharge, furloughs, &c., is a good and sufficient reason for the present plan. All I can then ask is that you keep in mind that the territory lying so remote as Arkansas is more naturally belonging to a division west of the Mississippi than this, more especially as soon I will be in immediate command of an army that will engross all my thoughts and action.

I dislike even to attempt to name a commander west of the Mississippi that could reconcile the discordant claims of Curtis, Rosecrans, Steele, and Banks. Of them I would prefer Steele, because he will fight, but his movements are too slow for this stage of the war.

Banks is entirely too much engrossed in schemes of civil experiments. These ought to be deferred till all large armies of the Confederacy are broken up and destroyed. Our efforts heretofore to cover trading schemes, local interests, and matters of civil reconstruction has almost paralyzed large armies by dividing them up into little squads easy of surprise and capture. . . .

But all these things are well known to you, and I should not refer to them. Though Steele is subject to my orders I must naturally leave him to act on his own judgment, confining my attention to the concentration of force now rapidly being made on the Tennessee from Chattanooga to Decatur.[27]

Duty well performed is seldom rewarded, certainly never adequately, by words. Far better, but extremely rare, it is when a mentor can see the examples he has set, and the principles he has tried to impart, being adopted *as their own* by those he sought to advance. Such was the satisfaction the former drunkard Ulysses Grant and once "insane" William Tecumseh Sherman may well have given Old Brains, albeit inadvertently, in the course of taking up their new and vastly more demanding duties.

5

As PART OF HIS PREPARATIONS for the Western armies' spring offensive, on April 3, 1864, General Sherman wrote Nathaniel Banks: "The thirty days for which I loaned you the command of General A. J. Smith will expire on the 10th instant." He was sending Brigadier General J. M. Corse with orders for Smith and to emphasize, "I must have A. J. Smith's troops now, as soon as possible."[28]

Cump wrote similar letters to Admiral Porter and General Steele. By

April 15, General Grant's anxiety had prompted him to telegraph Halleck: "Please send General Hunter to report to me. From the last dispatches from Major-General Banks, I fear he is going to be late in his spring movement, and I am desirous of sending an officer of rank with duplicates of [Banks'] orders, and with further instructions."[29]

General Sherman guessed that Steele might be at fault. "It seems to me his movement is very slow," he wired Grant that day, "and he may be so late in reaching Red River as to keep General Banks and A. J. Smith away behind time."[30]

Steele's apparent tardiness might delay the proposed Mobile operation, Cump meant. In any case, Grant instructed General Hunter in a letter dated April 17, 1864, to impress upon Banks "the importance of [his] commencing operations at the very earliest possible moment against Mo-bile, so that his movement may serve as co-operative with those of the other armies in the field. . . ."[31] And in the letter Hunter was to deliver to Banks, the general-in-chief opened with a reference to the Halleck Doctrine: "Owing to the difficulty of giving positive instructions to a distant commander respecting his operations in the field, and being exceedingly anxious that the whole army should act nearly as a unit, I send Major-General Hunter. . . ." And Grant closed by saying: "Hoping that General Hunter will find you back at New Orleans, with the work of concentration commenced. . . ."[32]

For two more days no one east of the Alleghenies could do more than wonder what was really happening up the Red River. Preparing for the coordinated, concurrent attacks Grant and Sherman had envisioned, and Halleck was supporting, took priority in Washington. On April 19, however, Brigadier General Mason Brayman in Cairo began relaying the substance of distressing letters and rumors he had received from the Red River Valley.[33] By April 21, though, Brayman was able to telegraph Secretary of War Stanton and General-in-Chief Grant:

> *General Corse, who was sent by General Sherman to recall General A. J. Smith's command from Red River, has returned. Our loss is 4,000 men, 16 guns, and over 200 wagons. Banks returned to Grand Ecore* [near Natchitoches], *badly injured. He refused to return Smith's command. The naval force is caught in low water, with shoals above and below.*[34]

Promptly, Grant made sure Halleck was informed:

> *You can see from General Brayman's dispatch to me something of*

General Banks' disaster. I have been satisfied for the last nine months that to keep General Banks in command was to neutralize a large force and to support it most expensively. Although I do not insist upon it, I think the best interests of the service demand that General Reynolds should be placed in command at once and that he name his own successor to the command of New Orleans.[35]

To this message the next day, April 23, General Halleck added this terse endorsement: "This telegram [was] shown to the President, by order of the Secretary of War. The President replied that he must delay acting upon it for the present."[36]

Now, it may well have been that Old Brains would have preferred to keep the lieutenant general isolated from the firestorm of controversy that seemed imminent. However, Grant's references to Banks and his sideshow indicated that he had placed no importance at all on the President's attempt to restore Louisiana and Arkansas to the Union through the political assignments he had given Banks and Steele. From April 23 onward, high on the list of Old Brains' concerns had to be acting as a moderator between a soldier who was correct in his military evaluations of the fiasco and a politician whose earlier mistakes seemed likely to blight his chances of being re-elected—and beyond that, of bringing about a just and lasting binding-up of the nation's wounds.

Before April 23 ended, however, from Nashville, General Sherman forwarded to General Halleck copies of letters Corse had brought him that Admiral Porter had written to Cump from Grand Ecore on April 14 and Alexandria, downstream, on April 16. In his first letter, Porter told his friend:

You will no doubt feel much disappointed at not having General A. J. Smith's division returned to you in the time expected, but you will be reconciled when I assure you that the safety of this army and my whole fleet depend on his staying here. His is the only part of the army not demoralized, and if he was to leave there would be a most disastrous retreat.

The army has been shamefully beaten by the rebels. There is no disguising the fact, notwithstanding the general commanding and his staff try to make a victory. Armies victorious don't often go back as this one has done.

Your part of it maintained its reputation and saved the army from being beaten in the two days' fight. It is too long a tale to write, but some of these days I will give you a full and fair account of it. . . . General Corse has heard it all and will tell you all about it.

I was averse to coming up with the fleet, but General Banks considered it necessary to the success of the expedition, and I now can't get back again, the water has fallen so much. This has been terrible work. . . .

I cannot express to you my entire disappointment with this department. You know my opinion of political generals. It is a crying sin to put the lives of thousands in the hands of such men, and the time has come when there should a stop be put to it.

This army is almost in a state of mutiny and not fit to go into a fight. They would follow A. J. Smith, though, anywhere. The more I see of that old gentleman the more I like him. He is a regular trump, and has no give-up in him.

I have been up as far as Loggy Bayou, and there was brought to a dead stand by a large steamer sunk in the channel, resting on each bank. It was providential, or I might have gone farther, and would have been cut off to a certainty. I am not sure that Banks will not sacrifice my vessels now to expediency; that is, his necessities.

I only wish, dear general, that you had taken charge of this Red River business. I am sure it would have had a different termination.[37]

In Admiral Porter's second letter, two days later, he added several thousands of words detailing "an affair the management of which would have been discreditable to a boy nine years of age." Porter's report was of necessity mostly hearsay, as he admitted; even so, the Union's war managers must have shared severe shocks when they read:

I hear that when the general commanding and staff arrived at Pleasant Hill [after their mauling at Sabine Crossroads on April 8] *he had lost all control of himself. I do not wonder at that. An educated soldier may be cool and pleasant enough in the hour of victory, but the true general is best known in the hour of defeat.*

General Banks lost all his prestige, and the men talked so openly of him that our officers had to check them and threaten to have them punished. . . .

You know I have always said that Providence was fighting this great battle its own way, and brings these reverses to teach us, a proud and unthankful people, how to be contented under a good Government, if peaceful times come again. I hope it will teach us not to place the destines of a great nation into the hands of political generals or volunteer admirals.[38]

It is a solace to the wretched to have companions in grief, Old Brains may well have recalled when he read Porter's last sentence. The admiral had made the same point in his first letter; it was impossible for the President to miss it. Yet all that could be hoped was that Abraham Lincoln would sin no more.

"We have more to fear from our friends," Banks had said during the first thrashing Stonewall Jackson gave him in the Shenandoah Valley Campaign, "than from the bayonets of our enemies." And apparently this was uppermost in his mind when he wrote General Sherman on April 14 to inform him that he would not return A. J. Smith's 10,000 troops as promised. "The enemy is very strong," Banks reported, "his army being not less that 25,000 men, many of them the best troops in the rebel service."[39]

In fact, Richard Taylor had no more than about 5,000 braves left after his superior, General Edmund Kirby Smith, stripped his command for the purpose of pursuing Frederick Steele, who had already abandoned the campaign and was trying to get his force back to Little Rock before they starved. Taylor's "army" may well have been the best in the Confederate service, but many of the Texans began the battle of Mansfield (Sabine Crossroads) with weapons they had brought from their farms, and some had none at all until they picked up the ones Yankees had discarded. But crediting Taylor with five times his true number was only a white lie compared with Banks' closing sentences:

Our affairs are in an entirely satisfactory condition, except that, from the low stage of the water and the unexpected strength of the enemy, we required more time than we had anticipated.

Believing you will consider favorably this representation of facts, I have the honor to be, with much respect, your obedient servant.[40]

Sherman had passed copies of Banks' letter, along with the two from Porter to Grant and Halleck, who surely shared his with the President.[41] That was on April 23. The next day, Cump wrote Old Brains on another subject:

I see a mischievous paragraph [in a newspaper] *that you are dissatisfied, and will resign; of course I don't believe it. If I did I would enter my protest.*

You possess a knowledge of law and of the principles of war far beyond that of any other officer in our service. You remember that I regretted your going to Washington for your own sake, but now that you are there you should not leave.

Stability is what we lack in our Government, and changes are always bad. Stand by us and encourage us by your counsels and advice. I know Grant esteems you, and I assure you I do.[42]

6

AS THE END OF APRIL APPROACHED, more and more "news" reached Washington from Louisiana and Arkansas, and for a time many of the messages Halleck and Grant exchanged would be devoted to the questions Nathaniel Banks' fiasco was generating. "I have just received two private letters," the general-in-chief telegraphed the chief of staff from Culpeper on April 25, "one from New Orleans, and one (anonymous) from the Thirteenth Corps, giving deplorable accounts of General Banks' mismanagement. His own report and these letters clearly show all his disasters to be attributable to his incompetency."[43] And that evening, he added:

I would send orders to General Steele to return to Little Rock; to General Banks to return himself immediately to New Orleans and make preparations to carry out his previous instructions [regarding Mobile] *the moment his troops returned; to place the senior officer under himself in command of the troops in the field, with instructions to see the gunboats safely out of Red River as soon as possible, and then return all the troops rapidly to where they belong. If before receiving these instructions he has taken Shreveport, then to leave General Steele and the navy in charge of the river, giving General Steele, if necessary, all of* [A. J.] *Smith's troops.*[44]

Again ignoring the President's political interests embedded in the Red River Expedition, the lieutenant general commanding the Union armies had—in effect—called for the virtual termination of that venture in favor of the Mobile operation. By so doing, Grant had presented General Halleck with precisely the kind of challenge Cump Sherman had nigh-begged him recently to keep facing; "stand by us," he had urged, and "encourage us by your counsels and advice."

As if in response to that appeal, on April 26 Halleck telegraphed Grant:

> *Your telegram of the 22d, asking for the removal of General Banks, was submitted to the President, who replied that he must await further information before he could act in the matter.*
>
> *General Steele was at Camden on the 20th, and was informed of General Banks' disaster. An order to him to return to Little Rock would probably reach him in five or six days. One to General Banks would not reach him in less than two or three weeks.*
>
> *This would cause a conflict in your proposed instructions to these officers, if Banks should have advanced on Shreveport, for Steele would then have returned to Little Rock. Would it not be better to send the instructions contained in your telegram to Banks, and a copy of them to General Steele, with orders to communicate with Banks or his successor in command, and to carry out the spirit of your instructions as in his judgment the condition of affairs at the time would require?*
>
> *I omitted to state that Admiral Porter says the failure of Banks' expedition and the withdrawal of our forces from Red River will result in the loss of nearly all of Louisiana and a part of Arkansas, where there is already a pretty strong Union sentiment.*
>
> *If General Banks is withdrawn from the field General Franklin will be the senior officer left.*[45]

Therein, Henry Halleck applied his characteristic precision in thought and expression directly but with tact. Twice he injected Lincoln's concerns. His examination of the complexity of the message delivery timetable reflected experience Grant had not yet acquired. And having identified a problem, he offered a solution.

"The way you propose to communicate orders to General Steele and General Banks will be better than as I directed," the general-in-chief conceded. And he continued:

> *General Franklin is an able officer, but has been so mixed up with misfortune that I would not select him for a large separate command, but he is so much better than General Banks that I will*

*feel safer with him commanding midst danger than the latter. I
submit this, however, to the President and Secretary of War, whether
the change shall be made. I am in hopes the whole problem will be
solved before orders reach.*[46]

"I do not see that better orders[47] could have been given," General
Grant wired the chief of staff after he received a copy of Halleck's directive
to Banks. "General Banks, by his failure, has absorbed 10,000 veteran
troops that now should be with General Sherman and 30,000 of his own
that would have been moving toward Mobile, without accomplishing any
good result."[48]

General Hunter, Grant's special courier, described Banks' actual results
in a letter written from Alexandria on April 28:

*I arrived here yesterday morning in eight and a half days from
Washington. I immediately had an interview with General Banks,
and delivered him your communications.*

*I regret very much to find affairs here in a very complicated,
perplexing, and precarious situation. You have, of course, had the
particulars of the fights. The situation at present is this: We have
some six, eight, or ten gun-boats, among them two monitors, above
the rapids, with no possibility of getting them out.*

*The whole question is, then, reduced to this: Shall we destroy
the gun-boats or lose the services at this critical period of the war of
the 20,000 men necessary to take care of them? My opinion is, of
course, to destroy the boats.*

*Why this expedition was ordered I cannot imagine. General
Banks assures me it was undertaken against his opinion and earnest
protest. The result is certainly a very sad one.*

*I shall communicate from day to day anything of interest
which may occur.*[49]

While Hunter's news, which did not add much to what Admiral
Porter had earlier relayed to Sherman, Halleck, Grant, and Lincoln, was on
its way to Culpeper, General Grant was revising his opinion about that
situation. On April 29 he telegraphed Halleck:

*On due reflection I do not see that anything can be done this spring
with troops west of the Mississippi, except on that side.*

I think, therefore, it will be better to put the whole of that territory into one military division, under some good officer, and let him work out of present difficulties without reference to previous instructions. All instructions that have been given have been given with the view of getting as many of these troops east of the Mississippi as possible.[50]

At 2:30 that afternoon the chief of staff replied:

Your telegram of 10.30 a.m. has been received and submitted to the Secretary of War. You do not name any officer for the trans-Mississippi command. Did you propose to leave Banks in the general command, or only of his present department, or to supersede him entirely?
    I will immediately write to you confidentially the difficulties in the way of removing General Banks, as I understand them.[51]

General Grant had hoped to launch the Union armies' fully coordinated spring offensives at about this time. Surely, striving to minimize delays was taking most of his time and attention. In any case, it was not until six o'clock that evening that he sent Halleck this message:

Of the four department commanders west of the Mississippi I would far prefer General Steele to take the general charge, but he cannot be spared from his special command; there is no one to fully take his place. I would leave General Banks in command of his department, but order him to his headquarters in New Orleans.
    If you could go in person and take charge of the trans-Mississippi division until it is relieved from its present dilemma, and then place a commander over it or let it return to separate departments, as now, leaving General Canby temporarily in your place, I believe it would be the best that can be done.
    I am well aware of the importance of your remaining where you are at this time, and the only question is which of the two duties is the most important.[52]

Unaware, as yet, that a message from Grant was on its way—one in which the lieutenant general commanding had in haste downgraded his mentor's value to him by suggesting that Old Brains' undistinguished classmate Edward R. S. Canby could fill his place—on that same evening, the chief of staff fulfilled his promise to write confidentially:

I fully agree with you, that after General Banks' long delay it will hardly be possible to get his troops east of the Mississippi time to be of any use in the spring campaign. Moreover, to withdraw any of his forces at the present time might lead to serious disasters and to a virtual closing of the navigation of the Mississippi River.

I submitted your telegram of 10.30 a.m. to the Secretary of War, who was of opinion that before asking the President for an order I should obtain your views in regard to the extent of the proposed division, the officer to command it, &c., and that I should write to you confidentially on the subject.

Do you propose to include Pope's, Curtis', and Rosecrans' commands, or only the present Departments of the Gulf and of Arkansas, with the Indian Territory? Is it proposed to give Banks the command of the division, or to leave him in the subordinate position of his present department, or to remove him entirely?

In either case the order must be definite. If Banks is superseded Franklin will be the ranking officer in the field, and Rosecrans, Curtis, and McClernand in the division. You have also heretofore spoken of Steele and Reynolds in connection with this command.

I think the President will consent to the order if you insist upon General Banks' removal as a military necessity, but he will do so very reluctantly, as it would give offense to many of his friends, and would probably be opposed by a portion of his Cabinet. Moreover, what could be done with Banks? He has many political friends who would probably demand for him a command equal to the one he now has. . . .

Before submitting the matter to the President, the Secretary of War wishes to have in definite form precisely the order you wish issued.[53]

Having delivered himself of that counsel, which neither General Canby nor any other officer in the United States' armies could possibly have provided, Old Brains turned his attention to answering Cump Sherman's letter to him dated April 24:

Newspaper stories about quarrels between the President, Secretary of War, General Grant, and myself, and my resigning are all "bosh." Not a word of truth in them.

There has not been the slightest difficulty, misunderstanding, or even difference of opinion between any of the parties, so far as I know, and the relations between Grant and myself are not only friendly and pleasant, but cordial.

I have never had the slightest intention of resigning so long as my services can be useful to the country. These malicious stories generally originate in such secesh journals as the [New York] *Herald and* World. *Of course my position here, both as General-in-Chief and as Chief of Staff, has been and is a disagreeable one, from which I can receive no credit, but sufficient abuse to satisfy any ordinary ambition.*

To this, however, I have become utterly callous. Grant very wisely keeps away from Washington, and out of reach of the rascally politicians and shoddy contractors who infest every department of the Government and abuse everybody who will not grind their axes.

Banks' operations in the West are about what should have been expected from a general so utterly destitute of military education and military capacity. It seems but little better than murder to give important commands to such men as Banks, Butler, McClernand, Sigel, and Lew. Wallace, and yet it seems impossible to prevent it.

If Banks and Steele fail to occupy the line of Red River and the troops are withdrawn as General Grant contemplated, I fear that we shall have serious trouble in Louisiana and Arkansas, and that the navigation of the Mississippi will be greatly disturbed, if not suspended.[54]

On April 30, the next day, General Grant returned to the question of who should command in a reorganized "trans-Mississippi division":

I do not propose removing General Banks, but would not increase his command. If you could not go to take temporary command until present difficulties are cleared up, I think General Steele would be the best man, and General Reynolds to take his place. The great objection to this is taking General Steele from where he is at this time.[55]

Halleck finally set the general-in-chief straight about the situation in Washington on May 2. At the end of a long message about shortages of manpower and supply vessels, he wrote:

General Canby has been assisting me in getting recruits, furloughed men, and troops out of the Northern States. He has been sick, and his duties in the War Department have nearly broken him down. He says his business is greatly behind in the office.

Wherever you and the Secretary of War think I can be of most service I am ready to go. I am willing to serve anywhere and everywhere.

Just at the present crisis it might not be well to derange the machinery here. There must be some military head here to keep things from getting into a snarl. There must be some common head to make the different bureaus act in concert and with promptness. It is impossible for the Secretary of War or his assistants to attend personally to these matters.[56]

So ended the possibility of General Halleck's change in assignment; but even on the eve of launching the Union armies' spring campaigns, Grant's mind was still on Banks. On May 3, 1864, he telegraphed Halleck:

This army moves to-morrow morning. Will occupy Germanna, Ely's, and Culpeper Mine Fords by daylight the morning of the 4th.

I will have to leave affairs west entirely with you. General Banks now proposes to keep A. J. Smith's force altogether, so as to give him sufficient strength to operate against Mobile. It is now too late for Smith's force to return to be of any use in the spring campaign, but I do think it is a waste of strength to trust General Banks with a large command or an important expedition.[57]

Old Brains' reply was immediate and confidential:

In regard to changes in commanders west of the Mississippi, or the superseding of General Banks by placing Steele, Reynolds, or some other officer in general command, the Secretary of War has copies of all your telegrams, and I believe they have all been read by the President. I have not, however, heard him say anything on the subject since his reply, which I sent you, to your first telegram immediately after the news of Banks' defeat.

General Banks is a personal friend of the President, and has strong political supporters in and out of Congress. There will undoubtedly be a very strong opposition to his being removed or superseded, and I think the President will hesitate to act unless he has a definite request from you to do so, as a military necessity, you designating his superior or superior in command. On receiving such a formal request (not a mere suggestion) I believe, as I wrote you some days ago, he would act immediately.

I have no authority for saying this, but give it simply as my own opinion, formed from the last two years' experience, and the reason, I think, is very obvious. To do an act which will give offense to a large number of his political friends the President will require some evidence in a positive form to show the military necessity of that act. In other words, he must have something in a definite shape to fall back upon as his justification.

You will perceive that the press in New Orleans and in the Eastern States are already beginning to open in General Banks' favor. The administration would be immediately attacked for his removal.

Do not understand me as advocating his retention in command. On the contrary, I expressed to the President months ago my own opinion of General Banks' want of military capacity. Whatever order you may ask for on this subject I will do my best to have issued.[58]

Chief of Staff Halleck succeeded in closing the case, as far as Washington was concerned, on May 7, 1864, in a letter of instructions to General Canby:

The Secretary of War directs that you immediately repair to the Military Division of West Mississippi and assume the direction of all military operations in the Departments of the Gulf and of Arkansas.

You will perceive from the dispatches sent to and received from Generals Grant, Sherman, Steele, and Banks that the main object of the recent military operations west of the Mississippi River was the occupation of Red River, so as to shorten our line of defense, secure the navigation of the Mississippi from interruption from the western side, and to prevent any large forces from penetrating into Arkansas, Missouri, or the Indian Territory. This would also enable us to dispense with the present difficult and expensive line of defense on the Arkansas River, and to diminish the military posts at Helena and New Madrid.

The failure to carry out this plan has, it is believed, resulted from General Banks' delay to co-operate in time with the movements of Generals Steele and A. J. Smith, and his meeting and fighting the enemy by detachments instead of his whole force in mass. You will perceive by Lieutenant-General Grant's dispatches that he has no confidence in General Banks' military capacity, and has consequently directed him to turn over the command of his troops to the senior officer in the field and return to New Orleans.

General Grant at one time ordered a part of the troops of the Department of the Gulf to New Orleans to operate against Mobile, but this project has been given up, and all troops in your division will be retained for duty west of the Mississippi. . . .

The enemy lives almost entirely upon the country, and we must hereafter imitate his example and avoid so far as possible encumbering our movable columns with too large trains. Existing orders give you all necessary authority on this subject.

You will perceive from a perusal of official dispatches that General Banks' course in scattering his troops by the occupation of so many points upon the Gulf coast, and in operating both upon the coast and by the line of Red River, has been against the advice and instructions sent to him by his superiors. Success can be gained only by concentration upon some important point, and avoiding all detachments and double lines of operations. . . .

At this distance from the theater of war it is not possible to give special instructions or to anticipate the condition of your command at the time you will reach it. You are therefore invested with all the power and authority which the President can confer on you, and you will act in all things as in your opinion may be best to secure the object in view, the restoration of the authority of the United States west of the Mississippi.[59]

General Halleck added a postscript—"I am directed to call your attention particularly to the importance of protecting the gun-boats in the Red River by the military forces under your command"—but that duty proved moot. Later in May, by building dams, former logger Lieutenant Colonel Joseph Bailey and about four thousand of Banks' troops succeeded in raising the water level in the rapids at Alexandria enough for Admiral Porter's trapped gunboat flotilla to reach the lower Red River. Dick Taylor pursued the fleeing Yankees to the west bank of Atchafalaya Bayou, where high water prevented Banks' troops from crossing. Again, Bailey saved the expedition's survivors—this time by using steamers for pontoons and laying a wooden road across their decks. On May 19, 1864, as the troops boarded transports on the Mississippi bound for New Orleans, General Canby relieved General Banks of command.[60]

All of which Stonewall Jackson, witnessing from Valhalla his pupil Richard Taylor's skillful employment of his late mentor's principles, must have found "delightful excitement." A contrary assessment of the Red River Expedition and of Napoleon P. Banks was filed from Alexandria on May 2 by Major General David Hunter, and it foreshadowed the findings of the Joint Congressional Committee on the Conduct of the War a year later. Wrote Hunter to General-in-Chief Grant:

> *You told me to write you fully with regard to affairs in this department. I may write too freely, but where great and vital interests are at stake you must excuse me if I am very free. Knowing that your time is very precious, I shall briefly state the conclusions to which I have arrived:*
>
> *First. The Department of the Gulf is one great mass of corruption. Cotton and politics, instead of the war, appear to have engrossed the army. The vital interests of the contest are laid aside, and we are amused with sham State governments, which are a complete laughing-stock to the people, and the lives of our men are sacrificed in the interests of cotton speculators.*
>
> *Second. The vicious trade regulations, or the vicious administration of them, have filled the enemy's country with all kinds of goods except military supplies, and these they have been smart enough to capture. If this course is continued we cannot look for a speedy termination of the war.*
>
> *Third. The best interests of the service require that General McPherson, or some other competent commander, should be sent immediately here. Port Hudson and Natchez are both threatened, and unless prompt action is immediately taken we shall lose the navigation of the Mississippi.*
>
> *General Banks has treated me with great politeness and kindness, and I regret greatly to say anything prejudicial to him as a soldier or a gentleman, but a strong sense of an important duty compels me to speak. The most intelligent of the officers of the army and navy will, I think, fully concur in all I have said. General Banks has not certainly the confidence of his army.*[61]

Such was the record, with which historian Ludwell Johnson must not have been entirely familiar when he wrote: "The suspicion arises that perhaps [Halleck] had sensed some possible disaster awaiting Banks in the lonely pine forests of Louisiana, especially since, by his own admission, he believed Banks to be unfit for command in the field."[62]

7

"THE CROSSING OF THE RAPIDAN EFFECTED," Lieutenant General Grant telegraphed the chief of staff from Germanna Ford on May 4, 1864.[63] With his "overland" campaign off to an on-time start, he would prove more diligent than any field army commander had ever been in keeping General Halleck informed. Grant's reports were terse, and they invited no encouragement, counsel, or advice—which was as it should have been in a professionally led force well-supplied.

In a welcome change from generals who gave more thought to excuses for failures that may not yet have happened than to preventing them, "Unconditional Surrender" Grant was candid. "So far there is no decisive result," he wired Halleck on the second day of fighting in the Wilderness, where General Lee and Old Jack had wrecked Fighting Joe Hooker's Army of the Potomac almost exactly a year earlier. "I do not think our loss exceeds 8,000. . . ."[64]

It would reach 17,500 before Grant withdrew,[65] but unlike Hooker he did not head back to safety across the fords; instead, he tried to beat Lee to Spotsylvania, southeast of the suburb of hell called the Wilderness. But General Lee got there first and fortified the ground between the Ny and the Po Rivers, obliging Grant to attack his lines straight ahead.[66]

"We have now ended the sixth day of very heavy fighting," Grant reported to General Halleck on May 11 from "Near Spotsylvania Court House." His loss he estimated at twenty thousand men. "I am now sending back to Belle Plain all my wagons for a fresh supply of provisions and ammunition, and propose to fight it out on this line if it takes all summer. . . . I am satisfied the enemy are very shaky, and are only kept up to the mark by the greatest exertions on the part of their officers, and by keeping them intrenched in every position they take."[67]

Well, yes. But much earlier General Halleck had said he believed Robert E. Lee to be the best of the Southern generals; Grant was discovering directly, for the first time, how correct Old Brains had been; and now General Lee was performing as splendidly on the defensive as he had, while Jackson lived, in his audacious offensives.

Grant's casualties on May 10 and 12 alone totaled nearly 11,000.[68]

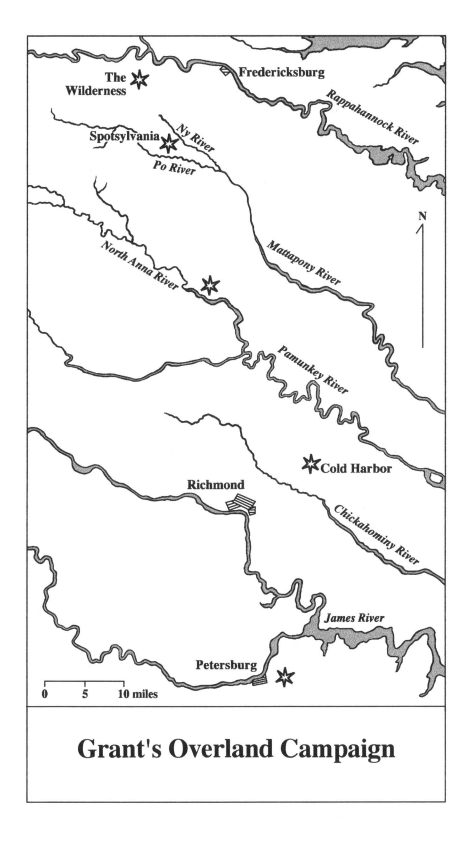

Grant's Overland Campaign

562 *Henry Halleck's War*

Another source put federal losses at "slightly less than 18,000" for the two-week fight near Spotsylvania Court House.[69]

When General Lee sensed that Grant was not going to fight it out with him on that line any longer, he dropped southward to a position on the North Anna River, too strong for Grant to attack. Their next encounter was near Cold Harbor, with General Lee still blocking Grant from the roads to Richmond and forcing him to attack his fortified lines. Grant lost more than seven thousand men in less than an hour (most of them in the first eight minutes, said some reports) during an assault through withering Confederate crossfire on the morning of June 3.[70]

From the campaign's outset, General Grant had refused to allow newspaper reporters to use the telegraph, so about all the Union's war managers in Washington knew of his progress came from the optimistic but vague comments he included in his initial messages to General Halleck. Ignoring Grant's sentences regarding his losses, Secretary of War Stanton's public statements (for example, "the brilliant success of the Army of The Potomac against the rebel army. . . ."[71])—absent any news to the contrary—misled the people in the North and enhanced their vulnerability to severe and angry shock when the appalling length of casualty lists became evident.

Abraham Lincoln had inadvertently contributed to the danger of the problem Stanton had created by responding to certain inquiries in a lighthearted manner. To members of Congress who wondered what was going on, he replied: "Well, I can't tell much about it. You see, Grant has gone into the Wilderness, crawled in, drawn up the ladder, and pulled the hole in after him, and I guess we'll just have to wait till he comes out before we know just what he is up to."[72]

Following the motto *Save the surface and you save all* may well have been irresistible politically—1864 being a presidential election year—but how would voters react once they had been shocked and saddened by the ever-increasing length of the casualty lists? How could they reconcile Stanton's early suggestions of victories in the light of General Lee's having forced Grant to withdraw from the Wilderness and then Spotsylvania and the North Anna to the slaughtering grounds at Cold Harbor, and having inflicted such appalling losses along the way, without Grant's having any accomplishment at all to offset all this killing and maiming?

General Halleck must have found the irony excruciating. For nineteen months his critics had done their best to destroy him by alleging that he was too spineless to give field army commanders direct orders. Now, Lincoln had found a general who would do precisely that, and more: Ulysses Grant had brought to the war in the east what no Union army's commander in that theater had ever displayed: a sense of duty so strong that he would pay *whatever price in casualties* the men in General Lee's army imposed in order to accomplish his mission. And because of this cold steel truth, if the dreaded lists grew much longer, either Lincoln would be swept out of office by a grieving and frustrated electorate in November or the proverbial guillotine would claim the head of Lieutenant General Grant.

Neither outcome was acceptable to Henry Halleck, apparently, for as early as May 17 he had broken his silence regarding Grant's (or Lincoln's?) sideshows being conducted by "Spoons" Butler south of Richmond and Franz Sigel in the Shenandoah Valley. Apparently, neither of the political generals' operations had distracted General Lee's attention one bit. To the general-in-chief, Old Brains wrote:

> *Instead of advancing on Staunton* [Sigel] *is already in full retreat on Strasburg. If you expect anything from him you will be mistaken. He will do nothing but run. He never did anything else. The Secretary of War proposes to put General Hunter in his place. Send him up immediately. . . . Butler has fallen back to-day. Do not rely on him. . . .*[73]

Henry Halleck had taken Franz Sigel's measure out in Missouri, and—like a country boy contemplating his first seidel of beer—he approached all political generals with long teeth, but a Confederate force that had included the Corps of Cadets of the Virginia Military Institute had routed Sigel at New Market.[74] But ridding the Union armies of Lincoln's mistakes was not the point: annihilating General Lee's army was, as Old Brains reiterated on May 23:

> *Permit me to repeat what I have so often urged, that in my opinion every man we can collect should be hurled against Lee, wherever he may be, as his army, not Richmond, is the true objective point of this campaign. When that army is broken, Richmond will be of very little value to the enemy.*
>
> *Demonstrations on that place exhaust us more than they injure the rebels, for it will require 2 men outside to keep 1 in Richmond. I once thought that this could be more than compensated for by destroying their lines of supply, but experience has proved that they can repair them just about as fast as we can destroy them; such at least was the case under Dix and Foster, and I think Butler's operations will have no better result.*

> *I have no doubt we shall soon have loud calls for re-enforcements* [from Hunter] *in West Virginia, but I shall not send any unless you so order, for I have very little faith in these collateral operations. The little good they accomplish seldom equals their cost in men and money.*
>
> *If you succeed in crushing Lee all will be well; if you fail, we immediately lose whatever we may have gained in West Virginia or around Richmond.*
>
> *I therefore propose to send to you everything I can get without regard to the calls of others, until you direct otherwise.*[75]

Butler's force, which had been trapped by Confederate defenders in a loop made by the James River below Richmond was (in Grant's phrase) "as completely shut off from further operations directly against Richmond as if it had been in a bottle strongly corked."[76] Once extricated, some of Butler's troops reinforced Grant at Cold Harbor.

Also on May 23, Old Brains passed along some gossip having to do with promotions to Regular Army ranks:

> *There are two vacancies. The law allows five. You filled an original vacancy; and I last year urged Sherman's name for Wool's place, but could not get him appointed.*
>
> *Your promotion makes a second vacancy, and I have urged the names of Meade and Sherman, and Hancock for Meade's place as brigadier.*
>
> *There is some obstacle in the way and I can't remove it. I am not certain what it is but can guess.*
>
> *Perhaps you will be enlightened a little by knowing what are some of the outside influences. I understand the names of Butler and Sickles have been strongly urged by politicians, in order they say to break down "West Point influence."*
>
> *It will not be difficult to draw conclusions. This is* entre nous.[77]

A letter Grant had written from the stalemate on the North Anna on May 26, however, may well have disturbed General Halleck because of the mixed signals it conveyed:

> *Lee's army is really whipped. The prisoners we now take show it, and*

the action of his army shows it unmistakably. A battle with them
outside of intrenchments cannot be had. . . . I may be mistaken, but
I feel that our success over Lee's army is already insured. . . .[78]

Old Brains was not ready to agree. Moreover, his misgivings were
supported by information he had obtained from other sources. Accordingly,
on May 27, a week before the sickening catastrophe at Cold Harbor, after
mentioning that he had sent between sixty thousand and seventy thousand
men to Meade's army since it crossed the Rapidan, he offered his superior
some unsolicited advice:

In a telegram . . . which I have just seen it is stated on the authority
of General Ingalls that you propose to break up your depots on the
Rappahannock about the first of next month, and remove them to
West Point, the White House, or some other place on the Pamunkey.
This would indicate that when Lee falls back behind the South
Anna you propose to make the Pamunkey your base of operations on
Richmond.

Permit me to repeat to you the opinions which have been
expressed to me within the last two years by officers who are thor-
oughly acquainted with the country, and who had much experience
with General McClellan in his Peninsular operations. They say that
any campaign against Richmond based on the Pamunkey, with West
Point, White House, or even New Castle, as the point of supplies,
will involve the defense of the line of the York and Pamunkey Rivers,
and the passage of the Chickahominy and its swamps. This will
leave Lee, if he falls back upon Richmond, the James River Canal,
and one or more of the railroads south of that river, as com-
munication by which to receive re-enforcements and supplies. Even
if your cavalry should cut these communications, they will soon be
reopened.

But should you occupy the sector less than 90 degrees between
the James and the Chickahominy, your right resting on the former
and your left on the Horse Pond or Meadow Bridge [i.e., the
northwest quadrant of a circle having Richmond as its center],
your flanks will be pretty safe, your line of advance will be over
favorable ground, you will hold the canal, and can, with your
cavalry, control the railroad lines south of the James River. Moreover,
they say this point is the most favorable for an attack, as the Tredegar

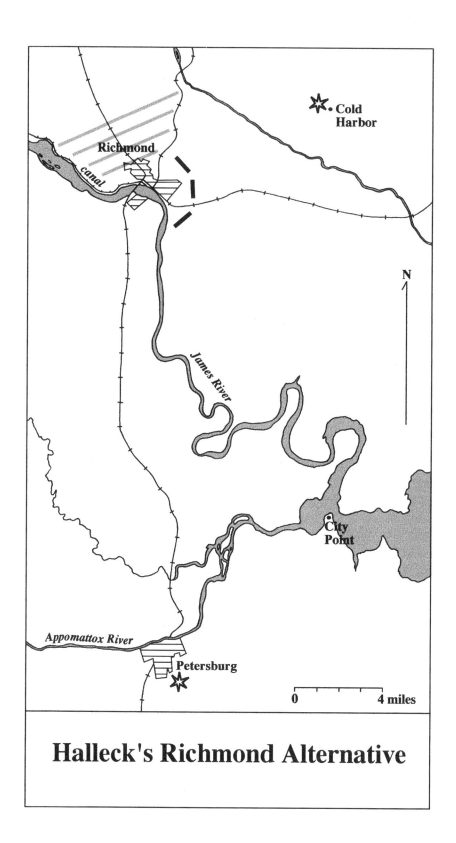

Cold Harbor

Richmond

canal

N

James River

City Point

Appomattox River

Petersburg

0   4 miles

Halleck's Richmond Alternative

Iron Works, the arsenal, the water-works, and all the flouring mills lie on the northwest side of the city, and exposed to a bombardment from that direction.

At this point General Halleck cited a great many of the disadvantages of relying on three river ports east of Richmond. Without saying as much, for it would be evident from any map, he seemed to assume the northwest quadrant's arc he thought Grant should occupy would be supplied by railroads coming southward from the Potomac. He continued:

Is it not safer to have your depot of supplies in your rear toward Washington than on the James or the York? I presume there were good reasons for abandoning the [Richmond, Fredericksburg and Potomac railroad] *at the time you did, but if you should wish to resume that line it can be immediately put in operation. It is completed to Falmouth, and the bridge to Fredericksburg can be restored in a few days. Although a little longer for land transportation than either of the others, it is much shorter and more convenient by water, and with our railroad facilities supplies could be forwarded much more rapidly, and I hardly think a larger force would be required to guard it.*

I simply make these suggestions for your consideration, but shall make no changes without your orders. I, however, must urge you not to put the Chickahominy between your army and its supplies, nor between you and Richmond. It is a most serious obstacle to be passed by a large army or by its supplies. Moreover, in the summer months, it is exceedingly unhealthy, as is also the James River below Richmond.[79]

Lengthy as General Halleck's suggestion certainly was, there were several important points he did not include—presumably because they would occur to the lieutenant general commanding. Among them:

- After having taken such horrifying casualties to get from the Rapidan to the North Anna, for Grant merely to reoccupy the lines east of Richmond from which General Lee drove McClellan two years earlier would surely enrage the Union electorate.
- For Grant to be operating from the south side of the James, with Lee between him and Richmond, would alarm the President since if Lee advanced toward Washington and Maryland again, Meade's Army of

the Potomac would be badly out of position to protect the Union capital.

On May 31, while Grant was deploying his forces near Cold Harbor and the plateau formed by Boatswain's Swamp (where Lee had wrecked Fitz-John Porter's corps in the battle called Gaines's Mill), General Halleck backed his proposal of May 27 by sending an emissary to the general-in-chief. Old Brains wrote:

> *I know of no one who has a more thorough knowledge of all the passes of the Chickahominy and of the approaches to Richmond than Brig. Gen. J. G. Barnard. Although I do not agree with General Barnard in all his opinions on the strategy of the campaign, I think he is a man of very great military ability, and that the information which he can give you will be very valuable. His mind is clear and his judgment excellent. Of course if you do not want him you will order him back to Washington.*[80]

Had General Halleck become inured that Grant was going to repeat the Young Napoleon's errors? Perhaps, but it may have been more likely that sending Barnard, formerly George McClellan's chief engineer, to Grant was merely another attempt by the chief of staff to carry out his duty to support the general-in-chief.

Actually, Henry Halleck was thinking about the entire situation and its opportunities as well as its problems. Not facing Lee himself, he could take longer and broader views—views which were, in fact, beyond Grant's ability to perceive dispassionately, much less to evaluate at the end of May. Indeed, Grant could not reach Halleck's proposed arc unless and until he could dispose of the Army of Northern Virginia or get around the northern end of its new line west of Cold Harbor. Accordingly, he deferred decision and concentrated on attacking Lee.

Grant's climactic assault was launched early on the morning of June 3, 1864. Cold Harbor would rival Fredericksburg as a federal disaster in numbers of casualties (roughly thirteen thousand before Grant withdrew), sheer pigheadedness of Union army leadership, and horror experienced by wounded bluecoats who were left to die where they had fallen. The main difference was the season.

Without referring to the fact that more than seven thousand of his men shot down two days earlier were dying or lying unburied between the lines, on June 5 the lieutenant general replied to Halleck's letter of May 27:

"A full survey of all the ground satisfies me that it would not be practicable to hold a line northeast [sic] of Richmond that would protect the Fredericksburg railroad, to enable us to use it for supplying the army," he began, raising the question: How could Grant possibly have made such a survey, with General Lee's army in the way? Then Grant, who must have forgotten Halleck's long discussion of such factors, added: "To do so would give us a long vulnerable line of road to protect, exhausting much of our strength in guarding it, and would leave open to the enemy all of his lines of communication on the south side of the James."

> *My idea from the start* [General Grant continued] *has been to beat Lee's army, if possible, north of Richmond, then, after destroying his lines of communication north of the James River, to transfer the army to the south side and besiege Lee in Richmond, or follow him south if he should retreat. I now find, after more than thirty days of trial, that the enemy deems it of the first importance to run no risks with the armies they now have. They act purely on the defensive, behind breast-works, or feebly on the offensive immediately in front of them, and where in case of repulse they can instantly retire behind them.*
>
> *Without a greater sacrifice of human life than I am willing to make, all cannot be accomplished that I had designed outside of the city. I have, therefore, resolved upon the following plan: I will continue to hold substantially the ground now occupied by the Army of the Potomac, taking advantage of any favorable circumstance that may present itself, until the cavalry can be sent west to destroy the Virginia Central Railroad from about Beaver Dam for some 25 or 30 miles west. When this is effected, I will move the army to the south side of James River, either by crossing the Chickahominy and marching near to City Point, or by going to the mouth of the Chickahominy on the north side and crossing there.*
>
> *To provide for this last and most probable contingency six or more ferry-boats of the largest class ought to be immediately provided.*
>
> *Once on the south side of the James River I can cut off all sources of supply to the enemy, except what is furnished by the* [James River] *canal. If Hunter succeeds in reaching Lynchburg that will be lost to* [Lee] *also. Should Hunter not succeed I will still make the effort to destroy the canal by sending cavalry up the south side of the river with a pontoon train to cross wherever they can.*

> *The feeling of the two armies now seems to be that the rebels can protect themselves only by strong intrenchments, while our army is not only confident of protecting itself without intrenchments, but that it can beat and drive the enemy wherever and whenever he can be found without this protection.*[81]

Given Cold Harbor's grim results, General Grant's last paragraph was unfortunate. But Halleck put the entire exploration of the alternatives behind him, as was indicated by his reversion on June 7 to the normal chief of staff's duty of reporting:

> *Your letter of the 5th, by Lieutenant-Colonel Babcock, was received last evening. General Meigs has been advised of your wishes in regard to ferry-boats. . . . Everything will be sent forward as soon as you direct. . . .*
> *Nothing has recently been heard of Generals Hunter* [who had relieved Sigel] *and Crook. Sherman is still doing well, but some apprehension has been felt about Forrest's movements to cut off his communications. General Canby has sent forces to Memphis to assist in driving Forrest out of the country. Nothing recently from Steele.*
> *I inclose a list of the troops forwarded from this department to the Army of the Potomac since the campaign opened—48,265 men. I shall send you a few regiments more, when all resources will be exhausted till another draft is made.*[82]

Having been unable to catch General Lee outside the Confederates' entrenchments or to whip him in assaults at hideous cost, the federal general-in-chief bypassed the Confederate capital, crossed the James, and drove westward to below Petersburg, the railroad hub not far south of Richmond. Again, General Lee blocked him. Grant resorted to siege operations.

It could hardly have been much of a surprise to Henry Halleck to have learned that while shredding Meade's ranks at Cold Harbor, General Lee had dispatched Major General Wade Hampton and his cavalry to spoil Little Phil Sheridan's raid west of Richmond. Moreover, Lee had sent Stonewall Jackson's old corps, led now by Jubal Early, to the Shenandoah Valley to rid it of David Hunter's Yankees and—if Early chose—to move down the Turnpike, cross the Potomac into Maryland, and to threaten Washington.

17 ★ Honor, Honor, Honor

G ENERAL GRANT WAS MADE COMMANDER of all the United States armies by the friends of the administration in Congress," according to an editorial in the New York *Herald,* "because they had no faith in the military abilities of General Halleck. . . ." Allegedly, Congress desired that his influence should no longer be felt in the armies' operations, and [the lawgivers] "are naturally dissatisfied at the manner in which the President has failed to carry out, and has even thwarted, their wishes."

Halleck, continued the writer, had been on trial for nearly two years without originating "the great plans that are to crush the rebellion." Therefore, "it is hardly to be expected that he will appreciate the great plans of another, and it is believed that he will be but too ready to criticize and carp at those plans. . . . Nor is it to be expected that a man of Halleck's caliber will have the moral elevation and greatness of soul to cooperate with one who, being his subordinate in the West, has come forward so rapidly, and finally pushed him from his place. . . ."

The *Herald's* remedy:

> *Congress must see that its work is only half done. It was not enough to elevate General Grant. General Halleck must be put out of the way; and until that is done, there is no hope that the conduct of the war will be different in the future from what it has been in the past.*[1]

Such spleen was vented in early April 1864, weeks before the Army of the Potomac's casualty lists arriving from the Wilderness, Spotsylvania, and especially Cold Harbor had provided grim evidence of the assininity of the newspaper's rush to judgment. In fact, the Union's conduct of the war *had* changed: It had *hardened.*

Even so, the author of the *Herald's* editorial had posed—or at least implied—a question well worth asking: How drastically had the North's efforts to quell the rebellion been impaired by Old Brains' proving "too ready to criticise and carp" when he learned of Lieutenant General Grant's plans?

Not in the *slightest.* On February 17, 1864, Halleck had said in a letter to Grant: "I write to you plainly and frankly, for between us there should be no reserve or concealment of opinions. As before remarked, I presume, under the authority of the President, the final decision of these questions will be referred to you. Nevertheless, I think you are entitled to have, and that it is my duty to frankly give, my individual opinion on the subject. . . ."[2]

But how closely had Halleck's performance *actually tracked* his stated intent? By mid-June the soldier Grant had supposedly "pushed from his place" had supported his successor so diligently that he had nigh-depleted the North of fresh cannon fodder.

And what effect had Old Brains' "plain and frank opinions"—the *Herald's* predicted criticisms and carpings—had on the lieutenant general commanding's actions and orders? Again, none.

In fact, the *Herald's* resident Halleck-hater ought to have asked: How drastically were the North's efforts to quell the rebellion impaired by General Grant's having paid *too little* attention to Old Brains' warnings—for one, that General Lee might try to take Washington even while he was blocking Grant from getting any nearer to Richmond than the ghastly killing grounds east of the Confederate lines at Cold Harbor?

Congress had desired to "replace the President's mediocre adviser by an able soldier," the New York *Herald* had assured its readers. "[They] desired that a technical strategist, a martinet and a Marplot, should not occupy the highest place in our armies while there was a man of genius to fill it."[3]

Henry Halleck—once described as "an oleagenous Methodist parson in regimentals"[4]—a *martinet*?

Conferring upon Ulysses Grant the rank of genius was, alas, an even more egregious deviation from reality. True, the skill and tenacity of Robert E. Lee and the devastating firepower of his Army of Northern Virginia had so far denied the Congressionally-anointed lieutenant general the opportunity to display the "genius" perceived by the *Herald.* Unfortunately for the Union, all that General Grant had achieved near term was the shift of

Meade's Army of the Potomac from the Rapidan to a stalemate south of the James at a cost in casualties that would move historian Allan Nevins to write:

> *As Americans thought of two hundred thousand graves of Northern boys staring at the sky, they were aware that another summer of faltering and defeat might be the last. Meanwhile, dwellers in the cities once more opened their newspapers daily to long lists of the slain and maimed, villagers and townspeople bleakly studied the sheets posted on bulletin boards, farm mothers opened War Department envelopes with trembling fingers.*[5]

If, as the Northern press now insisted, General Grant was a "butcher," so had been the chief of staff who had supported him by (among many other things of value to his superior) replacing his appalling losses. When Old Brains made the kind of commitment to Grant that he had set forth in his letter of February 17, 1864, he had put his personal *honor* at risk. That, of course, was nothing new for him. But the lieutenant general's having been unable to adopt Halleck's advice—to shift his forces around Lee's to a line along the northwest quadrant of a circle drawn from Richmond's center—resulted in a chain of events that raised the question: How far would Henry Halleck's sense of honor, *beyond* his sense of duty, permit him to aid and abet the efforts of a "genius" who, in going his own way, might be raising the stakes to heights the people of the Union, and presidential candidate Abraham Lincoln in particular, would no longer—and possibly should no longer—accept?

2

AS JULY 1864 OPENED, ULYSSES GRANT was discovering what his predecessor as general-in-chief had known all along: that the politicians Abraham Lincoln had appointed to high rank very early in the war had been mistakes that ought to be corrected. Nathaniel Banks had earned fresh disgrace by his display of incompetence during the Red River Expedition. Franz Sigel had been whipped and humiliated at the battle of New Market. Now it seemed that Major General Benjamin F. Butler, also known in Louisiana as "Spoons" and "Beast," might be returned to civilian life before Sigel.

From Old Brains, General Grant had learned that one must be extremely circumspect when trying to remove officers whose importance to a President seeking re-election transcended military realities. Such an awareness is evident in a letter the lieutenant general wrote Halleck on July 1, 1864:

> *Mr. Dana, Assistant Secretary of War, has just returned. He informs me that he called attention to the necessity of sending General Butler to another field of duty.*
>
> *Whilst I have no difficulty with General Butler, finding him always clear in his conception of orders and prompt to obey, yet there is a want of knowledge how to execute and particularly a prejudice against him as a commander that operates against his usefulness.*
>
> *I have feared that it might become necessary to separate him and General [W. F.] Smith. The latter is really one of the most efficient officers in service, readiest in expedients and most skillful in the management of troops in action. I would dislike removing him from his present command unless it was to increase it, but, as I say, may have it to do yet if General Butler remains.*
>
> *As an administrative officer General Butler has no superior. In taking charge of a department where there are no great battles to be fought, but a dissatisfied element to control, no one could manage it better than he.*
>
> *If a command could be cut out such as Mr. Dana proposed, namely, Kentucky, Illinois, and Indiana, or if the Departments of the Missouri, Kansas, and the States of Illinois and Indiana, could be merged together and General Butler put over it, I believe the good of the service would be subserved.*
>
> *I regret the necessity of asking for a change in commanders here, but General Butler not being a soldier by education or experience, is in the hands of his subordinates in the execution of all operations military. I would feel strengthened with Smith, Franklin, or J. J. Reynolds commanding the right wing of this army.*
>
> *At the same time, as I have here stated, General Butler has always been prompt in his obedience to orders from me and clear in his understanding of them. I would not, therefore, be willing to recommend his retirement.*[6]

Circumspection enhanced by circumlocution, Old Brains may well have thought as he read this letter. It would get Grant into no trouble, yet it presented him and, ultimately, candidate Lincoln with one more problem than either needed at that time.

Concurrently, "Baldy" Smith was protesting Grant's refusal to give him a leave of absence. "I consider it due you . . . to render some explanation," Butler's second in command began a long letter to the general-in-chief. After citing the Southern climate's threats to his health and ability to serve, hence his inability "to go out at all in the heat of the day even and visit my lines," Smith suggested that "some other with more ambition and no hostilities could better serve the country. . . ."

General Smith then inadvertently revealed his own confused state of mind by making references to his service under Burnside at Fredericksburg, and, more recently, under Butler:

> *I wish to say to you, unofficially, that from the time I joined the Department of Virginia until the campaign terminated disgracefully I gave to the work the utmost energies of mind and body. Then I wanted to be where I could be useful, and, thinking the more troops there were in this department the more blunders and murders would be committed, I went gladly to the Army of the Potomac with the most hearty good will and intentions. In looking back over the sneers and false charges and the snubbings I received there I only wonder, general, at my own moderation.*
>
> *I then came back, thinking that your presence here would prevent blunders, and that I could once more be useful. Two letters have been written to me [by Butler?] which I think any gentleman would be ashamed to acknowledge as emanating from him and for which there was not even the shadow of an excuse. This has induced me to believe that some one else would be of far more service here than I am. And as my only ambition is to be of service, I determined to present the just plea of my health to remove one of the obstacles to harmony in this army, and that, general, if you will look closely into the campaign, you will find to be one of the causes of want of success when you needed and expected it.*
>
> *In conclusion, general, I am willing to do anything and endure anything which will be of service to the country or yourself.*
>
> *Now I am through with the personal, and I want simply to call your attention to the fact that no man since the Revolution has had a tithe of the responsibility which now rests on your shoulders, and to ask you how you can place a man in command of two army corps, who is as helpless as a child on the field of battle and as visionary as an opium eater in council, and that, too, when you have such men as Franklin and Wright available to help you, to make you*

famous for all time and our country great and free beyond all other nations of the world. Think of it, my dear general, and let your good sense and not your heart decide questions of this kind.[7]

Of course *Smith* v. *Butler* would have to be decided in Washington, with Chief of Staff Halleck honor-bound to represent the general-in-chief. On July 3, 1864, Old Brains advised his client:

It was foreseen from the first that you would eventually find it necessary to relieve General B. on account of his total unfitness to command in the field, and his generally quarrelsome character. What shall be done with him has, therefore, already been, as I am informed, a matter of consultation.

To send him to Kentucky would probably cause an insurrection in that State and an immediate call for large re-enforcements. Moreover, he would probably greatly embarrass Sherman, if he did not attempt to supersede him, by using against him all his talent at political intrigue and his facilities for newspaper abuse.

If you send him to Missouri nearly the same thing will occur there. Although it might not be objectionable to have a free fight between him and Rosecrans the Government would be seriously embarrassed by the local difficulties, and calls for re-enforcements likely to follow. Inveterate as is Rosecrans' habit of continually calling for more troops, Butler differs only in demanding instead of calling.

As things now stand in the West I think we can keep the peace, but if Butler be thrown in as a disturbing element I anticipate very serious results. Why not leave General Butler in the local command of his department, including North Carolina, Norfolk, Fort Monroe, Yorktown, &c., and make a new army corps of the part of the Eighteenth under Smith?

This would leave B. under your immediate control, and at the same time would relieve you of his presence in the field. Moreover, it would save the necessity of organizing a new department. If he must be relieved entirely I think it would be best to make a new department for him in New England.

I make these remarks merely as suggestions. Whatever you may finally determine on I will try to have done. As General B. claims to rank me I shall give him no orders wherever he may go without the special direction of yourself or the Secretary of War.[8]

Honor is a concept with many definitions and still more interpretations, but few clear examples. Here, however, Old Brains was providing one. His counsel reflected his loyalty to Grant, Lincoln, and the Union without impairing the interests of General Butler.

But Spoons was not the only general whose military proficiency General Halleck found deficient. In another message to Grant on July 3, 1864—one foreshadowing much adversity for the Union to come—he warned:

> *General Sigel reports that Early, Breckinridge, and Jackson, with Mosby's guerrillas, are said to be moving from Staunton down the Shenandoah Valley. I ordered General Hunter up to the line of the* [Baltimore & Ohio] *railroad, but he has replied to none of my telegrams, and has made no report of his operations or present condition.*
>
> *Sigel has been ordered to telegraph directly to him, to inform him of the condition of affairs, and to ask for instructions. . . .*
>
> *The three principal officers on the line of the road are Sigel, Stahel, and Max Weber. You can, therefore, judge what probability there is of a good defense if the enemy should attack the line in force.*[9]

On the next day, Halleck had occasion to reply to an inquiry from Weber. "Nothing is known here of General Sigel's movements," he reported. "Everything should be prepared for the defense of your works, and the first man who proposes a surrender or retreats should be hung."[10]

Motivation-enhancing though a few neck-stretchings may have been to the troops serving under commanders thought to be unreliable, General Halleck's main concern soon shifted to the questions of where Jubal Early's divisions were, what they had been doing since they drove Hunter's forces out of Lexington and into the Alleghenies, and where they might appear next. General Grant was wondering, too, although his main interest was in whether "Ewell's corps"—Early's units—had returned to General Lee's trenches south of Petersburg.

"I have learned nothing which indicated an intention on the part of the rebels to attempt any northern movement," the lieutenant general wrote Halleck on July 4. "If General Hunter is in striking distance there ought to be veteran force enough to meet anything the enemy have, and if once put to flight he ought to be followed as long as possible."[11]

"We can learn nothing whatever of Hunter," the chief of staff telegraphed Grant the next day, adding:

The line from the Monocacy to Harper's Ferry has been cut, and the re-enforcements sent from here fell back to the Monocacy. General Howe has been sent there with about 2,800 men, to force his way to Harper's Ferry.

We have nothing reliable in regard to the enemy's force. Some accounts, probably very exaggerated, state it to be between 20,000 and 30,000. If one-half that number we cannot meet it in the field till Hunter's troops arrive.

As you are aware, we have almost nothing in Baltimore or Washington, except militia, and considerable alarm has been created by sending troops from these places to re-enforce Harper's Ferry. You probably have a large dismounted cavalry force, and I would advise that it be sent here immediately. It can be remounted by impressing horses in the parts of Maryland likely to be overrun by the enemy. All the dismounted fragments here we armed as infantry and sent to Harper's Ferry.[12]

Grant offered to send an army corps if the Confederates crossed into Maryland or Pennsylvania. However, General Halleck was not yet convinced that the situation required such action. Near midnight on July 5 he wired the general-in-chief:

I think your operations should not be interfered with by sending troops here. If Washington and Baltimore should be so seriously threatened as to require your aid, I will inform you in time. Although most of our forces are not of a character suitable for the field (invalids and militia), yet I have no apprehensions at present about the safety of Washington, Baltimore, Harper's Ferry, or Cumberland. These points cover our supplies, and raids between cannot effect any damage that cannot soon be repaired. If, however, you can send us your dismounted cavalry, we can use it to advantage, and, perhaps, soon return it remounted.[13]

On July 6 Jubal Early had been crossing the Potomac at Antietam Ford and Shepherdstown "for forty hours, in large force," or so Sigel reported to Halleck.[14] In fact, Early paused at the old Sharpstown battle ground so his veterans of that battle could show the newcomers in his ranks where Stonewall Jackson wrecked every Yankee unit McClellan had thrown at them. Before leaving Lexington, all of Early's men had filed past Old

Jack's grave and also toured the ruins of V. M. I., blackened by Hunter's arsonists.

By July 7 Early's tourists had made a sharp right turn and were advancing southeastward on the road to Frederick—and Washington. Calmly and methodically, General Halleck had already started to mobilize such strength as could be found in and around the capital and in Baltimore, as well.

"Some 8,000 or 10,000 men have been ordered to rendezvous at mouth of Monocacy as fast as they arrive from the Army of the Potomac," Old Brains instructed the commissary-general. "See that they are properly supplied with provisions."[15] And to Major General Lew Wallace, near the Monocacy, he telegraphed:

> *Impress all the horses fit for cavalry service in Maryland and border counties of Pennsylvania, liable to fall into the enemy's hands, paying loyal owners appraised value, not to exceed contract price, and send them to the Mouth of the Monocacy to remount dismounted cavalry, which will be sent to that point with equipments.*[16]

"There has been considerable alarm in Washington, Baltimore, and Pennsylvania," General Halleck advised Grant on July 7. By the next night he had more to say:

> *Latest dispatches state that a heavy column of the enemy has crossed the Monocacy and is moving on Urbana. Sigel and Couch say that scouts, prisoners, and country people confirm previous reports of the enemy's force—that is, some 20,000 or 30,000.*
>
> *Until more forces arrive we have nothing to meet that number in the field, and the militia is not reliable even to hold the fortifications of Washington and Baltimore. It is the impression that one-third of Lee's entire force is with Early and Breckinridge, and that Ransom has some 3,000 or 4,000 cavalry.*
>
> *None of the cavalry sent up by you has arrived nor do we get anything from Hunter. Troops sent from the James River should come here, not to Baltimore, where they cannot be supplied or equipped.*
>
> *If you propose to cut off this raid and not merely to secure our depots we must have more forces here. Indeed, if the enemy's strength is as great as represented, it is doubtful if the militia can hold all of*

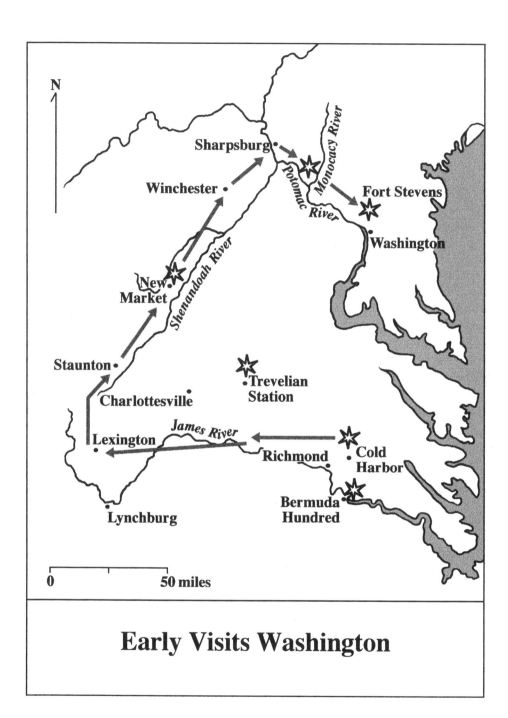

Early Visits Washington

*our defenses. I do not think that we can expect much from Hunter.
He is too far off and moves too slowly.*

    *I think, therefore, that very considerable re-enforcements
should be sent directly to this place.*[17]

However, General Grant had anticipated Halleck's implied request.
On July 7 he had telegraphed the chief of staff:

*The number of dismounted cavalry sent from here reaches nearly
3,000 men; the whole force sent about 9,000. . . . The dismounted
cavalry took with them such arms and accouterments as they had,
but they were not completely armed.*

    *Won't Couch do well to command until Hunter reaches? All of
General Sigel's operations from the beginning of the war have been
so unsuccessful that I think it advisable to relieve him from all duty,
at least until present troubles are over. I do not feel certain at any
time that he will not after abandoning stores, artillery, and trains,
make a successful retreat to some safe place.*[18]

General Grant's having returned to the problem of incompetent
commanders, Halleck responded:

*Sigel has been removed from Harper's Ferry and Howe sent to take
his place till Hunter arrives. Nothing heard from the latter to-day.
Of Couch, Ord, and Gillmore I think the latter the best and have
sent for him to-night.*

    *Early and Breckinridge are unquestionably in this raid, which
is probably larger than we first supposed. Their special object is not
yet developed.*[19]

True, yet by July 9 General Halleck was stripping the capital's bureaus
of clerks and having them armed and formed into units and reaching as far
north as Philadelphia for more defenders. To Major General George
Cadwalader he telegraphed:

*Organize a board to examine hospitals, and send immediately to
General Augur, at Washington, all convalescents capable of defending the forts and rifle pits. They will be given a temporary
organization for that purpose, and are not required to march. All
officers capable of such duty will be sent with them.*[20]

General Halleck's position in this emerging emergency was ambiguous but certainly limited. As chief of staff he had no command authority except over the bureaucrats and local defense forces, and as yet the general-in chief had not seen fit to expand his powers.

During earlier threats to Washington, Secretary of War Stanton had displayed a distressing tendency to panic. This time, though, he supported Halleck's efforts by ordering Quartermaster-General Montgomery Meigs to report to "Chief of Army Staff for such field duty as you can render in Washington and its vicinity. . . ."[21] Also to Stanton's credit was his refusal to go to pieces when informed by a civilian in New York that "Lee in person would move by force by Georgetown Heights on Washington."[22]

Near midnight on that eventful July 9, General Halleck received a message from Wallace that contained good news as well as the other kind:

> *I fought the enemy at Frederick Junction from 9 a.m. till 5 p.m., when they overwhelmed me with numbers. I am retreating with a foot-sore, battered, and half-demoralized column. Forces of the enemy at least 20,000. They do not seem to be pursuing.*
>
> *You will have to use every exertion to save Baltimore and Washington.*
>
> *I think the troops of the Sixth Corps fought magnificently. I was totally overwhelmed by a force from the direction of Harper's Ferry arriving during the battle. Two fresh regiments of the Sixth Corps are covering my retreat. I shall try to get to Baltimore.*[23]

Halleck's response: "I am directed by the President to say that you will rally your forces and make every possible effort to retard the enemy's march on Baltimore."[24]

Absent the command authority Grant had not yet granted him, Old Brains had been obliged to impose Lincoln's. Yet that faded into insignificance given Wallace's mentioning that Sixth Corps troops General Grant had sent northward from Meade's Army of the Potomac were engaged in the fight.

Of course, it remained to be seen what effect the sudden appearance of troops believed to have been engaged below Petersburg would have on Jubal Early's thinking and hence his future moves. At a minimum, however, General Halleck's unspectacular actions had contributed to the gaining of time in which even closer coordination of his efforts and Grant's could give the Confederate invader much more to ponder.

3

JOSEPH EGGLESTON JOHNSTON had never been among Stonewall Jackson's favorite generals. Even so, Old Jack would have been sad to witness Sherman driving Johnston's forces from one fortified position to another, from Dalton in northwestern Georgia steadily toward the Chattahoochie River and Atlanta beyond it.

General Sherman had launched his campaign at about the same time Grant crossed into the Wilderness. Blocked by Johnston, Cump used Jamie McPherson's army as his maneuvering element, while Thomas pressed Johnston directly and Schofield struck him from the north. Although Johnston could only defend, his troops inflicted heavy casualties before withdrawing from one flanked position to the next. By early July federal losses were numbered in five figures. "I begin to regard the death and mangling of a couple of thousand men as a small affair, a kind of morning dash," Sherman wrote his wife, "and it may be well that we become so hardened."[25]

Almost every day since early May, Cump had been sending succinct reports to General Halleck, who condensed them to a sentence or two in relaying them to the general-in-chief. An example is Sherman's message from roughly a dozen miles north of Atlanta on July 11, 1864:

> *The enemy is now all beyond the Chattahooochee, having destroyed all his bridges. We occupy the west bank for thirty miles, and have two heads of columns across; one at the shallow ford at Roswell, and the other at the mouth of Soap Creek (Phillips'). . . .*
>
> *The last works abandoned by the enemy were the strongest of all, embracing two detached redoubts and extending along the river hills for about five miles, having in its whole extent finished abatis and parapet, with glacis obstructed with chevaux-de-frise, and all manner of impediments. But the moment Johnston detected that I had ignored his forts, and had secured two good lodgments above him on the east bank, at Roswell Factory and at Phillips', he drew his forces across and burned all his bridges, viz, one railroad, one trestle, and three pontoons.*
>
> *We now commence the real game for Atlanta, and I expect pretty sharp practice, but I think we have the advantage, and propose to keep it.*[26]

So far, Sherman had succeeded in preventing Johnston from sending any reinforcements to General Lee. Grant, however, had failed to keep Lee from spoiling Franz Sigel's sideshow in the Shenandoah Valley—and now the forces Lee had sent north were creating serious problems for the Union's war managers in Washington. On the morning of July 10, for instance, A. Lincoln sent this message to some nervous citizens in Baltimore:

> *Yours of last night received. I have not a single soldier but who is being disposed by the military for the best protection of all. By latest accounts the enemy is moving on Washington. They cannot fly to either place. Let us be vigilant, but keep cool. I hope neither Baltimore nor Washington will be sacked.*[27]

Later that morning, though, General Halleck was able to inform a general in Baltimore: "The Navy Department has directed 500 sailors from New York to report to you for duty in the fortifications."[28] And to Cadwalader in Philadelphia, Old Brains telegraphed: "Send forward to Baltimore all convalescents fit for duty, armed or unarmed, as may be most expeditious."[29]

That afternoon the President wired his summary of the situation to General Grant:

> *Your dispatch to General Halleck referring to what I may think in the present emergency is shown me. General Halleck says we have absolutely no force here fit to go to the field. He thinks that with the 100-days' men and invalids we have here we can defend Washington, and scarcely Baltimore. Besides these there are about 8,000, not very reliable, under Howe, at Harper's Ferry, with Hunter approaching that point very slowly, with what number I suppose you know better than I.*
>
> *Wallace, with some odds and ends and part of what came up with Ricketts, was so badly beaten yesterday at Monocacy that what is left can attempt no more than to defend Baltimore. What we shall get in from Pennsylvania and New York will scarcely be worth counting, I fear.*
>
> *Now, what I think is that you should provide to retain your hold where you are, certainly, and bring the rest with you personally, and make a vigorous effort to destroy the enemy's force in this vicinity. I think there is really a fair chance to do this if the movement is prompt.*

>   *This is what I think, upon your suggestion, and is not an*
> order.[30]

What Abraham Lincoln thought, and wrote, revealed—inadvertently, of course—that his having made Ulysses Grant general-in-chief had amounted to the sowing of dragons' seed. As was their wont, members of Congress had contributed to the disaster. General Grant's inadequacies, also, were relevant. And so was the superior generalship of Robert Edward Lee. Halleck, having been relegated formally to the role of clerk, was precluded from preventing the damage—although in trying, he stretched the limits of propriety. And though it was skillfully covered-up, damage *was* done.

Lincoln had been too accommodating back in March when Grant insisted on remaining in the field, as far distant from Washington as he could drive Lee's army, leaving purely administrative duties to Halleck. On the surface, the unusual arrangement seemed to work. For the first time in the war, Union military operations in the field would be directed by a general-in-chief who was on the scene of the most important action; no longer would the Halleck Doctrine have to be applied in every case. And the President, given a general universally thought to be highly competent, could concentrate on getting re-elected.

Yet in the series of battles from the Wilderness through Cold Harbor, Grant had not proved competent enough to accomplish his mission: to destroy the Army of Northern Virginia. In the process of failing, the general-in-chief had completely drained the Union's reservoir of replacements for the tens of thousands of soldiers who had been thrown into, and had their bodies shredded by, murderous Confederate crossfires.

True, Grant had kept Lee from reinforcing Joe Johnston's army in Georgia. Yet, during the horror at Cold Harbor, with his back to Richmond, Lee had not hesitated to detach Jubal Early and Jackson's old divisions and launch them on the campaign that had now brought them to the northwestern fringe of Washington City.

Early had been able to advance almost all the way down the Shenandoah Valley and through southern Maryland, in large part because David Hunter was a third-rate officer so intimidated that he seemed to be avoiding prodding messages from Halleck as assiduously as he was the bayonets of Early's troops. Yet, how much competence had been displayed by the men who had placed such a weakling in harm's way—Lincoln and Grant?

Yes, but Jubal Early was leading the Confederate thrust mainly because he had survived. What if General Lee could have given the mission to Old Jack?

Moreover, Early was threatening a place in which there was a leadership vacuum. General Halleck's powers were limited to recruiting and forwarding to the District's ring of fortifications men who for various reasons had been exempt from shipment to Grant's trenches below Petersburg. The Union army's finest commanders—Halleck's lieutenants Sherman, Thomas, Schofield, McPherson—were rather busy hundreds of miles to the southwest trying to shatter Johnston's army just north of Atlanta. Yet, who could say that Old Brains had erred by sending every man he could find anywhere to replace Grant's casualties, in the process making Washington vulnerable to the Confederate sacking that now seemed imminent? Duty aside, would *honor* have permitted anything less?

Indeed, Washington's appalling weakness was evidence of how completely Lee had out-generaled Grant. In such circumstances, why had the commander-in-chief not *ordered* General Grant to come to Washington forthwith to take charge?

This situation was entirely different from the one prevailing on January 1, 1863, when Lincoln had (in effect) demanded that then-General-in-Chief Halleck go to Falmouth and settle the nasty squabbling among Ambrose Burnside's disaffected subordinates. Here, there was no command authority at all in Washington for Grant to undercut. This was strictly an *operational* matter—the kind of challenge Halleck had never hesitated to deal with, when necessary, on the scene.

Even so, Abraham Lincoln negated his implied appeal to Grant to perform as general-in-chief toward correcting the alarming result of his own and Grant's incompetence by adding one one-sentence paragraph too many to his message: "This is what I think, upon your suggestion, and not an order."

That night, General Grant replied: "I think, on reflection, it would have a bad effect for me to leave here, and with General Ord at Baltimore, and Hunter and Wright with the forces following the enemy up, could do no good."[31]

Why, after Lincoln had been compelled to "suggest" that the general-in-chief come to the beleaguered capital and take charge, had Grant apparently been oblivious to the reality that the Union's most important military operation in the East had shifted from Petersburg to Washington? And why had he not concluded *even earlier* that duty and honor required him to go there, analyze the situation first-hand, and grasp control of it?

What "bad effect" might Grant's leaving Petersburg's stalemate to save Washington from being sacked *possibly* have had? Was he implying that he could not trust General Meade to keep the Army of the Potomac from being mauled by Lee in his absence? Or was he inadvertently confessing that he was too afraid of what Lee might do next?

Whatever the reasoning behind Ulysses Grant's reply to his commander-in-chief, his decision would also be a factor in the continuation and proliferation of Confederate actions to jerk around the Union's forces in the East during the months to come. And in a presidential election year, this otherwise exceptionally fine soldier's display of obtuseness might cost the man who had empowered him more than Lincoln and the Union could afford.

4

THE NEXT DAY, JULY 11, to Brigadier General J. R. West, who had telegraphed General Halleck from Philadelphia to offer his services, Old Brains responded: "We have five times as many generals here as we want, but are greatly in need of privates. Anyone volunteering in that capacity will be thankfully received."[32]

By that time, however, the main body of Major General Horatio Wright's Sixth Corps was arriving, and the citizens of Washington thankfully received them.[33] So, surely, must have General Halleck, who earlier that day had ordered Quartermaster-General Montgomery Meigs to "send all your organized employees to report to Major-General McCook near Fort Stevens, with as little delay as practicable."[34]

Fort Stevens, in the northwest quadrant of the ring of fortifications General McClellan had placed around the District of Columbia in the war's early months, and the hastily assembled defense force Old Brains had assembled, were about all that stood between Jubal Early's divisions and the streets of the Union's capital. Yet, wrote historian Margaret Leech:

> *The city, which had no love for the grouchy bureaucrat, spitefully criticized Halleck. At his residence on Georgetown Heights, he kept great military state, with a guard of invalid soldiers and nightly bugle-blowing of tattoo and taps. Irritable persons suggested that it would be no serious loss if the rebels marched down Rock Creek and captured him.*[35]

To do that, though, Early's men would have been obliged to drive all the way to the War Department, where Old Brains was still trying to get orders to David Hunter, wherever he might be. Halleck—reflecting his confidence, thinking ahead—had directed the elusive major general to form a junction with units Wright would send up the Potomac northwestward from Washington, so as to block Early's escape to the Shenandoah Valley.[36]

In the updating Halleck gave the general-in-chief on the next day, July 12, he inserted a sly suggestion that Grant should not overlook an opportunity in his own front yard. His message also reflected his diligence in keeping his distant former subordinate informed:

> *Only about half of the Sixth Corps has landed and only one transport of the Nineteenth Corps. Till more arrive and are organized nothing can be done in the field.*
>
> *I think, however, that Washington is now pretty safe, unless the forces in some part of the intrenchments, and they are by no means reliable, being made up of all kind of fragments, should give away before they can be re-enforced from other points. A line thirty-seven miles in length is very difficult to guard at all points with an inferior force.*
>
> *The forces in our front seem to be those previously named. Prisoners and citizens say that parts of Hill's and Longstreet's corps are expected. If this be true the enemy in your front must be very weak indeed.*
>
> *Nothing heard of Hunter. The breaking of the wires to Baltimore and Harrisburg has cut off all communication with him and with General Howe at Harper's Ferry. It seems to be the impression here that the enemy is massing his forces to attack us to-morrow. The boldness of this movement would indicate that he is stronger than we supposed.*[37]

A. Lincoln added his weight to Chief of Staff Halleck's easily overlooked suggestion: "Vague rumors have been reaching us for two or three days that Longstreet's corps is also on its way to this vicinity. Look out for its absence from your front."[38]

Concurrently, Assistant Secretary of War Charles A. Dana, the reformed journalist Stanton had sent in 1863 to check on Grant's sobriety and who had become the general's strong supporter, was writing the general-in-chief to this effect:

> *No attack either on this city or Baltimore. . . .*
>
> *Nothing can possibly be done here toward pursuing or cutting off the enemy for want of a commander. . . .*

> [T]*here is no head to the whole, and it seems indispensable that you should at once appoint one. Hunter will be the ranking officer if he ever gets up, but he will not do. Indeed, the Secretary of War directs me to tell you in his judgment Hunter ought instantly to be relieved, having proven himself far more incompetent than even Sigel.*
>
> *He also directs me to say that advice or suggestions from you will not be sufficient. General Halleck will not give orders except as he receives them; the President will give none, and until you direct positively and explicitly what is to be done, everything will go on in the deplorable and fatal way in which it has gone on for the past week.*[39]

Also concurrently, Ulysses Grant was anticipating—albeit belatedly—the counsel Dana was attempting to give him. To General Halleck he had sent this directive:

> *Give orders assigning Maj. Gen. H. G. Wright to supreme command of all troops moving out against the enemy, regardless of the rank of other commanders. He should get outside the trenches with all the force he possibly can and should push Early to the last moment, supplying himself from the country.*[40]

"The enemy have disappeared along the entire line," Assistant Secretary Dana telegraphed to Grant on the morning of July 13.[41] Before leaving, however, the rebels looted Francis Blair's wine cellar and burned his son's house at the family's summer place in Silver Spring, Maryland. Such was the background for a memorandum from General Halleck to the Secretary of War in which Old Brains nigh-lost his temper:

> *I deem it my duty to bring to your notice the following facts: I am informed by an officer of rank and standing in the military service that the Hon. M. Blair, Postmaster-General, in speaking of the burning of his house in Maryland, this morning, said, in effect, that "the officers in command about Washington are poltroons; that there were not more than 500 rebels on the Silver Spring road, and we had 1,000,000 of men in arms; that it was a disgrace; that General Wallace was in comparison with them far better, as he would at least fight."*
>
> *As there have been for the last few days a large number of*

officers on duty in and about Washington who have devoted their time and energies, night and day, and have periled their lives in the support of the Government, it is due to them, as well as to the War Department, that it should be known whether such wholesale denouncement and accusation by a member of the Cabinet receives the sanction and approbation of the President of the United States.

If so, the names of the officers accused should be stricken from the rolls of the Army; if not, it is due to the honor of the accused that the slanderer should be dismissed from the Cabinet.[42]

And in reply to a message from Rear Admiral L. M. Goldsborough, temporarily serving with the navy's contingent at Fort Lincoln—"We require 500 cups and spoons. Can they be sent immediately?"[43]—General Halleck snapped: "Cups and spoons are not furnished by the Government to troops."[44]

General Grant reacted to the Confederates' withdrawal by recalling to Petersburg the troops he had sent northward, leaving it to still-missing David Hunter's troops to pursue Early up the Shenandoah Valley: "If the enemy has left Maryland, as I suppose he has," wrote the general-in-chief to Halleck on July 14, "he should have on his heels veterans, militiamen, men on horseback, and everything that can be got to follow to eat out Virginia clear and clean as far as they go, so that crows flying over [the Valley] for the balance of this season will have to carry their provender with them."[45]

Fine, but Hunter was nowhere to be found. Moreover, elements of Horatio Wright's Sixth Corps were moving northeastward up the Potomac to try to catch up with Early's rear guard. Grant was eager to retrieve his troops because he wanted to smash Lee's army before Early's forces could rejoin it—but no one could be certain that Early was indeed heading back up the Valley.

Old Brains' estimate of the situation was set forth in a remarkably candid letter he wrote Sherman on July 16. This was in reply to one from Cump that had opened with "Drop me a word now and then of advice and encouragement" and ended with "Write me a note occasionally and suggest anything that may occur to you, as I am really in the wilderness down here, but I will fight any and all the time on anything like fair terms, . . ." with a report on his recent operations in between.[46] Halleck wrote:

Yours of the 9th is just received. If I have written you no "encouragement or advice" it has been mainly because you have not wanted [needed] *either. Your operations thus far have been the admiration of all military men; and they prove what energy and skill combined can accomplish, while either without the other may utterly fail.*

In the second place, I must be exceedingly cautious about making military suggestions not through General Grant. While the general himself is free from petty jealousies, he has men about him who would gladly make difficulties between us. I know that they have tried it several times, but I do not think they will succeed. Nevertheless, I think it well to act with caution. I therefore make all suggestions to him and receive his orders.

In my present position I cannot assume responsibility except in matters of mere administration or in way of advice. The position is not an agreeable one, but I am willing to serve wherever the Government thinks I can be most useful.

As you will learn from the newspapers, we have just escaped another formidable raid on Baltimore and Washington. As soon as Hunter retreated southwest from Lynchburg the road to Washington was open to the rebels, and I predicted to General Grant that a raid would be made. But he would not believe that Ewell's corps had left his front till it had been gone more than two weeks and had already reached Maryland. He was deceived by the fact that prisoners captured about Petersburg represented themselves as belonging to Ewell's old corps, being so ordered no doubt by their officers.

We had nothing left for the defense of Washington and Baltimore but militia, invalids, and convalescents, re-enforced by armed clerks and quartermaster's employees. As the lines about Washington alone are thirty-seven and a half miles in length, laid out by McClellan for an army of 150,000, you may judge that with 15,000 such defenders we were in no little danger of losing the capital or Baltimore, attacked by a veteran force of 30,000. Fortunately the Sixth Corps, under Wright, arrived just in the nick of time, and the enemy did not attempt an assault.

Entre nous, I fear Grant has made a fatal mistake in putting himself south of James River. He cannot now reach Richmond without taking Petersburg, which is strongly fortified, crossing the Appomattox and recrossing the James. Moreover, by placing his army south of Richmond he opens the capital and the whole North to rebel raids. Lee can at any time detach 30,000 or 40,000 men without our knowing it till we are actually threatened.

I hope we may yet have full success, but I find that many of

Grant's general officers think the campaign already a failure. Perseverance, however, may compensate for all errors and overcome all obstacles. So may it be.

Be assured, general, that all your friends here feel greatly gratified with your operations, and I have not heard the usual growling and fault-finding by outsiders. I have twice presented in writing your name for major-general regular army, but for some reason the matter still hangs fire.[47]

5

DURING THE DAYS FOLLOWING Jubal Early's apparent withdrawal, telegrams General Halleck received or may have seen reflected gossip, rumors, and alarums that were strange, indeed. Some examples:

- Mr. Ashley, member of Congress from Ohio, tells me confidentially that in an interview the other day with Butler, that officer showed him the order directing him to report to Fortress Monroe, and said he would be damned if he paid any attention to it; he did not receive orders from staff officers. Mr. Ashley tells me also that he found a good deal of discontent and mutinous spirit among staff officers of the Army of the Potomac. A good deal of McClellanism, he says, was manifested, especially by officers of very high rank. He tells me also that Meade is universally disliked by officers of every sort.[48]
- Hunter's precise whereabouts is not yet known, but Garrett understands that he is moving with his forces to get east of the Blue Ridge to cut off the enemy. Hunter appears to have been engaged in a pretty active campaign against the newspapers in West Virginia. We also have semi-official reports of his having horse-whipped a soldier with his own hand. . . . The enemy will doubtless escape with all his plunder and recruits, leaving us nothing but the deepest shame that has yet befallen us.[49]
- Order Barnard to send an officer of engineers to make a careful measured survey of the rebel trenches at Fort Stevens. . . . In view of the [newspapers'] articles it will be well to have them recorded in official form and get it engraved and published in papers of large circulation. The physical signs are of a large force lying in ambush hoping to tempt an attack by our weak garrison to overthrow and follow them into the lines.[50]

Major General David Hunter surfaced at Harpers Ferry and delivered himself of a long combination of complaints and excuses addressed to Secretary Stanton. Hunter's two opening sentences:

I have the honor to express to you my sincere regret that His Excellency the President should have seen fit, in a telegram from General Halleck of yesterday's date, to have so far censured my conduct as to place before me the alternatives, either of turning over my command of troops in the field to one of my brigadiers, or volunteering to serve under a junior of my own rank; the difficulties in the latter alternative being increased by the too obvious inference from General Halleck's words, that my abandoning my command to the subordinate in question would be preferred. I am further censured by the President, through General Halleck, for not having made sufficiently frequent reports to Washington of the condition of affairs in my department. . . .[51]

And General Hunter concluded:

I cannot but feel that the action of the President in my case has been of a character to shake the confidence of my troops in me, and thereby to impair my usefulness; and as the interests of the service have ever been my highest aim to be pursued at any personal sacrifice, I have most respectfully to request that I may be relieved from command by some officer more enjoying the confidence of the President, and whose efficiency will not be impaired, as I cannot but feel that mine has been in the manner indicated.[52]

Assuming, perhaps—and incorrectly—that Stanton did not share his important incoming messages with both His Excellency and the chief of staff, Hunter shot himself in the other foot by telegraphing Lincoln directly:

I again most earnestly request to be relieved from the command of this department. Your order, conveyed through General Halleck, has entirely destroyed my usefulness. When an officer is selected as the scapegoat to cover up the blunders of others, the best interests of the country require that he should at once be relieved from command.[53]

General Hunter appealed also to the lieutenant general commanding all the Union armies:

I was not informed that I had any thing to do with the defense of Washington, and supposed General Halleck had made ample provision for this purpose. I hope, general, you will do me the justice to say that I have done my whole duty, and I beg that you will give me a command of some kind. If I am not deemed worthy of a corps, give me a division, a brigade, or a regiment. I have tried to do my whole duty, and if I have failed, I am much mortified.[54]

General Grant responded not to Lincoln but to Dana:

I am sorry to see such a disposition to condemn so brave an old soldier as General Hunter is known to be without a hearing. He is known to have advanced into the enemy's country toward their main army, inflicting a much greater damage upon them than they have inflicted upon us with double his force, and moving directly away from our main army. . . . I fail to see yet that General Hunter has not acted with great promptness and great success. Even the enemy give him great credit for courage, and congratulate themselves that he will give them a chance of getting even with him.[55]

Soldiers cherish loyalty. But they place even greater weight on *honor,* and here were violations of it by both Hunter and Grant: Hunter, by claiming that he "was not informed that I had any thing to do with the defense of Washington," and Grant for the doubtful basis for the information he provided Assistant Secretary of War Dana in supporting Hunter.

Did such things matter? Time would tell. A. Lincoln responded to General Hunter by attempting to dodge the blame for offending him: "You misconceive," he wrote. "The order you complain of was only nominally mine, and was framed by those who really made it, with no thought of making you a scapegoat."[56]

How honorable was this, one wonders, on the part of His Excellency? Hunter had already alleged that Henry Halleck, Lincoln's loyal lightning rod, had been the framer.

6

"IN MY OPINION," WROTE GENERAL GRANT to the President on July 19,

1864, "there ought to be an immediate call for, say, 300,000 men to be put into the field in the shortest possible time."[57] A. Lincoln replied: "Yours of yesterday about a call for 300,000 is received. I suppose you have not seen the call for 500,000 made the day before, and which I suppose covers the case." And there may have been some sly sarcasm in his next sentence: "Always glad to have your suggestions."[58]

Disenchantment setting in? Maybe, but not as far as Chief of Staff Halleck was concerned. To Grant's complacent "I do not think there is now any further danger of an attempt to invade Maryland"[59] Old Brains responded with one of his carefully reasoned advisories on July 19:

> *The recent raid into Maryland seems to have established several things, which it would be well for us to keep in mind:*
>
> *First. It has proved that while your army is south of the James River and Lee's between you and Washington, he can make a pretty large detachment unknown to us for a week or ten days and send it against Washington, or into West Virginia, or Pennsylvania, or Maryland.*
>
> *Second. General Hunter's army, which comprises all troops north of Richmond that can go into the field, is entirely too weak to hold West Virginia and the Baltimore and Ohio Railroad, and at the same time to resist any considerable rebel raid north of the Potomac.*
>
> *Third. We cannot rely upon aid from the militia of the Northern States. They will not come out at all, or will come too late, or in so small a force as to be useless.*
>
> *Fourth. The garrisons of Washington and Baltimore are made up of troops entirely unfit for the field and wholly inadequate for the defense of these places. Had it not been for the opportune arrival of the veterans of the Sixth Corps both cities would have been in great danger.*
>
> *So long as you were operating between Washington and the enemy your army covered Maryland and Pennsylvania, and I sent you all the troops from here and the North which could take the field or guard your depots and prisoners of war. But the circumstances have now most materially changed, and I am decidedly of opinion that a larger available force should be left in this vicinity.*
>
> *It may be answered that re-enforcements can be sent in time from the James River, as was done in this case. This answer would be decisive, if we here, or you there, could always be apprised of the*

number and position of the raiders, as well as the object upon which their march is directed.

But this cannot be done without a superior cavalry force, which we have not got and are not likely to have. The country is so stripped of animals that it is hardly possible to supply demands in the field.

If the enemy had crossed the Potomac below Harper's Ferry (and it is now fordable in many places), and had moved directly upon Washington or Baltimore, or if the arrival of the Sixth Corps had been delayed twenty-four hours, one or the other of these places, with their large depots of supplies, would have been in very considerable danger.

Will it be safe to have this risk repeated? Is not Washington too important in a political as well as a military point of view to run any serious risk at all?

I repeat that so long as Lee is able to make any large detachments, Washington cannot be deemed safe without a larger and more available force in its vicinity.

What you say of establishing schools of instruction here, at Baltimore, and at Harper's Ferry, will be applicable when we get troops to be instructed. But we are now not receiving one-half as many as we are discharging. Volunteering has virtually ceased, and I do not anticipate much from the President's new call, which has the disadvantage of again postponing the draft for fifty days. Unless our Government and people will come square up to the adoption of an efficient and thorough draft, we cannot supply the waste of our army.[60]

Obviously, and understandably, General Halleck was stating the case for holding Lee in place while increasing troop strength for the protection of the capital. Grant, on the other hand, was more interested by far in bringing the Army of the Potomac back to maximum combat effectiveness than he was in relieving the stress of Washingtonians. Old Brains held the high cards; the lieutenant general must have realized that, yet it took him a surprisingly long time to accept the realities.

Several times between (roughly) July 20 and 27 Grant changed his mind regarding whether Horatio Wright's Sixth Corps should return to Petersburg's trenches or remain near the Potomac. Nothing Meade had attempted recently had been successful, nor did possible future operations appear feasible unless he could overwhelm Lee by employment of the sheer weight of superior numbers. Moreover, Grant may have been overly impressed by the enormous advantage afforded by the Union's ability to move troops in steamers from the James up Chesapeake Bay and the lower Potomac in a short time and on short notice; absent the timely arrival of Wright's first regiments on July 11, Jubal Early's men might well have poured over Fort Stevens' ramparts and camped that night on the Executive Mansion's lawn. Yet shipments of larger units had proved more time consuming. There really could be no assurance that seaborne mobility could be substituted for having ample forces in both areas of operations—and Chief of Staff Halleck had reported that for the time being, the North had exhausted its ability to feed-in more soldiers.[61]

"Are you able to take care of the enemy," Abraham Lincoln had telegraphed General Hunter on July 22, "when he turns back upon you, as he probably will on finding that Wright has left?"[62] No, Hunter replied, and he added that Early had reportedly gone southward "suddenly upon the arrival of a courier from Richmond with orders to fall back upon that place." Hunter, whose entreaties had postponed his removal, closed by assuring His Excellency that no movement of the enemy "shall surprise us."[63]

Later that day, Hunter sent another message to Lincoln, one in which he asked if the Government wanted him to chase Early up the Shenandoah Valley, destroying the Confederates' crops as Grant had directed, or establish blocking positions in the Blue Ridge's gaps for Washington's protection.[64] Two points emerge: Hunter was not competent to conduct operations as Halleck had held that a general in command of a field army should, and Hunter was putting the question of what he should do to Lincoln: not to Halleck, certainly, and not even to General-in-Chief Grant.

Could these problems be solved through some sort of reorganization of departments and new leadership? In a letter delivered to the President by Brigadier General John A. Rawlins, his chief of staff, Grant made two suggestions that were in the circumstances remarkable and somewhat puzzling. In one, he suggested Major General William Franklin—whose performance to date (as Lincoln was all too well aware) had been as devoid of distinction as Nathaniel Banks'—as commander of the whole. In the other, he offered Major General George Gordon Meade, his commander of the Army of the Potomac, as the head of a "Military Division."[65]

Apparently, General-in-Chief Grant was nearing the bottom of his list of alternatives. And while he was waffling over where Wright's Sixth Corps ought to be, Jubal Early gave him some assistance by launching a raid down the Shenandoah Valley and up through western Maryland to Chambersburg, Pennsylvania, threatening points east.

In the letter Rawlins brought to Lincoln, General Grant had referred to the fact that during Early's earlier raid, interruptions in telegraphy "made it take from twelve to twenty-four hours each way for dispatches to pass. Under such circumstances, it was difficult for me to give positive orders or directions, because I could not tell how the conditions might change during the transit of dispatches."[66]

Clearly, General-in-Chief Grant was experiencing some of the frustration his predecessor had endured. Technological considerations aside, he was plagued (as have been all combat commanders, before him and ever since) by being unable to be everywhere he felt he needed to be at the same instant.

By default, it fell to Grant's superiors to prescribe the remedy he seemed to have been unable either to grasp or suggest. After giving notice to the general-in-chief, on July 27, 1864, Secretary of War Stanton issued this order to Major General Halleck:

> *Lieutenant-General Grant having signified that, owing to the difficulties and delay of communication between his headquarters and Washington, it is necessary that in the present emergency military orders must be issued directly from Washington, the President directs me to instruct you that all the military operations for the defense of the Middle Department, the Department of the Susquehanna, the Department of Washington, and the Department of West Virginia, and all the forces in those departments, are placed under your general command, and that you will be expected to take all military measures necessary for defense against any attack of the enemy and for his capture and destruction. You will issue from time to time such orders to the commanders of the respective departments and to the military authorities therein as may be proper.*[67]

7

THERE WAS LESS TO STANTON'S ORDER than met the eye, given that Abraham Lincoln was in deep political trouble. In part this reflected frustration due to the fact that under General-in-Chief Grant, the Union armies had suffered more than one hundred thousand casualties with only a stalemate south of Petersburg and costly skirmishing north of Atlanta as results. Also, the lieutenant general had proved lethargic at best in responding to Jubal Early's recent threat to Washington.[68]

Moreover, the order dated July 27 did not appear to have been well thought-out. In enhancing Ulysses Grant's rank and power, Lincoln had been able to shrink Halleck's role to that of a bureaucrat; now, by restoring a portion of Old Brains' authority to command, Lincoln and Stanton were in the position of cooks trying to restore a botched omelet to the pristine condition of the eggs.

Worse, the maneuver reeked of politics. By appearing to empower General Halleck, the President was most likely positioning him to serve again as a lightning rod to absorb the wrath of the Northern public and minimize the additional damage Early might do to candidate Lincoln's chances of being re-elected.

Henry Halleck's code of honor compelled him to carry out his pledge to support the Union war effort in every way he could. Not so clear, however, was what the partial restoration of his powers ordered by Lincoln through Stanton required of him in terms of duty. For him to join General Hunter at Harper's Ferry would have been Quixotic, for not much could be done by any commander given the report Hunter had telegraphed to him the day before:

> *I am very sorry to say that 7,000 men with General Crook, and about 1,500 with General Averell, in all about 8,500, are all that are fit to take the field. The cavalry and the dismounted men in the late fights behaved in the most disgraceful manner, their officers in many instances leading them off, and starting all kinds of lying reports, tending to demoralize the whole command, and it was only owing to the steadiness and good conduct of the infantry which came with us from the Kanawha that the army was saved from utter annihilation. Mulligan's brigade is not reported to have been efficient; was soon broken, and 500 or 600 of them fled toward Cumberland. The refuse force sent from Washington, representing twenty-seven different regiments is said to have done more injury than service.*[69]

Technically, Wright's troops did not belong to any of the departments Halleck controlled but they were moving in accordance with instructions given previously. Halleck made no reference to any change in his status in reporting the situation to Grant on July 28:

> *The main body of the enemy reported yesterday at 20,000 in Martinsburg, and that a column had gone toward Cumberland. If*

this be so, Wright and Crook will form a junction to-night at Harper's Ferry, with orders to cross and give battle. If the enemy crosses the river above Harper's Ferry, they are ordered to move against him by South Mountain; if the enemy crosses Blue Ridge, to cross below and meet him.[70]

And Halleck's message to the general-in-chief on July 31 did not differ significantly from those he sent before July 27:

It appears from General Averell's reports that while General Hunter was collecting his forces at Harper's Ferry to attack the enemy on the south side the rebel army crossed [the Potomac] on the morning of the 29th near Williamsport, and moved, by Hagerstown, into Pennsylvania. Their cavalry captured and partly destroyed Chambersburg yesterday.

We have no reliable information of the main body, but, if it crossed and moved as reported by Averell, it would be nearer Baltimore, Harrisburg, and York than Hunter was at Harper's Ferry. I consequently directed him to move east of South Mountain toward Emmitsburg, and sent last night, by railroad, to the Monocacy such of Emory's command as had arrived, where he would come immediately under Hunter's orders. They will probably effect a junction to-night.

The weather is so intensely hot that marches will be very slow. It is possible that the enemy's infantry is merely covering his cavalry raid. Enemy's cavalry force said to be very large. Ours is so weak and poor that it gives us very little information.[71]

On August 1, 1864, General Grant, fresh from a short conference at Fort Monroe with the commander-in-chief, indicated that cavalry was on the way northward—and something more:

I am sending General Sheridan for temporary duty whilst the enemy is being expelled from the border. Unless General Hunter is in the field in person, I want Sheridan put in command of all the troops in the field, with instructions to put himself south of the enemy and follow him to the death. Wherever the enemy goes let our troops go also. Once started up the Valley they ought to be followed until we get possession of the Virginia Central Railroad. If General Hunter is in the field give Sheridan direct command of the Sixth Corps and

cavalry division. All the cavalry I presume will reach Washington in
the course of to-morrow.[72]

This message contained some ambiguities, which Halleck sought to
have clarified on the next day. "If Sheridan is placed in general command I
presume Hunter will again ask to be relieved," he pointed out. And then, as
if returning to the general-in-chief the limited command authority Stanton
had granted him, he wrote: "Whatever you decide upon I shall endeavor to
have done."[73]

Halleck followed up this assurance on August 3:

General Sheridan has just arrived. He agrees with me about his
command, and prefers the cavalry alone to that and the Sixth Corps.

> *How would it do to make a military division of Departments*
of Pennsylvania, Washington, Maryland, and West Virginia, and
put Sheridan in general command, so far as military operations are
concerned?

> *Only about three regiments of Sheridan's cavalry have arrived,*
and he thinks it will not all be here for several days. It is important
to hurry it up, for if the enemy should make a heavy cavalry raid
toward Pittsburgh or Harrisburg, it would have so much the start
that it would do immense damage before Sheridan could possibly
overtake it.

> *He thinks that for operations in the open country of Penn-*
sylvania, Maryland, and Northern Virginia cavalry is much better
than infantry, and that the cavalry arm can be much more effective
there than about Richmond or south. He, therefore, suggests that
another cavalry division be sent here, so that he can press the enemy
clear down to the James River. They are now gathering in their crops
in the Valley counties, and sending them Richmond by canal and
railroad.

> *I concur with General Sheridan, and think that much greater*
damage can be done to the enemy by destroying his crops and com-
munications north of the James than on the south.[74]

Against such a background, providing indications that weaknesses
were being strengthened, documented by sheafs of messages Abraham
Lincoln habitually read during his frequent visits to the War Department's
telegraph office, it is indeed strange that the President reverted to the
curiously angry tone he had employed in his nigh-disastrous note to Halleck

back on January 1, 1863, in the telegram he sent to Lieutenant General Grant at around 6:00 p.m. on August 3:

> *I have seen your dispatch in which you say "I want Sheridan put in command of all the troops in the field, with instructions to put himself south of the enemy and follow him to the death. Wherever the enemy goes let our troops go also."*
>
> *This, I think, is exactly right as to how our forces should move, but please look over the dispatches you may have received from here even since you made that order, and discover, if you can, that there is any idea in the head of any one here of "putting our army south of the enemy," or of "following him to the death" in any direction.*
>
> *I repeat to you it will neither be done nor attempted, unless you watch it every day and hour and force it.*[75]

Well, yes, it was understandable that a presidential candidate losing the support of substantial numbers of his own political party might slip into a certain amount of negligence and overstatement. However, if Lincoln's purpose was to get General Grant's attention, he succeeded. "I will start for Washington in two hours," the general-in-chief wired the President, the next day.[76]

At midnight on August 3, though, Grant responded to Old Brains' report on his conversations with recently arrived Little Phil Sheridan in a rather curt manner: "Make such disposition of Sheridan as you think best."[77]

Whereupon his sense of honor drove General Halleck to erase the last vestige of the fiction that he had been in command of anything during the past week. To Grant on August 4 he telegraphed:

> *Had you asked my opinion in regard to Generals Hunter and Sheridan it would have been freely and frankly given; but I must beg to be excused from deciding questions which lawfully and properly belong to your office. I can give no instructions to either till you decide upon their commands. I await your orders, and shall strictly carry them out, whatever they may be.*[78]

So much for the New York *Herald*'s prediction that "it is hardly to be expected that [Halleck] will appreciate the great plans of another, and it is believed that he will be but too ready to criticise and carp at those plans. . . . Nor is it to be expected that a man of Halleck's caliber will have the moral elevation and greatness of soul to cooperate with one who, being his subordinate in the West, has come forward so rapidly, and finally pushed him from his place. . . ."

Honor was a concept to which the *Herald*'s editorial writer seemed oblivious. But to Henry Wager Halleck, Lincoln's "Marplot," demonstrably it was as vital as oxygen in the air he breathed.

18 ★ Halleck v. Grant, et al.

WILLIAM TECUMSEH SHERMAN'S CONDUCT of the campaign in Georgia was proof, if any were needed, that the Halleck Doctrine worked when "the General in command of an army in the field" was competent. This must have given General Halleck more than a few grains of comfort during the high summer of 1864, for satisfactions were far too few while disappointments were plentiful. Indeed, just as Sherman was mauling the Confederate Army of Tennessee, commanded now by Lieutenant General John Hood, northeast of Atlanta, he had the sad duty of informing the chief of staff on July 23 that Jamie McPherson "when arranging his troops, about 11 a.m., and passing from one column to another, unconsciously rode upon an ambuscade without apprehension and at some distance ahead of his staff and orderlies was shot dead."[1]

On July 24, Cump added: "The sudden loss of McPherson was a heavy blow to me. I can hardly replace him, but must have a successor." O. O. Howard was the general he suggested.[2]

"General Hooker is offended because he thinks he is entitled to [McPherson's] command," Cump reported to Halleck on July 27. "I must be honest and say he is not qualified or suited to it. [Hooker] talks of quitting. I shall not object. He is not indispensable to our success. He is welcome to my place if the President awards it, but I cannot name him to so important a command as the Army of the Tennessee."[3]

Jefferson Davis had relieved General Johnston for being too cautious; in Hood, he had an army commander who proved aggressive enough to keep Sherman's forces out of Atlanta for roughly five weeks. On September 3, however, Cump was able to telegraph Old Brains: "Atlanta is ours, and fairly won."[4] And on the next day, he wrote Halleck a long letter that opened:

> *MY DEAR FRIEND: I owe you a private letter, and believe one at this time will be acceptable to you. I appreciate your position and the delicate responsibilities that devolve on you, but believe you will master and surmount them all.*
>
> *I confess I owe you all I now enjoy of fame, for I had allowed myself in 1861 to sink into a perfect "slough of despond," and do believe if I could I would have run away and hid from the dangers and complications that surrounded us. You alone seemed to be confident, and opened to us the first avenue of success and hope, and you gradually put me in the way of recovering from what might have proved an ignoble end.*
>
> *When Grant spoke of my promotion as a major-general of the regular army, I asked him to decline in my name till this campaign tested us. Even when my commission came, which you were kind enough to send, I doubted its wisdom, but now that I have taken Atlanta as much by strategy as by force, I suppose the military world will approve it.*
>
> *Through the official bulletins you are better acquainted with all the steps of our progress than any other man in the country, but I will try and point out to you more clearly the recent achievement. . . .*

After a description of the last stages of his Atlanta campaign that might have served as an official rather than an informal one, Sherman turned to other matters:

> *I hope to God the draft will be made to-morrow; that you will keep up my army to its standard, 100,000 men; that you will give Canby an equal number; give Grant 200,000, and the balance keep on our communications, and I pledge you to take Macon and Savannah before spring, or leave my bones.*
>
> *My army is now in the very condition to be supplied with recruits. We have good corporals and sergeants, and some good lieutenants and captains, and those are far more important than good generals. They all seem to have implicit confidence in me. They*

observe success at points remote, as in this case of Atlanta, and they naturally say that the old man knows what he is about. They think I know where every road and by-path is in Georgia, and one soldier swore that I was born on Kenesaw Mountain.

George Thomas, you know, is slow, but as true as steel; Schofield is also slow and leaves too much to others; Howard is a Christian, elegant gentleman, and conscientious soldier. In him I made no mistake. Hooker was a fool. Had he staid [sic] *a couple of weeks he could have marched into Atlanta and claimed all the honors.*

I therefore think I have the army on which you may safely build. Grant has the perseverance of a Scotch terrier. Let him alone, and he will overcome Lee by untiring and unceasing efforts. . . .

To-morrow is the day for the draft, and I feel far more interested in it than any event that ever transpired. I do think it has been wrong to keep our old troops so constantly under fire. Some of those old regiments that we had at Shiloh and Corinth have been with me ever since, and some of them have lost 70 per cent in battle. It looks hard to put those brigades, now numbering less than 800 men, into battle. They feel discouraged, whereas if we could have a steady influx of recruits the living would soon forget the dead. The wounded and sick are lost to us, for once at a hospital they become worthless.

It has been very bad economy to kill off our best men and pay full wages and bounties to the [draftees] *and substitutes. While all at the rear are paid regularly, I have here regiments that have not been paid for eight months, because the paymaster could not come to them. The draft judiciously used will be popular, and will take as many opponents of the war as advocates, whereas now our political equilibrium at the North seems disturbed by the absence of the fighting element, whereas the voting population is made up of sneaks, exempts, and cowards. Any nation would perish under such a system if protracted.*

I have not heard yet of the Chicago nominations, but appearances are that McClellan will be nominated. The phases of "Democracy" are strange indeed. Some fool seems to have used my name. If forced to choose between the penitentiary and White House for four years, like old Professor Molinard, I would say the penitentiary, thank you, sir. If any committee would approach me for political preferment, I doubt if I could have patience or prudence enough to preserve a decent restraint on myself, but would insult the nation in my reply.

If we can only carry our people past this fall, we may escape the greatest danger that ever threatened a civilized people. We as soldiers best fulfill our parts by minding our own business, and I will try to do that.

I wish you would thank the President and Secretary for the constant support they have given me, and accept from me my personal assurance that I have always felt buoyed up by the knowledge that you were there.

And in closing, Cump wrote, "Your sincere friend."[5]
On September 16, Old Brains replied:

Your very interesting letter of the 4th is just received. Its perusal has given me the greatest pleasure. I have not written before to congratulate you on the capture of Atlanta, the objective point of your brilliant campaign, for the reason that I have been suffering from my annual attack of "coryza," or hay cold. It affects my eyes so much that I can hardly see to write.

As you suppose, I have watched your movements most attentively and critically, and I do not hesitate to say that your campaign has been the most brilliant of the war. Its results are less striking and less complete than those of General Grant at Vicksburg, but then you have had greater difficulties to encounter, a longer line of communication to keep up, and a longer and more continuous strain upon yourself and upon your army. . . .

I fully agree with you in regard to the policy of a stringent draft, but, unfortunately, political influences are against us, and I fear it will not amount to much. Mr. Seward's foolish speech at Auburn, again prophesying for the twentieth time that the rebellion would be crushed in a few months, and saying that there would be no draft, as we now had soldiers enough to end the war, &c., has done much harm in a military point of view. But these infernal old political humbugs cannot tell the truth even when it is for their interest to do so.

I have seen enough of politics here to last me for life. You are right in avoiding them. McClellan may possibly reach the White House, but he will lose the respect of all honest, high-minded patriots by his association with such traitors and copperheads as Belmont,

Vallandigham, Wood, Seymour, and Co. He could not stand upon the traitorous Chicago platform, but he had not the manliness to oppose it. A major-general in the United States service, and yet not one word to utter against rebels or the rebellion! I had much respect for McClellan before he became a politician, but very little after reading his sneaking and cowardly letter accepting the nomination.

Hooker certainly made a mistake in leaving before the capture of Atlanta. I understand that when here he said that you would fail, your army was discouraged and dissatisfied, &c. He is most unmeasured in his abuse of me. I inclose you a specimen of what he publishes in Northern papers wherever he goes. They are dictated by himself, and written by Wilkes, Butterfield, and such worthies.

The funny part of the business is that I had nothing whatever to do with his being relieved on either occasion. Moreover, I have never said anything to the President or Secretary of War to injure him in the slightest degree, and he knows that perfectly well. His animosity arises from another source. He is aware that I know something about his character and conduct in California, and fearing that I may use that information against him, he seeks to ward off its effects by making it appear that I am his personal enemy, am jealous of him, &c. I know of no other reason for his hostility to me. He is welcome to abuse as much as he pleases; I don't think it will do him much good or me much harm.

I know very little of General Howard, but believe him to be a true, honorable man. Thomas is also a noble old war horse. It is true that he is slow, but he is always sure.

I have not seen General Grant since the fall of Atlanta, and do not know what instructions he has sent you. I fear that Canby has not the means to do much by way of Mobile. The military effects of Banks' disaster are now showing themselves by the threatened operations of Price and Co. toward Missouri, thus keeping in check our armies west of the Mississippi.[6]

2

GENERAL HALLECK'S FAILURE TO COMMENT on Sheridan's campaign in the lower Shenandoah Valley may have been due to the fact that nothing much had happened there since General Grant placed Little Phil in command. As before, whenever the general-in-chief leaned toward returning troops to the stalemated Army of the Potomac's trenches, Jubal Early did enough demonstrating to remind panic-prone Washingtonians of his presence, and shipment orders were suspended.

At five o'clock on the morning of September 19, however, Sheridan's forces attacked Early's units east of Winchester. Though greatly outnumbered by the Yankees, the Confederates rallied and what Little Phil called "a most stubborn and sanguinary engagement" ensued.[7] By the end of the day, Sheridan had lost around five thousand men, Early perhaps thirty-five hundred. But Sheridan occupied Winchester, and the rebels were digging-in on Fisher's Hill, south of Strasburg.[8]

Three days later, Sheridan drove Early from Fisher's Hill up the Valley Turnpike south of Woodstock.[9] "I am now eighty miles from Martinsburg," he telegraphed Grant on September 24, "and find it exceedingly difficult to supply this army. . . . There is not sufficient in the Valley to live off the country."[10] Put differently, Sheridan ought not to be expected to continue his pursuit of Early. But "I will go on and clean out the Valley," he assured Grant on September 29. Recalling that the general-in-chief had expressed the hope that he could get far enough up the Valley to cut one of the last railroads connecting Richmond with points west, however, from Harrisonburg Sheridan warned:

> *It will be exceedingly difficult for me to carry the infantry column over the mountains and strike the* [Virginia] *Central road. I cannot accumulate sufficient stores to do so, and think it best to take some position near Front Royal. . . ."*[11]

Front Royal, of course, was almost all the way back down the Valley toward Washington.

"I have devastated the Valley from Staunton down to Mount Crawford, and will continue," Little Phil reported to General Grant on October 1, 1864. "The rebels have given up the Valley, excepting Waynesboro. . . . I think the best policy will be to let the burning of the crops of the Valley be the end of this campaign, and let some of this army go somewhere else."[12]

Also on October 1, 1864, General Sheridan wrote Old Brains in much the same vein:

> *Early was driven out of the Valley, and only saved himself by getting through Brown's Gap in the night, and has probably taken position at Charlottesville, and will fortify, holding Waynesborough and*

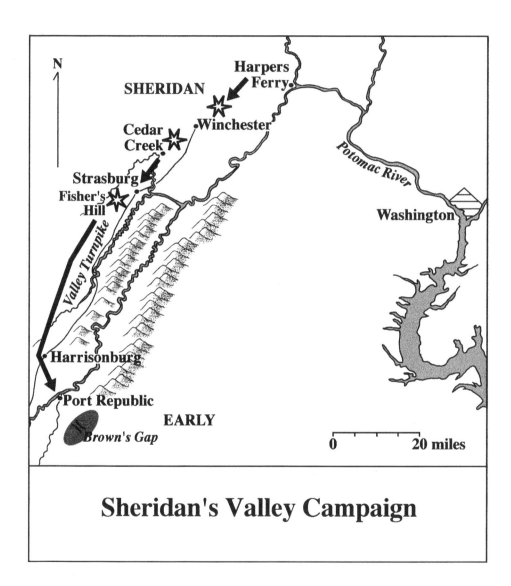

N

SHERIDAN

Harpers
Ferry

Winchester

Cedar
Creek

Strasburg

Fisher's
Hill

Valley Turnpike

Potomac River

Washington

Harrisonburg

Port Republic

EARLY

Brown's Gap

0   20 miles

Sheridan's Valley Campaign

Rockfish Gap. I strongly advise General Grant to terminate this campaign by the destruction of the crops in the Valley and the means of planting, and the transfer of the Sixth and Nineteenth Corps to his army at Richmond.

This is my best judgment. With Crook's force, the Valley can be held.

If this course is not deemed best, then the Orange and Alexandria Railroad should be opened. If it is, it will require an army corps at least to protect it. This force cannot be furnished from this army; and wherever these troops come from, it will be a loss of that number of men from the fighting force. . . .

What we have destroyed and can destroy in this Valley is worth millions of dollars to the rebel Government. A large number of the best farmers of the Valley are moving north, taking advantage of our presence to get out.[13]

Earlier, General-in-Chief Grant had ordered Halleck to cause the railroad connecting Manassas Junction and Strasburg to be restored. Also, as if in anticipation of Sheridan's comments, efforts were being made to reopen the Orange & Alexandria rail line. Such was the background for a curious message from Secretary of War Stanton to Grant on October 2:

The railroad and telegraph corps have reached Manassas. If they are to go to Front Royal, it will be loss of time and labor to proceed to the Rappahannock as ordered by General Halleck.

I understand you were leaving the route to be selected by Sheridan, and understand him as choosing the road to Front Royal; but Halleck does not so understand the matter. Wouldn't it be well for you to direct specifically the route from Manassas immediately?[14]

Concurrently, General Halleck was telegraphing Grant:

I have received no reply from General Sheridan in regard to his future line of supplies, but infer from his dispatch of September 29 to you that he will not go to Charlottesville. Our construction party has passed Manassas Junction, toward the Rappahannock. In view of Sheridan's last dispatch would it not be better to put the working party on the road toward Front Royal?[15]

Trouble in Washington's bureaucratic hell, Ulysses Grant may have suspected, but he came down on General Halleck's side. "Please direct the construction party at work on the railroad to open the road to Front Royal," he directed, whereupon Old Brains promptly instructed Quartermaster-General Meigs: "All work on the Orange railroad will cease, and the road to Front Royal be repaired."[16]

Absent re-election candidate Lincoln's involvement—helpful though Sherman's seizure of Atlanta had been to offset widespread dissatisfaction with his conduct of the war—Stanton seemed to have assumed the role of the Union's primary military mover and shaker, eclipsing Chief of Staff Halleck into irrelevance, or so the tone of his messages to General-in-Chief Grant suggested. Curiously, the thrust of Stanton's guidance seemed to be that the sooner Sheridan's forces could be returned to Meade's Army of the Potomac, the better.

"I will follow Sheridan's suggestion of bringing the Sixth and Nineteenth Corps [to Meade below Petersburg]," Grant replied to a telegram from Stanton on October 3, "and yours as to bringing them by rail from Front Royal."[17] In these circumstances, about all that General Halleck could do was remind the lieutenant general commanding of the adverse effect that the shift of the bulk of Sheridan's forces back to below Petersburg would have on anyone's ability to defend Washington, should General Lee—who, since Cold Harbor back in early June, had been jerking around Union forces—order Jubal Early to make at least one more strike at the Union's capital. This warning Old Brains gave in a long letter to Grant on October 4. And what he said to their superior officer, he shared with General Sheridan.[18]

Uncertain though General Halleck may have been about the results of the Sheridan-Stanton-Grant concurrence that this most recent Shenandoah Valley campaign had reached a successful end, Old Brains had ample cause to be proud of the young quartermaster to whom he had given the opportunity to move upward as a combat commander. Moreover, Little Phil's successes enabled the Union armies' chief of staff to return his attention to the question of what General Sherman ought to do next.

3

SHERMAN HIMSELF HAD RAISED THE QUESTION in a letter to Grant on September 20, 1864, by stating: "I would not hesitate to cross the State of Georgia with 60,000 men, hauling some stores and depending on the country for the balance. . . . If you can whip Lee and I can march to the Atlantic I think Uncle Abe will give us a twenty days' leave of absence to see the young folks."[19]

Earlier in that letter to Grant he had suggested that the general-in-chief cause Wilmington, North Carolina, and Savannah to be seized by other Union forces. "If I were sure that Savannah would soon be in our possession," Cump telegraphed Halleck on September 26, "I would be tempted to make for Milledgeville and Augusta, but I must secure what I have."[20]

On that same day Old Brains replied:

> *I do not know what General Grant's views are about Savannah, but I hardly think he intends to operate there. I should say your line was Columbus, Montgomery, and Selma, opening, in conjunction with Farragut and Canby, the Alabama River.*
>
> *Selma is a very important place. You are nearer to Montgomery than to Augusta, and the latter as far from Savannah as the former from Mobile. By holding Atlanta, Montgomery, and the Alabama River we can prevent any serious raids into Mississippi, Tennessee, and Kentucky, and at the same time cut off the rebel army from their grain-fields. . . .*
>
> *Your mode of conducting war is just the thing we now want. We have tried the kid-glove policy long enough.*[21]

Old Brains' approval of Sherman's way of waging war was by no means flattery. "The course which you have pursued in removing rebel families from Atlanta," he wrote Cump on September 28, "is fully approved by the War Department."[22]

Although General Halleck admitted that he had not had time to examine the exchanges of letters between Sherman, Atlanta's mayor, and Confederate Lieutenant General John Hood, in responding to Sherman's message Old Brains went on to reveal his innermost convictions regarding the conduct of the war to quell the rebellion at this stage:

> *Not only are you justified by the laws and usages of war in removing these people, but I think it was your duty to your own army to do so. Moreover, I am fully of opinion that the nature of your position, the character of the war, the conduct of the enemy, and especially of non-combatants and women of the territory which we have heretofore conquered and occupied, will justify you in gathering up all the*

forage and provisions which your army may require both for a siege of Atlanta and for your supply in your march farther into the enemy's country.

Let the disloyal families of the country thus stripped go to their husbands, fathers, and natural protectors in the rebel ranks. We have tried three years of conciliation and kindness without any reciprocation. On the contrary, those thus treated have acted as spies and guerrillas in our rear and within our lines. The safety of our armies and a proper regard for the lives of our soldiers require that we apply to our inexorable foes the severe rules of war.

We certainly are not required to treat the so-called non-combatants and rebels better than they themselves treat each other. Even here in Virginia, within fifty miles of Washington, they strip their own families of provisions, leaving them as our army advances to be fed by us or to starve within our lines. We have fed this class of people long enough. . . .

I would destroy every mill and factory within my reach which I did not want for my own use. This the rebels have done, not only in Maryland and Pennsylvania, but also in Virginia and other rebel States, when compelled to fall back before our armies. In many sections of the country they have not left a mill to grind grain for their own suffering families, lest we might use them to supply our armies.

We must do the same. I have endeavored to impress these views upon our commanders for the last two years. You are almost the only one who has properly applied them. I do not approve of General Hunter's course in burning private houses, or uselessly destroying private property—that is barbarous; but I approve of taking or destroying whatever may serve as supplies to us or to the enemy's armies.[23]

Old Brains' letter, Sherman wrote him on October 11, was "exceedingly to my liking because it is the judgment of history." By then Cump had decided to seek approval for the Atlantic and Savannah as his next campaign's objectives rather than the Gulf of Mexico and Mobile—his concern being that there should be a goal beyond, and beyond Savannah he might drive northward to the Carolinas and draw Lee out of the trenches below Petersburg.[24] "I am loath to remain on the defensive," he declared to Halleck, "and want to break up this line [the Western & Atlanta railroad] back to Chattanooga, leave Thomas to defend Tennessee, and collect my forces and go to the seashore, taking Macon, Milledgeville, and Savannah *en route*. I can do it." And in closing, he wrote:

> *Again let me say that I value your opinion of matters of importance above those of any other, because I know you to be frank, honest, and learned in the great principles of history. Both Grant and I are deficient in these and are mere actors in a grand drama, the end of which we do not see.*[25]

These words from his old shipmate on the *Lexington*'s seven-month voyage around Cape Horn to California and seeming career oblivion a decade and more earlier were in sharp contrast to most opinions regarding General Halleck. Recently he had contributed to the removal of Spoons (a.k.a. Beast) Butler from combat command. Mindful of Old Brains' having completed and published his translation of Baron Henri Jomini's *Vie Militaire et Politique de Napoleon*, which he had started on the *Lexington*, the outraged political general declared:

> *Now there is General H., what has HE to do? At a moment when every true man is laboring to his utmost, when the days ought to be forty hours long, General H is translating French books at nine cents a page; and, sir, if you should put those nine cents in a box and shake them up, you would form a clear idea of General H's soul!*[26]

Perhaps a more accurate appraisal of the state of General H's soul could have been obtained by recalling what he had written Grant as early as October 2:

> *Some time since, General Sherman asked my opinion in regard to his operations after the capture of Atlanta. While free to give advice to the best of my ability, I felt it my duty to refer him to you for instructions, not being advised of your views on that subject.*
>
> *I presume from his dispatches that you have corresponded upon the subject, and perhaps his plan of future operations has already been decided upon. . . .*
>
> *All I wish to say or know upon the subject is, that if any definite plans have been adopted it is desirable that the Secretary of War or myself should be informed of that plan as early as possible. . . . Now, if General Sherman is going to move east to connect*

*with the coast by the Savannah River, stores should not be shipped to
Mobile or Pensacola, but to Hilton Head. . . .*

    *It is exceedingly important that some definite conclusion
should be arrived at as early as possible, for the expenses of the water
transportation, and especially of the demurrage of large fleets, are
enormous.*[27]

"I must have alternatives," Cump wrote Halleck on October 19, "else,
being confined to one route, the enemy might so oppose that delay and
want would trouble me, but having alternatives, I can take so eccentric a
course that no general can guess at my objective." He would turn up
somewhere, Sherman assured his old friend, and then he added:

*This movement is not purely military or strategic, but it will illus-
trate the vulnerability of the South. They don't know what war
means, but when the rich planters of the Oconee and Savannah see
their fences and corn and hogs and sheep vanish before their eyes they
will have something more than a mean opinion of the "Yanks." Even
now our poor mules laugh at the fine corn-fields, and our soldiers
riot on chestnuts, sweet potatoes, pigs, chickens, &c.*

    *The poor people come to me and beg as for their lives, but my
answer is, "Your friends have broken our railroads, which supplied
us bountifully, and you cannot suppose our soldiers will suffer when
there is abundance within reach."*

    *It will take ten days to finish up our road; during which I will
eat out this flank and along down the Coosa, and then will rapidly
put into execution the plan. In the mean time I ask that you give to
General Thomas all the troops you can spare of the new levies, that
he may hold the line of the Tennessee during my absence of, say,
ninety days.*[28]

4

BY THE END OF OCTOBER'S FIRST WEEK, General Sheridan was again reflecting a desire to quit chasing Jubal Early up the Shenandoah Valley. The
whole country, he reported to Grant, had been made untenable for a rebel
army. "When this [raid] is completed the Valley, from Winchester up to
Staunton, ninety-two miles, will have little in it for man or beast."[29] That
being the case, Little Phil was nigh-totally dependent on wagon trains from

Martinsburg to supply his marauders. Guerrillas, he complained to Halleck on October 7, had attacked every party.[30]

Moreover, after the thinking of the lieutenant general commanding had reverted to returning troops to Meade's army, some misgivings developed—or so a message from Halleck to Sheridan on October 9 indicated: "General Grant directs me to say that you had better, at all events, retain the Nineteenth Corps and that the time of sending the Sixth Corps and a division of cavalry must be left to your judgment."[31] More confusion was introduced two days later when Grant wrote Halleck:

> *After sending the Sixth Corps and one division of cavalry here, I think Sheridan should keep up as advanced a position as possible toward the Virginia Central* [rail]*road, and be prepared with supplies to advance on to that road at Gordonsville and Charlottesville at any time the enemy weakens himself sufficiently to admit of it. The cutting of that road and the canal would be of vast importance to us.*[32]

Well, fine—but had Sheridan not declared the Valley devastated, and returned to the Winchester vicinity? And on October 12, he was advising Grant: "I have directed the Sixth Corps to march to Alexandria. . . . I will request General Halleck to have transportation ready for them through to Petersburg. . . . I believe that a rebel advance down this valley will not take place."[33]

Concurrently, through Chief of Staff Halleck, Secretary of War Stanton was venting his anxiety and vexation over dangers in the vicinity of Washington. "Your plan of putting prominent secessionists on trains is approved," Old Brains had written Major General C. C. Augur on October 11, "and you will carry it into effect. They should be so confined as to render escape impossible, and yet be exposed to the fire of the enemy."[34] And the next day he informed Brevet Brigadier General D. C. McCallum:

> *The Secretary of War directs that, in retaliation for the murderous acts of guerrilla bands, composed of and assisted by the inhabitants along the Manassas Gap Railroad, and as a measure necessary to keep that road in running order, you proceed to destroy every house within five miles of the road which is not required for our own purposes, or which is not occupied by persons known to be friendly.*
>
> *All males suspected of belonging to, or assisting, the robber bands of Mosby, will be sent, under guard, to the provost-marshal at*

> *Washington, to be confined in the Old Capitol prison. The women and children will be assisted in going north or south, as they may select. They will be permitted to carry with them their personal property and such provisions as they may require for their own use. Forage, animals, and grain will be taken for the use of the United States. All timber and brush within musketry fire of the road will be cut down and destroyed. Printed notices will be circulated and posted that any citizens found within five miles of the road hereafter will be considered as robbers and bushwhackers, and be treated accordingly.*
>
> *Copies of these instructions will be sent to General Augur and General Sheridan, with orders to give you all possible military aid for the accomplishment of these objects. The inhabitants of the country will be notified that for any further hostilities committed on this road or its employés an additional strip of ten miles on each side will be laid waste, and that section of country entirely depopulated.*[35]

Next, Stanton had Chief Clerk Halleck telegraph Little Phil: "The Secretary of War wishes you to come to Washington for consultation, if you can safely leave your command." That said, Old Brains added a sly suggestion: "General Grant's wishes about holding a position up the Valley as a basis [sic] against Gordonsville, &c., and the difficulty of wagoning supplies in the winter, may change your views about [calling off the reconstruction of] the Manassas Gap [rail]road."[36]

General Augur, who had been puzzled by Sheridan's having telegraphed him that he "will not want to use the Manassas Gap Railroad" and ordering Augur back to Manassas Junction, sought guidance from General Halleck. Old Brains replied: "Dispatches sent General Sheridan may change his views in regard to abandoning the railroad. Send the rolling-stock back to a safe position, place your troops in favorable places for defending [the] road, and wait for further orders."[37]

How long might it have been since Henry Halleck had been able to use such a direct tone? Most of his messages had opened with "General Grant wishes . . ." or "The Secretary of War directs. . . ." Worse, the lieutenant general commanding seemed too preoccupied with supervising George Meade to be consistent regarding exactly *what* he wished, and Philip Sheridan was no Cump Sherman. But Old Brains' reversion to his old style was short-lived. As if complying with instructions, he telegraphed Augur: "You will remain where you are until General Sheridan meets you, and then act according to his instructions."[38]

On October 14, 1864, Major General Halleck was in the position of the man sitting on the floor during a musical chairs game a moment after the piano player suddenly lifted his fingers from the keyboard. All of the other players were sending messages hither and yon to one another:

Stanton to Grant:

> *I requested Sheridan to come here immediately by rail, to confer with me. . . . I expect to make you a visit* [at City Point] *to-morrow with General Meigs, to confer on matters in hand, and am only awaiting Sheridan's arrival.*[39]

Grant to Sheridan:

> *What I want is for you to threaten the Virginia Central Railroad and* [James River] *canal in the manner your judgment tells you is best, holding yourself ready to advance if the enemy draw off their forces. If you make the enemy hold a force equal to your own for the protection of those thoroughfares, it will accomplish nearly as much as their destruction.*
>
> *If you cannot do this, then the next best thing to do is to send here all the force you can. . . .*[40]

Despite Stanton's having ordered Sheridan to Washington forthwith, Little Phil was still at Rectortown, southwest of the capital, on October 16. From there, he queried General Halleck: "Have you heard that any rebel force has been detached from Richmond? Cipher dispatches sent me yesterday or the day before, via this place, are lost."

Promptly Old Brains replied:

> *General Grant says that Longstreet brought with him no troops from Richmond, but I have very little confidence in the information collected at his headquarters. If you can leave your command with safety come to Washington, as I wish to give you the views of the authorities here.*[41]

Late that afternoon, though, Sheridan relayed to Halleck an intercepted Confederate message: "Be ready to advance on Sheridan as soon as my forces get up, and we can crush him if he finds out I have joined you." Little Phil added this comment:

> *This dispatch is not in accordance with all the information I have*

been able to gather heretofore; but I thought some information to corroborate it might have been in the cipher dispatches lost yesterday.

General Wright, in command, has made every preparation to meet the threat of Longstreet, if the [intercepted] *dispatch should prove true, and I am confident of good results.*

I would like to see you. Is it best for me to go to see you?[42]

Evidently Halleck thought it was, for on the next day, October 17, Assistant Secretary of War Charles Dana wired Stanton, by then conferring with General Grant at Fort Monroe, that Sheridan had been in Washington to see General Halleck. And Old Brains reported to the general-in-chief: "General Sheridan has just been here. He has not yet decided about the Manassas [Gap Railroad's restoration,] but will do so in a day or two."[43]

Whereupon—*again* apparently reflecting his inability to think beyond the interests of *his,* not Meade's, Army of the Potomac—the general-in-chief of the Union armies telegraphed Halleck:

General Sheridan should follow and break up Longstreet's force if he can, and either employ all the force the enemy now have in the Valley, or send his surplus forces here. With the Sixth Corps and one division of cavalry, I think my lines could be closed up to the Appomattox [River] *above Petersburg and the Danville road cut.*[44]

Given the events in mid-April 1865, Grant's posterity might well ponder how prescient he had been in October 1864.

While Sheridan was making his way from Washington back toward the forces he commanded, however, he paused for the night at Winchester. As he slept, Jubal Early—back down the Valley on Fisher's Hill—was approving an audacious plan to attack the Yankee camps north of nearby Cedar Creek.

Stonewall Jackson's map-maker, Jedidiah Hotchkiss, and Major General John Gordon had scouted the approaches from Fisher's Hill down the narrow path between the Shenandoah River's North Fork and the high ground just to the south of it, making it possible during the night for Early's men to pass along this route, often single-file, and cross the river suddenly enough to drive the Yankees, left by Sheridan several days earlier under the command of Horatio Wright, in utter panic, running as fast as they could northward.

Early's Confederates had struck the place where the federal commanders least expected an attack, catching many of the Yankees asleep or starting breakfast fires. By the middle of the morning on October 19, 1864, all of Sheridan's thirty-two-thousand-man army, except the Sixth Corps, had been wrecked. "Well, Gordon," Early said to his subordinate, "this is glory enough for one day."

John Gordon disagreed. "We have but one more blow to strike," he argued, "and then there will not be left an organized company of infantry in Sheridan's army." There was no use in doing that, Early replied, "they will all go, directly."

"That is the Sixth Corps, General," Gordon protested. "It will not go unless we drive it from the field."

"Yes, it will go too, directly." Later, Gordon wrote: "My heart went into my boots."[45]

General Gordon was right about the Sixth Corps. It held until Sheridan, who had galloped down from Winchester, got enough fugitives turned around to start a counterattack. To a discouraged general who had suggested a retreat, Little Phil snapped: "Retreat, Hell! We'll be back in our camps tonight!" And when his troops rallied, he yelled: "Run! Go after them! We've got the God-damnedest twist on them you ever saw!"[46]

Ten days later, Assistant Secretary of War Dana wrote General Rawlins, Grant's chief of staff:

> *I have lately been in the Shenandoah Valley, and send, for the general's consideration and yours, the result of my observations and of my conversations with Sheridan and other officers.*
>
> *The active campaign in the Valley seems to be over for this year. The enemy is so decidedly beaten and scattered, and driven so far to the south, that he can scarcely be expected to collect his forces for another attempt during the present season. Besides, the devastation of the Valley, extending as it does for a distance of about 100 miles, renders it almost impossible that either the Confederates or our own forces should make a new campaign in that territory; and when Sheridan has completed the same process down the Valley to the vicinity of the Potomac, and when the stores of forage which are yet to be found in Loudoun County and in some parts of Fauquier, and the animals that are still there are all destroyed or removed, the difficulty of any new offensive operations on either side will have been greatly increased.*[47]

5

"ABUNDANT STORES ARE COLLECTED at Hilton Head and Pensacola," General Halleck telegraphed Sherman on November 8, 1864. "I think you are now free to move as soon as you choose."[48]

The Pensacola supply facility was part of the program of deception Sherman desired and Old Brains supported. On November 10 Cump telegraphed Charles Dana, a reporter who became assistant secretary of war:

> *If indiscreet newspaper men publish information too near the truth, counteract its effect by publishing other paragraphs calculated to mislead the enemy—such as "Sherman's army has been much reinforced, especially in the cavalry, and he will soon move by several columns in circuit, so as to catch Hood's army;" "Sherman's destination is not Charleston, but Selma, where he will meet an army from the Gulf," &c.*[49]

One day later, General Grant complained to Stanton:

> *All the Northern papers of 10th (and especially the* New York Times*) contain the most contraband news I have seen published during the war. The* Times *lays out Sherman's programme exactly and gives his strength. It is impossible to keep these papers from reaching the enemy and no doubt by to-morrow they will be making the best arrangements they can to meet this move.*[50]

Stanton, in responding, added some twist:

> *I have seen with indignation the newspaper articles referred to, and others of like kind, but they come from Sherman's army and generally from his own officers and there is reason to believe he has not been very guarded in his own talk.*
>
> *I saw today, in a paymaster's letter to another officer, his plans as stated by himself. Yesterday I was told full details given by a member of his staff to a friend in Washington. Matters not spoken of aloud in the Department are bruited by officers coming from Sherman's army in every Western printing office and street.*
>
> *If he cannot keep from telling his plans to paymasters and his staff are permitted to send them broadcast over the land, the Department cannot prevent their publication.*[51]

While their superiors fumed and fussed, Generals Sherman and Halleck were ending one phase of Cump's next movement and entering another. Wrote Sherman:

> *My arrangements are now all complete, and the railroad cars are being sent to the rear. Last night we burned all foundries, mills, and shops of every kind in Rome, and to-morrow I leave Kingston with the rear guard for Atlanta, which I propose to dispose of in a similar manner, and to start on the 16th on the projected grand raid.*
>
> *All appearances still indicate that Beauregard has got back to his old hole at Corinth, and I hope he will enjoy it. My army prefers to enjoy the fresh sweet-potato fields of the Ocmulgee.*
>
> *I have balanced all the figures well, and am satisfied that General Thomas has in Tennessee a force sufficient for all probabilities, and I have urged him the moment Beauregard turns south to cross the Tennessee at Decatur and push straight for Selma.*
>
> *To-morrow our wires will be broken, and this is probably my last dispatch. I would like to have General Foster to break the Savannah and Charleston road about Pocotaligo about December 1. All other preparations are to my entire satisfaction.*[52]

On the next day, November 12, General Grant countered Stanton's waspish accusations of Sherman's responsibility for leaks of his plans to the press:

> *The publication referred to in my dispatch seemed to originate in an Indianapolis paper on the authority of army officers direct from Chattanooga. I will send a staff officer west in the morning to ascertain who these officers are, and order them here. I think I will send them to the Dry Tortugas for duty without commands for a while, as a warning to the others that they are not to report military movements in advance of their being made.*[53]

With Sherman disappearing into an information vacuum and Sheridan's defeat of Jubal Early at Cedar Creek all but closing out operations in the Shenandoah Valley, General Halleck turned most of his attention to the task of ordering troops from Missouri and many other places to Nashville. Major General Rosecrans, commanding at St. Louis, invited a second sacking by seeming slow to obey Old Brains' orders to send forces to

George Thomas. But horses turned out to be a larger problem for Thomas, hence for Halleck, than manpower.

Confederate Major General Nathan Bedford Forrest, his scalp intact despite all the forces Cump Sherman had sent out to lift it, had done about all the damage he could to Thomas' lines of communication west of Nashville by November 22, 1864, when General John Hood sent his troops across the Tennessee River with Columbia, Tennessee, as their first objective. Hood's West Point roommate John Schofield moved northward from Pulaski early enough to beat him. But from that point northward, Forrest's cavalry aided Hood's advance by turning up on one of Schofield's flanks or the other and forcing him to withdraw—first from the Duck River line at Columbia, then past Spring Hill to the town of Franklin, on the Harpeth River twenty miles, more or less, south of the position Thomas and Halleck were doing their best to strengthen at Nashville.

On November 30, 1864, the backs of General Schofield's infantrymen were to the Harpeth. Hood was determined to attack their hastily occupied line. Forrest and others tried in vain to persuade Hood to try another Jacksonian wide envelopment, led by Forrest.

General Thomas' cavalry commander, Brigadier General James H. Wilson, was north of the Harpeth, positioned to oppose Forrest whether he tried to cross east or west of Schofield's line. But John Hood, as had been Ulysses Grant at Cold Harbor, was adamant about making a frontal assault. In so doing he took a whopping sixty-two hundred casualties without achieving anything more than a temporary dent in his former roommate's line.

Schofield, having bought as much time as he could to enable Thomas to prepare Nashville's fortifications, moved into the positions Old Pap directed. In fact, the least flamboyant of Halleck's lieutenants had prevented Hood and even Forrest's cavalry from cutting him off short of Nashville.[54]

Such was the background for the message General Thomas sent the Union armies' chief of staff on December 1, 1864:

> *After General Schofield's fight* [at Franklin] *of yesterday, feeling convinced that the enemy very far outnumbered him, both in infantry and cavalry, I determined to retire to the fortifications around Nashville, until General Wilson can get his cavalry equipped.*
>
> *He has now but about one-fourth the number of the enemy, and consequently is no match for him. . . . I therefore think it best to wait here until Wilson can equip all his cavalry.*

If Hood attacks me here, he will be more seriously damaged than he was yesterday; if he remains until Wilson gets equipped, I can whip him and will move against him at once.[55]

Responding to a message from Grant, on December 3 Halleck telegraphed him:

Every available man from Hooker's and other western departments have [sic] *been sent to General Thomas. . . . All cavalry horses that could be procured in the Western States have been sent to Nashville, to the entire neglect of other departments. I believe that every possible effort has been made to supply General Thomas' demands and wants, so far as the means at the disposition of the Government permitted. General A. J. Smith's command was thirty-one days, after General Rosecrans received the orders, in reaching Nashville.*[56]

Thomas' message to General Halleck that evening was reassuring:

I have a good intrenched line on the hills around Nashville, and hope to be able to report 10,000 cavalry mounted and equipped in less than a week, when I shall feel able to march against Hood. I gave the order for the impressment of horses last night, and received the authority of the Secretary of War this morning.[57]

Old Brains added to the fund of knowledge regarding horses on December 5 in a telegram to the general-in-chief:

The records show that there have been issued at Louisville, Lexington, and Nashville since September 20, 22,000 cavalry horses. . . . If this number, without any campaign, is already reduced to 10,000 mounted men, as reported by General Wilson, it may be safely assumed that the cavalry of that army will never be mounted, for the destruction of horses in the last two months has there alone been equal to the remounts obtained from the entire West. None are issued to Rosecrans, Steele, or Canby.[58]

Also on December 5, from City Point General Grant was bordering on violating the Halleck Doctrine. To George Thomas he telegraphed:

Is there not danger of Forrest moving down the Cumberland to

*where he can cross it? It seems to me whilst you should be getting up
your cavalry as rapidly as possible to look after Forrest, Hood should
be attacked where he is. Time strengthens him, in all probability, as
much as it does you.*[59]

Concurrently, Thomas was reporting to Halleck: "The enemy has not
advanced at all since the 3d instant. If I can perfect my arrangements I shall
move against the advanced positions of the enemy on the 7th instant."[60]

On the next day, December 6, Thomas wrote General Grant:

*Your telegram of December 5 is just received. As soon as I can get up
a respectable force of cavalry I will march against Hood. General
Wilson has parties out now pressing horses, and I hope to have some
6,000 or 8,000 cavalry mounted in three days from this time.
General Wilson has just left me, having received instructions to
hurry the cavalry remount as rapidly as possible.*

*I do not think it prudent to attack Hood with less than 6,000
cavalry to cover my flanks, because he has, under Forrest, at least
12,000. I have no doubt Forrest will attempt to cross the river, but
I am in hopes the gun-boats will be able to prevent him.*[61]

Before Thomas' message reached City Point, however, the lieutenant
general commanding had shattered the Halleck Doctrine. That afternoon
he had ordered Thomas: "Attack Hood at once, and wait no longer for a
remount of your cavalry. There is great danger of delay resulting in a
campaign back to the Ohio River."[62]

Old Pap's reply was prompt and soldierly: "I will make the necessary
dispositions and attack Hood at once, agreeably to your order, though I
believe it will be hazardous with the small force of cavalry now at my
service."[63]

Why had Ulysses Grant, from hundreds of miles to the east, suddenly
and peremptorily superseded the judgment of the general commanding an
army in the field? Well, on the morning of December 7, Secretary Stanton
had telegraphed the general-in-chief: "Thomas seems unwilling to attack
because it is hazardous, as if all war was anything but hazardous. If he waits
for Wilson to get ready, Gabriel will be blowing his last horn."[64]

Equally shallow was Grant's reply: "You probably saw my order to
Thomas to attack. If he does not do it promptly, I recommend superseding
him by Schofield, leaving Thomas subordinate."[65]

As late as the next day, December 8, General Halleck had refrained from interfering in the matter of *Edwin M. Stanton and Ulysses S. Grant* v. *George H. Thomas.* In a long message to the general-in-chief sent early that afternoon, Old Brains noted that Missouri was "in no more danger of an insurrection than Chicago, Philadelphia, or New York" and respectfully suggested that Rosecrans could send five thousand men from St. Louis to Nashville.[66] Let it be done, Grant replied, adding:

> *I fear either Hood or Breckinridge will get to the Ohio River. . . . If Thomas has not struck yet, he ought to be ordered to hand over his command to Schofield. There is no better man to repel an attack than Thomas, but I fear he is too cautious to ever take the initiative.*[67]

6

COMMENTING ON JUBAL EARLY'S decision back in mid-July to withdraw from Fort Stevens, historian Margaret Leech wrote: "The alarms of war had vanished overnight, leaving a scene as empty of initiative as the brain of General Halleck."[68] True, since his demotion in mid-March to chief of staff of the Union armies, he had behaved as a model bureaucrat. In the circumstances, the demands of duty and honor required nothing less.

Evidently, however, General Grant's message seemed to cause Henry Halleck to stop being the kind of man poet T. S. Eliot, generations later, made immortal in "The Love Song of J. Alfred Prufrock," as these lines from it suggest:

> *There will be time, there will be time*
> *To prepare a face to meet the faces that you meet;*
> *There will be time to murder and create,*
> *And time for all the works and days of hands*
> *That lift and drop a question on your plate . . .*
> *And time yet for a hundred indecisions,*
> *And a hundred visions and revisions,*
> *Before the taking of a toast and tea.*
>
> *Do I dare*
> *Disturb the universe?*
> *In a minute there is time*
> *For decisions and revisions which a minute will reverse.*

No! I am not Prince Hamlet, nor was meant to be;
Am an attendant lord, one that will do
To swell a progress, start a scene or two,
Advise the prince; no doubt, an easy tool,
Deferential, glad to be of use,
Politic, cautious, but a bit obtuse;
At times, indeed, almost ridiculous —
Almost, at times, the fool.[69]

If so before, no longer. To General Grant, the Old Brains of earlier times telegraphed at nine o'clock on the evening of December 8, 1864:

If you wish General Thomas relieved from command, give the order. No one here will, I think, interfere. The responsibility, however, will be yours, as no one here, so far as I am informed, wishes General Thomas' removal.[70]

For Henry Halleck it was, all over again, the night at his quarters in mid-December 1862, when he had stopped pacing the floor and scratching his elbows and told Abraham Lincoln that if he wanted Ambrose Burnside to cancel the attack about to be launched against General Lee's impregnable defenses on and below Marye's Heights west of Fredericksburg, "you must issue it yourself."

Halleck's implied refusal to go on being *an attendant lord, deferential, glad to be of use,* seemed to have given Grant pause, for he replied merely:

I want General Thomas reminded of the importance of immediate action. I sent him a dispatch this evening which will probably urge him on. I would not say relieve him until I hear further from him.[71]

The dispatch to Thomas to which the lieutenant general commanding referred had taken this form:

It looks to me evident that the enemy are trying to cross the Cumberland River and are scattered. Why not attack at once? By all means avoid the contingency of a foot race to see which, you or Hood, can beat to the Ohio [River]. . . . Now is one of the finest opportunities ever presented of destroying one of the three armies of the enemy. Use the means at your command, and you can do this and cause a rejoicing that will resound from one end of the land to another.[72]

Fine, even admirable. Yet on the next day, December 9, 1864, Generals Grant, Thomas, and Halleck exchanged a flurry of messages. And most of those written by the lieutenant general indicated that his inclination to encourage Thomas had been ephemeral.

At 10:30 on that morning, Halleck had telegraphed Thomas:

General Grant expresses much dissatisfaction at your delay in attacking the enemy. If you wait till General Wilson mounts all his cavalry, you will wait till doomsday, for the waste equals the supply. Moreover, you will soon be in same condition that Rosecrans was last year—with so many animals that you cannot feed them. Reports already come in of a scarcity of forage.[73]

At 11 a.m., Grant to Halleck:

Dispatch of 8 p.m. last evening from Nashville shows the enemy scattered for more than seventy miles down the river, and no attack yet made by Thomas. Please telegraph orders relieving him at once and placing Schofield in command.[74]

As though he did not trust General Halleck to carry out an action he opposed, Grant also sent the same instructions directly to the Adjutant General's Office.[75]

At 1:00 p.m. General Thomas replied to Grant's message of encouragement sent the night before:

I had nearly completed my preparations to attack the enemy to-morrow morning, but a terrible storm of freezing rain has come on to-day, which will make it impossible for our men to fight to any advantage. I am, therefore, compelled to wait for the storm to break and make the attack immediately after.

Admiral [S. P.] Lee is patrolling the [Cumberland] river above and below the city, and I believe will be able to prevent the enemy from crossing. There is no doubt but that Hood's forces are considerably scattered along the river with the view of attempting a crossing, but it has been impossible for me to organize and equip the troops for an attack at an earlier time.

Major General Halleck informs me that you are very much dissatisfied with my delay in attacking. I can say only that I have done all in my power to prepare, and if you should deem it necessary to relieve me I shall submit without a murmur.[76]

At two o'clock on that Friday afternoon, General Thomas sent essentially the same message to General Halleck. Not having heard from Grant since that morning, at 4:10 p.m. Halleck gave him another chance to reconsider:

Orders relieving General Thomas had been made out when his telegram of this p.m. was received. If you still wish these orders telegraphed to Nashville they will be forwarded.[77]

Grant to Halleck, 5:30 p.m., Friday, December 9, 1864:

General Thomas has been urged in every way possible to attack the enemy, even to the giving the positive order. He did say he thought he would be able to attack on the 7th, but didn't do so, nor has he given a reason for not doing it. I am very unwilling to do injustice to an officer who has done as much good service as General Thomas has, however, and will, therefore, suspend the order relieving him until it is seen whether he will do anything.[78]

Grant to Thomas, 7:30 p.m:

I have as much confidence in your conducting a battle rightly as I have in any other officer; but it has seemed to me that you have been slow, and I have had no explanation of affairs to convince me otherwise.
    Receiving your dispatch of 2 p.m. from General Halleck, before I did the one to me, I telegraphed to suspend the order relieving you until we should hear further. I hope most sincerely that there will be no necessity of repeating the orders, and that the facts will show that you have been right all the time.[79]

And finally, at 11:30 p.m., the Rock of Chickamauga's response:

I can only say in further explanation why I have not attacked Hood that I could not concentrate my troops and get their transportation in order in shorter time than has been done, and am satisfied I have made every effort that was possible to complete the task.[80]

That message sent, General Thomas is said to have turned to cavalry commander James Wilson and remarked, "The Washington authorities treat me like a schoolboy, but if they let me alone I'll lick them yet."[81] Presumably, he meant he would defeat Hood's forces. But might the ambiguity have been intentional?

Earlier on December 9, General Thomas had issued this order to his senior commanders:

Owing to the severity of the storm raging to-day, it is found necessary to postpone the operations designed for to-morrow morning until the breaking-up of the storm. I desire, however, that everything be put in condition to carry out the plan contemplated as soon as the weather will permit it to be done, so that we can act instantly when the storm clears away.[82]

John Hood might well have issued the same directive. His army's situation, in fact, was even more discouraging. In the two weeks since he crossed the Tennessee, the number of his troops had gone down from thirty-eight thousand to about twenty-four thousand—a drop of roughly fourteen thousand—with desertions rivaling combat losses. All Hood could hope to do was lure Thomas into attacking him, but now the ice was so thick along his four-mile line that his men could not stab through it even with their sharp knives to deepen their trenches.[83]

In fact, Hood had outsmarted himself. Now that he had pursued Schofield from the Duck River and the Harpeth to the Cumberland and Thomas' line, he could not move northeastward and threaten the Ohio River country—or in any other direction—without Old Pap's army right behind him.

7

WHY, THEN, WAS GENERAL-IN-CHIEF GRANT insisting that Thomas attack? Was he living up to Cump Sherman's description of him to Halleck as having the perseverance of a Scotch terrier? Or, frustrated by General Lee for the better part of six months below Petersburg and southeast of Richmond, was Grant trying too hard to please the two politicians who were his only superiors?

Sherman's seizure of Atlanta in September was widely thought to have contributed materially to Lincoln's re-election in November. But there had been no more Union victories since Little Phil Sheridan had gallantly but narrowly saved the North from having to absorb another stunning, demoralizing whipping at Cedar Creek back on October 19. And the Congress was to reconvene on December 5, 1864.[84] How, then, given that Sherman had vanished (and that the less said about that until he reappeared, the better), could the President defend himself against the Radicals' inevitable charges that the Union armies had all gone into winter quarters?

Spur plodding George Thomas, Edwin Stanton must have suggested, for as far back as December's first week the Secretary of War had telegraphed General Grant:

> *The President feels solicitous about the disposition of Thomas to lay in fortifications for an indefinite period, "until Wilson gets equipment." This looks like the McClellan and Rosecrans strategy of do nothing, and let the enemy raid the country. The President wishes you to consider the matter.*[85]

Lieutenant General Grant's subsequent erratic, vacillating, and generally hectoring manner of dealing with Thomas suggests that he had become much easier to intimidate than Halleck had ever been. Concurrently, in daring to admonish his superior to stop and think before relieving the general in command of an army in the field, Henry Halleck—who, unlike Grant, had nothing left in terms of reputation to lose—had upheld moral standards along with military principles.

But this was hardly anything new.

Until late in 1861, as has been shown, almost everything Old Brains had done since the Mexican War was related to the law. Lieutenant Halleck had helped shape the constitution for Californians. After 1854 he had expanded the basis for jurisprudence in that state through his practice. During 1862, from the principles of equity laced with common sense, he had derived the Halleck Doctrine, which the Union's chief magistrate had been obliged to accept on that December night before the slaughter at Fredericksburg.

But in holding that the general commanding in the field is the best judge of conditions—put another way, that war managers in the rear echelon should abstain from seeking to direct operations on distant battlefields—Old Brains had assumed the consequent duty of *enforcing* it. And that, while he had been the Union's general-in-chief, he had done.

Ulysses Grant, however, had taken a different view of what a general-in-chief ought to do. His place, he decided, was with the field army capable of inflicting the greatest damage to the most powerful Confederate force. Being on the scene he could control George Meade directly; Cump Sherman, Grant knew, could command the Union's Western armies without any supervision at all.

But just as Lincoln had been forced to prod Grant into responding to Jubal Early's threat to Washington, the commander-in-chief may well have been wondering if he had, after all the trials and egregious errors, *indeed* found *his* general.

And so it was that only one man, Henry Wager Halleck, stood between Lincoln, Stanton, and Grant and their warped values and George H. Thomas—the general, as dedicated to duty, honor, and country as Old Brains, out there on the frozen field in central Tennessee.

8

"THE POSITION OF THE ENEMY appears the same to-day as yesterday," General Thomas telegraphed Chief of Staff Halleck late on the evening of December 11, 1864. "The weather continues very cold and the hills are covered with ice. As soon as we have a thaw, I will attack Hood."[86]

Fine, presumably, thought General Halleck, but not the equally distant lieutenant general commanding. To George Thomas, Grant thundered:

> *If you delay attack longer the mortifying spectacle will be witnessed of a rebel army moving for the Ohio River, and you will be forced to act, accepting such weather as you find. Let there be no further delay.*
>
> *Hood cannot stand even a drawn battle so far from his supplies of ordnance stores. If he retreats and you follow, he must lose his material and much of his army.*
>
> *I am in hopes of receiving a dispatch from you to-day announcing that you have moved. Delay no longer for weather or re-enforcements.*[87]

Solid soldier that General Thomas was, though all but one of the war managers in Washington thought him *stolid*, Old Pap replied:

I will obey the order as promptly as possible, however much I may regret it, as the attack will have to be made under every disadvantage.

The whole country is covered with a perfect sheet of ice and sleet, and it is with difficulty the troops are able to move about on level ground. It was my intention to attack Hood as soon as the ice melted, and would have done so yesterday had it not been for the storm.[88]

Adverse weather continued to plague Thomas on Monday, December 12. That night he telegraphed General Halleck:

I have the troops ready to make the attack on the enemy as soon as the sleet which now covers the ground has melted sufficiently to enable the men to march. As the whole country is now covered with a sheet of ice so hard and slippery it is utterly impossible for troops to ascend the slopes, or even move over level ground in anything like order.

It has taken the entire day to place my cavalry in position, and it has only been finally effected with imminent risk and many serious accidents, resulting from the number of horses falling with their riders on the roads. Under these circumstances I believe an attack at this time would only result in a useless sacrifice of life.[89]

On the next day, Tuesday, Old Pap was more hopeful: "At length there are indications of a favorable change in the weather," he wrote Halleck, "and as soon as there is I shall move against the enemy, as everything is ready and prepared to resume the offensive."[90]

General-in-Chief Grant had been strangely silent for the past day or two, but he had not been idle. At the time, Major General John A. Logan was passing through City Point and Grant had plans for him. Logan, an Illinois politician appointed to general officer rank by Lincoln, had served under Grant early in the war but had balked when Sherman failed to give him command of Fighting Joe Hooker's corps. Go to Nashville, Grant instructed Logan, and relieve General Thomas—provided he had not attacked Hood in the meantime.[91]

Whether or not General Halleck was aware of Logan's assignment, on Wednesday, December 14, he made one more effort to warn Thomas that Grant's patience was almost exhausted:

It has been seriously apprehended that while Hood, with a part of his forces, held you in check near Nashville, he would have time to operate against other important points left only partially protected. Hence, General Grant was anxious that you should attack the rebel force in your front, and expressed great dissatisfaction that his orders had not been carried out.

Moreover, so long as Hood occupies a threatening position in Tennessee, General Canby is obliged to keep large forces upon the Mississippi River, to protect its navigation and to hold Memphis, Vicksburg, &c., although General Grant had directed a part of these forces to co-operate with General Sherman. Every day's delay on your part, therefore, seriously interferes with General Grant's plans.[92]

Thomas replied a few hours later:

Your telegram of 12.30 p.m. to-day is received. The ice having melted away to-day, the enemy will be attacked to-morrow morning. Much as I regret the apparent delay in attacking the enemy, it could not have been done before with any reasonable hope of success.[93]

By the time General Thomas' telegram was on its way to Halleck, the lieutenant general commanding had decided to go to Nashville and attend personally to Old Pap's replacement. On Wednesday night he boarded a steamer bound for Washington, where he would catch a train for Nashville.[94] But he was still in the capital on Thursday, December 15, when General Halleck received this message:

I attacked the enemy's left this morning and drove it from the river, below the city, very nearly to the Franklin Pike, a distance about eight miles. . . . The troops behaved splendidly, all taking their share in assaulting and carrying the enemy's breastworks.

I shall attack the enemy again to-morrow, if he stands to fight, throwing a heavy cavalry force in his rear, to destroy his trains, if possible.[95]

Thereupon, Grant telegraphed General Rawlins at City Point: "I send you dispatch just received from Nashville. I shall not now go there."[96]

9

GEORGE THOMAS' VICTORY MESSAGE was not the only gratifying news
Henry Halleck received on Thursday, December 15, 1864. From on board
the dispatch boat *Dandelion* on Ossabaw Sound, roughly eighteen miles
south of Savannah, Cump Sherman had written Old Brains at near
midnight on December 13:

> *To-day, at 5 p.m., General Hazen's division of the Fifteenth Corps
> carried Fort McAllister by assault, capturing its entire garrison and
> stores. This opened to us the Ossabaw Sound, and I pulled down to
> this gunboat to communicate with the fleet.*
>
> *Before opening communication we had completely destroyed
> all the railroads leading into Savannah and invested the city. . . .
> Were it not for the swamps we could march into the city, but as it is
> I would have to assault at one or two places over narrow causeways,
> leading to much loss; whereas in a day or two, with my com-
> munications restored and the batteries in position within short range
> of the city, I will demand its surrender.*
>
> *The army is in splendid order, and equal to anything. Weather
> has been fine, and supplies abundant. Our march was most agree-
> able, and we were not at all molested by guerrillas. . . . We have on
> hand plenty of meat, salt, and potatoes; all we need is bread, and I
> have sent to Port Royal for that.*
>
> *We have not lost a wagon on the trip, but have gathered in a
> large supply of negroes, mules, horses, &c., and our teams are in far
> better condition than when we started. My first duty will be to clear
> the army of surplus negroes, mules, and horses, and suppose General
> Saxton can relieve me of these. . . .*
>
> *Full and detailed reports of the events of the past month will
> be prepared at a more leisure moment, and in the meantime I can
> only say that I hope by Christmas to be in possession of Savannah,
> and by the new year to be ready to resume our journey to Raleigh.
> The whole army is crazy to be turned loose in Carolina; and with
> the experience of the past thirty days I judge that a month's sojourn
> in South Carolina would make her less bellicose.*
>
> *The editors in Georgia profess to be indignant at the horrible
> barbarities of Sherman's army, but I know the people don't want our
> visit repeated. We have utterly destroyed over 200 miles of railroad,
> and consumed stores and provisions that were essential to Lee's and*

Hood's armies. A similar destruction of roads and resources hence to Raleigh would compel General Lee to come out of his intrenched camp. . . .

I regard Savannah as already gained.[97]

Actually, from December 8 onward both Halleck and Grant had been receiving reports from Major General J. G. Foster, commanding at the Union's Hilton Head, South Carolina, supply base, that Sherman was nearing Savannah.[98] This, of course, raised the question of what directives should next be given to Cump.

It appeared that George Thomas was well on the way to wrecking John Hood's (not long earlier, Joe Johnston's and before that Braxton Bragg's and Pierre Beauregard's and Albert Sidney Johnston's) tragically depleted Army of Tennessee. From the Union's point of view, of course, this was a consummation devoutly to be wished; it would leave General Lee's frustrating but pinned-in-place Army of Northern Virginia as the *only force of any consequence* that was still remaining to be shattered.

Indeed as far back as on December 6, General Grant had written Sherman: "I have concluded that the most important operation toward closing out the rebellion will be to close out Lee and his army. . . ."[99] His idea was that Cump ought to establish a base on the sea-coast and move the balance of his command to him by water, with all dispatch. "I want you here in person," Grant added. "Unless you see objections to this plan, which I cannot see, use every vessel going to you for purposes of transportation."[100]

Cump replied in one of the longest letters he ever wrote that he had been concentrating on capturing Savannah and using that port city as his base for the campaign he had intended to launch northward through the Carolinas, but that "since the receipt of yours of the 6th [of December] I have initiated measures looking principally to coming to you with 50,000 to 60,000 infantry. . . ." Clearly, General Sherman was recalling that a soldier's first duty is to obey, for in three subsequent passages he bade perhaps rueful farewells to his earlier hopes while assuring the lieutenant general commanding of his cheerful compliance. First:

General Slocum occupies Argyle Island and the upper end of Hutchinson's Island, and has a brigade on the South Carolina shore opposite, and he is very urgent to pass one of his corps over to that shore; but, in view of the change of plans made necessary by your order of the 6th, I will maintain things in statu quo *till I have got*

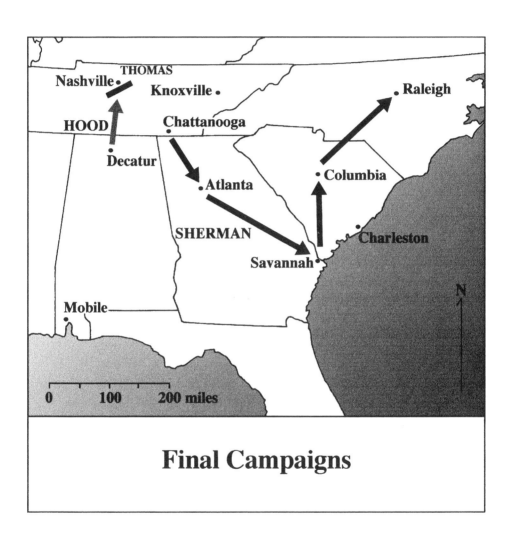

Final Campaigns

all my transportation to the rear and out of the way, and until I have sea transportation for the troops you require at James River, which I will accompany and command in person.

Next:

My four corps, full of experience and full of ardor, coming to you en masse, equal to 60,000 fighting men, will be a re-enforcement that Lee cannot disregard. Indeed, with my present command, I had expected upon reducing Savannah instantly to march to Columbia, S.C., thence to Raleigh, and thence to report to you; but this would consume, it may be, six weeks time after the fall of Savannah, whereas by sea I can probably reach you with my men and arms before the middle of January.

And finally:

Our whole army is in fine condition as to health, and the weather is splendid; for that reason alone, I feel a personal dislike to turning northward. I will keep Lieutenant Dunn [Grant's aide] *here until I know the result of my demand for the surrender of Savannah; but, whether successful or not, shall not delay my execution of your order of the 6th, which will depend alone upon the time it will require to obtain transportation by sea.*[101]

Was Cump's closing reference to the time it would take to assemble the hundred transports, more or less, a hint to General Halleck—who, presumably, saw copies of most messages—that it might be helpful if he abandoned the role of deferential, attendant lord and entered the case? Old Brains came close to doing that on December 18 in his reply to Sherman's letter to him dated December 13. "Should you capture Charleston," he wrote, "I hope that by some accident the place may be destroyed, and if a little salt should be sown upon its site it may prevent the growth of future crops of nullification and secession."[102]

In that message Halleck mentioned that "General Grant is expected here this morning and will probably write you his own views." Three days earlier, the general-in-chief had telegraphed: "Please communicate with Sherman, and direct him to send no troops from his army to Virginia until plan of campaign is fully agreed upon. My last instructions to Sherman contemplated his sending troops to operate against Richmond. . . ."[103] The conference in Washington set for December 18, then, was presumably for the purpose of discussing the two possible courses of action. In any event, in a letter to Sherman from the capital on that day, Grant wrote:

> *I did think the best thing to do was to bring the greater part of your army here and wipe out Lee. The turn affairs now seem to be taking has shaken me in that opinion. I doubt whether you may not accomplish more toward that result where you are than if brought here, especially as I am informed since my arrival in the city that it would take about two months to get you here, with all the other calls there are for ocean transportation.*
>
> *I want to get your views about what ought to be done and what can be done. If you capture the garrison of Savannah it certainly will compel Lee to detach from Richmond, or give us nearly the whole South. My own opinion is that Lee is averse to going out of Virginia, and if the cause of the South is lost he wants Richmond to be the last place surrendered. If he has such views it may be well to indulge him until everything else is in our hands.*[104]

On December 24, 1864, General Sherman provided Grant with his plans—then he revealed them to Old Brains, in a letter that opened with thanks for the "high encomiums you have passed on our recent campaign. . . . I am also very glad that General Grant has changed his mind about embarking my troops for the James River." After describing his next moves he commented:

> *I think the time has come now when we should attempt the boldest moves, and my experience is that they are easier of execution than more timid ones, because the enemy is disconcerted by them. . . . I think my campaign of the last month, as well as every step I take from this point northward, is as much a direct attack upon Lee's army as though I were operating within the sound of his artillery.*
>
> *I attach more importance to these deep incisions into the enemy's country, because this war differs from European wars in this particular. We are not only fighting hostile armies, but a hostile people, and must make old and young, rich and poor, feel the hard hand of war, as well as their organized armies.*
>
> *I know that this recent movement of mine through Georgia has had a wonderful effect in this respect. Thousands who had been deceived by their lying papers into the belief that we were being whipped all the time, realized the truth, and have no appetite for a repetition of the same experience. To be sure, Jeff. Davis has his*

people under a pretty good state of discipline, but I think faith in him is much shaken in Georgia; and I think before we are done, South Carolina will not be quite so tempestuous.

I will bear in mind your hint as to Charleston, and don't think salt will be necessary. When I move the Fifteenth Corps will be on the right of the Right Wing, and their position will bring them, naturally, into Charleston first; and if you have watched the history of that corps you will have remarked that they generally do their work up pretty well.

The truth is the whole army is burning with an insatiable desire to wreak vengeance upon South Carolina. I almost tremble at her fate, but feel that she deserves all that seems in store for her. Many and many a person in Georgia asked me why we did not go to South Carolina, and when I answered that I was en route for that State the invariable reply was, "Well, if you will make those people feel the severities of war, we will pardon you for your desolation of Georgia. . . ."

Of you I expect a full and frank criticism of my plans for the future, which may enable me to correct errors before it is too late. I do not wish to be rash, but want to give my rebel friends no chance to accuse us of want of enterprise or courage.[105]

As 1864 was nearing its end Chief of Staff Halleck was entitled to a few grains of comfort as he reviewed the year's challenges. Despite the awkwardness caused by the changes in their relationship, he had not only served his successor loyally but in a number of situations he had also done his best to save Grant from making potential mistakes, including these:

- Offending Lincoln by relieving Nathaniel Banks prematurely: *Prevented*
- Moving the Army of the Potomac south of the James, instead of taking positions northwest of Richmond: *Not acted upon, General Lee's acquiescence not having been forthcoming*
- Delaying his response to Lincoln's concern over Jubal Early's presence just northwest of Washington: *Corrected, barely*
- Violating the Halleck Doctrine by giving direct, peremptory orders to General Thomas and seeking his relief: *Prevented, barely*
- Moving the bulk of Sherman's army from Savannah to the trenches below Petersburg by sea, another probable violation of the Halleck Doctrine: *Blocked, by facts*

Paraphrasing the blind poet John Milton, *They also serve who only stand and say* No.

But by the end of the year, with A. Lincoln assured of another four-year term and the Union armies' conquest of the Confederacy merely a question of time, politics—which Henry Halleck had abhorred and avoided all his life—obliged him to respond to Cump Sherman's request that he give his old friend "a full and frank criticism of my plans for the future. . . ." On December 30 Old Brains said in a letter marked Confidential:

> *I take the liberty of calling your attention, in this private and friendly way, to a matter which may possibly hereafter be of more importance to you than either of us may now anticipate. While almost every one is praising your great march through Georgia and the capture of Savannah, there is a certain class, having now great influence with the President, and very probably anticipating still more on a change of Cabinet, who are decidedly disposed to make a point against you—I mean in regard to "Inevitable Sambo."*
>
> *They say that you have manifested an almost criminal dislike to the negro, and that you are not willing to carry out the wishes of the Government in regard to him, but repulse him with contempt. They say you might have brought with you to Savannah more than 50,000, thus stripping Georgia of that number of laborers and opening a road by which as many more could have escaped from their masters; but that instead of this you drove them from your ranks, prevented them from following you by cutting the bridges in your rear, and thus caused the massacre of large numbers by Wheeler's cavalry.*
>
> *To those who know you as I do such accusations will pass as the idle winds, for we presume that you discouraged the negroes from following you simply because you had not the means of supporting them and feared they might seriously embarrass your march. But there are others, and among them some in high authority, who think, or pretend to think, otherwise, and they are decidedly disposed to make a point against you.*
>
> *I do not write this to induce you to conciliate this class of men by doing anything which you do not think right and proper and for the interest of the Government and the country, but simply to call your attention to certain things which are viewed here somewhat differently than from your standpoint.*

I will explain as briefly as possible: Some here think that, in view of the scarcity of labor in the South, and the probability that a part, at least, of the able-bodied slaves will be called into the military service of the rebels, it is of the greatest importance to open outlets by which the slaves can escape into our lines, and, they say, that the route you have passed over should be made the route of escape and Savannah the great place of refuge. These I know are the views of some of the lending men in the administration, and they now express dissatisfaction that you did not carry them out in your great raid.

Now that you are in possession of Savannah, and there can be no further fears about supplies, would it not be possible for you to reopen these avenues of escape for the negroes without interfering with your military operations?

Could not such escaped slaves find, at least, a partial supply of food in the rice fields about Savannah, and occupation in the rice and cotton plantations on the coast?

I merely throw out these suggestions; I know that such a course would be approved by the Government, and I believe that a manifestation on your part of a desire to bring the slaves within our lines will do much to silence your opponents.[106]

On the next day, 1864's last, General Halleck went beyond warning Sherman. To Grant at City Point, he telegraphed:

I learn from a letter of General Foster that all able-bodied negroes brought in by Sherman are to be shipped to City Point. Permit me to suggest that they be armed, organized, and used in the Department of the South during the winter.

Our experience is that negroes brought North during the cold weather, from a warm climate, are almost useless; moreover, they suffer much from cold. To send them North at the present time would create a panic among them, and prevent others from coming in from the interior of the country. Rebel papers are already harping on this point in order to frighten their slaves.

The Secretary of War and General Meigs concur in these views.[107]

Henry Halleck had spent most of his adult life in California, half a continent away from slavery, and he had incurred the wrath of the eastern

Union's abolitionists back in 1861 by excluding fugitive slaves from his camps in Missouri. Strictly viewed, neither his military duty nor his honor obliged him to intervene.

Yet he did, with this result: "The Secretary of War directs," Old Brains telegraphed General Foster at Hilton Head on December 31, 1864, "that the order to send able-bodied or other negroes from your department to City Point be suspended, and that you organize all you can get for service there."[108]

19 ★ *The Treacherous Fog of Peace*

*J*ANUARY 1, 1865, WAS THE SECOND ANNIVERSARY of Major General Henry W. Halleck's decision to withdraw his request to be relieved as general-in-chief. In the interval his support had assisted Ulysses Grant and William Tecumseh Sherman in recovering from their discouraging defeats at Chickasaw Bluffs and Holly Springs, in winning decisive victories at Vicksburg and Missionary Ridge, and in Cump's capturing Atlanta and scourging Georgia from there to Savannah and the Atlantic. Despite his demotion Old Brains had helped Grant grow into an effective general-in-chief—at times, by bluntly obliging the lieutenant general commanding to stop and think. And as to Abraham Lincoln, the powerful if not actually rich man in trouble who had called him to Washington in July 1862, Halleck had saved him from making mistakes in *United States v. Confederacy* that might well have held his client to one term.

With the war's end almost imminent and no fresh opportunities to be of important service looming, January 1, 1865, might have been an excellent time for Halleck to have turned his desk over to Quartermaster-General Montgomery Meigs, or to any other senior officer who had demonstrated superior abilities as an administrator, and to have returned to his law practice and business interests in San Francisco. He would have left nothing of value behind except the project he had initiated during 1863: to collect and preserve the Official Records of the Union Armies,[1] another task his successor as chief of staff could superintend. Moreover, by resigning early in 1865 Old Brains would have been able to stop the erosion of his reputation; indeed, since he left California in the fall of 1861, at the pinnacle of his success, condemnation and denunciation and ridicule had been the only returns he had received on his heavy investments in devotion to duty, honor, and the Union.

Why then, should Old Brains have invited *more* abuse by remaining in Washington's political hell? Lincoln no longer needed him. Indeed, the President's attention had shifted to the future, to political questions such as:

- How to negotiate possibilities for peace with the Confederate government, whose existence—even after nearly four years of fierce and bloody warfare—he still refused to concede
- What terms should be insisted upon
- How the states that had been in rebellion, the "erring sisters," were to qualify for restoration to the bosom of the Union family

"After four exhausting years [Lincoln] was now master of the almost impossible job to which he had been elected," historian David Herbert Donald has written. "He was commander-in-chief of the largest military and naval forces the country had ever raised, and at last they were functioning with machine-like efficiency."[2]

Well, not quite—as the Union fiasco later called the Wilmington expedition, or Fort Fisher I, proved.

Wilmington, North Carolina, was the last port anywhere on the Confederacy's Atlantic or Gulf coasts that remained open to successful blockade runners. Grant had long wanted it seized and converted to a Union base for operations aimed at removing the Tarheel State's agricultural wealth from the resources still sustaining General Lee's determined resistance south of Richmond.

Thanks to George Thomas' smashing of John Hood's army at Nashville, which had occurred despite Grant's impatience, troops were available. So were the warships of the navy's North Atlantic Squadron, commanded by Rear Admiral David Dixon Porter whose support in the spring of 1863 had been of enormous value to General Grant in capturing Vicksburg and in reopening the Mississippi to Union navigation from Minnesota to the Gulf of Mexico and the world beyond.

But Wilmington, and Fort Fisher on the south bank of the Cape Fear River east of the port, were technically in the military department commanded by the last and perhaps least competent of A. Lincoln's original gaggle of political generals, "Spoons" Butler. Earlier, after Butler's waste of his troops' lives in the futile Bermuda Hundred sideshow southeast of Richmond, the lieutenant general and Halleck had relegated the former governor of Massachusetts to Fort Monroe where he could do less harm. But "Beast" Butler's reaction to news of the Fort Fisher task force's formation was to use his remaining political clout on Lincoln to obtain command of it.

This might have done no great damage except for General Butler's insistence on packing a steamer full of gunpowder, tugging the vessel as close as possible to Fort Fisher's masonry wall, igniting the explosives, and sending troops through the hole in the fort thus created. To the surprise of Grant and everyone else who had high regard for Porter's common sense, the admiral liked the idea.[3]

And so it was that before December 1864 ended, Butler's experiment had been tried. It had failed so miserably that, in a New Year's Day letter to Sherman, General Halleck wrote: "Thank God, I had nothing to do with it, except to express the opinion that Butler's torpedo ship would have about as much effect on the forts as if he should --- at them. I said about the same thing to the Secretary of War and General Grant before they consented to it."[4]

But no one had listened to Old Brains, or no one had possessed the courage to point out to the President that Ben Butler had sought the command of the Wilmington expedition merely because this might be his last chance to prevent his deplorable military reputation from being a liability in the political contests he would be entering after the war. Of course, General Halleck could oppose indulging Spoons with impunity; unlike Grant and Stanton, he had no reputation left to protect—and nothing he could do or say at this late point in the war could restore a single fragment of the shattered good name he had brought to Washington.

Indeed, Benjamin Butler was not the only general, political or otherwise, whose concern over reputation transcended almost every consideration. As 1864 was giving way to 1865, many other senior movers and shakers of the Union's war efforts were anticipating victory by giving much thought to how posterity would view their performances, and especially their achievements. In the process, the prevailing definition of *honor* deteriorated from "that which rightfully attracts esteem, as dignity and courage; especially, excellence of character; in men, integrity, uprightness" all the way down to "esteem due or paid to worth; . . . hence, fame, credit, good name."[5]

Or so it seemed as the scent of victory stimulated ambitions in some men and compelled others to seek revenge for what they had perceived as injustices blighting their reputations. In some instances along the way, their treatment by Halleck would be cited, and correctly, as the cause of their distress. Strict observer, upholder, and, when necessary, *enforcer* of principles as Old Brains had long been, it was hardly surprising that the man Abraham Lincoln had used earlier as a lightning rod when criticism was crackling would soon attract bolts of vituperation for *his own* sins of omission as well as commission. As it turned out, however, the most astonishing surprise would be the identity of the general whose animosity did more damage than any other to deprive Old Brains of satisfactions he ought to have been able to take with him when—finally—he left the rebellion completely quelled behind him and headed back westward.

2

THE MOST UNPOPULAR MAN in Washington[6] must have obtained a few grains of wry satisfaction when he read a message from General Grant to Secretary of War Stanton dated January 4, 1865:

> *I am constrained to request the removal of Maj. Gen. B. F. Butler from the command of the Department of Virginia and North Caro- lina. I do this with reluctance, but the good of the service requires it.*
>
> *In my absence General Butler necessarily commands, and there is a lack of confidence felt in his military ability, making him an unsafe commander for a large army. His administration of the affairs of his department is also objectionable.[7]*

And surely Halleck relished the privilege of sending Grant the result: "I send you by telegraph General Orders, No. 1, relieving General Butler from his command. It will not be entered on the files or published here until you have it delivered to him."[8]

Ulysses Grant quickly repaired the slight dents in his reputation by replacing Butler with Major General Alfred H. Terry and sending the same troops, supported this time by heavy gunfire from Porter's armada, back to capture Fort Fisher. Selecting Terry had been a stroke worthy of Grant's mentor, for—as Sherman gleefully pointed out—this solid soldier's success at Fort Fisher II disproved the allegations of Beast Butler, John McClernand, and others of that ilk that West Pointers deliberately conspired to insure the defeat of generals (such as Terry) who had not attended the United States Military Academy.[9]

Devoid of a good name of his own to protect, however, on December 30 of the year just ended, in a confidential letter, General Halleck had warned Cump Sherman to look out for his own reputation because "there is a certain class, having now great influence with the President . . . who are decidedly disposed to make a point against you—I mean in regard to 'Inevitable Sambo.'" On January 12, 1865, from Savannah, General Sherman replied:

> *I deeply regret that I am threatened with that curse to all peace and comfort—popularity; but I trust to bad luck enough in the future to cure that, for I know enough of "the people" to feel that a single mistake made by some of my subordinates will tumble down my fame into infamy.*
>
> *But the nigger? Why, in God's name, can't sensible men let him alone? When the people of the South tried to rule us through the negro, and became insolent, we cast them down, and on that question we are strong and unanimous. Neither cotton, the negro, nor any single interest or class should govern us.*
>
> *But I fear, if you be right that that power behind the throne is growing, somebody must meet it or we are again involved in war with another class of fanatics. Mr. Lincoln has boldly and well met the one attack, now let him meet the other.*
>
> *If it be insisted that I shall so conduct my operations that the negro alone is consulted, of course I will be defeated, and then where will be Sambo? Don't military successes imply the safety of Sambo and vice versa?*

Here, General Sherman referred to a tragic incident that occurred along Ebenezer Creek, not far west of Savannah on December 3, 1864:

> *Of course that cock-and-bull story of my turning back negroes that* [Confederate cavalryman Major General Joseph] *Wheeler might kill them is all humbug. I turned nobody back.* [Union Major General] *Jeff. C. Davis did at Ebenezer Creek forbid certain plantation slaves—old men, women, and children— to follow his column; but they would come along and he took up his pontoon bridge, not because he wanted to leave them, but because he wanted his bridge.*
>
> *He and Slocum both tell me that they don't believe Wheeler killed one of them. Slocum's column (30,000) reports 17,000 negroes. Now, with 1,200 wagons and the necessary* impedimenta *of an army, overloaded with two-thirds negroes, five-sixths of whom*

are helpless, and a large proportion of them babies and small children, had I encountered an enemy of respectable strength defeat would have been certain.

Tell the President that in such an event defeat would have cost him ten thousand times the effort to overcome that it now will to meet this new and growing pressure. I know the fact that all natural emotions swing as the pendulum. These southrons pulled Sambo's pendulum so far over that the danger is it will on its return jump off its pivot.

There are certain people who will find fault, and they can always get the pretext; but, thank God, I am not running for an office, and am not concerned because the rising generation will believe that I burned 500 niggers at one pop in Atlanta, or any such nonsense.

I profess to be the best kind of a friend to Sambo, and think that on such a question Sambo should be consulted. They gather round me in crowds, and I can't find out whether I am Moses or Aaron, or which of the prophets; but surely I am rated as one of the congregation, and it is hard to tell in what sense I am most appreciated by Sambo—in saving him from his master, or the new master that threatens him with a new species of slavery. I mean State recruiting agents. Poor negro—Lo, the poor Indian! Of course, sensible men understand such humbug, but some power must be invested in our Government to check these wild oscillations of public opinion. The South deserves all she has got for her injustice to the negro, but that is no reason why we should go to the other extreme.

I do and will do the best I can for negroes, and feel sure that the problem is solving itself slowly and naturally. It needs nothing more than our fostering care. I thank you for the kind hint and will heed it so far as mere appearances go, but, not being dependent on votes, I can afford to act, as far as my influence goes, as a fly wheel instead of a mainspring.[10]

Well worth noting, here, is the extraordinary candor reflected throughout Sherman's long reply to his old friend's admonition. Seldom, if ever, did either man confide in anyone else so freely or to that degree.

3

SET ASIDE THOUGH GENERAL HALLECK'S counsel had been in connection with Union combat operations such as the Fort Fisher embarrassment, on February 15, 1865, acting still as a mentor to Grant, he drew upon his business experience and desire for justice in the context of overall circumstances in writing at some length to give cogent counsel to the general-in-chief:

> *In reply to your telegram in regard to the payment of the troops before Richmond, I would remark that these troops have been paid generally to a later period than those in the West and South. Some are unpaid for seven or eight months.*
>
> *The fault is not in the Pay Department, but a want of money in the Treasury. There will be a change of the head in a few days, but whether that will help us any remains to be seen.*
>
> *Officers and members of Congress have suggested that the money be given to the Pay Department in preference to the Quartermaster's, Commissary's, and other supply departments. You will readily perceive by doing this we would necessarily cut off the supplies of our army.*
>
> *I understand that the Quartermaster's Department is already some $180,000,000 in debt, and that until a part, at least, of this is paid it will be almost impossible to purchase and transport supplies. The manufacturers cannot furnish cloth, or the tailors make clothes, or the shoemakers make shoes, or the railroads transport troops and supplies, much longer, unless paid a part, at least, of their claims. Some of the Western roads cannot pay their employés, and threaten to stop running their trains if they cannot be paid what the Government owes them. . . . What is here said of the Quartermaster's Department also applies to the Commissary, Medical, Ordnance, and other departments.*
>
> *If we pay the troops to the exclusion of the other creditors of the Government supplies must stop, and our armies will be left without food, clothing, or ammunition. We must equalize and distribute the Government indebtedness in such a way as to keep the wheels going. I give you these views as the result of various consultations with the heads of departments.*
>
> *What we want is some more great victories to give more confidence in our currency and to convince financial men that the war is near its close. In money matters these are the darkest days we have yet had during the war, but I hope that relief is not very distant.*[11]

They also serve, blind poet John Milton had declared, *who only stand and wait.*

So assumed General Sherman, for on April 5, from near Goldsboro, North Carolina, he wrote Halleck:

> *I send by Sergeant Rose my report. . . . The bearer has some things for Mrs. Sherman, but I don't know if she is in Chicago or South Bend. If John Sherman or Mr. Ewing are in Washington they will know. If you cannot put him in possession of the means of finding out, please telegraph to Mrs. Sherman so that the sergeant may go straight.*
>
> *We are all dead broke here; no paymaster, and none expected. The sergeant has a furlough to go to Iowa. If you can, give him an order of transportation, say to Burlington, Iowa, or give him $41 and charge to me; I expect to turn up somewhere, and having pay due since January 1, think my credit good for that amount. I like to hear from you.*[12]

While pre-war San Francisco banker Cump Sherman was reversing their earlier roles by seeking a line of credit from his storeship *Lexington* shipmate Halleck, their mutual friend from this war's earlier years was finally breaking through General Lee's thin lines below Petersburg. Grant's attacks led to the seizure of Richmond soon after the flight on the night of April 2 of Confederate President Jefferson Davis and his cabinet on a train followed by another containing the treasury's remaining monetary assets.[13]

On April 9 Generals Lee and Grant met in the parlor of Wilbur McLean's house at Appomattox Court House; when they parted the war was over for Army of Northern Virginia.[14] On the next day Halleck wrote Sherman:

> *We are now amidst the excitement of victory, speeches, &C, on the news of the surrender of Lee's army. I hope soon to hear of Johnston's to you, and of Mobile to Canby. They can have no possible hopes now, and it is utterly useless to waste any more blood.*
>
> *If Johnston will surrender as Lee has I presume you will give him the same terms. Beauregard, Bragg, and Hardee deserve no consideration. I congratulate you on your great marches and able combinations.*[15]

Two days later, from Smithfield, North Carolina, Cump telegraphed Grant: "The terms you have given Lee are magnanimous and liberal. Should Johnston follow Lee's example I shall of course grant the same."[16] And then, two nights later, to Sherman came a message dated April 14, 1865, from the commander of the Confederates facing him:

> *The results of the recent campaign in Virginia have changed the relative military condition of the belligerents. I am therefore induced to address you in this form the inquiry, whether, in order to stop the further effusion of blood and devastation of property, you are willing to make a temporary suspension of active operations, and to communicate to Lieutenant-General Grant, commanding the Armies of the United States, the request that he will take like action in regard to other armies; the object being to permit the civil authorities to enter into the needful arrangements to terminate the existing war.*[17]

Within an hour, Sherman replied:

> *I am fully empowered to arrange with you any terms for the suspension of further hostilities as between the armies commanded by you and those commanded by myself, and will be willing to confer with you to that end.*
>
> *I will limit the advance of my main column to-morrow to Morrisville, and the cavalry to the University, and expect that you will also maintain the present position of your forces until each has notice of a failure to agree.*
>
> *That a basis of action may be had, I undertake to abide by the same terms and conditions as were made by Generals Grant and Lee at Appomattox Court-House, on the 9th instant, relative to our two armies; and, furthermore, to obtain from General Grant an order to suspend the movement of any troops from the direction of Virginia.*
>
> *General Stoneman is under my command, and my order will suspend any devastation or destruction contemplated by him. I will add that I really desire to save the people of North Carolina the damage they would sustain by the march of this army through the central or western parts of the State.*[18]

But as General Sherman's response was being taken to Johnston, from Washington at two o'clock on the morning of April 15, 1865, General Halleck was telegraphing Major General E. O. C. Ord at Richmond:

Attempts have been made to-night to assassinate the President and Secretary of State. Arrest all persons who may enter your lines by water or land. Particulars will be given hereafter.[19]

4

BY APRIL 14, 1865—GOOD FRIDAY—General Grant had been in Washington only a short time, and he and his wife departed that evening for Burlington, New Jersey, to visit their children. Before he left, however, at the President's invitation he attended a cabinet meeting at which Lincoln commented on his recent trip to Richmond and expressed views regarding reconstruction that were in line with his "with malice toward none and charity for all" passage in his second Inaugural Address. Grant had reached Philadelphia and was changing trains when he learned that Lincoln had been shot. He returned to Washington as soon as he could get there.

Edwin McMasters Stanton was cursed with a tendency to become completely unhinged by the deaths of persons close to him. Abraham Lincoln's murder caused him to go into a perfect frenzy of activity. As if Andrew Johnson had not been about to be sworn-in as the next President of the United States, the panic-driven secretary of war—suspecting a gigantic, malignant Confederate conspiracy—took a number of measures aimed at capturing the perpetrators and securing the safety of officials not yet attacked. For a time, without authority, Edwin Stanton was running the Union government.[20]

By early in the afternoon on Saturday, April 15—Lincoln had died early that morning—Stanton had telegraphed a message to General Sherman:

President Lincoln was murdered about 10 o'clock last night in his private box at Ford's Theater in this city, by an assassin who shot him through the head with a pistol ball. About the same hour Mr. Seward's house was entered by another assassin, who stabbed the Secretary in several places, but it is thought he may possibly recover; but his son Frederick will probably die of wounds received from the assassin.

The assassin of the President leaped from the box, brandishing dagger, exclaiming, Sic semper tyrannis! and that now Virginia was revenged. Mr. Lincoln fell senseless from his seat, and continued in that state until twenty-two minutes after 7 o'clock, at which time he breathed his last.

General Grant was published to be at the theater, but fortunately did not go. Vice-President Johnson now becomes President, and will take the oath of office and assume the duties to-day.

I have no time to add more than to say that I find evidence that an assassin is also on your track, and I beseech you to be more heedful than Mr. Lincoln was of such knowledge.[21]

Certainly General Halleck was the author of that text, as is confirmed by the same steady, restrained tone evident in the message he sent Cump shortly thereafter:

It has been stated that when an assassin was chosen to kill Mr. Seward one also was sworn to murder you. His name was said to be Clark. He is about five feet nine inches high, rather slender, high cheek bones, low forehead, eyes dark and sunken, very quiet, seldom or never speaks in company unless spoken to, has a large dark-brown mustache and large long goatee, hair much darker than whiskers, complexion rather sallow; while in Paris, March 12, wore dark-gray clothes, a wide-awake slouched hat. . . .[22]

The round from John Wilkes Booth's pistol that killed Abraham Lincoln destroyed much more than a great and good man. That action opened a Pandora's Box of malevolent forces, many of which would plague the nation for as long as anyone living *thirteen decades* later could foresee. And soon after Edwin Stanton, among the first of them, shed the deceptive cocoon of subservient bureaucrat, he ordered General Halleck to Richmond as Military Division of the James.[23]

Lawyers Stanton and Halleck had been adversaries in California before the war. Back in 1862 Lincoln had called Old Brains to Washington for reasons of his own. Nothing short of astonishing was the fact that Halleck and Stanton had not only coexisted within the Union's high command for the better part of three years, but that they had so often cooperated.

At least two circumstances facilitated Stanton's summary ejection of Halleck from the Union's high command. General-in-Chief Grant would be making his headquarters in Washington from then on, so the position of chief of staff of the armies could be abolished. Also, conditions in Richmond were chaotic. Major General Ord described some of them in a report to Stanton on April 19:

There [are] *several thousand of the Army of Northern Virginia in Richmond. . . . They are without money or food. There are perhaps 25,000 women and children, of all colors, here in the same condition. Their money valueless, they can get no food. Two hundred or 300 men a day are arriving to give themselves up, lay down their arms, and be paroled under the order I have issued. Labor and bread these people must have. . . . There are thousands of colored people flocking into town and roaming through the country. They should be set to work. We cannot afford to feed them in idleness. . . .*[24]

Ord sent a similar message to General Grant, writing at the end: "It is important to get them away from here. If I am not authorized either to feed them or send them away by the most expeditious routes I cannot be responsible for the consequences."[25]

Grant replied:

We cannot undertake to bear all the hardships brought on individuals by their treason and rebellion. It was no part of the agreement that we should furnish homes, subsistence, or transportation to Lee's army. . . .

I did not by any means intend that this should be an excuse for all who choose to come within our lines and stay there, a public charge, or that men going to North Carolina or Georgia should be furnished a pleasant passage through the North and coastwise to their homes. . . .

General Halleck will start to Richmond to-morrow and he will take up and settle the present difficulties.[26]

In a message to Assistant Secretary of War Dana, Provost Marshal M. R. Patrick confirmed some of Ord's complaints but added:

Every boat brings from the North persons on business of various kinds, often very indiscreet in their conduct. I beg that the strictest orders may be given in regard to passes for Richmond until the city is cleared of the dangerous element that now fills it.[27]

And so it was that, for whatever reason, Old Brains would be the better part of a hundred miles away when Lieutenant General Grant would need him desperately.

5

BACK ON SATURDAY, APRIL 15, days before the news of Lincoln's assassination and of the North's shock and fear and orgy of mourning[28] could possibly have reached him, General Sherman had started on its way to Grant and Stanton a report on the progress he had made since he received Johnston's letter:

> *I send copies of a correspondence begun with General Johnston, which, I think, will be followed by terms of capitulation. I will accept the same terms as General Grant gave General Lee, and be careful not to complicate any points of civil policy.*
>
> *If any cavalry have started toward me caution them that they must be prepared to find our work done. It is now raining in torrents, and I shall await General Johnston's reply here, and will propose to meet him in person at Chapel Hill.*
>
> *I have invited Governor* [Zebulon B.] *Vance to return to Raleigh with the civil officers of his State. I have met ex-Governor Graham, Mr. Badger, Moore, Holden, and others, all of whom agree that the war is over, and that the States of the South must resume their allegiance, subject to the Constitution and laws of Congress, and that the military power of the South must submit to the national arms.*
>
> *This great fact once admitted, all the details are easy of arrangement.*[29]

So it may have seemed to Cump Sherman, and another message he started on its way through relays to Grant was in the same optimistic vein:

> *I have returned from a point twenty-seven miles up the railroad, where I had a long interview with General Johnston, with a full and frank interchange of opinions.*
>
> *He evidently seeks to make terms for Jeff. Davis and his cabinet. He wanted to consult again with Mr. Breckinridge at Greensborough, and I have agreed to meet him at noon to-morrow at the same place.*
>
> *We lose nothing in time, as by agreement both armies stand still and the roads are drying up, so that if I am forced to pursue we will be able to make better speed.*
>
> *There is great danger that the Confederate armies will dissolve*

and fill the whole land with robbers and assassins, and I think this is one of the difficulties that Johnston labors under. The assassination of Mr. Lincoln shows one of the elements in the rebel army which will be almost as difficult to deal with as the main armies.

Communicate substance of this to General Grant, and also that if General Sheridan is marching down this way to feel for me before striking the enemy. I don't want Johnston's army to break up in fragments.[30]

Three days later, on Tuesday, April 18, General Sherman had every reason to believe that General Halleck would be at his desk in Washington, as usual, when he sent him this letter:

I received your dispatch describing the man Clark detailed to assassinate me. He had better be in a hurry or he will be too late.

The news of Mr. Lincoln's death produced a most intense effect on our troops. At first I feared it would lead to excesses, but now it has softened down and can easily be guided. None evinced more feeling than General Johnston, who admitted that the act was calculated to stain his cause with a dark hue, and he contended that the loss was most serious to the people of the South, who had begun to realize that Mr. Lincoln was the best friend the South had.

I cannot believe that even Mr. Davis was privy to the diabolical plot, but think it the emanation of a set of young men of the South who are very devils. I want to throw upon the South the care of this class of men, who will soon be as obnoxious to their industrial classes as to us.

Had I pushed Johnston's army to an extremity these would have dispersed and would have done infinite mischief. Johnston informed me that Stoneman had been at Salisbury and was now about Statesville. I have sent him orders to come to me. General Johnston also informed me that Wilson was at Columbus, Ga., and he wanted me to arrest his progress. I leave that to you.

Indeed, if the President sanctions my agreement with Johnston, our interest is to cease all destruction. Please give all orders necessary according to the views the Executive may take, *and influence him, if possible, not to vary the terms at all, for I have considered everything and believe that the Confederate armies once dispersed we can adjust all else fairly and well.*[31] [Emphasis supplied.]

But by the time that letter reached Washington, General Halleck was in Richmond. Subsequent events suggested that Old Brains did not see it; but he might have caught up with the message Sherman sent, also on April 18, to whoever might be "COMDG. GENERAL ARMIES OF THE UNITED STATES IN VIRGINIA":

> *I have agreed with General Joseph E. Johnston for a temporary cessation of active hostilities, to enable me to lay before our Government at Washington the agreement made between us, with the full sanction of Mr. Davis and in the presence of Mr. Breckinridge, for the disbandment of all the armies of the Confederacy from here to the Rio Grande.*
>
> *If any of your forces are moving toward Johnston I beg you to check them where they are or at the extremity of any railroad where they may be supplied* until you receive orders from General Grant, *or until I notify you* that the agreement is at an end and hostilities resumed.[32] [Emphasis supplied.]

Friday, April 21, 1865, proved to be a day on which everything concerning Sherman and later Halleck that could go wrong, did go wrong. Their friendship's slide into hell began at around four o'clock that afternoon when Sherman's courier reached Washington and presented General Grant with some documents, including Cump's cover letter to him:

> *I inclose herewith a copy of an agreement made this day between General Joseph E. Johnston and myself, which, if approved by the President of the United States, will produce peace from the Potomac and the Rio Grande.*
>
> *Mr. Breckinridge was present at our conference in his capacity as major-general, and satisfied me of the ability of General Johnston to carry out to the full extent the terms of this agreement, and if you will get the President to simply indorse the copy and commission me to carry out the terms, I will follow them to the conclusion.*
>
> *You will observe that it is an absolute submission of the enemy to the lawful authority of the United States, and disperses his armies absolutely, and the point to which I attach most importance is that the dispersion and disbandment of these armies is done in such a manner as to prevent their breaking up into guerrilla bands. On the other hand, we can retain just as much of an army as we please. I*

agreed to the mode and manner of the surrender of arms set forth, as it gives the States the means of repressing guerrillas, which we could not expect them to do if we stripped them of all arms.

Both Generals Johnston and Breckinridge admitted that slavery was dead, and I could not insist on embracing it in such a paper, because it can be made with the States in detail. I know that all the men of substance South sincerely want peace, and I do not believe they will resort to war again during this century. I have no doubt that they will in the future be perfectly subordinate to the laws of the United States. . . .

The question of finance is now the chief one, and every soldier and officer not needed should be got home at work. I would like to be able to begin the march north by May 1.

I urge on the part of the President speedy action, as it is important to get the Confederate armies to their homes as well as our own.[33]

The way to value anything, someone has observed, *is to imagine the consequences of it being lost.* In the confusion generated by Lincoln's death and the Stantonian panic following it, General Grant had to decide promptly what to do. He had not been in Washington long enough to have an idea of where political quicksands might be. Halleck could have told him—but the secretary of war had put Old Brains beyond his reach.

Otherwise, Halleck might well have pointed out that the Sherman-Johnston agreement was doomed to be rejected because it encroached on political turf that had changed drastically in the wake of Lincoln's assassination. Hardly anything the late President had ever done had pleased the Radicals. Shortly before his murder they had been enraged by indications that he would be far too lenient in granting terms to the South.

Visiting Richmond on April 12 with four of the members of his Joint Congressional Committee on the Conduct of the War, ultra-Radical Senator Benjamin Wade became aware of an incorrect report that Lincoln had authorized Virginia's legislature to reassemble and begin the process of reconstruction. Benjamin B. French later wrote that Bluff Ben declared (in effect) that if Lincoln had done that, "By God, the sooner he was assassinated, the better."[34] In his diary, George W. Julian described a meeting of the committee in Washington on the day Lincoln died: "The hostility toward Lincoln's policy of conciliation and contempt for his weakness were undisguised; and the universal feeling among radical men here is that his death is a godsend."[35]

The Union's new President, Andrew Johnson, had once been a member of Senator Wade's committee.[36] And despite his apparent loyalty to Lincoln, Edwin Stanton had been currying favor from the Radicals since before he became secretary of war.

Moreover, General Sherman had said in at least two messages that he expected to offer Johnston the *same* terms that Grant had extended to General Lee at Appomattox. Now Cump had abandoned that intention. Was it the duty of the lieutenant general to go to Raleigh and bring Sherman back into conformity with the Appomattox terms? Maybe. But was there time for that?

No, General Grant decided. He forwarded the Sherman-Johnston document to Stanton and his Radical brethren. But the question would remain: What if he had corrected Cump's mistake within army authority *before* the politicians had blown it into an all-consuming, Union-wide firestorm?

That night, in a letter to General Sherman, Grant would tell him what happened next:

> *I read the agreement entered into between yourself and Johnston carefully myself before submitting it to the President and Secretary of War and felt satisfied that it could not possibly be approved. . . .*
>
> *Your agreement touches upon questions of such vital importance that as soon as read I addressed a note to the Secretary of War notifying him of their receipt and the importance of immediate action by the President, and suggested in view of their importance that the entire cabinet be called together that all might give an expression of their opinions upon the matter.*[37]

General Grant had underestimated the virulence of the reaction Johnson and his cabinet would have. Sherman's biographer, Lloyd Lewis, described the meeting:

> *That night at eight o'clock Stanton asked Grant to read Sherman's memorandum aloud to the hastily assembled President and Cabinet. As Grant concluded Stanton broke out in excited condemnation of the agreement.* [Secretary of the Navy Gideon] *Welles observed that* [Attorney General James] *Speed, "prompted by Stanton who seemed frantic . . . expressed his fears that Sherman at the head of his victorious legions had designs upon the government." In the stampede every one agreed that the President must not approve*

Sherman's action. It was decided that Grant, who was silent amid the denunciation of his friend, must immediately inform Sherman that his course was disapproved.[38]

Stanton forthwith put the meeting's findings, and a bit more, in the form of an order to Grant:

The memorandum or basis agreed upon between General Sherman and General Johnston having been submitted to the President, they are disapproved.

You will give notice of the disapproval to General Sherman and direct him to resume hostilities at the earliest moment. The instructions given to you by the late President Abraham Lincoln on the 3d of March by my telegraph of that date, addressed to you, express substantially the views of President Andrew Johnson. A copy is herewith appended.

The President desires that you proceed immediately to the headquarters of General Sherman and direct operations against the enemy.[39]

The telegram dated March 3, 1865, to which Stanton referred had been prompted by an inquiry from Grant as to whether he would be permitted to have a talk with General Lee to explore possibilities. Stanton had replied:

The President directs me to say to you that he wishes you to have no conference with General Lee, unless it be for the capitulation of General Lee's army or on some minor and purely military question. He instructs me to say that you are not to decide, discuss, or confer on any political question. Such questions the President holds in his own hands, and will submit them to no military conferences or conventions. Meantime, you are to press to the utmost your military advantages.[40]

Grant enclosed the message in the envelope containing the letter he wrote to Sherman that night before leaving Washington, the one in which he described his reactions and actions that afternoon after he had read the document. He concluded that letter:

The result was a disapproval by the President of the basis laid down, a disapproval of the negotiations altogether, except for the surrender of the army commanded by General Johnston, and directions to me to notify you of this decision. . . .

Please notify General Johnston immediately on receipt of this of the termination of the truce and resume hostilities against his army at the earliest moment you can, acting in good faith. . . .[41]

Next, at ten o'clock on that Friday night, Stanton telegraphed Halleck in Richmond:

The memorandum or basis of arrangement made between General Sherman and General Johnston are disapproved by the President, and General Sherman is ordered to resume hostilities.[42]

But the events of the next day suggested that the notification went astray.

6

ON THE NEXT DAY, SATURDAY, APRIL 22, 1865, General Halleck issued General Orders No. 1 in which he formally assumed command of "the military division which embraces the Department of Virginia, the Army of the Potomac, and such parts of North Carolina as may not be occupied by the command of Major-General Sherman."[43] Old Brains also acted quickly to expand the scope of the Official Records project he had initiated earlier; to General Ord he wrote:

All books, printed documents, maps, manuscripts, &c., found in any public office here, or belonging to Confederate of State authorities, will be carefully preserved. On no consideration will any person be permitted to appropriate or remove them. As soon as rooms can be prepared they will be collected together and inventoried. [Colonel] R. D. Cutts, who will soon arrive, will be placed in charge.[44]

Before noon, the general commanding relayed a report to Stanton that was to have extremely unfortunate consequences:

It is stated here by respectable parties that the amount of specie taken South by Jeff. Davis and his partisans is very large, including not

only the plunder of the Richmond banks, but previous ac-
cumulations. They hope, it is said, to make terms with General
Sherman or some other Southern commander by which they will be
permitted with their effects, including this gold plunder, to go to
Mexico or Europe. Johnston's negotiations look to this end. Would it
not be well to put Sherman and all other commanding generals on
their guard in this respect?[45]

That afternoon Stanton replied:

Your telegram of this morning indicates that Sherman's agreement
with Johnston was not known to you. His action is disapproved, and
he is ordered to resume hostilities immediately. But his order to
Stoneman will allow Davis to escape with his plunder. I will write
you the details.[46]

By mid-afternoon on that Saturday, Grant was at Fort Monroe, and
from there he telegraphed Halleck:

The truce entered into by Sherman will be ended as soon as I get to
Raleigh. Move Sheridan with his cavalry toward Greensborough,
N.C., as soon as possible. I think it will be well to send one corps of
infantry also, the whole under Sheridan.[47]

After telegraphing Meade, Halleck sent this order to Sheridan:

You will move with your cavalry immediately on Greensborough,
N.C. You will then act as circumstances may seem to require, unless
you receive instructions from General Grant, who is on his way to
Raleigh. General Meade has been directed to place an infantry corps
under your direction.
      It is said here that there is a large amount of specie on the road
between here and Charlotte. It is supposed to have been taken at
different points from the railroad and to be in wagons. The railroad
employes are said to know all about this, and will tell if forced to do
so. While pushing south with all possible dispatch look to these
things.[48]

At seven that evening, General Halleck reported to Grant: "Orders have been sent to Major-General Meade and Major-General Sheridan in compliance with your telegram of this date."[49]

On Sunday, April 23, newspapers in New York published the text of the Sherman-Johnston agreement and most of General Halleck's message to Stanton regarding the rebels' specie. The *New York Times,* for one, jumped to an alarming and thoroughly misleading conclusion: "It looks very much as if [Sherman's] negotiation was a blind to cover the escape of Jeff Davis and a few of his officials, with the millions of gold they have stolen from Richmond banks."[50] Was Sherman caught napping or was he too eager for the laurels of the peacemaker, wondered the New York *Herald,* adding: "Sherman has fatally blundered, for, with a few unlucky strokes of his pen, he has blurred all the triumphs of his sword."[51]

Elsewhere, the Chicago *Tribune* declared the next day that "Sherman has been completely over-reached and outwitted by Joe Johnston. . . . We cannot account for Sherman's signature on this astonishing memorandum except on the hypothesis of sheer insanity."[52]

There could have been only one source: Edwin McMasters Stanton. According to Sherman biographer Lloyd Lewis:

> *On April 22, Stanton decided to make a public statement regarding Sherman. . . . An erratic mixture of truths, half-truths, and false-hoods it was that Stanton gave the New York newspapers. . . . It implied that Sherman had willfully disobeyed Lincoln's order of March 3 directing Grant to hold no conferences with the enemy on political questions—the order Sherman in reality had never seen. Then Stanton quoted Halleck's wire of the twenty-second concerning Davis' flight with the gold, and from this he deleted the last sentence, which proved that Halleck had no suspicions of Sherman's honesty— the sentence reading, "Would it not be well to put Sherman and other commanding generals on their guard?"*[53]

7

ON SUNDAY, APRIL 23, 1865, Stanton was aware of the fierce condemnation of General Sherman his disclosures had caused. Halleck, Grant, and Sherman were not.

Grant had reached Beaufort, North Carolina, on his way to Raleigh. While waiting for a train he sent a short message to Stanton: "No news here from Sherman. I shall not telegraph him I am on the way."[54]

From Richmond at 7 p.m., General Halleck wired Sheridan: "Pay no attention to the Sherman and Johnston truce. It has been disapproved by the President. Try to cut off Jeff Davis' specie."[55]

And from Raleigh, while waiting for President Johnson's approval of the agreement, General Sherman wrote an "unofficial" letter to Johnston and Lieutenant General William J. Hardee that accompanied what he called "a bundle of papers" containing the "latest" news regarding the Lincoln assassination's aftermath.

"The feeling North on this subject is more intense than anything that has occurred before," Sherman commented, adding:

> *I believe this assassination of Mr. Lincoln will do the cause of the South more harm than any event of the war, both at home and abroad, and I doubt if the Confederate military authorities had any more complicity with it than I had. I am thus frank with you and have asserted as much to the War Department. . . . [If] any delay occurs it will result from the changed feeling about Washington arising from this new and unforeseen complication.*[56]

The delay ended abruptly early on Monday morning, April 24, 1865, when General-in-Chief Grant arrived and told Cump how matters stood—and why. Promptly, Sherman sent two messages to General Johnston. First, "You will take notice that the truce or suspension of hostilities agreed to between us will cease in forty-eight hours after this is received at your lines under first of the articles of our agreement."[57] That notice given, he followed it up:

> *I have replies from Washington to my communications of April 18. I am instructed to limit my operations to your immediate command and not to attempt civil negotiations. I therefore demand the surrender of your army on the same terms as were given General Lee at Appomattox, of April 9, instant, purely and simply.*[58]

By nine o'clock on that Monday morning, General Grant had started this message on the way to Secretary of War Stanton in Washington:

> *I reached here this morning, and delivered to General Sherman the reply to his negotiations with Johnston. He was not surprised, but*

rather expected their rejection. Word was immediately sent to Johnston terminating the truce, and information that civil matters could not be entertained in any convention between army commanders.

General Sherman has been guided in his negotiations with Johnston entirely by what he thought was precedent authorized by the President. . . .[59]

Monday, April 24, opened General Halleck's first full week as commander of the Military District of Virginia. New though he was to the war-ravaged region, however, he began at once to convert chaos to order. "I think the Tredegar Works should be put in operation to repair all ordnance here before it is removed North," he telegraphed the chief of ordnance in Washington. "This will give employment to mechanics whose families we must otherwise feed to prevent starvation."[60] Similarly, he wrote General Meigs:

The rebel army having stripped the country of all horses and mules the farmers have no means of putting in crops. I suggest the propriety of selling here all condemned animals instead of sending them to Washington. The farmers can get money to pay for them by selling tobacco and market stuff. We must either feed the poor or help them feed themselves.[61]

Colonel Cutts arrived, and Halleck issued General Orders No. 3 giving him authority for collecting and preserving Confederate documents in connection with the Official Records project.[62] Lawyer Halleck prepared the draft of an order opening trade and lifting travel restrictions for "loyal citizens and persons who have taken the prescribed oath under the amnesty proclamation of the President" and obtained lawyer Stanton's approval, subject to a few changes. Old Brains commented:

I think the [order will] *give great satisfaction, and afford immediate relief to Richmond and the surrounding country. I have had interviews with several prominent gentlemen from the surrounding country. They all say that the people are ready and anxious to return to the Union. They are very destitute of provisions, and unless they can be relieved many will resort to robbery. Most of them, however, can provide for themselves if trade is opened so that they can purchase provision and seeds.*[63]

On Tuesday, April 15, General Halleck provided another report to Stanton on the attitudes of Virginians:

> *I have had two interviews with Mr. Alex. Rives and other Union men who have held out against the rebellion. Mr. Rives says the Unionists fairly carried the State in 1861, and can do so now by an increased majority. He thinks that nearly all parties are now ready to abandon slavery, and that a popular vote would be strongly against it.*
>
> *He and others with whom I have conversed prefer the continuance of military authority for the present to the installation of the Peirpoint civil government. They seem to regard that as a kind of sham. All these men are adverse to our recognizing in any manner the rebel State authorities, and rejoice that the project of assembling the present legislature is abandoned.*
>
> *Rives says that the reopening of the mail routes and post-offices so that Northern newspapers can circulate among the people will have an excellent effect. They now have no newspapers of any kind, and are made to believe the most wild and absurd rumors.*
>
> *In this view I think the railroads to Lynchburg and Charlottesville should be opened. This can be done at a trifling expense by the military engineers while the armies are lying still. I regard the reopening of mail routes an important measure for pacification.*[64]

More evidence of Old Brains' mixture of compassion and pragmatism was reflected in the message he sent Stanton on Wednesday, April 26, 1865:

> *The people of Richmond have thus far conducted themselves with great propriety, and are most respectful to the United States authorities. The desire for the complete restoration of the Federal authority in the State seems to be very general here; nevertheless, so large a population entirely without employment and generally without any means is most undesirable, if not dangerous.*
>
> *I am, therefore, sending into the country all who have homes or friends to go to. As there are no means of conveyance here they will be taken to convenient points in public wagons.*
>
> *In this way I hope to soon diminish the issue of provisions. There are, however, thousands here who have a small supply on hand, but no means of purchasing more.*[65]

Just under four years earlier this man had left his highly successful careers as statesman, lawyer, businessman, and scholar-author behind him in San Francisco to contribute to the quelling of the rebellion. First from St. Louis and later from Washington, he had mentored and brought to high command and then supported two lieutenants who had advocated and then prosecuted *total* war. Even so, in a matter of only a few days he had reverted to the roles of state builder and conciliator.

Yet, none of Henry Wager Halleck's detractors, at the time or since, would pay any attention to the prudent and humane measures he took so soon after reaching Richmond. His abrupt banishment by Stanton to the Confederate capital's ruins, human as well as physical, was written-off as no more than a waypoint on his way to well-deserved oblivion.

8

AS LATE AS WEDNESDAY, APRIL 26, General Halleck was still unaware of the controversy over Sherman's agreement with Johnston that had been ignited by Stanton's "leak" to the New York newspapers in time for their Sunday editions. Inadvertent, certainly, was the assistance Old Brains gave the perfidious secretary of war toward destroying what was left of his reputation by sending him this message:

> *Generals Meade, Sheridan, and Wright are acting under orders to pay no regard to any truce or orders of General Sherman suspending hostilities, on the ground that Sherman's agreements could bind his own command only and no other. They are directed to push forward, regardless of orders from anyone except General Grant, and cut off Johnston's retreat.*
>
> *Beauregard has telegraphed to Danville that a new arrangement had been made with Sherman, and that the advance of the Sixth Corps was to be suspended till further orders.*
>
> *I have telegraphed back to obey no orders of General Sherman, but to push forward as rapidly as possible.*
>
> *The bankers here have information today that Jeff. Davis' specie is moving south from Goldsborough in wagons as fast as possible. I suggest that orders be telegraphed through General Thomas that Wilson obey no orders of Sherman, and notifying him and General Canby and all commanders on the Mississippi River to*

take measures to intercept the rebel chiefs and their plunder. The
specie taken with them is estimated here at from six to thirteen
millions.[66]

Halleck's message to Stanton had been sent at 9:30 on that Wednesday
night. Only half an hour later, from Raleigh, General Grant telegraphed
him:

> General Johnston surrendered the forces under his command,
> embracing all from here to the Chattahoochee, to General Sherman,
> on the basis agreed upon between General Lee and myself for the
> Army of Virginia. Please order Sheridan back to Petersburg at
> once. . . . Send copy of this to the Secretary of War.[67]

Presumably, Stanton was informed of Johnston's surrender and by
implication that hostilities would not be resumed almost as quickly as he
had received General Halleck's message on Wednesday night. Yet *again* he
released Old Brains' text. And on Friday, April 28, 1865, the New York
Herald informed its readers:

> Secretary Stanton, in an official dispatch, gives the important
> information that Generals Meade, Sheridan, Wright, Thomas, and
> Canby have all been instructed to pay no attention to General
> Sherman's truce arrangements with Joe Johnston and Breckinridge,
> but to continue pushing the enemy with their various commands,
> and endeavor to cut off Johnston's retreat from North Carolina.
>
> General Halleck, in a dispatch from Richmond to the War
> Department, suggests that General Wilson also be directed to obey no
> orders from Sherman, in consideration of the fact that it has been
> ascertained that the specie plundered from the Richmond banks by
> Jeff. Davis, and widely estimated at between six and thirteen
> millions of dollars, was recently being moved southward in wagons
> from Greensboro, N.C., as fast as possible.
>
> General Halleck likewise suggests that it would be advisable to
> make known this fact to General Canby and all the national
> commanders along the Mississippi River, so that they may be
> prepared to intercept the heavy supply of funds which the rebel chief
> is endeavoring to get out of the country with.[68]

Most of what the *Herald* reported was true, and sources were cited correctly. Yet a question lingered: Why was Edwin Stanton being so diligent in providing the press with documents that could not be interpreted or rewritten or read *accurately* by anyone, absent the overall operational context in which they had been composed?

Stanton's pattern of practices suggests that he saw the destruction of Sherman's and Halleck's reputations as a way of enhancing his own as President Andrew Johnson evaluated it. "Now he belongs to the ages," Stanton is said to have said immediately after Abraham Lincoln died. Also belonging to the ages were all of the generals and admirals and soldiers and sailors of all ranks who had fought, bled, and died to quell the rebellion.

Halleck, Sherman, even Grant, were history: Johnson was the future. Or so Edwin Stanton may have thought. In any case, his actions gave new meaning to the word *malice*.

20 ★ Sherman v. Halleck

$\mathcal{D}$URING APRIL AND MAY OF 1865, Henry Halleck's efforts were directed mainly toward ameliorating Virginians' suffering and privation; reinvigorating agriculture, trade, and industry; and, wherever possible, removing or at least easing military controls. His powers approached those of a dictator, yet he employed them sparingly and with benevolence. As it turned out, though, Old Brains' contemporaries as well as posterity would overlook the vigor and wisdom he put into reconciliation and restoration.

General Halleck's performance was all the more impressive given the damage Edwin Stanton's perfidy was doing to his reputation and Cump Sherman's. He had ample cause to be bitter. Even so, his messages on civil matters reflected the precision in thought and expression characteristic of his wartime dispatches, as is evident in these excerpts from communications he sent as commander of the Military Division of the James:

• April 28, 1865, to Stanton:

> *The Twenty-fifth (colored) Corps is reported to me as being poorly officered and in bad discipline, and altogether unfit for the military occupation of Virginia. Would it not be well to send this corps to the Rio Grande, in Texas, to cut off Davis' retreat into Texas? It is reported here that the officers forming his special escort are Texans and Californians, and that their ultimate destination is Sonora.[1]*

• Same date, to Stanton:

> *The number of staff and special officers here are too numerous by one-half. They do no good, but are a serious embarrassment to the course of business. I propose to send away at least one-half.[2]*

• Same date, to Stanton:

> *I forward General Orders No. 4. You will perceive from paragraph V that measures have been taken to prevent so far as possible the propagation of legitimate rebels.*
>
> *V. No marriage license will be issued until the parties desiring to be married take the oath of allegiance to the United States, and no clergyman, magistrate, or other party authorized by State laws to perform the marriage ceremony will officiate in such capacity until himself and the parties contracting matrimony have taken the prescribed oath of allegiance.*[3]

• April 28, to Major General Ord:

> *Churches which have been closed in Richmond on account of a refusal by the officiating clergyman to read the prescribed prayer for the President of the United States, will be opened for service by any other clergyman of the same denomination who will read such service.*[4]

• April 29, to Lieutenant General Grant:

> *General Ord represents that want of discipline and good officers in the Twenty-fifth Corps renders it a very improper force for the preservation of order in this department. A number of cases of atrocious rape by these men have already occurred. Their influence on the colored population is also reported to be bad. I therefore hope you will remove it to garrison forts or for service on the Southern coast and substitute a corps from the Army of the Potomac, say Wright's, temporarily.*
>
> *It seems very necessary to prevent the rush of the negro population into Richmond and to organize some labor system in the interior immediately as the planting season will be over in two or three weeks. Unless this is provided for there will be a famine in this State. For this purpose I shall occupy Fredericksburg, Orange or Charlottesville, Lynchburg, and a few other points.*
>
> *To perform this duty properly requires officers and men of more intelligence and character than we have in the Twenty-fifth Corps. I think that in a very short time the Twenty-fourth Corps can do all the duty required.*
>
> *Affairs here are settling down quietly. More than 5,000 people have offered to take the amnesty oath. Among these are many of Lee's*

paroled officers. Four offices have been opened for that purpose, and all are densely crowded.

The rebel feeling in Virginia is utterly dead, and, with proper management, can never be revived.[5]

• April 30, to Major General Meade:

You will move the Army of the Potomac, excepting General Wright's corps, from its present position to Manchester, preparatory to marching to Alexandria. . . .

No private property of any kind will be molested in the country passed over. In this respect the strictest discipline must be observed.

The Army of the Potomac has shown Virginians how they were to be treated as enemies. Let them now prove that they know equally well how to treat the same people as friends.

All condemned and captured horses, mules, harness, and wagons may be sold at such times and places en route, as you may deem most advantageous, to farmers. Implements that can be used for agricultural purposes may be sold in the same way.[6]

• May 3, 1865, to Stanton:

The special agent of the Treasury has to-day, I am informed, prohibited any wood or coal to be brought into this city for sale without a special permit from Washington. It is now perfectly evident that these agents are resolved that no one shall buy or sell even the necessaries of life except through themselves or their favorites.

This is increasing the price of provisions. Corn-meal, the only food of most of the colored population, bears a higher price to-day than under rebel rule. Those who have tobacco or other produce to exchange for provisions, seed, and agricultural implements, are told that they can sell only to particular persons, for none others will be permitted to ship such produce.

I know of no better system for robbing the people and driving them to utter desperation. If continued the military must feed the people or permit them to starve.[7]

• Same date, also to Stanton:

I understand that Treasury officers construe the executive order as annulling that clause of mine which makes spirituous liquors contraband in Richmond. I think the exclusion of such liquors at this time a military necessity. With so many rebel soldiers mingling with ours, and a colored population of over 20,000, mostly idle and destitute, the introduction of spirituous liquors will certainly lead to personal conflicts and perhaps riots. Such an element of disorder should not be introduced.[8]

• May 4, to Major General Wright:
All justices of the peace who take the amnesty oath and you deem reliable and worthy direct them to resume their functions to preserve order. Appoint to vacancies good, reliable men.

Hang up all guerrilla bands and all paroled prisoners who violate their parole. Keep the negroes on their plantations, and seek to arrange all differences between them and their masters so that crops may be cultivated. Local authorities will be arranged as soon as possible.[9]

• May 5, in General Orders No. 6:
III. All military officers of this division, and especially the commanders of the posts and districts, will be charged with the preservation of good order within their respective commands. They will use their influence to reconcile all differences between freedmen and their former masters, and will assure the freedmen that they will be required to labor for the support of themselves and families, but that they are free to select their own employers and make their own bargains. They must be made to understand that the Government will protect, but cannot support them.

All classes must be shown the absolute necessity of planting and cultivating crops this spring and the coming summer, in order to avoid want and starvation in the country. . . .

V. Interest, as well as humanity, requires that the former masters of the colored race should unite in devising the best measures for ameliorating their condition, and introducing some practical system of hired labor. To this end all military authorities will lend their aid.[10]

• Same date, to Major General Schofield:
The idea that slavery has ceased must be everywhere impressed, but the freedmen must be made to understand that they are not to be fed by us. They must work for a living. They should not be permitted to

leave the plantations and flock to the large cities, where they can get no labor.[11]

• May 7, to Stanton:

Is there any objection now to permitting exceptional cases of rebels who have taken the oath of allegiance to go North? There are cases here of real suffering and destitution, whose friends offer them support at the North. To let them go now will relieve the Government from the necessity of feeding them and also remove in part the idea that we have not kept faith on General Grant's agreement.[12]

• May 8, to Stanton:

It has been suggested that all obstacles to trade here, which now seem almost insurmountable, would be removed by a proclamation of the President that Virginia and North Carolina are no longer to be regarded as insurrectionary districts so far as domestic trade is concerned. This, I think, would greatly increase the revenue by causing produce to be brought in and subjected to internal taxes.[13]

• May 19, to Major Eckert:

It is respectfully recommended that telegraph lines in Virginia and North Carolina which are to be held for military purposes be also opened to private business and that those not to be so held be turned over to their companies for repair and operation.[14]

• May 24, to Major General Weitzel:

It is reported that various articles and stores were taken from the Davis house in Richmond while you were in command. You will cause any such articles held by any one in your command to be turned over to the quartermaster's department, to be returned to the place from which taken, and report to these headquarters any person who has taken from the said house or from any other public building any article whatever, whether papers, furniture, curiosities, or anything else.[15]

• May 27, in General Orders No. 8:

I. The attention of clergymen and magistrates, who are authorized by the laws of Virginia and North Carolina to perform marriage ceremonies, is respectfully called to the cases of colored men and women in their respective parishes and districts who have marital relations without contracting marital obligations. Such persons should be duly instructed in regard to their social and domestic duties, and especially in regard to their duty to support and educate their offspring. They must be made to understand that the laws of God, as well as the laws of their country, forbid their living together as man and wife without the solemnization of marriage. . . .

III. It is hoped that all persons interested in ameliorating the condition of the colored race and in improving their social character will use their influence in promoting the object in view.[16]

There were, of course, other matters that differed greatly from those with which General Halleck dealt during the war. For example, on May 18, Secretary of War Stanton telegraphed him:

General Grant is here with his wife, and is sick. It is not safe for him to be at a hotel, and he is reluctant to go into a private family. He would go into your house for a while if agreeable to you. Will you invite him to do so while your family are away?[17]

Before the day ended, Grant wired Old Brains: "Your very kind dispatch placing your house at Mrs. Grant's disposal during her stay is received. I have not seen Mrs. Grant since, but know she will be delighted to get out of the hotel for the few weeks she remains here."[18]

And almost a week earlier, General Halleck must have been delighted to learn that a major addition to the materials being collected for the Official Records was being made by Confederate General Joseph E. Johnston. From Charlotte, North Carolina, on May 8 Johnston had telegraphed Schofield:

It has just been reported to me that the archives of the war Department of the Confederate States are here. As they will furnish valuable materials for history, I am anxious for their preservation, and doubt not that you are too. For that object I am ready to deliver them to the officer you may direct to receive them.[19]

In fact, General Johnston's gift amounted to eighty-one boxes of papers weighing ten tons.[20] It was also timely, in at least two respects. Hastily prepared, emotion-driven trials of pro-Confederates accused of conspiring with John Wilkes Booth and assisting him in Lincoln's assassination were in progress in Washington; if justice rather than mere revenge were the object, the collection of Confederate papers might have material bearing. Also, in view of Stanton's erratic conduct, General Halleck may well have suspected that the entire Official Records project might be aborted during one of the secretary's mental equivalents of sunspots.

Such was the background for a letter Halleck wrote to Stanton on May 11, before the true dimensions of Johnston's contribution were known:

> *When I arrived here I found that very little care had been taken to secure and preserve the documents and archives of the rebel government. Many which had escaped the conflagration had been plundered and carried off by relic hunters. . . .*
>
> *It is very possible, however, that the papers which I have been able to preserve may furnish important links of testimony against prominent traitors. To avoid the risk of attempting to assort and classify them here I have directed Colonel Cutts to send them to Assistant Secretary Dana, as fast as they could be boxed, with a general description of the contents of each box. Over ninety large boxes have already been shipped. . . .*
>
> *Although many of the papers forwarded will probably prove worthless, yet there may be found among them much evidence in regard to plots of assassination, incendiarism, treason, &c. They therefore should be most carefully examined and preserved. At any rate, they will prove of great value to those who may hereafter write the history of this great rebellion. . . .*[21]

General Halleck urged Virginians to work, to take care of themselves and each other, and to avoid becoming dependent on the federal government. To the extent possible he evicted non-essential Northerners from the region and removed needless controls. While he asked for approvals occasionally, he did not look to Washington for guidance. In ravaged Virginia, as he had in Alta California after the Mexican War, Old Brains relied mainly on common sense and common decency. But he had not yet learned that the new regime looked upon the conquered Confederacy with malice toward all and charity for none—and that would prove to be his undoing.

2

LIKE GENERAL HALLECK IN RICHMOND, conciliation was much on Cump

Sherman's mind—or so it seemed on April 27, 1865, when he wrote General Johnston:

> *In addition to the points made at our interview of yesterday, I have further instructed General Schofield to facilitate what you and I and all good men desire, the return to their homes of the officers and men composing your army, to let you have of his stores ten days' rations for 25,000 men. . . .*
>
> *Now that war is over, I am as willing to risk my person and reputation as heretofore to heal the wounds made by the past war, and I think my feeling is shared by the whole army. I also think a similar feeling actuates the mass of your army, but there are some unthinking young men, who have no sense or experience, that unless controlled may embroil their neighbors. If we are forced to deal with them, it must be with severity, but I hope they will be managed by the people of the South.*[22]

On the next day, however, whatever satisfaction General Sherman had salvaged from Johnston's surrender was shattered. To Grant, on April 28, Cump wrote:

> *Since you left me yesterday I have seen the* New York Times *of the 24th, containing a budget of military news authenticated by the signature of the Secretary of War, which is grouped in such a way as to give very erroneous impressions.*
>
> *It embraces a copy of the basis of agreement between myself and General Johnston of April 18, with commentaries which it will be time enough to discuss two or three years hence, after the Government has experimented a little more in the machinery by which power reaches the scattered people of the vast area of country known as the South; but in the meantime I do think that my rank, if not past services, entitled me at least to the respect of keeping secret what was known to none but the cabinet until further inquiry could have been made, instead of giving publicity to documents I never saw and drawing inferences wide of the truth.*
>
> *I never saw or had furnished me a copy of President Lincoln's dispatch to you of the 3d of March until after the agreement, nor did Mr. Stanton, or any human being, ever convey to me its substance or anything like it. But, on the contrary, I had seen General Weitzel's invitation to the Virginia legislature, made in Mr. Lincoln's very*

presence, and had failed to discover any other official hint of a plan of reconstruction, or any ideas calculated to allay the fears of the people of the South, after the destruction of their armies and civil authorities would leave them without any government at all.

We should not drive a people into anarchy, and it is simply impossible for our military power to reach all the recesses of their unhappy country. I confess I did not wish to break General Johnston's army into bands of armed men, roving about without purpose and capable only of infinite mischief. But you saw on your arrival that I had my army so disposed that his escape was only possible in a disorganized shape, and, as you did not choose to direct military operations in this quarter, I infer you were satisfied with the military situation.

At all events, the instant I learned what was proper enough, the disapproval of the President, I acted in such a manner as to compel the surrender of General Johnston's whole army on the same terms you prescribed to General Lee's army when you had it surrounded and in your absolute power.

Mr. Stanton, in stating that my orders to General Stoneman were likely to result in the escape of "Mr. Davis to Mexico or Europe," is in deep error. . . . But even now, I don't know that Mr. Stanton wants Davis caught, and as my official papers, deemed sacred, are hastily published to the world, it will be imprudent for me to state what has been done in that respect.

As the editor of the Times has (it may be) logically and fairly drawn from this singular document the conclusion that I am insubordinate, I can only deny the intention. I have never in my life questioned or disobeyed an order, though many and many a time have I risked my life, my health, and reputation in obeying orders, or even hints, to execute plans and purposes not to my liking.

It is not fair to withhold from me plans and policy, if any there be, and expect me to guess at them, for facts and events appear quite different from different stand-points. For four years I have been in camp dealing with soldiers, and I can assure you that the conclusion at which the cabinet arrived, with such singular unanimity, differs from mine. I conferred freely with the best officers in this army as to the points involved in this controversy, and strange to say they were singularly unanimous in the other conclusion, and they will learn with pain and amazement that I am deemed insubordinate and wanting in common sense; that I, who, in the complications of last *year, worked day and night, summer and winter, for the cause and the Administration, and who have brought an army of 70,000 men in magnificent condition across a country deemed impassable, and placed it just where it was wanted almost on the day appointed, have brought discredit on our Government.*

I do not wish to boast of this, but I do say that it entitled me to the courtesy of being consulted before publishing to the world a proposition rightfully submitted to higher authority for proper adjudication, and then accompanied by other statements which invited the press to be let loose upon me. It is true that non-combatants, men who sleep in comfort and security whilst we watch on the distant lines, are better able to judge than we poor soldiers, who rarely see a newspaper, hardly can hear from our families, or stop long enough to get our pay.

I envy not the task of reconstruction, and am delighted that the Secretary has relieved me of it. As you did not undertake to assume the management of the affairs of this army, I infer that on personal inspection your mind arrived at a different conclusion from that of the Secretary of War.

I will therefore go on and execute your orders to their conclusion, and when done, will with intense satisfaction leave to the civil authorities the execution of the task of which they seem to me so jealous. But as an honest man and soldier, I invite them to follow my path, for they may see some things and hear some things that may disturb their philosophy.[23]

In a postscript to this uncommonly long but critically important letter, Sherman added: "As Mr. Stanton's singular paper has been published I demand that this also be made public, though I am in no manner responsible to the press, but to the law and my proper superiors."[24] Apparently Cump had not finished his venting of anger until after midnight, for at three o'clock in the morning of the following day, he sent this covering message to Grant's chief of staff, General Rawlins:

The tone of all the papers of the 24th is taken up from the compilation of the War Department of the 22d, which is untrue, unfair, and unkind to me, and I will say undeserved. . . .

The South is broken and ruined, and appeals to our pity. To ride the people down with persecutions and military exactions would be like slashing away at the crew of a sinking ship. I will fight as long as the enemy shows fight, but when he gives up and asks quarter I cannot go further.

This state of things appeals to our better nature, and it was an outrage to torture my forbearance into the shape the Secretary has done. He has either misconceived the whole case or he is not the man I supposed him. If he wants to hunt down Jeff. Davis or the politicians who had instigated civil war, let him use sheriffs, bailiffs, and catch-thieves, and not hint that I should march heavy columns of infantry hundreds of miles on a fool's errand.

The idea of Jeff. Davis running about the country with tons of gold is ridiculous. . . .

I doubt not efforts will be made to sow dissension between Grant and myself on a false supposition that we have political aspirations, or, after killing me off by libels, he will next be assailed. I can keep away from Washington, and I confide in his good sense to save him from the influences that will surround him there.

I have no hesitation in pronouncing Mr. Stanton's compilation of April 22 a gross outrage on me, which I will resent in time. He knew I had never seen or heard of that dispatch to General Grant till he sent it to me a few days ago by General Grant himself. . . .[25]

All of which recalls the question: What if General Halleck had still been in Washington on April 21 when Grant had to decide what he should do with the agreement that had just arrived. But by April 28 it was moot, of course. Yet Cump's anger and anguish and animosity would henceforth be directed as much toward Henry Halleck as the miscreant Stanton.

Sherman went from Raleigh to Savannah and then to Morehead City, North Carolina. From there on May 4, he sent General Grant a brief report on his inspection trip that included this barbed query: "Have you any reason why I should longer submit to the insult contained in Halleck's dispatch to the New York papers on the 28th?"[26]

Halleck's dispatch had been to Stanton only, of course, but Sherman had no way of knowing that. Grant stopped short of pointing that fact out in his reply the next day:

I do not know how to answer your dispatch asking whether you should submit to Halleck's insult contained in a dispatch published in the New York Herald *of the 28th. I never saw that dispatch except as published in the papers. I question whether it was not an answer, in Halleck's style, to directions from the Secretary of War, giving him instructions to do as he did.*[27]

Sherman continued to condemn Old Brains at every opportunity. In a message to General Schofield, he wrote:

At Hilton Head I got New York Papers of the 28th containing Halleck's perfidious order to disregard my truce. I will attend to him in time. Has it embarrassed you in your affairs? . . . If you are in telegraphic communication with General Wilson tell him I want him to do right regardless of the confusion likely from Halleck's impertinent interference with my business.[28]

And to the commander at New Berne he stated: "I have seen Halleck's perfidious and infamous order to disregard my truce. He is a brave general to pursue so fiercely an army that he knows did not intend to fight, but to surrender or run."[29]

On May 5 Sherman vented his resentment against targets beyond Halleck, but including him, in another message to Schofield:

[Our Government] *seems to fail us entirely at this crisis, for I doubt if any one at Washington appreciates the true state of affairs South. Their minds are so absorbed with the horrid deformities of a few assassins and Southern politicians that they overlook the wants and necessities of the great masses.*

> *You have seen how Stanton and Halleck turned on me because I simply submitted a skeleton as basis. Anything positive would be infinitely better than the present doubting, halting, nothing-to-do policy of our bewildered Government.*

> *After Stanton's perfidious course toward me officially I can never confer with him again, and therefore am compelled to leave you to approach him as best you can. Now that all danger is past, and our former enemy simply asks some practicable escape from the terrible vicissitudes of his position, it is wonderful how brave and vindictive former noncombatants have become. It makes me sick to contemplate the fact, but I am powerless for good, and must let events drift as they best may.*[30]

3

THAT DRIFT WOULD BE TOWARD WASHINGTON, for some genius in Andrew Johnson's administration had set bureaucratic wheels in motion toward a grand victory parade of Meade's Army of the Potomac down Pennsylvania Avenue to be held on May 23, followed the next day by a review of Sherman's "bummers." General Halleck ordered Meade's troops northward forthwith. But in order for Cump's veterans to participate in the celebration, they would have to reach Washington by going through Richmond, Old Brains' jurisdiction, first.

"When you arrive," Halleck telegraphed to Sherman on May 8, "come here directly to my headquarters. I have a room for you and will have rooms elsewhere for your staff."[31]

From Fort Monroe, Sherman promptly replied:

> *After your dispatches to the Secretary of War on April 26 I cannot have any friendly intercourse with you. I will come to City Point tomorrow and march with my troops, and I prefer that we should not meet.*[32]

And to a routine message to Schofield, Cump added: "Halleck invites me to his house in Richmond, but I declined emphatically."[33]

Because of the manifold problems within Richmond with which magistrate Halleck was attempting to cope, he had issued orders which had the effect of restricting Sherman's army to campgrounds south of the city and the James River around Manchester. Earlier, plans had been made for General Halleck to review units of Sherman's army as it marched through the former capital of the quelled rebellion. But on May 9, Old Brains' assistant adjutant general issued a one sentence order to General Ord: "General Halleck directs that all orders issued relative to receiving the army under General Sherman in Richmond be countermanded."[34]

Old Brains had never wasted his time and energy by trying to refute his critics or in carrying on running disputes. Usually, he made no response at all. Often he was not even aware of what was being said about him, and this appeared to be the case in the matter of Sherman's having turned against him. But Cump's abrupt rejection of his invitation prompted an exception. To him General Halleck wrote:

> *You have not had during this war nor have you now a warmer friend and admirer than myself. If in carrying out what I knew to*

be the wishes of the War Department in regard to your armistice I used language which has given you offense it was unintentional, and I deeply regret it. If fully aware of the circumstances under which I acted I am certain you would not attribute to me any improper motives.

It is my wish to continue to regard and receive you as a personal friend. With this statement I leave the matter in your hands.[35]

The next day, Sherman replied:

I received your cipher dispatch last evening, and have revolved it in my mind all night in connection with that telegraphic message of April 26 to Secretary Stanton, and by him rushed with such indecent haste before an excited public. I cannot possibly reconcile the friendly expressions of the former with the deadly malignity of the latter, and cannot consent to the renewal of a friendship I had prized so highly till I can see deeper into the diabolical plot than I now do.

When you advised me of the assassin Clark being on my track I little dreamed he would turn up in the direction and guise he did, but thank God I have become so blasé to the dangers to life and reputation by the many vicissitudes of this cruel war, which some people are resolved shall never be over, that nothing surprises me.

I will march my army through Richmond quietly and in good order, without attracting attention, and I beg you to keep slightly perdu, for if noticed by some of my old command I cannot undertake to maintain a model behavior, for their feelings have become aroused by what the world adjudges an insult to at least an honest commander. If loss of life or violence result from this you must attribute it to the true cause—a public insult to a brother officer when he was far away on public service, perfectly innocent of the malignant purpose and design.[36]

So ended all communication between Henry Wager Halleck and William Tecumseh Sherman, and with it a friendship that had lasted since their years as cadets at West Point, nearly thirty years before.

4

GENERAL SHERMAN'S ANIMOSITY seemed to increase as the month wore on. On May 12 he devoted nearly half of a letter to Major General John A. Logan, commander of the Army of the Potomac's Right Wing, to an attack on Halleck:

> *The manner of your welcome* [at Richmond] *was a part of a grand game to insult us—us who had marched 1,000 miles through a hostile country in midwinter. . . . And what has been our reward? Your men were denied admission to the city, when Halleck had invited all citizens (rebels, of course) to come and go without passes.*
>
> *If the American people sanction this kind of courtesy to old and tried troops, where is the honor, satisfaction, and glory of serving them in constancy and faith? If such be the welcome the East gives to the West, we can but let them make war and fight it out themselves. I know where is a land and people that will not treat us thus—the West, the Valley of the Mississippi, the heart and soul and future strength of America, and I for one will go there.*
>
> *I am not much of a talker, but if ever my tongue is loosed and free I think I can and will say some things that will make an impression resembling a bombshell of the largest pattern. . . . Men who are now fierce and who would have the Army of the Potomac violate my truce and attack our enemy, discomfited, disheartened, and surrounded, will sooner or later find foes, face to face, of different metal. Though my voice is still peace, I am not for such a peace as makes me subject to insult by former friends, now perfidious enemies.*[37]

As Sherman was writing Logan, Major General Oliver O. Howard was sending Cump a report from Washington that shed at least a little light on the controversy:

> *I saw the Secretary of War, who told me he sent for me in order to place me in charge of the Freedmen's Bureau. After I had conversed with him about that for some little time he inquired where you were and talked with me quite at length respecting your terms of settlement with Johnston.*
>
> *I told him that you were incensed at the publication that*

appeared over his signature. He said in reply that you put the Government entirely on the defensive by announcing in orders that terms had been agreed upon which would give peace from the Potomac to the Rio Grande, &c. This order appeared in the morning papers, and on account of it, in order to show the people why the Government broke the peace established, he deemed it proper to publish some of the reasons for disapproving the terms. He deprecated the spirit of the press, but said that he thought that he himself had had to bear his share of newspaper abuse. . . .[38]

General Sherman seemed to seize every opportunity to state his case to anyone. Such an instance was his letter from Washington to a West Point classmate, Major General Stewart Van Vliet, on March 21:

I have received several kind letters from you of late which I could not answer, as I was in motion. I am now getting ready for the review of Wednesday, after which I am to go before the war investigating committee, when, for the first time, I will be at liberty to tell my story in public.

Don't be impatient, for you will be amazed when the truth is narrated—how base Stanton and Halleck have acted toward me. They thought they had me down, and when I was far away on public business under their own orders, they sought the opportunity to ruin me by means of the excitement naturally arising from the assassination of the President, who stood in the way of the fulfillment of their projects, and whose views and policy I was strictly, literally following.

Thus far I have violated no rule of official secrecy, though sorely tempted; but so much the worse for them when all becomes revealed. You may rest assured that I possess official documents that not only justify but made imperative my course in North Carolina, and you may say as much to my friends.

Yesterday General Grant and President Johnson, who know all, received me with marked courtesy and warmth. Mr. Stanton dare not come into my presence. He is afraid to meet me. I would not let Halleck review my troops at Richmond. I bade him keep to his room as my army passed through Richmond, and he had to stay indoors.

I will insult Stanton in like public manner, but will not be drawn into an open, or even constructive, disrespect to the President or any "lawful authority of the United States." My motives in the past, as at present, are as pure as you know them to have been in all my life, but I do not deny that my soul revolts at perfidy and meanness in quarters however high and seemingly exalted. . . .

I will endeavor to come to New York, when I can tell you many things already known in all proper official circles, but which have been suppressed purposely, whilst the most silly, unfounded stories and suspicions have been sown broadcast to my personal injury and detriment. I have been down before in public favor as well as on the battle-field, but am blessed with a vitality that only yields to absolute death, and though terribly exposed have thus far escaped. . . .[39]

General-in-Chief Grant had remained aloof from *Sherman* v. *Halleck*, but he could do so no longer following an incident in Washington that had been ignited by the controversy. On May 27 he wrote Sherman:

General Augur has just been to see me on the matter of the conduct of men and officers of your command since coming north of the Potomac. He says that a deep feeling is exhibited by them, especially when a little in liquor, on account of the difficulties between yourself and Secretary Stanton. He has purposely avoided arresting them for fear of leading to violence and the charge that it is a hostility on the part of the Secretary to them and to yourself.

Yesterday many of the officers were at Willard's, drinking and discussing violently the conduct of Mr. Stanton, and occasionally would jump on the counter and give three groans for Mr. Stanton, then get down and take another drink.

Without giving any order in the matter, I think it will be advisable for you either to direct guards to be placed around the camps and prohibit officers and men from coming out except with passes from their division commanders or such other officers as you may direct, or move to the south side of the river. You can manage this without any order from me. . . .[40]

General Sherman replied:

I will see that no officers presume to misbehave because of the unfortunate difference between the Secretary of War and myself. Of that difference I can only say that every officer and man regarded the

Secretary's budget in the papers of April 24, the telegram of General Halleck indorsed by himself in those of the 28th, and the perfect storm of accusation which followed, and which he took no pains to correct, as a personal insult to me.

I have not yet seen a man, soldier or civilian, but takes the same view of it, and I could not maintain my authority over troops if I tamely submitted to personal insult, but it is none the less wrong for officers to adopt the quarrel, and I will take strong measures to prevent it.[41]

Yet Sherman took no measures to restrain himself. To John Schofield, on May 28, he wrote:

The army reached Alexandria May 19, and we met an order for the grand review. . . . Stanton offered to shake hands with me in the presence of the President, but I declined, and passed him to shake hands with Grant.

I have been before the war committee and gave a minute account of all matters connected with the convention, which will soon be published in full. Halleck tries to throw off on Stanton, and Stanton on Halleck, and many men want me to be patient under the infliction for the sake of patriotism, but I will not, the matter being more than official, a personal insult, and I have resented it, and shall continue to do so.

No man, I don't care who he is, shall insult me publicly or arraign my motives. Mr. Johnson has been more than kind to me, and the howl against me is narrowed down to Halleck and Stanton, and I have partially resented both.[42]

Also on May 28, Sherman said in a letter to General Grant:

I was hurt, outraged, and insulted at Mr. Stanton's public arraignment of my motives and actions, at his indorsing General Halleck's insulting and offensive dispatch, and his studied silence when the press accused me of all sorts of base motives, even of selling myself to Jeff. Davis for gold, of sheltering criminals, and entertaining ambitious views at the expense of my country. I respect his office, but cannot him personally till he undoes the injustice of the past.

I think I have soldierly instincts and feelings, but if this action of mine at all incommodes the President or endangers public har-

mony all you have to do is to say so and leave me time to seek civil employment and I will make room.[43]

5

SO MUCH FOR GENERAL SHERMAN'S CASE. All along, it had seemed that Old Brains would not offer any defense. But on June 7, 1865, for the first time he took official notice of Sherman's allegations and directed his response to Secretary of War Stanton:

I have just received the Army and Navy Gazette of May 30, containing an official publication of Major-General Sherman's letters of May 9 and 26, with other papers on the same subject, parts of which had been previously published in the newspapers. In these letters and papers General Sherman has made statements and reflections on my official conduct which are incorrect and entirely unjustified by the facts of the case.

First. He charges that I encroached upon his military command by directing a portion of my troops to march upon Greensborough in North Carolina.

By direction of the President, I was on the 19th of April last assigned to the "command of the Military Division of the James, which included such parts of North Carolina as were not occupied by the command of Major-General Sherman." At the time my troops were ordered to Greensborough General Sherman's troops did not occupy that part of North Carolina. It was occupied by the enemy, and consequently within my command, as defined by General Orders, No. 71, of the War Department.

But whether or not Greensborough, or any part of North Carolina, was in my command, General Sherman's remarks are equally without justification. On the 22d of April Lieutenant-General Grant notified me that Sherman's arrangements had been disapproved and orders given to resume hostilities and directed me to move my troops on Danville and Greensborough, precisely as I did move them, there to await his further orders. My instructions to Generals Meade, Sheridan, and Wright were just such instructions as General Grant had directed me to give.

The offense, or whatever he may please to call it, if any there was, of marching my troops within territory claimed by General

Sherman, was not mine, but General Grant's, and all the abuse which he has directed upon me for that act must fall upon the general-in-chief.

Second. *General Sherman charges that by marching my troops into North Carolina I violated his truce, which he was bound to enforce even at the cost of many lives by a collision of our respective armies.*

General Sherman had never sent me his truce. I had never seen it and did not know its terms or conditions. I only knew that his truce or "arrangement," whatever it was, had been disapproved and set aside by the President, and General Grant, in ordering the movement of my troops, simply notified me of this fact and of the renewal of hostilities.

Even if Sherman's truce had been binding on me, which it was not, I had no knowledge of the clause relating to forty-eight hours' notice. It is strange that he should seek to bind me by conditions of the existence of which I was ignorant, and of which he had taken no measures to inform me.

But even had I known them I could not have acted otherwise than I did. I simply carried out the orders of my superior officer, who had seen the truce and knew its terms. . . .

General Sherman reflects on me for not going in person to violate, as he is pleased to call it, a truce which he "was bound in honor to defend and maintain . . . even at the cost of many lives," and upon the marching powers of the troops which I sent into North Carolina.

In reply to this I can only say that I was not ordered to go with these troops, but to send them under their commanders to certain points, there to await further orders from Lieutenant-General Grant, precisely as I directed. The troops were mostly selected by General Grant, not by me, and as he had commanded them for a year he probably knew something of their capacity for marching and whether or not they would march their legs off "to catch the treasure for their own use."

Third. *Again, General Sherman complains that my orders of April 26, to push forward against Johnston's army, were given at the very time I knew that that army was surrendering to him.*

In making this statement he forgets time and circumstances. He must have known that I did not have, and could not possibly have had at that time, any official information of any new arrangements between him and Johnston for the surrender of the latter's army.

Neither General Sherman nor any one else could have sent me such official information otherwise than by sea, which would have required several days. I only knew from General Grant that Sherman's "arrangements" had been disapproved, that orders had been given to resume hostilities, and that I was directed by him to push forward my troops to Greensborough, where they would receive further orders. All other information from North Carolina came from rebel sources.

Fourth. *The burden of General Sherman's complaint on this subject is that I ordered Generals Sheridan and Wright to push forward their troops as directed by General Grant, "regardless of any orders from any one except General Grant."*

This was simply carrying out the spirit of my instructions from General Grant. He had notified me that orders had been given to resume hostilities, and had directed me to send certain troops to Greensborough to await his further orders.

As these troops approached the boundaries of North Carolina, Johnston, Beauregard, and other rebel officers tried, on the alleged grounds of arrangements with Sherman, to stop the movement ordered by General Grant. When informed of this I directed my officers to execute the commands which General Grant had given to me, regardless of orders from anyone except Grant himself. I respectfully submit that I could not have done less without neglecting my duty.

Fifth. *General Sherman sneers at my sending troops from the direction of Burkeville and Danville against Davis in North Carolina, as "hardly worthy of" my "military education and genius."*

However ridiculous General Sherman may consider these movements, they were made precisely as General Grant had directed them.

Sixth. *He complains that I did not notify him in regard to Davis and his stolen treasure.*

I had no communication open to him. My most direct way of communication with him was through the Department at Washington, and I sent all information to the Department as soon as it was received.

However "absurd" General Sherman may have considered the information, it was given by some of the most respectable and reli-

able business men in Richmond through a gentleman whose cha-racter and position would prevent me from pronouncing his statements "absurd," and of saying, without examination, "I don't believe a word of the treasure story."

Seventh. *In order to sustain his position that the movements of my troops, ordered by General Grant, were in violation of his truce which I was bound to observe even without knowing its terms, and that he would have been justified to resist "even at the cost of many lives," General Sherman refers to a chapter of International Law.*

His reference is most pointedly against his positions and doctrines, and the case given in illustration in Section 4 was one of which General Sherman was personally cognizant. In that case a subordinate commander refused to be bound by a truce of his superior commanding another department.

General Sherman was not even my superior. I contend that all my orders were justifiable by the laws of war and military usage, even if they had not been directed by superior authority.

Eighth. *General Sherman says that General Grant "reached the Chesapeake in time to countermand General Halleck's orders and prevent his violating my truce."*

This is not true. General Grant neither disapproved nor countermanded any orders of mine, nor was there at that time any truce. It had ceased by General Grant's orders to resume hostilities, and the subsequent surrender of Johnston's army, of which he then notified me, and recalled a part of the troops which he had directed me to send to Danville and Greensborough.

Ninth. *There is but one other point in General Sherman's official complaint that I deem it necessary to notice. I refer to the suggestion made to you in regard to orders to Generals Thomas and Wilson for preventing the escape of Davis and his cabinet.*

Although these officers were under the nominal command of General Sherman, yet after he left Atlanta they received their instructions and orders from yourself and General Grant direct, not through General Sherman. This is recognized and provided for by the regulations of the War Department and has been practiced for years.

I have transmitted hundreds of orders in this way and General Sherman was cognizant of the fact. The movements of Generals Thomas, Stoneman, Wilson, A. J. Smith, &c., while within General Sherman's general command have been directed in this way for more than six months. In suggesting that orders be sent to these officers directly, and not through General Sherman, I suggested no departure from well-established official channels. . . .

If his complaint is directed against the form of the suggestion, I can only say that I was innocent of any intended offense. My telegram was hurriedly written, intended for yourself, not the public, and had reference to the state of facts as reported to me.

It was reported that orders purporting to come from General Sherman had been received through rebel lines for General Wilson to withdraw from Macon, release his prisoners, and that all hostilities should cease. These orders threw open the door for the escape of Davis and his party.

This I knew was contrary to the wishes and orders of the Government, but I had no means of knowing whether or not Sherman had been so informed. I at the time had no communication with him or with General Grant, and I was not aware that either could communicate with our officers in the West except through rebel authorities, who of course could not be [relied] on. I repeat that my suggestion had reference only to the acts and wishes of the Government as known to me at the time, and was intended in no respect to reflect upon or be disrespectful to General Sherman.

If I had been able to communicate with General Sherman, or had known at the time the condition of affairs in North Carolina, there would have been no necessity or occasion for any suggestion to you, and most probably none would have been made.

After having refuted substantially all of General Sherman's allegations point-by-point and at considerable length, Old Brains' closing arguments were refreshingly brief:

With these remarks I respectfully submit that General Sherman's report, so far as he refers to me, is unjust, unkind, and contrary to military usage, and that his statements are contrary to the real facts of the case.

I beg leave further to remark that I have in no way, shape, or manner criticized or reflected upon General Sherman's course in North Carolina, or upon his truce, or, as General Grant styles it, "arrangement" with Johnston and Breckinridge, but have simply acted upon the orders, instructions, and expressed wishes of my superiors as communicated to me and as I understood them.[44]

Sadly, none of these words would have to have been written if only Cump Sherman could have accepted Old Brains' forthright apology back on May 9, 1865, when he read: "If in carrying out what I knew to be the wishes of the War Department in regard to your armistice I used language which has given you offense it was unintentional, and I deeply regret it."

6

GENERAL HALLECK SENT HIS BRIEF to Secretary of War Stanton on June 7. Three days later, Old Brains received this news: "In the new assignment of military commands the President has assigned you to the Military Division of the Pacific . . . with headquarters in San Francisco."[45]

Major General Alfred Terry had been designated as Halleck's successor at Richmond. To Terry on June 22 he wrote:

> *Where destitute colored people in the country cannot be cared for by their former masters or procure support by their labor for others, commanding officers of districts, in concert with officers of General Howard's bureau, will provide for their care and support at suitable places in the country.*
>
> *They will neither be brought nor permitted to come to this city, where they can obtain no labor and are liable to be contaminated by city vices. It is estimated by the governor that there is at present a colored population in Richmond of from 30,000 to 35,000—more, by far, than can obtain employment.*
>
> *All accessions to this population must necessarily be supported by the Government, but in the country they can at least partly support themselves, either by labor for others or by cultivating patches of land and raising vegetables for their own use and for the market. This policy is concurred in by General Howard and should be strictly enforced.*[46]

Was it not ironic that among Henry Wager Halleck's last directives issued from an eastern command should have been one on this subject, given the abuse heaped upon him at St. Louis by the press, driven as it was by abolitionists and Radicals, back in late 1861?

Yet there had been no change in Halleck's views. He considered blacks as individuals who should be as free as whites and who ought to make their own ways in the world. Radicals, especially those in the Republican party, looked upon the "freedmen" as potential voters. Much of the bitter fighting in Washington would be over who in the conquered South should be allowed to vote. Policy would be driven by the ultra-Radical Republicans' fear of losing control of Congress and by little else.

Inevitably, generals commanding military districts would be obliged to support reconstruction as prescribed by the victors in the struggle between President Johnson and the Radicals in the legislative branch. Virginia was especially vulnerable to punitive, coercive attention from Washington. Accordingly, Halleck—whose contempt for politicians had been intensified greatly during his three years of service there—would have been utterly miserable had he not been transferred.

In California, Old Brains would be a continent's width away from Washington's irritants. Hardly any of the measures enacted to impose federal controls on most aspects of Southern life were applicable to the West Coast. Halleck's main concerns would be rivers and harbors; he could revert to the duties he had performed as a young engineer and ignore the disasters occurring in the jurisdictions where Schofield, Sheridan, Wright, and many other generals were having to do the politicians' dirty work.

Yet it seems unlikely that Stanton and Grant meant the transfer as a favor to Old Brains. Both men were well aware of his strict, unyielding fidelity to principles and his intolerance of hypocrisy, deceit, and equivo-cation. He had never been a pleasant person to have around. And with the political winds blowing the Union in the direction opposite the one in which Halleck had been moving Virginia, the question would have been not *if* he would either resign or have to be sacked, but *how soon.*

Moreover, in General Halleck's response to Sherman's allegations, he had made it clear that he had found the performance of the general-in-chief to have been deficient. The Halleck-Grant bond had never been as strong as that between Old Brains and Cump. Its chances of lasting very long in peacetime had been, at best, slim. Stanton, of course, may well have wished Borneo had been a United States military district in need of a commander.

And so it was that in July 1865, Henry Wager Halleck returned to San Francisco—not to the practice of law or as a corporate executive or even as an author, but as a soldier who had done his best, and had seen much adversity, and was confident that those who took the time and trouble to read his messages in the *Official Records of the Union and Confederate Armies* would find him to have been an honorable man who did his duty to the utmost, and whose contributions to the quelling of the rebellion entitled him to a "Well done, be thou at peace."

Endnotes

INTRODUCTION

1. *War of the Rebellion: Official Records of the Union and Confederate Armies*, 109, / Series I, Volume LII, / 717.
2. Kenneth P. Williams, *Lincoln Finds a General*, V, 271.
3. *Ibid.*
4. Walter A. McDougall, Professor of History at the University of Pennsylvania, writing in the *National Review* in October 1997.
5. Alan C. and Barbara A. Aimone, *A User's Guide to the Official Records of the American Civil War*, 1, 5–6.
6. *O.R.*, 58, / XXXII, Part 2, / 407–408.
7. William Faulkner, "On Accepting the Nobel Award," in Harold F. Harding, editor, *The Age of Danger: Major Speeches on American Problems*, 397–398.

CHAPTER 1

1. For an account of how far from reality delegates to the Republican National Convention in Chicago were, see Murat Halstead, *Fire the Salute!*
2. Patricia L. Faust, editor, *Historical Times Encyclopedia of the Civil War*, 208–209.
3. David Herbert Donald, *Lincoln*, 44–45.
4. Emory M. Thomas, *The Confederate Nation*, 94–95, 104; William C. Davis, *Jefferson Davis: The Man and His Hour*, 329.
5. Gary W. Gallagher, editor, *Fighting for the Confederacy: The Personal Recollections of Edward Porter Alexander*, 23–24.
6. Bruce Catton, *The Coming Fury*, 302.
7. Faust, 429–430 (Lee) and 399 (Johnston).
8. James Grant Wilson, "General Halleck—A Memoir," in *Journal of the Military Service Institution of the United States*, Volume XXXVI, 537.
9. Ibid., 537–538; Dumas Malone, editor,

Dictionary of American Biography (DAB), Volume IV, 150; Stephen E. Ambrose, *Halleck: Lincoln's Chief of Staff*, 4–5.
10. *DAB*, IV, 150–151.
11. *Ibid.*, 150.
12. Association of Graduates, USMA, *Register of Graduates and Former Cadets, 1802–1996*, 261–267; Wilson, 538.
13. Two years earlier, while Halleck was a "yearling" at West Point, Union College awarded him the A.B. degree. It would add an L.L.D. in 1862. Wilson, 538.
14. *Ibid.*, 538–539; *DAB*, IV, 150–151.
15. *DAB*, IV, 150.
16. Lloyd Lewis, *Captain Sam Grant*, 66–67, based on a biographical sketch of Halleck by William E Marsh.
17. Lloyd Lewis, *Sherman: Fighting Prophet*, 56–58.
18. Wilson, 540.
19. *Ibid.*
20. *DAB*, IV, 151.
21. Clifford Dowdey, *Lee*, 64–66, 72–73, 79.
22. Wilson, 541.
23. *DAB*, IV, 150–151; Ambrose, 60.
24. Ambrose, 5–7.
25. Faust, 338–339; Steven E. Woodworth, *Jefferson Davis and his Generals*, 164–165.
26. Wilson, 541.
27. K. Jack Bauer, *The Mexican War 1846–1848*, 66–86.
28. *Ibid.*, 71–73.
29. *Ibid.*, 128–129, 169.
30. John F. Marszalek, *Sherman: A Soldier's Passion for Order*, 53–54.
31. Lewis, *Sherman: Fighting Prophet*, 75; William Tecumseh Sherman, *Memoirs of General W. T. Sherman*, 36–37.
32. Wilson, 541.
33. Marszalek, 55.
34. *Ibid.*, 56.

35. Wilson, 542.
36. Marszalek, 55–56.
37. Sherman, 40–41.
38. *Ibid.,* 44.
39. *Ibid.*
40. Bauer, 183–195.
41. Fremont's trouble-making in 1846–1847. is well covered by Bauer. For more about Fremont, see Allan Nevins, *Fremont: The West's Greatest Adventurer.*
42. Bauer, 195–196.
43. Hubert Howe Bancroft, *The Works of Hubert Howe Brancroft: History of California,* Volume VII, 452–453.
44. Bauer, 205–217.
45. *Ibid.,* 238–240.
46. *Ibid.,* 345–347.
47. Lewis, *Sherman: Fighting Prophet,* 78; Marszalek, 58.
48. William Henry Ellison, *A Self-Governing Dominion: California, 1849–1860,* 4–7.
49. *Ibid.,* 10, 6; Bancroft, VII, 445.
50. Ellison, vii.
51. *DAB,* VI, 373–374.
52. Ralph J. Roske, *Everyman's Eden: A History of California,* 264.
53. Ellison, 12.
54. *Ibid.,* 11–12.
55. Bancroft, V, 522–523n.
56. Ellison, 102–103.
57. *Ibid.,* 103–104.
58. Bancroft, VI, 534.
59. *Ibid.,* 535n.
60. *Ibid.,* 536–537.
61. *Ibid.,* 537.
62. Ellison, 115–116.
63. Ambrose, 8: "He had access to records of land titles, and in the confused state of transferring sovereignty from Mexico to the United States, the young officer succeeded in acquiring considerable land and valuable mineral rights."
64. Ellison, 15.
65. *DAB,* VIII, 608–609.
66. Ellison, 20.
67. *Ibid.,* 16.
68. Arthur Quinn, *The Rivals: William Gwin, David Broderick, and the Birth of California,* 21.

69. *Ibid.*
70. Ellison, 21.
71. *Ibid.*
72. Bancroft, VI, 276n.
73. *Ibid.,* 287–289, 287n.
74. *Ibid.,* 287n, 290n; Wilson, 542. Wilson said that Halleck "was substantially the author of it." Ambrose, 8, called much of the document his "personal handiwork."
75. Bancroft, VI, 290.
76. James A. B. Scherer, *Thirty-First Star,* 166–167.
77. Ellison, 38.
78. *Ibid.,* 38–39.
79. *Ibid.,* 43–45.
80. Bancroft, VI, 303–304.
81. *Ibid.,* 305.
82. Ellison, 54.
83. *Ibid.,* 55; *DAB,* IV, 151.
84. *Ibid.,* 98.
85. Bancroft, VI, 306–307, 307n.
86. Wilson, 542.
87. Ellison, 205; Roske, 248.
88. Ellison, 102–111; Bancroft, VI, 537–539.
89. Wilson, 542; Bancroft, VII, 656n.
90. Wilson, 542–543; Rolle, 304; Ambrose, 8. According to Ambrose, Halleck helped form the firm in the winter of 1849–1850; Wilson's account is used here.
91. Wilson, 542.
92. Ellison, 41–42.
93. Robert O'Brien, *This is San Francisco,* 32, 34.
94. *Ibid.,* 34–35.
95. Roske, 248.
96. Ellison, 112.
97. Wilson, 543.
98. Bancroft, III, 773–774.
99. Stanton's mental problems are covered in the early chapters of Benjamin P. Thomas and Harold M. Hyman, *Stanton: The Life and Times of Lincoln's Secretary of War.*
100. Ellison, 119–120.
101. Thomas and Hyman, 80–81.
102. Bancroft, VI, 213n, 253n, 657n, 715.
103. James D. Hart, *A Companion to California,* 49.
104. DAB, IV, 151; Mark M. Boatner, *The*

Civil War Dictionary, 369.

105. *DAB,* IV, 151.

106. *Webster's American Military Biographies,* 158.

107. *The National Cyclopedia of American Biography,* IV, 258.

108. Bancroft, VII, 267n.

109. Donald, 280–285.

110. General Johnston was waiting for the arrival of his successor, Union Brigadier General Edwin V. Sumner. Bancroft, VII, 467. Soon thereafter he departed for Texas. Boatner, 440.

111. Wilson, 553.

112. *DAB,* IV, 151.

113. *Ibid.,* 10.

CHAPTER 2

1. James G. Randall, *Lincoln the President,* I, 351–357; James M. McPherson, *Battle Cry of Freedom,* 274, 278–280.

2. David Herbert Donald, *Lincoln,* 285.

3. Herman Hattaway and Archer Jones, *How the North Won,* 35; Charles Winslow Elliott, *Winfield Scott: The Soldier and the Man,* 722–723.

4. Patricia L. Faust, *Historical Times Encyclopedia of the Civil War,* 98–99. (Butler), 38. (Banks), 456–457. (McClernand).

5. Shelby Foote, *The Civil War,* I, 89–90; E. B. Long with Barbara Long, *The Civil War Day-by-Day,* 65, 72–73.

6. Foote, I, 91–95; McPherson, *Battle Cry of Freedom,* 350–352.

7. *War of the Rebellion: Official Records of the Union and Confederate Armies,* 3, / Series I, Volume III, 466–467.

8. *Ibid.,* 469–470.

9. *Ibid.,* 477.

10. *Ibid.,* 478–479.

11. Allan Nevins, *Fremont: The West's Greatest Adventurer,* II, 589; *The War for the Union,* I, 338; Foote, I, 97.

12. *O. R., 3,* / III, 485–486.

13. The story of McClellan's studied insubordination has been told most recently by Sears, *George B. McClellan: The Young Napoleon,* 95–127.

14. *O. R., 3,* / III, 559, 537. Major General David Hunter held the command

from November 2, 1861, until Halleck arrived.

15. *O. R., 3,* / III, 568.

16. *Ibid.,* 540–549. The report has been edited.

17. Stephen E. Ambrose, *Halleck: Lincoln's Chief of Staff,* 13.

18. *O. R., 8,* / VIII, 369.

19. *Ibid.,* 370. Italics supplied.

20. James Grant Wilson, "General Halleck—A Memoir," in *Journal of the Military Service Institution of the United States,* Volume XXXVI, 548.

21. *O. R., 8,* / VIII, 389.

22. *Ibid.,* 389–390.

23. *Ibid.,* 382.

24. *Ibid.,* 392.

25. *Ibid.,* 374.

26. *Ibid.*

27. *Ibid.,* 390.

28. Lloyd Lewis, *Sherman: Fighting Prophet,* 149–155; Mark M. Boatner, III, *The Civil War Dictionary,* 751.

29. William T. Sherman, *The Memoirs of General W. T. Sherman,* 218–221.

30. *O. R., 3,* / III, 548.

31. John F. Marszalek, *Sherman: A Soldier's Passion for Order,* 161–163.

32. Lewis, 107.

33. Marszalek, 160.

34. *O. R., 3,* / III, 373.

35. *Ibid.,* 374.

36. *Ibid., 8,* / VIII, 398; Boatner 211. (Cullum), 369. (Hamilton), 451. (Kelton).

37. *O. R., 8,* / VIII, 817.

38. *Ibid.*

39. *Ibid.,* 818.

40. *Ibid.,* 395.

41. *Ibid.,* 401.

42. *Ibid.,* 827.

43. *Ibid.,* 379.

44. *Ibid.,* 381–382.

45. *Ibid.,* 391.

46. *Ibid.*

47. *Ibid.*

48. *Ibid.*

49. *Ibid.,* 392.

50. Lewis, 199.

51. *O. R., 8,* / VIII,, 201.

52. *Ibid.,* 819.

53. Sherman, 234–235.
54. *O. R., 8,* / VIII, 459.
55. Marszalek, 167–169.
56. Sherman, 238.
57. Earl Schenck Myers, editor-in-chief, *Lincoln Day-by-Day,* 79, entry for November 30, 1861.
58. *O. R., 7,* / VII, 451.
59. *Ibid., 5,* / V, 38.
60. T. Harry Williams, *Lincoln and the Radicals,* 58–64; Donald, 318–319.
61. *O. R., 8,* / VIII, 463.
62. *Ibid., 7,* / VII, 473.
63. *Ibid.,* 477.
64. *Ibid.,* 488.
65. *Ibid.,* 521.
66. *Ibid., 8,* / VIII, 701.
67. *Ibid., 7,* / VII, 524.
68. *Ibid.,* 526.
69. *Ibid.*
70. *Ibid.,* 527.
71. *Ibid.*
72. *Ibid.,* 532–533.
73. *Ibid.,* 533–534.
74. Ulysses S, Grant, *Ulysses S. Grant: Memoirs and Selected Letters,* 178.
75. *Ibid.,* 178–186.
76. *Ibid.,* 189.
77. Boatner, 768.
78. Grant, 189–190.
79. *O. R., 8,* / VIII, 820.
80. *Ibid.,* 821.
81. *Ibid.,* 822.
82. *Ibid.,* 475–476.
83. *Ibid.,* 431–432.
84. *Ibid.,* 823.
85. *Ibid.,* 490.
86. *Ibid.,* 826.
87. *Ibid.*
88. *Ibid.,* 827.
89. *Ibid.,* 828–829.
90. *Ibid.,* 496–497, 514–515.
91. *Ibid.,* 512–513.
92. *Ibid.,* 513.
93. Wilson, 544.
94. *Ibid.*
95. Stephen E. Ambrose, *Halleck: Lincoln's Chief of Staff,* 14–15.
96. *O. R., 8,* / VIII, 508–510.
97. *Ibid.,* 510.
98. *Ibid., 7,* VII, 547.
99. *Ibid.,* 530.

100. *Ibid.,* 530–531.
101. *Ibid.,* 531.
102. *Ibid.,* 548.

CHAPTER 3
1. *War of the Rebellion: Official Records of the Union and Confederate Armies, 7,* / Series I, Volume VII, 572.
2. *Ibid.,* 574.
3. *Ibid.,* 572.
4. *Ibid.,* 574.
5. *Ibid.,* 576.
6. *Ibid.,* 577.
7. *Ibid.,* 579.
8. *Ibid.*
9. *Ibid.,* 581.
10. *Ibid.,* 587.
11. *Ibid.,* 583.
12. *Ibid.,* 585.
13. *Ibid.,* 586.
14. *Ibid.,* 587.
15. *Ibid.,* 587–588.
16. *Ibid.,* 587.
17. *Ibid.,* 590.
18. *Ibid.,* 591.
19. Shelby Foote, *The Civil War,* I, 187.
20. *Ibid.,* 188–189.
21. *Ibid.,* 189–191.
22. *Ibid.,* 191.
23. *O. R., 7,* / VII, 594.
24. *Ibid.,* 585.
25. *Ibid.,* 599.
26. See, for example, Stephen E. Ambrose, *Halleck: Lincoln's Chief of Staff,* Chapter Three, 23–33.
27. *O. R., 7,* / VII,, 605.
28. *Ibid.,* 609.
29. *Ibid.,* 612.
30. *Ibid.,* 614.
31. *Ibid.,* 616.
32. *Ibid.,* 617.
33. *Ibid.*
34. *Ibid.*
35. Stephen W. Sears, *George B. McClellan: The Young Napoleon,* 85.
36. *Ibid.,* 89–91.
37. *O. R., 7,* / VII, 624.
38. *Ibid.*
39. *Ibid.,* 624–625.
40. *Ibid.*
41. *Ibid.,* 161.

42. *Ibid.*, 625.
43. *Ibid.*, 628.
44. *Ibid.*
45. *Ibid.*, 632–633.
46. Foote, I, 191–214, provides an excellent account of the fight for Fort Donelson.
47. *O. R., 7,* / VII, 636.
48. *Ibid.*, 637.
49. *Ibid.*
50. *Ibid.*, 640–641.
51. *Ibid.*, 641.
52. *Ibid.*, 645.
53. *Ibid.*, 646.
54. *Ibid.*, 647.
55. *Ibid.*, 648.
56. *Ibid.*
57. Earl Schenck Miers, editor-in-chief, *Lincoln Day-by-Day 1861–1865,* 96.
58. *O. R., 7,* / VII, 655.
59. *Ibid.*, 652.
60. *Ibid.*, 660.
61. *Ibid.*, 661.
62. *Ibid.*, 677.
63. Ulysses S. Grant, *Personal Memoirs and Letters of U. S. Grant,* 214–220.
64. *O. R., 7,* / VII, 679–680.
65. *Ibid.*, 680.
66. *Ibid.*, 682.
67. *Ibid., 8,* / VIII, 602.
68. *Ibid.*, 605.
69. *Ibid.*
70. *Ibid.*, 606.
71. *Ibid.*, 611.
72. *Ibid.*, 614.
73. *Ibid., 7,* / VII, 683–684.
74. This was fortuitous from the Union's point of view, for, unlike physicians and to Americans' sorrow, politicians are not obliged to observe even the first few words of the time honored Hippocratic Oath: *Primus non docere*—first, do no harm.
75. *O. R., 7,* / VII, 258–261.
76. *Ibid., 11,* / X, Part 2, 365.
77. Clifford Dowdey, *Lee,* 180–181.
78. *O. R., 11,* / X, Part 2, 30.
79. *Ibid.*, 32.
80. *Ibid.*, 37.
81. *Ibid.*, 42.
82. *Ibid.*, 41
83. *Ibid.*, 50, 53–54.
84. Patricia L. Faust, editor, *Historical Times Illustrated Encyclopedia of the Civil War,* 694–695.
85. *O. R., 11,* / X, Part 2, 38.
86. *Ibid.*, 57.
87. *Ibid.*, 57–58.
88. *Ibid.*, 59–60.
89. Foote, I, 277–292. For more on Curtis, see Faust, 198–199.
90. *O. R., 8,* / VIII, 629.
91. *Ibid.*
92. Long, 185; Faust, 527.
93. *O. R., 8,* / VIII, 614.
94. *Ibid.*, 633–634.
95. Canby was Halleck's classmate, graduating thirtieth in the thirty-one-man West Point Class of 1839. For more about Canby see Mark M. Boatner, *The Civil War Dictionary,* 118, and Faust, 111. For the New Mexico campaign, see Foote, I, 293–305.
96. *O. R., 8,* / VIII, 633.
97. *Ibid., 11,* / X, Part 2, 70–71.
98. *Ibid.*, 77.
99. *Ibid.*, 79.
100. *Ibid.*, 80.
101. *Ibid.*, 77.
102. *Ibid., 7,* / VII, 257–258.
103. *Ibid.*, 259–260.
104. *Ibid., 11,* / X, Part 2, 365.
105. *Ibid.*, 387.
106. *Ibid., 10,* / X, Part 1, 84.
107. Foote, I, 329.
108. *Ibid.*, 333–335.
109. Herman Hattaway and Archer Jones, *How the North Won,* 169.
110. *O. R., 10,* / X, Part 1, 98.
111. *Ibid., 11,* / X, Part 2, 98.
112. Foote, I, 313–314. His full account begins on 307.
113. *O. R., 8,* / VIII, 660.
114. James Grant Wilson, "General Halleck—A Memoir," in *Journal of the Military Service Institution of the United States,* Volume XXXVI, 549.
115. *Ibid.*, 556.
116. Stephen E. Ambrose, *Halleck: Lincoln's Chief of Staff,* 47.
117. Wilson, 554.
118. *O. R., 8,* / VIII, 657–658.
119. *Ibid., 10,* / X, Part 1, 98–99.

120. *Ibid.*, 98.
121. *Ibid.*, 99.
122. Foote, I, 372.
123. *O. R., 10,* / X, Part 1, 89, 90, 92.
124. *Ibid., 11,* / Part 2, 92.
125. *Ibid.*, 91.
126. *Ibid.*, 93.
127. *Ibid.*
128. *Ibid., 10,* / X, Part 1, 324. The report's full text is *Ibid.*, 323–326.
129. *Ibid.*, 113–114. This report's full text and that of McClernand's official report, is to be found at *Ibid.*, 113–123.
130. Foote, I, 339–340.
131. The exception was, of course, his suggestions to the authorities that Grant had reverted to his "bad habits."
132. Foote, 1, 374.

CHAPTER 4
1. *War of the Rebellion: Official Records of the Union and Confederate Armies, 10,* / Series I, Volume X, Part 1, 666–667.
2. David Herbert Donald, *Lincoln,* 352; Benjamin P. Thomas and Harold M. Hyman, *Stanton: The Life and Times of Lincoln's Secretary of War,* 195.
3. *O. R., 15,* / XII, Part 1, 525.
4. *Ibid., 10,* / X, Part 1, 667.
5. Stephen E. Ambrose, *Halleck: Lincoln's Chief of Staff,* 48–50.
6. Robert G. Tanner, *Stonewall in the Valley,* 225; Douglas Southall Freeman, *Lee's Lieutenants,* Volume I, 393–394.
7. *O. R., 10,* / X, Part 1, 665.
8. *Ibid.*
9. *Ibid.*
10. *Ibid.*
11. *Ibid.*
12. *Ibid.*, 666.
13. *Ibid.*
14. *Ibid., 15,* / XII, Part 1, 643.
15. Tanner, 264.
16. *O. R., 15,* / XII, Part 1, 644; Kenneth P. Williams, *Lincoln Finds a General,* I, 188.
17. *O. R., 15,* / XII, Part 1, 644.
18. *Ibid.;* Tanner, 346.
19. *O. R., 10,* / X, Part 1, 667.
20. *Ibid., 11,* / X, Part 2, 529–530.
21. *Ibid.*, 544.

22. *Ibid.*, 545–546.
23. *Ibid.*, 547.
24. Steven E. Woodworth, *Jefferson Davis and his Generals,* 104–105.
25. *O. R., 11,* X, Part 2, 223–224.
26. *Ibid.*, 225.
27. *Ibid.*
28. *Ibid.*, 225–226.
29. *Ibid.*, 226.
30. *Ibid.*
31. *Ibid.*, 227.
32. *Ibid.*
33. *Ibid., 10,* / X, Part 1, 667.
34. Woodworth, 104–106.
35. Douglas Southall Freeman, *R. E. Lee,* Volume II, 68–69; *Lee's Lieutenants,* I, 223–242.
36. Steven E. Woodworth, *Davis and Lee at War,* 147–148; William C. Davis, *Jefferson Davis: The Man and His Hour,* 424–425, offers a slightly different timetable.
37. Tanner, 234–310.
38. Stephen W. Sears, *George B. McClellan: The Young Napoleon,* 196–197.
39. Williams, I, 179.
40. *O. R., 10,* / X, Part 1, 668.
41. *Ibid., 11,* / X, Part 2, 231.
42. *Ibid.*, 232.
43. *Ibid.*
44. *Ibid., 10,* / X, Part 1, 669.
45. *Ibid.*
46. *Ibid.*
47. *Ibid.*, 669–670.
48. *Ibid.*, 670.
49. *Ibid.*
50. *Ibid., 11,* / X, Part 2, 240–241.
51. *Ibid.*, 634–635.
52. John F. Marszalek, *Sherman: A Soldier's Passion for Order,* 183–184.
53. *O. R., 11,* / X, Part 2, 233–234.
54. *Ibid., 25,* / XVII, Part 2, 76.
55. *Ibid., 11,* / X, Part 2, 277.
56. *Ibid.*, 279.
57. *Ibid.*, 282.
58. *Ibid., 23,* / XVI, Part 2, 62.
59. *Ibid., 17,* / XII, Part 3, 391–392.
60. J. C. Randall, *Lincoln the President,* II, 98–99.
61. Donald, 359.
62. Gideon Welles, *Diary of Gideon Welles, Secretary of the Navy Under Lincoln and*

Johnson, I, 108.

63. *O. R., 12,* / XI, Part 1, 48.
64. Randall, II, 104–105; Donald, 357–358.
65. Freeman, *R. E. Lee,* II, 108–109.
66. *Ibid.,* 110–112, 130–135; Clifford Dowdey, *The Seven Days,* 173–175.
67. *O. R., 17,* / XII, Part 3, 435.
68. *Ibid.,* 436–438.
69. *Ibid.,* 438.
70. *Ibid., 20,* / XIV, 260.
71. Excellent accounts of Gaines's Mill are to be found in Dowdey, 194–238; Freeman, *R. E. Lee,* II, 138–154. and *Lee's Lieutenants,* I, 517–530. For McClellan's conduct that day, see Sears, *George B. McClellan: The Young Napoleon,* 210–213.
72. *O. R., 12,* / XI, Part 1, 61; Stephen W. Sears, *The Civil War Papers of George B. McClellan,* 322–323.
73. Homer Bates, *Lincoln in the Telegraph Office,* 108–109; Williams, I, 210.
74. *O. R., 23,* / XVI, Part 2, 69–70.
75. *Ibid.,* 74–75.
76. *Ibid.,* 75.
77. *Ibid.,* 69–70.
78. *Ibid.,* 76.
79. *Ibid.,* 81–82.
80. *Ibid., 20,* / XIV, 269.
81. *Ibid., 23,* / XVI, Part 2, 88.
82. *Ibid.,* 89.
83. Donald, 361.
84. *Ibid.,* 357–358, 361.
85. *O. R., 23,* / XVI, Part 2, 95.
86. Halleck to McClernand, July 1, 1862: "Orders from Washington are suspended. Stop all movements of your troops." *O. R., 25,* / XVII, Part 2, 61.
87. *O. R., 23,* / XVI, Part 2, 95.
88. *Ibid., 25,* / XVII, Part 2, 83.
89. *Ibid.*
90. *Ibid.*
91. *Ibid., 23,* / XVI, Part 2, 104.
92. *Ibid.,* 122–123.
93. *Ibid.,* 128.
94. *Ibid.,* 100.
95. *Ibid.,* 117.
96. Ambrose, 61.
97. *O. R., 25,* / XVII, Part 2, 90.

CHAPTER 5
1. James Grant Wilson, "General Halleck—A Memoir," in *Journal of the Military Service Institution of the United States,* Volume XXXVI, 556.
2. *Ibid.*
3. *Ibid.,* 557.
4. *War of the Rebellion: Official Records of the Union and Confederate Armies, 14,* / Series I, Volume XI, Part 3, 282.
5. Stephen W. Sears, *George B. McClellan: The Young Napoleon,* 230.
6. *O. R., 14,* / XI, Part 3, 286.
7. Earl Schenck Miers, editor-in-chief, *Lincoln Day-by-Day 1861–1865,* 126–127; J. G. Randall, *Lincoln the President,* II, 100.
8. *O. R., 16,* / XII, Part 2, 22.
9. *Ibid., 23,* / XVI, Part 2, 143.
10. *Ibid.,* 150–151.
11. Wilson, 557.
12. *O. R., 23,* / XVI, Part 2, 151.
13. *Ibid., 25,* / XVII, Part 2, 100.
14. *Ibid., 11,* / X, Part 2, 65.
15. *Ibid., 25,* / XVII, Part 2, 100–101.
16. Ulysses S. Grant, *Personal Memoirs of U. S. Grant and Selected Letters,* 262–263.
17. Quoted by Stephen E. Ambrose, *Halleck: Lincoln's Chief of Staff,* 3.
18. *O. R., 23,* / XVI, Part 2, 167–168.
19. *Ibid., 14,* / XI, Part 3, 319.
20. *Ibid.,* 321–322.
21. *Ibid.,* 287–288.
22. Patricia L. Faust, editor, *Historical Times Encyclopedia of the Civil War,* 416.
23. *O. R., 14,* / XI, Part 3, 313–314.
24. Randall, II, 100.
25. *O. R., 17,* / XII, Part 3, 473–474.
26. Randall, II, 99–100.
27. Allan Nevins, *The War for the Union,* II, 154–155; Douglas Southall Freeman, *R. E. Lee,* II, 264.
28. Stephen W. Sears, *The Civil War Papers of George B. McClellan,* 348, note 1.
29. *Ibid.,* 346–347.
30. *Ibid.,* 354.
31. *Ibid.,* 354–355.
32. *Ibid.,* 360–361.
33. *Ibid.,* 364.
34. *O. R., 12,* / XI, Part 1, 73–74. This excerpt is from the controversial

"Harrison's Bar Letter," which McClellan included in an official report.

35. Sears, *The Civil War Papers of George B. McClellan*, 322–323.
36. Ibid., 371, Note 1.
37. *Ibid.,* 369, 370. Note 1.
38. *Ibid.,* 376–377.
39. *Ibid.,* 378, Note 1.
40. Miers, 129.
41. Sears, *George B. McClellan: The Young Napoleon,* 241.
42. Wilson, 557.
43. Shelby Foote, *The Civil War,* I, 594. General Halleck's report to Lincoln on his trip is to be found in O. R., *14,* / XI, Part 3, 337–338.
44. Wilson, 557.
45. *Ibid.*
46. *O. R., 14,* / XI, Part 3, 343.
47. *Ibid.,* 345–346.
48. Miers, 130.
49. *O. R., 17,* / XII, Part 3, 499–500.
50. Sears, *George B. McClellan: The Young Napoleon,* 239–242.
51. *O. R., 12,* / XI, Part 1, 80–81.
52. *Ibid.,* 81–82.
53. *Ibid.,* 82.
54. *Ibid.,* 82–84.
55. Sears, *The Civil War Papers of George B. McClellan,* 385.
56. *Ibid.,* 388.
57. *Ibid.,* 389–390.
58. Wilson, 557.
59. *O. R., 14,* / XI, Part 3, 359–360.
60. Herman Hattaway and Archer Jones, *How the North Won,* 222.
61. *O. R., 17,* / XII, Part 3, 499–500.
62. *Ibid.,* 521.
63. *Ibid.,* 524.
64. *Ibid.,* 547.
65. *Ibid.,* 554.
66. Foote, I, 596–602; Hattaway and Jones, 222–224.
67. Foote, I, 602–605.
68. Wilson, 557.
69. *O. R., 14,* / XI, Part 3, 378.
70. *Ibid.,* 379–380.
71. *Ibid.,* 236.
72. *Ibid.*
73. Foote, I, 571–585.
74. *O. R., 22,* / XVI, Part 1, 710–711. This letter was found by a Union patrol on August 8, 1862, and forwarded to General Buell, who passed it on to General Halleck. See *O. R., 25,* / XVI, Part 2, 296.
75. *Ibid., 22,* / XVI, Part 1, 711.
76. *Ibid., 23,* / XVI, Part 2, 278–279.
77. *Ibid.,* 307.
78. *Ibid.,* 314.
79. *Ibid.,* 314–315.
80. *Ibid.,* 344.
81. *Ibid.,* 360.
82. *Ibid.,* 360–361.
83. *Ibid.,* 375.
84. *Ibid.,* 421.

CHAPTER 6
1. *War of the Rebellion: Official Records of the Union and Confederate Armies, 18,* / Series I, Volume XII, Part 3, 575.
2. *Ibid.,* 576.
3. Shelby Foote, *The Civil War,* I, 605–607.
4. *O. R., 18,* / XII, Part 3, 591.
5. *Ibid.,* 601.
6. *Ibid.,* 606.
7. *Ibid.,* 605.
8. Stephen W. Sears, *The Civil War Papers of George B. McClellan,* 397.
9. *O. R., 18,* / XII, Part 3, 602.
10. *Ibid.*
11. *Ibid.,* 608.
12. *Ibid.,* 609.
13. Sears, 399.
14. *O. R., 18,* / XII, Part 3, 627.
15. *Ibid.,* 625.
16. *Ibid.*
17. *Ibid.,* 622.
18. Patricia L. Faust, editor, *Historical Times Encyclopedia of the Civil War,* 351.
19. *O. R., 18,* / XII, Part 3, 624.
20. Thomas Weber, *The Northern Railroads in the Civil War,* 147.
21. *Ibid.*
22. Foote, I, 608–610.
23. *O. R., 18,* / XII, Part 3, 623.
24. *Ibid.,* 622.
25. *Ibid., 23,* / XVI, Part 2, 395.
26. *Ibid.*
27. *Ibid.,* 404–405.
28. *Ibid.,* 406–407.
29. *Ibid.,* 416–417.

30. *Ibid.*, 428.
31. *Ibid.*, *18,* / XII, Part 3, 637.
32. *Ibid.*
33. Herman Haupt, *Reminiscences,* 80–83. The order from Halleck to which General Haupt referred may be *O. R., 18,* / XII, Part 3, 638.
34. Haupt, 90.
35. Kenneth P. Williams, *Lincoln Finds a General,* I, 295.
36. *O. R., 18,* / XII, Part 3, 632.
37. *Ibid.*, 630.
38. *Ibid.*
39. *Ibid.*
40. *Ibid.*
41. *Ibid.*, 645.
42. *Ibid.*
43. *Ibid.*, 645–646.
44. *Ibid.*, *12,* / XI, Part 1, 93–94.
45. *Ibid.*, 94.
46. *Ibid.*, *18,* / XII, Part 3, 646.
47. *Ibid.*
48. *Ibid.*, 646–647.
49. Foote, I, 610–613; more detailed accounts are to be found in Douglas Southall Freeman's *R. E. Lee* and *Lee's Lieutenants.*
50. *O. R., 18,* / XII, Part 3, 655.
51. *Ibid.*, 658.
52. *Ibid.*, *16,* / XII, Part 2, 65–66.
53. *Ibid.*, *18,* / XII, Part 3, 666.
54. *Ibid.*, 653.
55. *Ibid.*, 653.
56. *Ibid.*, 679.
57. *Ibid.*, 679–680.
58. *Ibid.*, 680.
59. Frank E. Vandiver, *Mighty Stonewall,* 355; Freeman, *Lee's Lieutenants,* II, 85–87, *R. E. Lee,* 301, 304–307.
60. *O. R., 18,* / XII, Part 3, 680.
61. Haupt, 94–96; Williams, I, 302; *O. R., 18,* / XII, Part 3, 680.
62. Foote, I, 617–620; Williams, I, 303–304.
63. *O. R., 18,* / XII, Part 3, 684.
64. *Ibid.*, 684.
65. Haupt, 100.
66. *Ibid.*,103.
67. Williams, I, 304, citing Haupt, *Reminiscences.*
68. *O. R., 18,* / XII, Part 3, 685.
69. Sears, 406.

70. *O. R., 18,* / XII, Part 3, 689.
71. *Ibid.*
72. *Ibid.*, 690.
73. *Ibid.*
74. *Ibid.*, 691.
75. *Ibid.*
76. Steven E. Woodworth, *Jefferson Davis and his Generals,* 125–185.

CHAPTER 7
1. G. F. R. Henderson, *Stonewall Jackson and the American Civil War,* 440–446.
2. *War of the Rebellion: Official Records of the Union and Confederate Armies, 18,* / Series I, Volume XII, Part 3, 697–698.
3. Ibid., 698.
4. Henderson, 442.
5. *O. R., 16,* / XII, Part 2, 72.
6. Kernstown was actually the first significant fight in Jackson's Valley Campaign. It was a battle of attraction that halted movement of Nathaniel Banks' and other Union troops eastward to support McClellan's Peninsula Campaign. For an account of Kernstown, see Robert G. Tanner, *Stonewall in the Valley,* 117–130.
7. *O. R., 18,* / XII, Part 3, 706.
8. *Ibid.*, 707.
9. Stephen W. Sears, *The Civil War Papers of George B. McClellan,* 411.
10. *O. R., 18,* / XII, Part 3, 708.
11. *Ibid.*
12. *Ibid.*, 709.
13. *Ibid.*
14. *Ibid.*, 710.
15. *Ibid.*
16. *Ibid.*, 720–721.
17. Douglas Southall Freeman, *R. E. Lee,* II, 256.
18. *Ibid.*, 312–316.
19. *O. R., 12,* / XI, Part 1, 97–98.
20. *Ibid.*, *18,* / XII, Part 3, 729.
21. Henderson, 454–458.
22. *Ibid.*, 454.
23. *Ibid.*, 452–453. Pope's orders to "bag Jackson" may be found in *O. R., 16,* / XII, Part 2, 72–73.
24. *O. R., 18,* / XII, Part 3, 732–733. On August 27, in an earlier letter to Burnside, Porter had written: "I wish

myself away from [Pope's Army of Virginia], with all our old Army of the Potomac, and so do our companions.... If you can get me away, please do. Make what use of this you choose, so it does good."—*O. R., 18,* / XII, Part 3, 699–700.

25. *Ibid.,* 733.
26. *Ibid., 12,* / XI, Part 1, 98.
27. *Ibid.*
28. Sears, 417.
29. *Ibid.,* 418. note 1.
30. *O. R., 12,* / XI, Part 1, 94.
31. *Ibid.,* 99–100.
32. Sears, 419.
33. *O. R., 12,* / XI, Part 1, 98.
34. *Ibid., 23,* XVI, Part 2, 441–442.
35. *Ibid.,* 447.
36. *Ibid.,* 447–448.
37. *Ibid., 18,* / XII, Part 3, 722.
38. *Ibid.*
39. *Ibid.,* 723.
40. *Ibid.*
41. *Ibid.,* 724.
42. Shelby Foote, *The Civil War,* I, 628–634. provides a good concise account. More details are provided in Henderson, and especially in Dr. Freeman's *R. E. Lee* and *Lee's Lieutenants.*
43. *O. R., 18,* / XII, Part 3, 741.
44. *Ibid.,* 742.
45. *Ibid.*
46. *Ibid.,* 744.
47. Foote, I, 636.
48. *Ibid.*
49. *O. R., 18,* / XII, Part 3, 741.
50. *Ibid.,* 751.
51. *Ibid.*
52. *Ibid.,* 742.
53. *Ibid.,* 744.
54. *Ibid.,* 745.
55. *Ibid.*
56. *Ibid.,* 747.
57. Foote, I, 634–642.
58. Ibid., 650–653; Steven E. Woodworth, *Jefferson Davis and his Generals,* 140–145.
59. *O. R., 18,* / XII, Part 3, 739–741.
60. Stephen E. Ambrose, *Halleck: Lincoln's Chief of Staff,* 80.
61. *O. R., 16,* / XII, Part 2, 78–79.

62. *Ibid., 12,* / XI, Part 1, 101–102.
63. *Ibid., 18,* / XII, Part 3, 771–772.
64. *Ibid., 12,* / XI, Part 1, 102.
65. *Ibid., 18,* / XII, Part 3, 769.
66. Sears, 423. McClellan's reference to prominent Democrat Aspinwall and his friends in New York is interesting when considered along with what British journalist Frederick Milnes Edge wrote in *Major-General McClellan and The Campaign on the Yorktown Peninsula,* published in London in 1865. Briefly, Edge suggested a conspiracy on the part of both Northern and Southern Democrats to find a Union general who was soft on slavery's abolition and to advance his career leading to his becoming their presidential candidate in 1864; according to Edge, George Brinton McClellan was their choice. Although Edge's allegations have been ignored by most historians, they do tend to explain some otherwise puzzling aspects of the Young Napoleon's behavior.
67. *O. R., 12,* / XI, Part 1, 102.
68. *Ibid.,* 102–103.
69. Ambrose, 76, citing David Herbert Donald, editor, *Inside Lincoln's Cabinet: The Civil War Diaries of Salmon P. Chase,* 148.
70. *O. R., 12,* / XI, Part 1, 103.
71. *Ibid.,* 103–104.
72. Earl Schenck Miers, editor-in-chief, *Lincoln Day-by-Day 1861–1865,* 136.
73. *O. R., 16,* / XII, Part 2, 81.
74. *Ibid.,* 82.
75. *Ibid.,* 82–83.
76. *Ibid., 18,* / XII, Part 3, 773.
77. *Ibid.,* 774. The date, time, and substances of this pair of messages do not agree with those found at *Ibid., 12,* / XI, Part 1, 102–103. The aide who responded to McClellan may have been mistaken or an error may have been made in editing the *O. R.*
78. *Ibid., 18,* / XII, Part 3, 787.
79. *Ibid., 14,* / XI, Part 3, 382–383.
80. *Ibid., 12,* / XI, Part 1, 104.
81. Sears, *The Civil War Papers of George B. McClellan,* 428.
82. *O. R., 12,* / XI, Part 1, 104.

83. Stephen W. Sears, *George B. McClellan: The Young Napoleon,* 257, citing *O. R., 16,* / XII, Part 2, 80.
84. *O. R., 12,* / XI, Part 1, 104–105.
85. Sears, *The Civil War Papers of George B. McClellan,* 427.
86. Foote, I, 515.
87. O. R., *28,* / XIX, Part 2, 646.
88. E. P. Alexander, *Military Memoirs of a Confederate,* 218.
89. *O. R., 18,* / XII, Part 3, 785.
90. *Ibid., 23,* / XVI, Part 2, 466.
91. *Ibid.,* 469.
92. *Ibid.,* 470.
93. Sears, *The Civil War Papers of George B. McClellan,* 428.
94. *O. R., 12,* / XI, Part 1, 105.
95. Margaret Leech, *Reveille in Washington,* 193. For such an able and meticulous historian to have conveyed such a negative judgment is an indication of how far-reaching and effective the anti-Halleck propaganda has been.
96. *O. R., 23,* / XVI, Part 2, 471–472.
97. *Ibid.,* 472.
98. *Ibid.,* 470–471.
99. *Ibid.,* 471.

CHAPTER 8
1. David Herbert Donald, *Lincoln,* 372.
2. *Ibid.* See also J. G. Randall, *Lincoln the President,* II, 110–114, and Shelby Foote, *The Civil War,* I, 647–649.
3. Donald, 372.
4. Stephen E. Ambrose, *Halleck: Lincoln's Chief of Staff,* 80–81. Ambrose cited George B. McClellan, *McClellan's Own Story,* Joint [Congressional] Committee on the Conduct of the War, *Report;* and Gideon Welles, *Diary of Gideon Welles, Secretary of the Navy Under Lincoln and Johnson.*
5. Margaret Leech, *Reveille in Washington,* 185.
6. James Grant Wilson, "General Halleck: A Memoir," in *Journal of the Military Service Institution of the United States,* XXXVI, 557. Halleck's letter was dated July 28, 1862, after his return from Harrison's Landing.
7. *War of the Rebellion: Official Records of the*

Union and Confederate Armies, 17, / Series I, Volume XII, Part 3, 796–797.
8. *Ibid.,* 797.
9. *Ibid.*
10. Wilson, 558.
11. Douglas Southall Freeman, *R. E. Lee,* II, 348–351.
12. Foote, I, 648–649.
13. *O. R., 28,* / XIX, Part 2, 169. The original order, according to the *O. R.,* was in Lincoln's handwriting.
14. In the wake of Second Bull Run, as the disaster would become known in the North, Ambrose Burnside had been considered for the role reluctantly restored to Little Mac, but nothing had come of that exercise. See Foote, I, 764.
15. Sears, *George B. McClellan: The Young Napoleon,* 263.
16. *O. R., 28,* / XIX, Part 2, 169.
17. Sears, *The Civil War Papers of George B. McClellan,* 431.
18. *O. R., 28,* / XIX, Part 2, 188.
19. Foote, I, 654–656.
20. *O. R., 23,* / XVI, Part 2, 483.
21. *Ibid.*
22. *Ibid.,* 495.
23. *Ibid.*
24. *Ibid.,* 496.
25. *Ibid.*
26. *Ibid.,* 497.
27. *Ibid.*
28. *Ibid.,* 500.
29. Sears, *George B. McClellan: The Young Napoleon,* 264.
30. *Ibid.,* 263.
31. For example, see *O. R., 28,* / XIX, Part 2, 174–175.
32. Wilson, 558.
33. *O. R., 28,* / XIX, Part 2, 183.
34. *Ibid.*
35. *Ibid.,* 182. For the formal order, see *Ibid.,* 188. As noted earlier, at McClellan's request General Halleck suspended the order as to Porter and Franklin. For McClellan's request see *Ibid.,* 189.
36. *Ibid.,* 188–189.
37. *Ibid.,* 189.
38. *Ibid.,* 182.
39. Homer Bates, *Lincoln in the Telegraph*

Room, 138–141.

40. Don E. Fehrenbacher, editor, *Abraham Lincoln: Speeches and Writings 1859–1865,* 339.

41. H. L. Trefousse, *The Radical Republicans: Lincoln's Vanguard for Social Justice,* 200.

42. Stephen W. Sears, *George B. McClellan: The Young Napoleon,* 265–269, and *The Civil War Papers of George B. McClellan,* 436–437, 437. Note 2.

43. Sears, *The Civil War Papers of George B. McClellan,* 438.

44. Freeman, II, 359–364.

45. *O. R., 28,* / XIX, Part 2, 211.

46. *Ibid.*

47. *Ibid.,* 228.

48. *Ibid.,* 229.

49. *Ibid.*

50. *Ibid.,* 230–231.

51. *Ibid.,* 231.

52. *Ibid.,* 253.

53. *Ibid.,* 253–254.

54. *Ibid.,* 254–255.

55. *Ibid.,* 255.

56. *Ibid., 23,* / XVI, Part 2, 506–507.

57. *Ibid.,* 507.

58. *Ibid.,* 506.

59. *Ibid.,* 508.

60. *Ibid.*

61. *Ibid.*

62. *Ibid.,* 505–506.

63. *Ibid.,* 509.

64. *Ibid.*

65. *Ibid.,* 515.

66. *Ibid.,* 516.

67. *Ibid., 28,* / XIX, Part 2, 253–254.

68. *Ibid.,* 267.

69. *Ibid.,* 268.

70. *Ibid.*

71. *Ibid.,* 276.

72. *Ibid.,* 277.

73. *Ibid.,* 270.

74. *Ibid.,* 271.

75. *Ibid.,* 272.

76. *Ibid.,* 273–274.

77. *Ibid.,* 277.

78. Mark M. Boatner, III, *The Civil War Dictionary,* 21.

79. *O. R., 28,* / XIX, Part 2, 278.

80. *Ibid., 27,* / XIX, Part 1, 43.

81. *Ibid.,* 44.

82. *Ibid., 28,* / XIX, Part 2, 189.

83. *Ibid.,* 254–255.

84. *Ibid.,* 281–282.

85. *Ibid.,* 280–281.

86. Stephen W. Sears, *Landscape Turned Red,* 112–113.

87. *O. R., 28,* / XIX, Part 2, 280. In some accounts, "unchallenged" appears as "unchanged," which makes more sense.

88. *Ibid.,* 281–282.

89. Among many excellent accounts of South Mountain are those of Freeman, *R. E. Lee,* II, and Sears, in *Landscape Turned Red.*

90. *O. R., 28,* / XIX, Part 2, 289.

91. Boatner, 20.

92. *O. R., 28,* / XIX, Part 2, 295.

93. *Ibid.*

94. See Sears, *Landscape Turned Red,* and Freeman, *R. E. Lee, II* and *Lee's Lieutenants, II.*

95. *O. R., 28,* / XIX, Part 2, 322.

96. Sears, *The Civil War Papers of George B. McClellan,* 469.

97. *O. R., 28,* / XIX, Part 2, 312.

98. *Ibid.,* 330.

99. *Ibid.,* 332.

100. *Ibid.,* 330.

101. *Ibid., 27,* / XIX, Part 1, 68.

102. *Ibid.*

103. *Ibid.,* 68–69.

104. Sears, *The Civil War Papers of George B. McClellan,* 473.

105. *Ibid.,* 476.

CHAPTER 9

1. Shelby Foote, *The Civil War,* I, 716–720.

2. *War of the Rebellion: Official Records of the Union and Confederate Armies, 23,* / Series I, Volume XVI Part 2, 530.

3. *Ibid.,* 538.

4. *Ibid.,* 539.

5. *Ibid.*

6. *Ibid.,* 542–543.

7. *Ibid.,* 546.

8. *Ibid.,* 549.

9. *Ibid.*

10. *Ibid.*

11. *Ibid.*

12. *Ibid.,* 554.

13. *Ibid.*
14. *Ibid.*
15. *Ibid.*
16. *Ibid.,* 555.
17. *Ibid.*
18. *Ibid.*
19. *Ibid.*
20. Foote, I, 714–715.
21. *O. R., 23,* / XVI, Part 2, 549–550.
22. Hudson Strode, *Jefferson Davis: Confederate President,* I, 307.
23. *O. R., 27,* / XIX, Part 1, 8.
24. *Ibid., 28,* / XIX, Part 2, 360.
25. Foote, I, 748–749; David Herbert Donald, *Lincoln,* 387.
26. Earl Schenck Miers, editor-in-chief, *Lincoln Day-by-Day 1861–1865,* 143.
27. *O. R., 25,* / XVII, Part 2, 282.
28. *Ibid.,* 209–210, 213, 214, 220, 222, 227, 235, 240, 245, 250. The date span is September 9–October 1, 1862.
29. Foote, I, 720–725.
30. *O. R., 25,* / XVII, Part 2, 239.
31. *Ibid.,* 251.
32. *Ibid.,* 286–287.
33. *Ibid.,* 290.
34. *Ibid.*
35. *Ibid., 28,* / XIX, Part 2, 394–395.
36. *Ibid., 23,* / XVI, Part 2, 564.
37. *Ibid.,* 566.
38. Foote, I, 726–740.
39. *Ibid.,* 730.
40. *O. R., 123,* / Series III, Volume II, 653.
41. *Ibid., 25,* / Series I, Volume XVII, Part 2, 274–275.
42. *Ibid., 23,* / XVI, Part 2, 611.
43. *Ibid.,* 612.
44. *Ibid.,* 619.
45. *Ibid.,* 623.
46. *Ibid.,* 634.
47. *Ibid.,* 636–637.
48. *Ibid.,* 638.
49. *Ibid.,* 640–641.
50. *Ibid.,* 650.
51. *Ibid.,* 651.
52. *Ibid.,* 646–647.
53. *Ibid.,* 652.
54. *Ibid.,* 643.
55. *Ibid., 25,* / XVII, Part 2, 296–297.
56. *Ibid., 23,* XVI, Part 2, 657.
57. *Ibid.,* 663.
58. Details may be found in Ludwell H. Johnson, *Red River Campaign: Politics and Cotton in the Civil War.*
59. *O. R., 122,* / Series III, Volume I, 870.
60. Foote, I, 533–538, 758.
61. *O. R., 123,* / Series III, Volume II, 706.
62. *Ibid.*
63. *Ibid., 23,* / Series I, Volume XVI, Part 2, 626–627.
64. Donald, 388.
65. *O. R., 27,* / XIX, Part 1, 13–14.
66. *Ibid.*
67. *Ibid., 28,* / XIX, Part 2, 464.
68. *Ibid.,* 484–485.
69. *Ibid.,* 485.
70. *Ibid.,* 490.
71. *Ibid.,* 490–491.
72. *Ibid.,* 496.
73. *Ibid.*
74. *Ibid.,* 497.
75. *Ibid.,* 497–498.
76. Stephen W. Sears, *The Civil War Papers of George B. McClellan,* 481.
77. *Ibid.,* 488.
78. *Ibid.,* 515.
79. Stephen W. Sears, *George B. McClellan: The Young Napoleon,* 329.
80. Sears, *The Civil War Papers of George B. McClellan,* 516.
81. *O. R., 27,* / XIX, Part 1, 84.
82. *Ibid.,* 84–85.
83. *Ibid.,* 7.
84. *Ibid.,* 7–9.
85. *Ibid., 123,* / Series III, Volume II, 703–704.
86. *Ibid.,* 691.
87. *Ibid.,* 712.
88. *Ibid.,* 736–737.

CHAPTER 10

1. *War of the Rebellion: Official Records of the Union and Confederate Armies, 28,* / Series I, Volume XIX, Part 2, 545.
2. *Ibid.*
3. *Ibid.,* 549.
4. Stephen W. Sears, *The Civil War Papers of George B. McClellan,* 485–486.
5. *Ibid.,* 519–520.
6. *O. R., 28,* / XIX, 2, 546.
7. *Ibid.,* 555.
8. *Ibid.,* 552–554.
9. *Ibid.,* 579. For details regarding the con-

ference at Warrenton, see Kenneth P. Williams, *Lincoln Finds a General,* II, 481–485, and Herman Haupt, *Reminiscences,* 158–166.

10. *O. R., 21, /* XV, 590.
11. *Ibid.,* 590–591.
12. *Ibid., 123, /* Series III, Volume II, 782.
13. *Ibid.*
14. *Ibid.,* 784.
15. *Ibid.,* 862.
16. *Ibid., 24, /* Series I, XVII, Part 1, 466.
17. *Ibid.,* 468–469.
18. *Ibid.,* 469.
19. *Ibid.*
20. *Ibid., 25, /* XVII, Part 2, 332.
21. *Ibid.,* 371–372.
22. *Ibid.,* 347.
23. *Ibid., 24, /* XVII, Part 1, 470.
24. *Ibid.,* 471.
25. *Ibid., 25, /* XVII, Part 2, 356.
26. *Ibid., 24, /* XVII, Part 1, 472.
27. *Ibid.,* 473.
28. *Ibid.*
29. *Ibid.,* 473–474.
30. *Ibid.,* 474.
31. *Ibid.*
32. *Ibid.,* 475.
33. *Ibid., 30, /* XX, Part 2, 59.
34. *Ibid.,* 117–118.
35. *Ibid.,* 118.
36. *Ibid.,* 123–124.
37. *Ibid.,* 141.
38. *Ibid., 28, /* XIX, Part 2, 579.
39. Douglas Southall Freeman, *R. E. Lee,* II, 425, 428.
40. Williams, II, 487–511.
41. *O. R., 31, /* XXI, 773–774.
42. *Ibid.,* 789–790.
43. *Ibid.,* 780.
44. *Ibid.,* 64.
45. Williams, *II,* 491.
46. Haupt, 176–177.
47. Shelby Foote, *The Civil War,* II, 38–42.
48. *O. R., 31, /* XXI, 65.
49. Allan Nevins, *The War for the Union,* II, 352–354; J. G. Randall, *Lincoln the President,* II, 242–243.
50. *O. R., 31, /* XXI, 66.
51. *Ibid.*
52. *Ibid.,* 66–67.
53. Williams, II, 519–520; Herman Hattaway and Archer Jones, *How the North Won,* 309, 291–293, 300.
54. Hattaway and Jones, 309–310.
55. Haupt, 308.
56. *O. R., 31, /* XXI, 46–47.
57. *Ibid., 30, /* XX, Part 2, 167.
58. *Ibid.,* 179.
59. *Ibid., 21, /* XV, 613.
60. *Ibid., 30, /* XX, Part 2, 218.
61. *Ibid.,* 194.
62. *Ibid.,* 282.
63. *Ibid., 31, /* XXI, 861, 865, 866.
64. *Ibid.,* 868–870.
65. *Ibid.,* 886.
66. *Ibid.*
67. *Ibid.,* 900.
68. *Ibid., 25, /* XVII, Part 2, 401.
69. *Ibid.,* 415.
70. *Ibid.,* 420.
71. *Ibid.*
72. *Ibid., 24, /* XVII, Part 1, 476.
73. *Ibid., 25, /* XVII, Part 2, 425.
74. *Ibid.*
75. *Ibid.,* 461–462.
76. *Ibid.,* 462.
77. *Ibid.,* 480.
78. *Ibid.*
79. *Ibid.,* 501–503.
80. Patricia L. Faust, editor, *Historical Times Encyclopedia of the Civil War,* 138–139.

CHAPTER 11

1. Accounts of the Lincoln-Burnside encounter early on the morning of January 1, 1863, differ. The one here is based on Stephen E. Ambrose, *Halleck: Lincoln's Chief of Staff,* 99. The issue is whether Halleck and Stanton were present. Subsequent communications in the *Official Records,* to be cited later, indicate that they were.
2. *War of the Rebellion: Official Records of the Union and Confederate Armies, 31, /* Series I, Volume XXI, 900.
3. *Ibid.,* 868–869.
4. *Ibid.,* 916–918.
5. Shelby Foote, *The Civil War,* II, 122.
6. *O. R., 31, /* XXI, 946–947.
7. *Ibid.,* 940.
8. Foote, II, 123.
9. *O. R., 31, /* XXI, 1006.
10. *Ibid.,* 941.

11. *Ibid.*, 940.
12. Foote, II, 80–103.
13. *O. R., 24,* / XVII, Part 1, 479.
14. *Ibid., 25,* / XVII, Part 2, 542.
15. Patricia L. Faust, *Historical Times Encyclopedia of the Civil War,* 138–139.
16. *O. R., 25,* / XVII, Part 2, 534.
17. *Ibid., 31,* / XXI, 943.
18. *Ibid.,* 944–945.
19. *Ibid.,* 945.
20. Gideon Welles, *Diary of Gideon Welles, Secretary of the Navy Under Lincoln and Johnson,* I, 383.
21. Foote, II, 123.
22. *O. R., 31,* / XXI, 953–954.
23. *Ibid.,* 954.
24. Foote, II, 128–130.
25. *O. R., 31,* / XXI, 989–999.
26. *Ibid.*
27. *Ibid.,* 1004–1005.
28. J. G. Randall, *Lincoln the President,* II, 254–255.
29. *O. R., 40,* / XXV, Part 2, 4.
30. Foote, II, 123.
31. *O. R., 40,* / XXV, Part 2, 504–506.
32. *Ibid.,* 9.
33. *Ibid.,* 139.
34. *Ibid.*
35. *Ibid.*
36. *Ibid.,* 158.
37. *Ibid.,* 209.
38. *Ibid.,* 210.
39. Foote, II, 233–234.
40. *Ibid.,* 232–237.
41. *Ibid.,* 235–237; Kenneth P. Williams, *Lincoln Finds a General,* II, 564, 566–567.
42. *O. R., 40,* / XXV, Part 2, 199–200.
43. John Bigelow, Jr., *Chancellorsville,* 142–161.
44. *O. R., 40,* / XXV, Part 2, 214.
45. Earl Schenck Miers, *Lincoln Day-by-Day 1861–1865,* 180.
46. *O. R., 40,* / XXV, Part 2, 236.
47. Foote, II, 315.
48. Douglas Southall Freeman, *Lee's Lieutenants,* II, 639.
49. In the present author's opinion, Chancellorsville is the most fascinating battle of the entire Civil War, and Bigelow's account of it is the best we have.
50. *O. R., 40,* / XXV, Part 2, 377.
51. *Ibid.*
52. *Ibid.,* 378.
53. *Ibid.,* 379.
54. *Ibid.,* 435.
55. *Ibid.*
56. *Ibid.,* 438.
57. *Ibid.*
58. Bigelow, 505.

CHAPTER 12
1. Stephen E. Ambrose, *Halleck: Lincoln's Chief of Staff,* 128.
2. George W. Cullum, *Report of the Third Annual Reunion of the Association of Graduates of the United States Military Academy,* 35–36.
3. *Dictionary of American Biography,* VI, 236–238.
4. *Ibid.*
5. *War of the Rebellion: Official Records of the Union and Confederate Armies, 118,* / Series II, Volume V, 671
6. *Ibid.,* 681–682.
7. For General Orders No. 100. in its entirety, *Ibid.,* 671–682.
8. *Dictionary of American Biography,* VI, 238.
9. *O. R., 118,* / Series II, V, 679.
10. *Ibid., 119,* / VI, 523–524.
11. Patricia L. Faust, *Historical Times Encyclopedia of the Civil War,* 16–17. (Andersonville), and 588, (Point Lookout).
12. *O. R., 25,* / Series I, XVII, Part 2, 550–551.
13. *Ibid.,* 553.
14. *Ibid.,* 555.
15. *Ibid.,* 553–554.
16. *Ibid.,* 566–567.
17. *Ibid.,* 579.
18. *Ibid., 36,* / XXIV, Part 1, 8–9.
19. *Ibid.,* 9.
20. *Ibid.*
21. *Ibid., 38,* / XXIV, Part 3, 18–19.
22. *Ibid., 36,* / XXIV, Part 1, 11.
23. *Ibid.,* 12–13.
24. *Ibid.,* 13.
25. *Ibid.,* 13–14.
26. *Ibid.,* 11.
27. *Ibid., 25,* / XVII, Part 2, 446.

28. *Ibid.,* 569.
29. Shelby Foote, *The Civil War,* II, 90–91; Peter Cozzens, *No Better Place to Die,* 166.
30. *O. R., 35,* / XXIII, Part 2, 37–38.
31. Foote, II, 123–124.
32. *O. R., 35,* / XXIII, Part 2, 23.
33. *Ibid.,* 75.
34. *Ibid.,* 75–76.
35. *Ibid.,* 54–58.
36. *Ibid.,* 107–109.
37. *Ibid.,* 95.
38. *Ibid.,* 111.
39. *Ibid.,* 138.
40. *Ibid.,* 155.
41. *Ibid.,* 143–144.
42. *Ibid.,* 147.
43. *Ibid.,* 162–164.
44. *Ibid.,* 193–194.
45. *Ibid., 38,* / XXIV, Part 3, 56–57.
46. *Ibid.,* 57.
47. Foote, II, 217.
48. *Ibid.*
49. *O. R., 36,* / XXIV, Part 1, 22.
50. *Ibid.,* 25.
51. *Ibid., 38,* / XXIV, Part 3, 151.
52. *Ibid.,* 49–50.
53. *Ibid., 36,* / XXIV, Part 1, 27–28.
54. Ambrose, 172.
55. George W. Cullum, in *Third Annual Reunion of the Association of Graduates of the United States Military Academy,* 34.
56. *O. R., 35,* / XXIII, Part 2, 255–256.
57. *Ibid.,* 279.
58. *Ibid.*
59. *Ibid.,* 284–285.
60. *Ibid.,* 300–304.
61. *Ibid., 38,* / XXIV, Part 3, 157–158.
62. *Ibid., 35,* / XXIII, Part 2, 307.
63. *Ibid., 36,* / XXIV, Part 1, 29–30.
64. *Ibid., 38,* / XXIV, Part 3, 240.
65. *Ibid.,* 242–243.
66. General Grant himself remains the best source for the Vicksburg Campaign, writing in *Ulysses S. Grant: Memoirs and Selected Letters,* compiled by Mary Drake McFeely and William S. McFeely.

CHAPTER 13
1. Darius N. Couch, in Robert U. Johnson and C. C. Buell, editors, *Battles and Leaders of the Civil War,* III, 161.
2. *War of the Rebellion: Official Records of the Union and Confederate Armies, 40,* / Series I, XXV, Part 2, 479.
3. *Ibid.,* 503–509.
4. *Ibid.,* 509.
5. *Ibid.,* 514.
6. *Ibid.,* 514–516.
7. *Ibid.,* 516.
8. *Ibid.,* 527–528.
9. *Ibid., 41,* / XXVI, Part 1, 494–495.
10. *Ibid.,* 492.
11. *Ibid.,* 498.
12. *Ibid.,* 500–501.
13. *Ibid.,* 503.
14. *Ibid.,* 525.
15. Fred Harvey Harrington, *Fighting Politician: Major General N. P. Banks,* 120–121.
16. *Ibid.*
17. Shelby Foote, *The Civil War,* II, 370–386.
18. Harrington, 118.
19. *O. R., 40,* / XXV, Part 2, 542.
20. *Ibid.,* 543.
21. *Ibid., 43,* / XXVII, Part 1, 30.
22. *Ibid.,* 31.
23. *Ibid.,* 31–32.
24. *Ibid.,* 34–35.
25. *Ibid.,* 35.
26. *Ibid.*
27. *Ibid.,* 39.
28. *Ibid.,* 39–40.
29. *Ibid.,* 41–42.
30. *Ibid.,* 43–44.
31. Herman Haupt, *Reminiscences,* 205–206.
32. *O. R., 43,* / XXVII, Part 1, 44–45.
33. *Ibid.,* 47.
34. *Ibid.,* 45.
35. *Ibid.,* 45–46.
36. *Ibid.,* 46.
37. *Ibid.,* 47.
38. *Ibid.,* 50–51.
39. *Ibid.,* 58.
40. *Ibid.,* 60.
41. *Ibid.*
42. *Ibid.*
43. Foote, II, 450–451.

44. *O. R., 43,* / XXVII, Part 1, 61.
45. Freeman Cleaves, *Meade of Gettysburg,* 129.
46. *O. R., 43,* / XXVII, Part 1, 61–62.
47. *Ibid.,* 62.
48. *Ibid.,* 69.

CHAPTER 14
1. *War of the Rebellion: Official Records of the Union and Confederate Armies, 45,* / Series I, Volume XXVII, Part 3, 474.
2. *Ibid.,* 476.
3. *Dictionary of American Biography,* IV, 400.
4. *O. R., 45,* / XXVII, Part 3, 514.
5. Louis M. Starr, *Bohemian Brigade: Civil War Newsmen in Action,* 215–218.
6. *O. R., 45,* / XXVII, Part 3, 515.
7. *Ibid.,* 523.
8. *Ibid.,* 528.
9. *Ibid.,* 546.
10. *Ibid.,* 550.
11. Herman Haupt, *Reminiscences,* 223–224.
12. Kenneth P. Williams, *Lincoln Finds a General,* II, 738.
13. *O. R., 43,* / XXVII, Part 1, 82.
14. *Ibid.,* 82–83.
15. *Ibid.,* 83.
16. *Ibid., 45,* / XXVII, Part 3, 519.
17. *Ibid.,* 567.
18. *Ibid., 43,* / XXVII, Part 1, 84.
19. *Ibid.*
20. *Ibid.,* 85.
21. *Ibid.*
22. *Ibid., 45,* / XXVII, Part 3, 609.
23. *Ibid.,* 623–624.
24. *Ibid.,* 625.
25. *Ibid.*
26. *Ibid., 43,* / XXVII, Part 1, 87.
27. *Ibid.,* 89.
28. Douglas Southall Freeman, *R. E. Lee,* III, 127.
29. *O. R., 43,* / XXVII, Part 1, 91–92.
30. *Ibid.,* 92.
31. *Ibid.*
32. *Ibid.*
33. *Ibid.,* 93.
34. Colin R. Ballard, *The Military Genius of Abraham Lincoln,* 170.
35. Williams, II, 751–752.

36. *O. R., 43,* / XXVII, Part 1, 93.
37. *Ibid.,* 105.
38. *Ibid.,* 104–105.
39. *Ibid.,* 106–107.
40. *Ibid.,* 108–110.
41. Mark M. Boatner III, *The Civil War Dictionary,* 420.
42. *O. R., 38,* / XXIV, Part 3, 563–564.
43. *Ibid., 41,* / XXVI, Part 1, 552.
44. *Ibid.,* 553.
45. Fred Harvey Harrington, *Fighting Politician: Major General N. P. Banks,* 122–125.
46. *O. R., 41,* / XXVI, Part 1, 564–565.
47. *Ibid.,* 602.
48. *Ibid.,* 624–625.
49. *Ibid.,* 652–653.
50. *Ibid.,* 659.
51. *Ibid.,* 661–662.
52. *Ibid.,* 664.
53. *Ibid.,* 666.
54. *Ibid.,* 672.
55. *Ibid.,* 673.
56. *Ibid.,* 651–652.
57. *Ibid.,* 682–683.
58. *Ibid.,* 682–683.
59. *Ibid.,* 695–698.
60. *Ibid.,* 311–312.
61. *Ibid.,* 303–306.
62. *Ibid.,* 288–289.
63. *Ibid.,* 289.
64. *Ibid.,* 742.
65. *Ibid.*
66. *Ibid., 35,* / XXIII, Part 2, 517.
67. *Ibid.,* 518.
68. *Ibid.,* 529.
69. *Ibid.,* 531.
70. *Ibid.*
71. *Ibid.,* 545.
72. *Ibid.*
73. *Ibid.,* 552.
74. *Ibid.*
75. *Ibid.,* 555.
76. *Ibid.,* 554–555.
77. *Ibid.,* 556.
78. *Ibid.,* 555–556.
79. Williams, I, 109.
80. *O. R., 35,* / XXIII, Part 2, 558.
81. *Ibid.,* 565.
82. *Ibid.,* 585–586.
83. *Ibid.,* 592.
84. *Ibid.*

85. *Ibid.*
86. *Ibid.*, 593.   .
87. *Ibid.*, 593–594.
88. *Ibid.*, 594.
89. *Ibid.*, 597.
90. *Ibid.*
91. *Ibid.*, 601–602.
92. *Ibid., 58,* / XXXII, Part 2, 407–408

CHAPTER 15
1. Steven E. Woodworth, *Jefferson Davis and his Generals,* in its entirety.
2. *War of the Rebellion: Official Records of the Union and Confederate Armies, 52,* / Series I, Volume XXX Part 3, 110.
3. Shelby Foote, *The Civil War,* II, 709.
4. *Ibid.,* 745–746.
5. Woodworth, 244.
6. *O. R., 50,* / XXX, Part 1, 33–40. This selection is from page 37.
7. Herman Hattaway and Archer Jones, *How the North Won,* 436. This work is the source also for much of this account of the Battle of Chickamauga.
8. *O. R., 48,* / XXIX, Part 1, 147. The account of the conference comes from Stephen E. Ambrose, *Halleck: Lincoln's Chief of Staff,* 152–154.
9. *O. R., 52,* / XXX, Part 3, 904–905.
10. *Ibid.,* 905.
11. *Ibid.*
12. *Ibid.,* 906.
13. *Ibid., 49,* / XXIX, Part 2, 278.
14. *Ibid.,* 328.
15. *Ibid.,* 328–329.
16. *Ibid.,* 332.
17. *Ibid.,* 345.
18. *Ibid.*
19. *Ibid.,* 346.
20. *Ibid.*
21. *Ibid.,* 354.
22. *Ibid.*
23. *Ibid., 38,* / XXIV, Part 3, 497–498.
24. *Ibid., 33,* / XXII, Part 2, 355.
25. *Ibid., 53,* / XXX, Part 4, 354–355.
26. *Ibid.,* 404.
27. Ulysses S. Grant, *Memoirs and Selected Letters,* 403.
28. *Ibid.,* 403–404.
29. *O. R., 53,* / XXX, Part 4, 404.
30. *Ibid., 54,* / XXXI, Part 1, 666.

31. *Ibid.,* 666–669.
32. *Ibid., 41,* / XXVI, Part 1, 291–292.
33. *Ibid.,* 767–768.
34. *Ibid.,* 788, 879–880.
35. *Ibid.,* 803–804.
36. *Ibid.,* 832–833.
37. Fred Harvey Harrington, *Fighting Politician: Major General N. P. Banks,* 133.
38. Foote, II, 859.
39. *Ibid.,* 845–859.
40. *O. R., 58,* / XXXI, Part 2, 25.
41. *Ibid.*
42. *Ibid.,* 46.
43. *Ibid., 49,* / XXIX, Part 2, 495.
44. Hattaway and Jones, 473–474.
45. Herman Haupt, *Reminiscences,* 43–44.
46. *Ibid.,* 44.
47. *Ibid.,* 262.
48. *Ibid.,* 264.
49. *Ibid.,* 264–267.
50. *O. R., 54,* / XXXI, Part 1, 757.
51. Patricia L. Faust, editor, *Historical Times Encyclopedia of the Civil War,* 282.
52. *O. R., 56,* / XXXI, Part 3, 502.
53. *Ibid.,* 529.
54. *Ibid., 111,* / LIII, 584.
55. *Ibid., 56,* / XXXI, Part 3, 457.
56. *Ibid., 109,* / LII, Part 1, 717.
57. David Herbert Donald, *Lincoln,* 471–473.
58. *O. R., 56,* / XXXI, Part 3, 376.
59. *Ibid., 41,* / XXVI, Part 1, 847.
60. *Ibid., 56,* / XXXI, Part 3, 497.
61. *Ibid., 41,* / XXVI, Part 1, 888–891.
62. *Ibid.,* 871.
63. *Ibid., 62,* / XXXIV, Part 2, 16.
64. *Ibid.,* 41.
65. *Ibid.,* 45–46.
66. *Ibid.,* 55–56.
67. *Ibid.,* 56.
68. Ludwell H. Johnson, *Red River Campaign: Politics and Cotton in the Civil War,* Chapter II, "Concerning Cotton," 49–78.
69. *O. R., 62,* / XXXIV, Part 2, 132–133.
70. *Ibid.*
71. Johnson, 48.
72. *O. R., 62,* / XXXIV, Part 2, 211–212.
73. *Ibid.,* 129.
74. *Ibid.,* 134.
75. Donald, 490–491.

CHAPTER 16

1. Kenneth P. Williams, *Lincoln Finds a General*, V, 374.
2. *War of the Rebellion: Offician Records of the Union and Confederate Armies, 58,* / Series I, XXXII, Part 2, 407–408.
3. *Ibid.,* 411–413.
4. *Ibid., 59,* / XXXII, Part 3, 18.
5. *Ibid.,* 49.
6. *Ibid.,* 58.
7. Bruce Catton, *Never Call Retreat,* 304.
8. Stephen E. Ambrose, *Halleck: Lincoln's Chief of Staff,* 162–163.
9. *O. R., 62,* XXXIV, Part 2, 293.
10. Ludwell H. Johnson, *The Red River Campaign: Politics and Cotton in the Civil War,* 82.
11. Herman Haupt, *Reminiscences,* 176–177.
12. *Ibid.*
13. Report of the Joint Congressional Committee on the Conduct of the War (CCW), *The Red River Expedition,* 19.
14. *O. R., 59,* / XXXII, Part 3, 289.
15. Curt Anders, *Disaster in Damp Sand: The Red River Expedition,* 27–31. See also Johnson, 42–48.
16. Anders, 38–124.
17. *O. R., 59,* / XXXII, Part 3, 92.
18. *Ibid.,* 221–222.
19. *Ibid.,* 245.
20. *Ibid.,* 245–246.
21. Anders, 42–43.
22. *O. R., 37,* / XXIV, Part 2, 179–180.
23. John G. Nicolay and John Hay, *Abraham Lincoln: A History,* VIII, 291.
24. *O. R., 59,* / XXXII, Part 3, 246.
25. *Ibid.*
26. *Ibid.*
27. *Ibid.,* 375–376.
28. *Ibid., 63,* / XXXIV, Part 3, 24.
29. *Ibid.,* 160.
30. *Ibid.*
31. *Ibid.,* 190.
32. *Ibid.,* 191–192.
33. *Ibid.,* 220–221.
34. *Ibid.,* 244.
35. *Ibid.,* 252–253.
36. *Ibid.,* 253.
37. *Ibid.,* 153–154.
38. *Ibid.,* 169–174.
39. *Ibid.,* 266.
40. *Ibid.,* 265.
41. *Ibid.,* 265–266.
42. *Ibid.,* 469.
43. *Ibid.,* 278.
44. *Ibid.,* 279.
45. *Ibid.,* 293.
46. *Ibid.,* 293–294.
47. *Ibid.,* 306.
48. *Ibid.,* 316.
49. *Ibid.*
50. *Ibid.,* 331.
51. *Ibid.*
52. *Ibid.*
53. *Ibid.,* 331–332.
54. *Ibid.,* 332–333.
55. *Ibid.,* 357.
56. *Ibid., 68,* / XXXVI, Part 2, 328.
57. *Ibid., 63,* / XXXIV, Part 3, 408.
58. *Ibid.,* 409–410.
59. *Ibid.,* 491–492.
60. Anders, 125–142.
61. O. R., *63,* / XXXIV, Part 3, 390.
62. Johnson, 82.
63. *O. R., 67,* / XXXVI, Part 1, 1.
64. *Ibid.,* 2.
65. Patricia L. Faust, editor, *Historical Times Encyclopedia of the Civil War,* 827.
66. *Ibid.,* 709.
67. *O. R., 67,* / XXXVI, Part 1, 4.
68. Mark M. Boatner, III, *The Civil War Dictionary,* 788–789.
69. William D. Matter, "Spotsylvania Court House," in Frances H. Kennedy, editor, *The Civil War Battlefield Guide,* 210.
70. Boatner, 163; Shelby Foote, *The Civil War,* III, 292.
71. *O. R., 68,* / XXXVI, Part 2, 694.
72. Benjamin F. Thomas and Harold M. Hyman, *Stanton: The Life and Times of Lincoln's Secretary of War,* 300; Horace Porter, *Campaigning With Grant,* 98.
73. *O. R., 62,* / XXXVI, Part 2, 840.
74. Foote, III, 247–250.
75. *O. R., 69,* / XXXVI, Part 3, 114.
76. Catton, 343–351.
77. *O. R., 69,* / XXXVI, Part 3, 115.
78. *Ibid.,* 206.
79. *Ibid.,* 245.
80. *Ibid.,* 375.

81. *Ibid.,* 598–599.
82. *Ibid.,* 665.

CHAPTER 17
1. New York *Herald,* April 2, 1864.
2. *War of the Rebellion: Official Records of the Union and Confederate Armies, 58,* / *Series I,* Volume XXXII, Part 2, 411–413.
3. *Herald,* April 2, 1864.
4. Shelby Foote, *The Civil War,* II, 128.
5. Allan Nevins, *The War for the Union,* IV, 34–35.
6. *O. R., 81,* / XL, Part 2, 558–559.
7. *Ibid.,* 595.
8. *Ibid.,* 598.
9. *Ibid., 71,* / XXXVII, Part 2, 15.
10. *Ibid.,* 38.
11. *Ibid., 81,* / XL, Part 2, 618.
12. *Ibid., 82,* / XL, Part 3, 3.
13. *Ibid.,* 4.
14. *Ibid., 71,* / XXXVII, Part 2, 85.
15. *Ibid.,* 100.
16. *Ibid.,* 108.
17. *Ibid.,* 119.
18. *Ibid., 82,* / XL, Part 3, 59.
19. *Ibid.,* 60.
20. *Ibid., 71,* / XXXVII, Part 2, 153.
21. *Ibid.,* 136.
22. *Ibid.*
23. *Ibid.,* 145.
24. *Ibid.*
25. John F. Marszalek, *Sherman: A Soldier's Passion for Order,* 259–272.
26. *O. R., 76,* / XXXVIII, Part 5, 113–114.
27. *Ibid., 71,* / XXXVII, Part 2, 173.
28. *Ibid.,* 174.
29. *Ibid.,* 187.
30. *Ibid., 82,* / XL, Part 3, 121.
31. *Ibid.,* 122.
32. *Ibid., 71,* / XXXVII, Part 2, 81, 196.
33. *Ibid.,* 207, 209.
34. *Ibid.,* 195.
35. Margaret Leech, *Reveille in Washington,* 342.
36. *O. R., 71,* / XXXVII, Part 2, 210.
37. *Ibid., 82,* / XL, Part 3, 175.
38. *Ibid.*
39. *Ibid., 71,* / XXXVII, Part 2, 223.
40. *Ibid., 82,* / XL, Part 3, 176.
41. *Ibid., 71,* / XXXVII, Part 2, 259.

42. *Ibid.,* 260–261.
43. *Ibid.,* 265.
44. *Ibid.*
45. *Ibid.,* 300–301.
46. *Ibid., 76,* / XXXVIII, Part 5, 91–92.
47. *Ibid.,* 150–151.
48. *Ibid., 71,* / XXXVII, Part 2, 331.
49. *Ibid.,* 331–332.
50. *Ibid.,* 333–334.
51. *Ibid.,* 339–340.
52. *Ibid.,* 340.
53. *Ibid.,* 365.
54. *Ibid.,* 366–367.
55. *Ibid.,* 332–333.
56. *Ibid.,* 365.
57. *Ibid.,* 384.
58. *Ibid.,* 400.
59. *Ibid.,* 350.
60. *Ibid.,* 384–385.
61. *Ibid.,* 385, 421–423, 444.
62. *Ibid.,* 423.
63. *Ibid.*
64. *Ibid.,* 423–424.
65. *Ibid.,* 433–434.
66. *Ibid.,* 433.
67. *Ibid.,* 463.
68. David Herbert Donald, *Lincoln,* 512–520.
69. *O. R., 71,* / XXXVII, Part 2, 467.
70. *Ibid.,* 478.
71. *Ibid.,* 527–528.
72. *Ibid.,* 558.
73. *Ibid.,* 573.
74. *Ibid.,* 582–583.
75. *Ibid.,* 582.
76. *Ibid., 90,* / XLIII, Part 1, 681.
77. *Ibid., 71,* / XXXVII, Part 2, 583.
78. *Ibid., 90,* / XLIII, Part 1, 681.

CHAPTER 18
1. *War of the Rebellion: Official Records of the Union and Confederate Armies, 76,* / Series I, Volume XXXVIII, Part 5., 234–235.
2. *Ibid.,* 240.
3. *Ibid.,* 271–272.
4. *Ibid.,* 777.
5. *Ibid.,* 791–794.
6. *Ibid.,* 856–857.
7. *Ibid., 90,* / XLIII, Part 1, 110.
8. Patricia M. Faust, editor, *Historical Times*

Encyclopedia of the Civil War, 835.

9. *O. R.., 90,* / XLIII, Part 1, 152.

10. *Ibid.,* 163.

11. *Ibid.,* 209.

12. *Ibid.,* 249.

13. *Ibid.,* 250.

14. *Ibid.,* 257.

15. *Ibid.,* 257–258.

16. *Ibid.,* 258.

17. *Ibid.,* 265–266.

18. *Ibid.,* 272–273.

19. *Ibid., 78,* / XXXIX, Part 2, 411–413.

20. *Ibid.,* 464.

21. *Ibid.,* 480.

22. *Ibid.,* 503.

23. *Ibid.*

24. *Ibid.,* 411.

25. *Ibid.*

26. Stephen E. Ambrose, *Halleck: Lincoln's Chief of Staff,* 172, citing George Agassiz, editor, *Meade's Headquarters 1863–1865,* 193.

27. *O. R., 78,* / XXXIX, Part 2, 25–26.

28. *Ibid.,* 357–358.

29. *Ibid., 90,* / XLIII, Part 1, 307.

30. *Ibid.,* 308.

31. *Ibid.,* 327.

32. *Ibid.,* 339.

33. *Ibid.,* 345.

34. *Ibid.,* 341.

35. *Ibid.,* 348.

36. *Ibid.,* 355.

37. *Ibid.,* 356.

38. *Ibid.,* 357.

39. *Ibid.,* 363.

40. *Ibid.*

41. *Ibid.,* 386.

42. *Ibid.*

43. *Ibid.,* 393.

44. *Ibid.,* 402.

45. Jeffry D. Wert, *From Winchester to Cedar Creek: The Shenandoah Campaign of 1864,* 142–216.

46. Ibid., 221–224; Shelby Foote, *The Civil War,* III, 570.

47. *O. R., 91,* / XLIII, Part 1, 487–488.

48. *Ibid., 78,* / XXXIX, Part 2, 697.

49. *Ibid.,* 727.

50. *Ibid.,* 740.

51. *Ibid.*

52. *Ibid.*

53. *Ibid.,* 749.

54. Faust, 285–286, 284–285; *Mark M. Boatner, III, The Civil War Dictionary,* 304–308.

55. *O. R., 94,* / XLV, Part 2, 4.

56. *Ibid.,* 28.

57. *Ibid.,* 29.

58. *Ibid.,* 55.

59. *Ibid.*

60. *Ibid.*

61. *Ibid.,* 70.

62. *Ibid.*

63. *Ibid.*

64. *Ibid.,* 84.

65. *Ibid.*

66. *Ibid.,* 95.

67. *Ibid.*

68. Margaret Leech, *Reveille in Washington,* 344.

69. T. S. Eliot, *The Complete Poems and Plays,* 3–7.

70. *O. R., 94,* / XLV, Part 2, 96.

71. *Ibid.*

72. *Ibid.,* 97.

73. *Ibid.,* 114.

74. *Ibid.,* 115.

75. *Ibid.,* 114.

76. *Ibid.,* 115–116.

77. *Ibid.,* 116.

78. *Ibid.*

79. *Ibid.,* 115.

80. *Ibid.*

81. Richard O'Connor, *Thomas: Rock of Chickamauga,* 310.

82. *O. R., 94,* / XLV, Part 2, 118.

83. O'Connor, 307–312.

84. David Herbert Donald, *Lincoln,* 552–553.

85. O'Connor, 307–308.

86. *O. R., 94,* XLV, Part 2, 143.

87. *Ibid.*

88. *Ibid.*

89. *Ibid.,* 155.

90. *Ibid.,* 168.

91. Foote, III, 684–685; Faust, 443.

92. *O. R., 94,* / XLV, Part 2, 180.

93. *Ibid.*

94. Foote, III, 685.

95. *O. R., 94,* / XLV, Part 2, 194.

96. *Ibid.,* 195.

97. *Ibid., 92,* / XLIV, 701.

98. *Ibid.,* 666, 699, for example.

99. William T. Sherman, *Memoirs of General*

W. T. Sherman, 682. in the Library of America edition.

100. *Ibid.*
101. *O. R., 92,* / XLIV, 726–728.
102. *Ibid.,* 741.
103. *Ibid.,* 715.
104. *Ibid.,* 740–741.
105. *Ibid.,* 798–800.
106. *Ibid.,* 836–837.
107. *Ibid.,* 840.
108. *Ibid.,* 847.

CHAPTER 19
1. Alan C. and Barbara A. Aimone, *A User's Guide to the Official Records of the American Civil War,* 1–10.
2. David Herbert Donald, *Lincoln,* 575.
3. Herman Hattaway and Archer Jones, *How the North Won,* 658–660.
4. War of the Rebellion: *Official Records of the Union and Confederate Armies, 99,* / Series I, Volume XLVII, Part 2, 3.
5. *Webster's New Collegiate Dictionary,* 397.
6. Mark M. Boatner, III, *The Civil War Dictionary,* 367.
7. *O. R., 96,* / XLVI, Part 2, 29.
8. *Ibid.,* 60.
9. Hattaway and Jones, 660.
10. *O. R., 99,* / XLVII, Part 2, 36–37.
11. *Ibid., 96,* / XLVI, Part 2, 561–562.
12. *Ibid., 100,* / XLVII, Part 3, 100–101.
13. Burke Davis, *To Appomattox: Nine April Days,* 107–109.
14. *O. R., 100,* / XLVII, Part 3, 140.
15. *Ibid.,* 150–151.
16. *Ibid.,* 177.
17. *Ibid.,* 206–207.
18. *Ibid.,* 207.
19. *Ibid., 97,* / XLVI, Part 3, 762.
20. Shelby Foote, *The Civil War,* III, 980–986; Benjamin F. Thomas and Harold Hyman, *Stanton: The Life and Times of Lincoln's Secretary of War,* 399, 399n. For details of Stanton's mental instability, see earlier chapters in Thomas and Hyman.
21. *O. R., 100,* / XLVII, Part 3, 220–221.
22. *Ibid.,* 221.
23. *Ibid., 97.* / XLVI, Part 3, 833.
24. *Ibid.,* 835.
25. *Ibid.,* 836.

26. *Ibid.*
27. *Ibid.,* 836–837.
28. Margaret Leech, *Reveille in Washington,* 395–403.
29. *O. R., 97,* / XLVI, Part 3, 836–837.
30. *Ibid., 100,* / XLVII, Part 3, 237.
31. *Ibid.,* 245.
32. *Ibid.,* 245.
33. *Ibid,,* 243.
34. H. L. Trefousse, *Benjamin Franklin Wade: Radical Republican From Ohio,* 246.
35. *Ibid.,* 249.
36. *Ibid.*
37. *O. R., 100,* / XLVII, Part 3, 263–264.
38. Lloyd Lewis, *Sherman: Fighting Prophet,* 550.
39. *O. R., 100,* / XLVII, Part 3, 263–264.
40. *Ibid.,* 263.
41. *Ibid.,* 263–264.
42. *Ibid.,* 264.
43. *Ibid., 97,* / XLVI, Part 3, 891.
44. *Ibid.,* 896.
45. *Ibid.,* 887.
46. *Ibid.*
47. *Ibid., 100,* / XLVII, Part 3, 276–277.
48. *Ibid., 97,* / XLVI, Part 3, 895.
49. *Ibid., 100,* / XLVII, Part 3, 277.
50. John F. Marszalek, *Sherman: A Soldier's Passion for Order,* 347.
51. Lewis, 552.
52. *Ibid.,* 553.
53. *Ibid.,* 551–552.
54. *O. R., 100,* / XLVII, Part 3, 286.
55. *Ibid., 97,* / XLVI, Part 3, 907.
56. *Ibid., 100,* / XLVII, Part 3, 287.
57. *Ibid.,* 293.
58. *Ibid.,* 294.
59. *Ibid.,* 293.
60. *Ibid., 97,* / XLVI, Part 3, 917.
61. *Ibid.,* 916.
62. *Ibid.,* 944.
63. *Ibid.,* 915.
64. *Ibid.,* 939.
65. *Ibid.,* 953.
66. *Ibid.,* 953–954.
67. *Ibid.,* 954.
68. *New York Herald,* April 28, 1865.

CHAPTER 20
1. *War of the Rebellion: Official Records of the*

Union and Confederate Armies, 97, /
Series I, Volume XLVI, Part 3, 989.

2. *Ibid.,* 990.

3. *Ibid.,* 990–991.

4. *Ibid.,* 1001.

5. *Ibid.,* 1005–1006.

6. *Ibid.,* 1016.

7. *Ibid.,* 1072.

8. *Ibid.,* 1073.

9. *Ibid.,* 1086.

10. *Ibid.,* 1091.

11. *Ibid., 100, /* XLVII, Part 3, 404.

12. *Ibid., 97, /* XLVI, Part 3, 1106.

13. *Ibid.,* 1110.

14. *Ibid.,* 1175.

15. *Ibid.,* 1206.

16. *Ibid.,* 1221.

17. *Ibid.,* 1162.

18. *Ibid.,* 1169.

19. *Ibid., 100, /* XLVII, Part 3, 443.

20. *Ibid.,* 519.

21. *Ibid., 97, /* XLVI, Part 3, 1132.

22. *Ibid., 100, /* XLVII, Part 3, 320.

23. *Ibid.,* 334–335.

24. *Ibid.,* 335.

25. *Ibid.,* 345–346.

26. *Ibid.,* 387.

27. *Ibid.,* 410.

28. *Ibid.,* 392–393.

29. *Ibid.,* 399.

30. *Ibid.,* 405.

31. *Ibid.,* 435.

32. *Ibid.*

33. *Ibid.,* 441.

34. *Ibid.,* 447.

35. *Ibid.,* 454.

36. *Ibid.,* 454–455.

37. *Ibid.,* 477–478.

38. *Ibid.,* 476.

39. *Ibid.,* 546–547.

40. *Ibid.,* 576.

41. *Ibid.,* 581–582.

42. *Ibid.,* 585–586.

43. *Ibid.,* 582–583.

44. *Ibid.,* 634–637.

45. *Ibid., 97, /* XLVI, Part 3, 1269.

46. *Ibid.,* 1291.

Bibliography

Aimone, Alan C. and Barbara A. *A User's Guide to the Official Records of the American Civil War.* Shippensburg, PA: White Mane Publishing Company, 1993.

Ambrose. Stephen E. *Halleck: Lincoln's Chief of Staff.* Baton Rouge: Louisiana State University Press, 1962.

Alexander, E. P. *Military Memoirs of a Confederate.* New York: Scribner's, 1907.

Anders, Curt. *Disaster in Damp Sand: The Red River Expedition.* Carmel, IN: Guild Press of Indiana, 1998.

Association of Graduates, USMA. *Register of Graduates, 1802–1996.* West Point, NY: 1996.

Ballard, Colin R. *The Military Genius of Abraham Lincoln.* Cleveland and New York: World, 1952.

Bancroft, Hubert Howe. *The Works of Hubert Howe Bancroft: History of California.* 7 vols. San Francisco: The History Company, 1888.

Basler, Roy P., editor. *The Collected Works of Abraham Lincoln.* 9 vols. New Brunswick: Rutgers University Press, 1953–1955.

Bates, Homer. *Lincoln in the Telegraph Room.* New York: Century, 1907.

Bauer, K. Jack. *The Mexican War.* New York: Macmillan, 1974.

Bigelow, John Jr. *The Campaign of Chancellorsville.* New Haven: Yale University Press, 1910.

Boatner, Mark M., III. *The Civil War Dictionary.* New York: McKay, 1959.

Catton, Bruce. *Never Call Retreat.* Garden City: Doubleday, 1965.

——, *The Coming Fury.* Garden City: Doubleday, 1961.

Cleaves, Freeman. *Meade of Gettysburg.* Norman: University of Oklahoma Press, 1960.

Cozzens, Peter. *No Better Place to Die.* Urbana and Chicago: University of Illinois Press, 1992.

———. *This Terrible Sound: The Battle of Chickamauga.* Urbana and Chicago: University of Illinois Press, 1992.

Davis, Burke. *To Appomattox: Nine April Days, 1865.* New York: Rinehart, 1959.

Davis, William C. *Jefferson Davis: The Man and His Hour.* New York: HarperCollins, 1991.

Donald, David Herbert. *Lincoln.* New York: Simon & Schuster, 1995.

Dowdey, Clifford. *Lee.* Boston: Little, Brown, 1965.

———. *The Seven Days.* Boston: Little, Brown, 1964.

Edge, Frederick Milnes. *Major-General McClellan and The Campaign on the Yorktown Peninsula.* London: Trubner & Co., 1865.

Eliot, T. S. *The Complete Poems and Plays.* New York: Harcourt, Brace, 1952.

Ellison, William Henry. *A Self-Governing Dominion: California, 1849–1860.* Berkeley and Los Angeles: University of California Press, 1950.

Faulkner, William. "On Accepting the Nobel Award," in Harding, Harold F., editor. *The Age of Danger: Major Speeches on American Problems.* New York: Random House, 1953.

Faust, Patricia L., Editor. *Historical Times Encyclopedia of the Civil War.* New York: Harper & Row, 1986.

Fehrenbacher, Don E., editor. *Abraham Lincoln: Speeches and Writings 1859–1865.* Second of 2 vols. New York: Library of America, 1989.

Foote, Shelby. *The Civil War.* 3 vols. New York: Random House, 1958, 1963, 1974.

Freeman, Douglas Southall. *Lee's Lieutenants.* 3 vols. New York: Scribners, 1942.

———. *R. E. Lee.* 4 vols. New York: Scribner's, 1934.

Fuller, J. F. C. *The Generalship of Ulysses S. Grant.* New York: Dodd, Mead, 1929.

Gallagher, Gary W., editor. *Fighting for the Confederacy: The Personal Recollections of Edward Porter Alexander.* Chapel Hill, NC: University of North Carolina Press, 1989.

Grant, Ulysses S. *Ulysses S. Grant: Memoirs and Selected Letters.* Compiled by Mary Drake and William S. McFeely. New York: Library of America, 1990.

Halstead, Murat. *Fire the Salute!* Kingsport, TN: Kingsport Press, 1960.

Harrington, Fred Harvey. *Fighting Politician: N. P. Banks.* Westport, CT: Greenwood Press, 1947.

Hart, James D. *A Companion to California.* Berkeley: University of California Press, 1987.

Hattaway, Herman and Archer Jones. *How the North Won.* Urbana: University of Illinois Press, 1983.

Haupt, Herman. *Reminiscences.* Milwaukee: Wright & Joy, 1901.

Henderson, G. F. R. *Stonewall Jackson and the American Civil War.* New York, McKay, 1961.

Johnson, Allen, and Dumas Malone, editors. *Dictionary of American Biography.* 12 vols. New York: Charles Scribner's Sons, 1960.

Johnson, Kenneth M. *San Francisco As It Is.* New York: Talisman Press, 1964.

Johnson, Ludwell H. *Red River Campaign: Politics and Cotton in the Civil War.* Baltimore: Johns Hopkins Press, 1959.

Johnson, Robert U., and C. C. Buel, editors. *Battles and Leaders of the Civil War.* 4 vols. New York: Century, 1887–1888.

Leech, Margaret. *Reveille in Washington.* New York: Harper, 1941.

Lewis, Lloyd. *Captain Sam Grant.* Boston: Little Brown, 1950.

——. *Sherman: Fighting Prophet.* New York: Harcourt Brace, 1932.

Marszalek, John F. *Sherman: A Soldier's Passion for Order.* New York: Free Press, 1992.

McClellan, George B. *McClellan's Own Story.* New York: Charles L. Webster, 1887.

Miers, Earl Schenck, editor-in-chief. *Lincoln Day by Day.* Dayton, OH: Morningside Press, 1991.

National Cyclopedia. New York: James T. White & Co., 1897.

Nevins, Allan. *Fremont: The West's Greatest Adventurer.* 2 vols. New York: Harper, 1928.

———. *The War for the Union.* 4 Vols. New York: Scribner's, 1959–1971.

Nicolay, John G. and John Hay. *Abraham Lincoln: A History.* 10 Vols. New York: Century, 1886–1890.

O'Brien, Robert. *This is San Fransisco.* New York: Wittlsey House-McGraw-Hill 1948.

O'Connor, Richard. *Thomas: Rock of Chickamauga.* New York: Prentice-Hall, 1948.

Quinn, Arthur. *The Rivals: William Gwin, David Broderick, and the Birth of California.* New York: Crown Publishers, 1994.

Randall, J. G. *Lincoln the President.* 4 vols. New York, Dodd Mead, 1945–1955.

Rolle, Andrew F. *California: A History.* New York: Thomas Y. Crowell, 1963.

Roske, Ralph J. *A History of California.* New York: Macmillan, 1968.

Royce, Josiah. *California: From the Conquest in 1846 to the Second Vigilance Committee in San Francisco.* New York: Alfred A. Knopf, 1948.

Scherer, James A. *Thirty-First Star.* New York: G. P. Putnam's Sons, 1942.

Sears, Stephen W. *George B. McClellan: The Young Napoleon.* New York: Ticknor & Fields, 1988.

———. *Landscape Turned Red.* New Haven and New York: Ticknor & Fields, 1983.

———. *The Civil War Papers of George B. McClellan.* New York: Ticknor & Fields, 1989.

Sherman, William T. *Memoirs of General W. T. Sherman* with Notes by Charles Royster. New York: Library of America, 1990.

Starr, Louis M. *Bohemian Brigade: Civil War Newsmen in Action*. Madison: University of Wisconsin Press, 1987.

Strode, Hudson. *Jefferson Davis: Confederate President*. 3 vols. New York: Harcourt Brace, 1955–1964.

Tanner, Robert G. *Stonewall in the Valley*. Garden City: Doubleday, 1976.

Thomas, Benjamin P. and Harold M. Hyman. *Stanton: The Life and Times of Lincoln's Secretary of War*. New York: Knopf, 1962.

Thomas, Emory M. *The Confederate Nation*. New York: Harper & Row, 1979.

Trefousse, H. L. *Benjamin Franklin Wade: Radical Republican From Ohio*. New York: Twayne Publishers, 1963.

——. *The Radical Republicans: Lincoln's Vanguard for Racial Justice*. Baton Rouge, LA: Louisiana State University Press, 1969.

U.S. Congress. Report of the Joint Congressional Committee on the Conduct of the War, 1863–1866. *Red River Expedition*. Millwood, NY: Kraus Reprint, 1977.

Vandiver, Frank E. *Mighty Stonewall*. New York: McGraw-Hill, 1957.

War of the Rebellion: Official Records of the Union and Confederate Armies. 70 vols. in 128. Washington, DC: Government Printing Office, 1880–1902.

Webster's American Military Biography. Springfield, MA: G. & C. Merriam Company, 1918.

Welles, Gideon. *Diary of Gideon Welles, Secretary of the Navy Under Lincoln and Johnson*. 3 vols. Boston: Houghton Mifflin, 1911.

Wert, Jeffry D. *From Winchester to Cedar Creek: The Shenandoah Campaign of 1864*. Carlisle, PA: South Mountain Press, 1987.

Williams, Kenneth P. *Lincoln Finds a General*. 5 vols. New York: Macmillan, 1949–1959.

Williams, T. Harry. *Lincoln and the Radicals*. Madison, WI: University of Wisconsin Press. 1965.

Wilson, James Grant. "General Halleck: A Memoir," in *Journal of the Military Service Institution of the United States.* Governor's Island, NY: Military Service Institution, 1905.

Woodworth, Steven E. *Davis and Lee at War.* Lawrence, KS: University Press of Kansas, 1995.

——. *Jefferson Davis and his Generals.* Lawrence, KS: University Press of Kansas, 1990.

Index